LEAVING CERTIFICATE

Biology *Plus*

Michael O'Callaghan

Special advisor: Angela Bury

The Educational Company of Ireland

First published 2013
The Educational Company of Ireland
Ballymount Road
Walkinstown
Dublin 12
www.edco.ie

A member of the Smurfit Kappa Group plc

ISBN 978-1-84536-557-8

The paper used in this book comes from Managed Forests in Northern Europe For every tree felled, at least one new tree is planted

Editors: Life Lines Editorial Services
Design: Design Image
Layout: Q2AMedia
Proofreader: Jennifer Armstrong
Cover design: Design Image
Cover photography: Mircea Bezergheanu, Dim Dimich, Mathagraphics/Shutterstock
Illustrations: Q2AMedia
Photograph acknowledgements: Alamy, Corbis, Imagefile, Science Photo Library, Shutterstock, Visuals
Unlimited

Web references in this book are intended as a guide for teachers. At the time of going to press, all
web addresses were active and contained information relevant to the topics in this book. However,
The Educational Company of Ireland and the authors do not accept responsibility for the views or
information contained on these websites. Content and addresses may change beyond our control and
pupils should be supervised when investigating websites.

05M18

Contents

Activities

Introduction

This book is written for the Leaving Certificate Biology course and includes a new and exciting revision resource for students at www.edco.ie/lcbiologyplus. The textbook is intended to be as close a fit as possible with the requirements of the Syllabus and Guidelines, and the digital revision resource includes an interactive testing facility with an assessment tracker that allows students to assess and follow their progress, chapter by chapter, throughout the Leaving Certificate Biology course.

In addition, teachers can gain access to the *Leaving Certificate Biology Plus* Interactive Textbook online and can access a bank of digital resources, including videos, animations and PowerPoint presentations by visiting www.edcodigital.ie. These materials can be used in class to demonstrate various aspects of the course in an engaging and dynamic way.

The *Leaving Certificate Biology Plus* textbook is closely aligned with the marking schemes of both the Ordinary and Higher level past examinations (higher-level material is clearly marked with a red bar and, where possible, is placed in separate chapters or at the end of the chapters). Learning objectives summarising the syllabus content are given at the start of each chapter.

Definitions play a key role in biology. Many definitions are given in brightly coloured panels throughout the chapters and are listed in the glossary at the back of the book. Biology is also a very visual subject. In this regard a large number of diagrams and photographs (many of which are electron microscope images) are included throughout, to support, complement and enhance the text. Numerous learning mnemonics and tips are also included to help students to recall key information.

The 22 mandatory activities for the course are included in coloured panels at the end of each relevant chapter. The activities are fully explained with the aid of labelled diagrams. Only those details required by students for the examinations are given, and where possible the results are indicated, if not stated directly. In addition, most of the mandatory activities are included as videos in an accompanying DVD, and are also available online.

A broad summary is included at the end of each chapter and is designed to be of help to students when revising for examinations. A large number of specially written revision questions and past exam questions are also given at the end of each chapter. These questions are based on the syllabus and are chosen to cover the sequence of material included in the chapters. In addition, every chapter concludes with a checklist of questions asked from 2004 to 2012 at both Ordinary and Higher level.

Finally, a QR code (quick response digitised square) is given to link to the digital support material available for each chapter, and a glossary of terms and comprehensive index are included at the back of the book.

Student Revision Website

To access the Student Revision Website, visit **www.edco.ie/lcbiologyplus** and enter the Unique Access Code: **BPN97826**

Laboratory Safety

Safety rules

The following rules are enforced to keep yourself and your classmates safe while in a school laboratory.

1 Do not enter the laboratory without permission.

2 Do not use any equipment unless permitted to do so by your teacher.

3 Make sure you know exactly what you are supposed to do. If in doubt, ask your teacher.

4 Make sure you know the position of all safety equipment in the laboratory, e.g. fire extinguishers, first-aid equipment, etc.

5 Always wear eye protection or gloves when instructed to do so.

6 Long hair must be tied back during practical classes.

7 Place your bag and other personal items safely out of the way.

8 Never handle any chemicals with bare hands.

9 Nothing must be eaten, tasted or drunk in the laboratory.

10 Any cut, burn or other accident must be reported at once to your teacher.

11 Always check that the label on the bottle is exactly the same as the material you require. If in doubt, ask the teacher.

12 Any chemical spilled on the skin or clothing must be washed at once with plenty of water and reported to your teacher.

13 Test tubes should never be overfilled. When heating a test tube ensure that the mouth of the test tube is pointed away from yourself and everyone else.

14 All equipment should be cleaned and put back in its correct place after use.

15 Always wash your hands after practical work.

16 Students should behave in a responsible manner at all times in the laboratory.

Safety symbols

The following labels appear on bottles in the laboratory. They also appear on many everyday chemicals such as cleaning products and solvents. These labels indicate chemicals that could be dangerous if not used or handled properly.

TOXIC

 Substances that can cause death if they are swallowed, breathed in or absorbed through the skin. Example: weedkiller.

HARMFUL OR IRRITANT

 Substances that should not be eaten, breathed in or handled without gloves. Although not as dangerous as toxic substances, they may cause a rash, sickness or an allergic reaction. Example: antifreeze.

OXIDISING

 Substances that provide oxygen, allowing other materials to burn more intensely. Example: hair bleach.

HIGHLY FLAMMABLE

 Substances that easily catch fire. Example: petrol.

CORROSIVE

Substances that attack and destroy living tissue, including skin and eyes. Example: oven cleaner.

WARNING

This sign is often used to draw attention to a warning of danger, hazards and the unexpected.

Recording and Reporting Practical Activities

General guidelines

- A folder or notebook should be used to record details of all the practical activities required by the syllabus.
- A table of contents of all the activities should be placed at the beginning of the notebook or folder.
- These records should be neatly and properly written so that they are clearly presented.
- Diagrams should be included whenever possible (and drawn in HB pencil).
- The main steps in any calculations (not including roughwork) should be included where appropriate.
- Where relevant, the results should be stated clearly. It is recommended to comment on the results where possible.
- The scale used in any graph should be suitable, the graph should be labelled, and the points on the graph should be clearly circled and joined.

Activity reports

The following headings should be included (where relevant) when writing up the report on each of the 22 mandatory activities specified in the syllabus.

- **Title and date.** A title and the date(s) on which the activity was carried out should be given.
- **Description of procedure.** A brief report should be written by each student to include (where possible):
  - A labelled diagram of the assembled apparatus
  - Reference to any adjustments to the apparatus that were required
  - Details of any measurements taken (including the units used)
  - Details of any safety procedures followed.
  - Refer to the use of a **control**, if one was carried out.
- **Results and observations.** The results or outcomes of each activity should be stated clearly. Reference should be made (where relevant) to any errors that may have arisen, and to any precautions that might be taken to reduce such errors.
- **Conclusions.** By interacting with other students, or groups of students, (where possible) a conclusion or conclusions should be stated.

Icons Explained

A number of icons are used in association with special text panels in this book. The meaning of each icon is listed below.

 The green arrow indicates a definition. As definitions make up about 25% of the marks in the Leaving Certificate Biology examination, they should be learned off by heart. A full list of all the definitions is given in the glossary on pages 491–496.

 The blue exclamation mark indicates something of special importance that should be noted.

 The yellow question mark indicates interesting facts related to the topic. This 'Did you know?' material does not have to be learned for the examination.

 The yellow pencil indicates a key diagram that you may need to draw in the examination. You can test yourself on these diagrams by visiting the *Leaving Certificate Biology Plus* website at www.edco.ie/lcbiologyplus.

 This is used to highlight the requirements of the syllabus. It is often used when there is a choice of material to be learned.

 This is used to emphasise the function of a particular structure.

 This indicates the material that is required only for the Higher level course.

 At the end of each chapter you can take an online test to assess your understanding and track your progress. There you will find a QR code; you can scan this code with your phone to be directed to an online test for that specific chapter (you will need to install a QR code scanner app first). Alternatively, you can visit the link that is also included at the end of each chapter.

Visit www.edco.ie/lcbiologyplus to find out more.

Unit 1
The Study of Life

Chapter 1 The scientific method

Learning objectives

- To define the term 'biology' and give examples of areas of biological study
- To understand the scientific method and describe its process
- To understand and describe the principles of experimentation
- To understand and describe the limitations of the value of the scientific method.

Science

Science is the organised and objective study of the physical, material and living world. The word *science* comes from the Latin word *scienta*, meaning knowledge.

Science is classified into three main subject areas: physics, chemistry and biology.

Biology

> Biology is the study of living things.

The word *biology* comes from the Greek words *bios*, which means life, and *logos*, which means knowledge.

Areas of study in biology

Originally biology consisted of botany (the study of plants), zoology (the study of animals) and microbiology (the study of small living things).

Biology later expanded to include the study of topics such as taxonomy (classification), anatomy (overall structure), physiology (overall function), cytology (cells), biochemistry (chemical reactions), ecology (relationships between living things and their environments) and genetics (inheritance).

As biology progresses, the areas of study become greater in number and more specific in content. For example, microbiology can be divided into three disciplines. These are bacteriology (bacteria), mycology (fungi) and virology (viruses).

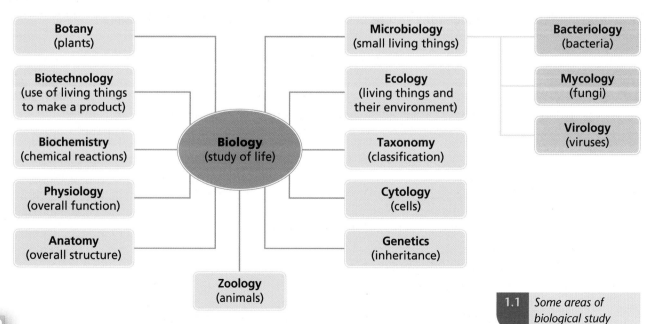

1.1 *Some areas of biological study*

The scientific method

The essence of science is knowledge of the physical world. This knowledge is obtained by asking relevant questions and then searching for the answers to these questions.

The scientific method is an attempt at using an organised approach to solving problems. The core of the scientific method involves asking questions and searching for answers.

Steps in the scientific method

The **scientific method** is a process of investigation in which problems are identified and their suggested explanations are tested by carrying out experiments.

1.2 *Biology is an experimental subject*

1. Observation

Observation is the most important part of the scientific method, especially when it is followed by asking the question 'Why?'. Observations may be obtained directly by our senses (seeing, hearing, etc.) or indirectly by the use of equipment such as microscopes and thermometers.

Observations that are properly taken and recorded provide the basis for all the facts relating to a problem.

2. Hypothesis

A hypothesis should (a) account for all the facts that have been observed and (b) lead to the prediction of new information.

3. Experimentation

The results of the experiment (or more often a series of experiments) will either support or contradict the hypothesis. The methods used for experimentation are outlined later in this chapter.

4. Collection and interpretation of data

The information that is obtained in the course of experiments is collected, recorded and analysed.

5. Conclusion

As in the saying 'it is the bottom line that counts', so in an experiment it is the conclusion that is often of greatest value. The data from an experiment is interpreted to reach a conclusion or result.

6. Relating the conclusion to existing knowledge

The conclusion of an experiment should tie in with the existing knowledge of the topic being examined.

On the basis of the conclusion(s) reached, the hypothesis is:
- Supported if the results agree fully
- Changed if the results agree only partly
- Rejected if the results contradict it.

Very often the conclusion reached in one experiment will lead to the need to design further experiments.

An **observation** is when something is noticed.

A **hypothesis** is an educated guess based on observations.

An **experiment** is designed to test a hypothesis.

Data consists of the measurements, observations or information gathered from experiments.

A **conclusion** is a summary of the results of an experiment.

THE STUDY OF LIFE

7. Reporting and publishing the results

The results of experiments should be written down and reported so that they can be examined and analysed by others. In this way new ideas are made available to all scientists. This adds to the growth of scientific understanding.

Experimental procedures and results are often published in scientific journals and magazines or on the world wide web. They may later be reported in newspapers and on television. One of the key concepts of the scientific method is that an experiment should be repeatable. If someone else follows the same procedures and gets the same results, then the conclusions are more likely to be valid. Experiments are published in order to allow them to be repeated.

Observation	
Hypothesis	Reject / Change / Accept
Theory / Experiment	
Principle / Result	
Interpretation	
Conclusion	

1.3 *Summary of the scientific method*

Theories and principles

The formation of a theory requires many years and involves many experimental results. The word *theory* means an idea that is uncertain but is widely accepted as a correct explanation. Theories may be altered but are rarely discarded.

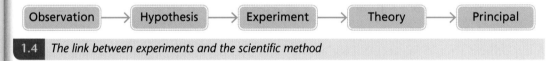

Observation → Hypothesis → Experiment → Theory → Principal

1.4 *The link between experiments and the scientific method*

Principles of experimentation

To ensure that experiments are conducted fairly the following concepts should be considered.

1. Careful planning and design

Experiments must be carefully planned and designed.

In most experiments, only a single factor (or variable) is tested. All other variables should be kept constant.

For example, it is observed that seedlings bend as they grow. The hypothesis is that they are growing towards light coming from one side. However, other variables, including temperature and wind (such as a draught), may be responsible for the bending response. An experiment might be designed to grow the seedlings in a black box with a hole in one side. In this case, the seedlings are seen to grow towards the light source, regardless of which way the box is turned.

In the example of the seedlings, careful planning and design would involve ensuring that temperature and wind do not influence the results (i.e. the experiment should be conducted in a draught-free room at a constant temperature).

A theory is a hypothesis that has been supported by many different experiments.

A principle or law arises from a theory that has been shown to be valid when fully tested over a long period of time.

An experiment is a test for a hypothesis.

A variable is a factor that may change in an experiment.

In the late 1700s an English doctor, **Edward Jenner**, observed that people working with cows did not get smallpox. However, they did get a similar, but milder, disease called cowpox. Smallpox (which has now been eliminated worldwide) caused huge skin disfigurement and sometimes death.

Often a hypothesis is stated in the form of an **If . . . , then . . .** statement. Jenner formed the hypothesis that **if** someone got cowpox and recovered, **then** that person was protected from smallpox. In other words he predicted that contracting cowpox protects humans against smallpox.

Jenner's experiment was to insert pus from a cowpox victim under the skin of a healthy boy. The boy got cowpox and recovered. Some time later Jenner inserted pus from a smallpox victim under the boy's skin. The boy did not get smallpox, even when the procedure was repeated.

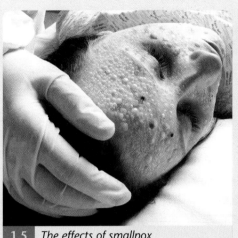

1.5 *The effects of smallpox*

Note that while Jenner's experiment was successful, it was also very dangerous. Such an approach would not be acceptable today on the grounds of safety.

Jenner's work was the first example of a vaccination programme in action. (The word **vaccination** comes from the Latin for cow, *vacca*.)

2. Ensure that the experiment is safe

It is important that safety is borne in mind when designing experiments.
The following safety features should be observed for classroom experiments:

- Tie back long hair
- Wear a laboratory coat
- Wear safety goggles when necessary
- Never place your fingers in your eyes or mouth unless you have washed your hands
- Avoid contact between electrical equipment and water
- Be aware of the safety information when using chemicals
- Report all accidents to a teacher.

3. Design a control experiment

A control is a comparison for the test experiment. There should be only one variable (or difference) between the test experiment and the control.

For instance, in the experiment to test whether seedlings are growing towards the light, the control could be to grow the same type of seedlings in a similar box, which does not have a hole to let in light. In other words, grow the seedlings in the dark and observe the results for the control seedlings.

Consider the hypothesis that a new drug reduces the effects of arthritis. A number of arthritic patients are x-rayed and their deformities noted. The drug is administered as a pill for 6 months. The patients are then x-rayed again and are found to have improved.

These improvements may not have been caused by the drug. They may have been caused by the attention paid to the patients or by some other factor.

Patients in a control group (who should be similar in age, gender, lifestyle, severity of disease and many other features) are given a harmless, tasteless pill at the same times as the patients in the experimental group. This pill is called a placebo. Neither the patients nor the medical staff know who is getting the placebo and who is getting the real drug. If the patients in the control (or placebo) group do not improve, and those taking the real pill do improve, then it may be the case that the drug improves arthritis.

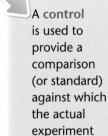

A control is used to provide a comparison (or standard) against which the actual experiment can be judged.

THE STUDY OF LIFE

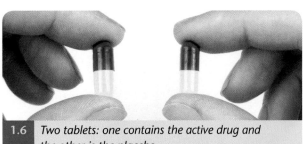

1.6   *Two tablets: one contains the active drug and the other is the placebo*

It has been found that the effect of a drug may be due to external factors such as the colour, size or number of tablets given in the test. For example, brightly coloured tablets may have a more beneficial effect, as may large tablets. For this reason the control group must have tablets of exactly the same colour, size and number as the test group.

4. Experiments must be fair

To ensure that experiments are as fair as possible the following four factors must be considered.

Sample size

Normally as large a sample as possible is tested. A large sample produces more reliable results.

When carrying out an experiment it is important that more than one person or object is tested. For example, when testing whether seedlings grow towards the light, a large number of seedlings are grown in each case.

In the same way, when testing a new drug to treat arthritis, if only one person was treated and recovered, the improvement may have been due to the person recovering of their own accord. However, if several hundred people were tested and all (or most) of them improved, then the result is more likely to be due to the drug given.

Random selection

When selecting a sample to be tested, the selection should be random. This is to prevent bias (or unfairness) by the person carrying out the experiment.

For instance, it would not be fair to grow and test seeds of only one size, or only normal-looking seeds, or only seeds that looked fully rounded. By testing a random selection of seeds (and seedlings) of different types, it is seen that the results apply to all seeds or seedlings.

In the same way, when testing the drug for arthritis, it would not be fair to select only males or only people over 50 years of age. If a certain type of sample is selected, the results may be influenced by the factor selected (e.g. the results may apply differently to females or those under 50 years of age).

Others must be able to replicate experiments

Experimental work is reported so that the information discovered is widely available to all. Once the work is properly reported it can be repeated by others. In this way the results can be shown to be always true and not caused by some unknown influence.

We often hear in the media of new 'wonder' cures. However, very often the work on which such cures is based is not published. Consequently the experiment(s) cannot be repeated or replicated by others.

For this reason, all experimental work is rigorously reported in scientific journals, so that other scientists can repeat the test and confirm or deny the results.

Guidelines for students on the recording and reporting of the 22 activities on this course are given on page vii.

Double blind testing

In a properly designed experiment neither the person being tested nor the tester should know who is receiving the real treatment or who is receiving the placebo.

A **replicate** is a repeat of an experiment.

Double blind means that both the investigator and the participant are unaware of the nature of the treatment the participant is receiving.

This means that the tester cannot influence the results of the experiment by consciously or unconsciously giving clues to the person being tested.

Limitations of the value of the scientific method

The scientific method is not always a perfect process. Its value is limited by the following five features.

1. The extent of our knowledge

The ability to form a hypothesis and design an experiment is dependent on the amount we know relating to our observations. It has often been said that more information would be discovered if we could only ask the correct questions. However, a basic amount of knowledge is required before the correct questions and hypotheses can be framed.

As time goes by, more knowledge is gained and more questions can be asked and, hopefully, answered. This is how science progresses.

2. The basis of investigation

If an investigation is badly designed or improperly carried out it will not yield results that are as valid as they should be.

The source of all scientific fact is careful observation and properly designed experiments. Experiments provide the information on which the conclusions are based.

Very often, control experiments are difficult to set up. This can lead to invalid experiments with dubious results. Sometimes hypotheses are based on such experiments.

For example, it is suggested that human activity (namely increased fossil fuel burning and deforestation) has increased carbon dioxide levels and that this, in turn, has caused global temperatures to increase.

The obvious control in this case would be a planet Earth on which there was no human activity. Of course, such a control is not possible. The lack of a suitable control may mean that factors apart from those proposed are causing the changes.

3. Interpreting results

If the results of an experiment are interpreted wrongly, then faulty conclusions and hypotheses may be drawn. It is important that the results of any experiment are analysed and considered in a proper manner. Sometimes it is very difficult to understand the results and form a valid conclusion.

Faulty interpretation of results occurred during the development of the drug **thalidomide** in the 1950s. This drug was used to treat morning sickness in human pregnancy.

Thalidomide was safely tested on many animals (including mammals such as rats and rabbits). The results of these tests were wrongly interpreted as suggesting that the drug was safe for humans. The problem was that the drug was not tested for its effects on human embryos in the womb. In fact, it caused major limb deformities in many babies born to women who took thalidomide during pregnancy. The drug was withdrawn in 1961.

1.7 *The effects of thalidomide*

4. Changes in the natural world

Sometimes the scientific method can lead to results that apply only to living things at one particular time. As living things are constantly changing (evolving), hypotheses must be constantly altered.

An example of this is the way in which antibiotics were thought to kill all bacteria. As a result, there was less research into new antibiotics. In recent times bacteria have emerged that are resistant to some or, more seriously, all antibiotics.

5. Accidental discoveries

New insights are often provided by accidental discoveries. Such findings have contributed enormously to the development of scientific thinking.

The discovery of the antibiotic **penicillin** in 1928 by Sir Alexander Fleming is a good example of an accidental discovery. Fleming carelessly left a petri dish of bacteria uncovered and it became contaminated by patches of a fungus. He noticed that the bacteria were killed in areas around the patches of fungus. He later confirmed that the chemical penicillin, produced by the fungus, had the ability to kill bacteria.

This accidental discovery had a huge effect on the treatment of bacterial infections. Notice that, although it was accidental, Fleming's discovery had much to do with his careful **observation** of the 'accident' and his accurate **interpretation** of the results. In addition, his discovery arose from his prior knowledge and work in the area of bacteriology.

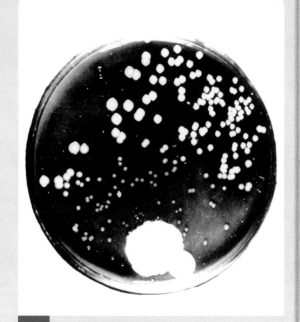

1.8 *Alexander Fleming's original petri dish: the small circles are bacteria and the large patch is the fungus*

Ethics relates to whether conduct is right or wrong.

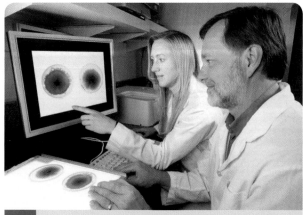

1.9 *Biotechnology: the orange fungus has a new gene to make vitamin A for people who are short of this vitamin*

Ethical issues

Sometimes there are arguments over whether the application of the scientific method is good or bad.

The main areas of disagreement tend to be based on issues such as:

- The use of captive animals in experiments
- The origin of life
- Whether or not evolution took place
- The way in which evolution may have taken place
- Medical issues such as contraception, abortion and assisted fertilisation
- Freezing human sperm and embryos
- Cloning animals
- The development and use of genetically altered plants and animals in agriculture
- The use of stem cells from embryos to form new tissues or organs
- Organ transplants, especially from animals to humans.

Summary

Science is the study of the physical, material and living world.

Biology is the study of living things.

The **scientific method** is based on:
- Making observations
- Forming a hypothesis
- Carrying out experiments
- Recording the results
- Forming a conclusion
- Discarding, changing or accepting the hypothesis based on the conclusions.

A **hypothesis** is an educated guess based on observations.

An **experiment** is a test for a hypothesis.

Data is the information gathered in experiments.

A **theory** is an explanation based on repeated hypotheses and experimentation.

A **principle** or **law** arises from a theory when it is seen always to be true under all conditions over a long period of time.

Experiments are based on:
- Careful planning and design
- Safe procedures
- Establishing a control (or comparison) which differs in only one variable from the real experiment
- Fair procedures such as:
  - Large sample size
  - Random selection
  - Reporting experiments publicly so they can be replicated
  - Double blind testing.

A **replicate** is when an experiment is repeated.

The **value of the scientific method** is limited by issues such as:
- Lack of basic knowledge
- Design of the experiment
- Difficulty in interpreting results
- Changes in nature
- Accidental discoveries.

Ethics refers to whether issues are right or wrong.

Revision questions

1 Define: **(a)** Science **(b)** Biology.

2 Name the area of biology studied by each of the following:
(a) Botanist **(c)** Biochemist **(e)** Zoologist
(b) Ecologist **(d)** Mycologist **(f)** Geneticist.

3 Jenner's work can be criticised on the grounds of **(a)** bad experimental design and **(b)** lack of safety. Explain these criticisms of his work.

4 Different humans have different heartbeat rates. List four variables (factors) that might cause such variations.

5 A test is given to a class of 20 pupils. The average result is 42%. Half the class is given homework for 2 weeks and the other half is not given homework. When re-tested, those given homework scored 58%.
(a) What hypothesis is being tested?
(b) Suggest a major flaw in this experiment.
(c) How could this flaw be corrected?
(d) Do the results, as given here, support the hypothesis that homework improves test results? Explain your answer.

6 List the three ways in which the results of an experiment may affect the hypothesis.

7 If the results of an experiment do not fully support the hypothesis, what should be done next?

8 Explain what is meant by:
(a) An observation **(e)** A theory
(b) A hypothesis **(f)** A principle
(c) An experiment **(g)** A replicate
(d) Data **(h)** A variable.

9 List four safety procedures that should be followed in a classroom experiment.

10 In terms of experimentation:
(a) What is a control?
(b) How should the control compare to the actual experiment?

11 State the need for each of the following experimental procedures:
(a) Large sample sizes
(b) Random selection
(c) Reporting the experiment
(d) Repeating the experiment.

12 **(a)** What do you understand by double blind testing?
(b) State the importance of this procedure.

13 **(a)** What is meant by ethical issues?
(b) Name three ethical issues associated with biology.
(c) Give a full account of the arguments surrounding any one of the issues you have named.

THE STUDY OF LIFE

Exam questions

Section A

14 Explain each of the following terms in relation to the scientific method.
  (a) Hypothesis   **(d)** Replicate
  (b) Control   **(e)** Theory
  (c) Data

(2005 HL Q 2)

15 Answer the following, which relate to the scientific method, by completing the blank spaces.
  (a) As a result of her observations a scientist may formulate a _____. She will then progress her investigation by devising a series of _____ and then carefully analysing the resulting _____.
  (b) Why is a control especially important in biological investigations?
  (c) If a scientist wished to determine the effect of a certain herbicide on weed growth she would include a control in the investigation. Suggest a suitable control in this case.
  (d) The use of replicates is an important aspect of scientific research. What, in this context, are replicates?
  (e) Suggest where a scientist may publish the results of her investigations.

(2008 HL Q 3)

Section B

16 **(a)** In relation to the scientific method, explain each of the following:
    (i) Experiment
    (ii) Theory.

(b) Scientists investigated the effect of a certain mineral on the growth of wheat. Use your knowledge of biology and laboratory procedures to answer the following questions.
   (i) Suggest a reason why the seeds used were all taken from one parent plant.
  (ii) The compost in which the wheat plants were grown was sterilised at the start of the investigation.
      1. Suggest a way in which the scientists may have sterilised the compost.
      2. State **one** reason why it was important to sterilise the compost.
 (iii) Why did the scientists divide the young wheat plants into two equal groups?
  (iv) During the investigation the scientists kept the two groups of plants under identical conditions. Why was this?
   (v) Name **two** conditions you think the scientists would have kept constant during the investigation.
  (vi) Why did the scientists repeat the investigation several times before publishing their results in a scientific journal?

(2011 HL Q 7)

Previous examination questions

Ordinary level	Higher level
2011 Q 8	2005 Q 2
	2008 Q 3
	2010 Q 8
	2011 Q 7
Latest questions at www.edco.ie/lcbiologyplus/examhelp	

Online test and assessment tracker

Scan the QR code and test yourself on chapter 1
www.edco.ie/lcbiologyplus

Chapter 2 The characteristics of life

Learning objectives

- To describe the diversity of living organisms and the features and characteristics that make them 'living'
- To define the terms 'life', 'metabolism' and 'continuity of life'
- To define and identify the 'characteristics of life': organisation, nutrition, excretion, response and reproduction.

The diversity of life

It is estimated that there are about 10 million different types of living things on Earth. These include:

- Microscopic organisms, such as: bacteria found on our skin and in decaying material; plankton in ponds and sea water; and single-celled organisms such as *Amoeba* found in freshwater ponds and pools
- Larger living things, including: fungi such as moulds and mushrooms; plants such as ferns, mosses, grasses, flowers and trees; and animals such as earthworms, insects, snails, fish, frogs, snakes, birds and humans.

> An **organism** is a living thing.
>
> **Metabolism** is the sum of all the chemical reactions in an organism.
>
> **Continuity of life** means that living things arise from other living things of the same type.

2.1 *Koala: an animal with a low metabolic rate*

Metabolism

Metabolism includes reactions and processes such as growth, movement, response, respiration and excretion.

Metabolic reactions are controlled by chemicals called enzymes. Organisms with a high metabolic rate, such as mice, are fast-acting. Those with a low metabolic rate, such as tortoises, are slow-acting.

Continuity of life

For centuries it was thought that living things could arise from non-living matter. People saw that maggots formed on rotting meat and frogs emerged from dried mud. The presumption was that the meat made the maggots and the mud formed the frogs.

It was not until the 1800s that it was first accepted that life originates only from living things of the same type. We now know that maggots develop from eggs laid in the meat by flies (with the maggots themselves turning into flies) and the frogs emerge from the mud because they had hibernated there during the winter.

Life

It is relatively easy to determine that a human, a dandelion and a ladybird are alive and that a rock is not. However, the distinction between living and non-living cannot be reduced to one single factor. It is in fact rather difficult to define life.

Life is said to consist of the possession of **all** of a series of five characteristics. The possession of any one, or a number, of these characteristics does not constitute life. They must **all** be present.

The five characteristics of life are necessary for organisms to maintain their metabolism and continuity of life. In particular, these characteristics allow organisms to carry out all the reactions necessary to survive and reproduce.

You might remember the characteristics using the phrase:

Our	Notes	Expand	Real	Results
Organisation	Nutrition	Excretion	Response	Reproduction

The characteristics of life

Organisation

Life is defined as the possession of all the following characteristics: organised, requiring nutrition and excretion, capable of responding and reproducing.

Life requires that living things are highly organised. The basic organisational feature of life is that living things are composed of cells.

Some organisms, such as bacteria and *Amoeba*, are single-celled (unicellular), whereas organisms such as trees and humans are composed of billions of cells. Cells contain all the chemicals that are necessary for life.

Organisation means that living things are composed of cells, tissues, organs and organ systems.

As Chapter 8 explains, cells are arranged into groups (called tissues) that perform similar functions. In turn, a number of tissues may be arranged into structures called organs. A series of organs forms an organ system. Each individual organism may be composed of a number of organ systems.

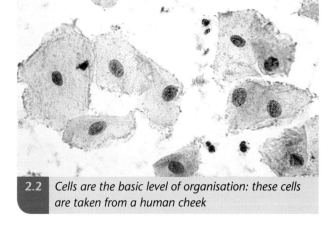

2.2 *Cells are the basic level of organisation: these cells are taken from a human cheek*

It is often said that structure relates to function. If any of the structures shown in the table to the left is damaged in any way, there is a loss of some basic function.

Nutrition is the way organisms obtain and use food.

Organisation in living things	
Structure	**Example in humans**
Cell	Stomach cell
Tissue	Lining of stomach
Organ	Stomach
Organ system	Digestive system
Organism	Human

Nutrition

Food is needed for energy and to supply the materials needed for normal life.

Plants, algae, some bacteria and plankton absorb chemicals from their surroundings and use sunlight energy to make food in a process called photosynthesis.

Animals, fungi, *Amoeba* and most bacteria take in their food from other organisms.

The Sun is the basic source of energy for all nutrition. Plants use sunlight directly to make food. The energy in plants is passed on to animals when they eat plants. In this way, energy is said to **flow** from the Sun to plants and then to animals.

$$Sun \xrightarrow{\text{energy}} Plants \xrightarrow{\text{energy}} Animals$$

2.3 *The flow of energy*

Excretion

Excretion is the removal of waste products of metabolism from the body.

In order to survive, organisms must maintain a fairly constant balance between their inside and outside environments. Excretion helps to provide this balance.

Many processes produce poisonous waste that could damage the organism if allowed to accumulate. It is important to remove (excrete) these toxic materials.

Plants have less need for excretion than animals because they make their own food and do not produce or take in as much waste. Plants excrete waste gases through openings called stomata on the underside of their leaves.

Advanced animals transfer waste internally from their cells to the blood. The liver is especially important in this process because it breaks down toxic material. The blood carries the waste to the excretory structures that take it out of the organism.

In humans these excretory structures are the skin, lungs and urinary system (i.e. kidneys and bladder). The main products excreted are carbon dioxide, salts and surplus water.

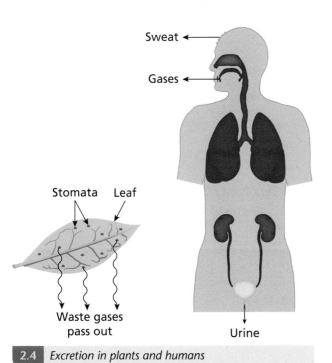

2.4 *Excretion in plants and humans*

Response

Living things have to respond in order to react to changes (or stimuli) in their internal and external environments (or surroundings). Response is also called behaviour.

Response is the way in which all living things react to changes in their environment.

2.5 *A plant responding to light*

Animals have fast responses, very often in the form of movement, to stimuli such as light, temperature, pressure, pain and sound. To allow for responses animals have structures such as eyes, ears, nose, tongue and skin.

Plant responses tend to be slower and less obvious than those of animals. Plants grow and move in response to factors such as water, light, gravity, touch and chemicals.

Most animals move very obviously from place to place. Plants move by changing their growth, e.g. stems bend towards light, roots grow down into the soil towards gravity, leaves turn to face the sun, the daisy opens and closes its petals in response to light (hence the name *daisy*, from *day's eye*).

THE STUDY OF LIFE

THE STUDY OF LIFE

Reproduction

All life develops only from living things. This means it is essential that organisms can produce offspring of their own type.

Reproduction may be sexual or asexual.

- Sexual reproduction occurs in most animals and plants. It involves the joining of two sex cells (called gametes) formed by two parents. The offspring will carry genetic information from both parents and will show features that are a combination of maternal (mother's) and paternal (father's) features.
- Asexual reproduction often involves simple organisms splitting into two or more identical offspring.

> **Reproduction** is the production of new individuals.
>
> **Sexual reproduction** involves the union of sex cells.
>
> **Asexual reproduction** does not involve the union of sex cells.

Living versus non-living

As stated earlier, there is no simple, clear-cut definition of life. Instead we say that living things must display a number of characteristics. Some of these are shared by non-living things, but only living things show all of them.

The difficulty of distinguishing living from non-living				
Characteristic	**Living**		**Non-living**	
	Human	**Oak tree**	**Rock**	**Flame**
Organised into cells etc.	✓	✓	✗	✗
Nutrition	✓	✓	✗	✓ (Needs a fuel)
Excretion	✓	✓	✗	✓ (Waste gases)
Response	✓	✓	✓ (Rolls when pushed)	✓ (Moves in wind)
Reproduction	✓	✓	✓ (Breaks if hit)	✓ (One flame lights a second)

Summary

Life and living things show all of the following characteristics:

- Organised into cells, tissues, organs, organ systems and organisms
- Nutrition
- Excretion
- Response
- Reproduction

Metabolism is the sum of all the chemical reactions in an organism.

The continuity of life means that life can arise only from living things of the same type.

Revision questions

1 Which of the characteristics of life are shown by:
   (a) A car
   (b) A burning match
   (c) A light bulb
   (d) A growing tree?

2 How does plant movement differ from animal movement?

3 What characteristic of life distinguishes a dead log from a rock?

4 One candle is used to light a second candle.
   (a) Is this reproduction?
   (b) How does it differ from reproduction in an organism?

5 There must have been one exception to the statement that life comes from life. What is the exception?

6 (a) List three stimuli in each case to which (i) plants and (ii) animals respond.
   (b) Name a stimulus that affects only animals.

7 Give a reason why animals tend to have complex excretory systems when compared with plants.

8 (a) What is metabolism?
   (b) Name three processes that form part of an organism's metabolism.

   (c) What kind of metabolic rate has a hyperactive child?
   (d) How does the metabolic rate of a frog differ between summer and winter?

9 It was once thought that swallows appearing in spring and mould appearing on bread were examples of life arising from non-life.
   (a) Explain the term 'continuity of life'.
   (b) Where do
       (i) the swallows and
       (ii) the mould come from?

10 (a) Life involves the interaction of five processes. Name these processes.
   (b) Give a brief description of each process.

11 Say whether the following statements are true or false. In the case of a false statement, give a reason why it is false.
   (a) Metabolism includes both digestion and respiration.
   (b) Energy is recycled between plants and animals.
   (c) The growth of bacteria on rotten meat is an example of the continuity of life.
   (d) Excretion does not occur in all forms of life.

Previous examination questions

Ordinary level	Higher level
n/a	n/a
[No questions asked on this chapter to date]	

Latest questions at www.edco.ie/lcbiologyplus/examhelp

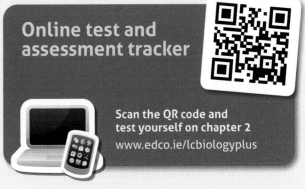

Online test and assessment tracker

Scan the QR code and test yourself on chapter 2
www.edco.ie/lcbiologyplus

Chapter 3 **Food**

Learning objectives

- To explain why living organisms need food
- To identify the different elements present in food
- To describe the roles of carbohydrates, proteins and lipids in structure and metabolism
- To define the terms 'anabolic reaction' and 'catabolic reaction' and give an example of each
- To describe the role of one water-soluble vitamin and one fat-soluble vitamin in metabolism and disorders associated with the deficiency of those vitamins
- To describe the requirement and use of two minerals present in plants and animals as dissolved salts or trace amounts
- To describe why water is important for living things
- To conduct tests for starch, fat, reducing sugar and protein.

The need for food

Nutrition is the way in which an organism obtains and uses food. Nutrients are the chemical substances, present in food, that are used by organisms. Nutrients are essential to maintain metabolism and continuity of life for all living organisms. In particular, nutrients are necessary:

- As a source of energy
- To make chemicals needed for metabolic reactions
- As the raw materials for the growth and repair of structures in the organism.

The elements present in food

Food is mainly made of 14 elements. Apart from carbon, hydrogen and oxygen, the rest of these elements are often called minerals.

- The six common elements found in food are: carbon (C), hydrogen (H), oxygen (O), nitrogen (N), phosphorus (P) and sulfur (S). The first four of these elements make up over 99% of the mass and atoms present in living organisms. Most of the chemical compounds found in living things are made from carbon atoms bonded together. Compounds made from carbon are said to be organic compounds.
- Five elements that are present as dissolved salts are: sodium (Na), magnesium (Mg), chlorine (Cl), potassium (K) and calcium (Ca).
- The three trace elements are: iron (Fe), copper (Cu) and zinc (Zn). Trace elements are elements that are only required in tiny amounts in the diet.

Biomolecules

 Biomolecules are chemicals that are made inside a living thing.

Biomolecules contain carbon and are also called biochemicals. The four major types of biomolecules found in food are: carbohydrates, lipids (fats, oils), proteins and vitamins.

Carbohydrates

Elements in carbohydrates

The elements present in carbohydrates are indicated by the name itself: carbon (C), hydrogen (H) and oxygen (O).

These elements are usually present in the ratio $Cx(H_2O)y$, where x and y are the same number (i.e. $x = y$). This means there is twice as much hydrogen as carbon or oxygen in a carbohydrate.

Glucose is a simple carbohydrate in which x and y are both equal to 6. The formula for glucose is $C_6H_{12}O_6$.

Types of carbohydrates

There are three types of carbohydrates: monosaccharides, disaccharides and polysaccharides.

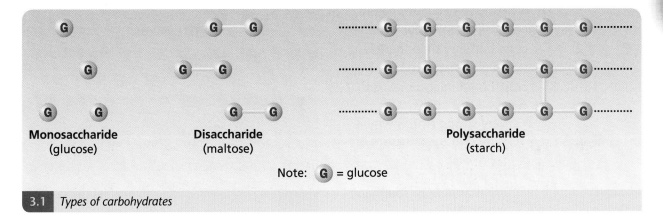

Monosaccharide (glucose) **Disaccharide** (maltose) **Polysaccharide** (starch)

Note: **G** = glucose

3.1 *Types of carbohydrates*

Monosaccharides

Monosaccharides are carbohydrates composed of a single sugar unit. A single sugar unit is a ring of carbon atoms. Monosaccharides are the simplest and smallest type of carbohydrate. They are sweet to taste and are soluble in water.

Glucose and fructose are examples of monosaccharides.

● Glucose is a very common molecule in biology. It is made by plants in photosynthesis and is the main molecule from which living things get their energy. It is commonly found in sweets, chocolate, fruit and soft drinks.

● Fructose has the same formula as glucose (however, its atoms are arranged differently). It is common in fruits and is much sweeter than glucose.

Disaccharides

Disaccharides are carbohydrates composed of two sugar units joined together. Like monosaccharides, they are sweet-tasting and soluble in water. Examples include maltose and sucrose.

● Maltose is found in germinating seeds and is composed of two glucose molecules joined together.

● Sucrose, or table sugar, is composed of a glucose joined to a fructose.

Polysaccharides

Polysaccharides are carbohydrates composed of many sugar units.

Polysaccharides are insoluble or only slightly soluble in water and are not sweet-tasting. They are very large molecules, often consisting of thousands of monosaccharides. Examples include starch, cellulose and glycogen.

Note that all monosac-charides and some disac-charides (e.g. maltose, but not sucrose) are reducing sugars.

- Starch (also called amylose) is made of many glucose molecules joined together. It is the carbohydrate stored by plants. Common examples of starch are bread, potatoes, rice and pasta.

  Starch is easily digested as the glucose molecules are arranged in a chain. To extract a glucose it is only necessary to break two bonds (see diagram 3.2).

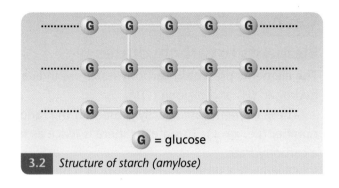

G = glucose

3.2 *Structure of starch (amylose)*

- Cellulose is also composed of many glucose molecules linked together. However, in cellulose there is much more cross-bonding than there is in starch (see diagram 3.3). This cross-bonding also means that cellulose is:
  - ▸ Very strong (this is why it is used in the structure of cell walls)
  - ▸ Very difficult to digest (we use it as fibre or roughage in our diet).

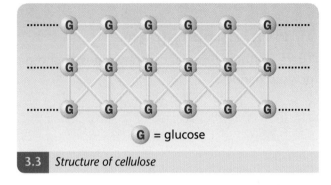

G = glucose

3.3 *Structure of cellulose*

- Glycogen is a complex polysaccharide. It is composed of large numbers of glucose molecules arranged in many-branched chains. Animals store glycogen in their liver and muscles.

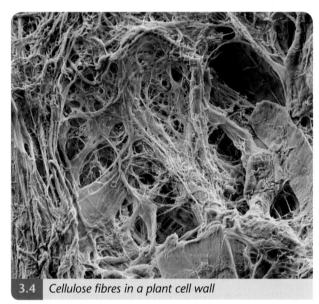

3.4 *Cellulose fibres in a plant cell wall*

Sources of carbohydrate

Common sources of carbohydrate in our diet are bread, potatoes, rice, pasta, sugars, fruits, sweets and cakes.

Structural role of carbohydrates

Cellulose is used to form plant cell walls.

3.5 *Foods rich in carbohydrate*

Metabolic role of carbohydrates

- Glucose is broken down in respiration to release energy. This energy is used to carry out many other metabolic reactions.
- Glucose is made in photosynthesis.

Lipids (fats and oils)

Elements in lipids

Lipids contain the elements carbon, hydrogen and oxygen. Unlike carbohydrates, the elements in lipids have no simple ratio. However, lipids have very little oxygen.

Fats are lipids that are solid at room temperature (20°C). Oils are lipids that are liquid at room temperature.

Structure of lipids

The smallest lipids are made of one molecule of glycerol linked to three fatty acid molecules. This structure is called a triglyceride. Different fats and oils have different types of fatty acids.

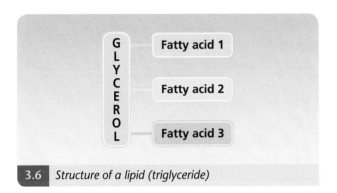

| 3.6 | *Structure of a lipid (triglyceride)* |

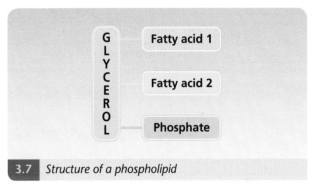

| 3.7 | *Structure of a phospholipid* |

Phospholipids are important in the structure of cell membranes (see Chapter 7).

Sources of lipids

Sources of lipids in our diet are butter, oils, margarine, cream, fat on meat and fried food. Lipids stain clothing.

Structural role of lipids

● Lipids are important food (or energy) stores in plants and animals. One gram of lipid contains twice as much energy as a gram of carbohydrate. This means that lipids can store twice as much energy compared with an equivalent amount of carbohydrate. This is especially important for animals that have to carry their stored energy around with them.

In animals, the stored lipids have secondary functions, such as heat insulation (fat under the skin) and protection of organs (fat around the heart and kidneys).

● Lipids combine with phosphorous to form phospholipids and with proteins to form lipoproteins. Both of these are important in the structure of cell membranes.

> Phospholipids are fat-like substances in which one of the fatty acids is replaced by a phosphate group or has a phosphate group added to it.

Metabolic role of lipids

Lipids can be broken down in respiration to release energy.

Proteins

Elements in proteins

Proteins contain the elements carbon, hydrogen, oxygen and nitrogen. They sometimes contain smaller amounts of sulfur and some may contain phosphorus and other elements. There is no ratio for the elements in a protein, but proteins are very large and complex, often containing tens of thousands of atoms.

Structure of proteins

Proteins are composed of amino acids. There are 20 common amino acids found in proteins.

The bond between amino acids is called a peptide bond. A peptide is made of a small number of amino acids (less than 20).

A polypeptide has more than 20 amino acids.

A protein is a long polypeptide (at least 200 amino acids). The amino acids that make up a protein can be thought of as the letters in an alphabet. By combining them in different sequences, nature can make a huge range of proteins.

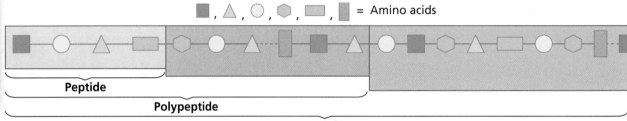

3.8 *Relationship between amino acids, peptides, polypeptides and proteins*

However, the way in which a protein works does not depend on the amino acid sequence alone. The manner in which the proteins are folded to take up three-dimensional (3-D) shapes is equally important.

> The importance of proteins folding in the correct way is seen when they fold incorrectly. Prions are proteins that do not fold correctly. They cause similar proteins to fold incorrectly and are responsible for brain and nervous system diseases such as bovine spongiform encephalopathy (BSE; in cattle), Creutzfeldt–Jakob disease (CJD; in humans) and scrapie (in sheep).

Fibrous proteins show little or no folding. They form long fibres and are strong and tough, e.g. keratin in hair, nails and feathers.

Globular proteins show lots of folding. They form rounded shapes, e.g. in egg white (albumen) and enzymes (see Chapter 9).

Sources of protein

Sources of protein include meat, fish, eggs, nuts, milk, peas and beans.

It is important to note that amino acids are not stored in the body. Surplus amino acids are taken to the liver and converted into urea, which is a toxic waste product. This process is called deamination. Urea is carried by the blood from the liver to the kidneys. In the kidneys, urea becomes part of urine and is excreted.

3.9 *Keratin: a protein found in hair and nails*

3.10 *Foods rich in protein*

Structural role of proteins

Fibrous protein such as keratin is found in skin and hair. Myosin is found in muscle.

Metabolic role of proteins

Proteins are used as enzymes to control reactions. They also form antibodies to fight infection. Some hormones are protein-based and are used to regulate body reactions.

Vitamins

Vitamins are complex carbon-based substances that the body cannot make. They are needed only in tiny amounts. Vitamins can be referred to by letters or by names based on their chemical structure.

Water-soluble vitamin

Vitamin C is called ascorbic acid. It is soluble in water. Common sources of vitamin C include vegetables and fresh fruits, especially citrus fruits such as oranges and lemons.

Metabolic role of vitamin C

Vitamin C is necessary for:
- The formation of connective tissue (tissue that surrounds body structures and holds them together) such as skin, gums, cartilage, ligaments and the cells that line the inside of blood vessels
- The growth and maintenance of bones and teeth
- Helping wounds to heal
- Helping the immune system to function properly.

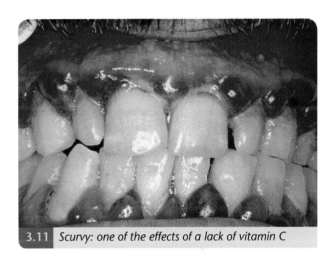

3.11 *Scurvy: one of the effects of a lack of vitamin C*

Deficiency of vitamin C

Disease: deficiency (lack) of vitamin C causes a disease called scurvy.
Symptoms: symptoms (or signs) of scurvy include poor healing of skin, bleeding under the skin (often seen as bruising) and bleeding gums with loose teeth.

Fat-soluble vitamin

There are a number of different types of vitamin D. The most common form is called calciferol. Vitamin D is soluble in fat.
   Good sources of vitamin D include liver, fish oils such as cod liver oil, milk and egg yolk. Vitamin D can be made by the action of ultraviolet rays on chemicals in the skin.

Metabolic role of vitamin D

Vitamin D helps to absorb calcium from the intestine. Therefore it is needed for healthy bone and tooth formation.

> **Syllabus** Although many vitamins are known, you are required by the syllabus to know only **one** water-soluble vitamin and **one** fat-soluble vitamin.

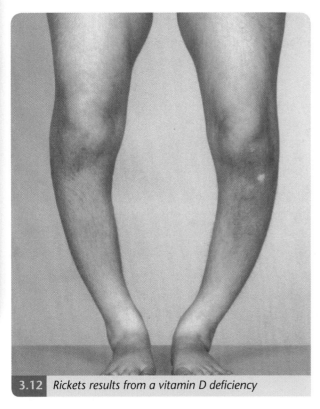

3.12 *Rickets results from a vitamin D deficiency*

Deficiency of vitamin D

Disease: a deficiency of vitamin D in children results in rickets. The adult equivalent of rickets is called osteomalacia.

Symptoms: the symptoms of both osteomalacia and rickets are weak, deformed bones that tend to break easily.

Minerals

Minerals are needed by plants and animals in small amounts for the following reasons:

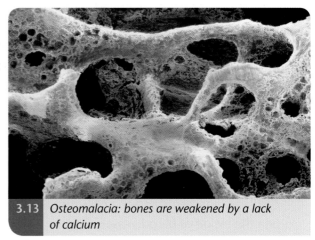

3.13 *Osteomalacia: bones are weakened by a lack of calcium*

Syllabus Although many minerals are used, you are required by the syllabus to know only **two** minerals used by plants and **two** used by animals.

● To form rigid body structures such as bone and the cement between plant cell walls (both contain calcium)
● To make soft body parts such as muscle (which requires nitrogen and sulfur)
● To form salts in cell and body fluids (tears, saliva and the liquid part of blood all contain sodium)
● To form biomolecules (such as haemoglobin, which is based on iron, and chlorophyll, which is based on magnesium).

Minerals needed by plants and animals				
	Mineral	**Symbol**	**Source**	**Use**
Plants	Magnesium	Mg	Salts in the soil	Helps form chlorophyll
	Calcium	Ca	Salts in the soil	Helps cell walls to attach to each other
Animals	Iron	Fe	Liver, meat, green vegetables	Helps form haemoglobin
	Calcium	Ca	Milk, cheese, dairy products	Helps form bones and teeth

Water

Water is the most abundant chemical in living things. It accounts for 99% of all the molecules in the human body. It comprises 60% of human body mass and 90% of the mass of most plants.

Life originated in water and living things are still dependent on water for their survival. Water is essential to life for three main reasons.

1. It is the liquid in which all metabolic reactions take place.
2. It provides the basis for transport systems in organisms.
3. It is the environment in which many organisms live.

Importance of water for living things

Component of cytoplasm and body fluids

Water is the most common chemical in cells. It is mainly found in the cytoplasm, which is the liquid that surrounds the nucleus in a cell.

In humans, about one-third of the body's water is found outside the cells. Some of this is in the form of tissue fluid, which surrounds all body cells, and the rest forms plasma, the liquid part of blood.

Good solvent

Water is a good solvent, i.e. it is able to dissolve a wide range of molecules.

- This allows chemical reactions to take place in water in the cytoplasm and in cell organelles.
- It also allows many molecules to be dissolved in water for transport in plants and animals.

Participates in chemical reactions

Water is directly involved in a number of biochemical reactions. These include:

- Photosynthesis: in which water is used to supply hydrogen ions and electrons
- Respiration: in which water is formed as an end product
- Digestion: in which water is needed to break down food. This is why we should take a drink when eating food.

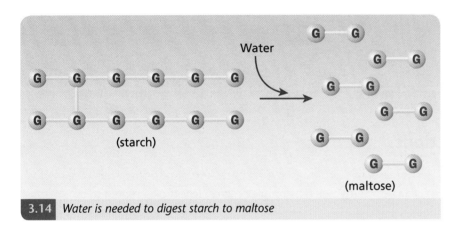

3.14 *Water is needed to digest starch to maltose*

Movement through membranes

Water can easily pass in or out through biological membranes (as will be described more fully in Chapter 13).

When cells absorb large amounts of water they become swollen. If cells lose water they shrivel and lose their shape. The loss of shape of cells can have serious results for the function of the cell. For example, if red blood cells lose shape, they absorb and carry less oxygen. If plant cells lose shape, the overall plant may also lose shape (a process called wilting).

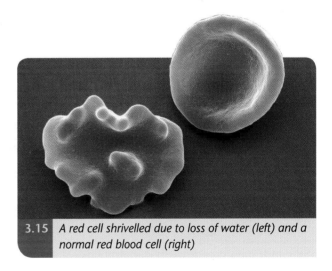

3.15 *A red cell shrivelled due to loss of water (left) and a normal red blood cell (right)*

Good absorber of heat

Water is a good absorber of heat energy. This means it is slow to heat up and slow to cool down. As a result:

- The oceans and other large bodies of water (and the organisms in them) have relatively stable temperatures
- The high water content of organisms helps to keep their temperature stable. This allows biological reactions to take place over a narrow temperature range (which means the reactions do not speed up or slow down due to the heating or cooling of the organism).

Energy transfer reactions

All the reactions taking place in an organism are referred to as its metabolism. Metabolic reactions can be divided into anabolic reactions and catabolic reactions.

Anabolic reactions

 Anabolic reactions use energy to convert smaller molecules into larger molecules.

Examples of anabolic reactions are the formation of muscle from amino acids (also called protein synthesis), the formation of cellulose from glucose and photosynthesis (where carbon dioxide and water are used to make a food such as glucose).

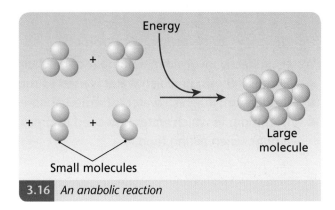

3.16 An anabolic reaction

 Anabolic steroids are drugs that are used (illegally) in sports to build up muscles.

Catabolic reactions

 Catabolic reactions release energy when a complex molecule is broken down to a simpler form.

Catabolic reactions include respiration (in which a molecule of food is broken down to release energy), the digestion of food and the decay of dead plants and animals.

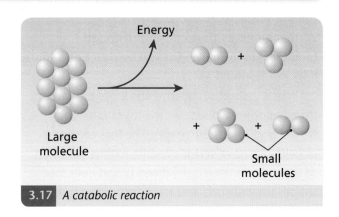

3.17 A catabolic reaction

Activity 1 To conduct qualitative tests for food

A qualitative test measures whether a substance is present or absent.

Activity 1a To test for reducing sugar

1. Dissolve glucose in water in a test tube.
2. Add an equal volume of Benedict's solution (which is blue).
3. In a second test tube mix equal volumes of water and Benedict's solution. This will act as a control.
4. Heat the test tubes in a boiling water bath.
5. If reducing sugar is present, the solution turns red (often called brick red).
6. If reducing sugar is not present the solution remains blue.

Note: Fehling's solution can be used instead of Benedict's solution.

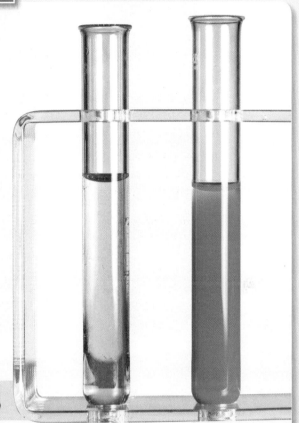

3.18 *Benedict's test for reducing sugar: a negative result (blue) and a positive result (red-orange)*

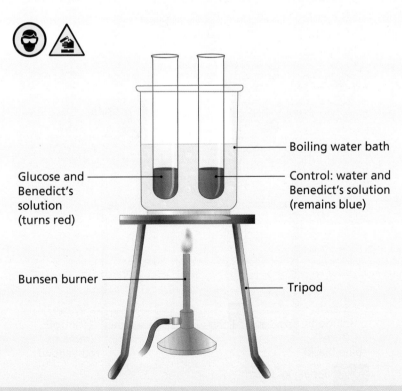

Boiling water bath

Glucose and Benedict's solution (turns red)

Control: water and Benedict's solution (remains blue)

Bunsen burner

Tripod

3.19 *Testing for reducing sugar*

THE STUDY OF LIFE

Activity 1b To test for starch

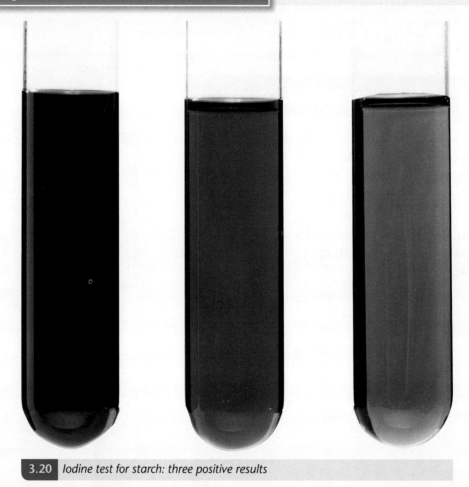

3.20 *Iodine test for starch: three positive results*

1. Add a few drops of iodine solution to some starch dissolved in water. (Iodine solution is a red-yellow colour.)
2. Add a few drops of iodine solution to some water. This acts as a control.
3. If starch is present the colour turns blue-black or purple.
4. If starch is absent the solution stays red-yellow.

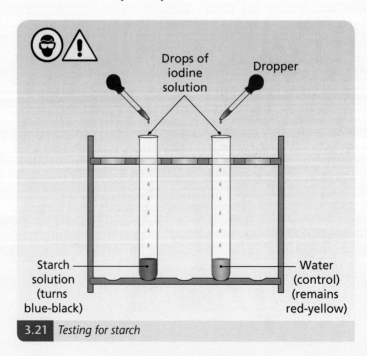

Drops of iodine solution

Dropper

Starch solution (turns blue-black)

Water (control) (remains red-yellow)

3.21 *Testing for starch*

Activity 1c To test for lipid

1. Label a piece of brown paper (or filter paper) as lipid.
2. Rub a small piece of butter or cooking oil (both lipids) on the paper.
3. Repeat the process using a few drops of water on a piece of paper labelled 'water'. (This acts as a control.)
4. Leave the two pieces of paper over a radiator to dry.
5. Lipid produces a permanent stain (or translucent spot) on the paper.
6. The water stain dries out.

Note: lipids can also be tested using Sudan III.

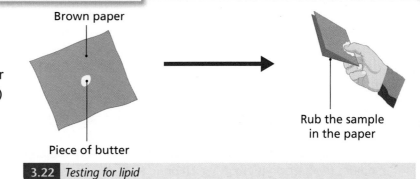

Brown paper

Piece of butter

Rub the sample in the paper

3.22 *Testing for lipid*

Activity 1d To test for protein

1. Dissolve a sample of soluble protein (e.g. egg white or milk) in water.
2. Add sodium hydroxide (colourless) until the solution clears.
3. Then add a few drops of dilute copper sulfate (blue).

Note: as an alternative to steps 2 and 3, add an equal volume of Biuret solution. This contains sodium hydroxide and copper sulfate and is blue.

3.24 *Biuret test for protein: a negative result (blue) and a positive result (purple)*

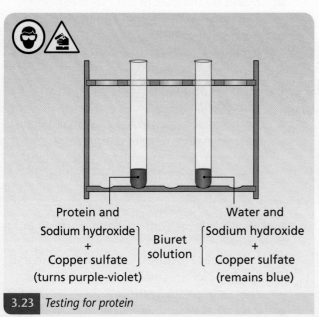

Protein and Sodium hydroxide + Copper sulfate (turns purple-violet)

Water and Sodium hydroxide + Copper sulfate (remains blue)

Biuret solution

3.23 *Testing for protein*

4. As a control, add sodium hydroxide and copper sulfate (or Biuret solution) to water.
5. The appearance of a purple-violet colour shows that proteins are present.
6. If protein is not present the colour remains blue.

Summary

Food provides the nutrients needed for organisms to get their energy and the materials they require to live.

Living things need 14 elements:
- The most common six elements are carbon (C), hydrogen (H), oxygen (O), nitrogen (N), phosphorus (P) and sulfur (S)
- The five elements in dissolved salts are sodium (Na), magnesium (Mg), chlorine (Cl), potassium (K) and calcium (Ca)
- The trace elements are iron (Fe), copper (Cu) and zinc (Zn).

Biomolecules are chemicals made inside living things.

The **biomolecules in food** are carbohydrates, lipids, proteins and vitamins.

Carbohydrates:
- Made of C, H and O in the ratio $Cx(H_2O)y$, where $x = y$
- Types: **(i)** monosaccharides (one sugar unit), e.g. glucose, fructose; **(ii)** disaccharides (two sugar units), e.g. sucrose, maltose; **(iii)** polysaccharides (many sugar units), e.g. starch, cellulose, glycogen
- Sources: bread, potato, rice, flour and sweets
- Structural role: cellulose forms cell walls
- Metabolic role: **(i)** glucose is made in photosynthesis; **(ii)** glucose releases energy in respiration
- Test: **(i)** reducing sugars – Benedict's or Fehling's solution; **(ii)** starch – iodine.

Lipids:
- Made of C, H and O
- Fats are solid and oils are liquid at room temperature
- Structure: glycerol and three fatty acids = triglyceride
- Sources: butter, cream, oils and fried food
- Structural role: **(i)** store energy; **(ii)** insulate; **(iii)** form membranes
- Metabolic role: release energy in respiration
- Test: brown paper.

Proteins:
- Made of C, H, O, N, (S, P)
- Structure: amino acids, peptides, polypeptides and protein
- Sources: meat, fish, eggs and milk
- Structural role: form structures such as skin, hair, nails and muscle

- Metabolic role: **(i)** enzymes; **(ii)** some hormones; **(iii)** antibodies
- Test: sodium hydroxide, then copper sulfate (the Biuret test).

Vitamin C (ascorbic acid):
- Water-soluble
- Sources: vegetables and fresh fruit
- Metabolic role: forms connective tissue, bones and teeth, helps healing and immune system
- Deficiency: scurvy (poor skin, bleeding, bad teeth and gums).

Vitamin D (calciferol):
- Fat-soluble
- Sources: liver, fish oils, milk, made in skin (ultraviolet rays)
- Metabolic role: helps absorb calcium for bones and teeth
- Deficiency: rickets in children, osteomalacia in adults (weak, deformed, brittle bones).

Minerals:
- Plants need calcium (absorbed from the soil) to hold cell walls together, and magnesium for chlorophyll
- Animals need calcium (in milk and cheese) for bones and teeth, and iron (in liver and green vegetables) for haemoglobin.

Water is important to living things because it:
- Makes up the bulk of the cytoplasm and is also found in tissue fluid and blood
- Is a good solvent that allows **(i)** cell reactions; **(ii)** transport
- Participates in chemical reactions
- Moves in and out of cells, giving them the correct shape
- Is a good absorber of heat (i.e. maintains its temperature despite temperature changes around it), which provides stable temperatures for living things and their reactions.

Metabolism is the sum of all the reactions in an organism:
- In anabolic reactions, energy is taken in and used to convert small molecules to larger ones, e.g. photosynthesis
- In catabolic reactions, larger molecules are broken down to smaller ones and energy is released, e.g. respiration.

Revision questions

1 Give the name and chemical symbol for:
   (a) The six most important elements in organisms
   (b) The five elements found in dissolved salts
   (c) Three trace elements.

2 (a) Explain what is meant by biomolecules.
   (b) Name four types of biomolecules found in food.

3 What elements are present in: (a) Table sugar (sucrose) (b) Meat (c) Butter?

4 (a) Distinguish between monosaccharides, disaccharides and polysaccharides.
   (b) Name one biomolecule from each of these three categories.

5 Name three polysaccharides and give one use for each of them.

6 A sample of urine when boiled with Benedict's solution turned red. What does this result tell you: (a) about the urine and (b) about the person from whom it was taken?

7 (a) Name the four elements in phospholipids.
   (b) Give one use for phospholipids.

8 (a) Describe how you would test milk for the presence of fat.
   (b) What observation indicates a positive result?

9 State one structural role and one metabolic role for: (a) Carbohydrates (b) Lipids (c) Proteins.

10 (a) What is meant by: (i) Metabolism (ii) Anabolism (iii) Catabolism?
   (b) State two examples of each process.

11 (a) Name two minerals required by plants.
   (b) State where plants get the named minerals.
   (c) Give one use for each mineral named.

12 (a) Name two minerals required by animals.
   (b) State where animals get the named minerals.
   (c) Give one use for each mineral named.

13 A picnic basket consists of brown bread, butter, apples, oranges, milk, ham, salmon, salt, cakes.
   (a) Name one good source from this list for:
       (i) Carbohydrate (ii) Protein (iii) Fat
       (iv) Vitamin C (v) Vitamin D
       (vi) Roughage (vii) Calcium
       (viii) Phosphorus.
   (b) Name three different carbohydrates and their sources from the above list.
   (c) Name a water-soluble and water-insoluble (i) carbohydrate and (ii) vitamin found in these foods.

14 (a) What is a solvent?
   (b) Give two biological benefits of water being a good solvent.

15 Name three reactions in which water plays a role.

16 Say whether the following statements are true or false. In the case of a false statement, give a reason why it is false.
   (a) Carbohydrates contain hydrogen and oxygen in the same ratio as water (H_2O).
   (b) Amino acids do not contain nitrogen.
   (c) Fish is a good source of protein and lipid, but not carbohydrate.
   (d) Amino acids are required to make fatty acids.
   (e) Keratin is a protein found in egg white.
   (f) The Biuret test indicates the presence of proteins.
   (g) Chewing food is an example of anabolism.

Exam questions

Section A

17 Answer five of the following by writing a word in the space provided.

   (a) Cellulose is an example of a structural _____.

   (b) Vitamins are either water-soluble or _____-soluble.

   (c) Fats are composed of oxygen, hydrogen and _____.

   (d) When an iodine solution is added to a food sample and remains red-brown in colour, _____ is absent.

   (e) When two monosaccharides unite they form a _____.

   (f) Removal from the body of the waste products of metabolism is called _____.

   (2005 HL Q 1)

18 Answer five of the following by filling in the blank spaces.
   (a) Biomolecules of the general formula $Cx(H_2O)y$ are examples of _____.

THE STUDY OF LIFE

(b) Give two functions of water in a living organism.

(c) Is energy release a feature of anabolic or catabolic reactions?

(d) How do fats differ from oils at room temperature?

(e) Name the test or give the chemicals used to detect the presence of protein in a food sample.

(f) Name a structural polysaccharide.

(2008 HL Q 1)

19 Answer **five** of the following:

(a) In carbohydrates, which two elements are in the ratio 2:1?

(b) Cellulose is a polysaccharide. Explain the term *polysaccharide.*

(c) Name a polysaccharide other than cellulose.

(d) Where precisely in a plant cell would you expect to find cellulose?

(e) Name a test or give the chemicals used to demonstrate the presence of a reducing sugar.

(f) In relation to the test referred to in (e) which of the following is correct?
   1. No heat needed.
   2. Heat but do not boil.
   3. Boil.

(2009 HL Q 1)

20 Answer **five** of the following by filling in the blank spaces.

(a) In relation to the human diet, what is meant by a trace element?

(b) Give an example of a trace element.

(c) State **one** way in which an oil differs from a fat.

(d) Vitamins may be divided into two groups depending upon their solubility. Name these **two** groups.

(e) What is a triglyceride?

(f) Give an example of a catabolic reaction in a cell.

(2010 HL Q 1)

21 Indicate whether each of the following statements is true (T) or false (F) by drawing a circle around T or F in each case.

Example: Polysaccharide molecules contain many sugar units. Ⓣ F

   (i) Cellulose is a protein. T F
   (ii) Iodine turns starch to a blue-black colour. T F
   (iii) Lipids are made of amino acids. T F
   (iv) All vitamins are fat soluble. T F
   (v) Eggs are a good source of fat in the diet. T F
   (vi) Nitrogen is a trace element. T F
   (vii) Glucose is a monosaccharide. T F

(2010 OL Q 2)

22 Answer **five** of the following:

(a) Which food type may be identified in the laboratory by the use of Sudan III or brown paper?

(b) Give one role for a **named** mineral in plants.

(c) What colour indicates a strong positive result of the Fehling's or Benedict's test for reducing sugar?

(d) Give a role of lipids in cells.

(e) Give a role of water in the human body other than as a component of cytoplasm and body fluids.

(f) How many common amino acids are found in proteins?

(2011 HL Q 1)

Section B

23 (a) (i) State one reason that your body needs protein.

   (ii) Name the element, other than carbon, hydrogen and oxygen, which is always found in protein.

(b) Answer the following questions in relation to tests that you carried out for protein.

   (i) Name two foods in which you found protein.

   (ii) What reagent or chemicals did you use to test for protein?

   (iii) Was heat necessary in the test that you carried out?

   (iv) What was the initial colour of the reagent or chemicals?

   (v) What colour change occurred if protein was present?

   (vi) Was there a colour change in the control?

(2007 OL Q 8)

24 (a) The main ingredient in a sports drink is water.

   (i) Give **one** reason why the body needs water.

   (ii) Give **one** way in which water is lost from the body.

(b) The composition of a **colourless** sports drink is to be investigated. Use your knowledge of food testing to answer the following:

   1. (i) Name the test **or** name the chemical used to test the sports drink for the presence of glucose (reducing sugar).

(ii) If glucose is present in the drink, what colour change would you expect to see? In your answer give the initial **and** final colour of the test solution.

(iii) Is heat necessary for this test?

2. **(i)** Name the test **or** give the chemicals used to test the sports drink for the presence of protein.

(ii) If protein is present in the drink, what colour change would you expect to see? In your answer give the initial **and** final colour of the test solution.

(iii) Is heat necessary for this test?

(2009 OL Q 7)

Section C

25 (a) **(i)** The same elements are found in carbohydrates and fats. Name these elements.

(ii) State one way in which carbohydrates differ from fats.

(iii) How do phospholipids differ from other lipids?

(b) Carbohydrates are classified as monosaccharides, disaccharides and polysaccharides.

(i) Name a monosaccharide and state a role for it in living organisms.

(ii) What is a disaccharide?

(iii) Cellulose is a polysaccharide. What is it formed from? State a role for cellulose in living organisms.

(iv) Name a polysaccharide that has a different role to cellulose. What is the role of the polysaccharide that you have named?

(v) Describe a test for a named polysaccharide.

(c) Answer the following in relation to a test for

1. A reducing sugar   2. A protein.

(i) Name the reagent(s) used.

(ii) State the initial colour of the reagent.

(iii) State whether the test requires heat.

(iv) What colour indicates a positive result?

(2004 HL Sample Q 10)

Previous examination questions

Ordinary level	Higher level
2004 Q 5, 10	2005 Q 1
2005 Q 5	2006 Q 7
2006 Q 3	2007 Q 1
2007 Q 1, 8	2008 Q 1
2008 Q 2	2009 Q 1
2009 Q 1, 7	2010 Q 1, 8
2010 Q 2	2011 Q 1
2011 Q 1	2012 Q 1
2012 Q 1, 9	

Latest questions at www.edco.ie/lcbiologyplus/examhelp

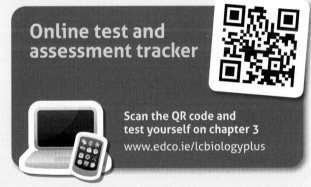

Online test and assessment tracker

Scan the QR code and test yourself on chapter 3
www.edco.ie/lcbiologyplus

Chapter 4 **Ecology**

Learning objectives

- To define the terms 'ecology', 'ecosystem', 'biosphere' and 'habitat'
- To define 'abiotic', 'biotic' and 'climatic' factors and give examples of each in relation to terrestrial and aquatic environments
- To define 'edaphic' factors and give examples in relation to terrestrial environments
- To describe how energy flows from the Sun along feeding pathways
- To explain, construct and use food chains, food webs and pyramids of numbers
- To explain the term 'niche'
- To define 'nutrient recycling' by organisms and describe the carbon cycle and nitrogen cycle
- To define 'pollution' and describe its effects and control, focusing on one particular human activity
- To define the term 'conservation' and describe it in relation to one of agriculture, fisheries or forestry
- To describe 'waste management', the problems associated with waste disposal, and the importance of minimising waste
- To describe how micro-organisms can be used in waste management and pollution control.

Ecology

Ecology is the study of the interactions between living things (organisms) and between organisms and their environment.

All the external factors that influence an organism are referred to as its **environment**.

Biosphere

> The **biosphere** is that part of the planet containing living organisms.

The biosphere extends from about 8 km deep in the oceans to 8 km high in the sky. It includes the air, the seas and soil and rock.

Ecosystem

> An **ecosystem** is a group of clearly distinguished organisms that interact with their environment as a unit.

The entire Earth is itself an ecosystem because no part of it is completely isolated from the rest. This global ecosystem forms the biosphere.

The biosphere consists of many large ecosystems. Conditions such as the climate, soil, plants and animals in each ecosystem are similar, even though they may be located in different regions around the planet.

Ecosystems can be very large. For example, deciduous forests once covered much of Europe. Nowadays, because of pressure on land for agriculture and housing, large areas of forest have been cleared. As a result, forests have been divided up into smaller units called woodlands. Woodlands are clearly distinguished ecosystems, as are grasslands, bogs, lakes, sand dune systems, salt-marshes, rocky seashores and hedgerows.

4.1 | *A rocky seashore*

4.2 | *A grassland*

The table below outlines some common ecosystems.

Examples of ecosystems		
Ecosystem	**Features**	**Sample locations**
Temperate deciduous forest	Warm summer, rain plentiful	Western Europe (includes Ireland), Eastern USA
Desert	Low rainfall	Sahara Desert, Gobi Desert
Tropical rain forest	High temperatures and high rainfall	Brazil, West Africa, parts of South-East Asia
Grassland	Mild temperatures, low rainfall	Steppes of Asia, pampas in South America, prairies in North America
Freshwater	Non-salty water	Rivers, lakes, wetlands
Marine	Salt water	Seashores and oceans

Habitat

Syllabus This book will concentrate on habitats in two sample ecosystems: a rocky seashore and a grassland. You need study only **one ecosystem** for examination purposes.

A **habitat** is the place where a plant or animal lives.

A habitat is also the place that we study to learn more about an ecosystem. As ecosystems can be very large, it is common to select a number of small, local areas or habitats to study. The study of the local habitat gives a representation of how an ecosystem functions.

A **population** is all the members of the same species living in an area.

We speak of a population of frogs in a pond or a population of primroses in a wood.

A **community** is all the different populations in an area.

For instance, all the plants, animals, fungi and micro-organisms living in a field or bog are a community.

THE STUDY OF LIFE

Environmental factors affecting organisms

The four categories of factors that influence the life and distribution of organisms are: abiotic, biotic, climatic and edaphic factors. Note that these four factors can affect living things by their variations (a) in levels and (b) from season to season. For example, the daily variation in temperature may affect the types of plants growing in an area. Plants are also affected by the changes in light and temperature from season to season. Note that the climatic factors and most of the edaphic factors are also abiotic factors.

Abiotic factors include altitude, aspect (the direction a surface faces), steepness, exposure, currents. Examples of the effects of abiotic factors:
- Higher altitudes are cooler, wetter and windier than lower altitudes; trees and other producers cannot live at higher altitudes
- North-facing slopes are cooler and darker than south-facing slopes; as a result, more plants grow on south-facing slopes.

Biotic factors include food, competition, predation, parasitism, pollination, seed dispersal and human intervention. Examples of the effects of biotic factors:
- The more food that is available, the greater the number of organisms that will survive; for example, the number of berries affects the number of blackbirds and the amount of plankton affects the number of mussels
- Competition means that plants and animals fight for scarce resources such as food, space, mates and shelter; for example, rabbits compete with each other for food, and barnacles and limpets compete for space on rocks.

Climatic factors include temperature, rainfall, humidity (the amount of water vapour in the air), day length, light intensity, wind and salinity (salt concentration).
- Temperature affects the rate of reactions in living things. This means that higher temperatures cause rapid plant growth in summer and lower temperatures cause hibernation in hedgehogs and frogs in winter.
- Rainfall provides the water that is essential for life. This means that only plants such as cacti can live in areas of low rainfall (deserts). Plants in tropical rain forests require high and regular rainfall (along with high temperatures).

Edaphic factors include soil pH, soil type and organic matter (humus) in the soil, along with the water, air and mineral content of the soil.
- Plants and animals are adapted to specific pH values in the soil. For example:
  - Acid soils (e.g. bogs) have a pH less than 7 and support bog moss and heather
  - Neutral soils have pH values close to 7 and are preferred by most plants
  - Alkaline soils have pH values greater than 7 and are preferred by lime-loving plants, e.g. birdsfoot trefoil and bee orchid.
- Soil type is determined by the size of soil particles:
  - Sandy soils have large soil particles. This gives the soil good drainage and air content. However, sandy soils may have low mineral and water content.

> Abiotic factors are non-living factors.
>
> Biotic factors are living factors.
>
> Climatic factors refer to weather over a long period of time.
>
> Edaphic factors relate to soil.

4.3 *Soil types: sandy soil, loam and clay soil (left to right)*

- ▸ Sandy soils have few earthworms (due to the lack of decayed organic matter, or humus). Marram grass growing in sand hills has to have long, deep roots to absorb moisture deep down in the soil.
- ▸ Clay soils have small particles. This means that the soil is impermeable to water and air. It also causes these soils to be waterlogged easily.
- ▸ Plants do not grow well in clay soils, as the soil is too wet and difficult for roots to penetrate.

Aquatic environments

Aquatic environments (e.g. ponds, lakes, oceans, rivers, streams) have special factors of influence.

- In land-based (terrestrial) ecosystems, the most important environmental factors are often temperature and rainfall, with light being relatively abundant.
- In aquatic environments, temperature is less important because it doesn't vary so rapidly, but although water is plentiful, lack of light may be a problem.

Special factors in aquatic environments

Light

Water interferes with the penetration of light. This means plants are limited to the upper layers of water and those that attach to the bottom can grow only in shallow waters.

Animals can be found at great depths. They feed off organisms that fall down from the upper layers.

> **Syllabus** Even if you are studying a land-based habitat you must be aware of the factors that relate to aquatic habitats.

Currents

Flowing water will cause plants to be carried away if they are not attached. Animals are better able to resist currents because they can move.

Wave action

Waves create currents. They also cause physical damage to organisms. Seaweeds avoid this by being flexible. Animals are often protected by a shell (e.g. limpets and barnacles).

Salt content

Most aquatic organisms are adapted to either freshwater or salt-water environments. If the external solution is unsuitable, they have problems with gaining or losing water (osmoregulation).

Some organisms (especially those in rock pools), can survive changes in salt content (salinity) due to rain or fresh water.

Oxygen concentration

The oxygen concentration in water is much lower than that of air. This affects the plant and animal life in water. The organisms must be able to extract oxygen from the water (e.g. they may have gills or large surface area to volume ratios).

4.4 *Barnacles (left), periwinkles (large shells) and spiral wrack (right)*

Energy flow

Every ecosystem requires a constant input of energy from an external source in order to function properly. The Sun is the primary source of energy for our planet.

Feeding allows energy to flow from one organism to another in an ecosystem.

Producers

Flora includes plants, seaweeds and plankton. All of these are producers. About 1% of sunlight is trapped by green plants and used to make food. The Sun's energy is stored by plants in the chemical bonds of molecules such as glucose and starch.

Plants break down most of these molecules to release energy. This process is called respiration. They use the energy to do work such as making new cells or repairing old ones. However, most of their energy is lost in the form of heat and only a small proportion (about 10%) is passed on to other organisms.

When an animal eats a plant or another animal, the food that is consumed contains energy. Feeding represents a flow of energy. This means that energy moves in one direction, i.e.

- *Sun → plant → animal 1 → animal 2 → etc.*
- *Sun → primary producer → primary consumer → secondary consumer → etc.*

Consumers

All animals are consumers.
Primary consumers feed on producers.
They include:

- Herbivores (animals that feed on vegetation)
- Decomposers (organisms that feed on dead organic matter such as bacteria and fungi)
- Detritus feeders (organisms that feed on small parts of dead and decomposing plants and animals such as mussels and earthworms).

4.5 *A caterpillar feeding on a leaf*

Secondary consumers are animals that feed on primary consumers. They include:

- Carnivores (meat-eaters)
- Scavengers (which feed on animals killed by other sources).

Tertiary consumers feed on secondary consumers. They are not always present. If no other organism feeds on them, they are called **top consumers**.

Organisms that feed on both plants and animals are called omnivores. Examples include gulls, blackbirds, badgers and humans.

Food chain

 A grazing **food chain** is a sequence of organisms in which each one is eaten by the next member in the chain.

In a grazing food chain the first organism is a producer or a green plant. An example of a grazing food chain is:

- *dandelion → butterfly → thrush → hawk*

Trophic level

A **trophic level** is a feeding stage in a food chain.

Producers form the first trophic level. Primary consumers are the second trophic level and secondary consumers form the third trophic level. Other examples of grazing food chains are given at the top of the opposite page:

Producers are organisms that carry out photosynthesis.

Flora is all the plants in an ecosystem.

Consumers are organisms that take in food from another organism.

Fauna is all the animals in an ecosystem.

Decomposers are organisms that feed on dead organic matter.

Detritus feeders are organisms that feed on small pieces of dead organic matter.

Grassland habitat

- grass → rabbit → fox
- buttercup → caterpillar → blackbird → fox

Seashore habitat

- algae → limpet → starfish → gull
- plankton → barnacle → whelk → crab

Scavengers, decomposers or detritus feeders can take food from each trophic level.

Sample food chains and trophic levels				
Trophic level	**1st**	**2nd**	**3rd**	**4th**
Stage	**Producer**	**Primary consumer**	**Secondary consumer**	**Tertiary (or top) consumer**
Grassland examples	Buttercup	Caterpillar	Blackbird	Fox
Seashore examples	Plankton	Barnacle	Whelk	Crab

Length of food chain

About 10% of the energy in each trophic level is passed on to the next level. The remaining 90% is used by the organisms or is lost as heat, waste or detritus. This means that the amount of energy (food) passing along a food chain decreases from one trophic level to the next. This limits the length of a food chain.

In the food chain shown in diagram 4.6, the rabbit does not have to travel too far to get food. The fox must range over a much larger area in order to get its food. If any consumer was to feed on foxes, it would have to use far too much energy hunting for its prey. This is why this food chain finishes with foxes.

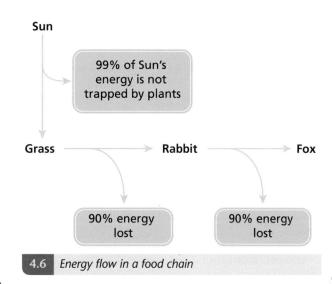

4.6 *Energy flow in a food chain*

Food web

Food chains and food webs are attempts to show the feeding inter-relationships in an ecosystem. They show the flow of energy through the ecosystem. Sample food webs are shown in diagrams 4.7 and 4.8.

A food web consists of two or more interlinked food chains.

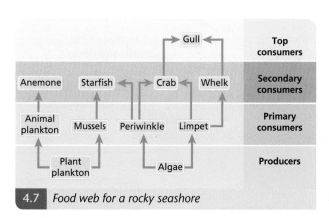

4.7 *Food web for a rocky seashore*

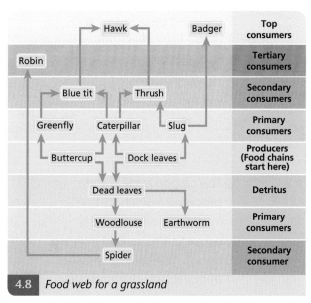

4.8 *Food web for a grassland*

Pyramid of numbers

The number of organisms at each trophic level in a food chain normally decreases as you move up the food chain. This is because of two factors:

- High energy loss at each trophic level (so there is less energy available to the organisms farther along the food chain)
- The organisms usually increase in size the further they are along the food chain (this is because organisms tend to feed on organisms smaller than themselves).

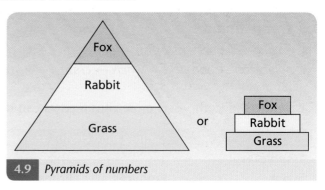

4.9 Pyramids of numbers

In the food chain *grass → rabbits → fox* there are many grass plants feeding a smaller number of rabbits, which support very few foxes. The relative number of organisms at each trophic level is shown in diagram 4.9.

Niche

The organism's niche (or way of life) includes what it eats, what it is eaten by and how it interacts with other organisms and with its abiotic environment.

Two species that have identical niches cannot survive for long in the same habitat. This is because they would both compete in some way (e.g. for food, space, nesting sites). This results in organisms occupying different niches.

- Swallows, thrushes and blackbirds prevent competition by occupying different niches in the same habitat. The swallow feeds on aerial insects, the thrush feeds on ground insects and snails, and the blackbird takes insects on trees, but mostly eats fruit and worms.
- Edible and flat periwinkles have different niches: edible periwinkles feed on algae scraped from rocks; flat periwinkles feed on larger seaweeds.

Nutrient recycling

Whereas energy flows in from the Sun and through the ecosystem, the nutrients that make up the bodies of living things are recycled and used time and time again. Such cycles are called biogeochemical cycles. Although many nutrients are recycled, we will focus on two: carbon and nitrogen.

The carbon cycle

The carbon cycle is the process by which carbon from the environment is converted to carbon in living things. The carbon in living things is later released back into the environment.

> A **pyramid of numbers** represents the number of organisms at each trophic level (or stage) in a food chain.

> The ecological **niche** of an organism is the functional role it plays in the community.

> **Nutrient recycling** is the way in which elements (such as carbon and nitrogen) are exchanged between the living and non-living components of an ecosystem.

Carbon dioxide

Combustion

Photosynthesis

Fossil fuels e.g. turf, coal, oil, petrol, gas

Weathering

Incomplete decay

Plant food

Respiration or death and decay

Consumed

Bones, teeth, shells, limestone

Animal food

Represents carbon
Represents processes

4.10 *The carbon cycle*

Carbon is an essential element for living things. It is normally exchanged between living things and their environment in the form of the gas, carbon dioxide.

Plants have been removing carbon dioxide from the atmosphere for millions of years. It is important that this gas is replaced in order to allow photosynthesis to continue.

Role of organisms in the carbon cycle

Three groups of organisms have roles to play in the carbon cycle:

● **Plants** remove carbon from the environment by photosynthesis and return it by respiration
● **Animals** obtain their carbon by eating plants; they release carbon dioxide by respiration
● **Micro-organisms** (such as fungi and bacteria) return carbon to the environment when they decompose dead plants and animals.

Global warming

In recent years there has been concern that the concentration of carbon dioxide in the atmosphere is rising. For example, the concentration of carbon dioxide 200 years ago was 0.028%. Now it has risen to 0.039%.

The main causes of the rise in carbon dioxide concentration are thought to be:

● Increased combustion of fossil fuels
● Deforestation.

Carbon dioxide is a 'greenhouse gas'. This means it allows heat radiation from the Sun to pass into the Earth's atmosphere, but does not allow reflected heat rays back out. (It is not the only gas that does this.)

Increased levels of carbon dioxide may contribute to global warming, i.e. a rise in the average temperature of the planet. Global warming may cause the following effects:

● Sea levels may rise due to ice melting and the expansion of hot water. This may cause increased flooding.
● Weather patterns may alter (e.g. more stormy weather), which in turn will affect wildlife and agriculture.
● Another major concern is that global warming may cause the Gulf Stream to reverse its direction of flow. This would cause very cold water to flow past Ireland and would have a huge impact on our climate.

The nitrogen cycle

Nitrogen is needed by living things to make proteins and other biomolecules. However, nitrogen gas in the air cannot be used, as it is unreactive.

The function of the nitrogen cycle is to take nitrogen from the air and make it available for use by living things. The nitrogen in living things is later converted to nitrogen in the air.

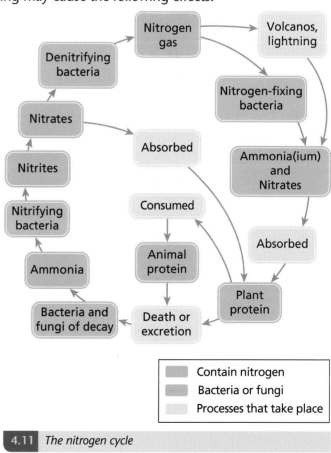

4.11   *The nitrogen cycle*

Refer to diagram 4.11 while reading the following account of the nitrogen cycle.

1. Living things need the element nitrogen (to make proteins, DNA, RNA and other biomolecules). Nitrogen gas (N_2) makes up about 79% of the air. However, this form of nitrogen is inert or unreactive and cannot be used by plants and animals.

2. **Nitrogen fixation** is carried out by volcanic action, lightning, industrial processes and by some bacteria. Nitrogen-fixing bacteria can be found free in the soil or they may be associated with the roots of certain plants. The latter group of bacteria live in nodules (swellings) on the roots of a group of plants called legumes. These include clover, soya beans, peas and beans.

Nitrogen fixation is an anaerobic process (i.e. it does not require oxygen) and the root nodules allow the bacteria to escape from oxygen.

The relationship between the bacteria and the legume is a form of symbiosis, i.e. two different species living closely together where at least one benefits. In this case

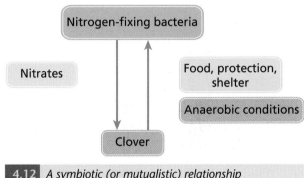

 4.12 *A symbiotic (or mutualistic) relationship*

both species benefit, because the bacteria get food and the plant gets nitrates, so the arrangement is technically called mutualism (although it is often simply called symbiosis).

Nitrates are converted (assimilated) into plant and animal protein, DNA and RNA.

3. **Decomposition** of dead organisms is carried out by bacteria and fungi of decay, which are mostly found in the soil. These organisms release nitrogenous compounds such as ammonia (NH_3) into the soil.

4. **Nitrification** is carried out by bacteria in the soil, called nitrifying bacteria. Nitrifying bacteria are chemosynthetic, i.e. they make their own food (normally in darkness in the soil) using energy from chemical reactions.

5. Some of the nitrate formed in the soil is absorbed and used by plants.

6. **Denitrification** is carried out by denitrifying bacteria in the soil. Denitrifying bacteria are anaerobic and live in swampy soil or deep down in the soil (where water collects to produce anaerobic conditions).

Role of organisms in the nitrogen cycle

● **Bacteria** play a central role in the nitrogen cycle. The four types of bacteria and their functions are:
  1. Nitrogen-fixing bacteria, which convert atmospheric nitrogen to nitrates
  2. Bacteria of decay, which convert nitrogen waste to ammonia
  3. Nitrifying bacteria, which convert ammonia to nitrates
  4. Denitrifying bacteria, which convert nitrates to nitrogen gas.

● **Fungi** also help to decay dead plants and animals and their wastes into ammonia in the soil.

● **Plants** absorb nitrates from the soil and use the nitrogen to form proteins.

● **Animals** consume plants and use their nitrogen to form animal protein.

Nitrogen fixation is the conversion of nitrogen gas into ammonia (NH_3), ammonium (NH_4^+) or nitrate (NO_3^-).

Nitrification is the conversion of ammonia and ammonium (NH_4^+) compounds to nitrite and then to nitrate.

Denitrification is the conversion of nitrates to nitrogen gas.

Human impact on ecosystems

Humans have been on Earth for about 200 000 years. This is a short period of time in relation to the age of the planet – four and a half billion years (4 500 000 000 years).

In this short time humans have had a huge effect on the Earth's resources and organisms in many ways. We will consider three ways that humans affect ecosystems: pollution, conservation and waste management.

Pollution

Most pollution arises from human activities such as dumping, littering, sewage disposal, electricity generation, transport, radioactive processes and noisy activities. Natural pollutants include volcanic emissions and smoke from natural forest fires. Pollution can affect air, fresh water, sea and soil or land.

There are many types of pollution.

- **Domestic pollution** includes household wastes.
- **Agricultural pollution** includes the use of sprays to control pests and weeds, the overuse of fertilisers and disposal of farmyard wastes such as slurry and silage effluent.
- **Industrial pollution** includes smoke that causes acid rain and wastes that may damage streams, rivers and lakes.

Ozone depletion – an example of air pollution

Ozone (O_3) is a gas that forms a protective layer in the upper atmosphere, between 10 and 45 km above the surface of the Earth. It helps to absorb and shield the Earth from incoming ultraviolet radiation.

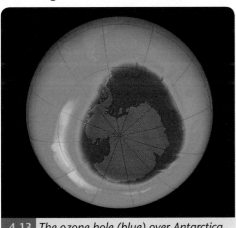

4.13 *The ozone hole (blue) over Antarctica in 2010*

Ozone depletion (or thinning) was first noted in 1984 as a 'hole' in the ozone layer over Antarctica. Since then a similar, but smaller, 'hole' has developed over the Arctic.

Ozone depletion is caused by a range of manufactured chemical pollutants. These include chlorofluorocarbons (CFCs) used in aerosols, refrigerators (Freon gas), insulating foams (Styrofoam) and industrial detergents.

Some fire extinguishers (halons) and agricultural sprays (fumigants) also destroy ozone, as do emissions from high-flying aircraft.

> **Pollution** is any harmful addition to the environment.
>
> **Pollutants** are harmful additions to the environment.

> **Syllabus** You are required to study the effects and control of any **one** pollutant, which must relate to the habitat studied.

Effects of ozone depletion

Ozone absorbs ultraviolet rays. Less ozone in the outer layers of the atmosphere allows more ultraviolet radiation to penetrate to the Earth's surface.

Increased ultraviolet levels have a number of effects, such as the following:

- Increased numbers of skin cancers, cataracts (in which the lens in the eye loses transparency) and weakened immunity
- Serious damage to crops and plant life
- Plankton depletion: there is great concern that plankton will be depleted. This would have huge effects on aquatic food chains and therefore on fish, penguins, birds, seals and whales. It might even result in less oxygen being produced for organisms to breathe.

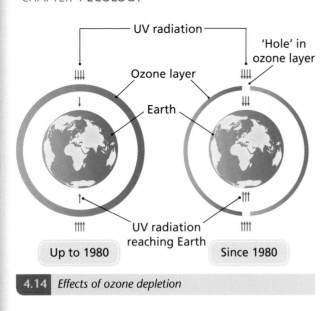

UV radiation

'Hole' in ozone layer

Ozone layer

Earth

UV radiation reaching Earth

Up to 1980

Since 1980

4.14 *Effects of ozone depletion*

Control of ozone depletion

- A reduction in the use of CFCs will eventually allow the ozone layer to be replenished. Ozone is formed naturally by the reaction of ultraviolet light with oxygen. CFCs are now being replaced with other chemicals such as hydrofluorocarbons (HFCs). These chemicals break down much faster than CFCs. This means they do not reach the upper atmosphere and therefore do not cause ozone to break down.
- Sprays or foam products that contain CFCs should not be used.
- Fridges should not be dumped in landfill sites. They should be returned to organisations that will dispose of their CFCs in an environmentally friendly way.

In recent years the hole in the ozone layer has stabilised. It looks like the control methods are allowing ozone to be replenished slowly.

Conservation

> Conservation is the wise management of the existing natural resources in an ecosystem, in order to maintain a wide range of habitats and prevent the death and extinction of organisms.

Modern humans exploit nature in order to live in the way they do. For example, they obtain fish from the sea, grow plant species such as grass and cereals in areas where they would not normally be found, remove timber for building and fuel, resulting in deforestation, and alter the environment for roads, homes, industry and recreation.

In all these cases an element of control must be exercised. This responsibility rests on the individual and on larger organisations. It is important that we slow down and prevent damage to ecosystems and habitats. Such damage is causing a huge loss of biological diversity.

4.15 *Killarney National Park: an example of conservation in an ecosystem*

The present rate of extinction is greater than at any time in the Earth's history. We have a duty to future generations to pass on the natural environment that we inherited.

The benefits of conservation

- It prevents organisms from becoming extinct.
- It maintains the balance of nature.
- It maintains a wide range of living things (biodiversity).
- Organisms may be found to be useful in the future.
- Organisms and habitats are enjoyable to see and visit.
- We have no right to wipe out other life forms.

> **Syllabus** You are required to outline any **one** conservation practice from the areas of agriculture, fisheries or forestry.

As an example of good conservation practices, we will examine the area of fisheries.

Fisheries

There are several problems associated with the fishing industry.
- Pollution of the rivers, lakes and the sea reduces the amount of fish in these waters. Once depleted, fish stocks may take many years to regenerate.

- Overfishing has reduced (and in some cases wiped out) fish stocks at sea. For this reason, fish quotas have been assigned to different countries to try to ensure that enough fish are left in the sea to replenish the stocks.
- The use of small-mesh nets can result in too many young (small) fish being caught. The ideal situation is to allow fish to reproduce for a number of years before being caught.

It is important to continuously monitor the environment in order to prevent problems such as these from developing and becoming too serious. In relation to fisheries this involves measures such as:

- Taking and analysing water samples
- Checking fish catches and fishing equipment
- Sampling fish stocks to calculate their numbers.

Example of conservation in fishing

The size of the mesh in fishing nets is crucially important. If the mesh size is too small, then young, small fish are trapped as well as older, larger fish. Removing too many young fish may reduce the ability of the fish to maintain a viable population size.

Fishing with large-mesh nets does not remove the young, small fish. This allows the fish numbers to be maintained.

Waste management

Modern life produces large amounts of waste material. It is important to manage these wastes wisely in order to conserve the environment and prevent excessive pollution.

Examples of waste management procedures in three different industries are outlined below. Note that in each case the basic principle is that the waste is recycled in a safe manner.

Agriculture

Many of our inland lakes have been (and are) depleted of fish. This has happened because of the lack of oxygen caused mainly by the release of slurry.

Slurry is liquefied waste material produced by animals. It contains high levels of minerals such as nitrogen and phosphorus. When slurry enters rivers or lakes the minerals it contains cause increased algal growth. This often results in algal blooms.

When the algae die they are decomposed by bacteria. This results in the absorption of oxygen and the water becomes depleted in oxygen. Aquatic animals and plants die when they cannot get sufficient oxygen.

The addition of nutrients to fresh water in this way is called eutrophication.

By controlling the release of nutrients into rivers and lakes the water quality can be improved. An example of this control involves storing slurry in leak-proof pits. The stored slurry is spread on dry land in summer. In this way it is not washed away into streams and rivers and the nutrients can be absorbed by plant roots and recycled by the plants. In time, lakes can be (and are) restocked with fish to return them to their original state.

4.16 *Dead fish due to eutrophication*

Fisheries

When fish are processed the waste materials consist of heads, tails, fins, intestines, dead (and decaying) fish and blood diluted by large amounts of water.

The solid wastes are highly alkaline and are first neutralised by the addition of formic acid. The product is pulped, dried and recycled as fertiliser or pig feed.

Forestry

Potential waste products in forestry include the tops of trees, small branches, tree stumps, roots and sawdust. These products are treated as follows.

- Small branches are spread on the forest floor to form a surface that can help machinery to move (especially in very wet land).
- These branches, along with the stumps and roots are allowed to rot naturally. The nutrients released into the soil by this rotting process 'feed' the next generation of trees, which grow much faster.
- Tops of trees and large branches are converted to sawdust, which is used to form processed wood products such as medium-density fibreboard (MDF).

Problems associated with waste disposal

- Wastes may contain many micro-organisms that could cause disease. If the waste is not properly treated, disease-causing micro-organisms may be spread by wind or enter drinking water supplies.
- Toxic chemicals released from wastes can easily be washed out and enter drinking water supplies. They may also have serious effects on plant and animal life in the environment.
- Nutrients released from waste can cause enrichment (eutrophication) of water supplies, which may lead to the death of plants and animals.
- Waste that is disposed of in landfill sites (dumps) can be unsightly, attract undesirable scavengers such as rats and gulls, and produce odours.
- Dumping waste at sea may lead to pollution of the sea, especially with the large amounts of waste now being generated by industrial societies.
- Incinerators burn waste at high temperatures. Incinerators can reduce a large amount of waste very rapidly and reduce the need for landfill sites. Sometimes they may even produce heat which can be used to generate electricity or to heat homes. However, there is a fear that poisonous gases may be released in the process.

An overall problem with waste disposal is the 'NIMBY' syndrome. This stands for *Not In My Back Yard* and refers to the fact that most people do not want waste disposal sites near where they live.

Role of micro-organisms in waste management and pollution control

Landfill sites

Most of our waste is disposed of in landfill sites. In these sites (dumps) the waste is covered with soil. Bacteria and fungi in the soil break down the organic (biodegradable) materials.

Sewage

Sewage is waste from toilets, bathrooms or industry and rainwater from drains.

- Primary sewage treatment involves physically screening or filtering waste and allowing it to settle. This removes large objects and solids.
- Secondary sewage treatment occurs when the waste is acted on by bacteria and fungi of decay. The liquid waste is aerated to allow this to happen. This biological treatment breaks down most of the organic matter.

The remaining sludge is disposed of and the cleaned water is treated with chlorine to destroy any remaining organisms.

- Tertiary sewage treatment is sometimes used to remove mineral nutrients (such as phosphates and nitrates).

4.17 *Sewage being agitated to allow it to gain oxygen to stimulate the growth of micro-organisms*

Control of waste production

Control of waste production can be achieved by implementing the three Rs: reduce, reuse, recycle.

Reduce

Individuals (and societies) can reduce their waste output by reducing their consumption of goods that they do not really need.

In addition, they could reduce the amount of packaging used unnecessarily (as happened in Ireland when a charge was placed on plastic bags). If consumers request less packaging then governments and industry may act to reduce these wastes.

Reuse

Some objects can be reused. For instance, glass bottles can be reused up to 40 times, after which they can then be broken down and recycled. Another example is the reuse of unwanted clothing by charities.

Recycle

Many modern materials can now be collected, treated and re-formed into new products. Examples include the recycling of paper, glass, different metals, plastics and organic waste.

Up to 40% of household rubbish is organic matter. This waste can be broken down by oxygen-requiring bacteria to form a dark-coloured material called compost or humus. This compost can be added to soil to improve the growth of plants.

Summary

Ecology is the study of the interactions between living things and their environment.

The **biosphere:**
- Is the part of the planet (air, water, soil) in which life is found
- Contains many ecosystems, e.g. desert, grassland, freshwater.

A **population** is all the members of the same species in an area.

A **community** contains many different populations.

A **habitat** is the place in which an organism lives. It is also the area studied when investigating an ecosystem.

The **distribution of organisms** is affected by four sets of factors:
- Abiotic (non-living) factors, which include altitude, aspect (i.e. north- or south-facing), steepness, currents, exposure

- Biotic (living) factors, which include food, competition, predation, parasitism, pollination, seed dispersal, human activity
- Climatic (long-term weather) factors, which include temperature, rainfall, humidity, day length, light intensity, moisture, wind, salinity (salt content)
- Edaphic (soil) factors, which include pH, particle size, organic matter, water/air/mineral content.

Aquatic (water) habitats have special problems compared with terrestrial (land) habitats, including:
- Light may not penetrate
- Currents move organisms
- Wave action moves and damages organisms
- Salt content means organisms adapt to fresh water or salt water
- Oxygen is in lower concentration.

The **Sun** is the main source of energy for the planet.

Energy flows in one direction, from the Sun through the producers and into the consumers.
- Producers make their own food.

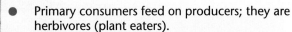

- Primary consumers feed on producers; they are herbivores (plant eaters).
- Secondary and tertiary consumers feed on animals; they are carnivores (meat eaters).

A **food chain** is a one-to-one series of organisms, with each organism feeding on the previous member.
- A grazing food chain starts with a producer.
- A food chain is limited in length by the loss of 90% of the energy at each trophic level.
- Each feeding stage is a trophic level, e.g. producers, primary consumers, etc.
- In most food chains the number of organisms decreases along the chain.

A **food web** is a series of interlinked food chains.

A **pyramid of numbers** is a representation of the number of organisms at each trophic level.

A **niche** is the role an organism plays in the community.
- Organisms with identical niches will compete with each other.

Energy flows through an ecosystem, whereas nutrients (minerals) are recycled.

In the **carbon cycle:**
- Carbon (dioxide) is removed from the environment by photosynthesis in plants
- Carbon (dioxide) is returned to the environment by:
  ‣ Respiration in plants, animals and micro-organisms
  ‣ Decay caused by micro-organisms
  ‣ Combustion
  ‣ Weathering.

The role of micro-organisms in the nitrogen cycle is summarised below:
- **Nitrogen-fixing bacteria:**
  ‣ Are found free in soil or in nodules in legumes
  ‣ Convert nitrogen gas to nitrates (NO_3).
- **Bacteria and fungi of decay:**
  ‣ Found in soil
  ‣ Convert dead organic matter into nitrogenous waste (e.g. ammonia).
- **Nitrifying bacteria:**
  ‣ Found in soil
  ‣ Convert nitrogenous waste (e.g. ammonia) into nitrates.
- **Denitrifying bacteria:**
  ‣ Found in soil
  ‣ Convert nitrates into nitrogen gas (N_2).

Three ways in which humans affect ecosystems are pollution, conservation and waste management.

Pollution is any harmful addition to the environment. It is caused by pollutants.

Ozone depletion is an example of air pollution.
- Ozone is a gas that absorbs ultraviolet radiation in the upper atmosphere.
- Ozone is broken down by manufactured chemicals such as CFCs.

- Ozone depletion results in increased skin cancers and cataracts, damage to plants and the immune systems of animals.
- Ozone depletion is being reduced by replacing CFCs with other chemicals (HFCs) which decompose before they reach the upper atmosphere and by not using sprays that contain CFCs.

Conservation is the wise management of existing resources in ecosystems, in order to maintain habitats and species.
Conservation problems in fishing include:
- Water pollution
- The use of nets with small mesh sizes
- Depletion of fish stocks due to overfishing.

Eutrophication is the addition of nutrients to fresh water. This leads to a lack of oxygen in the water.

Examples of **good conservation practices** are:
- The use of large mesh nets in fishing
- Storing slurry (liquid animal wastes) and spreading it on land in dry summer weather helps to prevent fish kills in rivers and lakes.

Waste management involves preventing pollution and conserving the environment. Where possible it involves recycling.
Examples of waste management are:
- In agriculture, slurry is stored and spread on dry land
- In the fishing industry, the waste parts of the fish are neutralised, pulped, dried and recycled as fertiliser or pig feed
- In forestry, any parts of trees not removed from the forest are allowed to decay and return nutrients to the soil.

Important problems in waste disposal are:
- Wastes may cause disease
- Poisonous chemicals from wastes can enter drinking water supplies or plants
- Waste nutrients can result in eutrophication and the death of aquatic plants and animals
- Landfill sites may be unsightly, smelly and attract undesirable wildlife
- Dumping at sea may lead to pollution of the sea
- Incinerators may release toxic fumes.

Micro-organisms break down organic waste in landfill sites.

Sewage treatment involves:
- Primary (physical) treatment, which removes particles from the waste by screening and sedimentation
- Secondary (biological) treatment, in which bacteria and fungi break down organic waste
- Tertiary treatment, if used, removes minerals from the waste.

The **amount of waste** we produce can be controlled by the three Rs.
- **R**educe the consumption of unnecessary materials.
- **R**euse as many materials as possible.
- **R**ecycle as much as possible.

Revision questions

1   Define: **(a)** Ecology **(b)** Biosphere **(c)** Ecosystem
    (d) Abiotic factors **(e)** Edaphic factors
    (f) Habitat.

2   **(a)** Give three examples of ecosystems.
    (b) For each example, **(i)** state the main factors that define it and **(ii)** give a geographical location where it is found.

3   **(a)** Name the ecosystem or habitat you have studied.
    (b) Name a producer and a consumer from your habitat.
    (c) The number of producers and consumers is determined by four categories of factors. Name these categories.
    (d) Give one example from each category that affects the number of **(i)** producers and **(ii)** consumers in your selected habitat.

4   Distinguish between climatic and edaphic factors, giving one example in each case as to how they might affect living things in a habitat.

5   **(a)** Distinguish between sand and clay.
    (b) Give one advantage and one disadvantage for each soil type.

6   **(a)** What is humus?
    (b) Suggest one way in which humus is of benefit to the soil.

7   Give a reason, based on feeding, why plants can survive only in the upper layers of water, but animals can be found at great depths.

8   Define each of the following and give one example from the ecosystem you have studied:
    (a) Producer **(b)** Decomposer **(c)** Primary consumer **(d)** Detritus feeder **(e)** Carnivore **(f)** Top consumer.

9   In the food chain:
    dandelion → butterfly → robin → falcon
    (a) What is the initial source of energy for the dandelion?
    (b) How many trophic levels are indicated?
    (c) Which way does energy flow?
    (d) What happens to the energy that does not pass to the next level?
    (e) Draw a pyramid of numbers to represent this food chain.
    (f) If a herbicide is sprayed to kill the dandelion, suggest an effect this might have on the top consumers.

10 Most food chains are limited to about four (or fewer) trophic levels. Explain why this is the case.

11 Suggest the effects on a food chain of:
    (a) Increasing the number of producers
    (b) Disease killing off the primary consumers
    (c) An immigration of more top consumers.

12 **(a)** Refer to diagram 4.18 showing the carbon cycle and name the processes represented by the letters A to H.

(b) Why are the levels of CO_2 thought to be rising worldwide?

(c) Give two possible results of a rise in CO_2 concentrations.

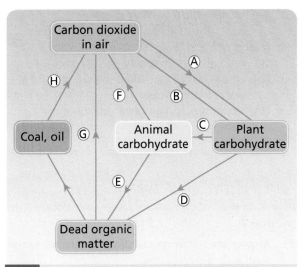

4.18

13 **(a)** Name three types of organism that have a role in the carbon cycle.
    (b) Outline the role of each type of organism in the carbon cycle.

14 **(a)** Why do plants and animals require nitrogen?
    (b) Why do plants not use atmospheric nitrogen?
    (c) In what form(s) do plants require nitrogen?
    (d) Name two processes that convert nitrogen gas into compounds that plants can use.

15 **(a)** Name four types of bacteria that play a role in the nitrogen cycle.
    (b) In the case of each bacterium, state:
    (i) where it is found **(ii)** what it acts on **(iii)** what it produces.
    (c) Three of these bacteria are beneficial and the other one is harmful. Explain why.

16 **(a)** What is meant by: **(i)** Pollution **(ii)** Pollutant?
    (b) Name any pollutant and state: **(i)** Its effect on the environment **(ii)** Any problem caused by this effect **(iii)** How the named pollutant can be controlled.

17 **(a)** What is meant by conservation?
    (b) Outline one conservation practice from the area of agriculture, fisheries or forestry.

18 **(a)** Define eutrophication.
    (b) State one cause of eutrophication.
    (c) Explain why this process kills aquatic life.

19 State one waste product and explain how it is dealt with in each case for **(a)** Agriculture **(b)** Fisheries **(c)** Forestry.

20 **(a)** Distinguish between primary and secondary waste treatment.

(b) Name four problems associated with waste disposal.

(c) Distinguish between physical and biological stages in waste management.

21 Name three practices that would result in the production of less waste.

22 Say whether the following statements are true or false. In the case of a false statement, give a reason why it is false.

(a) Animals are producers.

(b) Heavy rainfall can affect the salinity of the water in rock pools.

(c) Marram grass can grow only on a damp site.

(d) A trophic level denotes the height of an organism.

(e) A pyramid of numbers represents the relative numbers of organisms at each trophic level.

(f) Nitrifying bacteria produce nitrogen gas (N_2).

(g) The ozone layer causes global warming.

(h) Freon gas helps to produce ozone.

(i) Eutrophication is the reduction of minerals and nutrients in lakes.

(j) Chlorine is used in the sewage treatment process.

Exam questions

Section A

23 Answer the following questions in relation to the food web shown below.

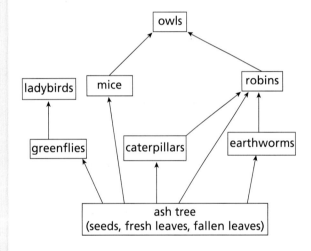

(a) Write out a food chain with four organisms in it.

(b) Name the primary producer in the web.

(c) Name **two** secondary consumers in the web.

(d) Name **two** herbivores in the web.

(e) Name **one** omnivore in the web.

(f) Name **one** carnivore in the web.

(2004 OL Q 6)

24 Answer the following questions in relation to your study of ecology.

(a) What is the biosphere?

(b) What is meant by a qualitative survey? (see page 66)

(c) Construct a grazing food chain containing at least four trophic levels.

(d) In your food chain in (c) identify each of the following.

1. A predator

2. A producer

3. A secondary (second order) consumer

4. A primary (first order) consumer.

(2006 HL Q 2)

25 The following food chain is from a hedgerow:

hawthorn leaves → caterpillar → blue tit → sparrowhawk.

Complete any **four** of the following by reference to this food chain.

(a) The primary consumer in this food chain is _____.

(b) If the number of sparrowhawks increases, the number of blue tits may _____.

(c) In this food chain the hawthorn leaves represent the _____.

(d) Name a carnivore from this food chain _____.

(e) The number of trophic (feeding) levels in this food chain is limited by the small transfer of _____ from one level to the next.

(2008 OL Q 1)

26 Explain each of the following terms from your study of ecology.

(a) Biosphere

(b) Ecosystem

(c) Habitat

(d) Symbiosis

(e) Biotic factor

(f) Food web

(g) Fauna

(2010 HL Q 5)

27 **(a)** **(i)** What does an ecologist mean by the term *conservation*?

(ii) Suggest a reason why nature reserves are important for conservation.

(b) **(i)** Explain the term *pollution*.

(ii) Pollution may result from domestic, agricultural or industrial sources. Select **one** of these areas **and** state an effect that may be produced by a **named** pollutant.

(iii) How may the pollution referred to in (ii) be controlled?

(c) In relation to the incineration of domestic waste, suggest:

(i) an advantage of the process.

(ii) a disadvantage of the process.

(2012 HL Q 4)

Section C

28 (a) (i) What is meant by nitrogen fixation?

(ii) Name a group of organisms involved in nitrogen fixation.

(2008 OL Q 10)

29 (c) (i) Explain what is meant by pollution.

(ii) Give an account of the effects of a named pollutant of domestic, agricultural or industrial origin.

(iii) Describe one way in which the pollution that you have indicated in (ii) might be controlled.

(iv) Outline the problems associated with the disposal of waste. Suggest two ways of minimising waste.

(2006 HL Q 10)

30 (a) Explain the following terms that are used in ecology: niche, edaphic factor, symbiosis.

(b) (i) What is the function of the nitrogen cycle?

(ii) What is meant by nitrogen fixation?

(iii) What is meant by nitrification?

(iv) Describe, using words and/or labelled diagrams, the events of the nitrogen cycle.

(2007 HL Q 12)

31 (c) (i) Waste management is a matter of growing concern in Ireland as the population expands. Outline three problems associated with waste disposal.

(ii) Give an example of waste produced in agriculture or fisheries or forestry and describe how it is managed.

(iii) Suggest two methods of waste minimisation.

(iv) Give one example of the use of micro-organisms in waste management.

(2008 HL Q 10)

32 (a) (i) Distinguish between a food chain and a food web. Include a clear reference to each in your answer.

(ii) What do ecologists mean by a *pyramid of numbers*?

(b) Organisms that are introduced into new environments outside their natural ranges are referred to as exotic species. In some cases these introductions have been deliberate and in other cases accidental e.g. when a species kept in captivity in a new country escapes and gives rise to a wild population. Worldwide, the great majority of deliberate attempted introductions have been unsuccessful.

(i) Suggest a reason for attempting to establish an exotic species in a new country.

(ii) Suggest **two** reasons why the great majority of attempted introductions have been unsuccessful.

(iii) Use your knowledge of the life cycle of flowering plants to suggest how an exotic plant may escape from captivity.

(iv) Use the knowledge that you have gained in your studies of ecology to suggest how the introduction of an exotic species may:

1. impact negatively on an existing community.

2. impact positively on an existing community.

(v) It has been stated that an exotic species has a good chance of becoming established in a new environment if there is a vacant niche.

1. Explain the term *niche* in this context.

2. Do you agree with the above statement?

3. Explain your answer.

(2012 HL Q 11)

Previous examination questions

Ordinary level	Higher level
2004 Q 6	2004 Q 5, 10
2005 Q 1, 10	2006 Q 2, 10c
2006 Q 1, 10	2007 Q 2, 12
2007 Q 2	2008 Q 10c
2008 Q 1, 10a	2009 Q 3, 11
2009 Q 2, 10, 12	2010 Q 5, 12
2010 Q 1, 10	2011 Q 3, 10
2011 Q 2, 11	2012 Q 4, 11
2012 Q 5, 10	

Latest questions at www.edco.ie/lcbiologyplus/examhelp

Online test and assessment tracker

Scan the QR code and test yourself on chapter 4
www.edco.ie/lcbiologyplus

Chapter 5 **Higher level ecology**

THE STUDY OF LIFE

Learning objectives

 ● To describe pyramids of numbers and their limitations

 ● To understand the inferences that can be made from the shape of a pyramid of numbers

HIGHER ▶ ● To understand factors that control populations and define 'competition', 'predation', 'parasitism' and 'symbiosis', with a description of one example in each case

 ● To describe predator–prey relationships

HIGHER ▶ ● To describe the effects of war, famine, contraception and disease on the human population.

Pyramids of numbers

A pyramid of numbers represents the number of organisms at each trophic level in a food chain.

Normally a pyramid of numbers is shown as a modified bar chart. In general the numbers of organisms decrease as you proceed up the chart, as shown in diagram 5.1.

Inference of pyramid shape

Two inferences can be drawn from the normal shape of a pyramid of numbers.
● The number of organisms declines as you go up a pyramid of numbers. This happens because of the large energy losses (about 90%) between each trophic level. This means there is less energy available to the organisms higher up the pyramid.

● The body size of the organisms usually increases as you go up a pyramid of numbers. This is mainly because bigger animals tend to eat smaller animals, e.g. hawks are bigger than thrushes.

Limitations of pyramids of numbers

● Pyramids of numbers do not take into account the size of the organisms. A large number of microscopic mites is represented by a wide rectangle. A single large rose bush is represented by a narrow rectangle. Therefore, two main shapes of pyramid are possible, a normal pyramid and an inverted pyramid.

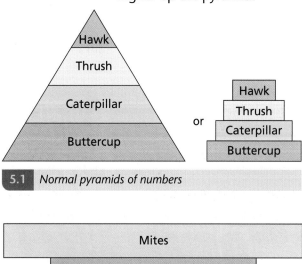

5.1 *Normal pyramids of numbers*

5.2 *Inverted pyramid of numbers*

HIGHER ▼

50

- Parasitic food chains often give rise to an inverted pyramid of numbers, e.g. many tiny mites can live on a single greenfly, as shown in diagram 5.2. Sometimes a pyramid of numbers may be partially inverted, as shown in diagram 5.3.
- The numbers of organisms can be so great that the pyramid cannot be drawn to scale. For example, millions of greenfly might live on a single oak or hundreds of millions of bacteria could live on a decomposing whale.

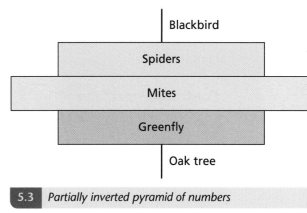

5.3 *Partially inverted pyramid of numbers*

Population control

A population comprises all the members of a species living in an area. We speak of a population of oak trees in a woodland, a population of rabbits in a locality or the population of humans on Earth.

A number of factors tend to reduce the population when numbers are high and increase the population when numbers are low. These factors mainly act on birth rates (causing more or fewer offspring to be produced) and death rates (causing more or fewer offspring to die).

In affecting birth and death rates, these factors help to maintain a balance in population numbers called the balance of nature. This allows the population to remain close to the number of organisms that the habitat can support.

Factors that control populations

The factors that control the size of a population include:

- Competition
- Predation
- Parasitism
- Symbiosis.

The ways in which these factors work to control the numbers of organisms is dealt with in the following sections.

Competition

Competition occurs when organisms actively struggle for a resource that is in short supply.

The consequence of competition is that the number of organisms is reduced. Plants compete for resources such as space, light, water and minerals. Animals compete for food, water, shelter, territory and reproductive rights (mates).

Intra-specific competition takes place between members of the same species.

For example, bladder wracks compete with each other for space on rocks or rabbits compete with each other for food.

Inter-specific competition occurs between members of different species.

For example, blackbirds and thrushes compete for insects and snails while grass and buttercups compete for light.

THE STUDY OF LIFE

Types of competition

There are two main types of competition: contest competition and scramble competition.

Contest competition

In **contest competition**, there is an active physical contest between two individual organisms.

Contest competition results in one individual getting the resource, while the second is left without it.

5.4 *Male deer competing (rutting) for mates*

A good example of contest competition is the way in which animals such as birds or deer select and defend an area or territory. This territory is used for feeding, nesting, reproduction and raising young. It is usually selected and defended by the male animal.

By displaying territorial behaviour, only the fittest animals can reproduce. This helps to improve the species. It also reduces population growth and helps conserve food supplies.

Scramble competition

In **scramble competition**, all of the competing individuals get some of the resource.

Scramble competition may mean that none of the individuals get as much of the resource as they need and they may not be able to grow and reproduce efficiently.

An example of scramble competition is the overcrowding of seedlings in flowerbeds. Unless some of the seedlings are removed, none of them will get sufficient resources and they all will grow poorly and fail to flower.

Scramble competition tends to reduce the numbers in a population.

Techniques to avoid competition

Syllabus You are required to know **one** adaptive technique to survive competition.

It is vital that species should avoid competition if they are to survive. They do this by adapting to their environments. These adaptations may involve changes in feeding habits, camouflage, protective coats, alterations to mouthparts and reproductive strategies.

- The caterpillar of the cabbage white butterfly chews on cabbage leaves, whereas the adult butterfly drinks nectar from flowers. In this way they avoid competition for food.
- Brown seaweeds called wracks have adapted so they can tolerate being out of water for different periods of time. This means they spread out from the upper to the lower shore and avoid competing for space and light.

Channel wrack can survive longest out of water and is found high up on a rocky seashore, followed by spiral wrack and bladder wrack, whereas serrated wrack can tolerate only short periods out of water and is found on lower rocks, where it is normally covered by the tide.

Predation

HIGHER ▼

> Predation is the catching, killing and eating of another organism.

Examples of predators and their prey include ladybirds and aphids, blackbirds and earthworms, hawks and mice, whelks and mussels.

The predator–prey relationship is used in the area of biological control of pests. This involves the use of one organism to control the numbers of another. For example, ladybirds are used to control aphids and certain types of bacteria are used to control the larvae of butterflies to prevent them from destroying crops (e.g. cabbage).

5.5 *Predator and prey: a ladybird feeding on an aphid*

Adaptations of predators and prey

Predators

Features that improve the efficiency of predators include the following:

- Hawks and other birds of prey have excellent sight so that they can locate their prey
- Ladybirds have strong mouthparts to enable them to chew aphids
- Whelks produce an acid that dissolves through the shell of mussels, limpets or barnacles.

Prey

Features that assist prey species to avoid being eaten include the following:

- Mice flee and hide to avoid being eaten
- Frogs are well camouflaged so that they are difficult to see and attack
- Ladybirds contain large amounts of formic acid, which is unpalatable to predators. Predators learn to avoid eating the brightly coloured ladybirds.

Parasitism

A parasite lives in or on the body of the host, to which it normally causes harm.

Exoparasites (also called ectoparasites) live on the outside of the host. Examples include fleas on a dog, mosquitoes or blood-sucking leeches on human skin and aphids such as greenfly on a rose bush.

Endoparasites live inside the host. Examples include liver flukes in sheep and cattle, potato blight fungus in potato plants, bacteria of disease in the human body and tapeworms in human intestines.

Parasites often weaken the host but do not kill it. Therefore, parasites usually do not significantly reduce the numbers of their host. However, in some cases (e.g. potato blight infection or disease-causing bacteria) they can reduce the numbers in a population.

A **predator** is an organism that catches, kills and eats another organism.

The **prey** is the organism that is eaten by the predator.

Parasitism occurs when two organisms of different species live in close association and one organism (the parasite) obtains its food from, and to the disadvantage of, the second organism (the host).

Symbiosis

> **Symbiosis** occurs when two organisms of different species live (and have to live) in close association and at least one of them benefits.

5.6 *Symbiosis: two types of lichens on a gravestone*

There are a number of different types of symbiosis, such as parasitism (in which the parasite gets the benefit of food but the host is harmed).

Another form of symbiosis is mutualism. In this case *both* organisms benefit from the association. Symbiosis is often taken to refer to mutualism. Examples of symbiosis (or mutualism) include:

● Cellulose-digesting bacteria in mammalian intestines, where the mammal gets digested food and the bacteria get shelter, warmth, moisture and food
● Bacteria in the large intestines of humans, where the bacteria produce vitamins B and K and get food and shelter
● Lichens (which are composed of an alga and a fungus), where the algae get protection, minerals and support, and the fungus gets food
● Nitrogen-fixing bacteria in the nodules of plants such as clover, where the bacteria gain food, shelter, anaerobic conditions and the clover gets nitrates.

Symbiosis increases the numbers of both organisms involved in the relationship.

Population dynamics

Population dynamics refers to the factors that cause population numbers to change.

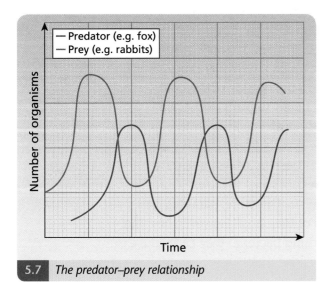

5.7 *The predator–prey relationship*

Predator–prey relationships

The numbers of predator and prey are inter-related. As the number of prey builds up, the number of predators will rise. This will result in more of the prey being killed and so their numbers will fall. This in turn will result in fewer predators and so their numbers will fall.

Eventually the numbers of prey will begin to rise again, starting the cycle once more. This repeated pattern is shown in diagram 5.7.

The variables or factors that contribute to predator–prey interactions include: availability of food, concealment and movement of predators.

Availability of food

A large number of prey can cause an increase in the number of predators. As the prey is killed off there is less food for the predators and the number of predators declines. This in turn allows the number of prey to rise again.

Concealment

The prey are prevented from being totally wiped out because, when their numbers are low, they may successfully conceal or camouflage themselves so that the predators can no longer locate them easily. This allows a small population of prey to survive and eventually to re-establish itself.

Movement of predators

If the number of prey is so small that the predator cannot easily catch sufficient food to survive, the predators normally move to areas where the prey is more numerous. This allows the prey in the old location to increase in number.

It is the balance between factors such as these that results in a repeated cyclical change in the numbers of predators and prey.

Human population growth

Since the origin of modern humans (some time in the last 200 000 years) our numbers initially increased slowly. By 400 AD, Chinese and ancient Roman records kept for tax purposes indicate that the world's population was about 100 million. By 1650 it was still below 500 million.

At the time of the Industrial Revolution (in the 1850s) the world's population was just above 1000 million (one billion). Since then the number of people in the world has grown very rapidly. In 2011 the number reached seven billion.

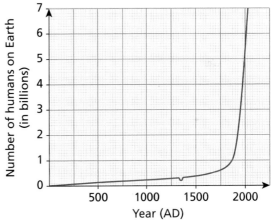

| 5.8 | *The human population explosion* |

The world population is now increasing by about 75 million people each year (this is equivalent to about 205 000 additional people each day, or 143 every minute). The rapid increase in human numbers in recent years is often referred as the 'population explosion'. The growth in human population is shown on the graph in diagram 5.8.

It is important to realise that although the world's population is rising continuously, the rate at which it is rising is slowing down. Future predictions are extremely difficult to make. Some experts predict that the world's population will stabilise at around 10 billion by the year 2100.

The increasing number of humans is not due to an increase in birth rates. In fact, birth rates are declining in many countries, especially in developed countries. In this context it should be noted that about 66% of the world's population lives in Asia. The increase in population has been caused by reduced death rates.

Factors affecting human population numbers

Some of the factors that influence human population numbers are war, famine, contraception and disease.

War

In general, war reduces human population numbers as a result of death. However, these effects can be temporary because an increase in birth rates (baby boom) often follows a war.

THE STUDY OF LIFE

HIGHER ▼

Famine

A lack of food leads to malnutrition and death due to disease or starvation. This was seen in the Great Irish Famine of 1845–1847, when about one million people died of starvation and disease.

Although some countries still suffer from famine, the cause is generally related to food distribution problems rather than absolute food shortages. Advances in agricultural techniques have so far allowed food supplies to match population growth.

Contraception

Increased availability of contraceptives has reduced birth rates since the 1960s. This is particularly evident in developed countries. For example, in much of Western Europe and the USA the average number of children born to a woman (the fertility rate) has fallen below 2.1. This is below the level needed to ensure that the population remains constant.

The fertility rate in developing countries has fallen from 6.1 in 1970 to about 3 today. Much of this decline can be attributed to increased use of contraceptives.

Disease

The ability to control and cure disease was mainly developed in the 20th century. The use of vaccines has reduced the incidence of diseases such as typhoid, cholera, diphtheria, tuberculosis, polio and many others. Smallpox was declared to have been eradicated worldwide in 1980 – the first disease ever wiped out by humans.

Improved sanitation and the use of insecticides have helped to control diseases such as malaria, yellow fever and sleeping sickness.

Safe anaesthetics, improved surgical methods and new drugs have combined to save many lives. The use of antibiotics (since 1940) has prevented many deaths caused by bacterial infections.

All of these disease-control methods have helped to reduce the death rate and increase human numbers. This is especially so in developed countries.

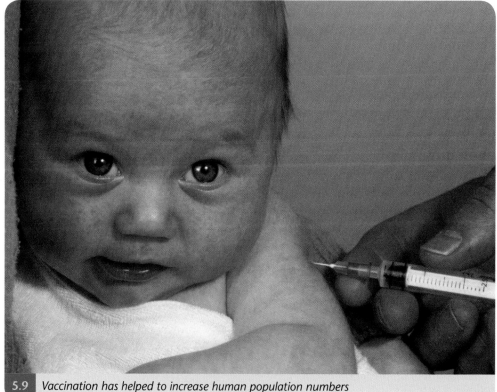

5.9 *Vaccination has helped to increase human population numbers*

Summary

HIGHER ▼

A **normal pyramid of numbers** indicates that:

- The number of organisms falls as you ascend each pyramid
- The body size of the organisms increases as you ascend each pyramid.

Some pyramids of numbers are not standard because:

- The size of the organisms can change the standard shape
- It may not be possible to represent large numbers of organisms correctly.

A **population** is made up of all the members of a species living in an area.

- The factors that control the numbers in a population act mainly on the birth and death rates.
- Factors controlling population size include competition, predation, parasitism and symbiosis.

Competition occurs when two or more organisms seek a scarce resource.

- Intra-specific competition takes place between members of the same species.
- Inter-specific competition involves different species.

Competition reduces population numbers.

The two main types of competition are:

- Contest competition, in which one organism gets the resource, whereas the second is left without
- Scramble competition, which means that all of those competing get some (but often not enough) of the resource.

Predation is the catching, killing and eating of another organism. A **predator** catches, kills and eats other organisms. **Prey** are the organisms that are eaten.

- Predation initially increases the number of predators and decreases the number of prey.
- The numbers of predators and prey often show repeated cycles of rising and falling numbers.

HIGHER ▼

A **parasite** is an organism that feeds from and harms another organism.

- Exo- or ectoparasites live on the outside of the host.
- Endoparasites live inside the host.
- Parasites sometimes reduce the numbers in a population, but often have little effect on host numbers.

Symbiosis occurs when two organisms from different species live (and are usually obliged to live) in close association for the benefit of at least one of the organisms.

Symbiosis (often called mutualism) increases the numbers of both species. Symbiosis includes:

- Parasitism (where one organism benefits but the other is harmed)
- Mutualism (where both organisms benefit).

Population dynamics refers to factors that cause changes in population numbers. Predator–prey numbers interact due to:

- Availability of food, which increases predator numbers when high but reduces them when low
- Concealment, which means that some prey survive by hiding from the predators
- Movement of predators, which means that predators move to new areas when prey numbers are low.

Human population growth has continued to rise rapidly since the 1900s because of falling death rates. Factors affecting human population numbers include war, famine, contraception and disease control:

- War normally reduces population numbers temporarily
- Famine reduces population numbers
- The increased use of contraceptives has reduced the birth rate and the rate of population growth, especially in developed countries
- Improved disease-control methods have reduced the death rate and caused an increase in human numbers.

Revision questions

HIGHER ▼

1 (a) Draw the pyramids of numbers you would expect for each of the following food chains:
    (i) grass → grasshopper → pheasant → fox
    (ii) oak tree → caterpillar → blackbird → hawk
    (iii) rose bush → caterpillar → mite
  (b) Name the type of pyramid in each case.
  (c) Account for the difference in shape between the pyramids in (i) and (iii) above.

2 (a) Draw a pyramid of numbers to show a dead whale, worms feeding off the dead flesh, parasitic lice feeding off the worms.
  (b) What factor(s) affect the shape of this pyramid?
  (c) Why is this pyramid difficult to draw to scale?

3 In the pyramid of numbers shown in diagram 5.10:
  (a) Name the producer.
  (b) Name the secondary consumer.
  (c) Name the organism at the third trophic level.
  (d) Why is the rectangle for rabbits larger than that for foxes?
  (e) Give a reason for the fox flea rectangle being so large.

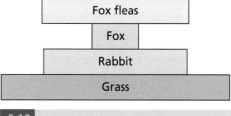

5.10

4 (a) Distinguish between contest and scramble competition.
  (b) Give one example of each of these types of competition.
  (c) State one way in which each type of competition can affect the numbers in the competing populations.

5 Naming one example in each case, describe what is meant by
(a) predation (b) predator (c) prey.

6 For a predator–prey relationship, give one reason for each of the following cases:
  (a) The number of prey controls the number of predators.
  (b) The number of predators controls the number of prey.

  (c) The predators rarely kill all the prey.
  (d) The predators survive even when the number of prey is small.

7 Name one adaptation in each case used by (a) predators and (b) prey, to improve their survival rates. Explain the benefit of each adaptation.

8 (a) What is meant by symbiosis?
  (b) Give two examples of symbiosis and in each case, state how the organisms benefit from the process.

9 Referring to diagram 5.11, answer the following:
  (a) Estimate human numbers in (i) 500 AD (ii) 1500 AD.
  (b) In what year did human numbers reach 1000 million?

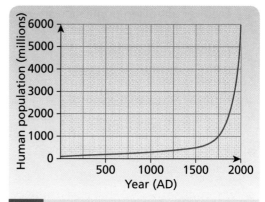

5.11

10 (a) Name and explain the effects of two factors that tend to reduce human numbers.
  (b) Account for the present increase in human numbers.

11 Name three disease-control techniques that have affected human population numbers in the last 100 years.

12 Say whether the following statements are true or false. In the case of a false statement, give a reason why it is false.
  (a) A parasite is an organism that provides food for a host.
  (b) There are always more predators than prey in a habitat.
  (c) Animals compete for mates, territory, shelter, light and food.
  (d) Bacteria living on human teeth are an example of symbiosis.
  (e) In a pyramid of numbers, the number of carnivores is always greater than the number of herbivores.
  (f) The herbivores in an ecosystem normally live long lives.

HIGHER ▼

Exam questions

Section B

13 (a) In ecology what is meant by a trophic level?

(b) Complete the pyramid of numbers by naming an organism in each case of A, B, C and D. (Note: the examiners gave no marks for naming D.)

A _____ B _____

C _____ D _____

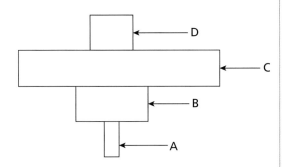

(c) Which letter represents the producer in the pyramid?

(d) Comment on the relative sizes of an individual producer and an individual primary consumer in the pyramid.

(2007 HL Q 2)

Section C

14 (c) (i) What term do ecologists use to describe an animal which kills and eats other animals?

(ii) What term is used to describe the animal that is killed and eaten?

(iii) If the population of the animals in (ii) declines suggest two possible consequences for the animals in (i).

(iv) Give four factors that influence the size of the human population.

(2007 HL Q 12)

15 (a) (i) What does an ecologist mean by competition?

(ii) Distinguish clearly between contest competition and scramble competition.

(b) Read the following extract, study the graph below and answer the questions that follow. "The application of pesticides to strawberry plants in an attempt to destroy cyclamen mites that were damaging the strawberries killed both the cyclamen mites and the carnivorous mites that preyed on them. But the cyclamen mites quickly re-invaded the strawberry fields while the mites that preyed on them returned much more slowly. The result was that the cyclamen mites rapidly increased in density and did more damage to the strawberries than if the pesticide had never been applied."

(Adapted from W. T. Keeton and J. L. Gould. 1993. *Biological Science.* New York: W.W. Norton & Co.)

(i) Which graph, A or B, represents the carnivorous mites? Explain your answer.

(ii) What term is used to describe the relationship between the cyclamen mites and the carnivorous mites?

(iii) Suggest two reasons why the cyclamen mites managed to quickly re-invade the strawberry fields.

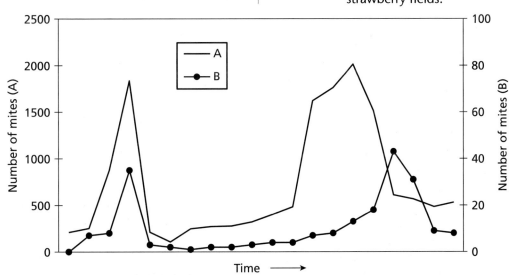

HIGHER ▼

(iv) Suggest an alternative to the use of pesticides for controlling the cyclamen mite population.

(v) Draw a pyramid of numbers to include each of the organisms mentioned in the extract above.

(vi) Apart from competition and the factor illustrated in the above example, state another factor that limits population growth.

(2008 HL Q 10)

16 (a) (i) Where are primary producers found in a pyramid of numbers?

(ii) Using named examples, construct a simple **inverted** pyramid of numbers.

(2010 HL Q 12)

17 (a) (i) Distinguish between *contest competition* and *scramble competition* by writing a sentence about each.

(ii) Name a factor, other than competition, that controls wild populations.

(b) What deduction is it possible to make from each of the following observations?

HIGHER ▼

(i) In a particular area the population of a predator did not decline following a big reduction in the population of its main prey.

(ii) Mortality levels resulting from infection by a particular virus tend to decline over the years.

(iii) Where some members of a species remain in the same general area throughout life and some members are migratory, mortality levels tend to be higher in the migratory part of the population.

(iv) There is a greater variety of herbaceous (non-woody) plants in areas where grazing species, such as rabbits, are more plentiful than in areas where grazing species are less plentiful.

(v) In some species of migratory ducks in the northern hemisphere it is found that the wintering grounds of the males lie further south than those of the females.

(2011 HL Q 10)

Previous examination questions

Ordinary level	Higher level
n/a	2004 Q 10
	2007 Q 2, 12c
	2008 Q 10
	2009 Q 3
	2010 Q 12a
	2011 Q 3, 10

Latest questions at www.edco.ie/lcbiologyplus/examhelp

Online test and assessment tracker

Scan the QR code and test yourself on chapter 5
www.edco.ie/lcbiologyplus

Diversity of organisms

Ireland offers a wide range of ecosystems. Depending on your location it is possible to study ecosystems such as a rocky seashore, a grassland, a hedgerow, a rock pool, a stream, a freshwater pond, an old wall, a woodland, a wasteland, an overgrown garden or a peatland.

The following sections will provide a general overview of the range of organisms in each of the two selected ecosystems. The inter-relationships of the organisms with each other and with the non-living (abiotic) parts of each ecosystem will also be outlined.

Rocky seashore ecosystem

Overview

A rocky seashore is a mixed ecosystem; i.e. it is both aquatic (water) and terrestrial (land). It is a harsh environment as there is no soil, wave action occurs, there are periodic tidal changes and there is an exposure to the sun and wind.

It is a particularly easy ecosystem to study because many of the organisms are stationary and cannot easily run away or hide below ground. It shows clear changes (called zonation) in organisms from the water's edge to the high rocks.

6.1 *Seaweeds on a rocky seashore*

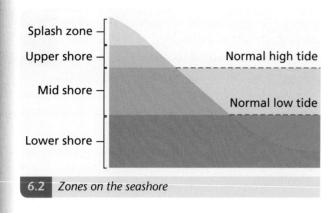

6.2 *Zones on the seashore*

Zones

A rocky seashore is normally divided into four zones, based on tidal movements.

- The **splash zone** is the area on the high ground that is rarely (if ever) covered by the tide.
- The **upper shore** is the area covered by high tides, but not by normal tides.
- The **mid shore** (or inter-tidal zone) is covered by the incoming tide and exposed at normal low tide.
- The **lower shore** is exposed only at very low tides. Very often the organisms here are similar to those found in rock pools.

Organisms found on the rocky seashore

In the following examples some of the adaptations of the organisms to their habitat are given in brackets.

Splash zone

Flora

- Sea pink (a flowering plant often found in crevices, has narrow leaves with many hairs to reduce water loss)
- Lichens (which may be black, orange, grey or green) can grow on bare rock above the water level

Fauna (animals)

- Black periwinkles (can crawl and act as herbivores on lichens and algae)
- Shore crabs (act as carnivores or scavengers, have strong pincers to open shells, have a flat body to shelter under rocks)

6.3 *Periwinkles*

Upper shore

Flora

- Sea lettuce (a green alga which contains lots of chlorophyll for maximum rates of photosynthesis at high light intensities)
- Channel wrack (a brown seaweed covered in mucilage to retain moisture, attached to rocks by a holdfast, fronds (similar to stems and leaves) are folded to form channels to hold water, can survive if out of the water 90% of the time)

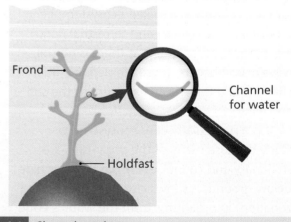

Frond

Channel for water

Holdfast

6.4 *Channel wrack*

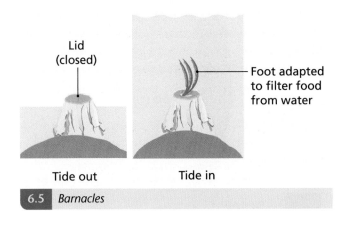

Lid
(closed)

Foot adapted
to filter food
from water

Tide out

Tide in

6.5   Barnacles

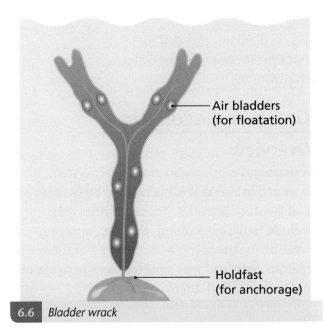

Air bladders
(for floatation)

Holdfast
(for anchorage)

6.6   Bladder wrack

6.7   Dog whelks (with barnacles attached)

Fauna

- Sand hoppers (detritus feeders on dead seaweed, nocturnal, hop rapidly to avoid being eaten)
- Barnacles (tiny animals attached to rocks, covered in shell plates, feed on plankton when covered by the tide; a lid closes over to protect when tide is out)

Mid shore

Flora

- Spiral wrack (a brown seaweed; all brown algae have a brown pigment to allow them to absorb light in dimly lit water, found on the upper reaches of the mid shore, fronds are twisted, survive out of water 60% of the time)
- Bladder wrack (a brown seaweed, has air bladders to allow it to float for maximum light, survives out of water 50% of the time)

Fauna

- Dog whelks (carnivores that bore through shells of barnacles, mussels and limpets)
- Limpets (herbivores, when tide is out feed on algae growing on rocks, attach to same place on the rocks when the tide comes in, ridges on shell prevent starfish from getting a grip and eating the limpet)
- Mussels (filter feeders on plankton when tide is in, attach to rocks by threads)
- Edible periwinkles (herbivores, scrape algae off rocks, heavy protective shell, can breathe out of water for a short time)

THE STUDY OF LIFE

Lower shore

Flora

- Serrated wrack (edges of fronds are jagged, does not tolerate being out of water for long)
- Corallina (a red alga, grows on rocks, red pigments allow it to absorb light at very low intensities, must be covered by water)

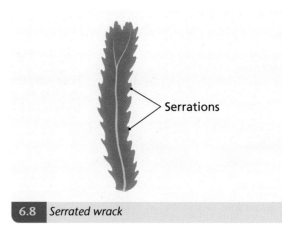

| 6.8 | *Serrated wrack* |

Fauna

- Sponges (attach to rocks, filter feeders on plankton and detritus)
- Flat periwinkles (feed on wrack, do not tolerate being out of water, breathe through gills, dislike high temperatures)

| 6.9 | *Wildflowers in a grassland* |

| 6.10 | *Dandelions and daisies* |

Grassland ecosystem

Overview

A grassland is usually an artificial ecosystem. It is an ecosystem that is maintained by human and livestock activities. These activities may include fertilising, cutting, draining, applying weedkillers, trampling and grazing. For these reasons grassland may not have a wide range of natural plant and, therefore, animal life.

Grasslands are often maintained as a monoculture (i.e. only one species of plant or grass is encouraged to grow). In comparison an unused meadow may have a wider range of living things.

Organisms found in grassland

Flora

- The defining species in a grassland are grasses. Sometimes only one species of grass is found, but often a number of grass species are growing.
- Clover is often grown in grasslands because it contains nitrogen-fixing bacteria. These form nitrates and reduce the need for the artificial addition of expensive fertiliser.
- Other plants that may be found in grasslands include buttercups, dandelions, daisies and nettles.
- If the ground has been disturbed you may find poppies, thistles and dock leaves.
- Near a hedge you may find hedgerow plants such as primroses and bluebells.

6.11 *A hedgehog feeding on a slug*

6.12 *A fox carrying its prey (a mouse)*

Fauna

- In the grass and soil you may find earthworms, snails, slugs, spiders and beetles.
- On the leaves of some of the plants you may find aphids (mostly small greenflies which drink sugar-water from the leaves), ladybirds (which eat aphids) and caterpillars (which chew the leaves).
- On the flowers you may find bees, wasps, butterflies and moths.
- Larger animals may include rabbits, badgers, foxes, hedgehogs, thrushes, blackbirds and hawks.

Scientific study of an ecosystem

It is not possible to study an entire ecosystem because of the large size. Instead, local areas of study (called habitats) are selected from within the ecosystem.

If the habitats are well chosen and if a number are chosen for the ecosystem, they provide a fair representation of the ecology of the overall ecosystem.

> A habitat is the place where a plant or an animal lives (and is also the local area of study).

Identify a number of habitats in the ecosystem

- In a rocky seashore the habitats normally comprise a number of strips. Each strip could be 1 metre wide, running from the high rocks down to the water's edge. Normally a square frame called a quadrat is placed at intervals along the strip. The organisms in each quadrat are then surveyed.
- In a grassland a number (normally 10) of sample areas are studied using a quadrat. The locations for each quadrat may be:
  - ▸ Chosen at random
  - ▸ Placed one after another in a line.

  The second method can be used to show how living things differ along a line or strip of land (e.g. from the base of a hedge out into a field or from a hill down to a wet piece of land).

The study of an ecosystem

The study of an ecosystem involves the five steps outlined below.

1. Mapping the habitat
2. Identifying the flora (plants) and fauna (animals) present
3. Estimating the number of flora and fauna
4. Measuring the environmental (abiotic) factors
5. Presenting the information gathered.

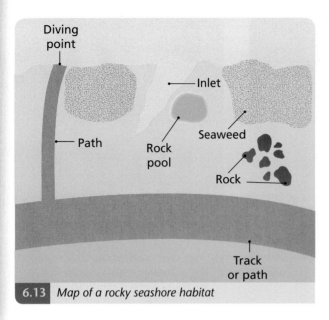

6.13 *Map of a rocky seashore habitat*

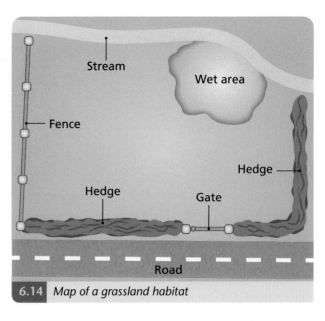

6.14 *Map of a grassland habitat*

Mapping the habitat

Although it is not essential to do so, a simple hand-drawn map (or photograph) of the habitat can be made. This helps to give an overall impression of the area being studied.

Identifying plants and animals

The methods used to identify organisms include the following:

- Get an expert to name them for you in the habitat
- Use guidebooks, photographs or diagrams
- Use an identification key, as described in Activity 2 at the end of this chapter.

A key can be used *in* the habitat. However, it is often necessary to collect plants and animals in the habitat and bring them back to the laboratory for identification. The methods used to collect organisms are outlined in Activity 3 at the end of this chapter.

When collecting organisms it is important to be sensitive to the ecology of the ecosystem. This involves the following rules.

- Follow the Countryside Code (i.e. ask permission to enter private land, close gates, cause no damage to fences, leave no litter)
- Only collect an organism if it is absolutely necessary and you cannot identify it in the habitat
- Return organisms to the habitat if possible
- Leave the habitat as you found it
- Be aware of dangers such as deep water, waves, thorns, stinging insects, bulls and aggressive dogs.

Qualitative vs. quantitative study

A **qualitative study** is carried out by identifying and naming the species directly in the habitat or by collecting and later naming the species.

A **quantitative study** of a habitat gives the numbers of each species that are in the habitat. A quantitative study provides a great deal more information than a qualitative study.

Activities 4a and 4b at the end of this chapter describe how to carry out quantitative studies of plants and animals in an ecosystem.

A **qualitative study** records the presence or absence of organisms.

A **quantitative study** records the numbers of organisms that are present.

Sources of error in an ecosystem study

The possible sources of error in studying an ecosystem can be considered under four headings.

Human error

When studying an ecosystem it is possible to make mistakes in measuring or recording information. This possibility is increased by the work being outdoors, perhaps in poor weather.

For example, there is an element of judgement to be made in deciding if a plant covers 20% or 30% of a quadrat. Equally, a quadrat may be located in an area that is easy to survey, but this area may not be typical of the ecosystem.

Changing conditions

Nature is never static or constant. Ecosystems are subject to changes, both natural (e.g. seasonal) or artificial (e.g. the effects of pollution). As a result, the findings of an ecosystem study may not apply all of the time to that ecosystem.

To allow for the influence of changing conditions it is best to study an ecosystem a number of times, e.g. in autumn, winter and spring.

Accidental discovery

Accidental discoveries have played a significant role in many areas of science. In the study of an ecosystem it is often possible that accidental discoveries will play an important role.

For example, if an animal is very shy it will be scared off by a class visit but may be discovered by an individual walking quietly in the ecosystem. Alternatively, a rare animal (such as a bird of prey) may be present in the area only on rare occasions or at night (e.g. owls).

Sample size

A single habitat may not be a fair representation of the entire ecosystem. For this reason, a number of habitats are studied within each ecosystem. The larger the number of habitats examined, the more accurately the results will reflect the overall ecosystem.

Equally, the size of each habitat studied is important. If the habitat is too small, many plants and animals will be left out of the study.

Influence of abiotic factors

The influences of three abiotic (non-living) factors on animal and plant life are given below.

Rocky seashore

Exposure

- The length of time that a plant can survive when exposed out of the water has a huge influence on where it can grow. There is usually a clear relationship between exposure to the air and the growth of the three species of wrack, as shown in diagram 6.15.

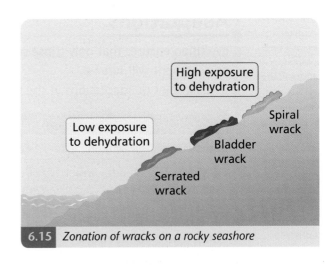

6.15 *Zonation of wracks on a rocky seashore*

- Limpets feed safely when out of water. As there are not enough algae on the upper shore, this restricts limpets to the mid shore (i.e. there are sufficient algae and they can feed when the tide is out).

- Mussels on the lower shore are usually bigger than those on the mid shore (because of being covered by the tide more often). This allows them to feed more often.

Air temperature

There can be up to four species of periwinkle found on a rocky seashore. Each of them has a tolerance for a different maximum temperature. This causes them to be limited to certain regions of the seashore, as shown in diagram 6.16.

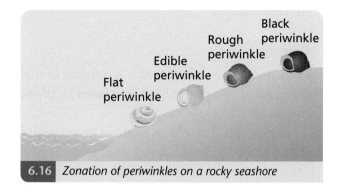

6.16 *Zonation of periwinkles on a rocky seashore*

Wave action

If you compare a sheltered shore with a shore exposed to greater wave action, you will note two main features:

- Different plants can be found higher up on the exposed site; this is because of increased cover by waves or by spray
- Plants with large fronds (e.g. wracks) suffer more damage and are replaced on exposed shores by species with narrow fronds, such as thong weed and corallina.

Grassland

Light intensity

Light intensity is lower near a hedge. This normally means that there is less grass growing at the base of a hedge compared with the middle of a field.

Soil type

Soils can be sandy, clay or loam-based. Sandy soils contain large soil particles and allow easy root penetration and good drainage. Clay soils have small particles, which results in difficult root penetration and poor drainage. Loam soils are a mixture of sand and clay and provide ideal conditions for grassland plants.

pH of soil

Most grassland plants prefer a neutral or slightly basic soil pH. Acid soils are mainly associated with boglands and support a totally different community of plants.

Adaptations

Evolution ensures that only those organisms that are suited (adapted) to their environment will survive.

Examples of adaptations in the two selected habitats are given in the following table.

> **Syllabus** Adaptations may be structural, competitive or behavioural. You are required to know only **one** adaptation by an organism in the ecosystem you studied.

> An **adaptation** is any alteration that improves an organism's chances of survival and reproduction.

Examples of adaptations			
Ecosystem	**Organism**	**Adaptation**	**Benefit**
Rocky seashore	Bladder wrack	Covered with mucilage	Retains moisture when tide is out
	Limpets	Shell	Protection and water retention
Grassland	Dandelions	Seeds have parachutes	Easily dispersed and not overcrowded
	Ladybirds	Brightly coloured	Easily seen and recognised (and avoided: ladybirds are full of acid)

Activity 2 To use simple keys to identify any five fauna and any five flora

Introduction

A wide range of keys is available for different ecosystems. There are separate keys for plants and animals on the rocky seashore, grassland, hedgerows and a variety of other ecosystems.

Other keys deal with seaweeds, flowering plants, trees, mushrooms, insects, spiders, etc.

Sample keys used for identifying organisms
Sample key 1

The simplest type of key is a 'spider' key. These are named because of their shape, as shown in diagram 6.17.

The key shown in diagram 6.17 can be used to name animals, as outlined in diagram 6.18.

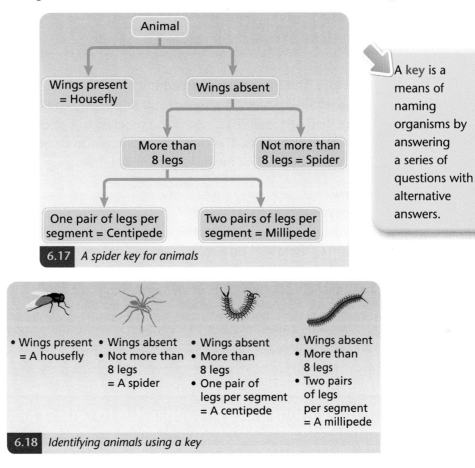

> A **key** is a means of naming organisms by answering a series of questions with alternative answers.

6.17 *A spider key for animals*

6.18 *Identifying animals using a key*

Sample key 2

The key shown below can be used to identify shelled animals at the seashore.

A key to identify seashore animals with shells		
Choice	**Questions**	**Go to**
1	Attached to rocks or similar	2
	Free moving	8
2	Worm-like (tubular)	3
	Not worm-like	4
3	Triangular shape	*Pomatoceros*
	Coiled tube	*Spirorbis*
4	Cone shaped, single shell	Limpet
	More than one shell	5
5	Two dark blue shells	Mussel
	More than two shells	6
6	Six shell plates in a pyramid	Barnacle
	Eight shell plates	*Chiton*

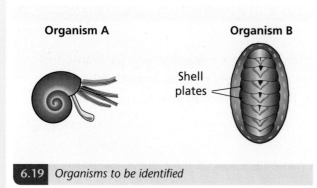

Organism A   **Organism B**

Shell plates

6.19 *Organisms to be identified*

As an example this key could be used to identify organisms A and B in diagram 6.19. Both organisms are found attached to rocks. The steps involved in identifying these organisms are outlined below.

Organism A

Choice number 1 = attached. This means you proceed to choice number 2.

Choice number 2 = worm-like tube. This means you proceed to choice number 3.

Choice number 3 = coiled tube. This means organism A is *Spirorbis*.

Organism B

Choice number 1 = attached. This means you proceed to choice number 2.

Choice number 2 = not a worm-like tube. This means you proceed to choice number 4.

Choice number 4 = more than one shell. This means you proceed to choice number 5.

Choice number 5 = more than two shells. This means you proceed to choice number 6.

Choice number 6 = eight shell plates. This means organism B is *Chiton*.

Presentation of results

By the end of this activity you should have:

- The names and drawings or photographs of five animals and five plants
- Related each organism to its habitat on a map of the ecosystem
- Stated how the organism gets its food
- Drawn a diagram of the reproductive parts of any flowering plant along with its method of pollination
- A detailed study of any one animal or plant to include: its height, mass and any other character that can be measured.

Activity 3   To use various pieces of apparatus to collect plants and animals in an ecosystem

Collecting plants

Plants are collected by breaking off a piece of the plant (preferably with flowers and leaves). Store them in labelled plastic bags.

Collecting animals

Animals that do not move, or move slowly, can be collected directly by hand. For other animals, a variety of devices are used, as shown in diagram 6.20.

Mammals can be collected using special live mammal traps. Earthworms can be collected by pouring water, to which washing-up liquid or mustard is added, on to the soil. The worms crawl to the surface and are collected, washed and stored.

Devices that may be used to collect animals

1. **Pooter:**
   ‣ Used to suck organisms into a jar
   ‣ Collects insects, spiders, sand hoppers.
2. **Beating tray:**
   ‣ Placed under a bush, hedge or tree and the plant is shaken or beaten to knock the organisms down onto the beating tray
   ‣ Collects insects, spiders, caterpillars.

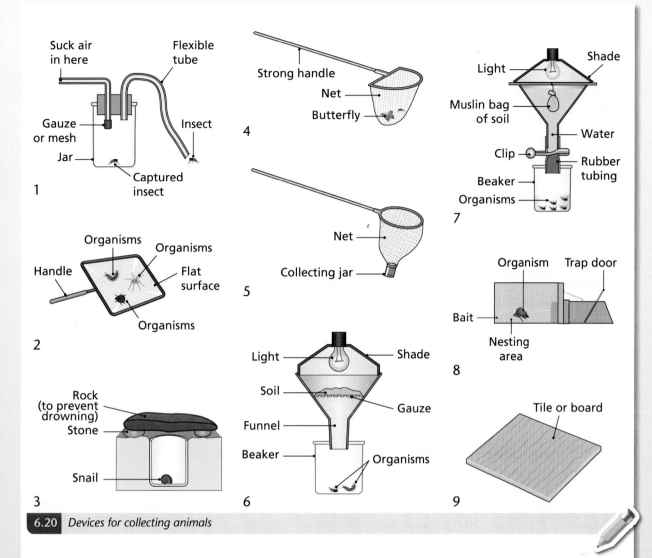

6.20 *Devices for collecting animals*

3. **Pitfall trap:**
   ‣ Placed in soil or sand and covered to prevent rain entering
   ‣ Collects crawling insects, snails, periwinkles.

4. **Sweep net:**
   ‣ Swept through long grass or at the edge of a hedge
   ‣ Collects insects and spiders.

5. **Plankton net:**
   ‣ Drawn through water from a rock or a boat
   ‣ Collects plankton.

6. **Tullgren funnel:**
   ‣ Heat from a bulb causes small organisms to move down out of soil into a collecting jar
   ‣ Collects centipedes, millipedes, small insects.

7. **Baerman funnel:**
   ‣ Heat from a bulb causes small organisms to move down out of wet soil; the clip is opened to release the organisms into a collecting jar
   ‣ Collects water snails, worms.

8. **Mammal trap:**
   ‣ Bait is placed in the trap, which is left in the habitat
   ‣ Animals can enter but are trapped by the trapdoor
   ‣ Collects shrews, mice.

9. **Cryptozoic trap:**
   ‣ Placed on (or supported just above) the soil and left for some time to collect animals that prefer dark or moist conditions
   ‣ Collects slugs, snails, worms.

THE STUDY OF LIFE

Activity 4a To carry out a quantitative survey of plants in an ecosystem

Select a suitable sample area of the ecosystem to study. This local area of study is called a habitat. Within any habitat there are two methods of calculating the numbers of each species.

Subjective estimates involve an individual judgement as to how numerous each type of species is in the habitat. This method is flawed because people may have different estimates for the same species in a habitat.

Objective estimates are better because they do not rely on individual judgements. A grid quadrat is often used to provide an objective estimate.

Quadrats

A quadrat is a square made of metal, wood or plastic. Quadrats can vary in size, but typically have sides of 1 m, 0.5 m or 0.25 m.

A quadrat is thrown randomly (by throwing a ball or stone over the shoulder and placing the quadrat where the object lands) into the habitat. Alternatively, quadrats can be laid out in a line across part of the habitat.

The species within each quadrat are examined as a guideline to what is present within the overall habitat.

The use of quadrats is limited by:
- The fact that fast-moving animals will not remain in a quadrat
- The size of the species, e.g. if used in a woodland they would indicate that there are no trees present (as no tree would be inside a quadrat).

Within each quadrat two sets of measurements are taken: percentage cover and frequency.

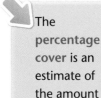

The **percentage cover** is an estimate of the amount of ground in a quadrat covered by each species.

Percentage cover

Within each quadrat the percentage cover of each species is estimated by using one of two methods.

Subjective estimate

The area of a quadrat covered by each species is calculated as a percentage of the total area of the quadrat.

For example, a pencil was thrown at random over the shoulder 10 times in a grassland habitat. A 0.5 m² quadrat was placed (centred) at each of the 10 locations. Within each quadrat the percentage of the area covered by each type of plant (i.e. the % cover) was estimated.

Sample results are shown in the table below. These results show that grass covered 70% of quadrat 1, 90% of quadrat 2, etc. Dandelions covered 15% of quadrat 1, but were not present in quadrat 3, etc.

Percentage cover of plants in a habitat (subjective estimate)												
Plant name	% cover in each quadrat										Total % cover	Average % cover
	1	2	3	4	5	6	7	8	9	10		
Grass	70	90	100	80	70	100	40	70	60	80	760	76
Dandelion	15	10	0	0	0	0	0	5	0	0	30	3
Buttercup	5	0	0	0	20	0	0	15	40	0	80	8
Daisy	10	0	0	0	10	0	0	5	0	20	45	4.5
Thistle	0	0	0	20	0	0	10	5	0	0	35	3.5

Objective estimate

A grid quadrat is a square frame subdivided by wires or string. The quadrat is placed over the pencil as before. Instead of calculating (estimating) the percentage of each quadrat covered by each type of plant, a more objective method is used.

Count the number of times each plant touches a point of intersection (grid point) of each small square. Then express this figure as a percentage of the number of grid points. For example, if dandelions touched the top right of 26 squares in the quadrat shown, then the % cover of dandelions in the quadrat would be calculated as:

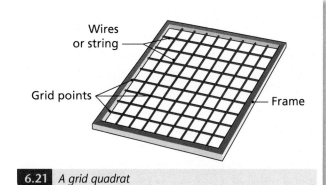

6.21 *A grid quadrat*

$$\frac{\text{No. points covered}}{\text{Total no. grid points}} \times \frac{100}{1} = \frac{26}{100} \times \frac{100}{1} = 26\%$$

A table prepared in this way will appear similar to the one shown below. The percentages are more accurate than those found by the subjective estimate shown in the previous table.

| Plant name | \multicolumn{10}{c}{% cover in each quadrat} | Total number of grid points covered | Total number of grid points | Average % cover |
	1	2	3	4	5	6	7	8	9	10			
Grass	74	92	100	84	67	100	37	70	55	77	756	1000	75.6
Dandelion	13	8	0	0	0	0	0	4	0	0	25	1000	2.5
Buttercup	4	0	0	0	23	0	0	16	40	0	83	1000	8.3
Daisy	9	0	0	0	10	0	0	5	0	21	45	1000	4.5
Thistle	0	0	0	16	0	0	9	5	0	0	30	1000	3

Percentage cover of plants in a habitat (objective estimate)

Frequency

 The **frequency** is the chance of finding a named species with any one throw of a quadrat.

To calculate the frequency of bladder wrack or serrated wrack it is sufficient to record whether they are present or absent in each quadrat, as shown in the table below.

The frequency is calculated as:

$$\frac{\text{No. quadrats containing the plant}}{\text{Total no. quadrats}} \times \frac{100}{1}$$

$$\text{Frequency for bladder wrack} = \frac{4}{10} \times \frac{100}{1} = 40\%$$

$$\text{Frequency for serrated wrack} = \frac{3}{10} \times \frac{100}{1} = 30\%$$

| Plant name | \multicolumn{10}{c}{Quadrat number} | Total | Frequency |
	1	2	3	4	5	6	7	8	9	10		
Bladder wrack	✓	✓	✓	✓	–	–	–	–	–	–	4	40%
Serrated wrack	–	–	–	✓	✓	✓	–	–	–	–	3	30%

Frequency of plants in habitat

This method is fast and easy to use. It has the disadvantage of being dependent on the organism and quadrat size and presumes that organisms are evenly distributed throughout the habitat.

Transects

Transects are used where changes along a gradient are suspected, e.g. across a rocky seashore or from one side of a field to another. They are non-random, because you decide where they should be placed. There are two types of transects.

Line transect

A line transect is a string or rope marked off at regular intervals, e.g. 50 cm or 1 m. The names of the plants or animals that touch the line are recorded. Line transects are of limited use, as they sample only a narrow strip of the habitat.

6.22 *A line transect*

Belt transect

Belt transects consist of two ropes parallel to each other with (usually) 1 m² squares made by tying lengths of string between the two ropes. They are laid down across the habitat to form a series of quadrats in a line (as shown in diagram 6.23).

Alternatively, the same effect can be achieved by placing one edge of a quadrat along a line transect. The contents of each square can be sampled in the same way as normal quadrats or grid quadrats (i.e. percentage cover and frequency).

6.23 *A belt transect*

The environmental conditions should be measured at each mark or quadrat along the transect.

Activity 4b To carry out a quantitative survey of animals in an ecosystem

Quadrats and transects are suited for estimating the numbers of plants and animals that do not move too fast (such as barnacles, limpets or mussels). The capture–recapture method is used to calculate the number of moving animals in a habitat.

Capture–recapture method

This method involves capturing a number of animals of the same species, marking them and releasing them unharmed. The animals should be marked in such a way as not to endanger them.

On a second visit (some day(s) later), a similar number of animals is collected. Some of these will be marked. The total number of animals can be calculated from the formula:

$$\text{No. animals in habitat} = \frac{\text{no. caught and marked on first visit} \times \text{no. caught on second visit}}{\text{no. marked on second visit}}$$

The capture–recapture method can be used for animals such as snails, crabs, periwinkles, woodlice (marked with paint), fish, whales, seals, deer (tagged) and birds (legs ringed).

Example 1

In a study 60 snails were caught and marked with paint on the lower edge of their shell. They were released into the habitat. Two days later 60 more snails were collected; 15 of these were marked. Calculate the number of snails in the habitat.

6.24 *A pitfall trap: note the Perspex rain cover*

Answer 1

$$\text{No. snails} = \frac{\text{no. caught and marked on first visit} \times \text{no. caught on second visit}}{\text{no. marked on second visit}} = \frac{60 \times 60}{15} = 240$$

Example 2

In attempting to estimate the number of wild deer in a woodland, 40 deer were trapped. A tag was placed in the ear of each deer and they were released. A week later 40 more deer were trapped, of which 16 had ear tags. A week later 40 more deer were trapped, of which 20 had ear tags.

Calculate:
(a) The population range of deer in this woodland
(b) The mean (average) population size of deer in this woodland.

Answer 2

(a) Compare the first and second visits.

$$\text{No. deer} = \frac{\text{no. caught and marked on first visit} \times \text{no. caught on second visit}}{\text{no. marked on second visit}} = \frac{40 \times 40}{16} = 100$$

Compare the first and third visits (for the calculations the third visit is now called the second visit).

$$\text{No. deer} = \frac{\text{no. caught and marked on first visit} \times \text{no. caught on second visit}}{\text{no. marked on second visit}} = \frac{40 \times 40}{20} = 80$$

The population range of deer in the woodland is 80 to 100 deer.

(b) Mean population size $= \dfrac{80 + 100}{2} = 90$ deer

The capture–recapture technique involves the following assumptions:
1. Marking must not harm the animals (e.g. make them more visible to predators)
2. Animals mix evenly in the habitat (i.e. they are not bunched, as in colonies of ants or shoals of fish)
3. Animals are restricted to a local area
4. Marked animals are given time to mix with the unmarked population.

Activity 5   To investigate three abiotic factors in a selected ecosystem

Abiotic factors are non-living factors that affect an organism's ability to live in a habitat. There is a wide range of abiotic factors, some of which are relevant only to particular habitats.

Samples of abiotic factors are given for the rocky seashore and a grassland ecosystem. Other possible abiotic factors might include the percentages of air, water and humus in the soil.

Syllabus You are required to investigate only **three** abiotic factors. The factors investigated will vary depending on the ecosystem studied.
In general abiotic factors should be measured at each habitat or quadrat studied.

Rocky seashore
Exposure to the air

The degree of exposure to the air (i.e. when the tide is out) can be judged by comparing the location of each organism on the upper, middle or lower shore.

Air temperature

Air temperature should be taken in the shade, using a thermometer. The temperature of rock pools should be taken at different depths.

Exposure to wave action

The effects of exposure to wave action can be investigated by examining habitats on exposed shores and comparing them with those on more sheltered locations.

Water current

The aspect (i.e. the direction it is facing) of the seashore can be determined with a compass. This may relate to prevailing currents and, in turn, the size of the waves.

Grassland
Air temperature

Air temperatures in different parts of the grassland are taken using a thermometer.

Soil pH

The soil pH is recorded using a pH meter or universal indicator. The indicator, along with some distilled water, is added to a small soil sample in a test tube. A little barium sulfate is added to cause soil particles to clump. This means the water is less cloudy. The colour is compared with the colour on the chart provided to find the exact pH.

Light intensity

Light intensity is measured with a photographic light meter. The readings are taken in different locations, varying from near a hedge to farther out into the grassland. Care should be taken to avoid mixing bright sunshine readings with cloud cover readings.

Aspect

If the grassland is sloping, its aspect (i.e. direction it is facing) can be discovered using a compass. Aspect will affect light intensity and temperature (i.e. both are higher on south-facing sides of grasslands). It also has a bearing on exposure to prevailing winds.

Wind speed

Wind speed and direction can be measured using an anemometer and wind gauge. The rate of rotation of the marker cup is measured.

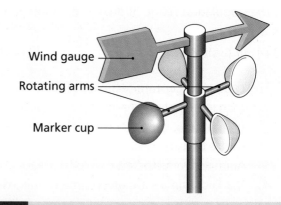

6.25 *An anemometer and wind gauge*

Reporting the results of the study of an ecosystem

1. A report outlining the main details and especially the results obtained in Activities 2, 3, 4a, 4b and 5 should be drawn up. This report should form part of a portfolio of work relating to these activities.

2. Include a title and the date or dates when each aspect of the work was carried out in this report.

3. Write a brief report to include:
   - A map of the ecosystem and habitats selected
   - The procedures used to collect organisms
   - Details of how the organisms were identified
   - An account of how the numbers of organisms were estimated, i.e. how quadrats were used and the results obtained and details of the capture–recapture method
   - Suitable diagrams.

Present the results for five fauna and five flora in the form of tables, histograms, pie-charts or other suitable methods. Present sample food chains, food webs and pyramids of numbers, based on your results. Sample food chains, food webs and pyramids of numbers are given in Chapter 4. Comment on any possible errors or difficulties that may have arisen such as:

- Mistakes made measuring and recording
- Not allowing for conditions to change in the ecosystem over time
- The effect of your intervention in the ecosystem (animals are scared off)
- Any accidental discoveries that might be made
- The habitats studied may not accurately reflect the overall ecosystem.

4. Local factors relevant to a particular habitat should be noted and investigated. These factors might include the effects of a local sewage works, factory, dump, town or village, harbour, road or path, crops in the field and spraying patterns.

Summary

Two sample ecosystems are featured in this chapter:

- Rocky seashore
- Grassland.

You are required only to study any **one** ecosystem, and to know **five** animals and **five** plants from your ecosystem.

Rocky seashore		
Zone	**Plants**	**Animals**
Splash	Sea pink, lichens	Black periwinkles, shore crabs
Upper shore	Channel wrack	Sand hoppers, barnacles
Mid shore	Spiral wrack, bladder wrack	Dog whelks, limpets
Lower shore	Serrated wrack, corallina	Mussels, edible periwinkles, sponges, flat periwinkles

Grassland					
Plants			**Animals** H = herbivore, C = carnivore, D = detritus feeder, O = omnivore		
Grasses	Daisies	Dock	Earthworms (D)	Caterpillars (H)	Rabbits (H)
Clover	Nettles	Primroses	Snails (H)	Ladybirds (C)	Badgers (O)
Buttercups	Poppies	Bluebells	Slugs (H)	Bees (H)	Foxes (C)
Dandelions	Thistles		Spiders (C)	Wasps (H, C)	Hedgehogs (O)
			Beetles (C, H, O)	Butterflies (H)	Thrushes (C)
			Aphids (H)	Moths (H)	Blackbirds (O)

The **study of an ecosystem** involves studying a number of sample habitats, as follows:

- Mapping
- Identifying plants and animals
- Estimating the numbers of plants and animals
- Measuring the environmental (abiotic) factors
- Presenting the information.

Collecting plants and animals involves some of the methods shown in the table overleaf.

THE STUDY OF LIFE

Collection methods		
Device	**Procedure**	**Collected**
Knife	Cut or prise	Plants, limpets
Trowel	Dig	Plants, animals in soil
Pooter	Suck	Insects
Beating tray	Shake bushes	Insects
Pitfall trap	Sink into soil or sand	Crawling animals
Sweep net	Sweep through grass	Insects
Plankton net	Sweep through water	Plankton
Tullgren funnel	Heat soil (using a lamp)	Small organisms from soil
Baerman funnel	Heat soil (using water)	Small organisms from mud
Mammal trap	Set the trap	Mammals
Water with washing-up liquid	Pour onto soil	Earthworms
Cryptozoic trap	Place on ground	Slugs, snails, worms, woodlice

A **habitat** is the place where an organism lives or the local area of study within an ecosystem.

A **suitable key** is used to identify and name organisms.

A **qualitative study** records the presence or absence of species.

A **quantitative study** records the number of each species. Quantitative studies can be:
- Subjective (i.e. a personal judgement is made as to the number)
- Objective (i.e. an independent method of calculating numbers is used).

Subjective methods are not recommended, because they depend on individual judgements, which may vary from person to person.

Errors may arise in the study of an ecosystem in the following ways:
- Mistakes may be made in judgement and recording
- Conditions change in the ecosystem over time
- Accidental discoveries may be made
- The habitats studied may not accurately reflect the overall ecosystem.

A **quantitative study of plants** in a habitat involves using:
- Quadrats, which are examined for:
  - Percentage cover of plants or stationary animals
  - Frequency.

- Transects:
  - Line transect (rope marked at intervals: record what touches the line)
  - Belt transect (equivalent to quadrats taken in a line: methods used are the same as for quadrats).

A **quantitative study of animals** in a habitat involves using:
- The capture–recapture method, i.e.

$$\text{No. animals} = \frac{\text{no. caught on first visit} \times \text{no. caught on second visit}}{\text{no. marked on second visit}}$$

Three abiotic factors are measured and their effects are related to the organisms that are present in one selected ecosystem as shown in the following table:

Examples of abiotic factors		
Ecosystem	**Sample factors**	**Measured by**
Rocky seashore	Exposure to air	Position on shore
	Air temperature	Thermometer
	Water current or wave action	Compare sheltered and exposed shores
Grassland	Air temperature	Thermometer
	Soil pH	pH meter or universal indicator
	Light intensity	Light meter

The **influence of the abiotic factors** measured is examined for one ecosystem, as in the following table:

Effects of abiotic factors		
Ecosystem	Abiotic factor	Influence
Rocky seashore	Exposure	Different species of wrack and animals are found on different zones of the shore
	Temperature	Periwinkles are arranged along a temperature gradient
	Wave action	High wave action forces plants higher on the shore and favours species with narrow fronds
Grassland	Air temperature	Temperature differences in different parts of the grassland will affect how well the plants (and animals) grow
	Soil pH	Soil pH will favour some plants and therefore some animals
	Light intensity	Plants grow better at higher light intensities

Organisms show many adaptations that allow them to survive in their habitat.

The **results of a study** can be presented in tables, lists, charts, graphs, diagrams, etc.

- The results of a study should include food chains, food webs and pyramids of numbers.
- The work carried out in Activities 2–5 should be presented in a portfolio.

Revision questions

1 **(a)** Name the ecosystem you have studied.
(b) From this ecosystem, name five flora and five fauna.
(c) For any one animal or plant in your study state: **(i)** Its range in height, weight, size, colour or any other measurable factor
(ii) Any adaptation it displays to the named ecosystem.

2 From your ecosystem (or habitat) give one example of each of the following:
(a) Producer **(b)** Herbivore **(c)** Carnivore
(d) Scavenger **(e)** Detritus feeder
(f) Top consumer.

3 **(a)** Give a food chain from your chosen ecosystem.
(b) Indicate each of the following on the food chain:
(i) Producer **(ii)** Consumer **(iii)** Herbivore
(iv) Carnivore **(v)** Third trophic level.

4 **(a)** Distinguish between an ecosystem and a habitat.
(b) Name the five main procedures carried out when studying an ecosystem.

5 Draw a food web for the habitat you have studied.

6 **(a)** Name two methods in each case used to collect: **(i)** Plants **(ii)** Animals.
(b) Draw labelled diagrams of three pieces of apparatus used for collecting animals.
(c) Explain how each piece of apparatus is used and give examples of what may be collected using the named apparatus.

7 Use this key to answer the questions that follow.

1	Segmented legs	2
	No legs	6
2	Three pairs of legs	Insect
	More than three pairs of legs	3
3	First and second pairs of legs equal	Harvest spider
	Legs not equal	4
4	Rounded body	Mite
	Elongated body	5
5	One pair of legs per segment	Centipede
	Two pairs of legs on most segments	Millipede

(a) Name the organisms shown in diagram 6.26.

Organism A   Organism B

6.26

(b) Using the information in the key above, state five features of centipedes.
(c) Name the following animal: it has a circular body with four pairs of segmented legs, the first pair being shorter than the second pair.

8 The following is part of a key used to identify animals from a freshwater pond.

1	Soft bodied	2
	Hard covering or shell on body	6
2	Tentacles at end of body	Hydra
	No tentacles on worm-like body	3
3	Body not divided into segments	4
	Body divided into segments	5
4	Body rounded, like a thread	Roundworm
	Body flat, like a ribbon	Flatworm
5	Suckers absent	16
	Suckers present	Leech
6	Limbs not present	7
	Limbs present	9
7	Two shells present	Freshwater mussel
	One shell present	8
8	Shell not spiralled	Freshwater limpet
	Shell spiralled	Pond snail

(a) Use the information in the key to draw a diagram of: **(i)** A leech **(ii)** A roundworm.

(b) Name the animal that fits the following description: it has no limbs but has a single shell, which is not spiralled.

(c) State two differences between a roundworm and a leech.

9 A woodland was 20 m wide and 30 m long. Ten quadrats (each 0.5 × 0.5 m) were thrown and the number of bluebells in each was counted. The results are shown below.

Quadrat number	Number of bluebells
1	4
2	2
3	0
4	0
5	2
6	6
7	4
8	2
9	0
10	0

Calculate: **(a)** The frequency of bluebells. **(b)** The total number of bluebells growing in the wood.

10 In estimating the number of periwinkles in a habitat 80 periwinkles were collected, marked and released. Sometime later 80 more periwinkles were collected in the same habitat. Only 64 of these were marked.
(a) Suggest one way to collect periwinkles for this study.
(b) Suggest one way to mark the periwinkles.
(c) What name is given to this method of calculating animal numbers?
(d) Calculate the number of periwinkles in the habitat.

11 A 2.5 hectare field was surveyed for clover plants using the quadrat method. A quadrat of side 0.5 m was used. The results of the survey are shown in the table below.

Quadrat number	1	2	3	4	5	6	7	8	9	10
Number of plants	6	2	2	2	4	0	2	5	5	2

(a) Estimate the number of clover plants in the field. (1 hectare = 10 000 m²)
(b) A survey of field mice was carried out in the field mentioned above using the capture–recapture method. The field mice were caught using small mammal traps, which were set at random points in the field. Forty field mice were captured, tagged and released at their capture points. One month later the traps were again set at the same locations and 40 field mice were caught. Five of these were found to be tagged. Estimate **(i)** the number of field mice in the field and **(ii)** the population density of the field mice in numbers per hectare.

12 Suggest any two reasons why your survey may not produce an absolutely accurate description of life in the selected ecosystem.

13 **(a)** List three abiotic factors measured in a **named** ecosystem.
(b) Suggest how each factor might influence the distribution of any named plant and any named animal.

Exam questions

Section B

14 (a) (i) What is meant in ecology by a **quantitative** survey?
   (ii) What is a quadrat frame?

(b) Answer the following questions in relation to a quantitative survey of plants that you carried out.
   (i) How did you use the quadrat frame to carry out the survey?
   (ii) Why did you use a number of quadrats or use the quadrat frame a number of times?
   (iii) How did you identify the plants?
   (iv) How did you present your results?
   (v) Is the quadrat method suitable for animal populations? Explain your answer.
   (2007 OL Q 9)

15 (a) (i) What is a habitat?
   (ii) What is an ecosystem?

(b) Answer the following questions by reference to a named ecosystem that you have investigated. Name the ecosystem.
   (i) List **three** abiotic factors that you investigated.
   (ii) For each of the three abiotic factors that you have listed describe how you carried out the investigation.
   (iii) In the case of a **named** organism give an adaptation feature that you noted.
   (iv) Briefly explain how the adaptation feature that you have given in (iii) is of benefit to the organism.
   (2008 HL Q 7)

Section C

16 (c) (i) Give an account of how you carried out a quantitative survey of a named plant species in an ecosystem that you have studied. In your answer describe how you recorded the results of your survey.
   (ii) As a result of a disease, a species of plant disappeared from an ecosystem. Suggest **three** possible effects of the disappearance of this plant on the populations of other plants and animals in the ecosystem.
   (2005 HL Q 12)

17 (c) Answer the following questions <u>in relation to a named ecosystem you have investigated.</u>
   (i) Name the ecosystem.
   (ii) Describe how you collected a **named** animal.
   (iii) State one way in which a **named** organism was adapted to the ecosystem.
   (iv) What is meant by an abiotic factor?
   (v) Give **two** abiotic factors that you investigated.
   (vi) In relation to the abiotic factors you have named, describe how you measured each one.
   (2007 OL Q 10)

18 (c) (i) In relation to a study of an ecosystem distinguish clearly between *qualitative* and *quantitative* surveys by writing a sentence about each.
   (ii) How were you able to identify the different plants in the ecosystem that you investigated?
   (iii) Describe how you carried out a quantitative survey of the major plant species.
   (iv) Give **two** possible sources of error that may have arisen in the course of your survey.
   (2011 HL Q 10)

19 (b) (i) All organisms in an ecosystem are influenced by <u>biotic</u> and <u>abiotic</u> factors. Explain the underlined words.
   (ii) Name any **two** abiotic factors from an ecosystem you have studied and describe how you measured **each** one.
   (iii) Keys may be used to identify animals. Use the following key [overleaf] to identify animals A, B and C. The animals are not drawn to scale.

A   B   C

Legs

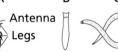
Antenna
Legs

1. Animal has a shell .... *Helix*.
   Animal does not have
   a shell ....Go to 2.
2. Animal has legs..............Go to 3.
   Animal does not
   have legs.......................Go to 4.
3. Animal has three
   pairs of legs................. *Tribolium*.
   Animal has more than three pairs
   of legs.......................*Pieris* larva.
4. Animal has long
   rounded body...........Nematode.
   Animal has flat body with two
   eye spots.....................Planarian.

(iv) All organisms are adapted to their
own habitat.
   1. Name **one** animal from the
      ecosystem you have studied.
   2. Describe **one** way in which it is
      adapted to its habitat.

(c) (i) Distinguish between a quantitative
and a qualitative survey by writing a
sentence about each.

(ii) 1. Name **one** plant from the
      ecosystem you have studied.
   2. Describe how you carried out a
      quantitative survey to determine
      its frequency.

(iii) As a result of pollution, a species of
plant disappears from an ecosystem.
Suggest **two** possible effects that
the disappearance of this plant
might have on the other plants
and animals living in the area.
(2012 OL Q 10)

20 (c) (i) Explain the terms:
   1. *Flora*
   2. *Fauna*.

(ii) Name **one** animal from your named
ecosystem **and** describe how you
carried out a quantitative study of
that animal.

(iii) Suggest **one** way in which marking
an animal might endanger it.

(iv) Ecosystems are subject to changes,
both natural and artificial. Mention
one of **each** type of change as it
applies to your named ecosystem.
(2012 HL Q 11)

Previous examination questions

Ordinary level	Higher level
2004 Q 8	2005 Q 12c
2005 Q 10b	2006 Q 9, 10b
2006 Q 8	2008 Q 7
2007 Q 9, 10c	2009 Q 11c
2008 Q 10b	2011 Q 10c
2009 Q 10b	2012 Q 11c
2011 Q 11b	
2012 Q 10b, c	

Latest questions at www.edco.ie/lcbiologyplus/examhelp

Online test and assessment tracker

Scan the QR code and
test yourself on chapter 6
www.edco.ie/lcbiologyplus

Unit 2
The Cell

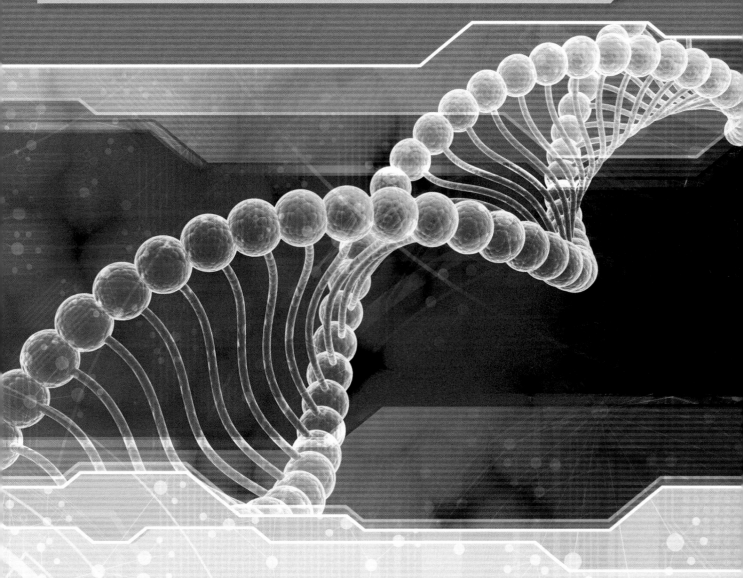

Chapter 7 **Cell structure**

Learning objectives

● To be familiar with the parts of the light microscope and be able to use it
● To be aware of the transmission electron microscope
● To recognise the components of plant cells and animals cells, as seen under a microscope, and describe their function
HIGHER ▶ ● To define and understand the terms 'prokaryotic' and 'eukaryotic'
● To prepare one plant cell and one animal cell (stained and unstained) and examine them using a light microscope.

Microscopes

A **compound microscope** uses two lenses, an objective lens and an eyepiece lens, as shown in diagram 7.1. The total magnification of the image is calculated by multiplying the power of the two lenses (see table below).

Magnification		
Eyepiece lens	**Objective lens**	**Total**
×5	×10	×50
×10	×40	×400

Compound microscopes use light to show the image. The maximum magnification that can clearly be achieved is about ×1000 for a compound microscope.

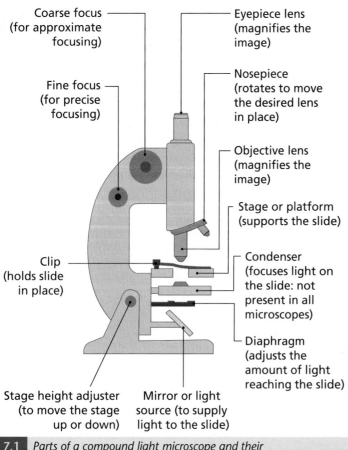

Coarse focus (for approximate focusing)

Fine focus (for precise focusing)

Clip (holds slide in place)

Stage height adjuster (to move the stage up or down)

Mirror or light source (to supply light to the slide)

Eyepiece lens (magnifies the image)

Nosepiece (rotates to move the desired lens in place)

Objective lens (magnifies the image)

Stage or platform (supports the slide)

Condenser (focuses light on the slide: not present in all microscopes)

Diaphragm (adjusts the amount of light reaching the slide)

7.1 *Parts of a compound light microscope and their functions*

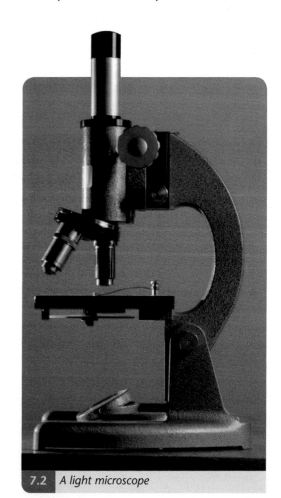

7.2 *A light microscope*

Cell structure as seen using a light microscope

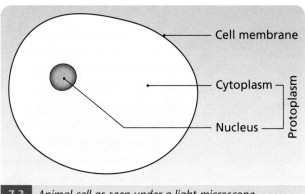

7.3   *Animal cell as seen under a light microscope*

Animal cells

Animal cells are surrounded by an outer membrane, called the cell or plasma membrane. This membrane surrounds the protoplasm.

The protoplasm of a cell is made up of the nucleus and the surrounding cytoplasm.

Many of the reactions in a cell take place in the cytoplasm.

> The protoplasm is all the living parts of a cell.
>
> The cytoplasm is the living material in a cell outside the nucleus.

Plant cells

Plant cells are enclosed by a rigid **cell wall** made of cellulose. Cellulose is a strong structural carbohydrate (or polysaccharide) and is the main component in paper and cotton wool.

The cell wall gives the cell strength and makes it less flexible. The **cell membrane** is usually found just inside the cell wall. The wall and membrane are often so close that the membrane is not seen clearly.

Vacuoles contain a fluid called cell sap. This is a solution of salts, sugars and pigments. Animal cells have no (or very few) vacuoles.

Plant cells also have a **nucleus** and **cytoplasm**. Plant cells that are green contain structures called **chloroplasts**. These are the structures in which photosynthesis takes place.

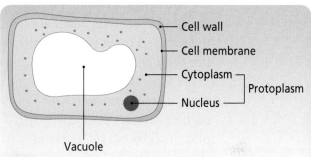

7.4   *Plant cell as seen under a light microscope*

> The vacuole helps to give the cell strength and shape and may also store materials.

Cell ultrastructure

Electron microscopes use a beam of electrons instead of light. As electrons are invisible, the image is often converted to an image on a TV screen.

There are two main types of electron microscope.

- A **transmission electron microscope** (TEM) sends a beam of electrons through a thin section of the specimen. This shows the internal structure of the specimen in great detail.
- A **scanning electron microscope** (SEM) uses a beam of electrons to provide a surface view of the specimen.

> Ultrastructure is the detail of a structure as seen using an electron microscope.

7.5   *An electron microscope*

THE CELL

Electron microscopes can give magnifications of 250 000 and higher. In addition, they can produce very clear images. This makes electron microscopes ideal for observing very small structures.

Ultrastructure of a generalised cell

Cell (or plasma) membrane

All membranes in biology are thought to have the same structure. They are composed of phospholipids and proteins.

The phospholipids, which have a water-loving phosphate group and a water-hating lipid group, are arranged into double layers (bilayers). The phosphates are on the exposed outer surfaces with the lipids in the middle.

In a membrane protein, molecules are completely or partially embedded in the phospholipid bilayer. Some of these proteins are attached to the bilayer; others are detachable and can move throughout the bilayer.

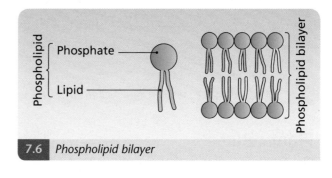

7.6 *Phospholipid bilayer*

Functions of membranes

The functions or roles of membranes include to:

- Retain the cell contents
- Recognise molecules that touch them
- Control what enters and leaves the cell
  - ▷ Membranes can allow the free passage of some molecules and prevent the passage of others; in this way they are said to be selectively (or semi-) permeable. For example, water and oxygen can pass freely across a membrane, but sodium ions and large proteins have to be moved across using energy.
- Give some support to the cell.

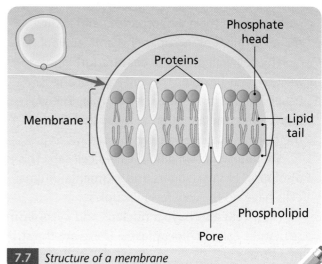

7.7 *Structure of a membrane*

Nucleus

A nucleus is surrounded by a double membrane with numerous nuclear pores. These allow the controlled entry and exit of molecules into and out of the nucleus.

The nucleus contains strands of deoxyribonucleic acid (DNA). DNA is arranged into structures called chromosomes (*chroma* means 'colour', *soma* means 'body'; so-called because DNA readily absorbs many stains and becomes darkly coloured under the microscope).

> The nucleus is the control centre of the cell.

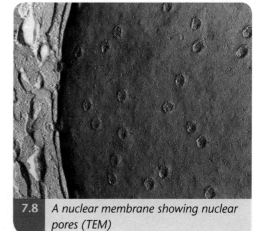

7.8 *A nuclear membrane showing nuclear pores (TEM)*

THE CELL

Every organism has a definite number of chromosomes in each nucleus (e.g. humans have 46). Genes are located randomly along chromosomes.

Genes are the structures that inform the cell how to make certain proteins. Genes control features such as the number of fingers, colour of eyes, production of enzymes and thousands more tasks. They are the units of inheritance.

When a cell is not dividing (i.e. most of the time), chromosomes are very elongated and interwoven. In this form they are called chromatin.

> Humans are thought to have between 20 000 and 25 000 genes in each cell.

> **Chromatin** is the name given to chromosomes when they are elongated and not dividing.

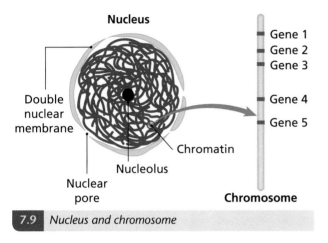

7.9 *Nucleus and chromosome*

Nuclear pores

Nuclear pores allow a type of RNA (ribonucleic acid) called mRNA (messenger RNA) to pass in and out of the nucleus. RNA is dealt with in Chapter 15.

Nucleolus

The nucleolus (plural nucleoli) is an area in the nucleus that stains very darkly.

> The nucleolus makes ribosomes.

Cytoplasm

The cytoplasm is the jelly-like liquid in a cell that surrounds the nucleus.

A number of small bodies called **organelles** (such as mitochondria, chloroplasts and ribosomes) are suspended in the cytoplasm.

Mitochondria

Mitochondria (singular is mitochondrion) are the sites of respiration.

> Mitochondria supply energy to the cell.

- Cells with many mitochondria (e.g. muscle and liver in animals, meristems in plants) produce lots of energy.
- Cells with few mitochondria (e.g. fat in humans, ground tissue in plants) produce less energy.

Mitochondria are surrounded by a double membrane. It is on the inner membrane, especially the infoldings, that energy is released. The more infoldings that are present the greater the surface area for cellular respiration, which results in the production of greater quantities of energy.

Each mitochondrion has its own loop of DNA.

> Active mitochondria convert to the inactive form if the cell rests for too long. This is why prolonged bed rest can cause tiredness when we try to resume normal life. Exercise causes the number of infoldings to increase again.

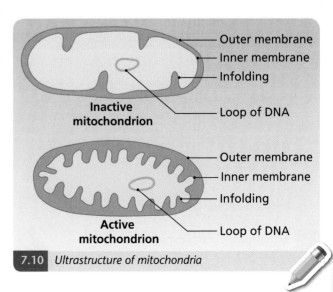

7.10 *Ultrastructure of mitochondria*

THE CELL

Chloroplasts (plants only)

> Chloroplasts are green structures in plants in which photosynthesis takes place.

Chloroplasts are surrounded by double membranes. They have membrane stacks, which contain the green pigment chlorophyll. They also have a loop of DNA. The detailed role of chloroplasts is examined in Chapter 11.

Cell wall (plants only)

> The function of cell walls is to support and strengthen the cell.

Plant cell walls are made of cellulose (which is a structural polysaccharide). Cell walls are fully permeable. This means that **all** molecules (big or small) can pass in or out through cell walls.

Ribosomes

> The function of ribosomes is to make proteins.

Ribosomes are very tiny, bead-like structures. They are made of RNA and protein. They work by combining a sequence of amino acids to form a protein.

Generalised cells

The ultrastructure of a general animal and plant cell is shown in diagrams 7.13 and 7.14.

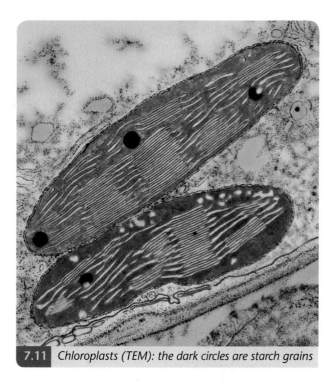

7.11 *Chloroplasts (TEM): the dark circles are starch grains*

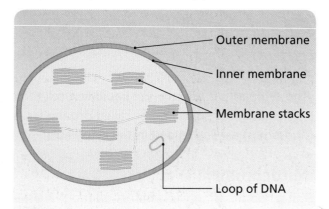

7.12 *Ultrastructure of a chloroplast*

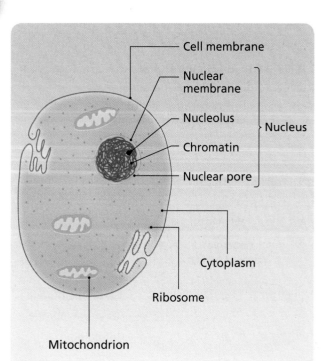

7.13 *Ultrastructure of an animal cell*

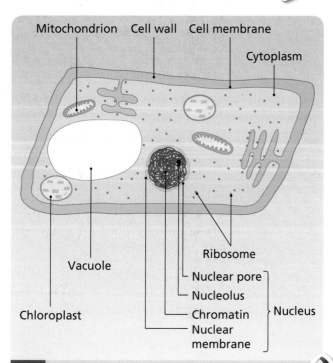

7.14 *Ultrastructure of a plant cell*

Differences between plant and animal cells	
Plant cells	**Animal cells**
Have a cell wall	Do not have a cell wall
May have chloroplasts (containing chlorophyll)	Do not have chloroplasts (or chlorophyll)
Have a large vacuole	Do not have a large vacuole

Prokaryotic and eukaryotic cells

Living things (also called organisms) can be placed into two categories depending on the structure and complexity of their cells: prokaryotes and eukaryotes.

Prokaryotic cells do not have a nucleus or membrane-enclosed organelles.

Prokaryotic organisms:
- Are single-celled
- Have a circular loop of DNA (not surrounded by a membrane, i.e. do not have a nucleus)
- Have small cells
- Do not have a membrane and enclosed structures such as mitochondria and chloroplasts
- Include bacteria.

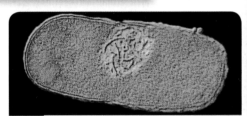

7.15 *A prokaryotic cell (TEM): note the absence of a membrane around the red chromosomes in this bacterial cell*

Eukaryotic cells have a nucleus and cell organelles, all of which are enclosed by membranes.

Eukaryotic organisms:
- Have a nucleus (i.e. DNA enclosed by a membrane)
- May have membrane-enclosed organelles such as mitochondria and chloroplasts
- Have large cells
- Include animals, plants and fungi
- Are more advanced than prokaryotes (i.e. life originated with prokaryotic cells and has evolved into eukaryotic cells).

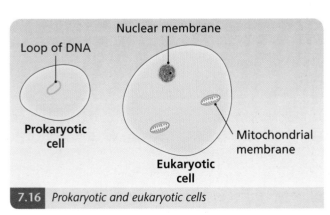

7.16 *Prokaryotic and eukaryotic cells*

Nuclear membrane

Loop of DNA

Prokaryotic cell

Mitochondrial membrane

Eukaryotic cell

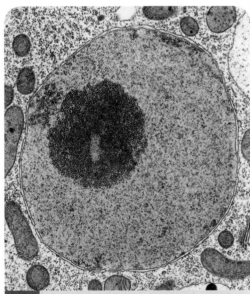

7.17 *A eukaryotic cell (TEM): a plant cell showing the pink nucleus surrounded by a double membrane; the nucleolus is brown*

THE CELL

Activity 6   To be familiar with and to use a light microscope

Examine a range of prepared slides as follows:

1. Make sure that the lenses are clean.
2. Lower the microscope stage as far as it will go.
3. Click the low-power objective lens into place.
4. Place a microscope slide on the stage. Ensure that the object to be viewed is in the centre of the opening in the stage.
5. Clip the slide into position.
6. View the stage from the side and use the coarse adjustment knob to move the low-power objective lens down so that it is just above the slide.
7. View the object through the microscope.
8. Adjust the coarse adjustment knob to move the stage down until the object is in focus. (Steps 6–8 prevent the slide from being damaged by the objective lens.)
9. Adjust the amount of light so that the object can be seen most clearly (this often involves reducing the amount of light). Depending on the type of microscope being used this may involve one or more of the following procedures:
   ▸ Adjusting the condenser to focus light on the object
   ▸ Adjusting the diaphragm to control the amount of light reaching the object
   ▸ Adjusting the angle of the mirror
   ▸ Using the concave side of the mirror
   ▸ Placing a sheet of paper between the bulb and the microscope to cause the light to be diffused.
10. When the object is focused under low power, move the slide so that the part of the object you wish to view is in the centre of what you can see (called your field of view).
11. Click the high-power objective lens into place.
12. The object should be almost in focus. If it is not, use the fine adjustment knob to focus it correctly. Be careful not to move the objective lens too close to the slide (as this would crack the slide).

Activity 7a   To prepare and examine plant (onion) cells, using a light microscope

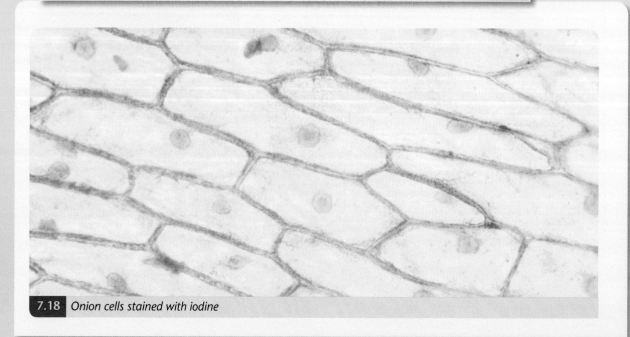

7.18   *Onion cells stained with iodine*

A Prepare the slide

1. Remove the outer, dry scaly leaves of an onion.
2. Use a forceps or your fingers to pull a strip of thin, transparent epidermis from the inner curve of a fleshy, inner leaf.
3. Place a small piece of the epidermal strip on a microscope slide.
4. Add a few drops of iodine solution. (This is a red-yellow stain. It stains the nucleus orange and the cytoplasm yellow. A mixture of potassium iodide and iodine gives a better result.)
5. Add a cover slip (this prevents the cells from drying out and prevents the lens from getting stained). Lower the cover slip at an angle (this eliminates air bubbles).
6. Blot off any surplus iodine, if necessary.
7. The cells can be viewed unstained by using a few drops of water instead of iodine solution at step 4 above.

B Examine under the microscope

1. The slide can be examined under the microscope in the same way as described in Activity 6.
2. The results will appear similar to those shown in diagram 7.18.
3. Draw diagrams of what you can see at low power and at high power.

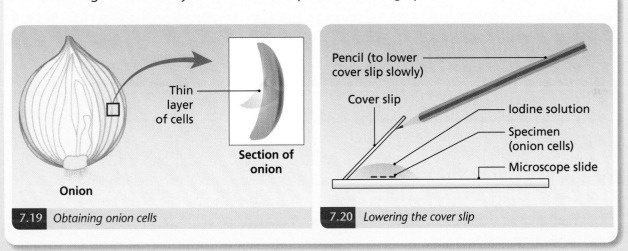

7.19 *Obtaining onion cells*

7.20 *Lowering the cover slip*

Activity 7b To prepare and examine animal (cheek) cells, using a light microscope

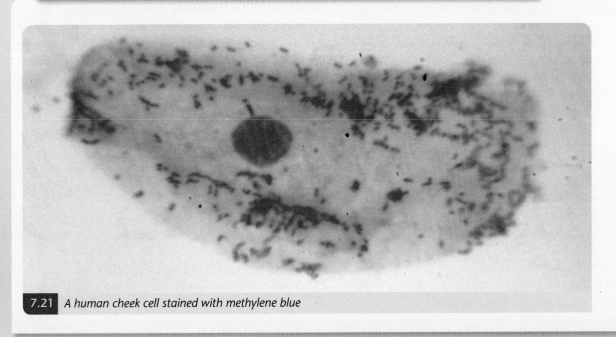

7.21 *A human cheek cell stained with methylene blue*

THE CELL

A Prepare the slide

1. Rinse your mouth out with water.
2. Scrape the inside of your mouth with a lollipop stick or a cotton wool bud (this will collect many cheek cells).
3. Spread the smear of cells thinly onto a glass slide.
4. Add a few drops of methylene blue (this stains the nucleus dark blue and the cytoplasm pale blue) and leave for a few minutes.
5. Add a cover slip at an angle (to eliminate air bubbles).
6. Blot off excess stain, if necessary.
7. The cells can be viewed unstained by using water instead of methylene blue at step 4.

B Examine under the microscope

1. The slide can be examined under the microscope in the same way as described in Activity 6.
2. The result will appear as shown in diagram 7.21.
3. Draw diagrams of the cells at low power and at high power.

Summary

THE CELL

Microscopes:
- Compound = two lenses
- Electron microscopes show ultrastructure:
  ‣ Transmission electron microscope (TEM) shows internal structures
  ‣ Scanning electron microscope (SEM) shows surfaces.

Cell (plasma) membrane:
- Surrounds the cell
- Controls the entry and exit of molecules to the cell.

Nucleus:
- Controls the cell
- Contains chromosomes, which have DNA (elongated, non-dividing chromosomes are called chromatin).

DNA:
- Stands for 'deoxyribonucleic acid'
- Is found in chromosomes or chromatin in the nucleus.

Nucleolus, located in nucleus:
- Makes ribosomes.

Vacuoles (plants only):
- Functions are to strengthen the cell and storage.

Mitochondria:
- Provide energy (through respiration)
- Are numerous in active cells

- May have many infoldings, which imply a large energy output.

Chloroplasts (plants only):
- Are green and carry out photosynthesis.

Cell wall (plants only):
- Is made of cellulose
- Provides support.

Ribosomes:
- Make protein.

Prokaryotic cells:
- Do not have a nucleus or membrane-enclosed organelles
- Are small and more primitive than eukaryotic cells
- Are found as bacteria.

Eukaryotic cells:
- Have a membrane-enclosed nucleus and cell organelles
- Are larger and more advanced than prokaryotic cells
- Are found as plant and animal cells, fungi and *Amoeba*.

Observing cells:
- Prepare and stain cells on a slide
- Examine under low power, then high power
- Stain plant cells using iodine solution
- Stain animal cells using methylene blue.

HIGHER ▼

Revision questions

1   (a)   Name the parts labelled A, B, C, D, E and F
          on the diagram of the microscope below.

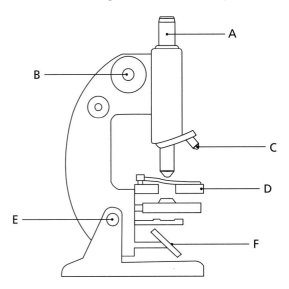

7.22

   (b)   Give the reason why this is an example of a
         compound microscope.
   (c)   What are the functions of the parts labelled
         B and C?
   (d)   If lens A is marked ×10 and and lens C is
         marked ×20, what is the total magnification
         of the image?

2   When using microscopes explain why:
   (a)   Thin specimens are used
   (b)   The specimen is placed in water
   (c)   Stains are sometimes used
   (d)   You should focus the objective lens
         upwards (away from the slide) first
   (e)   You use low power first, followed by
         high power
   (f)   A cover slip is used
   (g)   The cover slip is placed on the slide at
         an angle.

3   (a)   Name any stain you have used for
          microscopic examination.
   (b)   What was the stain used to highlight?
   (c)   What colour did the stain appear under the
         microscope?

4   (a)   Suggest any advantage of an electron
          microscope compared with a light
          microscope.
   (b)   What is meant by cell ultrastructure?

5   (a)   In what cell organelle are amino acids
          joined together?
   (b)   Name the food type formed in these
         organelles.

6   (a)   Name the material(s) that form the: (i) Cell
          wall (ii) Nucleus (iii) Cell membrane.
   (b)   What structure in animals carries out the
         function of the cell wall in plants?

7   (a)   Give the functions of: (i) Plasma membrane
          (ii) Cell wall (iii) Nucleus
          (iv) Vacuoles (v) Mitochondria
          (vi) Chloroplasts (vii) Ribosomes.
   (b)   Which of the structures named in part
         (a) are found only in plants?

8   (a)   Draw a labelled diagram of an animal cell
          as seen using the light microscope.
   (b)   What extra structures might be seen if a
         plant cell were drawn?

9   (a)   Draw a diagram to show the ultrastructure
          of an animal cell. Label at least six parts.
   (b)   Repeat part (a) for a plant cell.

10 (a)   Why do sperm cells have many
          mitochondria?
   (b)   Name a type of animal cell that has few
         mitochondria.

11 Distinguish between prokaryotic and
    eukaryotic cells on the basis of:
    (a) Nucleus (b) Cell organelles (c) Size
    (d) Examples in modern organisms.

Exam questions

Section A

12   Use ticks (✓) to show if the named structure is present in an animal cell, in a plant cell or in both. The first
     has been completed as an example.

Structure	Cytoplasm	Cell wall	Chloroplast	Nucleus	Vacuole
Animal cell	✓				
Plant cell	✓				

(2005 OL Q 2)

Section B

13 (a) (i) Name the parts of the light microscope labelled A and B.

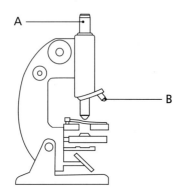

(ii) If the magnification of A is ×10 and the magnification of B is ×40, what magnification results when a slide is viewed using B?

(b) Answer the following in relation to preparing a slide of stained plant cells and viewing them under the microscope.

(i) From what plant did you obtain the cells?

(ii) Describe how you obtained a thin piece of a sample of the cells.

(iii) What stain did you use for the cells on the slide?

(iv) Describe how you applied this stain.

(v) What did you do before placing the slide with the stained cells on the microscope platform?

(vi) State **two** features of these cells that indicate that they are typical plant cells.

(2004 OL Q 7)

14 (a) State a function of each of the following components of a cell.

(i) Ribosome

(ii) Cell membrane

(b) Answer the following questions in relation to the preparation, staining and microscopic observation of a slide of an animal cell.

(i) What type of animal cell did you use?

(ii) After staining, a cover slip is placed on the slide. Give a reason for this.

(iii) How did you apply the cover slip? Why did you apply it in this way?

(iv) Describe the difference in colour or depth of colour, if any, between the nucleus and cytoplasm when the stained cell was viewed under the microscope.

(2006 HL Q 8)

Section C

15 (c) (i) State the precise location of the cell membrane in plant cells.

(ii) With what type of cell do you associate membrane-bound organelles?

(iii) What corresponding term is used to describe bacterial cells?

(2011 HL Q 14)

Previous examination questions

Ordinary level	Higher level
2004 Q 7	2006 Q 8
2005 Q 2	2010 Q 8
2006 Q 2	2011 Q 14c
2007 Q 3	2012 Q 12a
2010 Q 3	
2011 Q 9	
Latest questions at www.edco.ie/lcbiologyplus/examhelp	

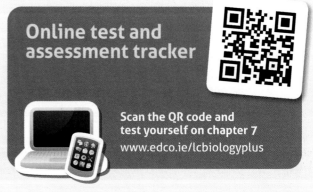

Online test and assessment tracker

Scan the QR code and test yourself on chapter 7
www.edco.ie/lcbiologyplus

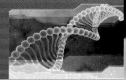

Chapter 8 **Cell diversity**

Tissues

> A **tissue** is a group of similar cells that are modified (or adapted) to carry out the same function(s).

Different types of tissues have different structures, but in all cases the structure of a tissue is designed to allow the tissue to perform its special task or function. A simple tissue has only one cell type. Complex tissue has more than one cell type.

Plant tissues

There are four main types of plant tissue: dermal, vascular, ground and meristematic tissue. These tissues will be discussed in detail in Chapter 23. In this chapter we will look briefly at dermal and vascular tissue.

Syllabus You are required to know **two** types of plant tissue.

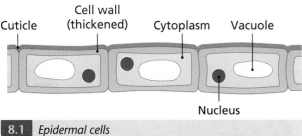

Cuticle | Cell wall (thickened) | Cytoplasm | Vacuole

Nucleus

8.1 *Epidermal cells*

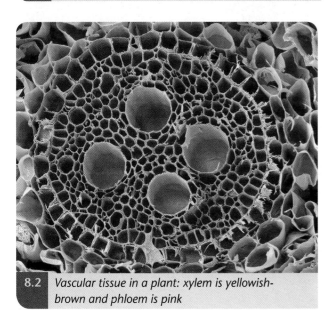

8.2 *Vascular tissue in a plant: xylem is yellowish-brown and phloem is pink*

Dermal tissue

Dermal tissue is normally a single layer of cells that surrounds the different parts of a plant. Epidermis is one type of dermal tissue.
- **Location**: epidermis is found as a covering on leaves, stems and roots.
- **Description**: epidermal cells often have a slightly thickened cell wall; sometimes the epidermis has a waterproof layer, called a cuticle, on its outer surface.
- **Function**: the main function of dermal tissue is to protect the plant.

Vascular tissue

Vascular tissue transports materials around a plant. It is a complex tissue because it consists of two types of cells: xylem and phloem.

THE CELL

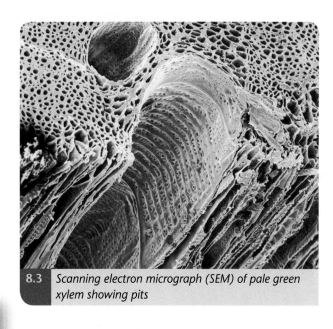

8.3 *Scanning electron micrograph (SEM) of pale green xylem showing pits*

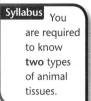

Xylem

- **Description:** xylem consists of hollow tubes with openings called pits that run continuously from the roots, up through the stem and into the leaves.
- **Function:** the main function of xylem is to transport water (and dissolved minerals) throughout the plant; a second function of xylem is to provide support.

Phloem

- **Description:** phloem also consists of a series of tube-like structures found in the leaves, stems and roots of a plant.
- **Function:** the function of phloem is to transport food from the leaves to the other parts of the plant.

Xylem and phloem are covered in more detail in Chapter 23.

Animal tissues

> **Syllabus** You are required to know **two** types of animal tissues.

There are four main types of animal tissue: epithelial, connective, muscular and nervous tissue. Epithelial tissue covers the internal and external surfaces of the body. Muscular tissue can contract and is found in muscles and many internal organs.

In this chapter, connective and nervous tissues are described in more detail.

Connective tissue

- **Description:** connective tissue consists of a number of cells spread out in a matrix (or material) that is produced by the connective cells.
- **Function:** connective tissue joins and supports other body structures.

Examples of connective tissue are adipose tissue (which stores fat, e.g. under the skin), cartilage, bone and blood. Blood is a connective tissue because it consists of red cells, white cells and platelets suspended in a matrix called plasma (see Chapter 25).

Nervous tissue

- **Description:** nervous tissue is composed of nerve cells called neurons.
- **Function:** neurons are adapted to carry electrical impulses to and from the brain and spinal cord. The detailed structure and functions of neurons are explained in Chapter 33.

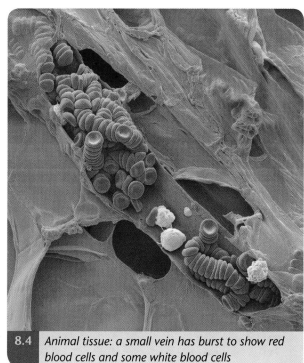

8.4 *Animal tissue: a small vein has burst to show red blood cells and some white blood cells*

Tissue culture

The growth of cells (or tissues) outside the body in an artificial environment is called **in vitro** growth (from the Latin *vitreus*, meaning glass). Tissue culture generally works on the basis that a sample of a tissue is removed from a plant or animal. The tissue sample is grown in glassware, or in a bath or bioreactor, under carefully controlled conditions.

Very often cells are grown in a bath of sterile fluid containing a source of nutrition. Sterile means that no micro-organisms are present. This is necessary as micro-organisms might grow faster than the desired cells and they might contaminate the product. Nutrients are needed to allow the cells to grow. It is common to also include hormones and other substances to enhance growth.

> Tissue culture is the growth of cells in or on a sterile nutrient medium outside an organism.

> **Syllabus** You are required to know **two** applications of tissue culture.

Applications of tissue culture

8.5 *Micropropagation: cereal plants growing on a sterile medium*

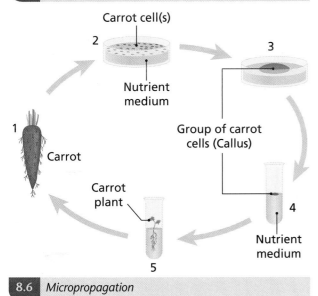

8.6 *Micropropagation*

Plant breeding

Micropropagation is the growth of large numbers of plants from very small plant pieces, often simply from plant tissues or cells.

In micropropagation, a desirable plant is cut into many small pieces (containing from one to a few thousand cells). The cells are grown or cultured in a laboratory on a suitable medium. In time they form a clump of similar cells called a callus.

The growing conditions are then changed so that the callus continues to grow. After some time a young plant embryo and then a young plant is formed. When the young plants are sufficiently large they may be planted out as normal small plants.

The formation of a new plant from a single cell or a small number of cells in this way shows that each nucleus has all the genes or instructions necessary to form an entire adult organism.

Benefits of micropropagation
- A large number of plants are produced in a short time.
- The plants grown in this way are genetically identical.
- It is an inexpensive way to produce large numbers of similar plants.

Cancer research

Antibodies are special proteins that react with (or join onto) one particular chemical (called an antigen). Antibodies are produced by white blood cells.

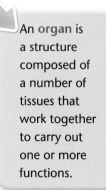

Cancer cells produce special antigens that are not present on any normal body cells. Using tissue culture, it is now possible to produce special antibodies (called monoclonal antibodies, or MABs) that will react with the antigens on cancer cells.

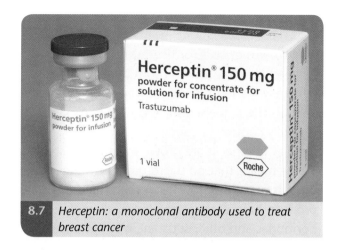

8.7 *Herceptin: a monoclonal antibody used to treat breast cancer*

Benefits of monoclonal antibodies for cancer

- MABs may change colour when they react with cancer antigens. In this way they are used to tell if a sample of cells is cancerous.
- If toxic drugs are attached to the MABs the drug is delivered only to cancer cells (i.e. the MABs will not join to normal cells).

Skin grafts

Tissue culture can be used to grow new skin for patients who have been badly burned. Previously, skin had to be taken from a healthy part of the body and transplanted onto the burned areas.

Very often the cells used to grow new skin are stem cells. These are the cells that can

8.8 *Skin grown outside the body*

develop into any body tissue. Originally stem cells were taken from embryos but now they can be taken from places such as bone marrow and umbilical cords.

Benefits of skin produced by tissue culture

- There is no need to remove skin from another part of the body.
- The new skin is identical to the patient's skin and is not rejected by their body.

An organ is a structure composed of a number of tissues that work together to carry out one or more functions.

8.9 *Plant organs: an avocado seed (the stone) surrounded by the fruit*

Organs

Plant organs include roots, stems, leaves, flowers, seeds and fruits.

Animal organs include the stomach, brain, lungs, liver, kidney and heart.

An example of a plant organ

A leaf contains three types of plant tissue:

1. Dermal tissue is found in the epidermis
2. Vascular tissue is found as xylem and phloem in the vascular bundle(s)
3. Ground tissue is found as the palisade and mesophyll cells.

All of these tissues combine so that the leaf can carry out the function of photosynthesis. A more detailed account of the leaf is given in Chapter 24.

An example of an animal organ

The heart is an organ designed to pump blood. It contains all four types of animal tissue:

1. The walls of the heart are made of cardiac muscle (muscular tissue)
2. The heart is enclosed in a membrane called the pericardium (epithelial tissue)
3. Blood and numerous blood vessels are present (connective tissue)
4. The heart is controlled by nervous tissue (the pacemaker).

The structure of the heart is described in Chapter 26.

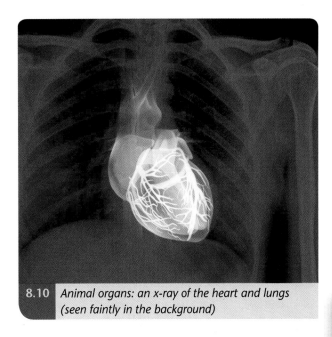

8.10 *Animal organs: an x-ray of the heart and lungs (seen faintly in the background)*

Organ systems

An **organ system** consists of a number of organs working together to carry out one or more functions.

Animals such as humans consist of 10 organ systems. These are the epithelial, skeletal, muscular, digestive, circulatory, respiratory, urinary, nervous, endocrine and reproductive systems. All of these organ systems, except the reproductive system, are essential for the survival of the individual.

While each organ system has its own functions, all the systems combine to allow the animal to survive and reproduce. All the organ systems combine to form the organism.

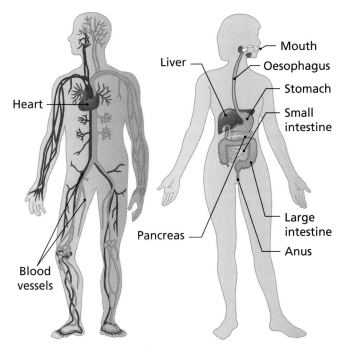

CIRCULATORY SYSTEM DIGESTIVE SYSTEM

8.11 *The circulatory and digestive systems*

Two examples of animal organ systems

- The **circulatory system** consists of the heart, blood vessels and blood. It also includes lymph vessels and lymph. Its **functions** are to transport materials around the body and to fight infection.

- The **digestive system** consists of the mouth, oesophagus, stomach, small intestine, large intestine and anus (in association with the liver and pancreas). Its **functions** are to take in food, break it down and transfer the digested food into the circulatory system so that it can be carried to all the cells in the body.

Biological organisation

An example of how cells, tissues, organs and organ systems are organised in an organism is shown in diagram 8.12.

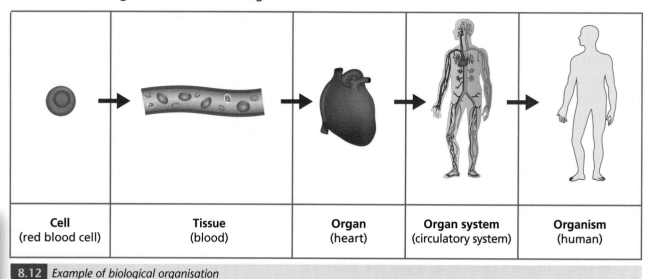

| Cell (red blood cell) | Tissue (blood) | Organ (heart) | Organ system (circulatory system) | Organism (human) |

 8.12 *Example of biological organisation*

Summary

A **tissue** is a group of similar cells modified to carry out the same function(s).

The **four basic plant tissue types** are: dermal, vascular, ground and meristematic tissues.
- Dermal tissue surrounds and protects the plant
  ▸ Epidermis.
- Vascular tissue transports materials throughout the plant:
  ▸ Xylem transports water and dissolved minerals
  ▸ Phloem transports food.

The **four basic animal tissue types** are: epithelial, connective, muscular and nervous tissues.
- Connective tissue consists of cells dispersed in a matrix, and it surrounds and supports body parts.
  ▸ Blood has red cells, white cells and platelets carried in plasma.
- Nervous tissue is adapted to carrying electrical impulses throughout the body.
  ▸ Neurons are nerve cells.

Tissue culture is the growth of cells in or on a sterile nutrient artificial medium outside the body.

In vitro means outside the body.

Micropropagation, the production of monoclonal antibodies and the growth of skin are forms of tissue culture.

- **Micropropagation:**
  ▸ Is the growth of large numbers of plants from cells of a parent plant
  ▸ Rapidly produces new genetically identical plants.
- **Monoclonal antibodies:**
  ▸ Combine with a specific, single type of antigen
  ▸ May be used to attach to and show the presence of antigens on cancer cells.
- **Growth of skin:**
  ▸ Patient's skin grown outside the body
  ▸ New skin is grafted onto the wound.

An **organ** is made of a number of tissues working together to carry out one or more functions.
- Plant organs include the root, stem and leaf.
- Animal organs include the brain, liver and heart.

An **organ system** contains a number of organs working together to carry out one or more functions.
- Animal organ systems include the circulatory and the digestive systems.

Multicellular living things are organised in the following manner:
- Cells → Tissues → Organs → Organ systems → Organism

THE CELL

Revision questions

1 (a) Define a tissue.
   (b) Name two types of plant tissue and state a function for each tissue named.
   (c) Name two types of animal tissue and state a function for each of the tissues named.

2 Distinguish between the two types of plant vascular tissue under the headings:
   (a) Names of tissue (b) Functions.

3 (a) What is meant by tissue culture?
   (b) Why is tissue culture sometimes called *in vitro* culture?

4 (a) Name two applications of tissue culture.
   (b) Name a product formed in each case.
   (c) Suggest one benefit of each named product.

5 (a) Define an organ.
   (b) Name a plant organ.
   (c) Give the main function of this organ.
   (d) Name two types of tissue found in the named plant organ.

6 (a) Name an animal organ.
   (b) State the function of this organ.

   (c) Name two types of tissue present in the named organ

7 (a) Define an organ system.
   (b) Name two animal organ systems.
   (c) Name one organ from each of the named organ systems.

8 State which of the following options, (i), (ii), (iii) or (iv), is the correct answer.
   (a) Which of the following is a tissue?
        (i) Blood vessel (ii) Leaf
        (iii) Epidermis (iv) Oesophagus
   (b) Which of the following is an organ?
        (i) Mesophyll (ii) Epidermis
        (iii) Pancreas (iv) Blood
   (c) Which of the following is an organ system?
        (i) Blood vessels (ii) Brain cells
        (iii) Leaf (iv) Nervous system
   (d) Micropropagation is an example of:
        (i) Leaf culture (ii) Cancer culture
        (iii) Spleen culture (iv) Tissue culture

Exam questions

Section A

9 (a) What is a tissue?
   (b) Name a tissue found in plants.
   (c) Give a function of the tissue referred to in part (b).
   (d) Name a tissue found in animals.
   (e) Give a function of the tissue referred to in part (d).
   (f) Explain what is meant by the term *tissue culture.*
   (g) Give **one** application of tissue culture.
                                    (2010 HL Q 4)

Section C

10 (a) (i) What is a tissue?
        (ii) Name **two** tissues found in animals.

   (b) Tissue culture is used to make a skin graft for patients who have been severely burned.
        (i)   What is meant by tissue culture?
        (ii) Name the gas needed to release energy to make a skin graft.
        (iii) Suggest the most suitable temperature to make skin cells grow.
        (iv) Suggest a reason why sterile conditions are needed in tissue culture.
        (v)   What type of cell division, mitosis or meiosis, is involved in tissue culture?
        (vi) Give **one** other application of tissue culture apart from skin grafting.
                                    (2007 OL Q 11)

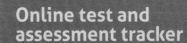

Previous examination questions

Ordinary level	Higher level
2007 Q 11, 14a	2010 Q 4
2009 Q 14	2012 Q 2
2012 Q 14c	

Latest questions at www.edco.ie/lcbiologyplus/examhelp

Online test and assessment tracker

Scan the QR code and test yourself on chapter 8
www.edco.ie/lcbiologyplus

Chapter 9 **Enzymes**

Metabolism

Metabolism is the sum of all the chemical reactions that take place within an organism. These reactions involve growth, movement, maintenance of a constant internal state, repair, response to stimuli and reproduction. Each of these changes requires that energy is released or absorbed. This means that metabolism is closely associated with energy conversions.

Metabolism is necessary to control the chemical and energy requirements of a cell. By doing this, metabolism maintains a balanced internal state (called homeostasis) within an organism.

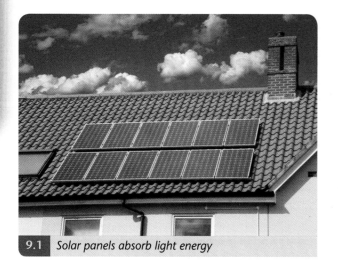

9.1 *Solar panels absorb light energy*

Sources of energy

Solar energy

The primary source of energy for life on Earth is sunlight. Some of the energy in sunlight (solar energy) is trapped by organisms that contain pigments which can absorb light. Chlorophyll is one of these pigments.

Producers such as green plants use solar energy to form the chemical bonds of carbohydrates and other biomolecules. This form of energy conversion is carried out by the process of photosynthesis.

Cellular energy

Solar energy is energy from the Sun.

Cellular energy is the energy stored in the bonds of biomolecules.

Cellular energy refers to sources of energy that are capable of being released by reactions within a cell, i.e. the energy stored in the bonds of biomolecules such as carbohydrates or lipids.

Some of the chemical energy stored in the bonds of biomolecules is transferred to consumers when they eat producers. The energy can then pass along the entire food chain.

Each organism breaks down energy-rich biomolecules in the process of respiration. This releases energy, some of which is used by the cells, while the rest is released into the environment as heat.

Enzymes

Enzymes are catalysts made of protein. This means that enzymes are often called biological (or organic) catalysts.

Enzymes are used to speed up chemical reactions and allow them to proceed at normal cell temperatures.

Enzymes are made of chains of amino acids which are then **folded** into a three-dimensional (3-D) shape. The 3-D shape of an enzyme means that it will fit neatly and react only with a substance of a shape that matches the enzyme. This is similar to the way in which a glove fits neatly on a person's hand, but not on his/her foot.

> ! Note that while all enzymes are proteins, not all proteins are enzymes.

> A **catalyst** is a substance that speeds up a reaction, without itself being used up in the reaction.

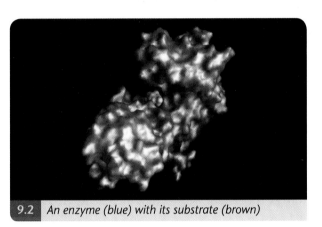

9.2   *An enzyme (blue) with its substrate (brown)*

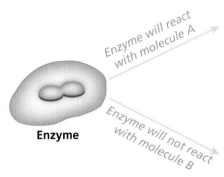

Enzyme will react with molecule A → **Molecule A**

Enzyme

Enzyme will not react with molecule B → **Molecule B**

9.3   *The importance of enzymes having the right shape*

Anything that changes the shape of an enzyme will reduce the efficiency of the enzyme to speed up a reaction. Changing the pH or temperature of a reaction will change the shape of enzymes, which in turn will affect the speed of the reaction.

Features of enzymes

As an example of a typical enzyme reaction consider the reaction in diagram 9.4.

- Enzymes are made of protein.
- Enzymes work because they have the correct **shape** to fit the substrate. This means the enzyme must have a complex, 3-D shape in order for it to fit with the substrate.
- Enzyme reactions are **reversible**. Just as a key can either open or close a lock, an enzyme can cause a reaction to proceed in either direction. This means any enzyme can be anabolic (forms more complex compounds) or catabolic (breaks down larger compounds).

	Amylase	
Starch (substrate)	→ (enzyme)	Maltose (product)

9.4   *A sample of an enzyme-controlled reaction*

The role of enzymes

Enzymes are necessary in plants and animals to control metabolic reactions. Of the vast range of enzymes controlling metabolic reactions, we will consider some catabolic enzymes and some anabolic enzymes.

Catabolic enzymes

- **Amylase** (sometimes called diastase) is an enzyme that converts starch into maltose. It is a catabolic enzyme, because it breaks down a substance into simpler parts.
  - ▸ Amylase is produced by the salivary glands in the mouth and by the pancreas. It converts starch to maltose.
  - ▸ When seeds germinate, the enzyme amylase converts starch in the seed into maltose.
- Other digestive enzymes (such as pepsin and lipase) are also catabolic enzymes, as are the enzymes used in respiration.

> **Enzymes** are proteins that speed up a reaction without being used up in the reaction.
>
> The **substrate** is the substance with which an enzyme reacts.
>
> The **product** is the substance(s) the enzyme forms.

THE CELL

103

Anabolic enzymes

- The enzyme **DNA ligase** is used in genetic engineering to join two pieces of DNA together (see Chapter 18).
- **DNA polymerase** is an enzyme found in both plants and animals that forms and repairs DNA. It is an anabolic enzyme, because it converts simpler molecules into a more complex form.
- The enzymes that control photosynthesis are also examples of anabolic enzymes. They convert water and carbon dioxide into glucose.

> A denatured enzyme has lost its shape and can no longer function.

Factors affecting enzyme activity

Enzymes work best under certain ideal conditions. Any change in these conditions will effect the rate of the reaction. These conditions include temperature and pH.

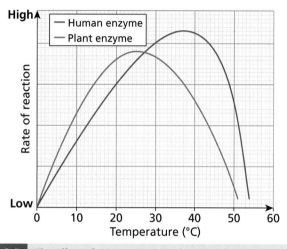

9.5   *The effect of temperature on the rate of reaction*

Temperature

The way in which temperature affects the rate of a reaction is shown in diagram 9.5.

At very low temperatures (0°C for pure water), ice forms. This means that cell contents become solid and enzymes cannot work.

As the temperature increases from 0°C, the rate of molecular movement increases. This causes substrate molecules and enzymes to 'collide' into each other more often. As a result the rate of reaction increases.

Human enzymes work best at 37°C (body temperature), whereas most plant enzymes work best at 20–30°C.

Above a certain temperature, enzymes begin to lose their 3-D shape. As a result the rate of reaction falls. When the shape of an enzyme is fully lost (usually above 50°C), the enzyme is said to be **denatured**. In this condition it has lost its ability to function.

Enzymes may also be denatured by other factors such as unsuitable pH, inhibitors and radiation.

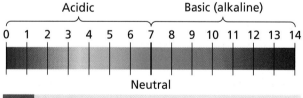

9.6   *The pH scale*

pH

The pH scale runs from 0 to 14. Values between 0 and 7 are acidic, pH 7 is neutral and values between 7 and 14 are basic (or alkaline).

Enzymes are very sensitive to changes in pH. As a result enzymes only work over a very narrow pH range. For most enzymes this is pH 6–8. Outside this range the activity of the enzyme falls quite rapidly. This is because the enzyme loses its shape, i.e. it becomes denatured. The optimum (or ideal) pH for most enzymes is pH 7.

Note: Pepsin, an enzyme in the stomach, works best at a pH of 2. This allows it to work efficiently in the acid conditions of the stomach.

The way in which pH affects the rate of reaction is shown in diagram 9.7.

Enzyme activity is also affected by the enzyme and substrate concentration, but these factors are beyond the scope of this course.

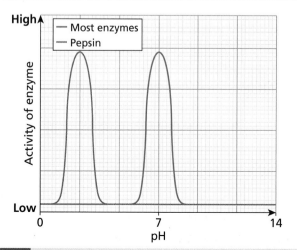

9.7   *The effect of pH on the rate of reaction*

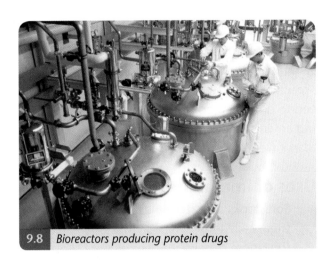

9.8 *Bioreactors producing protein drugs*

Immobilised enzymes

Traditionally, bioprocessing involved the use of micro-organisms, such as yeast and bacteria, to produce foodstuffs such as cheeses, yoghurts, breads, beers and wines.

In recent times bioprocessing has been developed to produce a vast range of products, including antibiotics, drugs, vaccines, methane gas (biogas), food colourings and flavours, vitamins, amino acids, sugar syrups, enzymes and perfumes.

From the early 1900s, but especially since the mid-1950s, the cells (micro-organisms) used in many of these bioprocesses have been replaced by purified enzymes.

The use of enzymes freely dissolved in a vessel to carry out a biological reaction (a bioreactor) is very wasteful. This is because the enzymes are removed from the vessel at the end of the process and it is not normally possible to isolate the enzymes for reuse.

> **Bioprocessing** is the use of enzyme-controlled reactions to produce a product.
>
> A **bioreactor** is a vessel or container in which living cells or their products are used to make a product.

THE CELL

To prevent this problem, enzymes are often immobilised or fixed so they remain in place. In this way they remain in the bioreactor and are easier to recover and reuse.

The immobilisation process forms enzymes in a similar state to the way in which they are found in nature, i.e. immobilised within cells rather than being free outside a cell.

9.9 *An immobilised car: immobilisation means it is fixed in place*

Methods of immobilising enzymes

Immobilised enzymes may be:
- Attached to each other
- Attached to insoluble supports
- Enclosed within a membrane or gel.

A range of different immobilisation techniques is used, as shown in diagram 9.10.

Adsorption means that the enzymes are physically attached to inactive (or inert) supports such as glass beads, ceramics, cellulose particles or artificial polymers.

In the case of trapping the enzyme in a gel, it is common to use sodium alginate as the gel. This material is prepared from algae and is permeable to the entry of the substrate and to the exit of the products. However, the enzyme is prevented from leaving the gel.

> **Immobilised enzymes** are enzymes that are attached, or fixed, to each other, or to an inert material.

PHYSICAL METHODS

Inert support

Adsorption | **Enclosed by a membrane** | **Enclosed in a gel**

Membrane | Gel

CHEMICAL METHODS

Inert support

Chemical bond

Bonded to inert support | **Bonded to each other**

(E) = enzyme

9.10 *Methods of enzyme immobilisation*

Advantages of immobilised enzymes

- Immobilised enzymes can be reused. This is an important consideration, because the cost of replacing enzymes can be rather high.
- Immobilised enzymes remain in the reaction vessel at the end of the process. This means the product does not need to be separated from the enzyme.
- Very often the process of immobilising an enzyme increases its stability.
- The production process is cheaper than if free enzymes are used.

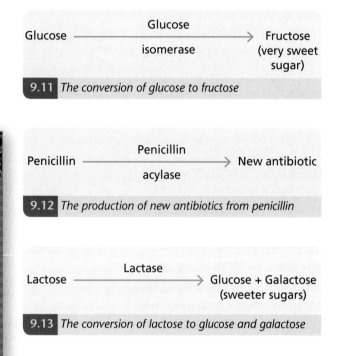

9.11 *The conversion of glucose to fructose*

9.12 *The production of new antibiotics from penicillin*

9.13 *The conversion of lactose to glucose and galactose*

Uses of immobilised enzymes

- Soft drinks are often sweetened with a sugar called fructose. Fructose is sweeter (but more expensive) than glucose. An immobilised enzyme called **glucose isomerase** is used to convert glucose to the sweeter-tasting fructose.
- **Penicillin acylase** is a very expensive enzyme used to alter the structure of the antibiotic penicillin. This allows the development of new antibiotics that may kill a wider range of bacteria. Penicillin acylase is used in an immobilised form in large bioreactors, so that it can be recovered and reused to reduce costs.
- **Lactase** is another expensive enzyme. It is immobilised in porous beads and used to convert lactose (a sugar found in a byproduct of cheese-making called whey) into two sweeter-tasting sugars (glucose and galactose). These products are used to replace condensed milk in the manufacture of soft toffee and caramel.

Enzyme experiments

In experiments measuring the rate of enzyme action (such as the following two activities) there are four factors to be considered: temperature, pH, enzyme concentration and substrate concentration.

In each of these experiments one factor is varied, while the other three must be kept constant. This is achieved by adopting the following procedures.

Varying the four factors in enzyme experiments		
Factor	Method used to keep factor constant	Method used to vary factor
Temperature	Use water bath(s) at the same temperature	Use water bath(s) at different temperatures
pH	Use the same pH buffer	Use pH buffers of different values
Enzyme concentration	Add the same volumes of enzyme	Not on the course
Substrate concentration	Add equal volumes of the same substrate	Not on the course

Activity 8 To investigate the effect of pH on the rate of enzyme activity

9.14 *Foam produced when hydrogen peroxide is broken down by catalase (in pieces of potato)*

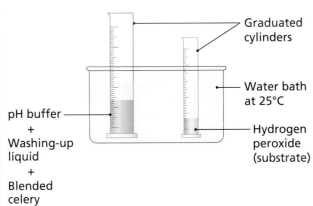

Graduated cylinders

Water bath at 25°C

pH buffer
+
Washing-up liquid
+
Blended celery (enzyme)

Hydrogen peroxide (substrate)

9.15 *Investigating the effect of pH on enzyme activity*

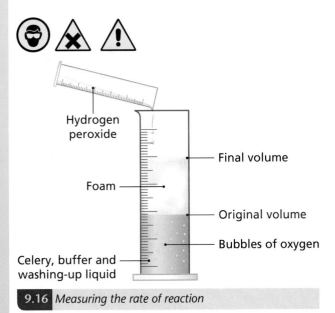

Hydrogen peroxide

Final volume

Foam

Original volume

Bubbles of oxygen

Celery, buffer and washing-up liquid

9.16 *Measuring the rate of reaction*

Introduction

Catalase is an enzyme that is found in a wide range of living things, e.g. liver, radishes, celery and potatoes. It converts the toxic substance hydrogen peroxide (H_2O_2) into water and oxygen.

When using catalase the oxygen forms foam (in association with washing-up liquid). The volume of the foam indicates the activity of the enzyme.

Syllabus The syllabus allows the use of any **one** of the following three enzymes: amylase, pepsin, catalase.

1. Place some pH buffer solution 4 in a graduated cylinder (pH buffer 4 ensures that the pH will remain at 4).

2. Using a dropper add one drop of washing-up liquid to the graduated cylinder (the washing-up liquid traps the oxygen that is released, forming foam).

3. Blend some stalks of celery in water in a blender. Filter this solution into a large beaker using coffee filter paper (filtration removes the blended cells and contents; coffee filter paper allows for fast filtration).

4. Add some of the filtrate to the graduated cylinder (the celery contains the enzyme catalase).

5. Add some hydrogen peroxide to a smaller graduated cylinder (hydrogen peroxide is the substrate).

6. Stand both graduated cylinders in a water bath (or a beaker of water) at 25°C for a few minutes (this ensures a constant temperature).

7. Remove the graduated cylinders from the water bath and pour the hydrogen peroxide into the graduated cylinder containing the blended celery.

8. Note and record the volume at the top of the foam after 2 minutes.

9. Calculate the volume of foam produced. This is done by subtracting the original volume of liquid in the graduated cylinder from the volume at the top of the foam after 2 minutes (the volume of foam indicates the rate of the reaction).

10. Repeat steps 1–9 using pH buffers 7, 10 and 13.

11. Record the results as shown overleaf; the first set of figures is filled in as an example.

THE CELL

Activity 8 results				
pH buffer	4	7	10	13
Original volume (cm³)	25			
Volume after 2 minutes (cm³)	25			
Volume of foam (cm³)	0			

12. Draw a graph of the results. Put pH on the horizontal axis and the volume of foam produced on the vertical axis. The graph should have a similar shape to that in diagram 9.7 (page 104).
13. Note that catalase is different to most enzymes as it has its maximum activity at pH 9 or 10.
14. As controls, repeat each procedure but do not add blended celery (i.e. no catalase is present) **or** add blended celery that has been boiled (to denature the catalase). In each case no foam is formed.

Activity 9 To investigate the effect of temperature on the rate of enzyme activity

1. Place some pH buffer 9 solution in a graduated cylinder (catalase works best at pH 9; the buffer ensures the pH remains constant at 9).
2. Using a dropper add one drop of washing-up liquid to the graduated cylinder (the washing-up liquid traps the oxygen that is released, forming foam).
3. Blend some stalks of celery in water in a blender. Filter this solution into a large beaker using coffee filter paper (filtration removes the blended cells and contents; coffee filter paper allows for fast filtration).
4. Add some of this solution to the graduated cylinder (the celery contains the enzyme catalase).

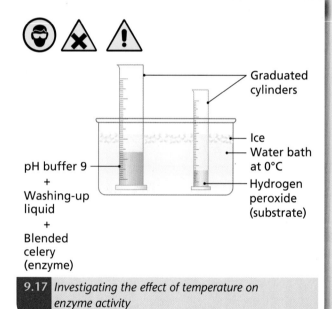

pH buffer 9
+
Washing-up liquid
+
Blended celery (enzyme)

9.17 *Investigating the effect of temperature on enzyme activity*

5. Add some hydrogen peroxide to a smaller graduated cylinder (hydrogen peroxide is the substrate).
6. Stand the graduated cylinders in a large beaker of ice-cold water until they are at 0°C.
7. Remove the graduated cylinders from the water bath and pour the hydrogen peroxide into the graduated cylinder containing the blended celery.
8. Note and record the volume at the top of the foam after 2 minutes.
9. Calculate the volume of foam produced, as shown in diagram 9.16 in Activity 8.
10. Repeat steps 1–9 at 10°C, 20°C, 30°C, 40°C, 50°C and 60°C.
11. Record the results as shown; the first set of figures is given as an example.

Activity 9 results							
Temperature (°C)	0	10	20	30	40	50	60
Original volume (cm³)	25						
Volume after 2 minutes (cm³)	25						
Volume of foam (cm³)	0						

12. Draw a graph of the results. Put temperature on the horizontal axis and the volume of foam produced on the vertical axis. The graph should have a similar shape to those in diagram 9.5 (page 104).

13. As controls, repeat each procedure but do not add blended celery (i.e. no catalase is present) **or** add blended celery that has been boiled (to denature the catalase). In each case no foam is formed.

Activity 10 To prepare an enzyme immobilisation and examine its application

Preparing the immobilised enzyme

The formation of alginate beads is a delicate process. All equipment must be clean before use. If possible all the water used in this activity should be distilled water.

In this activity yeast is immobilised. Yeast contains the enzyme sucrase. This means that the enzyme that is immobilised is **sucrase**.

1. Add some sodium alginate to water in a beaker.
2. Stir the mixture with a glass rod until it forms a smooth paste and leave it to soak for 5 minutes (sodium alginate is used to immobilise the yeast (and the enzyme)).
3. Add some yeast to water in a second beaker (the yeast contains the enzyme (sucrase) that is to be immobilised).
4. Stir the yeast solution and leave it for 5 minutes.
5. Dissolve some calcium chloride in water in a larger beaker.

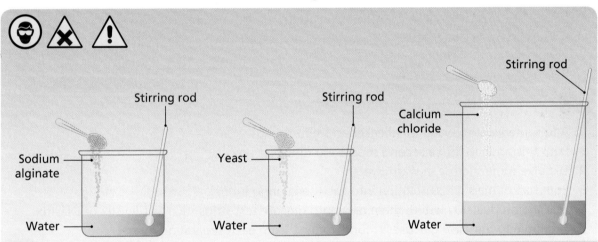

9.18 *Preparing solutions for an enzyme immobilisation*

6. Pour the yeast solution into the alginate paste and stir to mix thoroughly.
7. Draw some of the resulting mixture into a syringe (with no needle attached).
8. Slowly and steadily add a series of alginate and yeast drops from the syringe to the calcium chloride solution. Hold the syringe fairly high above the chloride solution and gently stir the solution as you add the drops (this prevents them from clumping). Beads of calcium alginate gel form, enclosing and immobilising some of the yeast cells.

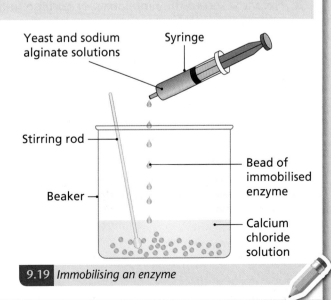

9.19 *Immobilising an enzyme*

9. Leave the beads in the calcium chloride solution for 15 minutes (this allows the beads to harden).

10. Place the beads in a sieve and rinse them under a tap of running water (this removes any yeast cells from outside the hardened beads). If necessary, the beads can be stored in water or dried on filter paper and stored in a refrigerator.

Examining the application of the immobilised enzyme

Yeast contains the enzyme sucrase. This enzyme converts sucrose into glucose and fructose. In this activity the ability of immobilised yeast and free yeast to convert sucrose into glucose is compared.

1. Pour the beads of immobilised enzyme into a separating funnel, as shown in diagram 9.21. A short piece of a drinking straw or a twisted-up paper clip should be used (to prevent the beads from blocking the outlet of the funnel).

Sucrose $\xrightarrow{\text{Sucrase}}$ Glucose and Fructose

9.20 *The conversion of sucrose to glucose and fructose*

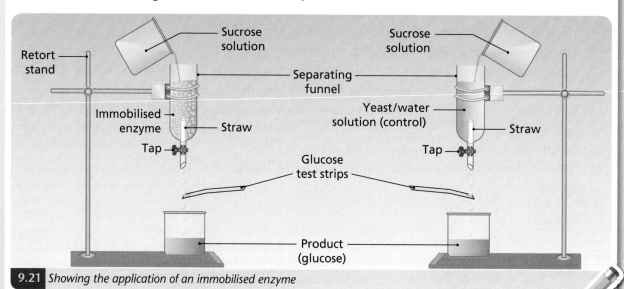

9.21 *Showing the application of an immobilised enzyme*

2. Add some yeast to water in a beaker and stir.
3. Pour this solution into a second separating funnel.
4. Dissolve some sucrose in warm water.
5. Pour half of the sucrose solution into each separating funnel.
6. Test the products by letting them drip onto glucose test strips such as Clinistix or Diastrix.
7. Continue to test until glucose is found coming from each separating funnel.
8. Note and record the time taken for glucose to first form. Note that in most cases glucose is formed more quickly in the separating funnel containing the non-immobilised yeast (the control). Immobilised yeast is slower to **start** forming glucose. This is because it takes longer for the sucrose to penetrate the alginate beads and for the glucose to emerge from the alginate beads. However, once they start producing glucose the immobilised enzymes (or yeast) can be reused very easily.
9. Observe the products in each beaker. Compare the cloudiness of each solution. (The non-immobilised yeast solution contains many yeast cells and is very cloudy or turbid. The product of the immobilised yeast is much clearer because there are no yeast cells present.)
10. Present the results as shown below.

Activity 10 results		
	Immobilised yeast (or enzyme)	**Non-immobilised yeast (or enzyme)**
Time taken (minutes) for glucose to form		
Cloudiness of product (cloudy or clear)		

Summary

Metabolism is all the chemical reactions in an organism.

Sunlight (solar) energy is the primary source of energy for life on Earth.

Cellular energy is contained in bonds found in molecules within cells.

A **catalyst** speeds up a reaction without being used up in the reaction.

An **enzyme** is a protein (or organic) catalyst.

Enzymes work because they have the 3-D shape to fit a particular molecule. Enzymes:
- Act on a substrate
- Form products
- Are made of protein.

Enzymes control metabolic reactions in plants and animals.
- Amylase is a catabolic enzyme that breaks starch down to maltose.
- DNA ligase is an anabolic enzyme that joins sections of DNA together.

Enzyme activity is affected by:
- Temperature
- pH.

Immobilised enzymes are attached to each other or to an inert material.

The **benefits of immobilised enzymes** are:
- They may be reused
- They are easy to separate from the product

- They are often more stable than the natural enzyme
- The process is cheaper.

Immobilised enzymes are used to:
- Produce fructose (sweetener) from glucose
- Convert penicillin to different forms
- Produce sweet-tasting sugars from lactose.

To investigate the **effect of pH on enzyme (catalase) activity**:
- Mix blended celery (catalase), hydrogen peroxide, pH buffer and washing-up liquid
- Note the volume of foam formed after 2 minutes at different pH values.

To investigate the **effect of temperature on the rate of enzyme (catalase) activity**:
- Mix blended celery (catalase), hydrogen peroxide, pH buffer 9 and washing-up liquid
- Note the volume of froth formed after 2 minutes at different temperatures.

Yeast contains the enzyme **sucrase**, which converts sucrose to glucose.

Sucrase is immobilised by:
- Mixing yeast solution with sodium alginate solution
- Adding beads of the mixture to calcium chloride solution
- Rinsing the hardened beads in a sieve.

The **application** of an immobilised enzyme is shown by:
- Adding sucrose solution to immobilised yeast (containing sucrase) in a separating funnel
- Testing for the production of glucose.

THE CELL

Revision questions

1 (a) What is metabolism?
   (b) Distinguish between anabolism and catabolism and give one example in each case.

2 (a) Distinguish between solar and cellular energy.
   (b) Name the biological process that converts: (i) Solar energy to cellular energy (ii) Cellular energy to energy that can be used in a cell.

3 Distinguish between: (a) An enzyme and a catalyst (b) A substrate and a product.

4 (a) Explain why the shape of an enzyme is important.
   (b) Explain why high temperatures may prevent an enzyme from working.
   (c) Name another factor that can affect the rate of enzyme action.

5 Name and give the function of (a) one anabolic and (b) one catabolic enzyme.

6 Give a reason for each of the following:
   (a) Amylase is inactivated in the mouth by very hot drinks.
   (b) Amylase works in the mouth but not in the stomach.
   (c) Pepsin works in the stomach, but amylase does not.
   (d) Putting food in a refrigerator slows bacterial action.
   (e) Putting food in a freezer stops bacterial action.

7 (a) Explain what is meant by:
       (i) Bioprocessing (ii) Immobilised enzymes (iii) A bioreactor.
   (b) Give two traditional (or older) and two modern examples of bioprocessing.
   (c) Suggest one problem with the use of freely dissolved enzymes in bioprocessing.

8 Explain, with the aid of a diagram, any three methods by which enzymes can be immobilised.

9 Give three benefits for using immobilised (compared to free) enzymes.

10 Give two uses for immobilised enzymes. In each case name the substrate, enzyme and product of the reaction.

11 In testing the effect of pH on enzyme activity:
   (a) Name a suitable enzyme.
   (b) What substrate would you use with this enzyme?
   (c) How do you ensure a constant temperature?
   (d) How do you vary the pH?
   (e) Name the end products of the reaction.
   (f) How is the activity of the enzyme measured?
   (g) Describe a suitable control.
   (h) (i) What result would you expect for the control?

   (ii) If the enzyme was pepsin, at what pH would you expect it to be most effective?

12 Answer the following questions with reference to investigating the effect of temperature on enzyme action.
   (a) Name the enzyme and substrate used.
   (b) Why is washing-up liquid used?
   (c) Why are the ingredients placed in a water bath before mixing them?
   (d) What factor was kept constant during this experiment?
   (e) Describe how the factor named in part (d) is kept constant.
   (f) What control is used in the experiment?
   (g) How is the activity of the enzyme measured?
   (h) (i) Explain why less foam forms at 10°C compared with 20°C.
       (ii) How did you know when the enzyme had completed its activity?

13 In preparing an enzyme immobilisation:
   (a) Name the enzyme that was immobilised.
   (b) Name the material that immobilises the enzyme.
   (c) Why is the immobilised enzyme:
       (i) Left in calcium chloride for some time
       (ii) Rinsed in a sieve?
   (d) Describe the appearance of the immobilised enzymes.

14 In examining the application of an immobilised enzyme:
   (a) Name the enzyme, substrate and product used.
   (b) How did you test for the presence of the product?
   (c) State one advantage of using immobilised enzymes.

Exam questions

Section A

15 The graph shows how the rate of reaction of a carbohydrate-digesting enzyme in the human alimentary canal varies with pH.

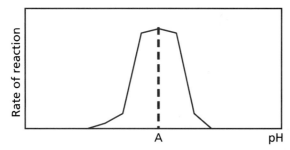

   (a) Name a carbohydrate-digesting enzyme in the human alimentary canal.
   (b) Where in the alimentary canal does this enzyme act?
   (c) State the enzyme's product(s).
   (d) What is the pH at A?
   (e) A is said to be the enzyme's _____ pH.
   (f) Suggest a temperature at which human enzymes work best.
   (g) What term best describes the shape of an enzyme?

   (2006 HL Q 3)

Section B

16 (a) (i) Is an enzyme a lipid, a protein or a carbohydrate?

(ii) Where in a cell are enzymes produced?

(b) As part of your practical activities you investigated the effect of temperature on the rate of activity of an enzyme.

(i) Name the enzyme that you used.

(ii) Name the substrate with which the enzyme reacts.

(iii) How did you vary the temperature?

(iv) How did you keep a constant pH during the investigation?

(v) How did you measure the rate of activity of the enzyme?

(vi) What was the result of your investigation?

(2007 OL Q 7)

17 (a) (i) To which group of biomolecules do enzymes belong?

(ii) Name a factor that influences the activity of an enzyme.

(b) In the course of your practical investigations you prepared an enzyme immobilisation. Answer the following questions in relation to that investigation.

(i) Describe how you carried out the immobilisation.

(ii) Draw a labelled diagram of the apparatus that you used to investigate **the activity** of the immobilised enzyme.

(iii) Briefly outline how you used the apparatus referred to in (b) (ii) above.

(2009 HL Q 9)

Section C

18 (a) What is metabolism? Describe briefly the part played by enzymes in metabolism.

(2004 OL Q 13)

19 (c) Enzymes can be immobilised and then used in bioprocessing.

(i) What is meant by *immobilisation*?

(ii) Name a substance that is used to immobilise enzymes.

(iii) Give **two** advantages of using immobilised enzymes.

(iv) Give **one** application of a named immobilised enzyme. In your answer, refer to substrate, enzyme and product.

(2007 HL Q 11)

20 (b) (i) What is meant by the term *metabolism*?

(ii) "Enzymes are essential for metabolism". Explain why this statement is true.

(iii) In each of the following cases state whether the process is anabolic or catabolic.

1. Protein synthesis.

2. Conversion of ADP to ATP.

3. Reactions in which product molecules are larger than substrate molecules.

(iv) State **one** way by which an enzyme may be denatured.

(v) Give **two** features of a denatured enzyme.

(vi) Apart from carbon, hydrogen and oxygen, there is one other element always present in the building blocks of enzymes. Name that element.

(2011 HL Q 14)

THE CELL

Previous examination questions

Ordinary level	Higher level
2004 Q 13a	2005 Q 7
2005 Q 8	2006 Q 3
2007 Q 7	2007 Q 7, Q 11c
2009 Q 15c	2008 Q 9
2010 Q 8	2009 Q 9
2011 Q 12c	2010 Q 14b
2012 Q 8	2011 Q 14b
	2012 Q 9

Latest questions at www.edco.ie/lcbiologyplus/examhelp

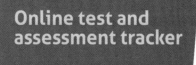

Online test and assessment tracker

Scan the QR code and test yourself on chapter 9
www.edco.ie/lcbiologyplus

Chapter 10 Higher level enzymes and energy carriers

Learning objectives

 ● To use the active site theory to explain the function and specificity of enzymes

 ● To define the term 'optimum activity' in relation to pH

 ● To describe the nature and roles of ATP and NADP$^+$

HIGHER ▶ ● To describe heat denaturation of proteins and investigate the heat denaturation of one particular enzyme.

THE CELL

HIGHER ▼

Active site

The active site is not a rigid shape. Instead it is a depression or pocket on the surface of the enzyme. The enzyme itself is a protein that has a complex three-dimensional (3-D) shape, as has the active site. Many enzymes are composed of two or more globular sections, called domains, joined together.

Very often the active site is larger than the substrate to which it combines. Each active site is specific to the substrate that it acts upon.

The substrate causes (or induces) the active site to change shape slightly when they come in contact. The active site then fits more precisely around the substrate. This process is called the **induced fit model** or the **active site theory** of enzyme action (see diagram 10.2).

The induced fit model of enzyme action can be compared to the way a bean bag, with a large hollow in it, will change shape to fit snugly around our body shape when we sit in it.

> The **active site** is the part of an enzyme that combines with the substrate.

10.1 *A computer graphic of an enzyme (blue) with the substrate (yellow) attached to the active site*

Mechanism of enzyme action – the induced fit model

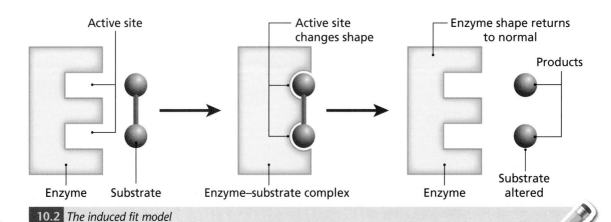

10.2 *The induced fit model*

1. The substrate combines with the 3-D active site of the enzyme.
2. The active site is induced or caused to change shape slightly by the substrate.
3. The substrate and enzyme form an enzyme–substrate complex. The bonds in the substrate are altered so that the substrate changes into the product(s).
4. The products leave the active site.
5. The active site returns to its original shape and can now accept a new substrate molecule.

These five steps happen very quickly. In some enzymes they take place more than 1000 times every second. For this reason, and because the enzyme is unchanged in the process, a small amount of enzyme can process a large number of substrate molecules in a short space of time.

> Enzyme specificity means that each enzyme will react with only one particular substrate.

Enzyme specificity

Most enzymes are said to be specific to a single substrate. This means that an enzyme will react with only one particular substrate. The reason for this is that each active site will fit or react with only a single substrate. Anything that alters the shape of the active site will reduce the ability of the enzyme to work effectively.

Optimum pH

The shape of the active site is particularly sensitive to pH. Each enzyme is adapted to have the correct shape at a particular pH value (e.g. pH 2 for pepsin and pH 6 to 8 for most other enzymes).

If the pH is unsuitable, then the enzyme changes shape and the active site will no longer accept a substrate molecule. Enzymes are said to have their optimum activity at specific pH values.

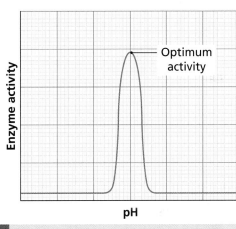

10.3 *Graph of optimum pH for enzyme activity*

Enzymes and temperature

Enzymes are less sensitive to temperature changes than they are to changes in pH. An increase in temperature causes increased molecular movement. As a result, substrate molecules collide more frequently with enzymes. This means that reaction rates rise as temperatures rise.

However, each enzyme and active site starts to change its shape and lose its efficiency above a certain temperature. This temperature is between 20°C and 30°C for most plant enzymes and 37°C for human enzymes (see the graph shown in diagram 9.5 on page 104).

> An enzyme's optimum pH means the pH value at which the enzyme works best.

Denaturation

Caused by

- High temperatures
- pH values outside the enzyme's optimum pH
- Some chemicals or radiation.

Explanation

When most proteins are heated above 40°C (or subjected to unsuitable pH values or treated with certain chemicals or radiation), they gradually lose their 3-D shape.

> A denatured enzyme has lost its shape and can no longer carry out its function.

THE CELL

115

Active site

Active site will not fit with substrate

Heat or

unsuitable pH

Denatured enzyme

Enzyme   Substrate

Substrate unchanged

10.4 *Denaturing an enzyme*

In the case of an enzyme, this means that the active site will lose its ability to react with its substrate. Such a change in shape and loss of biological activity is called **denaturation**. It is normally a permanent, or irreversible, process.

 High temperatures or fever in a human can be very serious, as they can affect the shape and the efficiency of enzyme reactions.

Energy carriers

In photosynthesis, some of the energy in sunlight is used to make food. In respiration, food is broken down to release energy. Energy is involved in both processes.

Molecules called ADP and ATP have vital roles in trapping and transferring energy in these processes (and in many other cell activities).

Molecules called NAD^+ and $NADP^+$ also have vital roles in trapping and transferring electrons and hydrogen ions in many cell reactions.

ADP and ATP

ADP

ADP is the abbreviation for adenosine **di**phosphate. ADP is found in the cells of all organisms.

ADP is made of the base adenine (this base is also found in DNA and RNA), a five-carbon sugar called ribose and two phosphate groups. The bond between the two phosphate groups is an unstable bond. These unstable bonds are represented by the symbol '~'.

ADP is a low-energy molecule.

ATP

ATP is an abbreviation for adenosine **tri**phosphate. ATP forms when another phosphate group is added to ADP. Extra energy is also added, in the form of the unstable bond between the last two phosphate groups.

The process of adding a phosphate group is called **phosphorylation**.

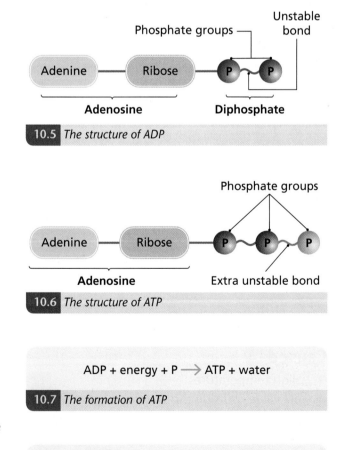

Phosphate groups — Unstable bond

Adenine — Ribose — P ~ P

Adenosine   Diphosphate

10.5 *The structure of ADP*

Phosphate groups

Adenine — Ribose — P ~ P ~ P

Adenosine   Extra unstable bond

10.6 *The structure of ATP*

ADP + energy + P ⟶ ATP + water

10.7 *The formation of ATP*

ATP + water ⟶ ADP + energy + P

10.8 *The breakdown of ATP*

HIGHER ▼

ATP is an energy-rich compound. It can be moved around inside a cell, i.e. it is an energy carrier. However, it cannot be stored for very long. The energy in ATP must be used immediately.

When ATP breaks down it releases energy and a phosphate, and forms ADP. The energy is released from the bond between the last two phosphate groups and is used to carry out most of the reactions in cells.

In respiration, glucose breaks down to form ATP. This ATP is used to provide energy in human cells for functions such as muscle movement, protein (and enzyme) production, urine formation and brain activity.

It is estimated that most cells break down about 10 million ATP molecules per second to release energy for metabolic reactions.

e^- = an electron, H^+ = a hydrogen ion or proton

$$NADP^+ + 1\ e^- \longrightarrow NADP$$
$$NADP + 1\ e^- \longrightarrow NADP^-$$
$$NADP^- + H^+ \longrightarrow NADPH$$

10.9 *The formation of NADPH from NADP$^+$*

NADP⁺ and NADPH

NADP⁺

NADP$^+$ (nicotinamide adenine dinucleotide phosphate) is a low-energy molecule, involved in photosynthesis.

A hydrogen atom (H) consists of a proton, symbolised as H^+, and an electron.

NADP$^+$ can accept a pair of high-energy electrons (combined with a hydrogen ion or proton) to form NADPH.

The reactions shown in diagram 10.9 can be simplified as shown in diagram 10.10.

The addition of electrons to a molecule is called reduction. NADP$^+$ is said to be reduced to NADPH.

$$NADP^+ + 2\ electrons + H^+ \longrightarrow NADPH$$
(low energy) \hspace{2cm} (high energy)

10.10 *A simplified equation to show the formation of NADPH from NADP$^+$*

NADPH

NADPH is an electron and hydrogen carrier. The energy and hydrogen it contains is used in photosynthesis to form glucose.

NADPH releases two high-energy electrons and a hydrogen ion or proton when it breaks down.

$$NADPH \longrightarrow NADP^+ + 2\ electrons + H^+$$
(high \hspace{1cm} (low
energy) \hspace{0.7cm} energy)

10.11 *The breakdown of NADPH*

$$NAD^+ + 1\ e^- \longrightarrow NAD$$
$$NAD + 1\ e^- \longrightarrow NAD^-$$
$$NAD^- + H^+ \longrightarrow NADH$$

10.12 *The formation of NADH from NAD$^+$*

NAD⁺ and NADH

NAD$^+$ is used in respiration as an equivalent low-energy molecule to NADP$^+$. In the same way, respiration uses NADH as an equivalent high-energy molecule to NADPH (see diagram 10.12).

These details are summarised in the table below.

Remember that photosynthesis (starting with the letter P) uses the molecules with the letter P, i.e. NADP+ and NADPH.

Energy carriers		
Process	**Molecules**	
	Low-energy	**High-energy**
Photosynthesis	ADP, NADP$^+$	ATP, NADPH
Respiration	ADP, NAD$^+$	ATP, NADH

THE CELL

Activity 11 To investigate the effect of heat denaturation on enzyme (catalase) activity

In this activity the enzyme used is catalase. This enzyme is obtained by blending celery. The reaction can be shown as:

Hydrogen peroxide	$\xrightarrow{\text{catalase}}$	Water + Oxygen
$2H_2O_2$	$\xrightarrow{\text{catalase}}$	$2H_2O + O_2$
(substrate)	(enzyme)	(products)

10.13 *The reaction to show the action of the enzyme catalase*

1. Place some stalks of celery in a blender and add some water. Turn on the blender to form a pulp. (Celery contains the enzyme catalase.)
2. Filter the pulped celery into a beaker using coffee filter paper (this will remove the cell parts; coffee filter paper allows faster filtration than laboratory filter paper).
3. Place some of this filtered solution into a large graduated cylinder and place in a water bath at 25°C (this is an ideal temperature for catalase activity).
4. Add some pH 9 buffer solution to the graduated cylinder (this ensures a constant pH; the optimum pH for catalase is 9).
5. Using a dropper add one drop of washing-up liquid (the washing-up liquid traps bubbles of oxygen, causing the formation of foam).

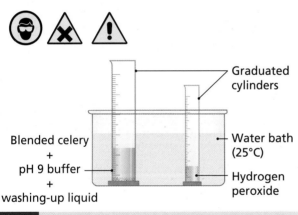

Blended celery
+
pH 9 buffer
+
washing-up liquid

Graduated cylinders

Water bath (25°C)

Hydrogen peroxide

10.14 *The effect of heat denaturation on enzyme activity*

6. Add some hydrogen peroxide to a smaller graduated cylinder. Place this in the water bath (hydrogen peroxide is the substrate).
7. Leave both solutions until they have reached 25°C (this ensures a constant temperature).
8. Add the hydrogen peroxide to the blended celery in the large graduated cylinder.
9. Note if foam is produced or not after 2 minutes.

10. Boil some of the filtered celery solution for 10 minutes (this denatures the enzyme catalase).
11. Repeat steps 3 to 9 using the boiled catalase solution (this acts as a control).
12. Results may be presented as:

Activity 11 results		
	Unboiled enzyme	Boiled enzyme (control)
Foam produced (yes or no)		

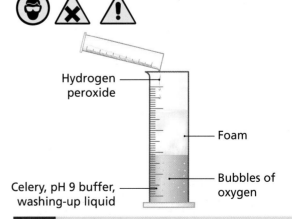

Hydrogen peroxide

Foam

Bubbles of oxygen

Celery, pH 9 buffer, washing-up liquid

10.15 *Investigating the activity of catalase*

Summary

The **active site** is the part of the enzyme that combines with the substrate.

In the induced fit model of enzyme action:
- The substrate causes the active site to change shape slightly
- The enzyme and substrate form a temporary enzyme–substrate complex
- The substrate is altered
- The enzyme remains unchanged and the active site returns to its original shape.

Most enzymes are specific to a single substrate, owing to the matching shapes of the substrate and active site.

The **shape of the active site** is sensitive to pH and temperature.

Enzymes (and other proteins) are denatured (lose their shape and activity) by high temperatures (and also by unsuitable pH and radiation).

ADP (adenosine diphosphate) is a low-energy molecule.

ATP (adenosine triphosphate) is an energy-rich molecule.

ATP is the source of energy used for most cell reactions.

ADP and ATP are interconvertible, i.e.
- ADP + energy + P → ATP + water
- ATP + water → ADP + energy + P

Phosphorylation is the addition of phosphate to a molecule.

NADP⁺ is a low-energy molecule; **NADPH** is a high-energy molecule. Both molecules are involved in photosynthesis.

NADP⁺ and NADPH are interconvertible, i.e.
- NADP⁺ + 2 electrons + H⁺ → NADPH
- NADPH → NADP⁺ + 2 electrons + H⁺

Respiration uses NAD⁺ (instead of NADP⁺) and NADH (instead of NADPH).

The **effect of heat denaturation** on catalase can be investigated by:
- Boiling catalase
- Testing if it will then form foam when it reacts with hydrogen peroxide.

THE CELL

Revision questions

1. (a) Explain what is meant by the following phrases:
     (i) The active site
    (ii) The enzyme–substrate complex
   (iii) Enzymes are specific.
   (b) What does the active site have to do with the specificity of enzymes?

2. (a) Explain, with the aid of labelled diagrams, the induced fit model of enzyme action.
   (b) In this model explain how the active site relates to the substrate:
     (i) Before the reaction starts
    (ii) When the enzyme–substrate complex is formed
   (iii) After the reaction is complete.

3. Suggest two reasons why a small amount of enzyme can speed up a reaction dramatically.

4. Draw simple graphs to show the effect on the activity of catalase of (a) pH and (b) temperature. Label the axes on each graph.

5. Explain why changes in (a) pH and (b) temperature affect the activity of an enzyme.

6. (a) What is meant by 'denaturation'?
   (b) Use a diagram to illustrate the effect of denaturation on an enzyme.
   (c) Name two factors that cause enzymes to be denatured.

7. In investigating the effect of heat denaturation on an enzyme:
   (a) Name the enzyme used
   (b) Name the substrate for this enzyme
   (c) State precisely how the enzyme was denatured
   (d) State what control was used
   (e) State what test was applied to determine the activity of the enzyme
   (f) State the result of the test on (i) the control and (ii) the denatured enzyme.

8. (a) Give the full name for: (i) ADP (ii) ATP.
   (b) Which of the following are high-energy molecules: NAD⁺, ATP, NADPH, NADP⁺, ADP, NADH?

9. (a) Draw a diagram to show where the available energy is located in a molecule of ATP.
   (b) What does ATP convert to when it releases its energy?
   (c) Give an equation to show the conversion of ADP to ATP.

119

Exam questions

Section B

HIGHER ▼

10 (a) **(i)** What is meant by an enzyme's optimum pH?

  (ii) What is a denatured enzyme?

(b) In the course of your studies you investigated the effect of denaturation by heat application on the activity of an enzyme.

  (i) Name the enzyme that you used.

  (ii) What substrate did you use?

  (iii) Describe how you carried out the investigation. In your answer you must refer to the way that you measured the enzyme's activity.

  (iv) State the results that you obtained.

  (2008 HL Q 9)

Section C

11 (a) **(i)** For what is ATP an abbreviation?

  (ii) What is the role of ATP in cells?

  (2007 HL Q 11)

12 (a) ATP and NAD/NADP⁺ play important roles in cell activities.

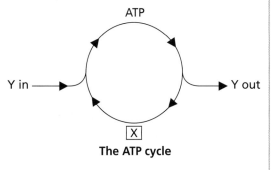

The ATP cycle

  (i) Name the substance X, formed by the loss of a phosphate group.

  (ii) The ATP cycle is kept going by Y. What is Y?

  (iii) Suggest a role for NAD/NADP⁺ in cell activities.

  (2009 HL Q 12)

13 (b) **(i)** What is an enzyme?

  (ii) What is meant by the *specificity* of an enzyme?

  (iii) Explain how the Active Site Theory may be used to explain the specificity of enzymes.

  (2010 HL Q 14)

HIGHER ▼

14 (b) **(i)** What is meant by the term *metabolism*?

  (ii) "Enzymes are essential for metabolism". Explain why this statement is true.

  (iii) In **each** of the following cases state whether the process is anabolic or catabolic.

   1. Protein synthesis.

   2. Conversion of ADP to ATP.

   3. Reactions in which product molecules are larger than substrate molecules.

  (iv) State **one** way by which an enzyme may be denatured.

  (v) Give **two** features of a denatured enzyme.

  (vi) Apart from carbon, hydrogen and oxygen, there is one other element always present in the building blocks of enzymes. Name that element.

  (2011 HL Q 14)

Previous examination questions

Ordinary level	Higher level
n/a	2004 Q 11a
	2007 Q 11a
	2008 Q 9
	2009 Q 12a
	2010 Q 14b
	2011 Q 14b
Latest questions at www.edco.ie/lcbiologyplus/examhelp	

Online test and assessment tracker

Scan the QR code and test yourself on chapter 10
www.edco.ie/lcbiologyplus

THE CELL

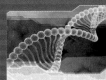
Learning objectives

- To define the term 'photosynthesis' and represent it as a balanced equation
- To describe simply the process of photosynthesis
- To describe the location of chlorophyll in cells
- To identify the sources of light, carbon dioxide and water for photosynthesis
- To describe the use of artificial light and added carbon dioxide for crop production in greenhouses
- **HIGHER ▶** To describe photosynthesis in detail as a two-stage process
- To investigate how light intensity OR carbon dioxide influence the rate of photosynthesis.

Introduction

The Sun is the ultimate source of energy for our planet. There are many forms of solar radiation. The most important types of solar radiation in biology are infrared rays (which help to heat the Earth), ultraviolet rays (which cause sunburn and cancer) and visible light rays.

Photosynthesis is the process by which green plants produce glucose and oxygen from carbon dioxide and water. Light is needed as a source of energy for this process. The green pigment (or dye) called chlorophyll is necessary as a catalyst for the process.

Photosynthesis takes place in plants, especially in the green parts, such as leaves, because they contain chlorophyll.

Cells need energy to carry out their reactions. This energy is needed in small, usable amounts and is best supplied by the breakdown of a molecule called adenosine triphosphate (ATP).

$$6CO_2 + 6H_2O + light \xrightarrow{\text{Chlorophyll}} C_6H_{12}O_6 + 6O_2$$
(Carbon (Water) (Glucose) (Oxygen)
dioxide)

11.1 *A balanced equation to show photosynthesis*

In photosynthesis, light energy is initially used to make ATP. ATP is then used to supply energy to make glucose. Plants can use glucose at a later stage to re-form ATP in order to provide cellular energy.

Animals consume glucose made by plants and convert it to ATP for their own use. This means that solar energy is the basic source of energy for all organisms on Earth.

Role of photosynthesis

Life on Earth depends on photosynthesis for the following reasons:
- Plants use it to make food
- Animals get their food from plants – thus, both plants and animals get food from photosynthesis
- Photosynthesis produces the oxygen that most living things need in order to obtain energy in respiration
- Photosynthesis was responsible for forming fossil fuels (e.g. turf, coal and oil). These fuels were formed over millions of years by the death and partial decay of plants and animals.

The main events in photosynthesis

1. Light is absorbed

Some of the sunlight that strikes a plant is trapped by chlorophyll. Chlorophyll is normally found in cell organelles called chloroplasts. Therefore it is in chloroplasts that photosynthesis takes place. The trapped sunlight provides the energy that a plant needs to make glucose.

2. Water is split

Some of the trapped sunlight energy is used in the chloroplast to split water molecules.

Every hydrogen atom is made of a hydrogen ion or proton (H^+) and an electron (e^-). Water has the formula H_2O. When two water molecules are split they form four protons, four electrons and a molecule of oxygen gas (O_2).

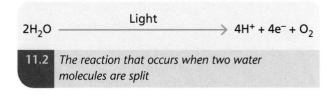

$$2H_2O \xrightarrow{\text{Light}} 4H^+ + 4e^- + O_2$$

11.2 *The reaction that occurs when two water molecules are split*

3. The products of the splitting of water

The three products formed when water is split are protons (H^+), electrons (e^-) and oxygen (O_2). These products behave as follows:

- The electrons are passed to chlorophyll
- The protons are released into a storage pool of protons in the chloroplast for later use
- The oxygen may pass from the chloroplast out into the cytoplasm and eventually out of the leaf into the atmosphere.
  Alternatively, the oxygen may be used within the cells of the leaf, in the process of respiration.

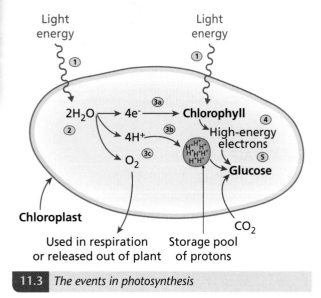

11.3 *The events in photosynthesis*

? The oxygen released by plants is the oxygen that humans and other organisms take in for respiration; photosynthesis maintains the Earth's oxygen levels.

4. Light energises electrons

Some of the sunlight energy trapped by chlorophyll is passed on to electrons in chlorophyll to form high-energy electrons.

5. Glucose is formed

The high-energy electrons from chlorophyll, along with protons from the pool of stored protons, are combined with carbon dioxide to form a carbohydrate (glucose, $C_6H_{12}O_6$). See diagram 11.3.

Sources of light, carbon dioxide and water for photosynthesis

Light

Sunlight is the normal source of light for photosynthesis. Light intensity levels must be of sufficient strength to allow photosynthesis to proceed.

Carbon dioxide

Plants have two sources of carbon dioxide: one is external, the other is internal.

External

Most of the carbon dioxide that a plant uses in photosynthesis enters the leaf from the atmosphere.

Internal

Some of the carbon dioxide used in photosynthesis is produced by the leaf cells in the process of respiration.

    The amount of carbon dioxide available to a plant is relatively low. This is due to the low levels of carbon dioxide in the atmosphere (only 0.04%). Low levels of carbon dioxide slow the rate of photosynthesis.

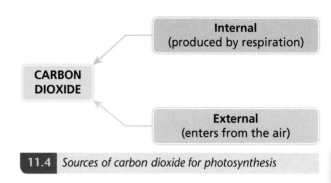

11.4 *Sources of carbon dioxide for photosynthesis*

Water

Water is absorbed from the soil by the roots of plants. This water then passes up through the plant stem and into the leaves, where it is used in photosynthesis.

Increasing the rate of photosynthesis

To increase the growth of crops grown in greenhouses humans can use two possible methods.

- Artificial light sources can be used. This is especially the case in countries that lie near the Earth's poles, because they receive very little sunlight in winter.
- Artificial sources of carbon dioxide (e.g. burning gas) are used in greenhouses to enhance carbon dioxide concentration and thus to increase crop growth.

Detailed study of photosynthesis

Photosynthesis is a process that takes place in two stages or phases: the light stage and the dark stage.

- Light stage (or the light-dependent stage)
  ▹ Dependent on light (reactions cannot take place in darkness)
  ▹ Energy provided by light allows the reactions to proceed
  ▹ Reactions occur so quickly that no enzymes are required.
- Dark stage
  ▹ Independent of light (reactions will take place in the presence or absence of light)
  ▹ Energy for the reactions is provided by ATP, which was made in the light stage
  ▹ Enzymes control the reactions (as a result temperature is a factor).

Light stage

The events of the light stage take place in the chloroplast.

    These events can be explained under the three headings of: light absorption, light energy transferred to electrons and the flow of electrons along pathways 1 and 2.

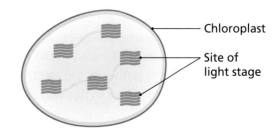

11.5 *Chloroplast, showing the site of the light stage*

HIGHER ▼

THE CELL

123

THE CELL

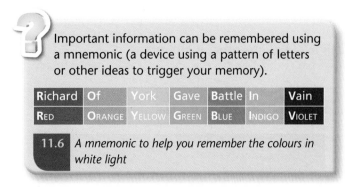

Important information can be remembered using a mnemonic (a device using a pattern of letters or other ideas to trigger your memory).

Richard	Of	York	Gave	Battle	In	Vain
Red	Orange	Yellow	Green	Blue	Indigo	Violet

11.6 *A mnemonic to help you remember the colours in white light*

Light is absorbed

White light is composed of different wavelengths (colours) of light. Each colour represents a different level of energy.

Chloroplasts contain a range of pigments, including chlorophyll. Each of the chloroplast pigments absorbs a different colour of light. By having a range of pigments, plants ensure that they can absorb a range of colours of light (i.e. as much light energy as possible).

In general, plants absorb all the colours of white light except green. Green light is normally reflected by plants. This is why most plants are green.

Light energy is transferred to electrons

Pigments are arranged in clusters in the chloroplast. Each cluster consists of:

- A variety of pigments
- A strategically placed chlorophyll molecule
- An electron acceptor.

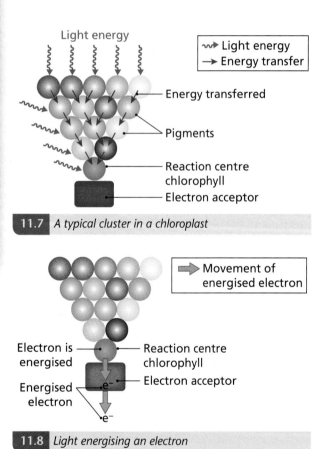

Light energy ⤳ Light energy → Energy transfer

— Energy transferred
— Pigments
— Reaction centre chlorophyll
— Electron acceptor

11.7 *A typical cluster in a chloroplast*

⇒ Movement of energised electron

Electron is energised — Reaction centre chlorophyll
Energised electron — Electron acceptor
e⁻
e⁻

11.8 *Light energising an electron*

The strategically placed chlorophyll molecule is called the reaction centre chlorophyll. There may be many chlorophyll molecules in a cluster, but only one is strategically located beside an electron acceptor.

In each cluster, the different pigments absorb light energy of different wavelengths (or colours). The function of the cluster is to absorb as much light as possible.

The different pigments transfer the absorbed energy from one to another until it reaches the reaction centre chlorophyll associated with the electron acceptor. Here the energy is transferred to electrons, causing them to become energised, or high-energy, electrons.

The energised electrons are passed from the chlorophyll to the electron acceptor. The energised electrons then flow from the electron acceptor along one of two different pathways.

Electron flow: Pathway 1

In pathway 1, the high-energy electrons pass from the reaction centre chlorophyll to an electron acceptor. They then pass from the electron acceptor to a series of other electron acceptors and back again to the chlorophyll molecule. All these molecules are located in the chloroplast.

In this pathway, the electrons are said to recycle (to chlorophyll). When the electrons return in this way they lose energy. The energy they release is trapped by ADP and a phosphate, and used to form ATP and water as shown:

$$ADP + energy + P \longrightarrow ATP + water$$

11.9 *ATP production*

Pathway 1 is said to be cyclic, because the electrons flow from chlorophyll to the electron acceptors and back again to chlorophyll. The method of making ATP used in pathway 1 is called **cyclic electron flow**.

Electron flow: Pathway 2

Sometimes two high-energy electrons at a time leave the reaction centre chlorophyll. They pass to an electron acceptor and along another series of electron acceptors. Again, all of these acceptors are in the chloroplast.

This time, the energised electrons do not return to chlorophyll. Instead, they lose some energy as they pass from acceptor to acceptor. The energy they release is used to make more ATP (see diagram 11.13).

Eventually the two electrons combine with $NADP^+$ to form $NADP^-$.

The chlorophyll molecule is now short of electrons. It gains new electrons from the splitting of water.

Recall that when two water molecules are split they form four protons ($4H^+$), four electrons ($4e^-$) and oxygen (O_2).

● The protons formed by the splitting of water are stored in a pool of protons in the chloroplast. One of these protons is now attracted to $NADP^-$ and combines with it to reduce it to NADPH as shown below.

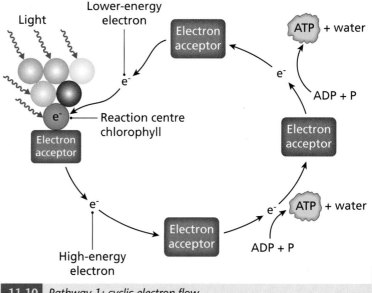

11.10 *Pathway 1: cyclic electron flow*

$$NADP^+ + 2 \text{ electrons } (2e^-) \longrightarrow NADP^-$$

11.11 *The formation of NADP$^-$*

$$NADP^- + H^+ \longrightarrow NADPH$$

11.12 *The formation of NADPH*

● Two of the electrons from the splitting of water replace the electrons lost by chlorophyll. This restores the number of electrons in the reaction centre chlorophyll.

● Oxygen gas formed by the splitting of water is used in one of two ways:
   ▶ Some is released out through the stomata into the atmosphere
   ▶ Some is used internally in the plant in respiration.

Photolysis is the splitting of water by light.

THE CELL

11.13 *Pathway 2: non-cyclic electron flow*

As a result of the events in pathway 2, electrons pass (two at a time) from a water molecule to chlorophyll. Here they are energised by light and flow to the electron acceptor.

From the first electron acceptor they move along a series of electron acceptors and are eventually used to form NADPH. As they flow, some of their energy is used to convert ADP into ATP.

In this pathway, the electrons start with water and end up in NADPH. The electrons do not recycle. For this reason, pathway 2 is called **non-cyclic electron flow**.

End products of the light stage

By the end of the light stage, three end products have formed: ATP, NADPH and oxygen.

The light stage	
Product	**Fate**
ATP	Supplies energy for the dark stage reactions
NADPH	Supplies protons and electrons for the dark stage reactions
Oxygen	Used for respiration **or** released into the atmosphere

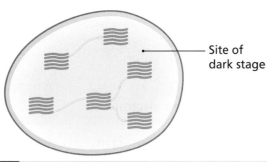

Site of dark stage

11.14 *Chloroplast, showing the site of the dark stage*

The events of the dark stage were discovered by Melvin Calvin, who received a Nobel prize for his work in 1961. The dark stage is sometimes called the Calvin cycle.

Dark stage

The dark stage reactions take place in a different part of the chloroplast from the light stage reactions.

The reactions of the dark stage are controlled by enzymes. This means that the dark stage is affected by temperature.

Carbon dioxide from the air or from respiration enters the chloroplast. Hydrogen ions (or protons, H^+) and electrons are released from NADPH to convert (or reduce) carbon dioxide to carbohydrate. (Recall that the addition of electrons is called reduction. For this reason it is said that carbon dioxide is reduced to glucose.)

The hydrogen ions (H^+) and electrons come from the breakdown of NADPH (made in the light stage).

The energy to form glucose comes from the conversion of ATP (made in the light stage) to ADP and phosphate.

$$NADPH \longrightarrow NADP^+ + 2\ electrons + H^+$$

11.15 *The breakdown of NADPH*

$$ATP + water \longrightarrow ADP + P + energy$$

11.16 *The conversion of ATP to ADP and phosphate*

All the $NADP^+$ and ADP molecules that are produced in the dark stage are reused in the light stage.

The dark stage is summarised by the reaction in diagram 11.17.

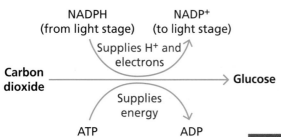

NADPH (from light stage) NADP⁺ (to light stage)

Supplies H^+ and electrons

Carbon dioxide ⟶ Glucose

Supplies energy

ATP (from light stage) ADP (to light stage)

11.17 *Events in the dark stage*

Activity 12 To investigate the influence of light intensity or carbon dioxide on the rate of photosynthesis

In this activity *Elodea* or pondweed is used. *Elodea* is an underwater plant, so it is possible to see the bubbles of oxygen released from the plant as they pass through the water.

Syllabus There is a choice of activity here. This account refers only to the influence of **light intensity** on the rate of photosynthesis.

The rate of photosynthesis is measured by counting the number of bubbles released in a given time.

1. Add excess sodium bicarbonate (also called sodium hydrogen carbonate) to some water in a test tube. This means that water is saturated with carbon dioxide (which ensures a constant concentration of carbon dioxide during the experiment).

2. Cut a section of *Elodea* and place it (cut end upwards) in the test tube. Set up the apparatus as shown in diagram 11.20 in a darkened room. (The water bath ensures that the temperature stays constant.) The lamp should be 1 metre from the apparatus.

3. Leave the apparatus for 5 minutes (to allow the *Elodea* to adjust to the conditions).

4. Count the number of bubbles of oxygen coming from the cut end of the stem per minute.

5. Repeat step 4 twice more.

6. Add the three numbers and divide by 3 to calculate the average number of bubbles per minute (this is a measure of the rate of photosynthesis).

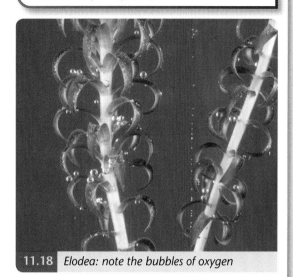

11.18 *Elodea: note the bubbles of oxygen*

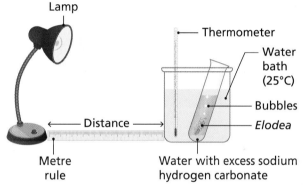

11.19 *To investigate the effects of light intensity on the rate of photosynthesis*

7. Increase the light intensity by moving the lamp closer to the apparatus.

8. Repeat steps 3 to 6 each time the lamp is moved (i.e. at 80 cm, 60 cm, 40 cm and 20 cm).

9. Record your results as shown in the following table (some values are included as samples).

Activity 12 results		
Distance (cm)	Number of bubbles/minute	Average number of bubbles/minute
100	8, 10, 9	9
80	12, 14, 13	13
60		
40		
20		

10. You will see that as the lamp is moved closer to the apparatus the rate of bubble production increases. However, at some point, the rate of bubble production ceases to increase. The plant is then said to be saturated with light.

$$\text{Light intensity} \propto \frac{10\,000}{(\text{distance})^2}$$

11.20 *The formula to use to convert from distance (in cm) to light intensity where the symbol means 'is proportional to'.*

THE CELL

The final table of results (based on the figures in step 9) will appear as:

Distance (cm)	Light intensity	Average number of bubbles/minute
100	1	9
80	1.56	13
60	2.78	
40	6.25	
20	20	

11. Draw a graph of the average number of bubbles/minute vs. light intensity (putting light intensity on the horizontal axis). The graph should appear as shown below.

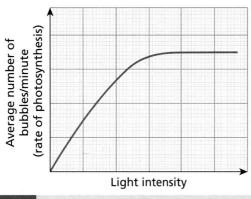

11.21 *Graph showing bubble rate against light intensity*

Note: This experiment can also be carried out using the apparatus shown in diagram 11.22.

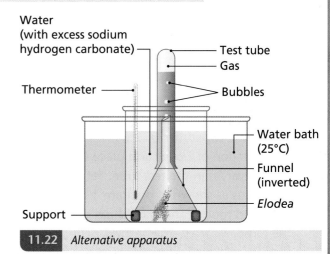

11.22 *Alternative apparatus*

In this case the rate of photosynthesis can be calculated by:
- ▸ Counting the number of bubbles/minute
- ▸ Measuring the volume of oxygen gas collected in the top of the test tube after a suitable length of time (e.g. 15 minutes).

In addition, the gas collected in the test tube can be shown to be oxygen, as it rekindles a glowing splint.

Summary

Photosynthesis:
- Is vital because it produces food and oxygen
- Takes place in the green parts of a plant
- Can be represented by the balanced equation:

$$6CO_2 + 6H_2O + Light \xrightarrow{\text{Chlorophyll}} C_6H_{12}O_6 + 6O_2$$

The **main events in photosynthesis** are:
- Light energy is absorbed by chlorophyll
- Water is split using absorbed sunlight energy
- The products of the splitting of water are electrons (passed to chlorophyll), protons (stored in the chloroplast) and oxygen gas (released or used for respiration)
- Sunlight energy is used to form high-energy electrons in chlorophyll
- The high-energy electrons, stored protons (hydrogen ions) and carbon dioxide are used to make glucose.

Sources of light, carbon dioxide and water for photosynthesis:
- Sunlight is the normal source of light for photosynthesis
- Carbon dioxide is obtained from the atmosphere or from the process of respiration in the leaf
- Water is obtained from the soil.

The **rate of photosynthesis** can be increased by:
- Using artificial light
- Increasing the carbon dioxide concentration.

The **light stage** requires light and takes place in the chloroplast.

The **events in the light stage** are:
- Light energy is absorbed by a range of pigments in the chloroplast
- The absorbed energy is transferred to a special chlorophyll, where it energises electrons.

THE CELL

HIGHER ▼

128

HIGHER ▼

- The energised electrons may return to chlorophyll, using their energy to make ATP (pathway 1), or may be taken away from chlorophyll and combined with $NADP^+$ and H^+ to form ATP and NADPH (pathway 2)
- Water is split to produce:
  ▸ Electrons, which replace those lost by the chlorophyll molecule
  ▸ Protons (H^+), which help to form NADPH
  ▸ Oxygen, which is used in respiration or released.

Electron flow:
- In cyclic electron flow, ATP is made using light energy, by a process that involves electrons from chlorophyll returning to chlorophyll (pathway 1)
- In non-cyclic electron flow, light energy is converted to ATP and NADPH by a process that involves electrons leaving chlorophyll but not returning to it (pathway 2).

The **end products of the light stage** are:
- ATP
- NADPH
- Oxygen.

The **dark stage** uses ATP and NADPH. The dark stage does not require light and takes place in the chloroplast.
The events of the dark stage are:
- NADPH releases H^+ and two electrons
- CO_2 combines with the H^+ and electrons
- Energy is provided by ATP converting to ADP
- Glucose is made
- ADP and $NADP^+$ return to the light stage.

To investigate the **influence of light intensity on the rate of photosynthesis**:
- The number of bubbles of gas released per minute from *Elodea* is counted to calculate the rate of photosynthesis.
- Excess sodium hydrogen carbonate ensures constant CO_2 concentrations.
- A water bath ensures a constant temperature.
- Light intensity is varied by altering the distance between the lamp and the apparatus.
- The results indicate that increasing light intensity increases photosynthesis, up to a point.

HIGHER ▼

THE CELL

Revision questions

1 (a) In what cell organelle does photosynthesis take place?
   (b) Name the most important pigment in this organelle.
   (c) Give a balanced equation for photosynthesis.
   (d) Name four substances necessary for photosynthesis.
   (e) Name the two main products of photosynthesis.

2 State two benefits of photosynthesis for:
   (a) Plants (b) Animals.

3 In photosynthesis water is split.
   (a) What supplies the energy to split water?
   (b) Name the three products formed when water is split.
   (c) State what happens to each of these products.
   (d) Which of the three products may be used directly by humans?

4 How do plants get (a) light (b) carbon dioxide and (c) water for photosynthesis?

5 Name any two methods that growers can use to increase their yield of greenhouse plants.

6 The following apparatus was used to investigate the effect of light intensity on photosynthesis.
   (a) Name a suitable plant for this experiment.

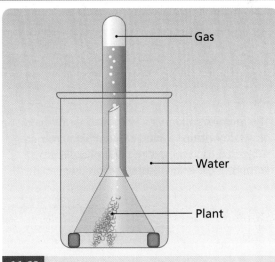

11.23

   (b) Name the gas produced.
   (c) State the normal test for this gas.
   (d) How can the CO_2 concentration in the water be kept constant?
   (e) What adaptation could be made to ensure that the temperature remained constant?
   (f) How could the light intensity be varied?
   (g) State one way in which the rate of photosynthesis could be measured.
   (h) Why should the experiment be carried out in a darkened room?

7   In carrying out the experiment outlined in the previous question, the following results were obtained.

The effect of light intensity on photosynthesis	
Light intensity	**Bubbles per minute**
0	0
1	6
2	14
3	26
4	38
5	40
6	40

(a)   Use graph paper to draw a graph of these results.

(b)   Explain, referring to specific numerical values, the results of the graph.

(c)   Estimate from your graph:
   (i)   The number of bubbles per minute produced at a light intensity of 2.5
   (ii)   The light intensity at which 30 bubbles per minute would be produced.

HIGHER ▼

8   Distinguish between the light and dark phases of photosynthesis on the basis of:
(a)   The need for light
(b)   The need for enzymes
(c)   The end products.

9   (a)   In what cell organelle is water split?
(b)   Name two products of the splitting of water that are necessary for the light stage.

(c)   What gas is produced when water is split?
(d)   State two possible fates of this gas.

10   (a)   What is the function of pigments in a chloroplast?
(b)   Why do chloroplasts have a range of such pigments?
(c)   In what cell organelle are these pigments located?

11   The light stage reactions involve a flow of energised electrons.
(a)   What molecule is necessary to allow these electrons to be energised?
(b)   What is the source of the energy used to energise them?
(c)   The energised electrons can follow pathway 1 or pathway 2. Distinguish between these pathways in terms of:
   (i)   The paths taken by the electrons
   (ii)   The end products of each route.

12   Give a brief, outline account of (a) the light stage and (b) the dark stage of photosynthesis.

13   Relate the following events to either the light or dark stage of photosynthesis:
(a)   Formation of ATP
(b)   Use of CO_2
(c)   Breakdown of NADPH
(d) O_2 production
(e)   Absorption of light
(f)   Photolysis
(g)   Production of ADP
(h)   Pathways 1 and 2
(i)   Formation of glucose.

HIGHER ▼

Exam questions

Section A

14   The following graph shows how the rate of photosynthesis varied when a plant was subjected to varying levels of light intensity or carbon dioxide concentration.

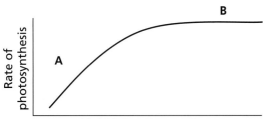

(a)   What is happening at A?
(b)   What is happening at B?
(c)   Suggest a reason for your answer in (b).
(d)   Where in a cell does photosynthesis take place?
(e)   Give **two** sources of the carbon dioxide that is found in the atmosphere.

(f)   Suggest **one** way in which the rate of photosynthesis of plants in a greenhouse could be increased.

(2005 HL Q 4)

Section B

15   (a)   State a precise role for **each** of the following in photosynthesis:
   (i)   Carbon dioxide
   (ii)   Water.

(b)   Answer the following questions in relation to an activity that you carried out to investigate the influence of light intensity or carbon dioxide concentration on the rate of photosynthesis.
   (i)   Name the plant that you used.
   (ii)   How did you vary light intensity or carbon dioxide concentration?
   (iii)   State a factor that you kept constant during the investigation.
   (iv)   How did you ensure that the factor that you mentioned in (iii) remained constant?

(v) How did you measure the rate of photosynthesis?

(vi) Using labelled axes, sketch a graph to show how the rate of photosynthesis varied with the factor mentioned in (ii) above.

(2007 HL Q 9)

Section C

16 (a) What is metabolism? Describe briefly the part played by enzymes in metabolism.

(b) The following equation summarises the process of photosynthesis.

$$\text{Gas A + Water} \xrightarrow[\text{Chlorophyll}]{\text{Energy}} \text{Glucose + Gas B}$$

(i) Name Gas A.
(ii) Name Gas B.
(iii) Name the energy source.
(iv) Plants obtain Gas A from the air. Name two processes that release this gas into the air.
(v) Suggest two possible fates for Gas B, following its production in the plant.
(vi) Where in a leaf would you expect to find cells with most chlorophyll?
(vii) What term is used to describe the nutrition of plants?

(c) The apparatus shown below may be used to investigate the effect of an environmental factor on the rate of photosynthesis.

(i) Name X and Y.
(ii) How would you measure the rate of photosynthesis?
(iii) Name an environmental factor that you would vary in this experiment.
(iv) Explain how you would vary the factor that you have named in (iii).
(v) Other environmental factors should be kept constant during the experiment. Name one of these factors.

(2004 OL Q 13)

17 (a) (i) During photosynthesis oxygen is produced.
1. From what substance is oxygen produced?
2. In which stage of photosynthesis is oxygen produced?
3. Give **two** possible fates of oxygen following its production.

(ii) Give an account of the role of **each** of the following in photosynthesis:
1. ATP
2. NADP.

(2008 HL Q 14)

18 (a) (i) Write the balanced equation for photosynthesis.
(ii) What is the main source of light for photosynthesis?
(iii) During photosynthesis water molecules are split into **three** products. Name **each** of these products.
(iv) Describe what happens to **each** of the products referred to in (iii).
(v) Name the structures in which photosynthesis occurs in plant cells.

(2009 OL Q 15)

19 (c) One laboratory activity that you carried out demonstrated the influence of light intensity or of carbon dioxide concentration on the rate of photosynthesis. Answer the following in relation to this activity:
(i) Explain how you measured the rate of photosynthesis.
(ii) Explain how you varied light intensity **or** carbon dioxide concentration.
(iii) State how you kept another **named** factor constant.
(iv) Draw a graph with labelled axes to show the results that you obtained.
(v) Briefly explain the trend in your graph.

(2009 HL Q 12)

20 (c) (i) Draw a labelled diagram of the apparatus you used to investigate the effect of light intensity **or** carbon dioxide concentration on the rate of photosynthesis.
(ii) How did you vary the light intensity **or** the carbon dioxide concentration?
(iii) How did you measure the rate of photosynthesis?
(iv) What is the relationship between the rate of photosynthesis and **either** the light intensity **or** the carbon dioxide concentration?
(v) Most Irish tomatoes are grown in greenhouses. State **two** ways a commercial producer could increase her/his crop yield of tomatoes.

(2010 OL Q 12)

21 (a) (i) Where in a plant cell does photosynthesis take place?
(ii) Give the alternative name of the first stage of photosynthesis.
(iii) During the first stage of photosynthesis energised electrons enter two pathways.
1. Where do the energised electrons come from?
2. Briefly describe the main events of **each** of these pathways.
(iv) 1. In the second stage of photosynthesis compounds of the general formula $Cx(H_2O)y$ are formed. What name is given to this group of compounds?

2. From which simple compound does the plant obtain the H used to make compounds of general formula $Cx(H_2O)y$?

(v) Name the simple compound that supplies the necessary energy for the second stage reactions.

(2010 HL Q 14)

22 (a) The graph shows the results of a classroom investigation into the factors affecting the rate of photosynthesis. The variable investigated was **either** light intensity **or** CO_2 concentration.

Indicate clearly which factor you choose to address and answer the following questions:

(i) Suggest a suitable plant for such an investigation.

(ii) How was the rate of photosynthesis measured?

(iii) Name a factor that must be kept constant during this investigation.

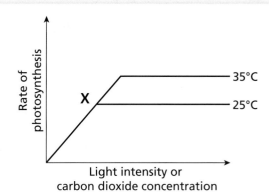

(iv) Explain how you would keep constant the factor referred to in (iii).

(v) Why is it necessary to keep that factor constant?

(vi) **1.** What happens to the rate of photosynthesis at X when the investigation is
   A. carried out at 25°C?
   B. carried out at 35°C?

2. Give a reason for **each** answer.

(2011 HL Q 14)

Previous examination questions

Ordinary level	Higher level
2004 Q 13	2004 Q 11
2005 Q 11	2005 Q 4
2006 Q 4	2006 Q 11
2008 Q 12	2007 Q 9
2009 Q 15a	2008 Q 14a
2010 Q 12c	2009 Q 12c
2011 Q 12a, b	2010 Q 8, 14a
	2011 Q 14a
	2012 Q 12b

Latest questions at www.edco.ie/lcbiologyplus/examhelp

Online test and assessment tracker

Scan the QR code and test yourself on chapter 11
www.edco.ie/lcbiologyplus

Chapter 12 **Respiration**

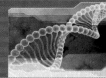

Learning objectives
- To define the term 'aerobic respiration' and represent it as a balanced equation
- To describe simply the aerobic respiration of glucose as a two-stage process
- To define the term 'anaerobic respiration' (fermentation) and represent it as a word equation
- To explain how micro-organisms are used in industrial fermentation
- **HIGHER ▶** To perform a detailed study of respiration, including glycolysis, Krebs cycle and the electron transport chain
- **HIGHER ▶** To describe ethanol or lactic acid fermentation
- To prepare and test the production of alcohol by yeast.

Introduction

External respiration is the process by which organisms exchange gases with their environment. External respiration takes place in the lungs of mammals, through the gills in fish, through openings in plant stems and on the bottom surface of leaves.

Internal respiration is the controlled release of energy from food. The food involved is usually glucose.

The process of internal respiration is controlled by enzymes. They allow energy to be released in small amounts, which can easily be trapped for later use. The energy is trapped in the form of a molecule called ATP (adenosine triphosphate).

Internal respiration can be either aerobic or anaerobic.

12.1 *Respiration produces energy*

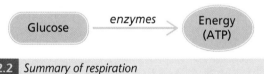

12.2 *Summary of respiration*

Aerobic respiration

Most living things get their energy from aerobic respiration and are therefore called aerobes. In this process, the energy stored in the bonds of a molecule such as glucose is released and used to make ATP.

When ATP later breaks down, it supplies energy for all the metabolic reactions in the cell (such as muscular movement, production of new cells and growth).

Aerobic respiration is a relatively efficient method of obtaining energy. About 40% of the energy in glucose is converted to ATP during aerobic respiration. This high efficiency is due to the substrate (glucose) being completely broken down.

The end products of aerobic respiration (carbon dioxide and water) have very low energies. Most of the energy that is not converted to ATP is lost as heat.

Aerobic respiration is the controlled release of energy from food using oxygen.

$$C_6H_{12}O_6 + 6O_2 \xrightarrow{enzymes} 6CO_2 + 6H_2O + energy$$
(glucose) (oxygen) (carbon dioxide) (water)

12.3 *A balanced equation to represent aerobic respiration*

THE CELL

133

Stages in aerobic respiration

Respiration may occur as either a one-stage or a two-stage process. Aerobic respiration is a two-stage process.

Stage 1

- Is an anaerobic process (this means it does not use or require oxygen in order to take place).
- Releases only a small amount of energy – as a result, it is inefficient as an energy-release system.

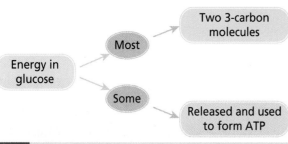

12.4 *A word equation to represent stage 1 of respiration*

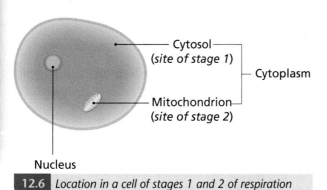

12.5 *Energy in stage 1 of respiration*

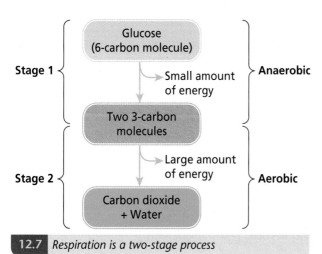

12.6 *Location in a cell of stages 1 and 2 of respiration*

Glucose → two 3-carbon molecules + a small amount of energy

- Takes place in the cytosol of the cell. The cytoplasm consists of all of the living parts of the cell surrounding the nucleus. The cytosol is the cytoplasm minus the cell organelles.
- Involves splitting glucose (a six-carbon sugar) into two three-carbon molecules. In doing this, a small amount of energy is released and used to produce a small number of ATP molecules.

In stage 1, glucose is incompletely or partially broken down. Much of the energy that was stored in the bonds of the glucose molecule is retained in the bonds of the two three-carbon molecules. This is why stage 1 produces only a low yield of energy.

Stage 2

- Is an aerobic process (it requires and uses oxygen).
- Releases a large amount of energy. This means it is efficient as an energy-release system.
- Takes place in the mitochondria.

The stage 2 reactions are very complex. They involve the breakdown of the three-carbon molecules (formed in stage 1) to carbon dioxide and water. One of the steps in this breakdown requires oxygen.

As stage 2 is a complete breakdown of the three-carbon molecules, it releases a large amount of energy (which is used to form a large number of ATP molecules). Very little energy remains in the carbon dioxide and water molecules.

Carbon dioxide and water are the end products of both stage 2 and of aerobic respiration.

12.7 *Respiration is a two-stage process*

THE CELL

Anaerobic respiration

Anaerobic respiration:
- Is also known as fermentation
- Does not use oxygen (note it can occur in the presence of oxygen, but it does not use oxygen)
- Is a stage 1 process (i.e. it does **not** involve stage 2)
- Takes place in the cytosol
- Releases a small amount of energy
- Initially involves the breakdown of glucose into two three-carbon molecules.

There are many different forms of anaerobic respiration. In each of them, the three-carbon molecules are converted to some other end products, but no extra energy is released.

Anaerobic respiration is a far less efficient process than aerobic respiration, because glucose is only partially broken down.

Two common types of fermentation are:
- Lactic acid fermentation (often simply called anaerobic respiration)
- Alcohol fermentation.

> **Anaerobic respiration** is the controlled release of energy from food without the use of oxygen.

> **Fermentation** is another name for anaerobic respiration.

Lactic acid fermentation

Lactic acid fermentation occurs in some bacteria and fungi (which are called anaerobes) and in human muscle when it is short of oxygen. In this process the three-carbon molecules are converted to lactic acid.

Lactic acid fermentation takes place in human muscle when the supply of oxygen to the muscle is not sufficient to meet its energy needs (i.e. when we are out of breath). Lactic acid builds up in the muscle, causing cramp and muscular stiffness. When the person rests, the lactic acid is taken to the liver by the blood and broken down.

Lactic acid (which can easily form a similar substance called lactate) is formed when:
- Bacteria cause milk to go sour
- Bacteria respire on cabbage to produce sauerkraut
- Silage is made
- Bacteria act on dairy products to make cheese and yoghurt.

Glucose $\longrightarrow$ 2 lactic acid + a small amount of energy

12.8 *A word equation to represent lactic acid fermentation*

Alcohol fermentation

Alcohol fermentation is another form of anaerobic respiration. It takes place in some bacteria, in fungi (such as yeast) and in plants when they are deprived of oxygen.

In this process the three-carbon molecules are converted to ethanol and carbon dioxide. This is also a partial breakdown of glucose. The end products of alcohol fermentation are ethanol and carbon dioxide. Ethanol is a high-energy product.

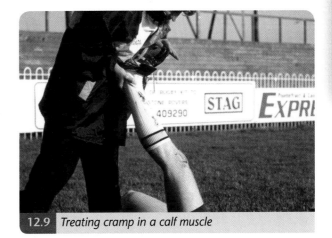

12.9 *Treating cramp in a calf muscle*

Glucose $\longrightarrow$ 2 ethanol + 2 carbon + a small amount
                              dioxide   of energy

12.10 *A word equation to represent alcohol fermentation*

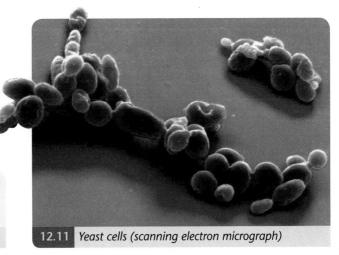

12.11 *Yeast cells (scanning electron micrograph)*

THE CELL

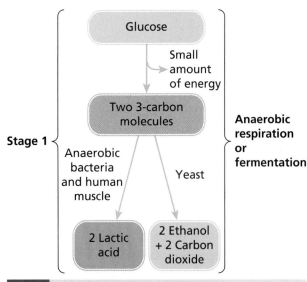

Stage 1

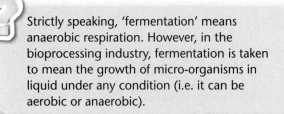

12.12 *The two types of anaerobic respiration*

Strictly speaking, 'fermentation' means anaerobic respiration. However, in the bioprocessing industry, fermentation is taken to mean the growth of micro-organisms in liquid under any condition (i.e. it can be aerobic or anaerobic).

Alcohol fermentation has been used for thousands of years in baking and in beer and wine production.

In baking, special yeasts are mixed with flour and liquid to form dough. Alcohol fermentation occurs in the dough. The alcohol evaporates, but the carbon dioxide produced causes the dough to rise, forming a lighter bread.

12.13 *Dough rising: unrisen dough is in the bottom and rising dough is shown above*

In modern baking, yeast (which cannot withstand the high temperatures of an oven) is often replaced with baking powder as a source of carbon dioxide.

Micro-organisms in industrial fermentation

Biotechnology is the use of living things or their components (especially cells and enzymes) to manufacture useful products or to carry out useful reactions.

Biotechnology can use micro-organisms, plants or animals to manufacture products. However, micro-organisms are the basis of most production techniques.

Fermentation is the foundation of much of the biotechnology industry. The production of substances using fermentation techniques is a form of bioprocessing (see Chapter 9).

Production method

In bioprocessing, the micro-organisms are placed in a container along with a suitable substrate on which they can react. The vessel in which the biological reactions take place is called a **bioreactor**.

Many different bioreactors are used, but a typical example is shown in diagram 12.15.

The contents of the bioreactor are mixed so that the micro-organisms are brought into contact with the substrate. Sometimes the mixing (or the reaction itself) produces foam. This is reduced by the use of a foam breaker.

The culture medium is the liquid (including a suitable substrate) in which the micro-organisms grow. In many bioreactors it is important to get as much oxygen dissolved in the culture medium as possible. For this reason air (or oxygen) is pumped into the vessel. The air passes through a device called a sparger, which forms small air bubbles that dissolve more readily into the culture medium.

THE CELL

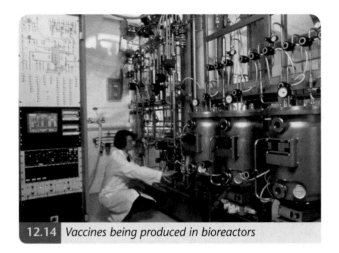

12.14 *Vaccines being produced in bioreactors*

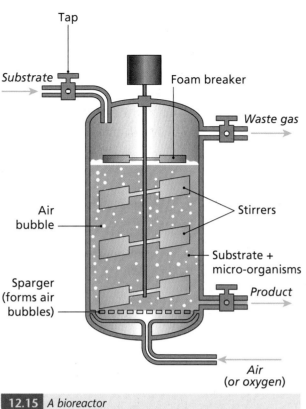

12.15 *A bioreactor*

Apart from using the correct micro-organism and substrate, the quality and yield of the product depend on a number of other factors. These include the materials and design of the bioreactor, elimination of micro-organisms that would contaminate the process, the correct rate of mixing, and control of environmental factors such as temperature and pH.

Micro-organisms used in bioprocessing

There is a very wide range of micro-organisms used in industrial fermentations. New micro-organisms are continuously being developed and used. Many of these are produced using genetic engineering techniques (see Chapter 18).

In general, the main organisms used are bacteria and fungi, especially different yeast strains. Note that very often different organisms may be used to produce the same end product (e.g. antibiotics are produced by bacteria, fungi and yeast).

Very old examples of bioprocessing include the use of yeast in the production of alcohol and of carbon dioxide in baking. Some modern examples of bioprocessing are given in the following table.

Microorganism	Product	Use
Bacteria	Ethanol	Beer, wine, paint, perfume, polish
	Acetone	Solvent (e.g. nail varnish remover)
	Amino acids and vitamins	Food additives (e.g. in breakfast cereals)
	Yoghurt	Food
	Methane gas	Fuel (called biogas)
	Antibiotics	To kill other bacteria
	Enzymes	Washing powders (act as stain removers)
	Drugs	Maintain health
	Hormones	Maintain health
Yeasts	Ethanol	Beer, wine, solvent
	Carbon dioxide	Causes dough to rise
	Single-cell protein	Edible protein
Other fungi	Citric acid	Food and drink additive (e.g. soft drinks)
	Antibiotics	To treat bacterial infections

Bioprocessing with immobilised cells

When micro-organisms are used in a bioreactor they are removed, along with the product, at the end of the process. They then have to be separated from the product and new micro-organisms must be grown to replace those lost. This is wasteful and costly.

To prevent these problems, micro-organisms are often fixed or immobilised in the bioreactor. Whole cells are immobilised in the same way as enzymes (see Immobilised enzymes in Chapter 9).

Detailed study of respiration

Aerobic respiration

Aerobic respiration is a two-stage process (as outlined earlier in this chapter). We will now look at these stages (especially stage 2) in more detail.

Glycolysis is the conversion of glucose into two molecules of pyruvic acid.

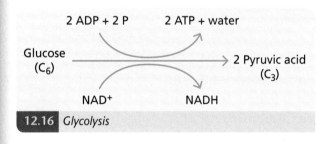

$$2\ ADP + 2\ P \qquad 2\ ATP + water$$

$$Glucose\ (C_6) \longrightarrow 2\ Pyruvic\ acid\ (C_3)$$

$$NAD^+ \qquad NADH$$

12.16 *Glycolysis*

$$NAD^+ + 2e^- + H^+ \longrightarrow NADH$$

12.17 *The formation of NADH as a result of the breakdown of pyruvic acid*

The reactions in Krebs cycle were first discovered by German biochemist (Sir) Hans Krebs (1900–81) and others in 1937. For his work in this area he shared the Nobel Prize in 1953.

12.18 *Sir Hans Krebs*

Stage 1

Stage 1 reactions are called glycolysis. Glycolysis:

● Takes place in the cytosol of the cell
● Does not require oxygen (it is anaerobic)
● Forms two ATP molecules
● Produces pyruvic acid as an end product (pyruvic acid can easily form a charged molecule called pyruvate).

Stage 2

In stage 2 a complex series of reactions take place, some of which require oxygen. If oxygen is present, pyruvic acid enters a mitochondrion. Here it loses a carbon dioxide molecule to form a two-carbon (C_2) molecule called acetyl coenzyme A (often shortened to acetyl CoA).

Pyruvic acid also loses two high-energy electrons and a proton (H^+). These combine with NAD^+ to form NADH, as shown in diagram 12.17. Each NADH will enter an electron transport system, as outlined later.

Krebs cycle

Acetyl CoA now enters into a series of reactions called Krebs cycle.

In Krebs cycle, acetyl CoA is broken down to carbon dioxide and protons (H^+) in a number of reactions (see diagram 12.20). The energy that was in acetyl CoA is released in a number of steps in the form of high-energy electrons. These electrons (along with protons, H^+) are picked up by NAD^+ to form NADH. The NADH molecules enter an electron transport system.

HIGHER ▼

At one point in Krebs cycle a single ADP (and a phosphate) is converted to ATP and water.

$$NAD^+ + 2e^- + H^+ \longrightarrow NADH$$

12.19 *The formation of NADH as a result of the breakdown of acetyl CoA*

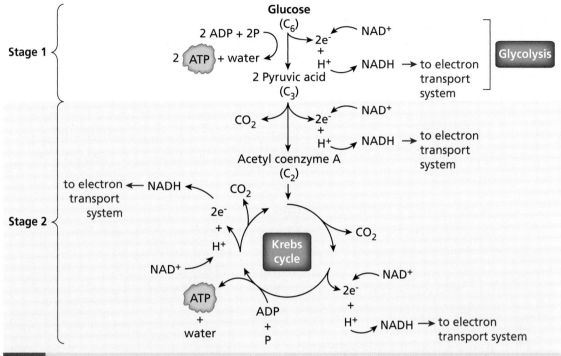

12.20 *The events in both stages of respiration*

Electron transport system

The electron transport systems, or chains, are located on the inner membrane of the mitochondrion. Infoldings of the inner membrane increase the surface area and allow larger numbers of these systems to fit on the membrane.

Each electron transport system consists of a number of molecules, mostly proteins. High-energy electrons are passed from NADH to the first of these molecules, as shown in diagram 12.21, overleaf.

As the electrons pass from molecule to molecule within each system they lose some of their energy. This is similar to the way water loses energy as it flows down a waterfall. Some of the energy released by the electrons is used to form ATP. The rest of the energy is lost as heat.

At the end of each system, low-energy electrons are removed by combining them with oxygen and hydrogen (H^+) to form water.

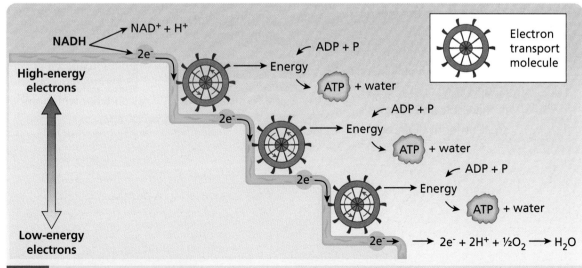

12.21 *The electron transport system*

THE CELL

> Certain chemicals, such as cyanide, are fatal because they prevent some of the proteins in the system from receiving or passing on electrons. This means that ATP is not produced.

Importance of the electron transport system

The importance or significance of the electron transport system is that it produces the energy-rich carrier ATP. It converts the energy in NADH to a more useable form of energy (ATP).

The electron transport system cannot work in the absence of oxygen. This is because oxygen is essential at the end of the system to remove the low-energy electrons. If oxygen is absent electrons cannot flow along the system and so no further ATP is produced. Aerobic organisms die due to a lack of available energy (ATP), in the absence of oxygen.

Summary of aerobic respiration

Aerobic respiration involves stage 1 and stage 2 reactions (see diagram 12.20).
- Stage 1 (glycolysis) is anaerobic and releases very little energy.
- Stage 2 includes Krebs cycle reactions and the electron transport systems. These are aerobic and release a large amount of energy as a result of the complete breakdown of glucose.

Anaerobic respiration

Anaerobic respiration starts with the stage 1 (glycolysis) reactions. This means that glucose is converted into two molecules of pyruvic acid. ATP and NADH are produced in this process (see diagram 12.16).

In the absence of oxygen, pyruvic acid is converted (or reduced) to either lactic acid (in animals and some bacteria) or ethanol and carbon dioxide (in plants and yeast). In both these forms of anaerobic respiration (also called fermentation) Krebs cycle cannot proceed and no further ATP is produced.

All the reactions in lactic acid fermentation and in alcohol fermentation are stage 1 reactions. These reactions take place in the cytosol and do not involve Krebs cycle or the electron transport systems.

In conclusion, both types of fermentation only involve stage 1 (glycolysis). Stage 1 is anaerobic and releases a small amount of energy.

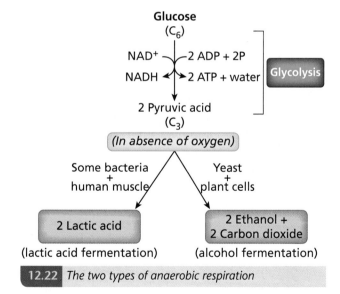

12.22 The two types of anaerobic respiration

Activity 13 To prepare and show the production of alcohol by yeast

Preparation of alcohol

1. Prepare a glucose solution by dissolving glucose in water.
2. Boil the solution in a conical flask for 5 minutes (this eliminates gases from the solution, forming anaerobic conditions).
3. When the solution cools, add some dried yeast.
4. Cover the liquid in the flask with oil (this prevents oxygen from re-entering the solution).
5. Set up either of the two pieces of apparatus as shown in diagram 12.23.
6. The airlock is needed to prevent micro-organisms entering and to allow carbon dioxide to pass out.
7. Limewater or water may be used in the airlock (limewater turns milky in the presence of carbon dioxide).
8. The apparatus is placed in a water bath at 30°C (this is an ideal temperature for the maximum rate of respiration).
9. Bubbles of carbon dioxide will be seen in the limewater. Fermentation is complete when the bubbles stop forming (often after a few days).
10. As a control, the same apparatus is used without adding any yeast cells (or adding boiled yeast). In this case, no bubbles form and the limewater remains clear.

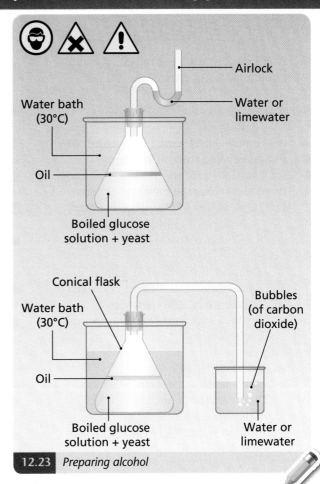

12.23 *Preparing alcohol*

To show the production of ethanol (the iodoform test)

1. Filter the solution (to remove yeast cells).
2. Place some of filtrate into a test tube.
3. Add an equal volume of potassium iodide solution. Note this is a colourless solution.
4. Add sodium hypochlorite solution (note that the solution turns a brown-orange colour and then becomes colourless).
5. Place the test tube in a water bath at 50–60°C for 4 or 5 minutes.
6. Remove the test tube and allow it to cool.
7. The appearance of pale yellow crystals (of a chemical called iodoform) indicates that ethanol is present.
8. As a control use water instead of the filtered solution. Yellow crystals do not form.

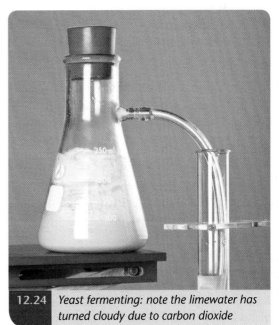

12.24 *Yeast fermenting: note the limewater has turned cloudy due to carbon dioxide*

To show that alcohol is produced

To test for alcohol, acidified potassium dichromate is added to the filtered solution. The test tube is placed in a warm water bath. If alcohol is present the colour changes from orange to green.

Syllabus According to EU regulations the use of potassium dichromate should be discontinued in schools. This test remains as a theoretical part of the syllabus but students are not required to carry out the test.

Summary

External respiration is the process of gas exchange or breathing.

Internal respiration is the release of energy (ATP) from food using enzymes.

Aerobic respiration:
- Uses oxygen
- Is a complete breakdown of glucose
- Releases a large amount of energy
- Is a two-stage process
- Is represented by the balanced equation:
  $C_6H_{12}O_6 + 6O_2 \rightarrow 6CO_2 + 6H_2O + energy$

Stages in aerobic respiration:
- Stage 1
  - Does not use oxygen (it is anaerobic)
  - Takes place in the cytosol of the cell
  - Releases very little energy
  - Splits glucose into two three-carbon molecules.
- Stage 2
  - Uses oxygen (it is aerobic)
  - Takes place in the mitochondrion
  - Releases a large amount of energy
  - Converts the three-carbon molecules formed in stage 1 to carbon dioxide and water.

Anaerobic respiration (or fermentation):
- Does not use oxygen
- Is a partial breakdown of glucose
- Releases a small amount of energy
- Is a stage 1 process
- Takes place in the cytosol
- Is represented by the word equations:
  Glucose → 2 lactic acid + some energy
  Glucose → 2 ethanol + 2 carbon dioxide
  + some energy

Stage 1 in anaerobic respiration is the same as stage 1 in aerobic respiration, except that the three-carbon molecules are converted to:
- Lactic acid in lactic acid fermentation (takes place in some bacteria and human muscle)
- Ethanol and carbon dioxide in alcohol fermentation (takes place in some bacteria and yeast).

Biotechnology is the production of useful products using living cells or their parts.

A large range of micro-organisms, especially bacteria and yeast, are used in industry to carry out different anaerobic or fermentation reactions.

The production of substances by fermentation is an example of bioprocessing.

A bioreactor is a vessel in which bioprocessing takes place.

Immobilised cells are attached to each other or to an inert solid.

Stage 1
The stage 1 reactions are called glycolysis and take place in the cytosol.

In glycolysis:
- Glucose is split into two molecules of pyruvic acid (or pyruvate)
- No oxygen is used
- ATP and NADH are formed.

Stage 2
In the presence of oxygen, stage 2 proceeds in the mitochondrion. Stage 2 involves both Krebs cycle reactions and the electron transport system.

Pyruvic acid loses carbon dioxide and high-energy electrons (in the form of NADH), forming acetyl CoA.

In Krebs cycle:
- Acetyl CoA goes through a cycle of reactions
- Acetyl CoA is converted to carbon dioxide and hydrogen
- High-energy electrons and protons (H^+) are released to form several NADHs
- ADP is converted to ATP.

In the electron transport systems (located on the inner membrane of the mitochondrion):
- NADH releases high-energy electrons
- The electrons are passed from molecule to molecule along the system
- The electrons release energy as they pass along
- The energy is used to form ATP
- At the end of the system, low-energy electrons combine with oxygen and hydrogen to form water.

Aerobic respiration involves both stage 1 (anaerobic, low energy release) and stage 2 (aerobic, high energy release).

Anaerobic respiration only involves stage 1 and is a low-energy release process.

HIGHER ▼

THE CELL

There are **two forms of anaerobic respiration:**
● In lactic acid fermentation, glycolysis is followed by the conversion of pyruvic acid to lactic acid
● In alcohol fermentation, glycolysis is followed by the conversion of pyruvic acid to ethanol and carbon dioxide.

To prepare alcohol:
● Mix glucose and water
● Boil the solution
● Add yeast
● Cover with oil
● Leave in a warm place.

To show the production of ethanol:
● Add potassium iodide
● Add sodium hypochlorite
● If pale yellow crystals form, ethanol is present.

To show the production of alcohol (**Note:** This reaction should no longer be carried out):
● Add acidified potassium dichromate
● Warm in hot water
● If the colour turns from orange to green then alcohol is present.

Revision questions

1 (a) Distinguish between internal and external respiration.
 (b) State a location for each in humans.

2 (a) Why is respiration essential for all living things?
 (b) Name the normal respiratory substrate.

3 Give (a) **two** similarities and (b) **two** differences between aerobic and anaerobic respiration.

4 Name the end products of:
 (a) Aerobic respiration
 (b) Alcohol fermentation
 (c) Lactic acid fermentation.

5 (a) Give a balanced equation for aerobic respiration.
 (b) Give word equations to represent:
  (i) Anaerobic respiration in yeast
  (ii) Anaerobic respiration in human muscle.

6 Aerobic respiration is a two-stage process. Say whether each of the following statements relates to stage 1 or stage 2.
 (a) Requires oxygen
 (b) Takes place in the cytosol
 (c) Occurs in the mitochondrion
 (d) Releases a large amount of energy
 (e) Produces carbon dioxide and water
 (f) Is a partial breakdown of glucose
 (g) Is anaerobic.

7 (a) Under what conditions do humans respire anaerobically?
 (b) What is the end product of this process?
 (c) What is the effect of this product on muscles?
 (d) State one possible fate of this product in a person.

8 (a) What is: (i) Biotechnology (ii) Bioprocessing (iii) A bioreactor?

 (b) Name any one organism used in industrial fermentation and state the product of this fermentation.

9 Micro-organisms are used to produce large quantities of the products listed below. State one commercial application for each of them.
 (a) Methane gas
 (b) Enzymes
 (c) Vitamins
 (d) Single-cell proteins
 (e) Citric acid.

10 Alcohol fermentation is the oldest known form of industrial fermentation.
 (a) Name an organism that carries out this process.
 (b) Name two industries based on this process.
 (c) State the end product of this process used in each of the industries named.
 (d) Outline one use for each of the products named in part (c).

11 (a) Give a word equation for glycolysis.
 (b) Name the end products of glycolysis.
 (c) State the location in a cell for glycolysis.

12 State what happens to the products of glycolysis:
 (a) In the presence of oxygen
 (b) In the absence of oxygen.

13 With regard to Krebs cycle:
 (a) State its location in a cell.
 (b) Name the end products.
 (c) Name the molecule that continuously enters the cycle.
 (d) Name the energy-rich compound that links the cycle with the electron transport system.

HIGHER ▼

14 (a) What is the benefit to a cell of the electron transport system?
(b) What is the fate of the electrons that pass through the system?
(c) State the precise location of the electron transport systems in a cell.

15 Respiration may be a one or a two-stage process. Distinguish between these stages in terms of:
(a) The need for oxygen
(b) The amount of energy released
(c) Whether one or both occur in **(i)** aerobic and **(ii)** anaerobic respiration.

16 Aerobic respiration can be represented as a two-stage process as shown in diagram 12.25.

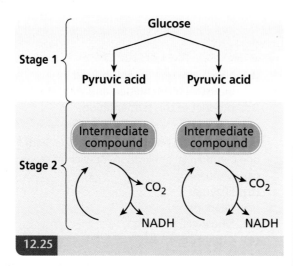

12.25

(a) Name the two stages shown as 1 and 2.
(b) Name the intermediate compound shown.
(c) What is the fate of the **(i)** carbon dioxide and **(ii)** NADH, produced at stage 2?
(d) Name two places on the diagram where ATP is produced.

17 The apparatus in diagram 12.26 may be used to demonstrate aerobic respiration. Air is drawn through the apparatus by attaching it to a vacuum pump at X. Sodium hydroxide is placed in flask 1 to remove carbon dioxide.
(a) What is the purpose of removing carbon dioxide?
(b) Limewater is put in flasks 2 and 3. Suggest a reason for putting it in each flask.

(c) What is the purpose of a control in an experiment? Suggest a suitable control for this experiment.
(d) If the animal in the apparatus were replaced by a plant, and the experiment carried out in daylight, would you expect a similar result? Explain your answer.

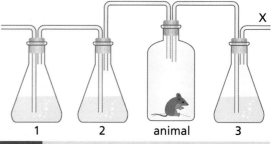

12.26

18 Choose which of the options (i), (ii), (iii) or (iv) represents the correct answer in each case below.
(a) Krebs cycle reactions occur in:
  (i) Chloroplasts
  (ii) Cytosol
  (iii) Mitochondria
  (iv) Yeast.
(b) The largest ATP (energy) output results from:
  (i) Glycolysis
  (ii) Aerobic respiration
  (iii) Anaerobic respiration
  (iv) Stage 1 reactions.
(c) Respiration is essential because it:
  (i) Releases energy
  (ii) Uses glucose
  (iii) Requires enzymes
  (iv) Involves stage 1.
(d) In preparing alcohol, anaerobic conditions are achieved by:
  (i) Using a water bath
  (ii) An airlock
  (iii) Boiling the substrate solution
  (iv) Using a conical flask.
(e) During anaerobic respiration, lactic acid may be directly produced from:
  (i) Glucose
  (ii) Ethanol
  (iii) Pyruvic acid
  (iv) ATP.

THE CELL

Exam questions

Section A

19 (a) What is the first stage process of respiration called?

(b) In this first stage there is a release of ATP as glucose is converted to another substance. Name this other substance.

(c) To what is the substance you have named in (b) converted under anaerobic conditions in:
1. Yeast?
2. A human muscle cell?

(d) Under aerobic conditions the substance that you have named in (b) is converted to an acetyl group and in the process a small molecule is released. Name this small molecule.

(e) The acetyl group now enters a cycle of reactions. What name is given to this cycle?

(f) Where in the cell does this cycle take place?

(2006 HL Q 4)

20 (a) Write a balanced equation to represent aerobic respiration.

(b) The first stage of respiration takes place in the cytosol. What is the cytosol?

(c) Does the first stage of respiration release a small or large amount of energy?

(d) What is fermentation?

(e) Where in the cell does the second stage of aerobic respiration take place?

(f) Is oxygen required for the second stage of aerobic respiration?

(g) Suggest a situation in which some cells in the human body may not be able to engage in the second stage of aerobic respiration.

(2008 HL Q 5)

21 Choose each term from the following list and place it in **Column B** to match a description in **Column A**. The first one has been completed as an example.

Alcohol, Oxygen, Water, Mitochondria, Lactic acid, ~~Large~~

Column A	Column B
The amount of energy released in aerobic respiration.	Large
(i) A substance required for aerobic respiration.	
(ii) A product of anaerobic respiration in muscles.	
(iii) A product of aerobic respiration.	
(iv) A product of anaerobic respiration in yeast.	
(v) The cell structures in which Stage 2 of aerobic respiration takes place.	

(2011 OL Q 5)

22 Cellular respiration may occur in one stage or two stages.

(a) Give **two** differences, other than location, between Stage 1 and Stage 2.

(b) Where in a cell does Stage 1 occur?

(c) What term is used to describe respiration in which only Stage 1 occurs?

(d) Name a chemical end product of the type of respiration referred to in (c).

(e) In Stage 2 of respiration electrons pass along an electron transport chain, releasing energy. In what molecule is this energy stored in the cell?

(f) To what are these electrons transferred at the end of the electron transport chain?

(2011 HL Q 6)

Section B

23 (a) Yeast cells produce ethanol (alcohol) in a process called fermentation. Is this process affected by temperature? Explain your answer.

(b) Answer the following in relation to an experiment to prepare and show the presence of ethanol using yeast.
(i) Draw a labelled diagram of the apparatus that you used.
(ii) Name a substance that yeast can use to make ethanol.
(iii) What substance, other than ethanol, is produced during fermentation?
(iv) Describe the control that you used in this experiment.
(v) Explain the purpose of a control in a scientific experiment.
(vi) How did you know when the fermentation was finished?
(vii) Why were solutions of potassium iodide and sodium hypochlorite or potassium dichromate added to the reaction vessels after a certain period of time?
(viii) Name a substance produced during aerobic respiration that is not produced during fermentation.

(2004 HL Q 7)

Section C

24 (b) (i) What name is given to the first stage of respiration?
(ii) Where in a cell does this first stage take place?
(iii) To what substance is glucose normally converted in this first stage of respiration?
(iv) Is oxygen required for this conversion?
(v) Name a compound to which the substance that you have named in (iii) may be converted, in the absence of oxygen.

(vi) In aerobic respiration, the product of the first stage moves to the mitochondrion. Outline subsequent events in the total breakdown of this product.

(2007 HL Q 11)

25 (b) (i) What name is given to the first stage of respiration?

(ii) The first stage ends with the formation of pyruvate (pyruvic acid). In **anaerobic** conditions, what is produced from this pyruvate:
  1. In muscle cells?
  2. In yeast cells?

(iii) If conditions are **aerobic**, pyruvate next passes to an organelle in which the second stage of respiration takes place. Name this organelle.

(iv) In this organelle pyruvate is broken down to CO_2 and a two-carbon compound. Name this two-carbon compound.

(v) This two-carbon compound passes directly into a series of reactions in the second stage of respiration. Name this series of reactions **and** give **one** product, other than electrons, of these reactions.

(vi) The electrons released from the above reactions pass along a transport chain and in the process energy is released.
  1. To what use is this energy put?
  2. At the end of the transport chain what happens to the electrons?

(2009 HL Q 12)

26 (a) (i) What is meant by *metabolism*?

(ii) Give **two** reasons why living things need energy.

(b) (i) Which biological process is represented by the following word equation:
glucose + oxygen → carbon dioxide + water + energy?

(ii) The above process occurs in two stages, Stage 1 and Stage 2, that take place in different parts of the cell. Say where in the cell Stage 1 occurs **and** where in the cell Stage 2 occurs.

(iii) Does the whole process release a large amount or a small amount of energy?

(iv) Write a word equation to show what happens when **yeast** breaks down glucose in the absence of oxygen.

(v) Give **one** industrial application of this process.

(vi) When **muscles** break down glucose in the absence of oxygen, one main product is produced. Name this product.

(2010 OL Q 12)

Previous examination questions

Ordinary level	Higher level
2005 Q 11c	2004 Q 7
2006 Q 13	2005 Q 11c
2007 Q 12	2006 Q 4
2008 Q 3	2007 Q 11b
2009 Q 15b	2008 Q 5
2010 Q 12a, b	2009 Q 12a, b
2011 Q 5	2011 Q 6
2012 Q 14a	2012 Q 12c

Latest questions at www.edco.ie/lcbiologyplus/examhelp

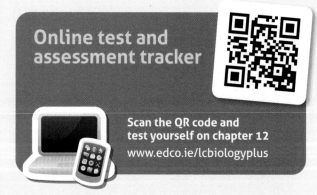

Online test and assessment tracker

Scan the QR code and test yourself on chapter 12
www.edco.ie/lcbiologyplus

THE CELL

Chapter 13 Diffusion and osmosis

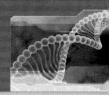

Selective permeability of membranes

All the membranes in a cell (all biological membranes) are similar in structure and in the way they operate. This means that the cell or plasma membrane is the same as the membranes around organelles such as mitochondria or chloroplasts.

A membrane is said to be **permeable** to a substance if the substance can pass through it and **impermeable** if it cannot pass through.

Biological membranes are selectively permeable, as are materials such as cellophane, visking tubing and dialysis tubing. These membranes allow molecules such as water, oxygen and carbon dioxide to pass through freely. They do not, however, allow sugars, proteins and salts to pass through easily.

Although membranes are impermeable to some substances, cells have specialised mechanisms in their membranes to allow these substances to pass through when necessary. For example, glucose has to pass in through the plasma or cell membrane to allow for respiration. Equally, proteins have to pass out through membranes in the form of hairs, nails and hormones.

Diffusion

Diffusion is said to take place along a concentration gradient. Everyday examples of diffusion include the way the smell of perfume, bread baking or the unpleasant effects of a stink bomb can spread through a room.

Examples of diffusion in biology are carbon dioxide diffusing into a leaf, oxygen diffusing out of a leaf, oxygen diffusing from the blood into a cell and carbon dioxide diffusing out of a cell.

Diffusion is caused by the kinetic energy of the molecules. These molecules are moving randomly and will tend to spread out if they can. This movement does not need external energy so diffusion is said to be passive.

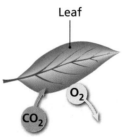
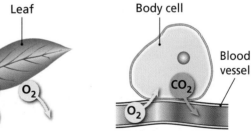

13.1 *Examples of diffusion*

> A selectively **permeable membrane** allows some but not all molecules to pass through.
>
> **Diffusion** is the spreading out of molecules from a region of high concentration to a region of low concentration.

13.2 *Diffusion: the dark blue solution is spreading out into the pale blue solution*

THE CELL

Osmosis

> Osmosis is the movement of water molecules across a semi-permeable membrane from a region of high water concentration to a region of low water concentration.

Before dealing with osmosis it is important to understand the following terms.

- A **solvent** is a liquid that dissolves other substances. Water is the most common biological solvent.
- A **solute** is a substance that has been dissolved. Salt dissolved in water is an example of a solute.
- A **solution** is a mixture of a solute and solvent. Salt water is an example of a solution.

Osmosis is a special type of diffusion. Like diffusion it is also passive (i.e. it requires no external energy).

Another way to define osmosis is to say it is the movement of water (solvent) across a semi-permeable membrane from a region of low solute concentration to a region of high solute concentration. The fact that both definitions are the same should be clear from diagram 13.3.

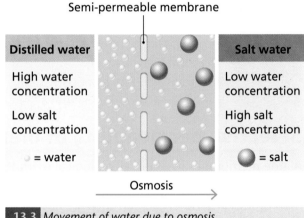

13.3 *Movement of water due to osmosis*

Osmosis and animal cells

Animal cells are enclosed only by a cell (or plasma) membrane. They do not have cell walls (unlike plant cells).

Animal cells in a solution that is the same concentration as their cytoplasm

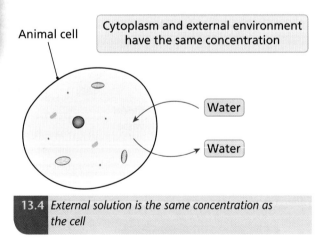

13.4 *External solution is the same concentration as the cell*

If an animal cell is in a solution that is the same concentration as its cytoplasm, water will move in and out through its cell membrane at the same rate. The volume of the cell will remain the same.

Sea water has the same concentration as the cytoplasm of many animals that live in the sea. Also the cells of most land animals are surrounded by tissue fluid that has the same concentration as the cells.

In the same way, one of the functions of the kidneys is to ensure that plasma, the liquid portion of our blood, has the same concentration as our blood cells.

Animal cells in less concentrated solution

If an animal cell is in a solution that is less concentrated than the cell, water will move into the cell as a result of osmosis. The cell will enlarge and may burst and die.

Amoeba is a single-celled organism that lives in freshwater pools and ponds (see Chapter 22). Fresh water is less concentrated than the cell contents of *Amoeba*.

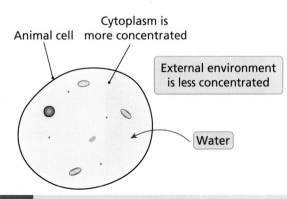

13.5 *External solution is less concentrated than the cell*

This means that *Amoeba* must have a method of controlling osmosis or it will enlarge and burst.

The osmoregulation system in *Amoeba* consists of a contractile vacuole. The contractile vacuole expels water, which prevents the cell from bursting.

Amoeba species that live in sea water do not have contractile vacuoles. This is because the sea water has the same concentration as their cells. Hence excess water does not enter their cells.

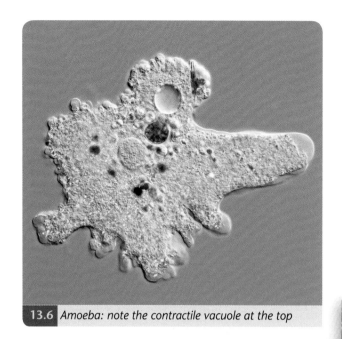

13.6 *Amoeba: note the contractile vacuole at the top*

Animal cells in more concentrated solution

If an animal cell is in a solution that is more concentrated than the cell, water will move out of the cell as a result of osmosis. This will cause the cell to shrivel (a condition known as crenation) and possibly die.

This sometimes happens to aquatic animals if their environment becomes too salty. It also happens to red blood cells if they are in a very salty solution.

Osmosis and plant cells

Plant cells are enclosed by a cell membrane, which in turn is surrounded by a strong cell wall. Cell walls are **fully permeable** to water, gases and many solutes (e.g. salts and sugars). The cell wall gives a certain amount of strength to a plant cell.

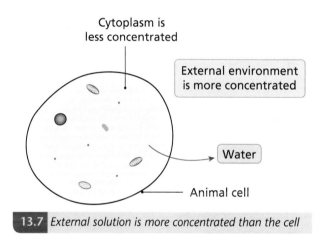

13.7 *External solution is more concentrated than the cell*

Plant cells in less concentrated solution

If a plant cell has a higher concentration of solutes than its surroundings, water moves into the cytoplasm and vacuole of the cell by osmosis. This is how plant roots absorb water from the soil.

Water enters the vacuole, which swells slightly and pushes the cytoplasm out against the cell wall. The cell wall is relatively rigid and prevents the cell from swelling.

Turgor pressure gives a plant cell great strength. In this state, the cell is said to be turgid. Plants that do not have wood, such as most house plants or lettuce, get their strength because their cells are fully turgid.

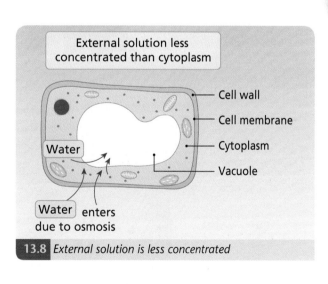

13.8 *External solution is less concentrated*

Turgor, or **turgor pressure**, is the outward pressure of the cytoplasm and vacuole against the cell wall of a plant.

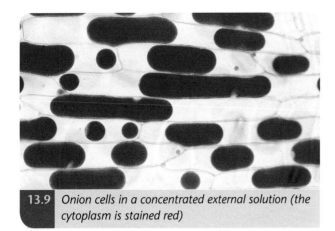

13.9 *Onion cells in a concentrated external solution (the cytoplasm is stained red)*

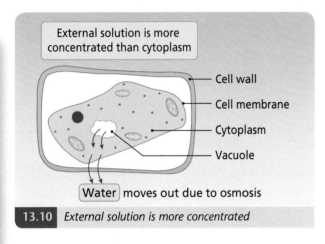

External solution is more concentrated than cytoplasm

Cell wall

Cell membrane

Cytoplasm

Vacuole

Water moves out due to osmosis

13.10 *External solution is more concentrated*

13.11 *A normal houseplant and one that has wilted*

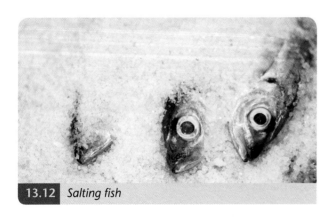

13.12 *Salting fish*

Plant cells in more concentrated solution

If the cytoplasm of a plant cell has a lower concentration of solutes than the surroundings, then the cell is less concentrated than its surroundings. Equally, the surroundings are more concentrated than the cell contents.

In this case, water moves out of the cell as a result of osmosis. The vacuole and cytoplasm shrivel and the cell membrane moves away from the cell wall. The more concentrated solution fills the space between the cell membrane and the cell wall. The cell loses turgor pressure.

As a result the cell is not as strong as it was and is said to be flaccid (limp). The loss of water from the cytoplasm and the movement of the cell membrane away from the cell wall is called **plasmolysis**.

When all the cells of a plant are plasmolysed the plant is said to wilt. This can be seen when lettuce becomes limp due to soaking in salty salad dressing. It is also seen when cut flowers lose water as a result of evaporation.

Plasmolysed cells can be restored to normal by placing them in a less concentrated solution. This is called deplasmolysis.

Osmosis and food preservation

Bacteria and fungi are similar to plants in that they are also enclosed by walls. Osmosis is often used to prevent micro-organisms such as bacteria and fungi from growing on food. This prevents them from producing harmful toxins (poisons) and from decaying the food.

Examples of food preservation techniques based on osmosis are:

- Foods such as fish and meat (bacon) may be soaked in a very salty solution. Any micro-organisms in or on the food will lose water and die as a result of osmosis.
- Fruit can be preserved in the form of jams and marmalades by using a high sugar concentration. This dehydrates micro-organisms and prevents them from growing.

THE CELL

Activity 14 To demonstrate osmosis

Note: Visking tubing is a selectively permeable membrane. Water can pass freely through visking tubing, but sucrose cannot.

1. Soak two strips of visking tubing in water (this softens them).
2. Tie a knot in one end of each of the strips.
3. Dissolve a large amount of sucrose in warm water in a beaker. This forms a concentrated sucrose solution (warm water is a better solvent than cold water).
4. Almost fill one piece of visking tubing with distilled (or tap) water. Tie a knot to seal the contents (this bag acts as a control).
5. Almost fill the second piece of visking tubing with sucrose solution. Tie a knot to seal the contents.
6. Dry each tube. Note the 'fullness' (or turgidity) of each tube and record its mass.
7. Place each tube of visking tubing in a container of distilled (or tap) water, as shown in diagram 13.13.
8. Leave the apparatus for about 30 minutes.
9. Remove the bags, dry them and note and record the 'fullness' and mass of each bag.

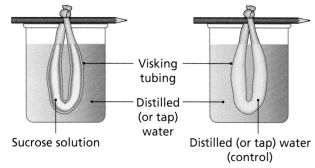

13.13 *To show osmosis*

10. Record the results as follows:

Contents of tube	Sucrose solution	Distilled or tap water
Mass at the start (g)		
Final mass (g)		
Change in fullness or turgidity (more, less or the same turgidity)		

The expected results are:

● The visking tubing containing the sucrose solution will have filled with water so that it has gained mass and is more full (this is due to water entering the tubing as a result of osmosis).

● The visking tubing containing the distilled water shows no change in mass or 'fullness' (i.e. it has not gained or lost water).

Summary

All **biological membranes** are similar.

Selectively permeable membranes allow some substances to pass through easily, but other substances cannot pass through easily.

Diffusion is:
● The movement of molecules from high to low concentration
● Passive (needs no external energy).

Osmosis is:
● The movement of water from a high water concentration to a low water concentration through a semi-permeable membrane
● A special case of diffusion
● Passive.

Animal cells in a solution that is:
● The same concentration as their cytoplasm stay the same size
● Less concentrated than their cytoplasm gain water, swell and may burst

- More concentrated than their cytoplasm lose water, shrivel and may die.

Amoeba survives in a less concentrated (freshwater) environment because of its contractile vacuole, which eliminates water.

Plant cells in a solution that is:
- Less concentrated than their cytoplasm gain water and become turgid and strong
- More concentrated than their cytoplasm lose water and become weak.

High salt and sugar concentrations:
- Can be used to remove water from micro-organisms by osmosis
- Are used as food preservation techniques.

To show osmosis:
- Place bags of visking tubing almost filled with **(a)** distilled water and **(b)** concentrated sucrose solution, in distilled water
- Bag **(a)** stays the same in mass and turgidity
- Bag **(b)** increases in mass and turgidity as water enters as a result of osmosis.

Revision questions

1. Explain the following terms as they relate to membranes:
   (a) Permeable
   (b) Impermeable
   (c) Selectively permeable.

2. Give two examples in each case of diffusion in:
   (a) Plants (b) Animals. In each case, name:
      (i) The substance that diffuses
      (ii) Where it is moving from
      (iii) The place to which it moves.

3. Explain the meaning of each of the following, giving a named example in each case:
   (a) Solute (b) Solvent (c) Solution.

4. (a) What is osmosis?
   (b) Explain briefly why osmosis is a special case of diffusion.
   (c) How do osmosis and diffusion differ?

5. (a) Why should blood plasma have the same concentration as blood cells?
   (b) What organ carries out this function?
   (c) What is the likely result if blood plasma became less concentrated than the blood cells?

6. (a) What is *Amoeba*?
   (b) Where does *Amoeba* normally live?
   (c) Name the structure that *Amoeba* uses to carry out osmoregulation.
   (d) Why do seawater *Amoebae* not have the structure named in (c)?

7. Diagram 13.14 represents a plant cell.

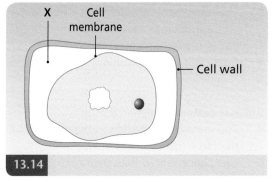

13.14

   (a) What term describes the condition of the cell?

   (b) What does this result tell us about the solution outside the cell?
   (c) The solution at X has the same concentration as the external solution. What does this tell us about the cell wall?

8. (a) What is turgor pressure?
   (b) Why is turgor pressure not associated with animal cells?

9. (a) What happens to red blood cells in distilled water?
   (b) Explain why plant cells in distilled water do not behave in exactly the same way.

10. Thirty cubes of equal size were cut from a fresh potato. They were weighed and the average weight was calculated. Ten cubes were placed in distilled water, ten in a 10% salt solution and ten in a 1% salt solution. After 1 hour all the cubes were again weighed. The results were:

Sample	Average weight of each cube (g)
Fresh potato	7.2
Cubes in distilled water	9.3
Cubes in 10% salt solution	4.1
Cubes in 1% salt solution	7.2

   (a) What process accounts for the gain or loss in weight?
   (b) Why were ten cubes used in each case?
   (c) What does this tell you about the salt concentration of the potato cytoplasm?

11. The apparatus shown in diagram 13.15 was set up and left for 15 minutes. Note that iodine molecules can pass through visking tubing. Give a reason for each of the following results:
   (a) The volume of liquid in the visking tubing increased.
   (b) The contents of the visking tubing turned blue-black.
   (c) The colour of the distilled water and iodine changed.

(d) The liquid in the beaker did not turn blue-black.

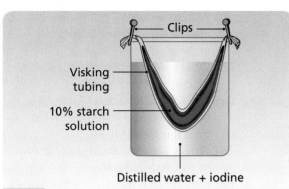

Clips

Visking tubing

10% starch solution

Distilled water + iodine

13.15

12 **(a)** Why does salting fish help to preserve it?
   (b) Suggest why fungus does not easily grow on the surface of jams.

13 The experiment in diagram 13.16 demonstrates osmosis.

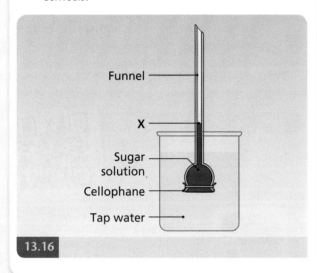

Funnel

X

Sugar solution

Cellophane

Tap water

13.16

(a) Why is cellophane used?
(b) What do you expect will happen to the level of liquid at X?
(c) Which solution is less concentrated?
(d) If extra sugar is added to the solution in the funnel how will the final result change?
(e) What causes the changes in water levels?

14 Three cellophane bags were half filled with a 2% sugar solution. The bags were then placed in three different solutions as shown in diagram 13.17.

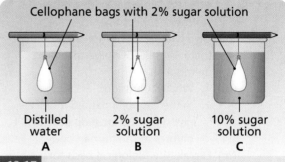

Cellophane bags with 2% sugar solution

Distilled water
A

2% sugar solution
B

10% sugar solution
C

13.17

(a) Which solution is **(i)** more concentrated **(ii)** less concentrated and **(iii)** the same concentration, with reference to the contents of the bags?
(b) Explain, giving reasons, what will happen to the mass of each bag.

Exam questions

Section B

15 **(a)** **(i)** What is osmosis?
   (ii) What is a selectively permeable (semi-permeable) membrane?
   (b) **(i)** Draw a labelled diagram of the apparatus that you used to demonstrate osmosis.
   (ii) Describe how you carried out the experiment to demonstrate osmosis.
   (iii) How were you able to tell that osmosis had taken place?
   (2005 OL Q 7)

16 **(a)** **(i)** Define the term osmosis.
   (ii) Give an example of osmosis in plants.
   (b) Answer the following questions in relation to practical work you carried out to investigate osmosis.

   (i) Draw a labelled diagram of the apparatus you used in the investigation.
   (ii) Describe how you used this apparatus to carry out the investigation.
   (iii) State the result(s) of your investigation.
   (2009 OL Q 8)

Section C

17 **(a)** **(i)** Water enters the roots of plants by osmosis. Explain what is meant by osmosis.
   (ii) Describe how you demonstrated osmosis as part of your practical activities.
   (2008 OL Q 15)

18 (c) (ii) Water enters the outermost cells of the root by osmosis. What does this tell you about the cell sap of these outermost cells?

(iii) Osmosis has been described as a special case of diffusion. Explain why.

(iv) Describe an investigation that you carried out to demonstrate osmosis.

(2008 HL Q 14)

19 (c) (i) In relation to membranes in cells, explain what is meant by *selective permeability*.

(ii) Give two locations in a cell at which there is a selectively permeable membrane.

(iii) 1. What is diffusion?
2. In the case of a named molecule, give a precise location at which it diffuses in the human body.

(iv) Explain the biological basis for the use of high sugar or high salt concentrations in the preservation of food.

(2010 HL Q 14)

20 (c) (i) State the precise location of the cell membrane in plant cells.

(ii) With what type of cell do you associate membrane-bound organelles?

(iii) What corresponding term is used to describe bacterial cells?

(iv) The cell membrane is described as being *selectively permeable*. What does this mean?

(v) Why is diffusion alternatively known as *passive transport*?

(vi) Osmosis may be described as "a special case of diffusion". Explain why.

(vii) Describe, with the aid of a labelled diagram, how you demonstrated osmosis in the laboratory.

(viii) Name the structure by which *Amoeba* gets rid of excess water that has entered by osmosis.

(2011 HL Q 14)

Previous examination questions

Ordinary level	Higher level
2005 Q 7	2008 Q 14c
2008 Q 15a	2010 Q 14c
2009 Q 8	2011 Q 14c
	2012 Q 15c

Latest questions at www.edco.ie/lcbiologyplus/examhelp

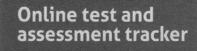

Online test and assessment tracker

Scan the QR code and test yourself on chapter 13
www.edco.ie/lcbiologyplus

154

Chapter 14 **Cell division**

Cell continuity

Cell continuity means that all cells develop from pre-existing cells.

Cell continuity gives rise to the continuity of life, which was discussed in Chapter 2.

When a new cell forms (from an existing cell) it goes through the following three phases:
- It produces or synthesises all the materials it will need
- It grows larger
- It reproduces to form new cells.

Cell continuity implies that most cells spend a lot of time producing the chemicals and substances they need to survive and grow. They are not actively dividing into new cells during this phase of their life. Cells spend a relatively short time engaged in cell division.

Chromosomes

When a cell is not dividing, the chromosomes exist as long, thin threads called chromatin. At cell division, chromatin contracts to form a number of clearly distinguishable chromosomes.

Every species has a definite number of chromosomes in each cell. For example, humans have 46 chromosomes in each body cell.

Each chromosome is composed of hundreds, or even thousands, of genes. These genes are arranged along the chromosome as shown in diagram 14.2.

Chromosomes are coiled threads of DNA (which forms genes) and protein that become visible in the nucleus at cell division.

14.1 *A human chromosome (SEM)*

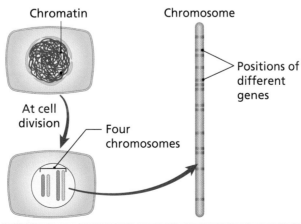

14.2 *Chromatin, chromosomes and genes*

THE CELL

A gene is a section of DNA that contains the instructions for the formation of a protein.

Genes

Many of the proteins produced by genes are enzymes. As these enzymes control the activities of the cell, it can be said that genes (or chromosomes) control the cell. Genes are also said to be units of inheritance.

All the genes in an organism make up its **genome**. In humans, genes control features such as eye colour, production of skin pigment (melanin), number of fingers, the shape of the face and about 20 000 to 25 000 other features. In plants, genes control petal colour, leaf shape, fruit taste and many more features.

Haploid and diploid cells

A **haploid cell** has one set of chromosomes, i.e. it has only one of each type of chromosome in the nucleus.

A **diploid cell** has two sets of chromosomes, i.e. it has two of each type of chromosome in the nucleus.

Haploid is symbolised by the letter 'n', and the number of chromosomes in the cell is given as n = 2 or n = 3 etc. In diagram 14.3, all the cells shown are haploid because in each case there is only one of each *type* of chromosome.

In humans, eggs and sperm are haploid cells and each one contains 23 chromosomes (i.e. n = 23).

Diploid is symbolised as '2n', and the total number of chromosomes in the cell is given as 2n = 4 or 2n = 6, etc.

The diploid number for humans is 46 (2n = 46). This means that each human cell has 23 chromosomes that were obtained from the person's mother and 23 that were obtained from the father.

In a diploid cell the chromosomes are in pairs. As each pair of chromosomes has similar genes, they are called **homologous pairs**.

In diploid cells, one chromosome from each homologous pair is derived from the mother and the other one from the father. This is shown in diagram 14.5, in which the maternal and paternal chromosomes are shown in different colours.

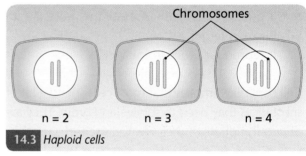

14.3 *Haploid cells*

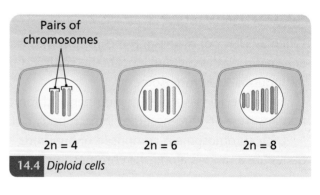

14.4 *Diploid cells*

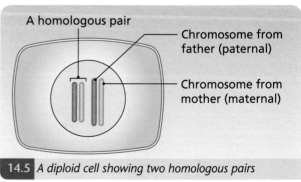

14.5 *A diploid cell showing two homologous pairs*

A **homologous pair** is two chromosomes of similar size with the same sequence of genes.

THE CELL

The cell cycle

A small number of cells, such as nerve and red blood cells, do not divide when they reach full size. Most cells, however, grow until they reach a certain size and then divide.

The cell cycle describes the life cycle of a cell. At its simplest, the cell cycle is divided into a period when the cell is not dividing, called interphase, and a period when the cell divides, called mitosis (or meiosis).

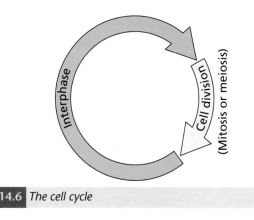

14.6 *The cell cycle*

The **cell cycle** is the changes that take place in a cell during the period between one cell division and the next.

Interphase is the phase in the cell cycle when the cell is not dividing.

Interphase is the longest phase in the cell cycle, often accounting for over 90% of the cycle.

During interphase, the chromosomes are very elongated. It is not possible to distinguish individual chromosomes in the nucleus during interphase. Instead, they appear as a mass of material called chromatin, as shown in diagram 14.2. Although cells are not dividing during interphase, they are very active in the following ways during this phase.

- In the early part of interphase the cell is very active, producing new organelles such as mitochondria or chloroplasts. It also forms many chemicals that are needed for growth, especially enzymes and other proteins.
- Towards the end of interphase (just before the cell divides), the chromosomes produce identical copies of themselves. The duplication (or doubling) of a chromosome produces a chromosome with two strands. The two strands have identical genes, as shown in diagram 14.7.

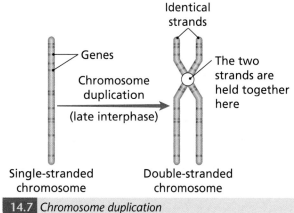

14.7 *Chromosome duplication*

Mitosis

Mitosis is a form of nuclear division in which one nucleus divides to form two nuclei, each containing the same number of chromosomes with identical genes.

Each of the new nuclei formed in mitosis becomes enclosed within a cell called a daughter cell, even when the process occurs in male cells.

The two daughter cells each have the same number of chromosomes. Not only do they have the same number of chromosomes, but the genes on the chromosomes in each cell are identical to each other.

Mitosis takes place in cells that are not associated with the reproductive system. These cells are called somatic cells.

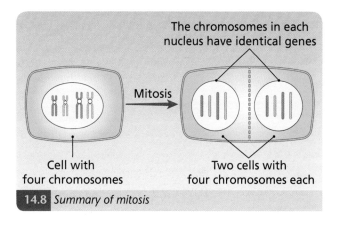

14.8 *Summary of mitosis*

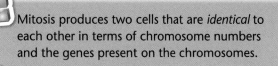

Mitosis produces two cells that are *identical* to each other in terms of chromosome numbers and the genes present on the chromosomes.

Stages of mitosis

Mitosis is a continuous process that is often described as if it had four definite stages or phases. Each stage runs smoothly into the next and it is often difficult to say exactly when any stage starts and ends.

The account of mitosis that follows refers to an animal cell with four chromosomes, i.e. an animal cell with a diploid number of four (2n = 4).

Stage 1

- At the end of interphase, and early in stage 1, chromosomes contract. They gradually become visible in the nucleus as short, thickened strands.
- Each chromosome appears as a double strand.
- Fibres begin to appear in the cytoplasm of the cell.
- The nuclear membrane starts to break down.

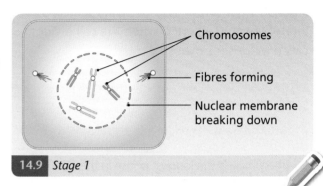

14.9 Stage 1

Stage 2

- The nuclear membrane is fully broken down.
- The chromosomes move so that they line up across the middle of the cell.
- Two fibres attach to each of the chromosomes.

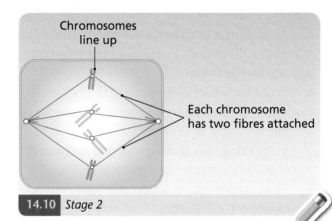

14.10 Stage 2

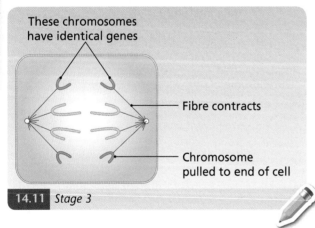

14.11 Stage 3

Stage 3

- The fibres contract. This means that each chromosome is pulled apart.
- The two strands within each chromosome are pulled to opposite ends of the cell.
- Each of the strands in a double-stranded chromosome has identical genes. As a result of the chromosomes splitting at this stage, an identical set of genes is pulled to each end of the cell.

Stage 4

- A nuclear membrane forms around each of the two sets of chromosomes.
- The chromosomes elongate within each nucleus and become chromatin.

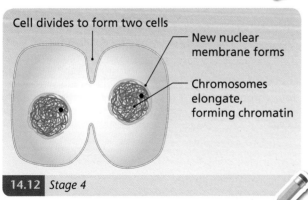

14.12 Stage 4

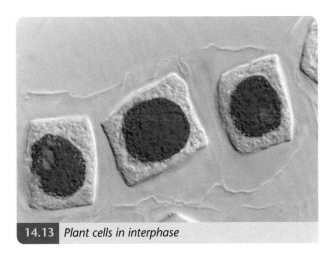

14.13 *Plant cells in interphase*

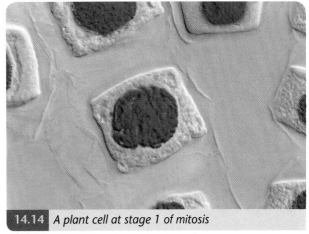

14.14 *A plant cell at stage 1 of mitosis*

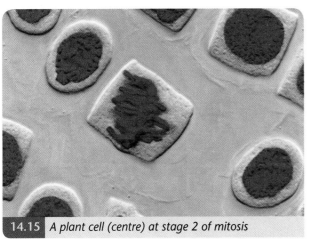

14.15 *A plant cell (centre) at stage 2 of mitosis*

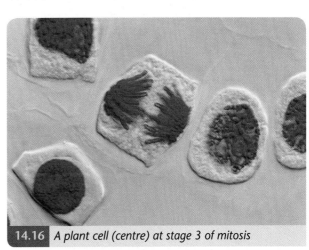

14.16 *A plant cell (centre) at stage 3 of mitosis*

Cell division

Once mitosis is complete, the original cell divides to form two cells. These daughter cells will contain the same number of identical chromosomes as each other. In addition, each daughter cell will have some (about half) of the cell organelles and biomolecules that were in the parent cell.

Function of mitosis

Unicellular organisms

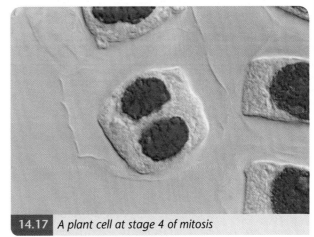

14.17 *A plant cell at stage 4 of mitosis*

In single-celled (unicellular) organisms mitosis increases the number of individuals and is used as a **method of reproduction.** This is the case in organisms such as *Amoeba* and bacteria.

Reproduction that does not involve the joining of two cells is called asexual reproduction. In other words, asexual reproduction only involves a single parent or cell. Mitosis is the basis of asexual reproduction.

Multicellular organisms

In many-celled (multicellular) organisms mitosis is responsible for **growth and repair of cells.** In these organisms mitosis produces new cells, not new individuals.

Mitosis is responsible for the single-celled zygote growing into an embryo.

Even when a person is fully grown, mitosis is essential to replace old and damaged cells. This is seen when new blood cells are produced, when skin damaged by a cut is repaired or when torn muscles are healed.

Mitosis is also responsible for growth and repair in plants.

THE CELL

Cancer

 Cancer is a group of disorders in which certain cells lose their ability to control both the rate of mitosis and the number of times mitosis takes place.

Normally the rate of mitosis and cell division is carefully controlled. This means that just enough new cells are formed to allow for normal growth and repair.

However, sometimes a cell (or a group of cells) loses the ability to control the rate of mitosis. A mass of cells forms, called a tumour. Tumours may be benign or malignant.

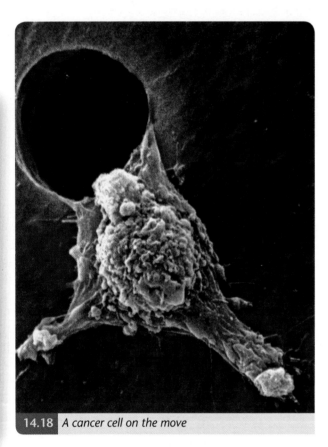

14.18 *A cancer cell on the move*

Benign tumours

Benign means 'kind'. In a benign tumour the cells stop dividing after some time. Benign tumours are not life-threatening. They do not invade other tissues.

Examples of benign tumours are warts (caused by a virus) and skin 'tags' (small blobs of raised skin). Most breast tumours are benign. Benign tumours can be surgically removed.

Malignant tumours

Cancer results in an uncontrolled multiplication of abnormal cells. These abnormal cells form a malignant tumour.

Malignant tumours, called 'cancers', may be life-threatening. This is because they can invade other cells and can move from one place to another in the body. This movement (or migration) of malignant cells is called metastasis.

Cancer cells continue to divide indefinitely. For this reason they are said to be 'immortal'.

Causes of cancer

Cancer is caused when normal genes are altered to form cancer-causing genes (called **oncogenes**). These alterations are brought about by cancer-causing agents called carcinogens. Some common **carcinogens** are cigarette smoke, asbestos fibres, dioxins, pesticides, ultraviolet radiation and some viruses.

It is important to realise that most cancers can be cured. This is especially so if they are discovered and treated early. Treatment includes surgery, radiation (to burn out the cancer) and the use of chemicals that slow down mitosis (chemotherapy).

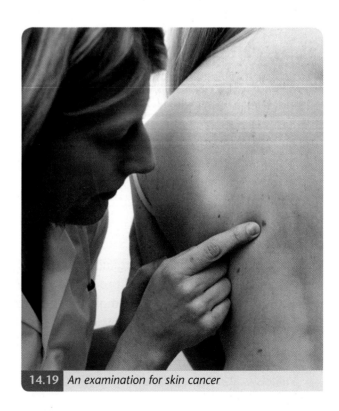

14.19 *An examination for skin cancer*

THE CELL

Meiosis

 Meiosis is a form of nuclear division in which the four daughter nuclei contain half the chromosome number of the parent nucleus.

Immediately after meiosis, the daughter nuclei are enclosed by cells.

When meiosis takes place in a diploid cell, all daughter cells will be haploid. If these cells are capable of joining with another haploid cell from the opposite sex, they are called sex cells or **gametes**.

Most human cells have 46 chromosomes. Meiosis occurs in the ovaries and testes to produce gametes called eggs and sperm, respectively. As a result of meiosis, there are 23 chromosomes in each egg or sperm.

Functions of meiosis

Meiosis has two basic functions in multicellular organisms:
- It allows for sexual reproduction, involving gametes, while still maintaining the parental chromosome number
- It allows for new combinations of genes to be formed, which will give rise to variations among organisms.

Meiosis allows for sexual reproduction

In sexual reproduction, two haploid (n) cells join to form a diploid (2n) zygote. These haploid cells are called gametes or sex cells.

In animals, the gametes are the sperm and egg. In flowering plants, the gametes are the male gamete nuclei and the egg and polar nuclei. The zygote will contain the normal number of chromosomes.

Meiosis is essential for sexual reproduction because it halves the chromosome number. This means that the normal chromosome number is restored at fertilisation.

The role of meiosis in humans is outlined in diagram 14.20. The normal human chromosome number per cell is 46. Meiosis halves this number to 23 in the gametes. Fertilisation restores the chromosome number to 46.

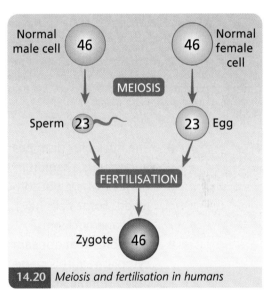

14.20 *Meiosis and fertilisation in humans*

Meiosis allows for variation

The cells resulting from meiosis are not identical. Their genes vary due to the exchange of genetic material which takes place during meiosis.

The variation in the genes (genetic variation) produced in meiosis results in variations or differences in the organisms resulting from the re-assortment of genetic material due to sexual reproduction. This is why brothers (or sisters), while they may resemble each other, are rarely identical.

Variations produced in this manner are part of the basis of evolution, as detailed in Chapter 17.

The differences between mitosis and meiosis	
Mitosis	**Meiosis**
The daughter cells have the same number of chromosomes as the parents	The daughter cells have half the number of chromosomes of the parents
The daughter cells have identical genes on their chromosomes	The daughter cells have different genes on their chromosomes
Two cells are formed	Four cells are formed

THE CELL

Detailed study of mitosis

The account of mitosis that follows is for a similar cell to that outlined earlier in this chapter (i.e. an animal cell with four chromosomes).

The sequence of the four stages of mitosis (Prophase, Metaphase, Anaphase and Telophase) may be recalled by using the first letters of either of the following phrases:

Passed My Algebra Test   or   **Party Monday And Tuesday**

THE CELL

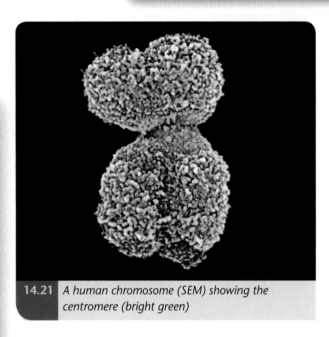

14.21 *A human chromosome (SEM) showing the centromere (bright green)*

- The nucleolus disappears. The nucleolus is a region in the nucleus where ribosomes are made. Some cells have more than one nucleolus.
- The fibres that appear in the cytoplasm at this stage are called spindle fibres. All the spindle fibres collectively form a structure called the spindle.
- The nuclear membrane starts to break down.

The **centromere** is the point at which the chromosomes are attached in a double-stranded chromosome.

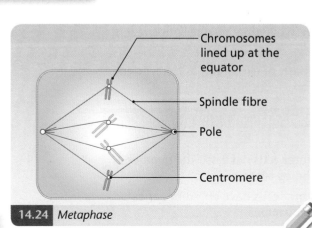

Chromosomes lined up at the equator

Spindle fibre

Pole

Centromere

14.24 *Metaphase*

Prophase

- At the end of interphase and early in prophase chromatin starts to contract.
- Chromosomes become visible as double-stranded structures. The point at which the strands are held together is called a **centromere**.

  The two strands in a chromosome have identical genes. In fact, each strand is a chromosome.

Double-stranded chromosome

Centromere

Each strand (or chromosome) has identical genes

14.22 *A double stranded chromosome*

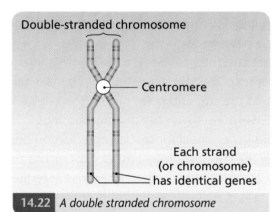

Double-stranded chromosome

Spindle fibres forming

Nuclear membrane and nucleolus breaking down

14.23 *Prophase*

Metaphase

- In metaphase the nuclear membrane completes its breakdown.
- A spindle fibre from each end (or pole) of the cell attaches to each centromere.
- The chromosomes line up across the middle, or equator, of the cell.

Anaphase

- The spindle fibres contract. This causes the centromeres to split.
- One strand (or chromosome) from each double-stranded chromosome is pulled to opposite poles of the cell. This means the cell has eight chromosomes at this stage. The four chromosomes pulled to each pole have identical genes.
- Anaphase is the shortest phase in mitosis. It often lasts only a few minutes, compared with up to 30 minutes for each of the other phases.

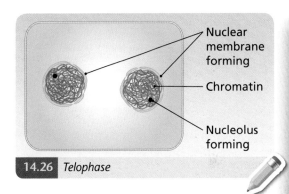

Spindle fibre contracts

Pole

Chromosome pulled to pole

14.25 *Anaphase*

Telophase

- The four chromosomes at each pole begin to lengthen and become hard to distinguish.
- The spindle fibres break down.
- One or more nucleoli (singular: nucleolus) begin to re-form.
- A nuclear membrane forms around the chromatin at each end of the cell.
- At the end of mitosis the original nucleus has divided into two identical nuclei.

Nuclear membrane forming

Chromatin

Nucleolus forming

14.26 *Telophase*

Cell division

Cell division follows immediately after mitosis. The process of cell division proceeds differently in animal and plant cells.

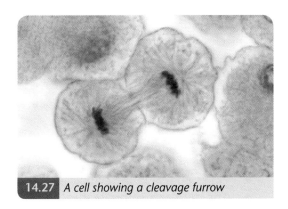

14.27 *A cell showing a cleavage furrow*

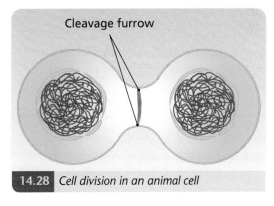

Cleavage furrow

14.28 *Cell division in an animal cell*

Cell division in animal cells

Cell division occurs in animals by a process called cleavage. A shallow groove, called a **cleavage furrow**, appears around the cell, lining up with the position occupied by the equator during metaphase.

The cleavage furrow becomes deeper, until it eventually divides the cytoplasm and the cell splits into two.

Cell division in plant cells

In plant cells, the rigid cell wall prevents a cleavage furrow from forming. Instead, a number of small membrane-enclosed sacs, called vesicles, gather in the area between the two nuclei. The vesicles contain the material, mainly cellulose, which forms the new cell walls, as shown in diagram 14.30.

THE CELL

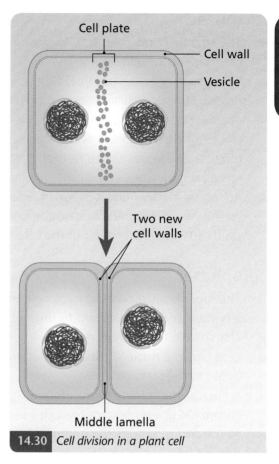

Animal cell → cleavage furrow forms
Plant cell → cell plate forms

These vesicles form a structure called the **cell plate**. The cell plate enlarges and its membranes join with the cell membrane of the original cell.

Two cell walls form from the cell plate, one for each of the daughter cells. The region between two adjacent plant cell walls is called the **middle lamella**.

HIGHER ▼

Cell plate

Cell wall

Vesicle

Two new cell walls

Middle lamella

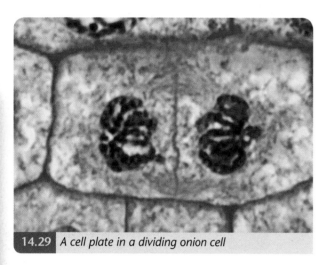

14.29 *A cell plate in a dividing onion cell*

14.30 *Cell division in a plant cell*

Summary

Cell continuity means that cells develop from existing cells.

Chromosomes are made of DNA and protein.
- Chromatin is chromosomes in an elongated form.
- Chromosomes contain genes.

A **gene** is a section of DNA that controls the formation of a protein.

A **haploid cell** (n) has one set of chromosomes.

A **diploid cell** (2n) has two sets of chromosomes.

The **cell cycle** is the changes that occur in a cell between one cell division and the next. The cell cycle includes:
- Interphase, when the cell is not dividing
- Cell division (mitosis or meiosis).

Interphase is an active phase because:
- New cell organelles are formed
- Single-stranded chromosomes form double-stranded copies of themselves.

Mitosis means that:
- A nucleus divides into two
- The chromosome number in each resulting nucleus remains the same as in the parent nucleus.

Mitosis can be divided into four stages:
- In stage 1:
  ▸ Double-stranded chromosomes become visible in the nucleus
  ▸ Fibres appear in the cytoplasm
  ▸ The nuclear membrane starts to break down.
- In stage 2:
  ▸ The nuclear membrane breaks down fully
  ▸ Chromosomes line up along the middle of the cell
  ▸ Two fibres attach to each chromosome.
- In stage 3:
  ▸ The fibres contract
  ▸ One strand from each double-stranded chromosome is pulled to each pole.
- In stage 4:
  ▸ The chromosomes elongate
  ▸ A nuclear membrane forms around each set of chromosomes.

Immediately after mitosis the cell divides into two new cells.

The **functions of mitosis** are:
- It allows single-celled organisms to reproduce
- In multicellular organisms it allows for growth and repair.

A **tumour** results when one or more cells lose the ability to control the rate of mitosis.
- Benign tumours are not life-threatening.
- Malignant tumours are called cancers.

Cancer occurs when cells lose the ability to control the rate and the number of times mitosis takes place.

The **group of disorders called cancers** are dangerous because:
- The cells never stop dividing
- They invade other tissues
- They may spread from one body part to another.

Cancers are caused by agents called carcinogens.

Meiosis halves the number of chromosomes in each resulting nucleus.

Gametes are haploid cells that are able to fuse with another gamete of the opposite sex.

The **functions of meiosis** are:
- To halve the number of chromosomes so that the normal number may be restored at fertilisation (i.e. to allow for sexual reproduction)

- To produce chromosomes with genetic variations that will result in variations in the organisms produced by sexual reproduction.

The **stages of mitosis** are:
- Prophase
  - Chromatin contracts
  - Chromosomes are seen as two strands held together at the centromere
  - The nucleolus disappears
  - Spindle fibres appear
  - The nuclear membrane breaks down.
- Metaphase
  - The nuclear membrane is broken down
  - Two spindle fibres attach to each centromere
  - The chromosomes line up along the equator of the cell.
- Anaphase
  - The spindle fibres contract
  - An equal number of identical chromosomes is pulled to each pole.
- Telophase
  - The chromosomes elongate to form chromatin
  - The spindle fibres break down
  - Nucleoli re-form
  - Two nuclear membranes form.

Cell division follows both mitosis and meiosis.
- In animal cells, a cleavage furrow forms and deepens to produce two new cells.
- In plant cells, vesicles gather to form a cell plate, which forms new cell walls.

HIGHER ▼

THE CELL

Revision questions

1 Explain what is meant by:
   (a) Cell continuity
   (b) The continuity of life
   (c) The cell cycle.

2 With regard to chromosomes:
   (a) What substances are they made of?
   (b) Where in the cell are they located?
   (c) What is their function?
   (d) How many chromosomes are present in a normal human cell?

3 (a) What is a gene?
   (b) Name the substance of which genes are made.
   (c) Use a diagram to explain the relationship between genes and chromosomes.
   (d) State the function of genes.

4 Draw simple diagrams to show each of the following cells:
   (a) The chromosomes are single-stranded and the cell has a haploid number of four.

(b) The chromosomes are single-stranded and the cell has a diploid number of six.

(c) The chromosomes are double-stranded for a cell where n = 3.

(d) The chromosomes are double-stranded for a cell where 2n = 4.

5 (a) Name the main periods in the cell cycle.

(b) Explain why interphase is not a resting phase in the cell cycle.

6 Refer to diagram 14.31 and answer the following:

14.31

(a) How many centromeres are shown in the diagram?

(b) Is the cell shown haploid? Give a reason for your answer.

(c) Name two events that should occur immediately before the stage of mitosis shown.

(d) Draw a labelled diagram of the cell immediately after the stage of mitosis shown.

(e) When this cell has finished mitosis, how many chromosomes will be in each nucleus?

7 Distinguish between interphase and mitosis under the headings:

(a) Duration

(b) Chromosome appearance

(c) What happens to organelles and chromosomes.

8 With regard to mitosis, state:

(a) Why the nuclear membrane must break down

(b) Why fibres form

(c) How the chromosomes are pulled apart

(d) How many chromosomes will be in each resulting nucleus.

9 Explain why the cells in a person's body are all identical genetically.

10 A cell has a chromosome number of 4. Draw a labelled diagram to show this cell in the second stage of mitosis.

11 (a) What is a tumour?

(b) Distinguish between benign and malignant tumours.

(c) What is cancer?

(d) Give two reasons why cancer cells are said to be abnormal cells.

12 (a) What are carcinogens?

(b) Name two common carcinogens.

13 A cell has 46 chromosomes. How many chromosomes will be in the nuclei as a result of:

(a) Mitosis

(b) Cancer

(c) Meiosis?

14 If meiosis did not occur, why would sexual reproduction be a problem?

15 A chimpanzee has 48 chromosomes per cell. How many chromosomes are in each of the following:

(a) Chimpanzee eggs

(b) Chimpanzee sperm

(c) Chimpanzee zygote

(d) Chimpanzee mouth cell?

16 Name the stages in mitosis associated with the following events:

(a) The formation of spindle fibres

(b) Nuclear membrane formation

(c) Contraction of spindle fibres

(d) Lining up of chromosomes

(e) Movement of chromosomes to the poles

(f) The division of the nucleus.

17 Draw a labelled diagram of a plant cell at metaphase of mitosis. Show the chromosome number as 2n = 6.

18 State which of the following options, (i), (ii), (iii) or (iv), is the correct answer.

(a) In human liver cells, the correct chromosome number is: (i) 23 (ii) 24 (iii) 92 (iv) 46.

(b) Genes are made from: (i) Chromosomes (ii) DNA (iii) Chromatin (iv) Proteins.

(c) The cell cycle consists of: (i) Four stages (ii) Three states (iii) Two stages (iv) Thousands of stages.

(d) Chromatin consists of: (i) Cytoplasm (ii) Centromeres (iii) Chromosomes (iv) Spindle fibres.

(e) A cleavage furrow develops after: (i) Prophase (ii) Metaphase (iii) Anaphase (iv) Telophase.

(f) A cell plate develops in: (i) Metaphase (ii) Plant cells (iii) Cancer cells (iv) Animal cells.

HIGHER

HL

Exam questions

Section A

19 The diagram shows a stage of mitosis.

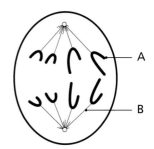

(a) Name A and B.

(b) What is happening during this stage of mitosis?

(c) How many cells are formed when a cell divides by mitosis?

(d) For what purpose do single-celled organisms use mitosis?

(2005 OL Q 4)

20 Study the diagram of a stage of mitosis in a diploid cell and then answer the questions below.

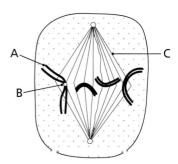

(a) Name A, B and C.

(b) What stage of mitosis is shown?

(c) What is the diploid number of this nucleus which is undergoing mitosis?

(e) Some cells in the human body undergo meiosis. Give one function of meiosis.

(2007 HL Q 3)

21 The diagram represents the cell cycle.

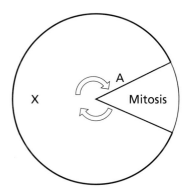

(a) What stage of the cycle is represented by X?

(b) Give the names of the two processes involving DNA which take place during stage X.

(c) For convenience of study, mitosis is divided into four stages. List these in order, starting at A.

(d) In which of the stages of mitosis that you have listed in (c) would you expect to see the spindle fibres contracting?

(e) Explain the term diploid number.

(f) What term is used to describe a group of disorders of the body in which cells lose the normal regulation of mitosis?

(2008 HL Q 2)

22 Indicate whether the following are true (**T**) or false (**F**) by drawing a circle around **T** or **F** in each case.

Example: The cells produced by meiosis are haploid.   ⓣ   F

The cells produced by mitosis are identical.	**T**	**F**
Meiosis gives rise to variation.	**T**	**F**
Mitosis always produces four new cells.	**T**	**F**
Meiosis is never involved in gamete formation.	**T**	**F**
Single-celled organisms use mitosis for reproduction.	**T**	**F**

(2009 OL Q 4)

23 The diagram shows a cell undergoing cell division.

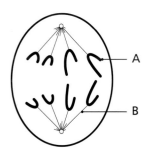

(a) Genes are found on structure A. Name structure A.

(b) What is the function of structure B?

(c) Tissues grow by cell division. Name the type of cell division by which tissues grow.

(d) Organs are found in both plants and animals. What is meant by the term *organ*?

(e) Name **one** organ found in plants.

(2011 OL Q 3)

24 Use your knowledge of mitosis to answer the following questions:

(a) What is the role of mitosis in single-celled organisms?

(b) What medical term is used for the group of disorders in which certain cells lose normal control of mitosis?

(c) Suggest a possible cause of one of the group of disorders referred to in (b).

(d) Name the stage of mitosis in which the chromosomes are located at the equator of the cell and before they begin to separate.

(e) To what are the chromosomes attached in the stage of mitosis referred to in (d)?

(f) Towards the end of mitosis, in what type of cell does a cell plate form?

(g) Give one way in which mitosis differs from meiosis.

(2011 HL Q 2)

Previous examination questions

Ordinary level	Higher level
2005 Q 4	2005 Q 5
2009 Q 4	2007 Q 3
2011 Q 3	2008 Q 2
2012 Q 14c	2009 Q 5
	2011 Q 2

Latest questions at www.edco.ie/lcbiologyplus/examhelp

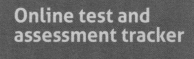

Online test and assessment tracker

Scan the QR code and test yourself on chapter 14
www.edco.ie/lcbiologyplus

Chapter 15 **DNA and RNA**

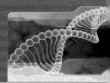

Learning objectives

- To define the terms 'heredity', 'gene' and 'gene expression' and give examples
- To explain the structure and function of chromosomes and the difference between coding and non-coding DNA
- To understand the structure of DNA, including complementary base pairing, and the genetic code
- To describe the process of DNA replication
- To define and describe DNA profiling and give examples of two applications
- To understand the meaning of 'genetic screening', giving examples
- To understand the structure of RNA and how it differs from DNA
- To describe protein synthesis, including the role of messenger RNA
- HIGHER ▶ To describe DNA structure and the process of protein synthesis in detail
- To describe how to isolate DNA from a plant tissue.

Heredity

Heredity is the passing on of features from parents to offspring by means of genes.

Heredity is also called **genetic inheritance**.

- Humans inherit features such as the number of fingers, the production of nails and the ability to form tears.
- Plants inherit features such as the number of petals, the colour of the petals and the shape of the leaves.

Genes

A **gene** is a section of DNA that causes the production of a protein.

Many of the proteins produced by genes are enzymes. Genes are said to control a cell because many of the enzymes they produce control cell activities. Genes are the units (or structures) of heredity.

Gene expression

Gene expression is the way in which the genetic information in a gene is decoded in the cell and used to make a protein.

In other words, gene expression refers to the way in which genes work. It describes the sequence of events that occur so that a gene on a chromosome in the nucleus can cause the production of, for example, an enzyme in the cytoplasm of the same cell.

Characteristics are traits or features that are inherited genetically.

Characteristics arise from the interaction of heredity and the environment.

It is the expression of genes that produces the characteristics or traits that are inherited. Characteristics such as those listed earlier arise from the interaction between the genes that are inherited (heredity) and the environment.

● A child may inherit genes for tallness, for instance, but if the child's diet lacks the correct nutrients, the genes may not be able to cause tallness, i.e. the genes may not be expressed.

● In the same way, leaf cells have genes to control the production of the green pigment, chlorophyll. However, if the plant grows in a dark place these genes do not work and chlorophyll is not made.

Chromosomes

Chromosomes are composed of about 60% protein and 40% DNA.

The protein is responsible for holding the DNA in a tightly packed configuration so that it can fit into the nucleus. For example, a typical human chromosome has a DNA strand that could extend to about 6 cm long. This is far too large to fit into a nucleus that is much smaller than the full stop at the end of this sentence.

To enable DNA to fit into a nucleus, it is heavily coiled and folded, very similar to an elastic band twisted repeatedly until it forms a solid ball. Proteins are responsible for holding the DNA in its folded state.

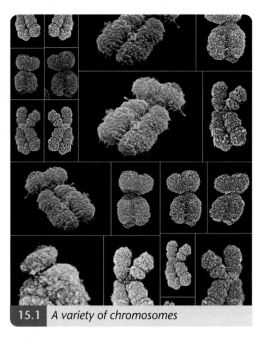

15.1 *A variety of chromosomes*

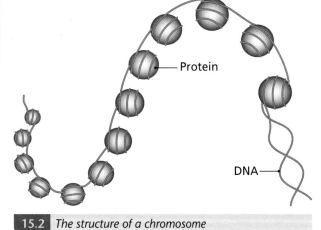

Protein

DNA

15.2 *The structure of a chromosome*

Non-coding DNA

Genes are arranged along the DNA of a chromosome in a line. Sometimes a number of genes are located close together on the chromosome. Other genes are widely separated along the chromosome.

This means that large sections of the chromosome are not made up of working genes. In fact it is known that about 97% of the DNA in a human cell does not consist of genes. This DNA is said to be non-coding (i.e. it does not carry the code for the formation of a protein).

The non-coding DNA was often called **junk DNA**. Recent research indicates that large amounts of this DNA may act as a genetic control panel switching genes on and off.

Non-coding DNA is of two types:
● Some of it occurs **between** genes
● Some of it is found **within** genes.

Non-coding DNA is DNA that does not cause the production of a protein.

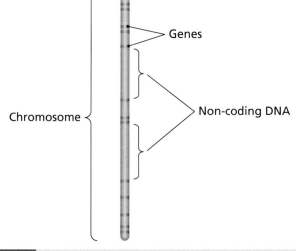

Genes

Chromosome

Non-coding DNA

15.3 *Genes on a chromosome*

The sequence of non-coding DNA varies greatly from one person to another. It is the DNA in these non-coding sections that is used to prepare DNA profiles.

Structure of DNA (deoxyribonucleic acid)

There are only four different chemicals, called 'bases', used in DNA. The four bases are known by the first letter of their names:

- Adenine (A)
- Thymine (T)
- Guanine (G)
- Cytosine (C).

Each of the four bases can only join or bond with one other base:

- A joins with T
- G joins with C.

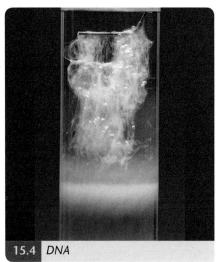

15.4 *DNA*

The pairs of bases, A/T and G/C, are said to be complementary base pairs.

The four bases, and the way they combine, can be recalled using the phrase:

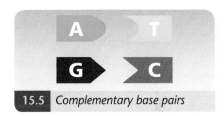

15.5 *Complementary base pairs*

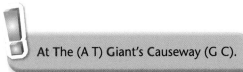

At The (A T) Giant's Causeway (G C).

The DNA molecule is made of two attached strands, similar to the two sides of a ladder (as shown in diagram 15.6). The strands are held together by the complementary bases.

The pattern of complementary base pairing means that if one strand of a DNA molecule has the sequence TAGCAT, then the sequence on the partner strand must be ATCGTA.

The double-stranded DNA is twisted to form a spiral structure, with each of the side strands forming a spiral or helix. DNA is arranged in this way to form a double helix shape.

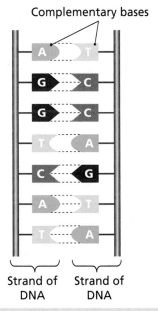

15.6 *Simplified structure of DNA*

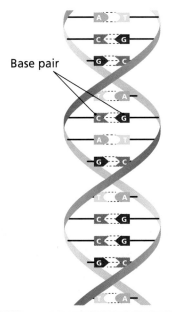

15.7 *DNA double helix*

THE CELL

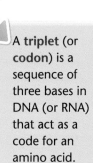

THE CELL

> The **genetic code** is the sequence of bases in DNA that provide the instruction for a cell (using RNA) to form a protein.

The genetic code

A chromosome consists of many base pairs arranged into a double helix. For example, the DNA in the longest human chromosome (number 1) contains about 300 million base pairs. A gene is a sequence of many bases. The precise sequence of bases is called the genetic code.

A gene works, or is expressed, when this code is sent into the cytoplasm (using another molecule called RNA; see page 177) to form a protein.

Genes are made of DNA. A gene is a section of DNA that instructs a cell to form a particular protein molecule.

Proteins are made up of combinations of hundreds or thousands of amino acids joined together in a specific sequence. Up to 20 different types of amino acids are used in proteins. This means that a gene must carry a different code to control the assembly of each of the 20 different amino acids.

DNA codes for each amino acid by using a sequence of three consecutive bases. Such a sequence of three bases is called a **triplet** (or **codon**).

For example, the DNA triplet CAA is the code for an amino acid called valine, and CGA is the triplet for an amino acid called alanine. If these triplets form part of a gene they will cause a protein to form with the relevant amino acids in sequence, as outlined in diagram 15.8.

Triplets are similar to the way in which Morse code uses a sequence of three dots or dashes to specify a letter.

A gene consists of a long stretch of triplets or codons that code for a specific sequence of amino acids, allowing for the production of a particular protein.

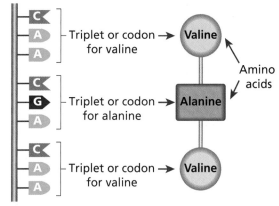

15.8 *DNA triplet code for particular amino acids*

> A **triplet** (or **codon**) is a sequence of three bases in DNA (or RNA) that act as a code for an amino acid.

Replication of DNA

At the end of mitosis each new cell has single-stranded chromosomes. Before these cells can divide again, the DNA in each chromosome must produce an exact copy of itself. This means that the single-stranded chromosomes must become double-stranded chromosomes. This process is called DNA replication and it takes place in the nucleus during interphase (see diagram 15.10).

15.9 *DNA replication*

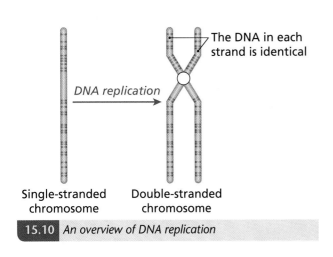

Single-stranded chromosome   Double-stranded chromosome

15.10 *An overview of DNA replication*

Mechanism of DNA replication (see diagram 15.11)

1. The double helix unwinds (or uncoils).
2. An enzyme breaks the bonds between the base pairs. The two strands of the original double helix separate.
3. DNA bases that are normally present in the cytoplasm enter the nucleus. The incoming bases attach to the exposed complementary bases (i.e. base pairing occurs).
4. In this way, each side of the DNA molecule acts as a mould or template for the new DNA that is formed.
5. Each new double strand rewinds to form a double helix. Note that each new DNA double helix is:
    ▸ Half new DNA and half original DNA
    ▸ Identical to the original DNA double helix and to the other new double helix formed.

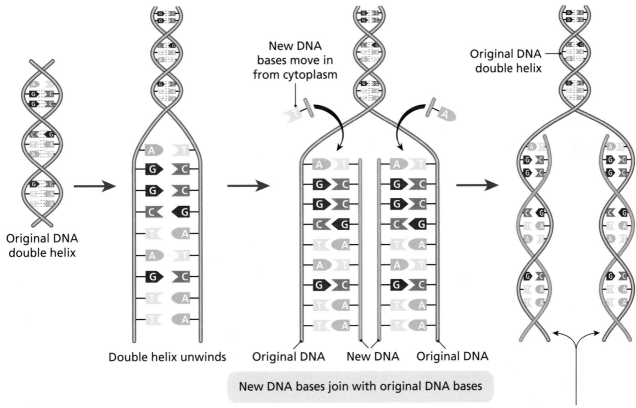

New DNA bases move in from cytoplasm

Original DNA double helix

Original DNA double helix

Double helix unwinds   Original DNA   New DNA   Original DNA

New DNA bases join with original DNA bases

Each new double helix is identical to the original

The original DNA double helix forms two identical copies

15.11 *DNA replication*

Significance of DNA replication

Each new DNA double helix (chromosome) will have exactly the same sequence of bases as the original (as shown in diagram 15.11).

DNA is able to produce **exact** copies of itself (hence the term 'replication' is used to describe its manner of reproducing). This allows the same DNA to be passed on to each new generation of cells, as outlined in diagram 15.12.

For example, a human zygote is a single cell with 46 chromosomes. These chromosomes contain a certain sequence of bases. The same sequence of bases is passed on, in the form of new chromosomes, to each body cell in a person due to DNA replication (and mitosis).

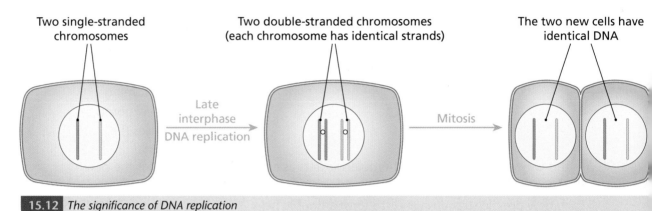

Two single-stranded chromosomes

Two double-stranded chromosomes (each chromosome has identical strands)

The two new cells have identical DNA

Late interphase DNA replication

Mitosis

15.12 *The significance of DNA replication*

DNA profiling

Method of preparing a DNA profile

Preparing a DNA profile involves four steps:

1. The DNA is released from cells
2. The DNA is cut into fragments of different lengths
3. The DNA fragments are separated according to their sizes
4. The patterns produced by the fragments are compared or analysed.

15.13 *A DNA profile*

The following describes these four procedures in more detail.

1. DNA is released

In order to produce a DNA profile, cells are broken down to release their DNA (as in Activity 15).

If the amount of DNA available is too small to work with, it can be increased or amplified. A common technique used to amplify small quantities of DNA is a process called the polymerase chain reaction (PCR).

2. DNA is cut into fragments

The isolated DNA is cut into fragments using special enzymes. These enzymes are called **restriction enzymes.** They were first isolated from bacteria, where they are used to destroy the DNA of invading viruses.

Different restriction enzymes cut DNA at specific base sequences. For example, one restriction enzyme will always cut DNA at the base sequence GAATTC, whereas another only cuts at the sequence GATC.

The sections of DNA that are cut will be of different lengths because the base sequences being cut may be close together or far apart on the DNA strands.

> **A DNA profile** (also called a DNA or genetic fingerprint) is a method of making a unique pattern of bands from the DNA of a person, which can then be used to compare with the DNA profile of another person.

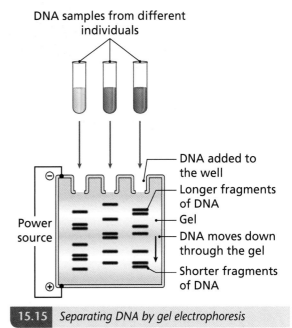

DNA samples from different individuals

DNA added to the well

Longer fragments of DNA

Gel

DNA moves down through the gel

Shorter fragments of DNA

Power source

15.14 *Adding DNA to a gel for electrophoresis*

15.15 *Separating DNA by gel electrophoresis*

3. The fragments are separated

The sections of DNA that have been cut are separated on the basis of their size. They are separated by a process called gel electrophoresis. This involves placing the invisible DNA fragments in a small glass tank containing a sugar-based gel. An electric current is applied along the gel. The current draws the negatively charged DNA to one end of the gel.

Small DNA fragments move faster through the porous gel than do the larger fragments. In this way bands of small fragments are separated from bands of larger fragments.

When the electrophoresis is finished a permanent record of the results is obtained. This may involve adding radioactive material, which combines with DNA fragments to produce a fluorescent image. A photographic copy of the final pattern of DNA bands is then obtained.

4. Patterns are compared

In the same way that no two people have the same fingerprints, it is highly unlikely that any two people will have the same DNA profile (unless they are identical twins).

If the pattern of bands from two different DNA samples is the same, then the two samples must have come from the same person.

Profile taken at crime scene	Victim's profile	Suspect's profile

These profiles match, indicating the suspect was at the crime scene

15.16 *Forensic use of DNA profiles*

Applications of DNA profiles (DNA fingerprints)

Crime

DNA profiles are often used in forensic (legal) cases. If biological material such as blood, hair, saliva or semen is left at the scene of a crime it can be collected and a DNA profile prepared.

- If the pattern of the DNA profile from the crime scene is compared with those of the victim and a suspect, it may be seen that it matches that of the suspect but not that of the victim. This would be strong evidence to associate the suspect with the crime scene.
- Of course the profile may not match that of the suspect, which might eliminate the suspect from the inquiry.

Forensic medicine is the way in which medical knowledge is used in legal situations.

THE CELL

175

The bands differ in thickness due to there being more or less bands of this length present, e.g. a thick band represents many DNA fragments of a particular length. This is visible in diagram 15.17.

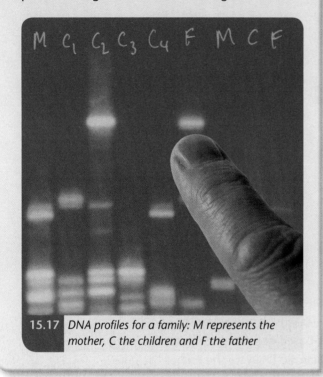

15.17 *DNA profiles for a family: M represents the mother, C the children and F the father*

Mother	Child	Man

All the child's bands match with the mother's or the man's.
The man is the father of the child.

15.18 *Using DNA profiles to determine the father of a child: a match*

Mother	Child	Man

Some of the child's bands match with the mother's.
The rest of the child's bands do not match with the man's.
The man is not the father of the child.

15.19 *Using DNA profiles to determine the father of a child: no match*

Medical

DNA profiles can be used to determine whether a particular person is, or is not, the parent of a child. In this way the paternity (father) or maternity (mother) can be established.

This information can apply in property or financial inheritance cases, or in immigration cases where a person can enter a country if his/her parent or child is already in that country.

To decide if a man is the father of a child, blood samples are taken from the child, the mother and the man. DNA profiles are prepared and examined.

- If all the bands in the child's profile match with bands in either the mother's or the man's profile, then the man is shown to be the natural father of the child (see diagram 15.18).

- If some of the child's bands match those of the mother, but the rest do not match with the man's bands, then the man is not the father of the child (see diagram 15.19).

Genetic screening

Sometimes the process of DNA replication does not work exactly as it should. In these cases, a gene (or a number of genes) may be incorrectly copied. In addition, DNA can be altered by mutations (see Chapter 17).

If genes are altered in any way they will not carry the correct code for the protein that they were intended to produce. This may have severe effects on a person who inherits such genes.

Genetic screening often involves adding a radioactive section of DNA (called a DNA, or genetic, probe) to a sample of DNA from the person being tested. The DNA probe will only attach to a normal gene. If the probe does not attach then the gene is altered.

Genetic screening can be carried out in two main ways: adult screening and foetal screening.

THE CELL

Genetic disorders caused by defective genes include:
- Albinism (in which the pigment melanin cannot be made)
- Cystic fibrosis (in which there is a build-up of mucus in the lungs and intestines)
- Haemochromatosis (in which too much iron accumulates in the body and has to be removed by regular bleeding)
- Cancer.

Adult screening

Screening is sometimes carried out on adults who, although they do not suffer from a genetic disorder, may carry a defective gene in each of their cells. People who carry defective genes, without having the disorder themselves, are said to be carriers for the condition.

It is now possible to identify (or genetically screen) individuals who are carriers for many disorders such as sickle cell anaemia, the most common form of cystic fibrosis, and the likelihood of getting heart disease or some forms of cancer.

The benefits of these tests is that it gives people information regarding the chances of them having a child with the disorder or it allows them to prepare for a disease that might affect them.

> **Genetic screening** means testing DNA for the presence or absence of a particular gene or an altered gene.

Embryonic or foetal screening

In this type of screening, cells can be removed from the embryo, placenta or the fluid around the foetus. These cells can be tested to detect if the embryo or foetus has any one of a number of genetic disorders.

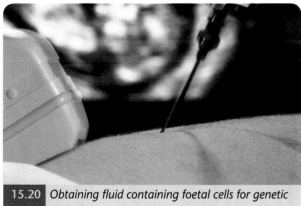

15.20 *Obtaining fluid containing foetal cells for genetic screening*

Ethics of genetic screening

Ethics relates to whether behaviour is proper or improper. Genetic screening may cause ethical problems.

If the results of genetic tests become public, the people concerned may suffer embarrassment or be treated unfairly. For example, they may be isolated and treated as if they had a disease even if they do not. Employers and insurance companies may be reluctant to get involved with them.

Another issue is whether a person would wish to know that they have a genetic disorder that will develop in later years. This is especially problematic if the disorder is untreatable.

In relation to genetic screening in the embryo or foetus, would knowledge of a genetic disorder help to prepare the family for the future, or encourage a termination of the pregnancy?

THE CELL

RNA (ribonucleic acid)

DNA and RNA are both nucleic acids. However, RNA differs from DNA in the following ways:
- RNA is based on the sugar ribose (whereas DNA is based on the sugar deoxyribose)
- RNA (ribonucleic acid) consists of four bases, like DNA. However, RNA contains the base uracil instead of thymine. This means that the bases in RNA are A, U, G and C. The bases A and U are complementary, as are the bases G and C.

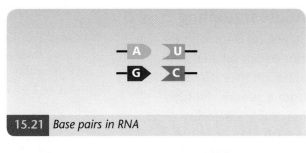

15.21 *Base pairs in RNA*

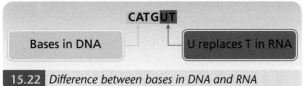

15.22 *Difference between bases in DNA and RNA*

The difference between the bases in DNA and RNA are simplified in diagram 15.22.

- The sequence of bases in RNA is determined by the sequence of bases in DNA. The bases in RNA are complementary to those in a section of DNA. For example, if a strand of DNA has the sequence GGAATC, then the RNA produced will have the sequence CCUUAG.
- RNA is a single-stranded molecule, unlike DNA, which is a double strand (helix).
- RNA can move out of the nucleus into the cytoplasm. DNA is always in the nucleus.

Structural differences between DNA and RNA	
DNA	**RNA**
1 Contains the sugar deoxyribose	Contains ribose
2 The bases are AT GC (thymine)	The bases are AU GC (uracil)
3 Double-stranded (i.e. double helix)	Single-stranded

Protein synthesis

Genes control cell activities by producing proteins, many of which are enzymes. Proteins are composed of amino acids. It is important that the amino acids are assembled in the correct sequence, in order to produce the correct protein.

To understand the vital role carried out by genes (or DNA), it is essential to understand how genes work (i.e. how genes are expressed). This means it is necessary to know how DNA makes proteins.

The main steps in this process are as follows:

1. The sequence of bases on a DNA strand carries instructions in the form of a code to make a particular protein.
2. The bases in DNA and RNA work in groups of three. Each group of three bases causes one particular amino acid to become part of the protein being made.
3. The DNA strands separate (see diagram 15.23). This step takes place in the nucleus.
4. RNA bases attach to the exposed bases on one side of the DNA. This means that the code has been **transcribed** from DNA to a complementary strand of RNA. The RNA strand formed in this way is called messenger RNA (mRNA).
5. The mRNA strand detaches from the DNA and moves out of the nucleus into the cytoplasm.

> **Transcription** is the copying of a sequence of genetic bases from DNA onto messenger RNA (mRNA).

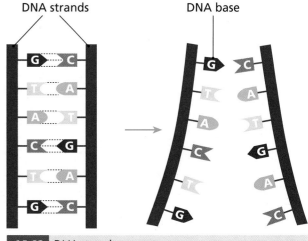

15.23 *DNA strands separate*

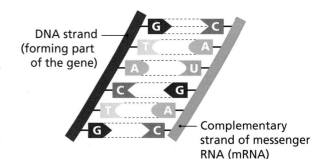

15.24 *Transcription*

THE CELL

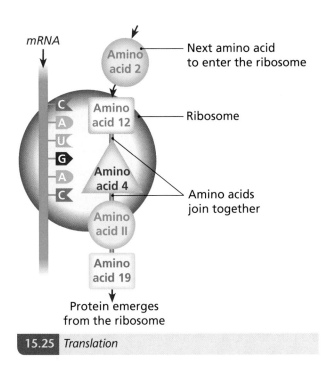

mRNA

Amino acid 2 — Next amino acid to enter the ribosome

Amino acid 12 — Ribosome

Amino acid 4 — Amino acids join together

Amino acid II

Amino acid 19

Protein emerges from the ribosome

15.25 *Translation*

6. The mRNA passes through a ribosome. As it passes through, each group of three bases causes a particular amino acid to be attached to the protein that is made in the ribosome.

7. In this way, the code on the mRNA is **translated** into the correct sequence of amino acids in a ribosome.

8. The protein becomes folded as it emerges from the ribosome. This allows the protein to carry out its particular function.

Translation is the conversion of a sequence of genetic bases on messenger RNA into a sequence of amino acids.

HIGHER ▼

Detailed structure of DNA

The structure of DNA was worked out by **James Watson** and **Francis Crick** in 1953. They shared the Nobel prize in 1962 with Maurice Watkins for their discovery. Their findings were based on the earlier research of Rosalind Franklin, who unfortunately died in 1958.

The discovery of the structure of DNA is considered to be one of the outstanding advances in biology in the 20th century. DNA is made up of units called nucleotides. These are arranged into very long chains called polynucleotides.

The detailed structure of DNA can be considered under three headings: nucleotides, base pairs and double helix.

Nucleotides

A nucleotide consists of three parts: a phosphate group, a sugar and a nitrogen-containing base. These are linked together as shown in diagram 15.26.

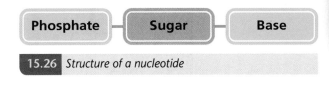

| Phosphate | Sugar | Base |

15.26 *Structure of a nucleotide*

The sugar in DNA is deoxyribose (i.e. a five-carbon sugar, similar to ribose but lacking an oxygen atom). RNA contains the sugar ribose.

The phosphate group is PO_4, but this is normally represented as P. The phosphate and deoxyribose groups form the sides of the DNA strand.

As there are four bases this means that there are four distinct nucleotides. The nucleotides join together, with a bond between the phosphate group of one and the sugar of the next, forming a polynucleotide.

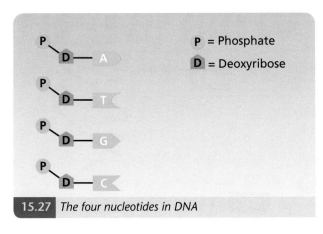

P = Phosphate
D = Deoxyribose

15.27 *The four nucleotides in DNA*

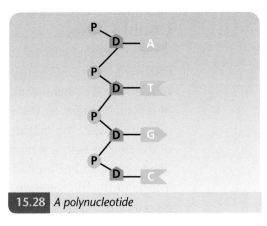

15.28 *A polynucleotide*

THE CELL

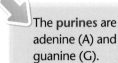

The **purines** are adenine (A) and guanine (G).

The **pyrimidines** are thymine (T) and cytosine (C).

Purines and pyrimidines

Of the four nitrogenous bases in DNA, two are classified as purines (double-ring molecules) and two as pyrimidines (single-ring molecules).

Base pairs

The bases join together in a very specific manner. Adenine and thymine each form two weak hydrogen bonds. This allows them to bond together. In a similar way, guanine and cytosine each form three hydrogen bonds, so they can pair together.

The purine bases can be remembered by the phrase: The Attorney General is **Pure**

The pyramidines can be remembered because: The pyrimidines contain the letter 'y' i.e. thymine and cytosine.

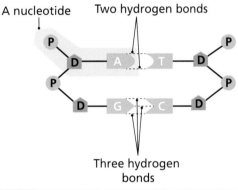

15.29 *Base pairs in DNA*

The bases can be thought of as having opposite or complementary shapes, just like adjoining pieces of a jigsaw. Note that each base pair has a purine and a pyrimidine.

The forces holding the bases together are **hydrogen bonds**. These are weak bonds formed when a slightly positive hydrogen is attracted by another slightly negative atom (e.g. nitrogen or oxygen).

Very often the phosphates and sugars are left out when drawing a simplified version of DNA. In this case, only the base pairs are shown, as seen in diagram 15.30.

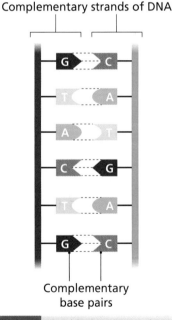

15.30 *Simplified structure of DNA*

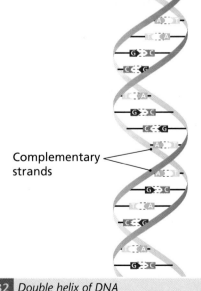

15.31 *Watson and Crick with their model of DNA in 1953*

Double helix

Francis Crick and James Watson discovered that DNA consisted of two helical or spiral chains of polynucleotides, as shown in diagram 15.32. The outside strands of the double helix are made of deoxyribose and phosphate. The 'rungs' of the molecule are the base pairs on the inside.

Complementary strands

15.32 *Double helix of DNA*

THE CELL

HIGHER ▼

Protein synthesis (extended study)

The process of protein formation proceeds as follows.

Initiation: starting the process

1. The DNA double helix unwinds at the site of the gene that is going to produce a protein.

Transcription: rewriting the code from DNA to RNA

2. RNA bases, which are present in the cytoplasm, move across the nuclear membrane. The RNA bases will match up with the complementary bases on the DNA strand.

3. The enzyme RNA polymerase causes the sequence of RNA bases to join together to form messenger RNA (mRNA). Each mRNA molecule has complementary bases to those on the DNA strand from which it was transcribed. A sequence of three bases of DNA or RNA is called a triplet or codon. Codons may cause three possible outcomes.

   ▶ A start codon indicates the beginning of a gene (but is not involved in the production of the protein)

   ▶ Most codons in a gene specify particular amino acids

   ▶ A stop codon indicates the end of a gene (but is not involved in the production of the protein).

4. Every gene has **one** start codon, **many** codons specifying amino acids and **one** stop codon.

Translation: the production of a protein according to the RNA code

5. mRNA moves from the nucleus to the cytoplasm.

Gene (in reality a gene has many more bases than are shown here)

15.33 *The double helix unwinds at the site of the gene*

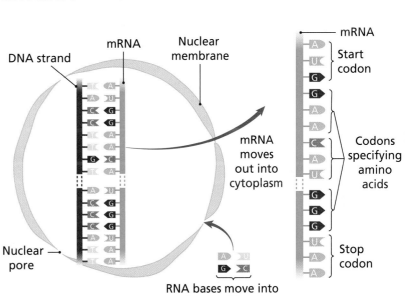

15.34 *Transcription*

DNA strand · mRNA · Nuclear membrane · Nuclear pore · mRNA moves out into cytoplasm · RNA bases move into nucleus and bond to complementary DNA bases · mRNA · Start codon · Codons specifying amino acids · Stop codon

THE CELL

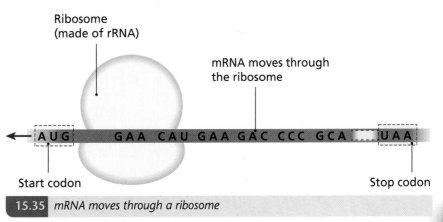

Ribosome (made of rRNA)

mRNA moves through the ribosome

AUG   GAA CAU GAA GAC CCC GCA   UAA

Start codon

Stop codon

15.35 *mRNA moves through a ribosome*

> An **anticodon** is a sequence of three bases (a triplet) on tRNA that are complementary to a sequence of three bases on mRNA.

THE CELL

6. Ribosomes are made up of ribosomal RNA (rRNA) and protein.
7. The mRNA strand forms weak bonds with the rRNA in a ribosome. This will be the site of protein synthesis.

AA 6 —— Amino acid
—— tRNA
CUU —— Anti-codon

AA 12 —— Amino acid
—— tRNA
GUA —— Anti-codon

15.36 *Each tRNA molecule has a specific amino acid*

8. The cytoplasm contains a supply of transfer RNA (tRNA) molecules. Each tRNA carries:
   ▶ A special triplet or anticodon
   ▶ A particular amino acid, which is specific to the anticodon.
9. tRNA molecules are attracted to the mRNA that is in the ribosome. Each anticodon on a tRNA is complementary to a codon on the mRNA. The tRNA molecules enter the ribosome.
10. The first tRNA molecule will be attracted to the mRNA just after the start codon (see left-hand side of diagram 15.37). In doing this it brings a particular amino acid to the ribosome.

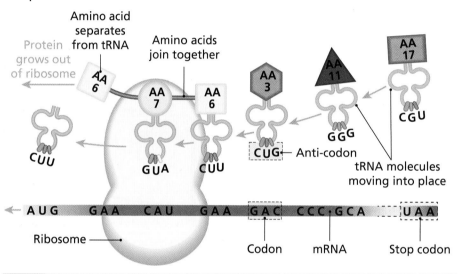

Protein grows out of ribosome

Amino acid separates from tRNA

Amino acids join together

AA 6 — CUU
AA 7 — GUA
AA 6 — CUU
AA 3 — CUG — Anti-codon
AA 11 — GGG
AA 17 — CGU
tRNA molecules moving into place

Ribosome

← AUG GAA CAU GAA GAC CCC•GCA UAA

Codon mRNA Stop codon

15.37 *Translation – forming a protein*

11. In the ribosome, amino acids are detached from the tRNA molecule and are bonded together to form part of the new protein.
12. tRNA molecules leave the ribosome without any attached amino acids. As they leave they pull the mRNA strand through the ribosome.
13. tRNA molecules continue to bind with mRNA until a stop codon is reached. At this point:
    ▶ The mRNA code sequence is complete
    ▶ The new protein is produced.
14. Once the protein is formed it folds to allow it to have the correct shape.

Functions of the three types of RNA	
Type of RNA	**Function**
mRNA (m = messenger)	● Complementary strand to DNA ● Carries instruction for the production of a protein from DNA to a ribosome
tRNA (t = transfer)	● Has a complementary anticodon to mRNA codon ● Carries an amino acid to the ribosome
rRNA (r = ribosomal)	● Forms part of the structure of a ribosome ● Forms a weak bond with mRNA in the ribosome.

Activity 15 To isolate DNA from a plant tissue

1. Add some sodium chloride (salt) to a small volume of washing-up liquid dissolved in water (the salt will cause the DNA molecules to clump together, and the washing-up liquid will dissolve the cell and nuclear membranes and release DNA from the cells).
2. Cut an onion (or kiwi fruit) into small cubes (this allows the washing-up liquid to reach more cells).
3. Add the chopped onion to a beaker containing the salt/detergent solution and stir the mixture.

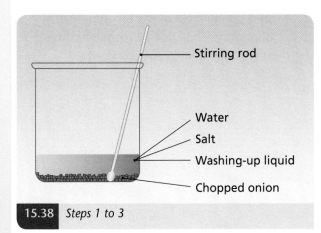

Stirring rod

Water
Salt
Washing-up liquid
Chopped onion

15.38 *Steps 1 to 3*

5. Cool the mixture by placing the beaker in an ice water bath for 5 minutes, stirring frequently (this slows down the breakdown of the DNA).

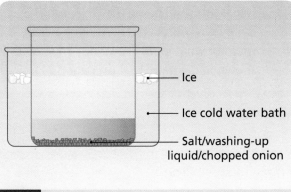

Ice

Ice cold water bath

Salt/washing-up liquid/chopped onion

15.40 *Step 5*

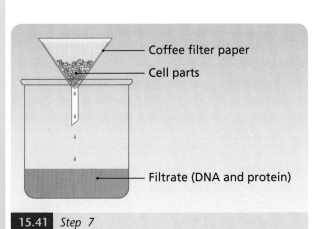

Coffee filter paper
Cell parts

Filtrate (DNA and protein)

15.41 *Step 7*

4. Put the beaker in a water bath at 60°C for 15 minutes. (This temperature inactivates (denatures) enzymes that would normally digest DNA. If left any longer than 15 minutes DNA itself would break down.)

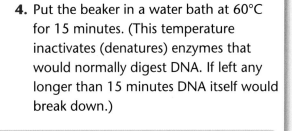
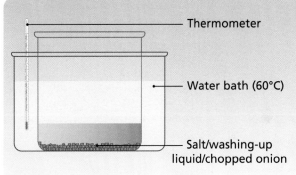

Thermometer

Water bath (60°C)

Salt/washing-up liquid/chopped onion

15.39 *Step 4*

6. Pour the mixture into a domestic food blender and blend it for only 3 seconds on high speed. (This breaks down the cell walls and releases DNA. Blending it for too long would break down the DNA strands.)
7. Filter the mixture through coffee filter paper into a second beaker. Do not add the foam from the top of the mixture to the filter paper. (Cell parts are retained in the filter paper. The filtered material, called filtrate, contains DNA and proteins. Normal laboratory filter paper is not used as its pores are too small and the process would be very slow.)
8. Use a syringe, without a needle, to place some of the onion filtrate into a boiling tube.
9. Add a few drops of protease enzyme (such as pepsin) to the contents of the boiling tube and mix well (the protease breaks down the proteins around the DNA).

THE CELL

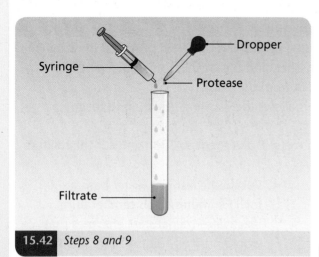

15.42 *Steps 8 and 9*

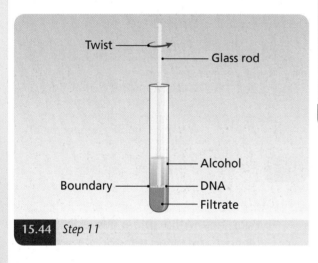

15.44 *Step 11*

10. Pour some ice-cold ethanol or methylated spirits (stored in a freezer overnight) carefully down the side of the boiling tube. The ethanol should form a layer on top of the onion filtrate. (Alcohol removes water from DNA, which causes DNA to float to the top of the water. DNA is insoluble in ice-cold alcohol and so it precipitates at the alcohol–filtrate boundary. The DNA forms white threads at the alcohol–filtrate junction).

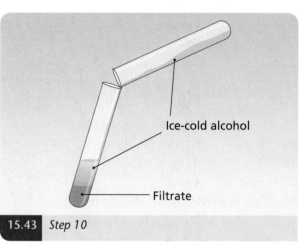

15.43 *Step 10*

11. Gently twist a small glass rod or a wire loop in the alcohol. Strands of DNA should attach to the rod or wire. Do not mix the two layers or damage the DNA, which is very easily broken (DNA forms a clear mesh of what looks like stringy mucus, as shown in diagram 15.4 on page 171).

Summary

Heredity (or genetic inheritance) is the passing on of features from parents to offspring by means of genes.

Characteristics arise from the interaction of genes and their environment.

Chromosomes are made of DNA and protein.

A **gene** is a section of DNA that controls the production of a protein.
- Genes comprise only about 3% of the DNA in human cells. The rest of the DNA is said to be non-coding DNA.

Gene expression is the way in which a gene works to produce a protein.

DNA is a long, double-stranded molecule.
- The bases in DNA are adenine (**A**) and thymine (**T**), guanine (**G**) and cytosine (**C**).
- The genetic code consists of a sequence of bases in DNA (or RNA) that cause the production of a protein.
- Each group of three bases is the code for an amino acid.
- A sequence of bases that produces a protein is called a gene.

DNA makes exact copies of itself. This process is called DNA replication and it involves:
- Each new strand being half new DNA and half original DNA
- Each new strand being identical to its partner and to the original DNA strand.

A **DNA profile** (or DNA or genetic fingerprint) is a unique pattern of bands of DNA from a person's cell(s).

- These bands can distinguish one person's DNA from another person's.

DNA profiles are obtained by:

- Releasing DNA from cells
- Cutting the DNA into fragments using restriction enzymes
- Separating the fragments according to their size.

DNA profiles can be used to:

- Establish whether biological tissue at a crime scene matches or does not match a suspect
- Determine whether a person is or is not the parent of a child.

Genetic or DNA screening means that a person's DNA can be tested to show the presence of abnormal or altered genes (which may cause disease).

| Differences between DNA and RNA ||
DNA	RNA
Has the sugar deoxyribose	Has the sugar ribose
Contains the base thymine (T)	Contains the base uracil (U)
Double-stranded (double helix)	Single-stranded
Found in the nucleus	Found in the nucleus and cytoplasm

DNA (or a gene) makes protein as follows:

- The DNA strands separate
- The bases on DNA link up with complementary bases to form mRNA (the code is **transcribed**)
- mRNA enters a ribosome
- The correct sequence of amino acids is linked together in the ribosome to form a protein (the code is **translated**)
- The protein folds into the correct shape.

HIGHER ▼

The detailed structure of DNA consists of:

- Nucleotides, which contain phosphate, deoxyribose sugar and a base. The four bases are:
  - The purines adenine (**A**) and guanine (**G**)
  - The pyridimines thymine (**T**) and cytosine (**C**).
- Nucleotide pairs (also called base pairs), i.e. A=T or G≡C, join together due to hydrogen bonding
- A double helix, in which the phosphates and sugars form the sides of the molecule and the base pairs are like rungs inside the double helix.

The details of protein synthesis are as follows:

- Enzymes open up the DNA at the site of a gene
- The DNA code is transcribed onto a complementary mRNA strand
- mRNA enters a ribosome in the cytoplasm
- Every tRNA has a complementary triplet to the triplets on the mRNA
- tRNA molecules enter the ribosome
- Each tRNA has a specific amino acid
- The amino acids are attached to each other at the ribosome to form a protein
- The protein folds into shape.

To **isolate DNA** from onion cells:

- Chop up onion tissue in a salt/detergent mixture (to clump DNA and break down cell membranes)
- Heat in a water bath (to stop enzymes damaging DNA)
- Place in an ice-cold water bath (to prevent damage to DNA)
- Filter the mixture (to remove cell parts); proteins and DNA form the filtrate
- Add protease enzyme to the filtrate (to break down the protein)
- Add ice-cold ethanol (to precipitate the insoluble DNA).

THE CELL

THE CELL

Revision questions

1 (a) What is heredity?
   (b) Name the key chemical that is inherited by organisms.
   (c) Name three inherited characteristics in (i) Humans (ii) Plants.

2 (a) Distinguish between a gene and gene expression.
   (b) What do you understand by 'characteristics'?
   (c) Characteristics are formed by the interaction of two factors. Name these factors.

3 (a) Name the materials of which chromosomes are made.
   (b) Give a function for each of these materials.
   (c) Show, by means of a diagram, the relationship between genes and chromosomes.
   (d) Explain what is meant by (i) coding, and (ii) non-coding, DNA.

4 (a) What do the letters 'DNA' stand for?
   (b) What name is given to the overall shape of DNA?
   (c) Explain how a very long DNA molecule can fit into a tiny nucleus.

5 One strand of a DNA molecule has the base sequence GATTCGTAA.
   (a) What is the sequence of bases on the complementary DNA strand?
   (b) How many triplets are in this sequence of DNA?

6 (a) Name the bases in DNA.
   (b) What is a DNA triplet?
   (c) How do DNA triplets relate to a gene?

7 (a) What is meant by non-coding DNA?
   (b) State two places in a chromosome where non-coding DNA may occur.

8 (a) What is meant by DNA replication?
   (b) What is the importance of DNA replication?
   (c) At what stage of the cell cycle does DNA replication occur?
   (d) Where in a cell does DNA replication occur?

9 (a) What is genetic profiling?
   (b) Give an outline account of how a genetic profile (or 'fingerprint') is obtained.
   (c) On a genetic profile, what does each band represent?
   (d) Explain why some of the bands are thicker than others.

10 (a) Give two applications for genetic profiling.
   (b) After a violent crime, genetic profiles were carried out on the victim's blood, the defendant's blood and some blood stains obtained from the clothing of the defendant. The results are given in diagram 15.45.

Victim's blood	Blood from clothing	Defendant's blood

15.45

   (i) What conclusions can be drawn from these results?
   (ii) Do these results prove the innocence or guilt of the defendant? Explain your answer.

11 (a) What is genetic screening?
   (b) Name one human condition that may be identified in this way.
   (c) State one possible benefit and one problem associated with genetic screening.

12 (a) Outline two structural differences between DNA and RNA.
   (b) If a stretch of DNA has the base sequence ATTGGCATT, what will the base sequence be on the complementary RNA strand?
   (c) Distinguish between transcription and translation in protein formation.

13 (a) What is a gene?
   (b) In what part of the cell are genes located?
   (c) What material do genes produce in order to control the activities of a cell?

14 (a) What is meant by base pairing in DNA?
   (b) Draw a diagram of a stretch of DNA comprising eight nucleotides to indicate base pairing involving all the possible base pairs (there is no need to draw a double helix).
   (c) Who discovered the double helix structure of DNA?

HIGHER ▼

HIGHER ▼

15 Outline the functions of each of the following in protein synthesis:
  (a) Start codon   (d) tRNA
  (b) Stop codon   (e) Protein folds
  (c) Ribosome   into shape.

16 (a) What is the full name for RNA?
   (b) Name three types of RNA.
   (c) State two places in a cell where RNA might be found.
   (d) What is meant by the phrase 'DNA codes for messenger RNA'?

17 (a) Name the bases present in DNA.
   (b) What is a triplet?
   (c) How do triplets relate to genes?
   (d) Draw a labelled diagram of a section of DNA to show the six bases ATTGCA (there is no need to show deoxyribose, phosphates or a double helix). On the same diagram show:
     (i) The complementary strand of mRNA
     (ii) The two tRNA molecules that attach to the mRNA strand.

18 In isolating DNA from plant tissue, give a reason for each of the following:
  (a) Using washing-up liquid
  (b) Using salt
  (c) Heating the salt, detergent and chopped tissue to 60°C
  (d) Using ice-cold water
  (e) Not blending the tissues for too long
  (f) Using protease enzyme
  (g) Adding ice-cold alcohol.

19 Choose which of the options (i), (ii), (iii) or (iv) represents the correct answer in each case below.
  (a) A codon contains:
     (i) Three base pairs
     (ii) Three bases
     (iii) Three triplets
     (iv) Three genes.
  (b) DNA is insoluble in:
     (i) Washing-up liquid
     (ii) Boiling water
     (iii) Salt water
     (iv) Ice-cold ethanol.
  (c) When the sequence of bases on DNA is coded onto an mRNA molecule, this is called:
     (i) Translation
     (ii) Replication
     (iii) Transcription
     (iv) Genetic fingerprinting.
  (d) DNA fragments can be obtained using:
     (i) Bacteria
     (ii) Protein synthesis
     (iii) Restriction enzymes
     (iv) Ribosomes.
  (e) DNA fingerprinting can be used to determine if a person:
     (i) Has a disease
     (ii) Is or is not the parent of a child
     (iii) Has faulty RNA
     (iv) Is a carrier for a disease.
  (f) During protein synthesis, the ribosome translates the code on mRNA, with the help of:
     (i) Restriction enzymes
     (ii) tRNA
     (iii) DNA
     (iv) A double helix.

HL ▼

THE CELL

Exam questions

Section A

20 The diagram represents a part of a DNA molecule. A and C represent nitrogenous bases.

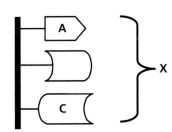

Complete the following in relation to DNA.
  (a) Name the nitrogenous bases whose first letters are A and C.
  (b) The structure labelled X is called a
     _____.
  (c) Where in the cell would you expect to find most DNA?
  (d) DNA contains the instructions needed to make protein. These instructions are called the _____ code.

(2008 OL Q 5)

THE CELL

Section B

21 **(a)** Explain each of the following terms in relation to DNA.
  (i) Replication
  (ii) Transcription

  (b) As part of your practical activities you extracted DNA from a plant tissue. Answer the following questions in relation to this experiment.
  (i) What plant did you use?
  (ii) It is usual to chop the tissue and place it in a blender. Suggest a reason for this.
  (iii) For how long should the blender be allowed to run?
  (iv) Washing-up liquid is normally used in this experiment. What is its function?
  (v) Sodium chloride (salt) is also used. Explain why.
  (vi) What is a protease enzyme?
  (vii) Why is a protease enzyme used in this experiment?
  (viii) The final separation of the DNA involves the use of alcohol (ethanol). Under what condition is the alcohol used?

(2005 HL Q 8)

22 **(a)** **(i)** How are the two strands of a DNA molecule joined together?
  (ii) What is 'junk' DNA?

  (b) Answer the following questions by referring to the procedures that you used to isolate DNA from a plant tissue.
  (i) Having obtained a plant tissue e.g. onion
    1. What was the first procedure that you followed?
    2. What was the reason for that procedure?
  (ii) Washing-up liquid is then used in the isolation. Give a reason for its use.
  (iii) Salt (sodium chloride) is also used in the isolation. Give a reason for its use.
  (iv) **1.** What is a protease?
    2. Why is a protease necessary when isolating DNA?
  (v) The final stage of the isolation involves the use of freezer-cold ethanol.
    1. Describe how it is used.
    2. For what purpose is it used?

(2011 HL Q 9)

Section C

23 **(a)** Copy the diagram into your answer book and then complete it to show the complementary base pairs of the DNA molecule. Label all parts not already labelled.

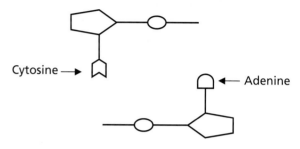

Cytosine →

Adenine ←

  (b) The genetic code incorporated into the DNA molecule finds its expression in part in the formation of protein. This formation requires the involvement of a number of RNA molecules. List these RNA molecules and briefly describe the role of each of them.

(2004 HL Q 13)

24 **(b)** **(i)** Name the four bases that are found in DNA.
  (ii) These bases form a triplet code. What is meant by a triplet code?
  (iii) The triplet code is transcribed into mRNA. What does this statement mean?
  (iv) To which structures in the cell does mRNA carry the code?

(2005 OL Q 13)

25 **(c)** **(i)** Explain briefly what is meant by a gene.
  (ii) Where in the nucleus would you find genes?

(2007 OL Q 11)

26 **(a)** **(i)** The DNA molecule is composed of two strands held together by paired bases.
    1. Which base can link only to thymine?
    2. Which base can link only to cytosine?
  (ii) Name the type of bonding which occurs between members of a base pair.

  (b) **(i)** Explain what is meant by the term DNA profiling.
  (ii) Give a brief account of the stages involved in DNA profiling.
  (iii) Give two applications of DNA profiling.
  (iv) What is genetic screening?

(c) 'The same amount of DNA is present in nuclei of cells taken from the liver, heart, pancreas and muscle of a rat.'

   (i) Use your knowledge of DNA and mitosis to explain this statement.

   (ii) Name a cell produced by the rat which will contain a different amount of DNA in its nucleus to those mentioned above.

   (iii) Briefly outline how you isolated DNA from a plant tissue.

(2007 HL Q 10)

27 (b) (i) DNA is made of units called nucleotides. Draw a labelled diagram of a nucleotide to show its three constituent parts.

   (ii) Which of the labelled parts in your diagram in (i) may vary from nucleotide to nucleotide?

   (iii) The genetic code is contained within the DNA of chromosomes. Briefly describe the nature of this code.

   (iv) What is meant by non-coding DNA?

   (v) Give one structural difference between DNA and RNA.

   (vi) Name a cell organelle, apart from the nucleus, in which DNA is found.

(2008 HL Q 14)

28 Part **(a)** deals with DNA structure and replication.

   (a) (i) Name the base in DNA that pairs with cytosine.

   (ii) What are the two main events in the replication of DNA?

Part **(b)** deals with protein synthesis.

   (b) (i) Explain the terms *transcription* and *translation*.

   (ii) In which structures in the cell does translation occur?

   (iii) How many bases in sequence make up a codon in mRNA?

   (iv) Each mRNA codon specifies one of three possible outcomes during protein synthesis. Name these **three** possible outcomes.

   (v) What does the letter 't' stand for in tRNA?

   (vi) During translation one end of a tRNA molecule attaches to an mRNA codon. What is usually attached to the other end of the tRNA molecule?

(2010 HL Q 10)

Previous examination questions

Ordinary level	Higher level
2004 Q 12c	2004 Q 13a, b
2005 Q 13b	2005 Q 8, 10b
2007 Q 4, 11c	2006 Q 7b(iii), 12a
2008 Q 5	2007 Q 10
2009 Q 11c	2008 Q 14b
2010 Q 7, 11a, c	2009 Q 10c
2011 Q 10c	2010 Q 8b(iii), 10a, b
2012 Q 11c	2011 Q 9
	2012 Q 10a

Latest questions at www.edco.ie/lcbiologyplus/examhelp

Online test and assessment tracker

Scan the QR code and test yourself on chapter 15
www.edco.ie/lcbiologyplus

THE CELL

Chapter 16 **Genetic crosses and heredity**

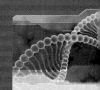

Learning objectives

- To define the term 'gamete', describe how gametes are formed and understand their role in sexual reproduction
- To define the terms 'fertilisation', 'allele', 'homozygous', 'heterozygous', 'genotype', 'phenotype', 'dominance', 'recessive' and 'incomplete dominance'
- To study inheritance to the first filial (F_1) generation of a single unlinked trait in a cross
- To study sex determination
- **HIGHER ▶** To describe the work of Gregor Mendel and how it led to his two laws of genetics as applied to monohybrid and dihybrid crosses
- **HIGHER ▶** To state and explain the law of segregation
- **HIGHER ▶** To state and explain the law of independent assortment
- **HIGHER ▶** To use the Punnett square technique to study inheritance of two unlinked traits to the second filial (F_2) generation
- **HIGHER ▶** To define and explain the terms 'linkage' and 'sex linkage'
- **HIGHER ▶** To describe non-nuclear inheritance.

Gametes

All body cells except reproductive cells are called **somatic** cells. Somatic cells include cheek, liver, muscle, blood, leaf, stem and root cells.

The somatic cells in most organisms are diploid (or 2n), which means they contain a double set of chromosomes. If these cells were to join together, the number of chromosomes in the resulting cell would be double the normal number.

In meiosis the number of chromosomes in the nucleus is halved. This means that in meiosis the diploid number is reduced to a haploid number of chromosomes. If the haploid cells formed in meiosis are capable of fusing together, they are called gametes, or sex cells.

Gametes transmit genes from one generation to another in sexual reproduction. In humans, the gametes are the sperm and egg.

The zygote normally grows (by mitosis) to form a new organism.

Gametes are haploid cells that are capable of fusion.

Fertilisation is the union of two gametes to form a single cell called a zygote.

Genetic crosses

The mechanism of genetic crosses is best understood by the use of sample questions and their answers. Explanations for new terms are provided as they arise in each question.

Question 1

In cats, black coat (B) is dominant over white coat (b). Give the genotypes and phenotypes for the offspring of a cross involving two cats whose genotypes are (BB) and (bb).

16.1 *Genetic crosses produce variations in coat colour in shorthorn cattle*

Explanation of some terms

Genes are represented by letters. Usually the first letter of the dominant trait is used (e.g. B). Normally two different types of the same gene exist, i.e. a dominant version (symbolised by a capital letter, e.g. B) and a recessive version (small letter, e.g. b). These different (or alternative) versions are called alleles.

Alleles are found at the same position (or locus) on similar chromosomes.

Dominant means the allele that prevents the recessive allele from being expressed.

Recessive means the allele is prevented from being expressed by a dominant allele.

Alleles are different (or alternative) forms of the same gene.

The **locus** of a gene is its position on a chromosome.

When a dominant and a recessive allele occur together it is the dominant allele that works. This means that cats that are BB or Bb are both black.

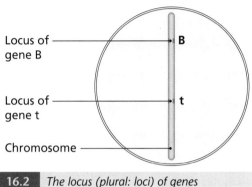

Locus of gene B

Locus of gene t

Chromosome

16.2   *The locus (plural: loci) of genes*

Recessive alleles *recede* in the presence of a dominant allele. This means that cats that are Bb are black, although they contain the recessive allele (b) for white coat. For a cat to be white it has to be bb.

Normally each characteristic is controlled by a gene that has a pair of alleles. For example the gene for coat colour in the cat has two alleles: B and b. In this case the genotypes may be BB, Bb or bb.

Genotype means the genetic make-up of an organism, i.e. the genes that are present.

Phenotype means the physical make-up, or appearance, of an organism.

THE CELL

In Question 1 the phenotype is the coat colour of the cat (i.e. the phenotype is either black or white coat).

Genes are the instructions to the cell that help to produce the phenotype. However, genes are influenced by the environment. It is the interaction of the genes with the environment that produces the phenotype.

Genotype + environment = phenotype

For instance, most people are born with the gene for the pigment melanin. However, the amount of melanin they produce will depend on their exposure to ultraviolet rays.

Amazingly, even gender can be influenced by the environment. In some reptiles and fish the sex of the individual will vary depending on heat or light acting on the genotype. Indeed, some organisms change from male to female every second year.

The relative importance of the genotype (nature) and the environment (nurture) has been argued for generations, especially with regard to intelligence.

This **nature versus nurture** argument has not been fully settled. Present-day opinion suggests that phenotype (e.g. intelligence) is a combination of inherited genes and the upbringing of the child.

When working out genetic crosses you should realise that:
- A pair of alleles is present in the cells of an organism for each characteristic
- Only one allele for each characteristic is carried in each gamete
- As a result of gametes fusing, a pair of alleles is present in the progeny.

These rules are applied in diagram 16.3. When writing the letters it is essential to distinguish *clearly* between capital and small letters.

Answer 1

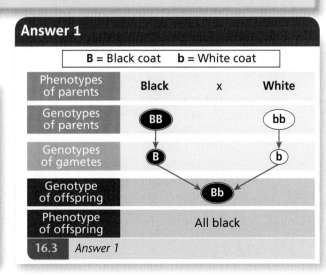

	B = Black coat	b = White coat	
Phenotypes of parents	**Black**	x	**White**
Genotypes of parents	BB		bb
Genotypes of gametes	B		b
Genotype of offspring		Bb	
Phenotype of offspring		All black	

16.3   *Answer 1*

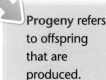

Progeny refers to offspring that are produced.

Homozygous means that two alleles are identical.

Heterozygous means that the alleles are different.

Question 2

In pea plants, green pods (G) are dominant to yellow pods (g). Show by means of diagrams the genotypes and phenotypes of the F₁ progeny that result from crossing two heterozygous plants.

Explanation of other terms

The F_1 progeny means the first generation of offspring. F_1 is short for 'first filial generation'.

Remember *homo* means 'the same as'; think of 'homosexual'.

Homozygous dominant = GG; homozygous recessive = gg. 'Pure breeding' is another term for homozygous.

Hetero means 'different', as in 'heterosexual'.

Heterozygous is also called hybrid. The genotype Gg (or gG) is heterozygous.

Answer 2

G = Green pod   g = Yellow pod

| Genotypes of parents | Gg | x | Gg |

Genotypes of gametes — Punnett square:

	G	g
G	GG	Gg
g	Gg	gg

(Note : the letters in the Punnett square are the F₁ genotypes, not the gametes.)

A **Punnett square** is a grid used to show the ratio of the genotypes of the progeny in a genetic cross.

Genotypes of F₁ progeny: GG Gg Gg gg

Phenotypes of F₁ progeny: **3 green pods : 1 yellow pod**

16.4   *Answer 2*

Question 3

In flies, long wing is dominant to short wing. A homozygous dominant fly is crossed with a homozygous recessive fly.

(a) What letter should represent long wing?

(b) Give the genotype of the homozygous dominant parent.

(c) State the phenotype of the homozygous dominant parent.

(d) Give the genotypes of all the gametes produced.

(e) If 100 flies are produced, how many would you expect to be:
 (i) Long winged
 (ii) Homozygous dominant?

Answer 3

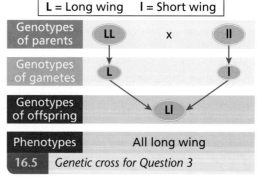

L = Long wing   l = Short wing

| Genotypes of parents | LL | x | ll |

Genotypes of gametes: L ... l

Genotypes of offspring: Ll

Phenotypes: **All long wing**

16.5   *Genetic cross for Question 3*

The cross in this case can be represented as shown above. Normally the first letter of the dominant trait is used to represent the gene.

The specific answers are:

(a) Long wing = L

(b) Genotype of homozygous dominant parent = LL

(c) Phenotype of homozygous dominant parent = long wings

(d) Gamete genotypes = L and l

(e) (i) Expect 100 long-winged.
 (ii) Expect none of the flies to be homozygous dominant.

Question 4	**Answer 4**

In the fruit fly, *Drosophila*, body colour is controlled by two alleles. The allele for grey body (G) is dominant to the allele for black body (g).

If two heterozygous flies are crossed, show by diagrams that the ratio of flies with grey bodies to flies with black bodies is 3:1.

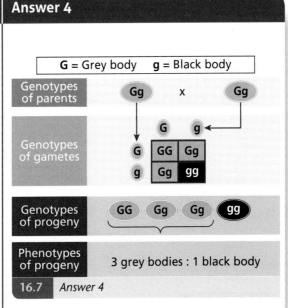

	G = Grey body **g** = Black body
Genotypes of parents	Gg x Gg
Genotypes of gametes	

	G	g
G	GG	Gg
g	Gg	gg

Genotypes of progeny	GG Gg Gg gg
Phenotypes of progeny	3 grey bodies : 1 black body

16.7   *Answer 4*

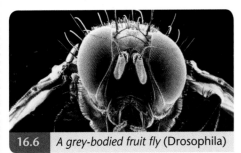

16.6   *A grey-bodied fruit fly* (Drosophila)

Incomplete dominance

Normally the characteristic controlled by a dominant allele is displayed in the heterozygous genotype. The characteristic controlled by a recessive allele is normally only displayed in the homozygous recessive genotype.

Incomplete dominance (also called codominance) is relatively rare.

Examples of incomplete dominance

- One example of incomplete dominance occurs in shorthorn cattle. In this case the genotype RR produces a red coat and the genotype rr produces a white coat. The heterozygous condition Rr gives a roan coat (patches of red and patches of white coat, as shown in diagram 16.1).
- Another example of incomplete dominance is flower colour in snapdragons. In this case RR produces red flowers, rr produces white flowers, but Rr produces pink flowers.

> **Incomplete dominance** means that neither allele is dominant or recessive with respect to the other. Both alleles are equally expressed in the heterozygous genotype to produce an intermediate phenotype.

THE CELL

Question 5	**Answer 5**

Flower colour in snapdragons shows incomplete dominance, i.e. the heterozygous condition (Rr) is pink. Give the phenotypes and genotypes for the progeny of the following crosses:

(a) A white-flowered plant and a red-flowered plant

(b) Two pink-flowered plants.

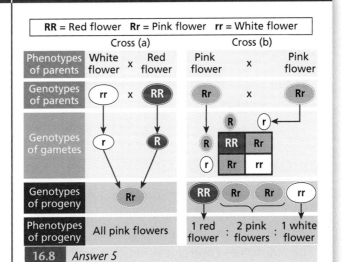

	RR = Red flower **Rr** = Pink flower **rr** = White flower

	Cross (a)	Cross (b)
Phenotypes of parents	White flower x Red flower	Pink flower x Pink flower
Genotypes of parents	rr x RR	Rr x Rr
Genotypes of gametes	r R	

Cross (b) gametes:

	R	r
R	RR	Rr
r	Rr	rr

Genotypes of progeny	Rr	RR Rr Rr rr
Phenotypes of progeny	All pink flowers	1 red flower : 2 pink flowers : 1 white flower

16.8   *Answer 5*

Pedigree studies

Question 6	Answer 6
In humans, the ability to produce the skin pigment melanin is controlled by a dominant allele (N). Lack of pigment (albinism) is controlled by the recessive allele (n). The pedigree for a family is represented below.	N = Normal pigment, n = Albino

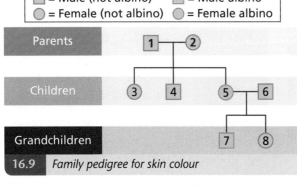

□ = Male (not albino)   ■ = Male albino
○ = Female (not albino)   ● = Female albino

Parents — 1 — 2

Children — 3   4   5   6

Grandchildren — 7   8

16.9   *Family pedigree for skin colour*

(a) Give the genotypes of persons 1, 2 and 5.
(b) Could person 6 be homozygous dominant? Give a reason for your answer.
(c) How many children had the parents 1 and 2?
(d) Give all the possible genotypes for person 4.

Answer 6

N = Normal pigment, n = Albino

(a) Persons 1 and 2 have normal pigment but their child (person 5) is an albino, nn. This means that persons 1 and 2 must both be Nn. Person 5 must be nn, i.e. albino.

(b) Person 6 cannot be homozygous dominant. If person 6 was NN then **all** his children would have normal pigment. However, one of his children (person 7) is albino, nn. Thus, person 6 must be Nn.

(c) Parents 1 and 2 had three children (i.e. persons 3, 4 and 5).

(d) Person 4 could be NN or Nn.

Summary of the ratios of genetic crosses

Note: In the first three crosses (or rows) below it is assumed that B (black coat) is dominant over b (white coat). In the final cross the assumption is that RR = red coat, Rr = roan coat and rr = white coat.

Ratio	Example	Explanation
1 : 0 or 100%	All offspring are black or 84 out of 84 of the offspring are black	BB × BB BB × Bb BB × bb
1 : 1 or 50% : 50%	Equal numbers of black and white offspring were produced or 164 black and 159 white	Bb × bb
3 : 1 or 75% : 25%	35 black and 11 white or 124 black and 41 white	Bb × Bb
1 : 2 : 1 or 25% : 50% : 25%	19 red, 40 roan and 22 white offspring	Rr × Rr (where alleles show incomplete dominance)

Sex determination

The nucleus of each human somatic (or non-gamete-forming) cell has 46 chromosomes (i.e. 2n = 46). These 46 chromosomes consist of 44 non-sex chromosomes called **autosomes** and two sex chromosomes.

The autosomes control features that are independent of whether a person is male or female. Examples of such gender-neutral features are skin colour, number of arms, production of saliva and digestive enzymes.

The two sex chromosomes are called the X and Y chromosomes. They contain genes that control gender in most species. The X chromosome is longer than the Y chromosome.

Humans

In humans every individual somatic cell nucleus should have two sex chromosomes. If these are XX the individual is female; if they are XY the individual is male.

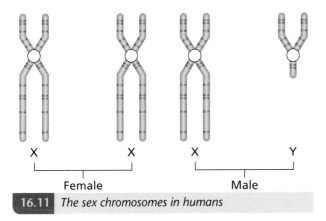

X   X   X   Y

Female   Male

16.11 *The sex chromosomes in humans*

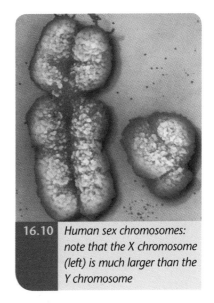

16.10 *Human sex chromosomes: note that the X chromosome (left) is much larger than the Y chromosome*

The arrangement of XX for females and XY for males has the following two consequences:
- It is the male who determines the sex of the child
- The ratio of male to female births should be equal (1:1).

Question 7	Answer 7
Show using diagrams why the father determines the sex of a child in humans.	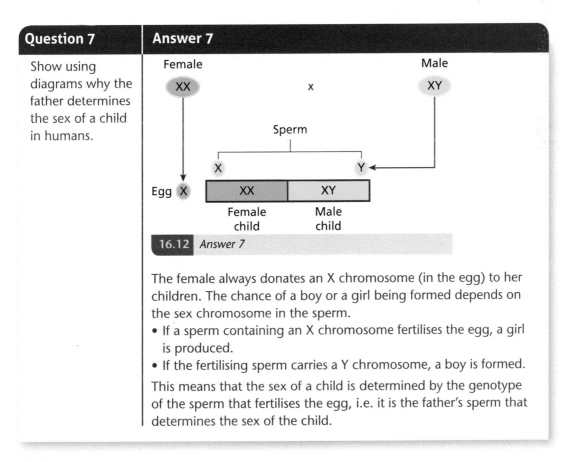

16.12 *Answer 7*

The female always donates an X chromosome (in the egg) to her children. The chance of a boy or a girl being formed depends on the sex chromosome in the sperm.
- If a sperm containing an X chromosome fertilises the egg, a girl is produced.
- If the fertilising sperm carries a Y chromosome, a boy is formed.

This means that the sex of a child is determined by the genotype of the sperm that fertilises the egg, i.e. it is the father's sperm that determines the sex of the child.

Other species

The pattern of sex determination in some species is the reverse of that in humans. For example, in birds, butterflies and moths males are XX and females are XY.

Ratio of male to female births in humans

Diagram 16.12 shows that the chance of an XX (girl) or XY (boy) offspring being formed is 50% (i.e. 1:1). This is because equal numbers of sperm containing an X

THE CELL

Despite the ratio being equal in theory, the numbers of male and female births is not equal. Large-scale worldwide studies suggest that boys are more likely to be born than girls (the figures are close to 106:100). This imbalance may occur to compensate for the fact that more males die early in life than females. The exact reason for the imbalance is not known.

chromosome and sperm containing a Y chromosome are produced. Therefore, if a woman is pregnant it is equally likely that her child will be a boy or a girl.

The work of Gregor Mendel

Gregor Mendel is known as the 'father of genetics'. He was born in Austria in 1822 and became an Augustinian monk at the age of 21. Having twice failed his teacher's qualifying examination, he turned to the study of the edible or garden pea plant.

Mendel carried out numerous experiments on garden pea plants. He investigated the inheritance of seven characteristics of these plants, such as stem height, flower colour and seed shape.

These experiments involved removing the pollen-producing structures (called anthers) from some flowers and transferring pollen from other flowers to the treated flowers by hand. The treated flowers were then covered with bags to prevent any more pollen from reaching them. The seeds that formed were collected and grown in carefully labelled containers. The appearance (phenotype) of the resulting plants was studied and recorded.

16.13 *Gregor Mendel (1822–1884)*

The success of Mendel's work was largely due to two main features.

- He only studied features (or characteristics) that displayed two forms (or traits). For instance, the plants were either tall or small and the pods were either green or yellow.
- He counted the number of plants with each type of trait. He was able to detect mathematical ratios such as 1:1 or 3:1 from the numerical data he obtained.

The law of segregation (Mendel's first law) states that:
- Inherited characteristics are controlled by pairs of alleles.
- These alleles segregate (or separate) from each other at gamete formation, with only one member of the pair being found in each gamete.

Mendel's research was carried out around 1860 and resulted in two basic laws of inheritance (called Mendel's first and second laws). His results were ignored until 1900, when a number of researchers discovered the significance of his studies.

Mendel's first law

Mendel's first law is called **the law of segregation**.

16.14 *Mendel studied the production of pea characteristics, such as round or wrinkled peas*

Example of the law of segregation

If, for a species of plant, T = tall and t = small, the height of the plant is controlled by a pair of alleles, e.g. TT, Tt or tt.

When gametes are formed, only one allele can enter each gamete (the alleles segregate or separate). This is shown in diagram 16.15.

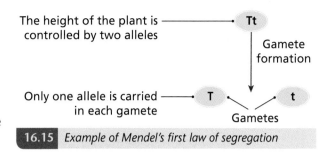

The height of the plant is controlled by two alleles

Only one allele is carried in each gamete

16.15 *Example of Mendel's first law of segregation*

Chromosomal basis of Mendel's first law

1. In diploid organisms, chromosomes occur in matching pairs (called homologous pairs).
2. Pairs of alleles occupy the same position (locus) on a homologous pair.
3. During meiosis, homologous chromosomes separate and go into different cells.
4. As a result, pairs of alleles also separate (see diagram 16.16).

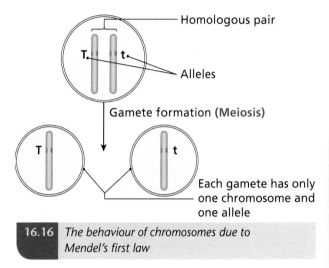

16.16 *The behaviour of chromosomes due to Mendel's first law*

Monohybrid and dihybrid crosses

> A **monohybrid cross** involves the study of a single characteristic.

Examples of monohybrid crosses involve features such as eye colour, seed shape or coat colour. Each characteristic can display two variations or phenotypes. This means that a characteristic such as eye colour can display two phenotypes, such as brown eyes or blue eyes.

All the examples of genetic crosses given in this chapter so far are monohybrid crosses.

> A **dihybrid cross** involves the study of two characteristics.

For example, Question 8 (on page 198) is a dihybrid cross because it involves two characteristics: plant size (tall or small) and pod colour (green or yellow).

Mendel's second law

Mendel carried out a range of dihybrid crosses. Having analysed his results, he formulated his second law, **the law of independent assortment**.

The second law means that in an organism with the genotype AaBb **either** of the As can combine with **either** of the Bs to form gametes. As a result, the four gamete types shown in diagram 16.17 are equally likely to be formed.

> The law of independent assortment states that:
> ● When gametes are formed ...
> ● either of a pair of alleles ...
> ● is equally likely ...
> ● to combine with either of another pair of alleles.

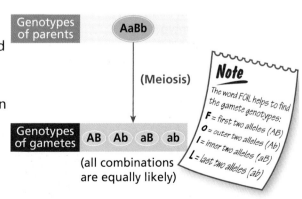

Genotypes of parents — **AaBb**

(Meiosis)

Genotypes of gametes — AB   Ab   aB   ab

(all combinations are equally likely)

Note
The word FOIL helps to find the gamete genotypes:
F = first two alleles (AB)
O = outer two alleles (Ab)
I = inner two alleles (aB)
L = last two alleles (ab)

16.17 *Example of Mendel's second law of independent assortment*

THE CELL

Chromosomal basis of Mendel's second law

As alleles are located on homologous chromosomes, Mendel's second law can be restated as:

- At gamete formation …
- either of a pair of homologous chromosomes …
- is equally likely …
- to combine with either chromosome of a second homologous pair.

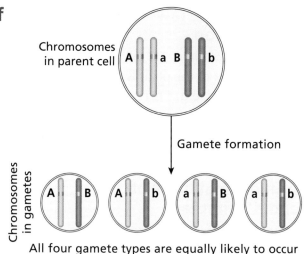

Chromosomes in parent cell

Gamete formation

Chromosomes in gametes

All four gamete types are equally likely to occur i.e. the ratio is 1 : 1 : 1 : 1

16.18 *The behaviour of chromosomes due to Mandel's second law*

Examples of dihybrid crosses

Question 8	Answer 8

Question 8

In pea plants, tall plant (T) is dominant over small plant (t). In addition, green pod (G) is dominant over yellow pod (g).

A tall plant with green pods (homozygous for both traits) is crossed with a small plant with yellow pods.

(a) Why is this a dihybrid cross?

(b) Show using diagrams the genotypes and phenotypes of the progeny of this cross.

Answer 8

(a) This is a dihybrid cross because two characteristics are studied, i.e. plant height and pod colour.

(b)

T = Tall plant	G = Green pod
t = Small plant	g = Yellow pod

Phenotype of parents	Tall plant and green pod (homozygous for both)	X	Small plant and yellow pod
Genotype of parents	TTGG	X	ttgg
Genotype of gametes	TG		tg
Genotype of progeny		TtGg	
Phenotype of progeny	All tall plants and green pods		

16.19 *Answer 8*

Progeny genotypes: TtGg. Progeny phenotypes: all tall plants and green pods.

Question 9	Answer 9

Question 9

In guinea pigs, black coat (B) is dominant to white coat (b). Also short hair (S) is dominant to long hair (s).

(a) Show the genotypes and phenotypes of the F₁ progeny for a cross involving a black-coated, short-haired guinea pig (heterozygous for both traits) and a white-coated, long-haired guinea pig.

(b) State the expected ratio of the offspring.

Answer 9

(a)

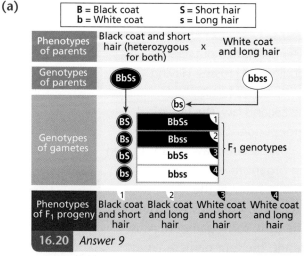

B = Black coat	S = Short hair
b = White coat	s = Long hair

Phenotypes of parents	Black coat and short hair (heterozygous for both)	X	White coat and long hair
Genotypes of parents	BbSs		bbss

Genotypes of gametes: BS, Bs, bS, bs × bs

F₁ genotypes:
1. BbSs
2. Bbss
3. bbSs
4. bbss

Phenotypes of F₁ progeny	Black coat and short hair	Black coat and long hair	White coat and short hair	White coat and long hair
	1	2	3	4

16.20 *Answer 9*

(b) The offspring are expected to occur in equal numbers (i.e. the ratio is 1:1:1:1).

HIGHER ▼

Question 10	Answer 10

Question 10

A homozygous purple-flowered, short-stemmed plant was crossed with a red-flowered, long-stemmed plant. All the F₁ offspring were purple-flowered with short stems.

(a) State the dominant and recessive traits.

(b) Explain, using diagrams, why the F₁ plants all had the same phenotypes.

(c) Give the expected phenotype ratios if an F₁ plant is selfed.

Answer 10

(a) This cross may be summarised as shown in diagram 16.21:

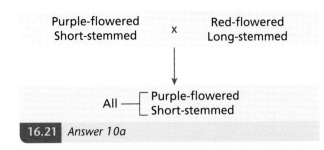

16.21 *Answer 10a*

The dominant traits appear in the F_1 generation. This means the dominant traits are purple-flowered and short-stemmed. (Red-flowered and long-stemmed are the recessive traits.) Normally the first letter of the dominant trait is used to represent the gene. The alleles in this cross should be represented as:

P = Purple-flowered   S = Short-stemmed
p = Red-flowered   s = Long-stemmed

(b)

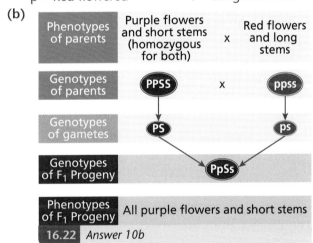

16.22 *Answer 10b*

(c) Selfing means you cross a genotype with the same genotype. In this case the F_1 genotype is PpSs and this is crossed with another plant with the genotype PpSs. If two F_1 offspring are crossed the organisms produced are called the F_2 progeny (i.e. the second filial generation).

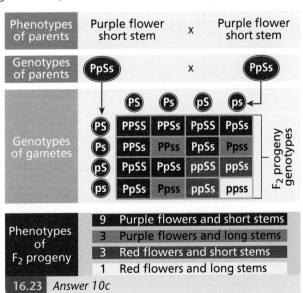

16.23 *Answer 10c*

THE CELL

Expected ratios arising from Mendel's second law

In a dihybrid cross where one parent is heterozygous for both characteristics and the second parent is homozygous recessive (e.g. BbSs × bbss), if the offspring are produced in the ratio 1:1:1:1 then independent assortment has occurred.

Also if both parents are heterozygous (e.g. PpSs × PsSs) and the offspring are in the ratio 9:3:3:1 then, again, independent assortment has occurred.

Chromosome diagrams

The **locus** of a gene is its position on a chromosome. The locus (plural: loci) of a gene is shown in diagram 16.24.

Alleles occupy similar loci on homologous chromosomes, as shown in diagram 16.25.

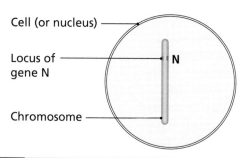

16.24 *The locus of a gene*

> Linkage means that genes are located on the same chromosome.

Linkage

Linked genes tend to be passed on together (forming a linkage group) to the next generation, i.e. they do **not** show independent assortment.

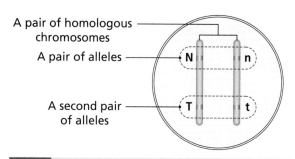

16.25 *Alleles on chromosomes*

Example of linked genes

In diagram 16.26:

- There are four chromosomes
- The alleles R and S are linked, as are the alleles r and s
- Nothing is linked to the alleles T and t
- R and r (along with S and s as well as T and t) are alleles
- R and S are *not* alleles, nor are R and s nor R and T.

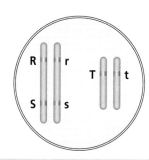

16.26 *A simple chromosome diagram showing linkage*

Question 11	Answer 11
Draw simple chromosome diagrams to illustrate the following cells. In each case show the gametes that might be produced. (a) The genes are not linked and the genotype is AaBb. (b) The genes are linked (A to B and a to b) and the genotype is AaBb.	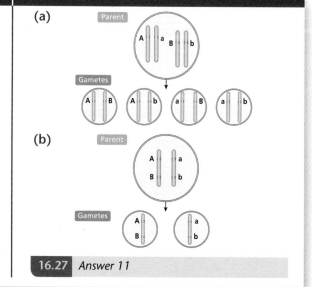

16.27 *Answer 11*

Note that in Answer 11:
(a) The four gamete types are equally likely, i.e. the ratio is 1:1:1:1.
(b) The genes are linked. In this case only two types of gametes are formed, i.e. the only gametes are (AB) and (ab). This is a contradiction of the law of independent assortment. For this reason we can say that linkage **contradicts** Mendel's second law of independent assortment.

Question 12

Draw simple chromosome diagrams to show each of the following cells. In each case indicate the gametes that each cell might produce.
(a) The genotype is RrTt, the genes are not linked.
(b) The genotype is RrTt, the genes are linked (R to T and r to t).
(c) The genes are not linked; the cell is homozygous for R and heterozygous for T.
(d) The genes are linked and the cell is homozygous dominant for both genes.

Answer 12

16.28 *Answer 12*

The ratio of offspring in linked crosses

In parts (a) and (b) of Question 12 the parents have the same genotypes (i.e. both are RrTt). However, different types of gametes are formed in each case.

The ratios of the **genotypes of the gametes** produced by linked crosses are different from those produced in non-linked crosses. This results in linked crosses producing different ratios of **offspring** than might otherwise be expected.

Sex linkage

Sex linkage means that a characteristic is controlled by a gene on a sex (or X) chromosome.

The sex chromosomes in humans are the X and Y chromosomes. The X chromosome carries a large number of genes. The Y chromosome is much shorter than the X and carries very few genes.

The main gene isolated on the Y chromosome is the **SRY** gene. This stands for the **S**ex-determining **R**egion of **Y**. It, and a small number of other genes on the **Y** chromosome, control the development of the testes. These genes are thought to control maleness.

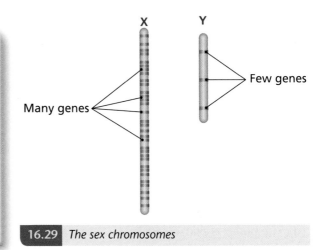

16.29 *The sex chromosomes*

Sex-linked characteristics are also said to be X-linked. Examples of sex-linked characteristics are:

- Colour blindness
- Haemophilia (inability to clot blood)
- Duchenne muscular dystrophy (where the muscles waste away, resulting in early death)
- Eye colour in *Drosophila* (the fruit fly, often used in genetics experiments).

All these characteristics are controlled by genes, or alleles, located on the X chromosome. In males there is no corresponding allele on the Y chromosome.

In sex-linked characteristics, the recessive phenotype is more likely to occur in males, i.e. males suffer more often from sex-linked characteristics (as shown in the following examples).

Examples of sex-linked characteristics

Colour blindness

Normal individuals can detect three colours of light (red, green and blue). The allele for normal vision (N) is dominant. Colour blindness (n) usually means an inability to distinguish red from green. The gene for colour vision is located on an X chromosome.

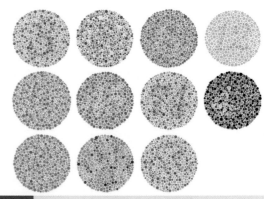

16.30 *Test for colour blindness: a person with normal vision can distinguish the number or pattern in each disc*

THE CELL

Females

Females can have three distinct genotypes with respect to colour vision. These are shown in diagram 16.31. Note that these genotypes can be represented as shown in the diagram or as XNXN or XXNn or XnXn.

For a female to be colour-blind, she needs **two** copies of the recessive allele (n). As recessive alleles are usually relatively scarce, it is rare to have two recessives. The incidence of colour-blind females in Ireland is about 0.2%.

Normal vision (homozygous dominant) Normal vision (heterozygous, called a carrier) Colour-blind (homozygous recessive)

16.31 *The alleles for colour vision in females*

Males

Males have only one allele for colour vision. This is on the X chromosome. The Y chromosome has no allele for colour vision.

This means there are only two genotypes for males, as shown in diagram 16.32. These genotypes can also be given as XNY– or XYn–.

Males only need **one** recessive allele in order to be colour-blind. This means that males are more likely to be colour-blind than females. The incidence of colour blindness in Irish males is about 8%. Most of these males have some degree of colour vision. Complete colour blindness is very rare in Ireland.

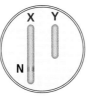

Normal vision Colour-blind

16.32 *The alleles for colour vision in males*

Haemophilia

Haemophilia is a bleeding disorder caused by the lack of a particular blood protein. Haemophiliacs suffer from frequent bleeding, often into the joints. Without treatment, some haemophiliacs may bleed to death after a small cut.

Haemophilia is caused by a gene located on the X chromosome. The allele (N) for the production of the clotting protein is dominant. The recessive allele (n) does not carry the correct genetic code for the production of the protein.

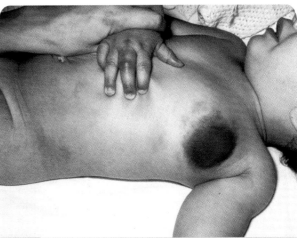

16.33 *A baby with haemophilia: notice the bruising caused by this bleeding disorder*

As with all sex-linked traits, haemophilia is more common in males (0.01%) than in females, where it is extremely rare. Males only need a single copy of the recessive allele (n) to be haemophiliac, but females need two copies of the recessive allele.

The ancient Jews did not insist on circumcision for sons whose families had a history of haemophilia. The royal families of Europe show a high frequency of haemophilia.

Haemophilia is treated by giving sufferers the missing protein. Unfortunately, in Ireland in the 1980s, some of the protein treatments given to haemophiliacs contained viruses for diseases such as hepatitis B and C and AIDS.

In recent years, the treatments are screened (checked) and treated to remove these viruses. The development of an artificially produced (genetically engineered) version of the protein totally eliminates any fear of contamination.

THE CELL

Question 13	Answer 13
The gene for haemophilia is located on an X chromosome. Normal blood clotting (N) is dominant over haemophilia (n). Show the genotypes and phenotypes of the offspring of a cross between a mother who is a carrier and a father who is normal for this trait.	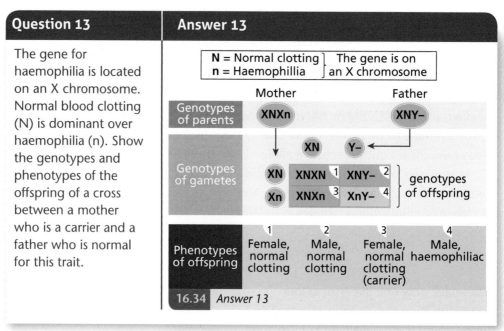

16.34   *Answer 13*

Summary of the ratios of (dihybrid) genetic crosses

Note: In the crosses below it is assumed that B (black coat) is dominant over b (white coat) and L (long tail) is dominant over l (short tail).

Ratio	Example	Explanation
1 : 0 or 100%	All offspring were black-coated with long tails	BBLL × bbll or BBll × bbLL (other explanations exist, but the two shown are the most commonly asked)
1 : 1 : 1 : 1 or 25% : 25% : 25% : 25%	All four offspring genotypes were formed in equal numbers or Black coat, long tail = 18 Black coat, short tail = 17 White coat, long tail = 19 White coat, short tail = 17	BbLl × bbll (where the genes are not linked)
1 : 1	Equal numbers of black-coated, long-tailed and white-coated, short-tailed or Black coat, long tail = 76 White coat, short tail = 75	BbLl × bbll (where the genes are linked)
9 : 3 : 3 : 1	Black coat, long tail = 176 Black coat, short tail = 62 White coat, long tail = 59 White coat, short tail = 20	BbLl × BbLl

Non-nuclear inheritance

Most of the DNA (and genes) in a cell is located in the nucleus. However, non-nuclear or extra-nuclear genes are present as small circles of DNA in mitochondria and chloroplasts. Both of these organelles reproduce by themselves and pass on their genes to the resulting organelles.

In plants, mitochondria and chloroplasts are normally passed on to the next generation in the cytoplasm of the egg. Pollen does not contain these organelles.

In animals, mitochondria are in the tail of the sperm. Only the head of the sperm joins with the egg (the tail stays outside the egg). This means that mitochondria from the sperm are not passed on to the zygote.

Mitochondria and chloroplasts are said to follow a maternal line of inheritance, i.e. they are inherited from the female in the cytoplasm of the egg.

For example, mitochondrial DNA (mtDNA) in humans is inherited only from the mother. A number of rare human disorders are inherited only from the mother because they are controlled by non-nuclear genes located on mtDNA. These disorders normally involve a lack of energy (ATP) and affect systems with high energy demands, such as the muscular and nervous systems.

Summary

Somatic cells are body (or non-sexually reproductive) cells.

Gametes (sex cells) are haploid cells capable of fusion.

Fertilisation is the union of two gametes to form a zygote.

Genetics is the study of the mechanisms of heredity and variation.

Alleles are different (or alternative) forms of the same gene.
- A dominant allele stops a recessive allele from working.
- A recessive allele does not work in the presence of a dominant allele.

Genotype means genetic make-up.

Phenotype means physical make-up or appearance.

The **phenotype is formed** by the action of the environment on the genotype.

Progeny means the offspring of a cross.

F_1 means the first filial generation, i.e. the first generation of offspring.

Homozygous means two alleles are the same.

Heterozygous means two alleles are different.

Incomplete dominance means there is no dominant or recessive allele and the heterozygous condition produces an intermediate phenotype.

A **pedigree** is a diagram that shows the genetic history of a family.

Autosomes are chromosomes that do not determine sexuality.

The **sex chromosomes** are the X and Y chromosomes. In humans:
- XX = female
- XY = male.

Gregor Mendel is known as the 'father of genetics'.
- He studied pea plants.
- He only studied characteristics that showed one of two traits.
- He counted the numbers of offspring produced.

Mendel's first law (the law of segregation) states that:
- Inherited traits are controlled by two alleles
- The alleles separate at gamete formation, with each gamete only having one allele.

A **monohybrid cross** involves the study of only one characteristic.

A **dihybrid cross** involves two characteristics.

Mendel's second law (the law of independent assortment) states that:
- Either of a pair of alleles …
- is equally likely …
- to combine with either of another pair of alleles …
- when gametes are being formed.

Linkage means genes are on the same chromosome and are likely to be passed on together to the next generation.
● Linkage contradicts Mendel's second law of independent assortment.

A **cross** between AaBb and aabb produces different results depending on whether the genes are linked or not linked.
● If the genes are not linked, four genotypes are found in equal numbers (i.e. 1:1:1:1).
● If the genes are linked, the two genotypes will be AaBb and aabb (i.e. 1:1).

The **locus** of a gene is its position on a chromosome.

The **sex chromosomes** are the X and Y chromosomes:
● The X chromosome contains many genes
● The Y chromosome is shorter and has very few genes.

A **sex-linked** (or X-linked) **trait** is controlled by a gene on the X chromosome.
● In sex-linked traits, the recessive phenotype is more common in males than in females.

Non-nuclear DNA:
● Is found in chloroplasts and mitochondria
● Is passed on only from the female
● Allows organelles to reproduce independently of the cell.

Revision questions

1 Explain what is meant by:
   (a) Somatic cells
   (b) Gametes
   (c) Diploid
   (d) Haploid
   (e) Fertilisation.

2 Name the process in each case responsible for converting: **(a)** Diploid cells into haploid cells **(b)** Haploid cells into diploid cells.

3 In corn plants, yellow seed (Y) is dominant to green seed (y). A pure breeding (homozygous) yellow-seeded corn plant is crossed with a green-seeded corn plant.
   (a) Using diagrams show the F_1 genotype and phenotype.
   (b) From your diagrams state:
       (i) The genotypes of the parents
       (ii) The genotypes of the gametes
       (iii) The genotype and phenotype of the F_1 generation.
   (c) State the genotypes of the gametes that could be produced by the F_1 progeny.

4 In humans, the gene for brown eyes (B) is dominant to that for blue eyes (b). If both parents are heterozygous for the trait:
   (a) Give the genotypes of the parents.
   (b) Give the genotypes of the gametes produced.
   (c) Give the possible genotypes and phenotypes of the children.

   (d) What percentage of the children would you expect to be:
        (i) Homozygous dominant
       (ii) Homozygous recessive
      (iii) Heterozygous
       (iv) Homozygous?

5 In a flower, red petal is dominant to white petal. A plant, homozygous for the dominant allele, is crossed with a plant with white petals.
   (a) Suggest suitable symbols for the two alleles.
   (b) Give the genotypes of each parent.
   (c) Give the genotypes of the gametes produced by each parent.
   (d) Give the genotype of the F_1 progeny.
   (e) Give the phenotype of the F_1 progeny.

6 In peas, green seed (G) is dominant to yellow seed (g). A pea plant, pure-breeding for green seed, is crossed with a yellow-seeded plant. Find the genotypes and phenotypes produced in this cross.

7 In cats, black coat (B) is <u>dominant</u> to white coat (b). The <u>genotype</u> of the male cat is <u>heterozygous</u>. The female cat has the <u>phenotype</u> white coat. Half of the progeny of these two cats are <u>homozygous</u> <u>recessive</u>.
   (a) Explain the meaning of each of the six underlined terms.
   (b) Show this cross diagrammatically.

(c) Use each of the underlined terms at least once to label your diagrams.

(d) What is the phenotype of the kittens that are not homozygous recessive?

8 In humans, normal skin colour (N) is dominant to albinism (n).

(a) State the phenotypes of individuals who are:
  (i) Homozygous dominant
  (ii) Homozygous recessive
  (iii) Heterozygous.

(b) Give the genotypes of the three individuals at (a) above.

(c) Show by diagrams how two parents with normal skin colour can have an albino child.

(d) An albino man has a daughter with normal skin colour. The daughter marries another albino man. Show by diagrams the percentage chance of their child having normal skin colour.

9 In a species of organism the allele D is dominant over the allele d. Diagram 16.35 shows the genotypes of two members, A and B, of the species of organism.

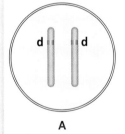
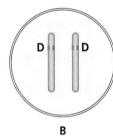

A   B

16.35

(a) Do these two organisms have the same phenotype? Explain your answer.

(b) Give the possible genotypes of the gametes produced by each organism.

(c) If A was crossed with B, could any of the offspring have the genotype dd? Explain your answer.

10 In cucumber plants, the character non-bitter fruit (n) is recessive to bitter fruit (N). If two heterozygous plants are crossed, show using diagrams that the ratio of bitter to non-bitter fruit is 3:1.

11 In shorthorn cattle, coat colour shows a lack of dominance; the heterozygous condition is roan. Show the genotypes and phenotypes of the progeny for each of the following crosses:

(a) A red male and a white female
(b) Two roan parents.

12 Coat colour in collies shows incomplete dominance. The gene for black coat (B) shows equal dominance with the gene for white coat (b). The heterozygous condition is called mixed coat.

(a) State the genotypes of a:
  (i) Black collie
  (ii) White collie.

(b) State the genotypes and phenotypes of the F₁ offspring that would result from crossing a black collie and a white collie.

(c) State the genotypes and phenotypes of the progeny of a cross between two mixed-coated collies.

13 Blue eyes are recessive to brown eyes. Diagram 16.36 shows the pedigree for eye colour in a family.

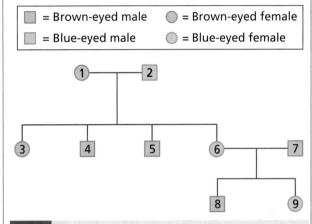

16.36

Answer the following, using B to represent the dominant allele.

(a) What is the relationship between persons:
  (i) 3 and 5
  (ii) 3 and 7
  (iii) 1 and 8?

(b) What are the genotypes of persons 1, 6 and 8?

(c) If person 8 married a brown-eyed female, could they have any blue-eyed children? Explain your answer by means of diagrams.

14 Name the sex chromosomes in human:
(a) Males (b) Females (c) Eggs (d) Sperm.

15 'A mother's chromosomes cannot determine the gender of her child.' Is this statement valid? Support your answer by including a diagrammatic cross.

16 Explain, giving an example in each case, what is meant by:
(a) Allele
(b) Genotype
(c) Phenotype
(d) Homozygous
(e) Heterozygous
(f) Dominant
(g) Recessive
(h) Incomplete dominance
(i) Autosomes.

17 Some of the results of Mendel's crosses carried out on pea plants are given below.

Trait	Original cross	F₁ progeny
Seed form	Round × wrinkled	Round
Seed colour	Yellow × green	Yellow
Flower position	Axial × terminal	Axial
Pod form	Inflated × constricted	Inflated

(a) Use suitable letters to show the genotypes of each of the following:
   (i) A green-seeded plant
   (ii) Homozygous dominant for seed form
   (iii) Heterozygous for flower position
   (iv) Homozygous recessive for pod form.

(b) Give the phenotypes for the plants at (ii) and (iv) above.

(c) Give the genotypes of the gametes that could result from (ii) and (iv) above.

(d) Two plants, each with inflated pods, were crossed: 75% of the progeny had inflated pods and 25% had constricted pods. What does this indicate about the genotypes of the parent plants?

(e) Show the results you would expect for the F₂ generation for the original cross involving seed form.

18 **(a)** State Mendel's first law of segregation.

(b) Show how this law applies to a cell with the genotype Tt.

19 **(a)** State Mendel's second law of independent assortment.

(b) Show how it applies to a cell with the genotype TtRr.

(c) What is the expected ratio of the gametes produced by the cell in part (b)?

20 In pea plants, the trait tall (T) is dominant to short (t) with regard to plant height. Yellow (Y) is dominant to green (y) with regard to seed colour.

(a) Give the genotype of a pea plant that is heterozygous for both height and seed colour. State the genotypes of the gametes that this plant could produce.

(b) Give the genotype of a pea plant that is homozygous for tallness and has green seeds. State the genotype of the gametes that this plant could produce.

(c) Show the phenotype(s) and genotype(s) of the progeny that could result from a cross between the plants described in (a) and (b) above.

21 In peas, the character round seed (R) is dominant over wrinkled seed (r) and yellow seed (Y) is dominant over green (y). Describe the genotypes and phenotypes found in the F₂ generation of the cross RRYY × rryy, when the F₁ generation is self-fertilised.

22 In the flour beetle, *Tribolium castaneum*, black eye (P) is dominant over pearl eye (p) and brown body (B) is dominant over sooty body (b). The genes governing these characters are located on different chromosomes.
A black-eyed, brown-bodied beetle, heterozygous for both genes, was crossed with a beetle with pearl eyes and sooty body. Describe the genetic constitution of the gametes formed and the genotypes and phenotypes of the progeny produced in this cross.

23 In snapdragons, flower colour can be red (RR), white (rr) or, in the heterozygous condition, pink. Also, tall (T) is dominant over dwarf (t).
A dwarf, red-flowered snapdragon plant was crossed with a homozygous tall, white-flowered snapdragon plant. State:
(a) The genotypes of the parents
(b) The genotypes of the gametes
(c) The possible genotypes and phenotypes of the offspring.

24 In shorthorn cattle, the colours red and white show incomplete dominance. In addition, the polled condition (without horns) is dominant over the horned condition. Show the results of a cross between a horned roan male and a polled white female. (**Note**: this question involves two crosses).

25 Draw simple chromosome diagrams to illustrate each of the following, given that the allele A is dominant over a and that the allele B is dominant over b.
(a) The genes for A and B are not linked and the organism is heterozygous for both genes.
(b) The genes are linked, A to B and a to b, and the organism is heterozygous for both genes.
(c) The genes are not linked and the organism is heterozygous for A and homozygous for B.

26 In humans, tongue rolling is governed by a single pair of allelic genes, R and r. The allele R is the dominant allele that allows tongue rolling; the allele r does not. Another pair of allelic genes, which are not linked to the tongue-rolling gene, govern hair colour. In this second pair, brown hair, B, is dominant to red hair, b. Answer the following using the above information.

(a) Draw a simple chromosome diagram to show the genotypes of all the possible gametes that a person, who is heterozygous in respect of tongue rolling and hair colour, can produce.

(b) State briefly how these gamete genotypes demonstrate the principle of independent assortment.

(c) State the phenotype of the person. What other genotypes would give rise to this phenotype?

27 Draw a large diagram of a cell nucleus with two pairs of chromosomes, each pair of chromosomes to be visibly distinguishable from the other pair. Indicate on the chromosomes the alleles A/a and R/r so that the nucleus is heterozygous for both genes and the genes are not linked.

28 An organism of genotype SsTt was crossed with one of genotype sstt. Show the progeny genotypes that could be produced if:

(a) The genes were linked

(b) The genes were not linked.

In each case, indicate the expected ratio of each genotype.

29 (a) What is meant by sex linkage?

(b) Give two examples of sex-linked traits in humans.

30 Colour blindness is caused by a gene located on an X chromosome. Normal vision (N) is dominant to colour blindness (n). Two parents with normal vision have a colour-blind son.

(a) Give the genotypes of both parents and their son.

(b) Did the son inherit the recessive allele from the mother or the father?

(c) What is the chance of this couple having a colour-blind daughter? Explain your answer using diagrams.

31 In humans, red–green colour blindness is a sex-linked trait. A colour-blind man and his wife have two sons. One of the sons is colour-blind and the other is not.

(a) What is the genotype of the mother? Outline your reasoning.

(b) If a future child of this couple is male, what is the chance that he will be colour-blind? Outline your reasoning.

32 Explain the meaning of the following terms:

(a) Sex-linked

(b) Linked genes

(c) Locus.

33 (a) Distinguish between nuclear and non-nuclear DNA.

(b) State two places where non-nuclear genes may be found.

(c) 'Non-nuclear DNA is only inherited from our mothers.' Explain why this statement is true for humans.

Exam questions

Section A

34 In tomato plants the allele responsible for purple stem (P) is dominant to that for green stem (p) and the allele for cut leaf (C) is dominant to the allele for potato type leaf (c). A plant with a purple stem and cut leaves was crossed with a plant with a green stem and potato type leaves. A total of 448 seeds was obtained. When the seeds were germinated four types of progeny resulted and they had the following phenotypes:

110 purple stem and cut leaves
115 green stem and potato type leaves
114 purple stem and potato type leaves
109 green stem and cut leaves

(a) What were the genotypes of the tomato plants that gave rise to these progeny?

(b) Do the progeny of this cross illustrate the Law of Independent Assortment? Explain your answer.

(2004 HL Q 3)

35 In each of the following cases read the information provided and then, **from the list below**, choose the correct percentage chance of obtaining the indicated offspring in each case.

0%   10%   25%   50%   75%   100%

(a) In the fruit fly *Drosophila* the allele for full wing is dominant to the allele for vestigial wing. One parent was homozygous in respect of full wing and the other parent was heterozygous. What is the % chance of obtaining offspring with **full** wing?   % = ☐

(b) In roses there is incomplete dominance between the allele governing red petals and the allele governing white petals. Heterozygous individuals have pink petals. A plant with pink petals was crossed with a plant with white petals. What is the % chance of obtaining offspring with **white** petals? % = ☐

(c) In Dalmatian dogs the allele for brown spots is recessive to the allele for black spots. The two parents were heterozygous in respect of spot colour. What is the % chance of obtaining offspring with **black** spots?   % = ☐

(d) Red hair in humans is recessive to all other hair colours. A red-haired woman and a black-haired man, whose own father was red-haired, started a family. What is the % chance of obtaining offspring with **red** hair?   % = ☐

(2010 HL Q 2)

36 In pea plants the allele for tall (T) is dominant over the allele for dwarf (t).
A heterozygous tall plant is crossed with a dwarf plant.
Complete the blank spaces below.
Genotypes of parents   (Tt)   X   (tt)
(a) Possible gametes   ( )( ) X   ( )
(b) Genotypes of offspring   ( )   ( )
(c) Phenotypes of offspring ____   ____

(2012 OL Q 6)

Section C

37 (a) Explain the following terms that are used in genetics: dominance, genotype, phenotype.

(b) In Aberdeen Angus cattle, the polled (P) condition (absence of horns) is dominant to the horned (p) condition. A heterozygous polled bull was crossed with a horned cow. Use the following layout in your answer book to find the possible genotypes and phenotypes of the calves that may result from this cross.

	Heterozygous polled bull	Horned cow
Genotypes of parents	....	....
Gametes	....	....
Genotypes of calves	....	....
Phenotypes of calves	....	....

(2004 OL Q 12)

38 (b) The diagram shows some of the chromosomes in the nucleus of a cell taken from a small mammal.

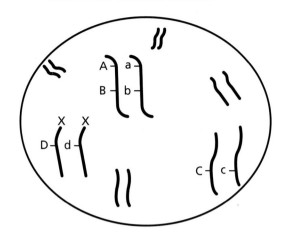

(i) What is the sex of this individual?
(ii) How many loci are marked in the diagram?
(iii) "A is linked to B but not to C." Is this statement correct? Explain your answer.
(iv) Is D linked to d? Explain your answer.
(v) What term is used to describe the allele pair Dd?
(vi) Draw a diagram, similar to the one above, but in which A, B and C are homozygous and the cell is taken from an individual of the opposite sex.

(2006 HL Q 12)

39 (a) (i) What is a chromosome?
(ii) The <u>haploid number</u> of chromosomes is found in the human egg and sperm. Explain the underlined term.

(b) Hair colour in humans is genetically controlled. The <u>allele</u> for brown hair (B) is <u>dominant</u> to the allele for red hair (b).
(i) Explain the underlined terms.
(ii) For hair colour Seán is heterozygous (Bb) and Máire is homozygous (bb).
   1. What colour is Seán's hair?
   2. What colour is Máire's hair?
(iii) Use a Punnett square or other means to show the following:
   1. the genotypes of all the gametes that Seán and Máire can produce.
   2. the genotypes of the children that Seán and Máire may have.
(iv) What is the probability that one of their children may have red hair? (Give your answer as a ratio or a percentage.)

(2008 OL Q 11)

40 (a) Explain the following terms which are used in genetics: homozygous, recessive, phenotype.

(b) In the fruit fly, *Drosophila*, the allele for grey body (G) is dominant to the allele for ebony body (g) and the allele for long wings (L) is dominant to the allele for vestigial wings (l). These two pairs of alleles are located on different chromosome pairs.

   (i) Determine all the possible genotypes and phenotypes of the progeny of the following cross: grey body, long wings (heterozygous for both) X ebony body, vestigial wings.

   (ii) What is the significance of the fact that the two allele pairs are located on different chromosome pairs?

(c) Haemophilia in humans is governed by a sex-linked allele. The allele for normal blood clotting (N) is dominant to the allele for haemophilia (n).

   (i) What is meant by sex-linked?

   (ii) Determine the possible genotypes and phenotypes of the progeny of the following cross: haemophilic male X heterozygous normal female.

(2008 HL Q 11)

41 (b) In the sweet pea plant the texture and colour of the testa (seed coat) are governed by two pairs of alleles, which are not linked. The allele for smooth (S) is dominant to the allele for wrinkled (s) and the allele for yellow (Y) is dominant to the allele for green (y).

   (i) State the Law of Segregation **and** the Law of Independent Assortment.

   (ii) Using the above symbols, and taking particular care to differentiate between upper case and lower case letters:

   1. give the genotype of a pea plant that is homozygous in respect of seed texture and heterozygous in respect of seed colour.

   2. state the phenotype that will result from the genotype referred to in 1.

   (iii) What phenotype will be produced by the genotype SsYy? Give another genotype that will produce the same phenotype. Do not use a genotype that you have already given in response to part (ii) 1.

   (iv) If the allele for smooth were linked to the allele for green and the allele for wrinkled were linked to the allele for yellow, give the genotypes of the **two** gametes that parent SsYy would produce **in the greatest numbers**.

(2012 HL Q 10)

Previous examination questions

Ordinary level	Higher level
2004 Q 12a, b	2004 Q 3
2005 Q 13a	2005 Q 10b, c
2006 Q 11a, b	2006 Q 12b
2007 Q 4, 11c	2007 Q 5
2008 Q 11a, b	2008 Q 11
2009 Q 11a, b	2009 Q 10a, b
2010 Q 4, 11b	2010 Q 2, 10c
2011 Q 10a, b	2011 Q 13b, c
2012 Q 6	2012 Q 10b

Latest questions at www.edco.ie/lcbiologyplus/examhelp

Online test and assessment tracker

Scan the QR code and test yourself on chapter 16
www.edco.ie/lcbiologyplus

THE CELL

Learning objectives

- To show a knowledge of the diversity of life and to define 'species'
- To understand how sexual reproduction and mutations can be the source of variation
- To describe two agents that can increase mutation rates
- To define the term 'evolution'
- To describe the Theory of Natural Selection, giving one source of evidence.

Classification

There is a vast variety of living things on our planet. There is no way of counting, never mind studying, every single individual organism alive today.

Organisms are classified according to similarities in structure, function and development. These similarities exist because organisms are related to each other, having arisen from common ancestors by evolution. The basic unit of classification is the species.

Benefits of classification

- To simplify the study of organisms (it is far simpler to study the features of a group such as flowering plants, than to learn the details of every type of flowering plant, about 250 000 in total).
- To allow scientists to communicate with each other.

17.1 *A horse and a mule: a mule is the offspring of a male donkey and a female horse. Horses and donkeys are different species as their offspring, the mule, is not able to reproduce*

Classification means placing objects into groups based on similar characteristics.

Taxonomy is the science of classifying organisms.

A **species** is a group of similar organisms that are capable of naturally interbreeding with each other to produce fertile offspring.

Species

All domestic (tame) dogs are members of the same species. All such dogs can interbreed with each other to produce offspring, which themselves can reproduce.

Domestic cats are members of a different species from dogs. Dogs and cats cannot naturally interbreed with each other. For the same reason, oak and ash trees are different species.

17.2 *A liger: the sterile offspring of a male lion and a female tiger*

So far, about 1.5 million species have been identified on Earth. Interestingly, insects alone make up about 750 000, or half, of all known species. Thousands of previously unidentified species are discovered every year. It is estimated that the total number of all species on Earth ranges between 5 and 100 million.

Variation within a species means that in a group of successfully interbreeding organisms the individual members show different characteristics.

Variation within species

All living humans are members of the same species. Despite their many similarities humans may differ in features such as hair colour, skin colour and height. In the same way, individual plants of the same species (such as roses) may differ in traits such as flower colour, leaf shape or size of thorns.

These differences mean that each individual organism (such as a person) is unique. The individual variations do not hinder the ability of the organisms to interbreed successfully.

There are two types of variation: acquired and inherited.

Acquired variation

Acquired variations are not inherited but are learned or developed during life.

Acquired variations are not genetically controlled. They are differences that form during life. Examples include the ability to walk, speak a language, ride a bicycle or use a computer.

17.3 *A father and son: tongue rolling is genetically inherited*

Inherited variation

Examples of inherited variations are blood groups, eye/ear/hair colour, attached or detached earlobes, freckles and ear shape.

Inherited variations are controlled by genes.

Causes of inherited variations

Inherited variations arise as a result of sexual reproduction and mutations.

Sexual reproduction as a cause of variation

Sexual reproduction is responsible for most of the variations that arise in each generation of offspring. Sexual reproduction causes genetic variation for three reasons.

1. Variations arise because of the independent assortment of chromosomes during meiosis. Human cells have 46 chromosomes. This means there are about 8 million different combinations of chromosomes available as a result of meiosis.

2. During meiosis, a process called crossing over takes place (details

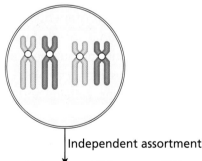

Independent assortment

Four different combinations of chromosomes may form from a cell with four chromosomes

17.4 *Variation due to independent assortment in a cell with only four chromosomes*

THE CELL

of crossing over are not required). This allows genes to be exchanged between chromosomes. This produces chromosomes that are a combination of the genes the mother and father inherited from their parents.

213

3. Finally, at fertilisation, owing to the random assortment of chromosomes in the egg and in the sperm, a vast range of variation is possible when a sperm and egg join.

Mutations

A mutation is a spontaneous (or sudden) change in the amount or structure of DNA.

Mutations can arise anywhere at random on a chromosome. This means that any gene, or group of genes, can be affected by mutations. However, cells contain enzymes that have a great ability to repair damage to DNA. This means that the number of mutations that survive is very low.

If a gene is altered it is very likely that the change in its sequence of bases will mean that the correct protein is no longer formed. The new version of a gene formed in this way by mutation is called a recessive allele.

Many mutations produce no change in the characteristics of a diploid organism. This is because the dominant allele on the second homologous chromosome can still produce the original protein.

Harmful mutations

However, many mutations are harmful. Mutations in somatic (non-reproductive) cells may not be harmful. This is because the gene that is altered may not be active in the particular body cell affected. For example, if a skin cell suffers a mutation in a gene for saliva production, the cell will not suffer because saliva is not produced by skin cells.

Some somatic mutations are harmful. If the mutation causes an increase in the rate of mitosis, then a tumour may result.

Mutations in a gamete are often very serious. This is because the mutation may be inherited by the zygote and passed on to *all* the cells in the developing child. This may give rise to genetic defects in the child or even in the following generation.

Beneficial mutations

A very small number of mutations may be beneficial in that they produce an even better protein than the original one. These mutations are a source of evolution.

Causes of mutations

Mutagens are agents that cause mutations.

Mutations may arise naturally when DNA fails to produce exact copies of itself or when it fails to repair properly. Mutations such as these are called **spontaneous mutations**.

If mutagens are present, the spontaneous rate of mutation is speeded up. A mutagen that causes cancer is called a carcinogen. The main categories of mutagens are:

- Ionizing radiation such as x-rays, gamma rays, cosmic rays and ultraviolet (UV) radiation
- Chemicals such as formaldehyde, tobacco smoke, dioxins, caffeine and many drugs, preservatives and pesticides
- Some viruses.

To protect against mutation when being x-rayed, a heavy lead shield is used to absorb stray x-rays.

A high sun protection factor cream should be used when sunbathing. This may reduce the risk of developing skin cancer in later life as a result of exposure to UV rays from the Sun.

Tobacco smoke contains about 400 harmful substances, which are responsible for 90% of lung cancer deaths (they also cause many other diseases). Even passive smokers have a 35% increased risk of developing lung cancer.

17.5 *A patient wearing a lead apron for protection against x-rays*

THE CELL

Types of mutation

Gene (or point) mutations

Very often gene mutations are caused by changes in a single pair of bases. The altered gene is called an allele. Examples of gene mutations are:

- Cystic fibrosis (the inability to remove mucus from the lungs)
- Haemophilia (the inability to form proper blood clots)
- Albinism (lack of the skin pigment melanin)
- Cancers
- Sickle-cell anaemia.

A gene (or point) mutation is a change in a single gene.

Sickle-cell anaemia as an example of a gene mutation

Sickle-cell anaemia is an inherited blood disorder caused by a mutation in the haemoglobin gene. The mutated gene forms a recessive allele.

A single copy of this mutation is found in about 10% of black Africans (who are healthy), but up to 1% have a double copy (i.e. they are homozygous recessive) and suffer from the disorder. It is also fairly common in people born near the Mediterranean.

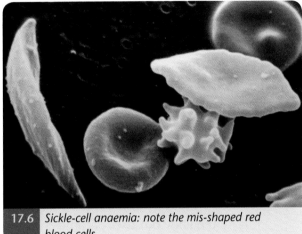

17.6 *Sickle-cell anaemia: note the mis-shaped red blood cells*

A person with two copies of the recessive allele produces haemoglobin with one incorrect amino acid. This results in an insoluble form of haemoglobin that causes the red blood cells to take on a curved or sickle shape. This causes the breakdown and clumping of red blood, which in turn leads to paleness, weakness, heart failure, severe pains, damage to the brain and other organs and, very often, death.

Apart from treating the symptoms of the disorder, the most common treatment involves total blood transfusions. Such a treatment is only temporary and is not easily available in many parts of Africa. There is some hope that bone marrow transplants may someday provide a permanent cure for sickle-cell anaemia.

Chromosome mutations

A **chromosome mutation** is a large change in the structure or number of one or more chromosomes.

Humans normally have 46 chromosomes in each somatic (non-reproductive) cell. If they gain a chromosome they will have 47, and if they lose a chromosome they will have 45 (i.e. 2n = 47 or 2n = 45).

Example of a chromosome mutation

Down syndrome (formerly called Down's syndrome) is an example of a chromosome mutation caused by the presence of one extra chromosome. The syndrome is usually caused by three number 21 chromosomes so that 2n = 47 (whereas usually a person has only two number 21 chromosomes).

This disorder often arises from a fault in meiosis where the egg has two number 21 chromosomes (instead of one), with the sperm adding one more. The presence of the single extra chromosome produces a range of physical and mental features associated with Down syndrome.

17.7 *Man with Down syndrome*

THE CELL

215

Down syndrome is more common in children born to older mothers. The exact reason for this is not yet known.

> Evolution is the way in which living things change genetically to produce new forms of life over long periods of time.

Evolution

Up until the early 1800s many people believed that species were fixed and unchanging. Since the start of the 19th century a number of theories of evolution have been suggested.

The most widely accepted modern theory of the mechanisms by which evolution takes place is based on the work of **Charles Darwin**.

Darwin initially studied theology but later became a naturalist. He formulated many of his ideas aboard a research ship, the HMS *Beagle*. Much of his work was done in the Galapagos Islands, which are located in the Pacific Ocean, west of South America.

Darwin's theory was first presented in 1858, largely due to pressure from another naturalist, **Alfred Russel Wallace**, who had come up with the same ideas as Darwin while living in Borneo.

In 1859 Darwin published these ideas in his book *On the Origin of Species by Means of Natural Selection*. Since then this theory has been known as 'natural selection'.

Although almost everyone accepts that evolution takes place (i.e. that living things have changed over many millions of years), not everyone agrees that these changes take place by natural selection. For instance, many people believe that the changes were due to some form of divine intervention.

It is important to realise that natural selection does not contradict mainstream religious beliefs and is widely accepted by most religions.

Mutation
(sudden change in DNA)

Gene (point) mutation
(a change in only one gene e.g. sickle cell anaemia)

Chromosome mutation
(many genes are changed e.g. Down syndrome)

17.8   *Summary of mutations*

17.9   *Charles Darwin (1809–1882)*

17.10   *Alfred Russel Wallace (1823–1913)*

Theory of natural selection

The theory of evolution by means of natural selection is based on three observations and two conclusions derived from these observations. These ideas are outlined below.

Observation 1: overbreeding

Darwin noted that organisms produce large numbers of offspring. For example, trees produce thousands of seeds and oysters lay millions of eggs.

Observation 2: population numbers remain constant

The number of organisms of the same species (called a population) in an area will continue to increase until the environment can no longer support any more. Then the number of organisms stays more or less the same.

Conclusion 1: there is a struggle for existence

If more offspring are formed and the environment cannot support all of them, then there must be competition for scarce resources. This means that animals compete for food, water, shelter and mates. Plants compete for space, light, water and minerals.

Observation 3: inherited variations occur in populations

The members of a population or species show genetic or inherited differences. These variations may arise from sexual reproduction, mutations or genetic engineering (variations arising due to the environment are not passed on, e.g. broken legs, learned abilities).

Conclusion 2: natural selection

Those organisms that have variations that enable them to adapt better to their environment will survive and reproduce. They will pass their variations on to the next generation. Organisms with unfavourable variations will not survive and they will not be able to pass on their variations to the next generation.

Natural selection is also called survival of the fittest, but this expression is misleading. Natural selection is not about fitness in terms of physical or mental abilities. Instead, it relates to the suitability of a species (or organism) to its environment. The essence of natural selection is how well adapted organisms are to their environment.

> **Natural selection** is the process by which those organisms with genetically controlled characteristics that allow them to be well adapted to their environments will survive and reproduce to pass on their genes to following generations.

Speciation

> **Speciation** is the production of new species as a result of evolution.

If organisms are created that can obtain more food, resist disease or produce more offspring, then they will be 'selected' by nature. This means they may live longer and reproduce more often and so be allowed to pass on their genes.

In time, the accumulation of slight changes results in the formation of organisms that can no longer interbreed. A new species is said to have formed, and speciation is said to have occurred.

The formation of new species does not mean that evolution ceases to take place. Evolution is a continual process and is taking place in all species (including humans) at present.

THE CELL

Evidence for evolution

Syllabus Evidence in support of evolution comes from three main areas:
- The study of fossils
- Comparative anatomy (comparing structures in different organisms)
- The study of embryos.

The syllabus requires evidence from only **one** of these sources.

The rest of this chapter will outline how fossil evidence may be used to indicate evolution (particularly in relation to the height of horses).

The study of fossils

One of the best sources of evidence for evolution is **palaeontology** (the study of fossils).

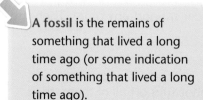

A fossil is the remains of something that lived a long time ago (or some indication of something that lived a long time ago).

17.11 *A 30-million-year-old fossil fly in amber (solidified tree resin)*

Examples of fossils include entire organisms, shells, bones, teeth, seeds, pollen grains, leaf prints, footprints and even the remains of faeces.

Fossil evidence for evolution

The information outlined below indicates that organisms have changed over time. It does not prove that these changes were due to natural selection.

- **Fossils can be aged.** This can be carried out by reference to the depth at which they are found in a rock or soil formation, or by measuring the amount of radioactive decay. This allows fossils to be compared according to a timescale.

- **Fossils show changes when compared with modern organisms.** These changes can be related to the time difference between when the fossilised organisms existed and the present.
  - Some fossilised organisms no longer occur as living organisms (they are extinct, e.g. the dodo and dinosaurs).
  - In other cases, there is no fossil record of modern species. This could be due to the modern organism being recently formed and therefore having no fossil record.

17.12 *Dinosaur footprint: 120 million years old*

- **The more modern fossils show increased complexity.**
- **Very often the fossil evidence can be linked to environmental change,** i.e. organisms had new environments to which they had to adapt.
  For example, 65 million years ago dinosaurs and many plants became extinct.
  At this time a layer of dust (rock) containing the element iridium was laid down.
  Iridium is rare on Earth but common in meteorites.

This suggests there may have been a huge meteorite impact, creating large amounts of dust. The dust is thought to have reduced the amount of heat and light entering the Earth's atmosphere from the Sun. This may have resulted in the sudden, mass extinction of plants and animals.

Evolution of the horse

The fossil record of the modern horse is very well documented. It covers a time span of about 60 million years and involves many hundreds of species, most of which are now extinct.

There are many trends to be seen in the evolution of modern horses. The following account deals with one change: the height of the animal.

- The ancestor of the modern horse developed about 60 million years ago. These animals were about the size of a fox (0.4 m high).
- Fossils from about 30 million years ago show that the ancestors of the horse were larger (about the size of a German shepherd, 0.6 m high).

- Fossils from 15 million years ago show the existence of creatures that were the size of a Great Dane (1 m high).
- The modern horse first evolved about 1 million years ago. Modern horses are normally about 1.6 m high.

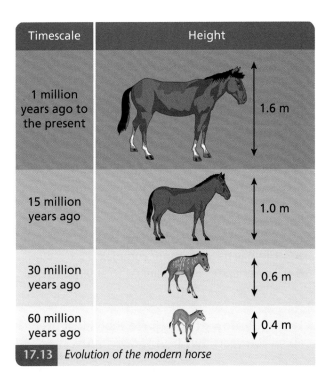

Timescale	Height	
1 million years ago to the present		1.6 m
15 million years ago		1.0 m
30 million years ago		0.6 m
60 million years ago		0.4 m

17.13 *Evolution of the modern horse*

17.14 *Artist's impression of the first horse, 60 million years ago*

THE CELL

Summary

Classification means placing organisms into similar groups.

Classification is necessary in order to:
- Simplify the study of organisms
- Allow scientific communication.

Taxonomy is the study of classification.

A **species** is a group of organisms capable of interbreeding naturally to produce fertile offspring.
- The members of a species, although similar in some respects, may show many differences.

Variation means that the members of a species show different characteristics.
- Acquired variation is learned during life.
- Inherited variation is caused by genes.

Inherited variations are caused by sexual reproduction and by mutations.

Sexual reproduction causes genetic variation due to:
- The way in which the chromosomes enter into gametes at meiosis
- Crossing over, which happens during meiosis

- The way in which sperm and eggs with many combinations of chromosomes may combine at fertilisation.

A **mutation** is a change in the amount or structure of DNA.

Mutations may produce:
- New alleles
- Beneficial phenotypes
- No noticeable effect (i.e. no phenotype change)
- Genetic defects in the offspring.

Mutations in a gamete are more serious than mutations in a somatic cell.

Mutations may be:
- Spontaneous (i.e. arise naturally)
- Caused by mutagens.

Mutagens include some types of radiation, some chemicals and some viruses.

A gene (or point) mutation is a tiny change in a single gene (often it involves only a single incorrect base).
- Sickle-cell anaemia is caused by a gene mutation.

Chromosome mutations are larger changes in the structure or number of one or more chromosomes.
- Down syndrome is caused by three number 21 chromosomes.

Evolution is the way in which genetic changes produce different types of organisms over long periods of time.

Darwin's (and Wallace's) theory of natural selection attempts to explain the mechanism by which evolution occurs. The theory of natural selection states:
- **Observation 1:** Organisms overbreed.
- **Observation 2:** Population numbers tend to remain static.
- **Conclusion 1:** Not all organisms in a population can survive, so there is a struggle for existence.
- **Observation 3:** Inherited variations arise in a population.
- **Conclusion 2:** Nature selects those organisms most suited (or best adapted) to their environment.

Evolution leads to the formation of new species (called speciation).

Fossils provide evidence for evolution.

Palaeontology is the study of fossils.

A **fossil** is the remains of an ancient organism.

Fossils can be formed as: entire organisms, preserved parts, seeds, pollen grains, imprints.

Fossil evidence indicates:
- Life has changed over time
- Life has become more complex
- The changes can be linked to environmental change.

The evolution of the horse shows that over 60 million years they have grown in size.

Revision questions

1 Explain what is meant by:
   (a) Classification
   (b) Taxonomy.

2 (a) What is a species?
   (b) Name two animal and two plant species.
   (c) Why are lions and tigers considered to be different species?

3 The members of a species show variations.
   (a) Name three variations that are visible in
      (i) Humans (ii) A named plant.
   (b) Why are all humans considered to be in the same species?

4 Pick out the four pairs of organisms in the following list that belong to the same species: house fly, giraffe, greyhound, black cat, zebra, horse chestnut tree, long-eared hamster, tiger, red tulip, guinea pig, ash tree, long-haired hamster, tortoiseshell cat, cheetah, yellow tulip, moth, highland terrier.

5 (a) What is meant by biological variation?
   (b) Distinguish, giving two examples in each case, between acquired and inherited variation.

6 Name two causes of inherited variation.

7 (a) What is a mutation?
(b) Explain why many mutations may not be serious.
(c) What are mutagens?
(d) Name two types of mutagen.
(e) Why should sun creams with a high protection factor be used during sunbathing?

8 Ozone is a gas that absorbs ultraviolet radiation in the atmosphere.
(a) Why does a reduction in the amount of ozone in the atmosphere represent a threat to human life?
(b) What are the likely consequences of depleting ozone levels on the rate of evolution?

9 (a) Distinguish between gene and chromosomal mutations.
(b) Give one example from each of the categories of mutations named in part (a) and give details of the effects of the named condition.

10 (a) What is evolution?
(b) Name the two scientists who first proposed the theory of evolution by natural selection.

11 A population of rabbits living on an island experience a struggle for existence.
(a) What two observations did Darwin make to suggest a reason for such a struggle?
(b) Suggest four resources for which the rabbits might struggle.

12 (a) What is a fossil?
(b) Give four examples of different types of fossil that have been discovered.
(c) State two methods used to date fossils.

13 Explain three ways in which the theory of evolution is supported by the study of fossils.

14 Outline any way in which fossils show how the modern horse has evolved.

15 State the significance of each of the following in the theory of evolution by natural selection.
(a) Organisms produce more offspring than their environment can support.
(b) Organisms show genetically controlled variations.
(c) A variation that does not improve the organism's ability to reproduce is of no value in terms of evolution.
(d) Organisms that reproduce asexually (using only mitosis) tend to evolve more slowly.

Exam questions

Section A

16 (a)

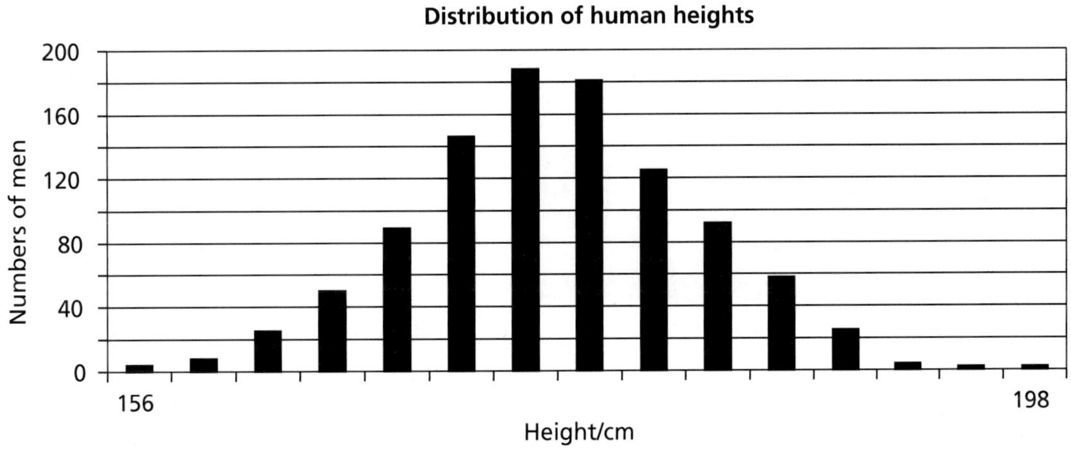

The diagram above shows the distribution of heights in a group of men between the ages of 18 and 23.
(i) What term is used by biologists to describe differences within a population with respect to features such as height?
(ii) State two factors that could be responsible for the differences shown.
(iii) Would you expect a similar distribution if the students were weighed instead of being measured for height? Explain your answer.
(iv) What is a mutation?
(v) State one cause of mutation.

(b) Give an example of a condition, found in the human population, that results from a mutation.

(2004 HL Q 2)

17 (a) In genetics, what is meant by the term *variation*?

(b) Variation can result from mutation. Name **one** other cause of variation.

(c) Name **two** types of mutation.

(d) Name **two** agents responsible for increased rates of mutation.

(e) Briefly explain the significance of mutation in relation to natural selection.

(2012 HL Q 6)

Section C

18 (c) (i) Explain the term *species*.

(ii) Within a species a considerable degree of variation is usually seen.

   1. What is meant by variation?

   2. State **two** causes of variation.

(iii) What is the significance of inherited variation in the evolution of species?

(iv) State **two** types of evidence used to support the theory of evolution. [Note that the examiners required only one source of evidence.]

(2009 HL Q 10)

19 (b) Read the paragraph and answer the questions that follow.

The rabbit in the photograph has no pigment in its skin, fur or eyes. This is due to an inherited condition known as albinism. Such animals are unable to produce melanin, a protein pigment that gives colour to the skin, eyes, fur or hair. This condition makes an animal more likely to be preyed upon.

Albinism is caused by genetic mutation. The gene that causes albinism (lack of pigment) is a recessive gene. If an animal has one gene for albinism and one gene for pigmentation, it will have enough genetic information to make pigment and the animal will not have this disorder. However, if both genes are recessive the result is albinism. At least 300 species of animal have albino individuals e.g. rabbits, turtles, squirrels, deer and frogs.

(i) What are the main characteristics of albinism?

(ii) What is meant by the term *recessive* gene?

(iii) What is a mutation?

(iv) Mutations can lead to variation in organisms. Variations that make an organism better adapted to its environment can lead to evolution.

   1. What is meant by *evolution*?

   2. Name **one** of the scientists who first explained how evolution occurs by natural selection.

   3. Give **one** source of evidence for evolution.

(v) People with albinism should always apply a high-factor sunscreen when going outdoors and must avoid strong sunshine. Suggest a reason for these precautions.

(2012 OL Q 11)

Previous examination questions

Ordinary level	Higher level
2005 Q 13c	2004 Q 2
2008 Q 11c	2006 Q 12a, c
2009 Q 3	2009 Q 10c
2012 Q11b	2011 Q 13a
	2012 Q 6

Latest questions at www.edco.ie/lcbiologyplus/examhelp

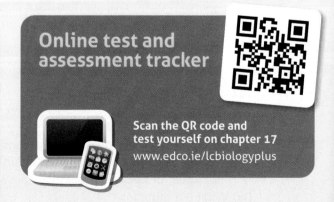

Online test and assessment tracker

Scan the QR code and test yourself on chapter 17
www.edco.ie/lcbiologyplus

Learning objectives

- To define genetic engineering
- To explain the process of genetic engineering, including isolation, cutting, transformation (ligation), introduction of base sequence changes and expression
- To describe three applications of genetic engineering, one in a plant, one in an animal and one in a micro-organism.

> Genetic engineering is the artificial manipulation or alteration of genes.

Introduction

The process of genetic engineering normally involves cutting a small section of DNA (usually containing a single gene called the target gene) from one organism and inserting it into the DNA of a second organism. In this respect it is really a 'cut and paste' process.

The altered DNA is called **recombinant DNA** because it recombines after the small section of DNA is inserted into it. The recombinant DNA is placed back into an organism.

18.1 *A genetically engineered organism: it is half sheep and half goat*

The organism with the altered DNA is called a genetically modified organism (GMO). If this organism reproduces asexually, the altered DNA is also reproduced, so that all of the offspring get a copy of the recombinant DNA containing the target gene.

The organism with the altered DNA produces the substance for which the target gene codes, given the correct nutrients and conditions.

Alternative names for genetic engineering

Genetic engineering is known by a number of other names. These include genetic manipulation, genetic modification, recombinant DNA technology, genetic splicing ('to splice' means to join two overlapping strands together) and gene cloning.

Gene cloning refers to the idea that many identical copies (clones) of the target gene are formed when the organism reproduces. Genetic engineering is the basis for most of the developments in the area of biotechnology.

Genetic engineering breaks the species barrier

Genetic engineering means that DNA from different species can be joined together. This often results in combinations of DNA that would never be possible in nature.

18.2 *A transgenic mouse: the mouse has a jellyfish gene that causes it to glow (the glow gene can also be added to cancer cells to detect their presence in an organism)*

This is because the two organisms would be prevented from reproducing together as they are from different species. For this reason, genetic engineering is not a natural process.

Examples of the cross-species transfer of genes are:

- Human genes can be inserted into bacteria
- Bacterial genes can be inserted into plants
- Human genes can be inserted into other animals.

Substances used in genetic engineering

Certain tools and materials are needed in order to cut and paste pieces of paper. These include the original document, the new material that is to be pasted on to the original document, scissors and some glue or paste.

In much the same way, genetic engineering requires the following materials and tools:

- **A source of DNA.** This is the DNA (or the gene) that is taken from one organism to be placed into the DNA of a second organism. The inserted or target DNA can be thought of as 'foreign' DNA.
- **A cloning vector.** A cloning vector is a special kind of DNA that can accept foreign DNA and replicate (reproduce exactly) itself and the foreign DNA. The most common cloning vector is a bacterial plasmid. This is a small loop of DNA found in bacteria (in addition to the larger loop of DNA that acts as a bacterial chromosome).

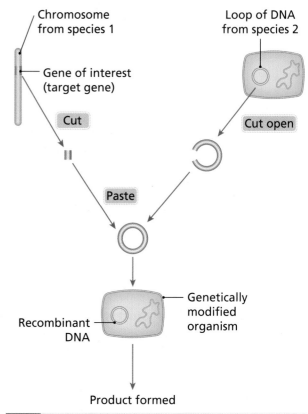

18.3 *Genetic engineering: a cut-and-paste process*

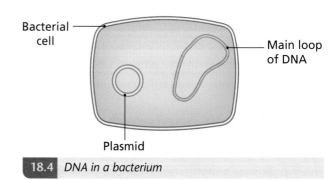

18.4 *DNA in a bacterium*

- **Restriction enzymes.** These are enzymes that cut DNA at specific places. They act as the genetic 'scissors'.
- **DNA ligase.** DNA ligase is an enzyme that is used to combine the foreign DNA with the plasmid DNA. In this way DNA ligase acts as the genetic 'glue' or 'paste'.

Restriction enzymes

Restriction enzymes will cut DNA only at particular sites. Each restriction enzyme is specific to a particular sequence of DNA bases and will only recognise that specific sequence, cutting the DNA at those bases only. For example, one restriction enzyme will cut DNA whenever the base sequence GAATTC arises.

When DNA from two different organisms is cut using the same restriction enzyme, the cut ends from both sources will be complementary. If the cut sections are mixed together, they will form base pairs and combine to produce recombinant DNA.

DNA ligase

DNA ligase is an enzyme that is used to stick DNA molecules from different sources firmly together. In this case it acts as an anabolic enzyme. DNA ligase will only work if the DNA from the two sources has been cut with the same restriction enzyme. In this case, the ends of the cut DNA will be complementary to each other.

The process of genetic engineering

Genetic engineering is used in a vast and rapidly growing number of applications. The techniques used in most of these applications include the six steps outlined in the following sections. The examples will refer to a human gene being inserted into a bacterium. The human gene is the target gene.

Isolation

> **Isolation** is the removal of the chromosome (containing the target gene) from the human cell and the plasmid DNA from the bacterium.

This is carried out in a similar manner to the way in which DNA is isolated from plant tissue (see Activity 15, page 183).

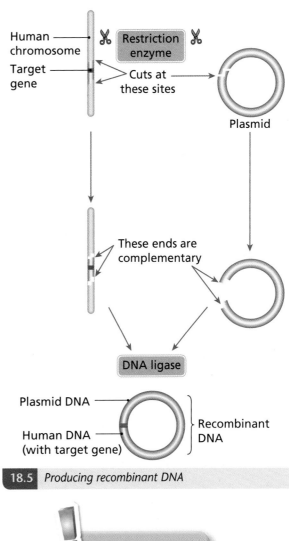

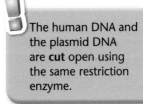

18.5 *Producing recombinant DNA*

> ! The human DNA and the plasmid DNA are **cut** open using the same restriction enzyme.

Cutting

Normally the plasmid will be cut open at a single site. The human DNA (chromosome) will be cut into many sections. Only one of these sections will contain the target gene.

Diagram 18.5 shows a single plasmid and a single chromosome being cut. In reality large numbers each are cut at this stage.

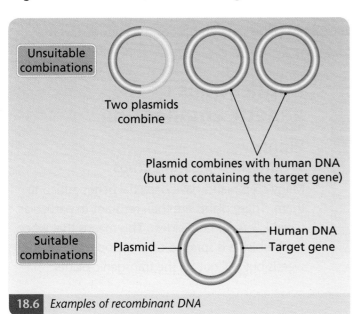

18.6 *Examples of recombinant DNA*

Ligation

The cut plasmids are mixed with the human DNA sections. This allows the cut ends to combine. The intention is that the cut ends of the plasmid should combine (by base pairing) with the complementary ends of the human DNA that contains the target gene. This happens, but many other unsuitable combinations also form. For example,

> **Ligation** is the joining of two sections of DNA to form a single strand.

THE CELL

the plasmids may stick to each other, a plasmid may stick to several human DNA sections in a row, or a plasmid may stick to a section of human DNA that does not carry the target gene (see diagram 18.6).

Splicing is the joining of overlapping sections together. Ligation is the joining of the overlapping cut ends of the DNA sections. Ligation is also called DNA splicing.

DNA ligase is used to form the bonds within the recombinant DNA (i.e. between the plasmid DNA and the human DNA). In this way the target gene becomes part of the plasmid DNA.

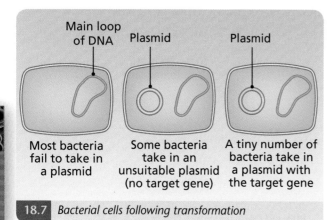

Most bacteria fail to take in a plasmid

Some bacteria take in an unsuitable plasmid (no target gene)

A tiny number of bacteria take in a plasmid with the target gene

18.7 *Bacterial cells following transformation*

Transformation

Transformation is the uptake of DNA into a cell.

The bacteria are treated in such a way that they can take in plasmids (composed of recombinant DNA) from a surrounding solution.

The vast majority (up to 99%) of the bacterial cells normally fail to take up the plasmids or only take up a plasmid that does **not** contain the target gene. These bacteria will be of no further use because they do not contain the target gene. Special techniques are used to identify the small number of bacteria that have taken up a plasmid containing the target gene (i.e. the bacteria containing the recombinant DNA).

Cloning

Cloning is the production of identical copies of the bacterium (containing the target gene).

The bacteria containing the target gene are grown (or cloned) using a nutrient medium. As the bacteria reproduce, they produce copies of the plasmid with the target gene.

Expression

Expression is the formation of the product by the organism with the recombinant DNA.

Expression normally takes place in a bioreactor. Once the product has been formed (or expressed) in sufficient amounts, it has to be separated from the culture and the bacteria that produced it.

18.8 *Spraying weed-killer on herbicide-resistant soya plants*

Applications of genetic engineering

Plants
Weed-killer-resistant crops

Many crop plants have bacterial genes added to them. These plants are then resistant to particular weed-killers (or herbicides). This means that when the herbicide is sprayed on the crop it will kill the weeds but will not kill the transgenic plants.

18.9 *Transgenic sheep: these sheep produce a protein to treat emphysema*

Animals

Sheep produce a protein to treat emphysema

Some people have a faulty gene that means they cannot produce a protective protein in their lungs. This leads to the collapse of the alveoli, in a condition known as emphysema.

A working human gene for this protein (known as AAT) has been inserted into sheep DNA. The sheep can then produce the protein in their milk.

Syllabus You are required to know **three** applications: one involving a plant, one an animal and one a micro-organism.

Micro-organisms

Bacteria make insulin

One of the first genetically engineered proteins to be produced commercially was human insulin. This involved inserting the gene for human insulin into a bacterium (called *E. coli*). The bacterium then produced large quantities of insulin. This meant that people with diabetes (who have a shortage of insulin) could inject themselves with human insulin.

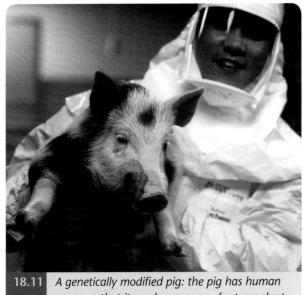

18.10 *Insulin-producing bacteria: insulin is made in the orange parts*

Prior to this development insulin was obtained from animals. This caused problems because many diabetics are allergic to animal insulin.

Ethical issues in genetic engineering

The use of genetically modified organisms provides undoubted benefits. Nevertheless, these techniques raise safety and ethical issues for people and the environment. These issues centre on concerns such as:

- The release of GMOs into the environment
- The use of GMOs as a food source
- The concern that animals will suffer as a result of being genetically modified
- The fear that humans (especially human zygotes) may be genetically modified.

18.11 *A genetically modified pig: the pig has human genes so that it produces organs for transplant into humans*

THE CELL

Summary

Genetic engineering is the artificial manipulation or alteration of genes.
- Genetic engineering allows genes from different species to be combined.

Genetically modified organisms (GMOs) are living things whose DNA has been altered artificially.

Transgenic organisms contain genes from another species.

To form recombinant DNA, the following are required:
- A source of DNA called the target gene
- A piece of DNA (called a cloning vector) that can accept the target gene and replicate
- A restriction enzyme to cut DNA at specific places
- The enzyme DNA ligase to cause the target gene to join with the DNA of the cloning vector and form recombinant DNA.

The **most common cloning vector** is a plasmid.
- A plasmid is a small circle of DNA found in bacteria.

Restriction enzymes cut DNA whenever they find a specific sequence of bases.
- Restriction enzymes cut DNA in such a way that the cut ends of the DNA will stick to each other.

The **process of genetic engineering** using bacteria involves the following steps:
- **Isolation** of a chromosome (containing the target gene) and a plasmid
- **Cutting** the chromosome and plasmids with a restriction enzyme
- **Ligation** (or joining) of the target gene into the plasmid
- **Transformation** of bacterial cells, i.e. getting bacterial cells to take up plasmids
- **Cloning** or reproducing identical copies of the new genetically engineered bacterium
- **Expression** or production of the required product by the bacteria with the recombinant DNA.

Applications of genetic engineering include:
- Inserting a bacterial gene for herbicide resistance into crop plants, so that the herbicide kills weeds but does not affect the plant
- Inserting a human gene for a lung-protecting protein into sheep DNA so that the sheep produce the protein in their milk
- Inserting the gene for human insulin into a bacterium, which then produces human insulin for use by diabetics.

Genetic engineering raises many **ethical** and **moral** questions regarding procedures that may be considered right or wrong.

Revision questions

1 Explain what is meant by the following terms:
   (a) Genetic engineering
   (b) Target gene
   (c) Recombinant DNA
   (d) Splicing
   (e) Transgenic.

2 Suggest one reason why genetic engineering is not a natural process.

3 Give one use for each of the following:
   (a) A cloning vector
   (b) A restriction enzyme
   (c) DNA ligase
   (d) A plasmid.

4 Explain the meaning of each of the following terms in relation to forming a genetically modified bacterium containing the gene for human growth hormone (HGH):
   (a) Isolation
   (b) Cutting
   (c) Ligation

   (d) Transformation
   (e) Expression.

5 Explain, with the aid of a diagram, why genetic engineering can be considered to be a 'cut-and-paste' process.

6 Give one example and state a benefit for each of the following:
   (a) Inserting a human gene into a bacterium
   (b) Inserting a bacterial gene into a plant
   (c) Inserting a human gene into an animal.

7 Human growth hormone (HGH) is produced in the pituitary gland. People who do not produce sufficient amounts of HGH do not grow properly. The gene for HGH can be extracted from a human chromosome and inserted into a loop of DNA in a bacterium, as shown in diagram 18.12. This procedure allows the hormone to be produced by bacteria using genetic engineering techniques.

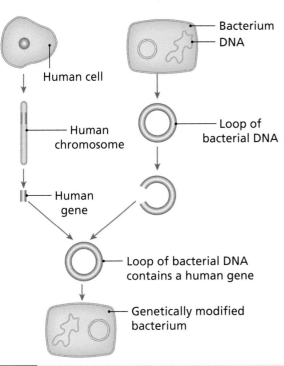

Human cell

Human chromosome

Human gene

Bacterium

DNA

Loop of bacterial DNA

Loop of bacterial DNA contains a human gene

Genetically modified bacterium

18.12

(a) What is a hormone?

(b) Where in the body is the pituitary gland located?

(c) What are chromosomes made of?

(d) What biomolecules are used to extract a gene from a chromosome?

(e) Explain why the same biomolecule must be used to extract the gene and to open the loop of DNA in the bacterium.

(f) What substances should be added to a bioreactor to enable bacteria to grow?

8 Choose which of the options (i), (ii), (iii) or (iv) represents the correct answer in each case below.

(a) Genetic engineering:
   (i) Is a natural process
   (ii) Only takes place in micro-organisms
   (iii) Happens when cells divide
   (iv) Involves combining DNA from different species.

(b) The most common cloning vector used in genetic engineering is:
   (i) RNA
   (ii) An enzyme
   (iii) A plasmid
   (iv) DNA ligase.

(c) Which of the following is not associated with genetic engineering?
   (i) Translation
   (ii) Transformation
   (iii) Cloning
   (iv) Expression.

(d) Genetically modified organisms:
   (i) Are always harmful
   (ii) Are always micro-organisms
   (iii) May be beneficial
   (iv) Arise naturally.

THE CELL

Exam questions

Section A

9 (a) What is *genetic engineering*?

(b) Name **three** processes involved in genetic engineering.

(c) Give an example of an application of genetic engineering in each of the following cases:
   1. A micro-organism
   2. An animal
   3. A plant

(2009 HL Q 6)

Section C

10 (a) (i) What is meant by genetic engineering?
   (ii) State **two** applications of genetic engineering, one involving a micro-organism and one involving a plant.

(2005 HL Q 10)

11 (c) (i) What is genetic engineering?
   (ii) Give **one** example of genetic engineering involving an animal and **one** example involving a plant.

(2006 OL Q 11)

Previous examination questions

Ordinary level	Higher level
2006 Q 11c	2005 Q 10a
	2009 Q 6
	2012 Q 10c

Latest questions at www.edco.ie/lcbiologyplus/examhelp

Online test and assessment tracker

Scan the QR code and test yourself on chapter 18
www.edco.ie/lcbiologyplus

Unit 3
The Organism

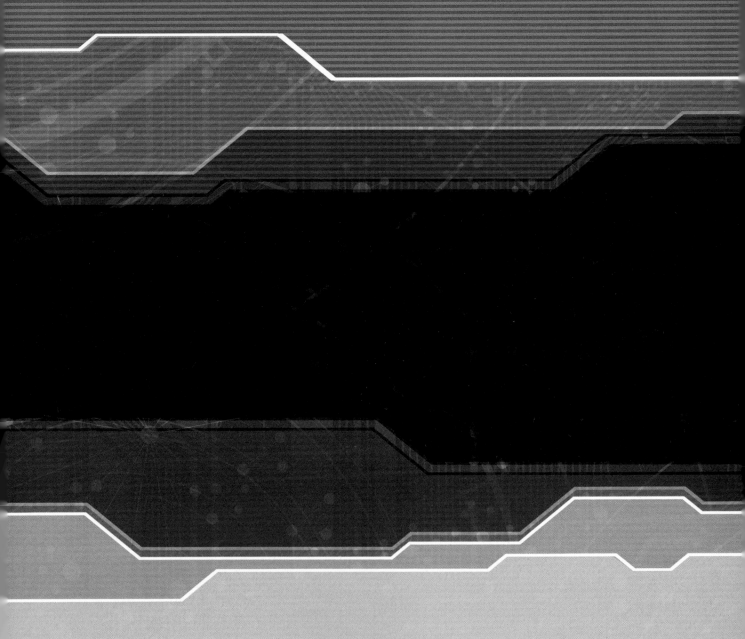

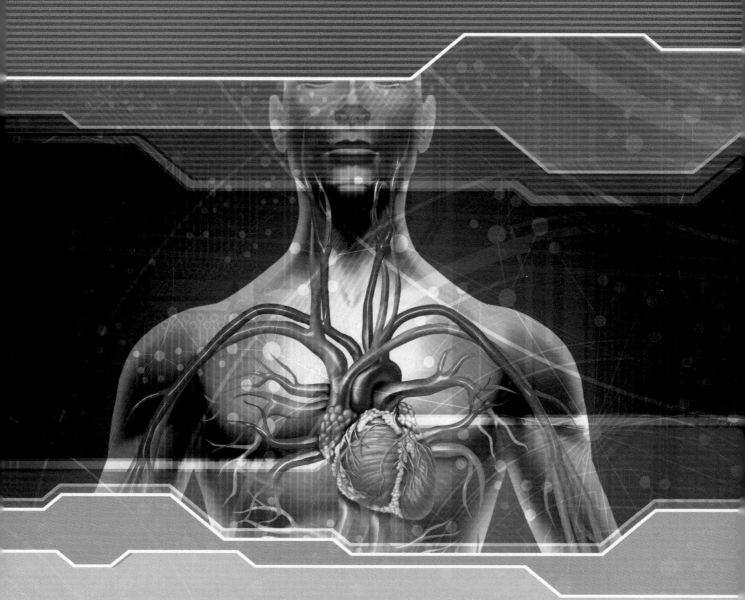

Chapter 19 The five kingdoms of life

Learning objective
- To describe the five-kingdom classification of living things: Monerans, Protists, Fungi, Plants and Animals.

Introduction

There is a need to classify the vast range of living things into different groups or categories. The original classification system was developed by the Greek philosopher and naturalist Aristotle around 350 BC. This system divided living things into two kingdoms: plants and animals. This division was later based mainly on the presence or absence of cell walls.

With the discovery of microscopic organisms, especially bacteria and fungi, the two-kingdom system was found to be increasingly unsatisfactory.

> **?** Viruses are not allocated to any of the five kingdoms because it is unclear whether or not they are living things. Viruses will be discussed in Chapter 38.

> **?** In 1969 American biologist Robert Whittaker proposed that life should be divided into five kingdoms.

In recent times the five-kingdom system of classification has gained widespread acceptance. The five kingdoms are: **Monera**, **Fungi**, **Protista**, Plantae **(plants)** and Animalia **(animals)**.

Each of these kingdoms is subdivided into many other categories, with each successive category containing organisms that are more and more alike. This is similar to the way in which the pupils in a school are classified into years, classes and individuals.

The final and most basic unit of biological classification is the species. The organisms in a species are similar enough to be able to interbreed successfully.

Monera (Prokaryotae)

The organisms in the Kingdom Monera are also called Prokaryotes. This kingdom includes about 10 000 identified species of bacteria.

It is thought that there may be up to four million species of bacteria on Earth. Bacteria were the first organisms on Earth (about 4000 million years ago) and were the only organisms for about 2000 million years.

Monerans are found everywhere on Earth. They are in the air, soil, water, animal bodies, acidic environments, alkaline environments, deserts and mountain tops. They are too small to be seen, but their numbers are absolutely colossal. They are by far the most numerous organisms on Earth.

> **?** There are more bacteria on the skin of one person than the total number of humans that have ever lived.

Although some bacteria cause disease, the vast majority are essential to life on Earth. One of their main roles is to decompose dead organisms. In this way they return minerals to the soil for use by other organisms.

We can get an idea of the importance of bacteria from the fact that if all the other four kingdoms of life were wiped out, bacteria could still survive. However, if bacteria were to become extinct, life on Earth would cease within about 30 years.

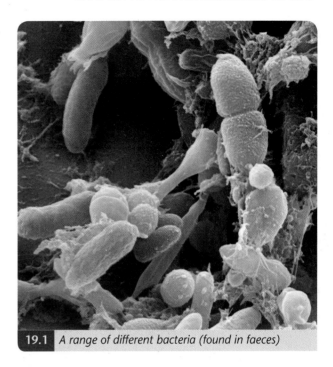

19.1 | *A range of different bacteria (found in faeces)*

Main features of monerans

- They do not have a membrane-enclosed nucleus, i.e. they do not possess a distinct nucleus
- They do not have membrane-enclosed organelles such as mitochondria or chloroplasts
- They are mainly small, microscopic and single-celled organisms
- They normally reproduce asexually

Fungi

More than 100 000 species of fungi have been identified, but it is thought that this represents only one-tenth of all the fungi on Earth. Examples of fungi include mushrooms, moulds, mildews and yeasts.

Fungi are essential for life on Earth because (like bacteria) they break down dead organisms and allow minerals to recycle.

Many fungi are of economic value. For example, some are edible, some produce antibiotics, and yeasts are used in baking and for producing alcohol. Some fungi cause diseases to plants, humans and other animals.

It is thought that fungi and animals evolved from a common ancestor about 700 million years ago. In many respects, fungi are more closely related to animals than to plants.

19.2 | *Fungus growing on a strawberry*

Main features of fungi

- They do not make their own food but get their nutrients by absorbing food from an outside source
- They are mainly multicellular
- They are composed of threads called hyphae, which combine to form a visible, fluffy mass called a mycelium
- Their cell (or hyphal) walls are made of a carbohydrate called chitin
- They reproduce by spores

THE ORGANISM

Protista (Protoctista)

The kingdom Protista is also called Protoctista. This kingdom contains about 60 000 species, including plant-like algae (both microscopic algae and plankton as well as larger, visible seaweeds), single-celled animal-like organisms such as *Amoeba* (see Chapter 22) and fungus-like slime moulds.

The first of these organisms evolved about 2000 million years ago. They were the ancestors of the fungi, plants and animals that evolved many millions of years later.

Protists are found almost anywhere water is present. For example, they occur in damp soil, decaying organic material, puddles, pools, ponds, lakes and oceans. In larger bodies of water they are often found on or in the mud at the bottom.

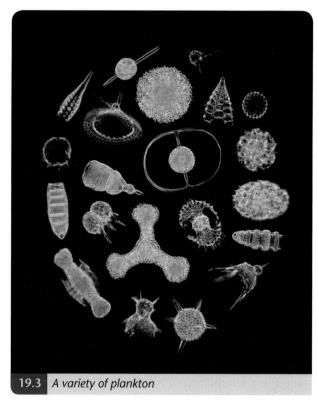

19.3 *A variety of plankton*

Plankton and larger algae account for more than half of all the photosynthesis that takes place on Earth.

The protists are a very varied group of organisms. In fact, they are so diverse that it is difficult to state the general features of the organisms in this kingdom.

Protists are often considered to be simple organisms that cannot be identified with any of the other four kingdoms.

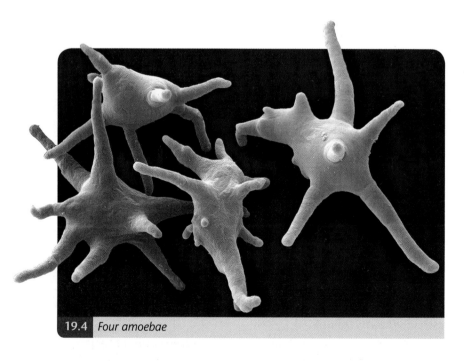

19.4 *Four amoebae*

Main features of protists

- They have a membrane-enclosed nucleus, i.e. a true nucleus
- They are mainly single-celled, but those that contain many cells are simple organisms (i.e. they do not form tissues)

Plants

It is thought that plants evolved from green algae about 500 million years ago. The evolution of plants allowed life to exist for the first time on land.

The major groups of plants are mosses, ferns and seed-producing plants. The seed-producing plants consist of non-flowering plants such as pine trees and flowering plants such as grasses, cereals, flowers and many trees.

Flowering plants comprise the greatest number of plant species (about 250 000), compared with about 30 000 species for all the other types combined.

The emergence of plants on land provided food for the animals that were to evolve soon after them on land.

19.5 *Wildflowers*

Main features of plants

- They are complex, multicellular organisms
- They are photosynthetic
- Their cell walls are made of cellulose
- Their cells often contain large vacuoles
- They are non-motile
- They reproduce asexually and sexually
- They protect the embryo for a time within the structure of the parent plant

Animals

The first animals evolved in the sea about 700 million years ago. Animals later evolved to live in fresh water, and eventually they emerged to live on land.

Animals range from simple sponges and jellyfish, through flatworms, roundworms and segmented worms, to snails, insects and animals with backbones (vertebrates) such as fish, birds and humans.

Trying to define an animal is not easy. There is such a variety of animal species that there is normally an exception to every general animal feature.

Main features of animals

- They are multicellular organisms that take in food (i.e. they do not make their own food)
- They do not have cell walls
- They have a nervous system (to allow fast responses)
- They have a muscular system (to allow movement)
- They normally reproduce sexually
- They have large eggs that cannot move by themselves (i.e. are non-motile)
- They have small sperm that can swim (i.e. are motile) by using a tail or flagellum (plural flagella)

19.6 *A bonobo: genetically the closest species to humans*

THE ORGANISM

235

Summary

Living things were originally divided into two kingdoms: plants and animals.

Life is now classified into the following five kingdoms:
- Monera (or Prokaryotes), Fungi, Protists (or Protoctists), Plants and Animals.

Monera include bacteria and their main features are:
- They lack a true nucleus and membrane-enclosed organelles
- They are microscopic and single-celled
- They reproduce asexually.

Fungi include mushrooms, moulds, mildews and yeasts and their features are:
- They absorb their food from outside
- They are composed of multicelled hyphae, which form mycelia
- They have walls made of chitin
- They reproduce by spores.

Protists include plankton, seaweeds, amoebae and slime moulds and their features are:

- They have a true nucleus (i.e. it is surrounded by a membrane)
- They are single-celled or simple multicelled organisms.

Plants include mosses, ferns and seed-producing plants (some without and some with flowers). Their features include:
- They are complex and multicellular
- They make their own food by photosynthesis
- They have cellulose cell walls
- Their cells have large vacuoles
- They do not move
- They reproduce asexually and sexually
- They protect the embryo for a short time.

Animals have most of the following features:
- They are multicellular and take in their food
- They have no cell walls
- They have nervous and muscular systems
- They reproduce sexually
- They have large non-motile eggs and small motile sperm.

Revision questions

1 (a) Name the kingdoms in the old two-kingdom system of classification.
   (b) What was the main basis for placing organisms in either of these kingdoms?
   (c) State one major problem associated with the old two-kingdom system.

2 (a) Name the five kingdoms.
   (b) Name the four kingdoms in which the organisms have a membrane around their nucleus.

3 Place each of the following organisms into its correct kingdom: (a) Mushroom (b) Frog (c) Daisy (d) Bacterium (e) Alga (f) *Amoeba* (g) Yeast (h) Pine tree (i) Tulip (j) Seaweed (k) Sponge.

4 With which kingdom is each of the following features associated?
   (a) Cellulose cell walls
   (b) Absence of a true nucleus
   (c) Reproduction by spores
   (d) Possessing a nervous system
   (e) Complex, photosynthetic organisms
   (f) Composed of hyphae
   (g) Lacking mitochondria.

Previous examination questions

Ordinary level	Higher level
n/a	n/a

[The questions asked on this chapter are usually small sections of questions relating to each individual kingdom.]

Latest questions at www.edco.ie/lcbiologyplus/examhelp

Online test and assessment tracker

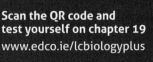

Scan the QR code and test yourself on chapter 19
www.edco.ie/lcbiologyplus

THE ORGANISM

Chapter 20 **Monera (Bacteria)**

Learning objectives

- To describe the distribution of bacteria and fungi in nature
- To describe the basic structure of bacterial cells, including plasmid DNA
- To describe the three main types of bacteria
- To describe the reproduction and nutrition of bacteria, and the factors affecting their growth
- To understand the economic importance of bacteria and give two examples of beneficial bacteria and two examples of harmful bacteria
- To define the terms 'pathogenic' and 'antibiotic' and describe the use and potential abuse of antibiotics in medicine
- **HIGHER ▶** To describe the prokaryotic nature of bacteria
- **HIGHER ▶** To explain the growth curves of micro-organisms and describe batch and continuous flow food processing.

Micro-organisms

The study of micro-organisms (also called microbes) is called microbiology.

Micro-organisms are so small that they can only be seen individually with the help of a microscope. They include bacteria, some fungi, and some protists such as plankton and slime moulds.

 Micro-organisms are small living things.

Distribution of bacteria and fungi in nature

Bacteria occupy a wide range of habitats in both terrestrial (land) and aquatic (water) environments. Fungi are mostly confined to terrestrial habitats.

Bacteria are found in salt water, fresh water, soil, dust, air, plants and animals. They can be found in extreme environments, such as hot springs where the temperatures are over 100°C, ponds of high salt concentration, sewage, swamps and human intestines. Some species can even exist in the human stomach at a pH of 2, and some are found in sulfur springs with a pH as low as 1.

Bacteria can survive under extreme pressures and temperatures, and may be found anywhere from deep-sea vents to mountain tops.

Size of bacteria

Bacteria are very small, single-celled organisms. They range in size from 0.1 to 10 μm in length. (There are 1 000 000 micrometres (μm) in a metre and 1000 micrometres in a millimetre. Micrometres were formerly called microns).

Up to 10 000 bacteria could fit across the full stop at the end of this sentence.

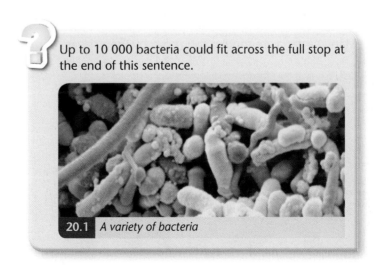

20.1 *A variety of bacteria*

THE ORGANISM

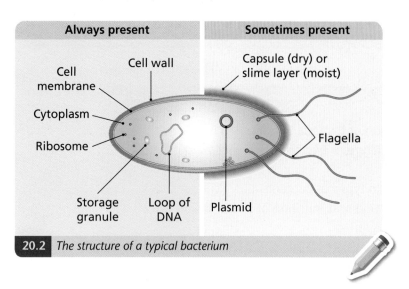

Always present	Sometimes present

Cell membrane
Cell wall
Cytoplasm
Ribosome
Storage granule
Loop of DNA
Plasmid
Capsule (dry) or slime layer (moist)
Flagella

20.2 *The structure of a typical bacterium*

Basic structure of a bacterial cell

Cell membrane

Bacteria are surrounded by a cell membrane, outside of which is a strong cell wall.

Cell wall

The cell wall is made of a complex mixture of sugars and protein. It prevents bacteria from swelling with water and bursting when they are in solutions that are less concentrated than their cytoplasm (which is normally the case).

Capsule

Outside the wall there may be further protection in the form of a semi-solid capsule or a more liquid slime layer.

Chromosome

Bacteria have one bacterial chromosome consisting of a circular strand of DNA (deoxyribonucleic acid), without any surrounding membrane. The chromosome does not contain any associated protein.

Plasmid

Most bacteria have one or more small DNA loops, called plasmids, in the cytoplasm. Plasmids contain genes that are responsible for bacterial resistance to antibiotics and are used in genetic engineering.

Bacterial genes are located on both the chromosome and the plasmid(s). This means that their genome (or genomic material) consists of a chromosome and one or more plasmids.

Cytoplasm

The material surrounding the chromosome is called the cytoplasm. It contains ribosomes, numerous storage granules (for food or waste), but no mitochondria or chloroplasts.

Flagella

Many bacteria are motile (can move by themselves) because they have one or more flagella.

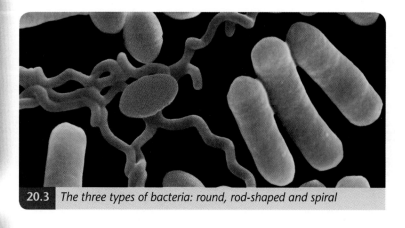

20.3 *The three types of bacteria: round, rod-shaped and spiral*

Bacterial types

Bacteria are classified into three groups depending on their shape: round, rod-shaped and spiral.

Although only a small number of bacteria cause disease, the different types of bacteria associated with some common diseases are shown in diagrams 20.5, 20.7 and 20.9.

THE ORGANISM

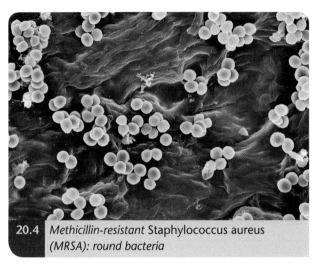

20.4 *Methicillin-resistant* Staphylococcus aureus *(MRSA): round bacteria*

Round

Round bacteria can be found in pairs, chains or clusters, as shown in diagram 20.5.

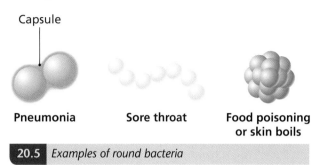

Capsule

Pneumonia | Sore throat | Food poisoning or skin boils

20.5 *Examples of round bacteria*

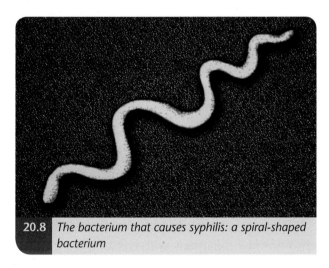

20.6 E. coli: *rod-shaped bacteria*

Rod

Rod-shaped bacteria may contain spores.

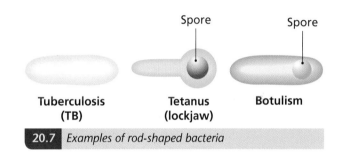

Spore | Spore

Tuberculosis (TB) | Tetanus (lockjaw) | Botulism

20.7 *Examples of rod-shaped bacteria*

 The bacterium responsible for botulism produces a toxin that inhibits muscular contraction. **Bo**tulinum **tox**in is better known as **Botox**.

Spiral

Spiral bacteria are called vibrio when they are shaped like a comma.

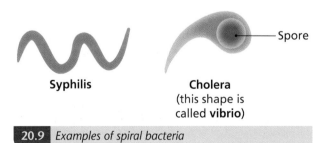

Spore

Syphilis | Cholera (this shape is called **vibrio**)

20.9 *Examples of spiral bacteria*

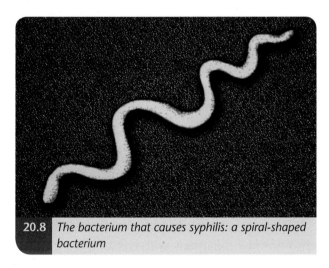

20.8 *The bacterium that causes syphilis: a spiral-shaped bacterium*

THE ORGANISM

Reproduction

Bacteria reproduce asexually, by a method called **binary fission**.

When a bacterial cell gets to a certain size the DNA strand (chromosome) copies itself. This means that there are now two identical strands of DNA. The cell elongates with a strand of DNA attached to each end. Finally, the cell splits into two similar-sized cells.

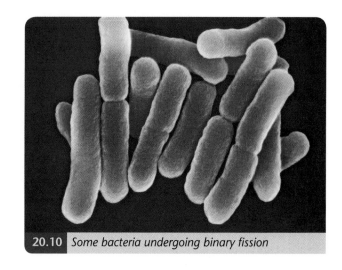

20.10 *Some bacteria undergoing binary fission*

Bacteria can divide every 20 minutes if conditions are suitable. This means a single bacterium could produce over a million bacteria in 7 hours. This is why bacterial infection can produce symptoms so quickly.

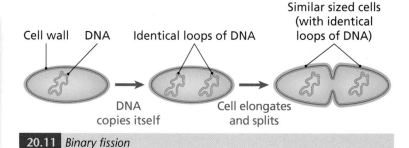

Cell wall   DNA   Identical loops of DNA   Similar sized cells (with identical loops of DNA)

DNA copies itself   Cell elongates and splits

20.11 *Binary fission*

Mutations in bacteria

Bacteria reproduce asexually, so their offspring are genetically identical. This means that they do not display the genetic variety that arises in plants and animals as a result of sexual reproduction. Although bacteria would be slow to evolve due to their method of reproduction, they can evolve very fast due to the speed at which new mutations can spread within the rapidly growing bacteria.

The short life cycles of bacteria mean that any new variation produced by a mutation can be passed on very quickly to a large number of bacteria. This is how bacteria evolve (and will continue to evolve) resistance to new antibiotics.

Endospores

Some bacteria can withstand harsh and unfavourable conditions by producing **endospores**.

Endospores form when the bacterial chromosome replicates, with one of the new strands becoming enclosed by a tough-walled endospore formed inside the parent cell. The parent cell then breaks down and the endospore can remain dormant for a long time.

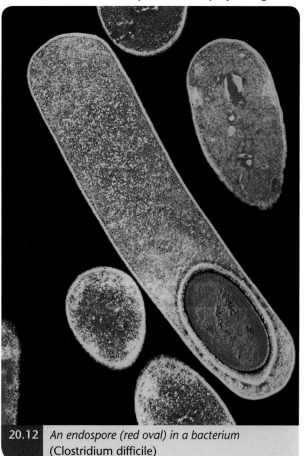

20.12 *An endospore (red oval) in a bacterium (Clostridium difficile)*

When conditions are suitable the endospore absorbs water and the tough wall breaks down. The chromosome is copied and a normal bacterium forms again. This bacterium can then reproduce by binary fission.

Endospores are very difficult to kill. They can withstand lack of food and water, high temperatures and most poisons. They are normally not even killed by boiling water. Some endospores can survive for hundreds of years.

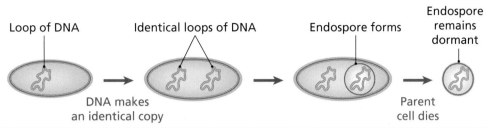

| Loop of DNA | Identical loops of DNA | Endospore forms | Endospore remains dormant |

DNA makes an identical copy

Parent cell dies

20.13 *Formation of an endospore*

Nutrition

Nutrition is the way an organism gets its food. Food supplies the energy and chemicals needed for survival and growth.

Bacteria get their food in four different ways. These four methods are grouped in pairs, under the headings **autotrophic** and **heterotrophic**.

Autotrophic

Autotrophic means an organism makes its own food.

The source of the energy needed to make food can be either sunlight (i.e. photosynthesis) or energy released from chemical reactions (i.e. chemosynthesis).

Photosynthetic bacteria often have chlorophyll on membranes within the cell (i.e. not in chloroplasts) and use the same type of light as plants.

Some photosynthetic bacteria have different pigments than plants and use mostly red light (almost invisible to humans). Some do not use water, but live on hydrogen sulfide gas (the gas found in stink bombs). These are called purple sulfur bacteria.

Chemosynthesis is the production of food using energy released from chemical reactions.

Chemosynthetic bacteria make food using energy from reactions involving ammonia, sulfur compounds and iron compounds. Examples of chemosynthetic bacteria are nitrifying bacteria in the nitrogen cycle.

Heterotrophic

Heterotrophic means an organism takes in food made by other organisms.

Most bacteria are heterotrophic. These bacteria secrete enzymes into their environment and absorb the digested food. They are divided into two groups: saprophytes and parasites.

Saprophytes are organisms that take in food from dead organic matter.

Saprophytes are also called decomposers because they cause the source of their food to decay. This allows mineral recycling. Examples are bacteria of decay in the soil.

Some saprophytic bacteria can even use petrol and oil products as a food source. These bacteria are used to clean up oil spills.

THE ORGANISM

Parasites are organisms that take in food from a live host and usually cause harm.

Examples of parasitic bacteria include those that cause diseases, such as pneumonia, shown in diagram 20.5.

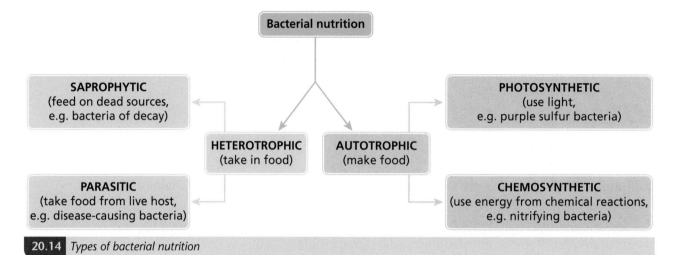

20.14 *Types of bacterial nutrition*

Factors affecting the growth of bacteria

The growth of bacteria is affected by five factors. Too much or too little of any one of these factors will slow down, or stop, the growth of the bacteria.

Factors that slow down a process when in short supply are called **limiting factors**. Most of these factors relate to the way in which bacterial enzymes work.

Bacterial growth factors include temperature, oxygen concentration, pH, external solute concentration and pressure.

Temperature

The rate of bacterial reactions is affected by temperature.

● Although most bacteria grow well at temperatures between 20°C and 30°C, some bacteria can tolerate much higher temperatures without their enzymes being denatured.

● Low temperatures slow down the rate of bacterial growth.

Genes from high-temperature bacteria are often added to bacteria that are used in biotechnology. This allows bioreactors to be run at higher temperatures, which results in faster bacterial metabolism and a higher rate of product formation.

Oxygen concentration

● **Aerobic bacteria require oxygen for respiration.** Most bacteria are aerobic. A low concentration of oxygen can often slow down bacterial growth, especially in liquids. Cultures in bioreactors often have oxygen bubbled through them and are stirred constantly to maintain high concentrations of oxygen. *Streptococcus* bacteria that cause sore throats are aerobic bacteria.

● **Anaerobic bacteria do not require oxygen to respire.** *Clostridium* is an anaerobic bacterium that causes tetanus or botulism.

- **Facultative anaerobes can respire with or without oxygen.** *Escherichia coli* are facultative anaerobes found in the intestines.
- **Obligate anaerobes can only respire in the absence of oxygen.** *Clostridium tetani* causes tetanus (or lockjaw) by infecting deep cuts, where there is a poor oxygen supply.

pH

Bacterial enzymes are designed to work at specific pH values. Bacterial enzymes placed in an unsuitable pH are denatured.
- Most bacteria grow at or near neutral pH (i.e. pH 7).
- However, some bacteria can tolerate very low (acidic) or very high (alkaline) pH values.

A bacterium called *Helicobacter* is found in the stomach of about half the Irish population. This bacterium can tolerate a pH of 2 and often causes stomach ulcers.

External solute concentration

The growth of bacteria is affected by the external solute concentration. This is because bacteria gain or lose water by osmosis.
- If the external solution has a higher solute (e.g. salt or sugar) concentration than the bacterial cytoplasm, water will move out of the bacteria. This dehydrates the bacteria and stops their enzymes from working. This is the principle behind the methods of food preservation such as salting and sugaring (as used for bacon and marmalade or jam).
- If the external solution has a lower solute (e.g. salt or sugar) concentration than the bacterial cytoplasm, water will enter the bacteria. The cell walls of bacteria can normally prevent bacterial cells from bursting in these circumstances. Most bacteria live in less concentrated solutions.

Pressure

- The growth of most bacteria is inhibited by high pressures. This is because the bacterial walls are not strong enough to withstand the high pressure.
- However, some bacteria can withstand very high pressures, such as those found in deep-sea vents.

The use of bacteria in biotechnology often requires that they are able to grow in pressurised bioreactors. To allow this to happen, pressure-tolerant bacteria are formed by genetic engineering techniques.

Economic importance of bacteria

Syllabus You are required to know **two** economic benefits and **two** economic disadvantages of bacteria.

Benefits

- Some bacteria are used to convert milk to products such as butter, yoghurt and cheese.
- Other bacteria are involved in the production of vinegar, silage, pickles and antibiotics.
- Genetically modified bacteria are used to make products such as insulin, drugs, enzymes, amino acids, vitamins, food flavourings, alcohols and a growing range of new substances.

THE ORGANISM

Disadvantages

- Bacteria cause food to decay. For example they cause milk to turn sour.
- Bacteria cause human, animal and plant diseases such as tuberculosis, whooping cough, septic throats, meningitis (one type), typhoid, cholera, diphtheria, dysentery, food poisoning, mastitis and brucellosis.

 Bacteria in the mouth convert sugars to acid, which then dissolves the outer layer of enamel on teeth, causing tooth decay.

Antibiotics

Pathogenic bacteria are bacteria that cause disease.

Antibiotics are chemicals produced by micro-organisms that stop the growth of, or kill, other micro-organisms without damaging human tissue.

Antibiotics are normally used to control bacterial infection, but they can treat some fungal diseases. Note that antibiotics do **not** affect viruses.

Originally antibiotics were isolated from fungi. Now antibiotics are mostly produced by genetically engineered bacteria.

Since the 1940s antibiotics have been widely used to treat bacterial infections. Many new antibiotics have been discovered, e.g. streptomycin, neomycin and tetracycline.

Antibiotic resistance

When an antibiotic is used to treat a bacterial infection, most of the bacteria are killed. However, antibiotic-resistant bacteria have developed (and continue to do so) by mutations.

These bacteria are not affected by the antibiotic that is being used. This means that new antibiotics must be produced continually to treat newly resistant bacteria.

If a person is taking antibiotics, then all the bacteria in that person are killed. If one antibiotic-resistant bacterium arises by mutation or enters that person's body, then this resistant bacterium has no competitors.

The gene for antibiotic resistance is usually located on a plasmid. Bacteria can pass copies of their plasmid onto other bacteria. In this way antibiotic resistance can pass from one bacterium to another.

The antibiotic penicillin was first isolated in 1928 from a fungus by Sir Alexander Fleming.

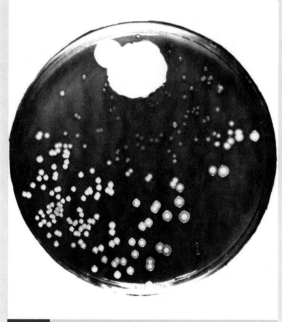

20.15 *The petri dish made famous by Alexander Fleming: penicillin fungus is at the top and the colonies of bacteria are at the bottom*

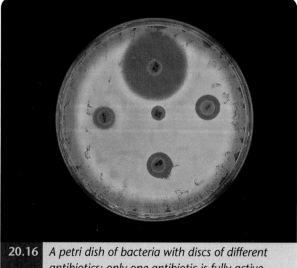

20.16 *A petri dish of bacteria with discs of different antibiotics: only one antibiotic is fully active against the bacteria*

THE ORGANISM

The antibiotic-resistant bacteria can reproduce very fast and take over a person's body. The person will then develop an infection for which the antibiotic is not an effective treatment.

In recent times bacterial strains have emerged that are resistant to almost all known antibiotics. These bacteria are said to be **multi-resistant**. Examples of such 'superbugs' are MRSA and *C. difficile*. These bacteria are becoming widespread, especially in hospitals.

Potential abuse of antibiotics in medicine

- The overuse of antibiotics in medicine results in the increased growth of antibiotic-resistant bacteria (because they have no competition). This happens when doctors prescribe antibiotics unnecessarily (e.g. for virus infections). In some countries it is even legal to buy antibiotics over the counter (without a doctor's prescription).
- The failure of some patients to complete their treatment of antibiotics allows the bacteria to survive and re-grow. This leads to the need for more antibiotics (along with the increased risk of the growth of resistant bacteria).

Bacteria are prokaryotes

HIGHER ▼

Bacteria belong to the Kingdom Monera. The organisms in this kingdom are also called prokaryotes. As outlined in Chapter 7, prokaryotes are organisms that lack a membrane-enclosed nucleus or membrane-enclosed cell organelles such as mitochondria and chloroplasts.

Apart from the Kingdom Monera, all other kingdoms contain eukaryotes (i.e. organisms whose nuclei and organelles are enclosed by membranes).

Growth curve

Binary fission results in a very fast increase in bacterial numbers. The growth curve for a typical population of bacteria growing on nutrient agar in a warm environment is shown in diagram 20.17. Note that the numbers of bacteria are represented on a logarithmic or exponential scale. This is to allow huge numbers of bacteria to be represented on the graph.

The graph can be divided into five phases, labelled A, B, C, D and E. These phases are explained as follows.

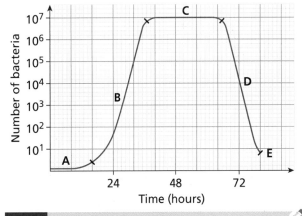

20.17 *Growth curve for bacteria*

Lag phase (A)

During the lag phase the bacterial numbers remain constant. The bacteria are adapting themselves to their new environment. For example, they may be producing new enzymes to digest the nutrients on which they are to grow.

Log phase (B)

In the log phase the bacterial numbers increase rapidly. The bacteria are reproducing at their maximum rate. The number of bacteria is doubling in every new generation. This is as a result of ideal conditions (e.g. plenty of food, moisture, space or oxygen).

The log phase is also called the exponential phase.

THE ORGANISM

Stationary phase (C)

In the stationary phase there is no increase in bacterial numbers. The production of new bacteria is compensated for by the death of equal numbers of bacteria. The rate of growth slows down because of factors such as:

- Lack of food
- Lack of space
- Lack of moisture
- Lack of oxygen
- The build-up of toxic waste products.

Decline phase (D)

In the decline (or death) phase the number of bacteria falls rapidly.

Bacteria numbers fall when the death rate is greater than the rate of reproduction. The slow rate of reproduction is caused by the same factors that caused the stationary phase.

Survival phase (E)

In the survival phase a small number of bacteria survive by remaining dormant as spores. Spores can survive for a long time by remaining dormant until conditions are suitable again.

Food processing

The production of useful products using enzymes was discussed in Chapter 12. Modern bioprocessing methods involve the use of bacteria (and other organisms) to produce a wide range of foods and related products. These include dairy products such as yoghurts and cheeses, artificial sweeteners, amino acids, vitamins, flavourings, flavour enhancers and alcohol products such as wines and beers.

There is a growing trend towards the use of micro-organisms themselves as a food source, especially as a source of protein. The use of bacteria (as well as yeasts, other fungi and algae) to produce edible forms of protein is called **single-cell protein** (SCP) production.

There are two main methods of production: batch culture (or fermentation) and continuous flow culture (or fermentation).

> **Batch culture** is the growth of cells in a sealed container (or bioreactor) over a short period of time and under ideal conditions until all the nutrients are used up.

THE ORGANISM

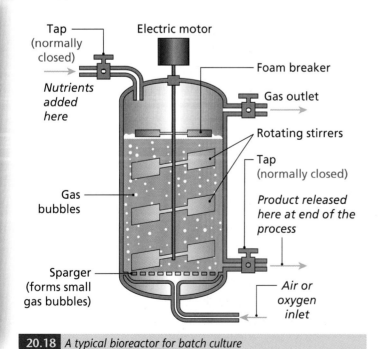

Tap (normally closed)

Nutrients added here

Electric motor

Foam breaker

Gas outlet

Rotating stirrers

Tap (normally closed)

Product released here at end of the process

Gas bubbles

Sparger (forms small gas bubbles)

Air or oxygen inlet

20.18 *A typical bioreactor for batch culture*

Batch culture

In batch culture, a fixed amount of sterile nutrient is added to the micro-organisms in the bioreactor. The other conditions include suitable temperatures, pressure, aeration and pH.

The micro-organisms go through the lag, log and stationary (but rarely the decline and survival) stages of a typical growth curve. As this happens the nutrients are used up and the product is formed. The product normally forms at the log or stationary stage.

The process is often stopped before the decline phase because there is very little product formed at this stage. In addition, there is a danger of the micro-organism bursting or of unwanted side products forming at this stage.

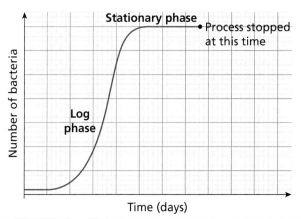

20.19 *The number of bacteria in batch culture*

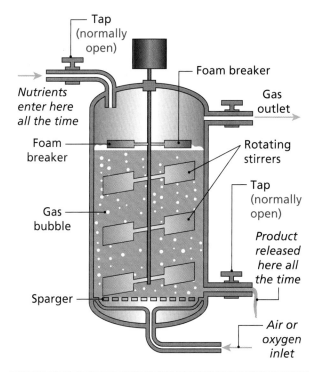

20.20 *A typical bioreactor for continuous flow processing*

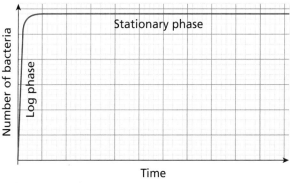

20.21 *The number of bacteria in continuous flow processing*

The container or bioreactor (see diagram 20.18) may or may not have oxygen added (depending on whether the micro-organisms are aerobic or anaerobic). Also the mixture is usually, but not always, stirred.

At the end of the production run the bioreactor is emptied. The product is then separated from the solution and purified. The bioreactor is cleaned, re-sterilised and the process can then be repeated.

Yoghurt and many antibiotics are made by batch culture.

Continuous flow

In continuous flow culture, nutrients are continuously fed into the bioreactor. At the same time the culture medium (containing some micro-organisms) is continuously withdrawn. In this way the volume of material in the bioreactor remains constant.

In continuous flow culture the micro-organisms are maintained more or less constantly in the log stage of growth. This means they are growing rapidly and producing the product at a fast rate.

Factors such as pH, temperature, the rate of stirring and the concentrations of nutrients, oxygen and waste products are kept constant. For this reason the organisms are said to grow under steady-state (unchanging) conditions.

Maintaining constant conditions is very difficult. For this reason continuous flow processing is limited to a small number of applications. These include the production of single-cell protein (and some methods of waste water treatment).

A **bioreactor** is a vessel or container in which living cells or their products are used to make a product.

Continuous flow food processing is the growth of cells in an open container (or bioreactor), where nutrients are added and the end products are removed all the time at a rate that maintains the volume of liquid and the number of cells.

THE ORGANISM

247

Summary

Micro-organisms:
- Are small living things
- Include bacteria, some fungi and plankton
- Are found in a wide range of habitats.

Bacteria:
- Are microscopic
- Are single-celled
- Have a cell wall
- Do not have a nucleus or membrane-enclosed organelles
- Have a single loop of DNA and a smaller loop called a plasmid.

Bacterial shapes are round, rod-shaped or spiral.

Bacterial reproduction is asexual, by binary fission.

Bacteria evolve rapidly by mutating.

Endospores are tough-walled spores capable of surviving harsh conditions.

Nutrition can be:
- **Autotrophic** (make their own food):
  - Photosynthetic (use light as an energy source to make food)
  - Chemosynthetic (use chemical reactions as an energy source to make food).
- **Heterotrophic** (take in food):
  - Saprophytic (feeding from a dead source)
  - Parasitic (feeding from a live host).

Bacterial growth is affected by:
- Temperature
- Oxygen concentration
- pH
- External solute concentration
- Pressure.

Aerobic bacteria use oxygen; **anaerobic bacteria** do not use oxygen for respiration.
- Obligate aerobes are obliged to use oxygen.
- Facultative aerobes have the facility to use or not to use oxygen.

The **economic benefits of bacteria** include:
- The manufacture of products such as yoghurt and cheese
- The use of genetically engineered bacteria to produce insulin, drugs and enzymes.

The **economic disadvantages of bacteria** include:
- They cause human, animal and plant diseases
- They cause food decay.

Pathogenic bacteria are bacteria that cause disease.

Antibiotics are chemicals made by fungi or bacteria to kill or stop the growth of bacteria (but not viruses).
- Bacteria can develop immunity (resistance) to antibiotics by mutations.
- Multi-resistant bacteria have evolved that are not affected by most antibiotics.

Prokaryotes do not have membrane-enclosed nuclei or organelles.
- Bacteria are prokaryotes.

Bacterial growth shows five phases:
- The lag phase (no increase in numbers)
- The log phase (numbers increase very rapidly)
- The stationary phase (no increase in numbers)
- The decline phase (rapid fall in numbers)
- The survival phase (some bacteria survive as spores).

Bacteria are used in food processing to form many types of food products.

Batch culture means that:
- A certain amount of nutrient is added to the micro-organisms in a bioreactor
- The bacteria go through the lag, log and stationary stages of growth
- The process is stopped
- The bioreactor is emptied and sterilised so that the process can be repeated.

Continuous flow culture means that:
- Nutrients are continuously added to the bioreactor
- Bacteria and product are continuously removed
- The bacteria are maintained at the log stage of growth
- Conditions in the bioreactor are kept constant.

Batch culture is used more often than continuous flow culture.

HIGHER ▼

THE ORGANISM

Revision questions

1 (a) What are micro-organisms?
   (b) Name three types of micro-organism.
   (c) State six habitats where micro-organisms may be found.

2 Diagram 20.22 represents a bacterium.

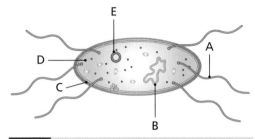

20.22

   (a) Name the parts labelled A to E and give **one** function for each part.
   (b) State the shape of the cell in the diagram.
   (c) Name the other two bacterial shapes.

3 (a) Name the method of reproduction used by bacteria.
   (b) Describe, with the aid of labelled diagrams, this method of reproduction.

4 (a) Name the method by which bacteria evolve.
   (b) Give one reason why bacteria evolve so rapidly.
   (c) Suggest one disadvantage of bacterial evolution.

5 (a) What is an endospore?
   (b) Under what conditions do endospores develop?
   (c) State one advantage of endospores.
   (d) Suggest why endospores are not methods of reproduction.

6 Distinguish between the following pairs of terms:
   (a) Heterotrophic and autotrophic
   (b) A saprophyte and a parasite
   (c) Photosynthesis and chemosynthesis
   (d) Aerobic and anaerobic bacteria.

7 (a) Name the kingdom in which bacteria are placed.
   (b) Why are bacteria referred to as prokaryotes?
   (c) Why are fungi considered to be eukaryotes?

8 Diagram 20.23 represents the number of bacteria growing on an agar dish over a period of time.

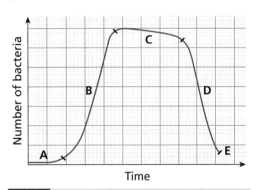

20.23

   (a) Name the phases labelled A to E.
   (b) State what is happening to the number of bacteria at each phase.
   (c) Give a reason for the events in each phase.
   (d) Does the graph show that all the bacteria die?
   (e) Explain your answer to part (d) and give a reason why the bacteria behave as shown.

9 (a) Name two methods of food processing using bacteria.
   (b) Explain what is meant by:
       (i) A bioreactor
       (ii) Steady-state conditions.

10 Distinguish between batch and continuous flow culture in terms of:
   (a) How the nutrients are added
   (b) The stage(s) of growth at which the bacteria are found
   (c) The length of time for which the process can continue
   (d) When the products are obtained.

HIGHER ▼

Exam questions

Section C

11 (b) (i) Draw and label a diagram to show the basic structure of a typical bacterial cell.
       (ii) Other than being prokaryotic, state two ways in which a typical bacterial cell differs from a typical human cell (e.g. cell from cheek lining).
       (iii) Describe how some bacteria respond in order to survive when environmental conditions become unfavourable.
       (iv) What is meant when a bacterium is described as being pathogenic?
       (v) What are antibiotics? Use your knowledge of the Theory of Natural Selection to explain the possible danger involved in the misuse of antibiotics.

(2005 HL Q 15)

THE ORGANISM

12 **(b)** Answer the following in relation to bacteria.
  (i) Distinguish between photosynthetic and chemosynthetic bacteria. Give an example of each type.
  (ii) Name two forms of heterotrophic nutrition found in bacteria.
  (iii) What are antibiotics? For what purpose are they used?
  (iv) Explain what is meant by antibiotic resistance and suggest how it may develop.
  (2006 HL Q 15)

13 **(c)** The diagram shows a bacterial growth curve.
  (i) A and B represent the labels on the axes. What does each of them stand for?

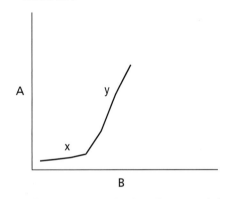

  (ii) What term is applied to the part of the curve labelled x? What is happening during x?
  (iii) What term is applied to the part of the curve labelled y? What is happening during y?
  (iv) Copy the diagram into your answer book and continue the curve to show the next phase. Explain why you have continued the curve in this way.

  (v) Distinguish between batch and continuous flow food processing using micro-organisms in the food industry.
  (2008 HL Q 15)

14 **(b)** The diagram shows the structure of a typical bacterial cell.
  (i) Name the bacterial cell parts A, B and C.
  (ii) What is the function of C?
  (iii) Name any **two** of the main bacterial types (shapes).

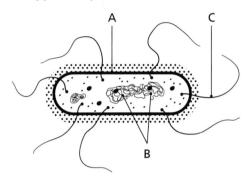

  (iv) By which method do bacterial cells reproduce?
  (v) Some bacteria are *anaerobic*. What does this mean?
  (vi) What are *pathogenic* bacteria?
  (vii) Give **two** examples of the economic importance of bacteria.
  (2009 OL Q 12)

15 **(c)** Suggest a biological explanation for the following observation:
  (ii) Doctors are reluctant to prescribe antibiotics to patients suffering from common cold-like symptoms.
  (2010 HL Q 15)

Previous examination questions

Ordinary level	Higher level
2005 Q 6b	2005 Q 15b
2007 Q 13a, b	2006 Q 15b
2009 Q 12b	2007 Q 14b(v), (vi)
2012 Q 13a, b	2008 Q 15c
	2010 Q 15c(ii)

Latest questions at www.edco.ie/lcbiologyplus/examhelp

Online test and assessment tracker

Scan the QR code and test yourself on chapter 20
www.edco.ie/lcbiologyplus

Chapter 21 **Fungi**

Introduction

There are over 100 000 different species of fungi, including mushrooms, mildews, moulds and yeasts. The study of fungi is called mycology.

Unlike bacteria, fungi have cells containing a nucleus and other cell organelles enclosed in a membrane. For this reason, they are described as eukaryotic.

Fungi also have cell walls, usually made of a carbohydrate called chitin, and they normally have tubes called hyphae. The hyphae form a visible mass called a mycelium.

21.1 *Hyphae (white threads) forming a mycelium (the black dots are reproductive structures)*

A **hypha** is a tube or filament in a fungus.

A **mycelium** is a (usually) visible mass of hyphae.

Nutrition

Fungi do not have chlorophyll and are heterotrophic (i.e. they take in food). They are either:

● Parasites (absorbing food from live hosts) or
● Saprophytes (absorbing food from dead organic matter).

Parasitic fungi

Parasitic fungi mostly take their food from plants. The fungus penetrates between the cells of the plant from which it absorbs food. Some fungal parasites live on animals causing disease, e.g. athlete's foot and ringworm.

● Obligate parasites (e.g. fungi causing mildews, smuts and rust diseases) can live only on live hosts and do not normally kill their host.
● Facultative parasites (e.g. fungi causing soft rots in fruit) may kill the host and feed on the dead remains.

An **obligate parasite** can only take its food from a live host.

A **facultative parasite** can get its food from a live or a dead host.

THE ORGANISM

251

21.2 *Morel: an edible fungus*

21.3 *The destroying angel: a poisonous fungus*

21.4 Rhizopus *growing on bread*

Saprophytic fungi

Most fungi are saprophytes. They are commonly found in the soil and on rotting leaves, trees and dead animals. Examples are mushrooms and moulds.

Saprophytic fungi act as decomposers. As the material is digested, minerals are released and recycled. For this reason saprophytic fungi are vital in the environment.

Edible and poisonous fungi

Some fungi are edible, but many are highly poisonous. Wild fungi should only be eaten with great caution, because it is very difficult to distinguish edible fungi from the poisonous species.

Edible fungi

Edible fungi include the standard field mushroom and morels. Both of these fungi grow above the ground.

Another edible fungus is the truffle. These highly priced fungi are formed underground, normally near the roots of trees.

> **?** Truffles have a very distinctive smell, and in the past pigs were used to 'sniff them out'. In more recent times dogs have been trained to find truffles.

Poisonous fungi

Poisonous fungi are numerous. Some species can cause death if only a single fungus cap is eaten.

The most common poisonous mushrooms are the death cap and the destroying angel (both fungi are *Amanita* species). These fungi damage cells in the lining of the intestine and liver. Death normally results from liver failure.

Common bread mould (*Rhizopus*)

Nutrition

The common bread mould is a saprophyte of starchy foods, e.g. bread, vegetable peelings and stored fruits such as apples.

The fungus secretes enzymes out into the starchy substrate. Digestion takes place outside the fungus and the digested nutrients are then absorbed.

Structure

Bread mould fungus appears as black circular patches. It is often called a pin mould because the reproductive structures look like pins sticking out from the surface.

Rhizopus consists of threadlike structures called hyphae (singular: **hypha**). These have no cross walls (i.e. they are **aseptate**) and are multinucleate, each nucleus being haploid.

A mass of hyphae is called a **mycelium**. The hyphae digest and absorb the substrate on which they grow. A **stolon** is an aerial hypha which allows the fungus to spread more rapidly. **Rhizoids** are hyphae that grow into the substrate and provide extra surface area for absorption.

Life cycle of *Rhizopus*

Asexual reproduction

After a few days' growth, some hyphae grow up from the surface of the substrate. These are called **sporangiophores**. Their tip swells to produce a **sporangium** whose contents divide by mitosis to form numerous spores. Each spore has at least one haploid nucleus.

The base of the sporangium is a wall called the **columella**. The columella surrounds a swollen area called the **apophysis**.

In dry conditions, the black sporangium dries out and opens to release many spores. Each spore blows away and grows into a new hypha and mycelium if it lands on a suitable substrate.

Sexual reproduction

Rhizopus exists as two separate strains called plus and minus strains. Both strains look identical but sexual reproduction can only occur between a plus and minus strain.

Sexual reproduction occurs as follows (refer to diagram 21.7).

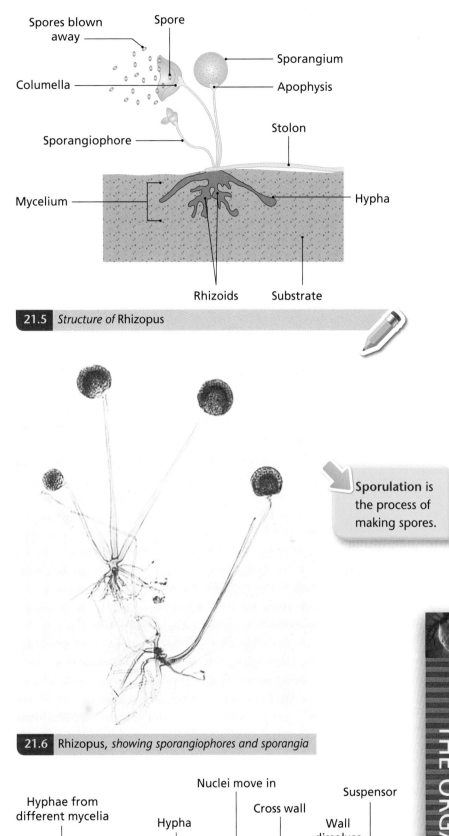

21.5 *Structure of* Rhizopus

21.6 Rhizopus, *showing sporangiophores and sporangia*

> **Sporulation** is the process of making spores.

21.7 *Sexual reproduction in* Rhizopus

THE ORGANISM

253

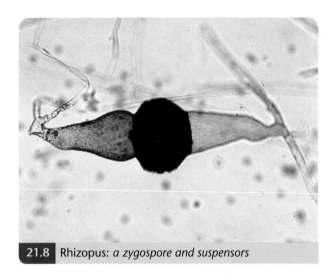

21.8 Rhizopus: *a zygospore and suspensors*

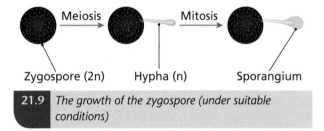

21.9 *The growth of the zygospore (under suitable conditions)*

Zygospore (2n) Hypha (n) Sporangium

Meiosis Mitosis

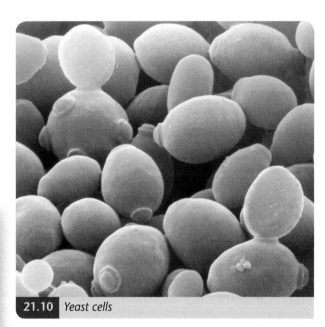

21.10 *Yeast cells*

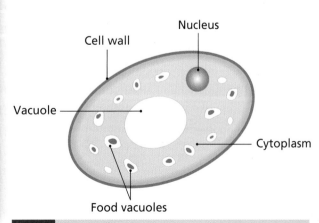

21.11 *Structure of yeast*

Cell wall
Nucleus
Vacuole
Cytoplasm
Food vacuoles

1. Hyphae from opposite strains grow close together.
2. Swellings form opposite each other.
3. The swellings touch.
4. Nuclei (which are the sex cells, or gametes) move into each swelling, forming **progametangia**.
5. Cross walls form to produce gametangia (singular: gametangium), which are held in place by suspensors.
6. The walls between the gametangia dissolve.
7. Many fertilisations produce a number of diploid zygote nuclei.
8. A tough-walled, black zygospore forms around these nuclei.
9. The zygospore (which is diploid) can remain dormant for a long time.
10. When conditions are suitable the zygospore germinates by meiosis.
11. A haploid hypha grows out of the zygospore and produces a sporangium at the tip.
12. The sporangium releases many haploid spores, which blow away to produce new hyphae and mycelia.

Yeast

Structure

Yeasts are single-celled (unicellular) fungi. Many different fungi can be induced to form a yeast stage.

Yeast cells are round or oval. They are tiny cells and are only clearly seen using an electron microscope.

Yeast cells have thin walls made of the carbohydrate chitin and a dense cytoplasm that contains many food storage vacuoles. This is why the cytoplasm appears granular or grainy. Usually one large vacuole is present. Each cell has one nucleus.

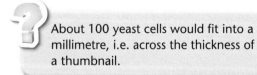 About 100 yeast cells would fit into a millimetre, i.e. across the thickness of a thumbnail.

Yeasts respire anaerobically, breaking down sugars and producing ethanol and carbon dioxide, according to the equation:

$$\text{Glucose} \rightarrow 2 \text{ ethanol} + 2 \text{ carbon dioxide}$$

Reproduction

Asexual reproduction in yeast occurs by **budding**. The parent cell divides by mitosis and one nucleus and some cytoplasm enters a small bud. This bud may separate to form an individual yeast cell.

Sometimes the bud remains attached to the parent cell. In this case each new bud may divide again. Eventually a colony can form. This often occurs when yeasts are growing rapidly. The colony is temporary and later divides to form single cells again.

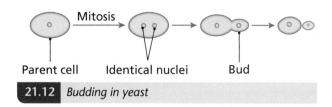

21.12 *Budding in yeast*

Parent cell   Identical nuclei   Bud

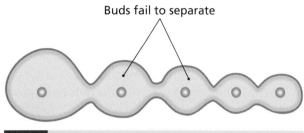

Buds fail to separate

21.13 *Formation of a yeast colony*

Economic importance of fungi

Benefits

- Yeasts are used to produce alcohols such as beers and wines.
- Fungi such as mushrooms can be grown as a source of food.

Disadvantages

- Fungi destroy a wide range of materials. These include:
  - ▶ Food (yeasts grow on fruits and sweet liquids; bread mould grows on bread)
  - ▶ Crops (potato blight fungus destroys potatoes; smuts and rusts are fungal diseases of cereals)
  - ▶ Paper (mildew grows on damp paper)
  - ▶ Timber (dry rot and Dutch elm fungus both grow on wood).
- Fungal diseases of plants, humans and animals can result in financial losses. These diseases include athlete's foot, ringworm, thrush and fungal nail infections.

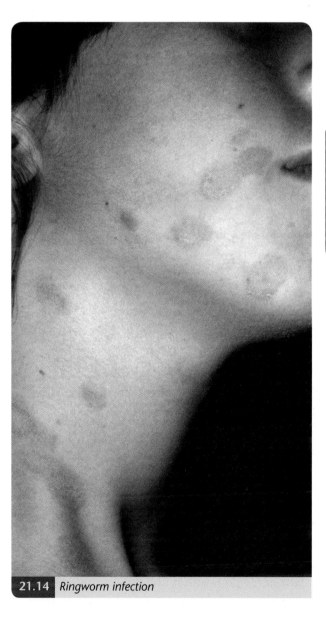

21.14 *Ringworm infection*

Syllabus You are required to know **two** economic benefits and **two** economic disadvantages of fungi.

THE ORGANISM

255

General precautions when growing micro-organisms

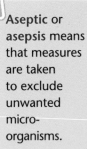

In general you should assume that all micro-organisms are potentially harmful, unless it is stated or proven otherwise.

Aseptic or asepsis means that measures are taken to exclude unwanted micro-organisms.

Sterile means that all micro-organisms are destroyed, i.e. there is nothing living.

Aseptic techniques

Aseptic techniques involve the creation of a germ-free environment in as far as is possible. Aseptic methods include the following procedures:

1. Wash your hands before and after each experiment
2. Wash the bench with disinfectant before and after each experiment
3. Do not put fingers, food, drink or equipment in or near your mouth
4. Keep all containers closed where possible
5. (i) Open all containers for the shortest possible time and (ii) open lids the shortest possible distance (minimal opening)
6. When micro-organisms are in a petri dish, seal the dish with adhesive tape.

Sterile techniques

1. Sterilise all equipment before use or use equipment that is already sterile. This can be done by placing the equipment (except plastic) in a pressure cooker (or autoclave) at 120°C for 15 minutes or by placing it in an oven at 160°C for an hour.
2. Pass the neck of test tubes, needles or loops through the flame of a bunsen burner.
3. Flame all test tube necks, needles and loops again after they are used.
4. At the end of the experiment immerse all equipment and cultures in sterilising fluid.

The material can then be put in a dustbin or, in the case of glassware and metal, cleaned and reused as usual.

Activity 16 To investigate the growth of leaf yeast using agar plates

Micro-organisms are widely found in nature. This activity shows that, although they are not visible to the naked eye, leaves have many yeasts growing on their surfaces. These yeasts do not harm the leaves.

1. Cut a small branch containing some leaves from an outdoor plant – privet, ash or sycamore leaves are ideal. (These will be tested for the presence of leaf yeasts.)
2. Wash your hands with an aseptic soap solution. (This reduces the chance of micro-organisms being on your hands.)
3. Wash the bench or worktop with disinfectant. (Again this eliminates micro-organisms.)
4. Sterilise a forceps by heating it in the flame of a bunsen burner for a few seconds. (This means there will be no micro-organisms on the forceps.)
5. Obtain two sterile petri dishes containing prepared sterile nutrient agar. (Agar is a material derived from seaweed. It is used to form a solid growth medium. The nutrient agar provides food for micro-organisms to grow.)
6. Use the forceps to pick up one of the leaves, which should be small enough to fit across a petri dish. (This prevents micro-organisms getting onto the leaf from your hands.) Alternatively, for large leaves, you may flame a cork borer or scissors, allow it to cool and use it to cut a number of leaf discs.

Forceps

Hottest part of bunsen flame

Bunsen burner

21.15 *Flaming a forceps*

7. Place a small spot of petroleum jelly (such as Vaseline) on the inside lid of the petri dish. (This will be used to attach the leaf to the lid of the petri dish.)

8. Reflame the forceps and allow it to cool.

9. Barely open the lid of one of the petri dishes in terms of (a) the distance it is opened and (b) the time for which it is opened. Use the forceps to attach the **upper** surface of the leaf to the lid of the petri dish. Make sure that the leaf does not touch the agar. Close the lid of the petri dish. The lower surface of the leaf is now facing down onto the agar. (There are more micro-organisms on the lower surface of the leaf than on the upper surface. The upper surface is covered by a cuticle which prevents the growth of micro-organisms. Leaf yeasts can expel their spores onto the surface of the agar.)

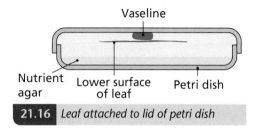

21.16 *Leaf attached to lid of petri dish*

10. Reflame the forceps. (This will kill any micro-organisms on it.)

11. Seal a sterile nutrient agar petri dish containing no leaf. (This dish will act as a control or comparison. The only difference between the two petri dishes is that one contains a leaf and the other does not.)

12. Seal the petri dishes with tape or parafilm. (This prevents them from opening by accident.)

13. Label the petri dishes on the undersurface with a marker. (This allows the dishes to be identified, without further blocking the view of the agar surface.)

14. Leave the petri dishes at room temperature or in an oven or incubator at 25°C. (Leaf yeasts grow well at room temperature, but a higher temperature will speed up their growth.)

15. The dishes should be incubated upside down. (This prevents condensation forming on the lids.)

16. Observe the surfaces of the agar each day for three or four days (to see if any yeast colonies are forming.)

17. The expected results are:
   - The dish with the leaf should show pink yeast colonies on the surface of the agar. These colonies may form a pattern similar to the shape of the leaf. Very few other micro-organisms will grow on the agar, unless part of the leaf is touching the agar. (The yeast can expel spores from a distance onto the agar; most other micro-organisms cannot grow across the space.)
   - There should be no growth in the control dish. (This shows that the yeasts did not arise from any other source except the leaf.)

21.17 *Leaf yeast on nutrient agar*

 The growth of leaf yeasts is inhibited by air pollution. If the leaves are collected from a location with polluted air (such as a town or city) there may be few, or no, yeasts on the agar.

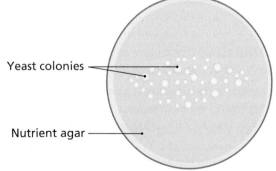

21.18 *Leaf yeast colonies growing on agar*

18. At the end of the experiment dispose of the agar and yeasts by sterilising it in an autoclave or pressure cooker for 15 minutes. Alternatively it can be immersed in sterilising fluid (such as Milton) and then put in a bin.

THE ORGANISM

Summary

Fungi:

- Are eukaryotic
- Reproduce by spores
- Are heterotrophic (i.e. do not have chlorophyll)
- Have cell walls made of chitin
- Consist of hyphae, forming a mycelium.

Fungi can be:

- Parasites of plants (mildews, soft rots) and animals (athlete's foot, ringworm)
- Saprophytes that cause decay (decomposers).

Edible fungi (mushrooms and truffles) are hard to distinguish from poisonous fungi (death cap fungus and destroying angel).

Rhizopus (black bread mould):

- Is a saprophyte
- Has tubes called hypha(e) (forming a visible mycelium)
- Reproduces asexually by spores
- Reproduces sexually when nuclei from different mycelia fuse to form zygospores. These remain dormant until conditions are suitable for growth.

Yeast:

- Is a single-celled fungus
- Reproduces asexually by budding
- Respires anaerobically to form ethanol and carbon dioxide.

Economic benefits of fungi include:

- Yeasts produce alcohol
- Mushrooms are edible.

Economic disadvantages of fungi include:

- They destroy food (*Rhizopus* destroys bread), crops and a wide range of other materials
- They cause human (athlete's foot and ringworm), animal and plant diseases.

General precautions that should be taken when working with micro-organisms include:

- Use aseptic techniques to exclude unwanted micro-organisms
- Use sterile equipment where possible
- Flame any relevant equipment before and after use
- Dispose of all material safely.

The presence of yeast on leaves can be shown by:

- Attaching the top surface of a leaf to the lid of a petri dish containing nutrient agar
- Observing the pink colonies of yeast that form on the agar
- As a control use a nutrient agar plate with no leaf (no yeast colonies form in the control).

Revision questions

1. (a) Name two characteristics of fungi that distinguish them from animals.
   (b) Name one feature of fungi, in each case, that they share with (i) Plants (ii) Animals.

2. What is the ecological benefit of fungi growing on dead leaves?

3. (a) Why are fungi obliged to be heterotrophic?
   (b) Name the two modes of heterotrophic nutrition used by fungi.

4. (a) Why may it be dangerous to eat wild fungi?
   (b) Give one example in each case of an edible and a non-edible fungus.

5. Explain what is meant by:
   (a) Hypha (b) Mycelium
   (c) Aseptate (d) Multinucleate.

6. Sexual reproduction in *Rhizopus* never occurs between hyphae of the same mycelium.
   (a) Explain why this statement is true.
   (b) Give an illustrated account of sexual reproduction in *Rhizopus*.

7. Give an account of yeast under the headings:
   (a) Structure (b) Reproduction
   (c) Respiration.

8. List (a) two similarities, and (b) two differences, between yeast and *Rhizopus*.

9. Outline the economic importance of fungi.

10 When investigating the growth of leaf yeasts, give a reason for each of the following:
(a) Flaming the forceps
(b) Using petroleum jelly
(c) Using a control
(d) Labelling the petri dishes on their undersurface
(e) Soaking the petri dishes in sterilising fluid at the end of the investigation.

11 Suggest a reason for each of the following:
(a) It may be dangerous to eat wild mushrooms.
(b) Some fungi inhibit the growth of bacteria.
(c) Athlete's foot is not treated with antibiotics.
(d) Fungus does not grow well on the surface of jams.
(e) *Rhizopus* normally forms zygospores when all its food is used up.
(f) *Rhizopus* does not grow well on biscuits.

(g) Leaf yeasts are more common on the undersides of leaves (compared with the upper surfaces).
(h) Leaf yeasts are more abundant on leaves in rural rather than city environments.
(i) Leaf yeasts are more common on older leaves than younger leaves.

12 Choose which of the options (i), (ii), (iii) or (iv) represents the correct answer in each case below.
(a) On nutrient agar, leaf yeast colonies appear: (i) White (ii) Salmon or pink (iii) Creamy (iv) Fuzzy.
(b) Spores of *Rhizopus* are contained in a structure called a: (i) Sporangium (ii) Gametangium (iii) Colony (iv) Apophysis.
(c) *Rhizopus* is: (i) Autotrophic (ii) Parasitic (iii) Saprophytic (iv) Photosynthetic.
(d) Yeast is: (i) Unicellular (ii) A bacterium (iii) Multicelled (iv) Poisonous.

Exam questions

Section A

13 The diagram shows a yeast cell which is undergoing asexual reproduction.

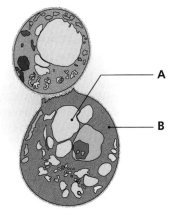

A.B. Dowsett/Science Photo Library

(a) Name A and B.
(b) What type of asexual reproduction is shown in the diagram?
(c) Which type of division, mitosis or meiosis, is involved in this form of reproduction?
(d) If yeast cells are kept under anaerobic conditions, alcohol (ethanol) and another substance are produced.
    (i) What are anaerobic conditions?
    (ii) Name the other substance produced.
                                    (2006 OL Q 6)

Section B

14 (a) (i) Name a fungus, other than yeast, that you studied during your course.
        (ii) Give **one** way in which the fungus that you have named in (i) differs from yeast.
    (b) Answer the following questions in relation to your investigation of the growth of leaf yeast.
        (i) It was necessary to use a nutrient medium. What is a nutrient medium?
        (ii) Name the nutrient medium that you used.
        (iii) The nutrient medium should be sterile. Explain the underlined term.
        (iv) Describe, in words and/or labelled diagram(s), how you conducted the investigation.
        (v) What was the result of your investigation?
                                    (2007 HL Q 8)

15 (a) Draw a labelled diagram of a single, reproducing, yeast cell.
    (b) Answer the following questions in relation to your investigation into the growth of leaf yeast.
        (i) From what plant did you obtain the yeast?
        (ii) Name the nutrient medium on which you grew the yeast.

(iii) Outline the steps you followed to get the yeast cells onto the nutrient medium.

(iv) How long did it take for the yeast to become visible on the nutrient medium?

(v) How did you recognise the yeast?

(vi) Describe **one** aseptic technique you carried out during this investigation.

(2011 OL Q 7)

Section C

16 (c) The diagram shows part of the mycelium of *Rhizopus*.

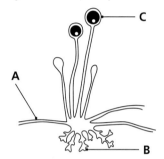

(i) Identify A, B, C.

(ii) State a function of B.

(iii) State a function of C.

(iv) What term is used to describe the nutrition of *Rhizopus*? Explain the importance of this type of nutrition in nature.

(v) To what kingdom does *Rhizopus* belong?

(vi) Name another organism that you have studied in your biology course that belongs to the same kingdom as *Rhizopus*.

(2005 OL Q 15)

17 (c) Saprophytic and parasitic fungi are widespread in nature.

(i) Explain each of the underlined terms.

(ii) State a role of each of these types of fungus in the overall scheme of nature.

(iii) Give **one** example of a beneficial fungus and one example of a harmful fungus.

(iv) State a function for each of the following structures that are found in fungi: rhizoid, sporangium, gametangium, zygospore.

(2005 HL Q 15)

18 (a) (i) Decomposition is essential for the addition of nutrients to the soil. Explain the underlined term.

(ii) Name two groups of micro-organisms in the soil which are responsible for decomposition.

(2009 OL Q 12)

19 (c)

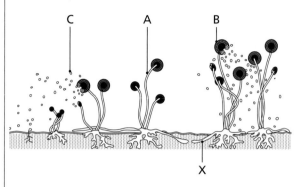

(i) Identify the organism shown in the diagram.

(ii) To which kingdom does this organism belong?

(iii) Name the parts labelled A, B and C.

(iv) 1. Give a role, other than anchorage, for structure X.

2. Describe how X carries out this role.

(v) Which term describes the mode of nutrition of this organism.

(vi) The cells of this organism are described as eukaryotic. Give **two** characteristic features of eukaryotic cells.

(vii) What corresponding term is used to describe bacterial cells?

(2009 HL Q 14)

20 (c) *Rhizopus* is a type of mould often found growing on stale bread.

(i) Draw a diagram of *Rhizopus* **and** on it label a hypha, a sporangium and a sporangiophore.

(ii) Explain how *Rhizopus* gets its food.

(iii) What form of heterotrophic nutrition does *Rhizopus* have?

(iv) Outline the importance of this type of nutrition in nature.

(v) To what kingdom does *Rhizopus* belong?

(vi) Name **one** economically harmful member of this kingdom.

(vii) Mushrooms also belong to this kingdom. A restaurant owner decides to collect and cook wild mushrooms from a local forest. Suggest **one** reason why this may not be a good idea.

(2010 OL Q 15)

THE ORGANISM

21 (c) The diagram below shows part of the mycelium of the fungus *Rhizopus*.

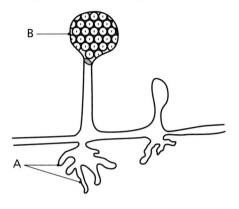

(i) Give the name **and** state a function of the part labelled A.

(ii) Name part B **and** explain why the reproduction associated with it is asexual.

(iii) The nutrition of *Rhizopus* is described as being *saprophytic*.

   1. What does the term *saprophytic* mean?

   2. Explain the importance of saprophytic nutrition in the overall scheme of nature.

(iv) Saprophytic nutrition is a form of *heterotrophic* nutrition. What does the term *heterotrophic* mean?

(v) Name another form of nutrition employed by some fungi.

(vi) Give **two** examples of harmful members of the kingdom Fungi.

(2011 HL Q 15)

Previous examination questions

Ordinary level	Higher level
2005 Q 15c	2004 Q 15c
2006 Q 6	2005 Q 9, 15c
2007 Q 13c	2006 Q 6c
2008 Q 7, 15c	2007 Q 8
2009 Q 12a	2009 Q 14c
2010 Q 15c	2011 Q 15c
2011 Q 7	2012 Q 8, 14c
2012 Q 13c	

Latest questions at www.edco.ie/lcbiologyplus/examhelp

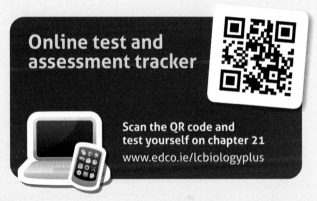

Online test and assessment tracker

Scan the QR code and test yourself on chapter 21
www.edco.ie/lcbiologyplus

Introduction

Amoeba is in the Kingdom Protista. It is a microscopic organism that lives at the bottom of shallow freshwater ponds and streams. (Other species of *Amoeba* are found in sea water.)

Each *Amoeba* consists of just a single cell about 0.1 mm in diameter (about five *Amoeba* cells would fit across the full stop at the end of this sentence). *Amoeba* is heterotrophic (takes in food) and is omnivorous, i.e. it eats other single-celled protists, plants and animals.

It is important to realise that *Amoeba* can carry out all the life processes of larger organisms, even though it is only a single cell.

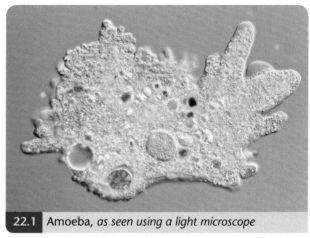

22.1 Amoeba, *as seen using a light microscope*

Structure of *Amoeba*

The living material in the cell (protoplasm) is surrounded by a flexible membrane. The shape of the cell is constantly changing to allow it to move from place to place. The nucleus can move about within the cytoplasm, which itself is constantly flowing within the cell.

The outer cytoplasm (ectoplasm) is clear and relatively stiff. The inner cytoplasm (endoplasm) is grainy due to food vacuoles and waste materials. The endoplasm is more fluid than the ectoplasm and contains food vacuoles, fat droplets and crystals of waste products.

There is usually a single, large contractile vacuole present. Sometimes a number of these vacuoles are found.

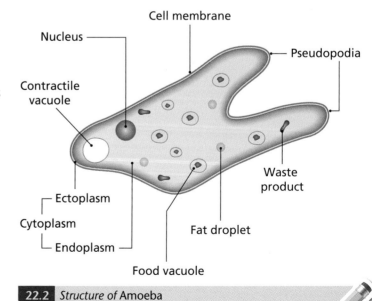

22.2 Structure of Amoeba

Functions of cell structures
- The cell membrane keeps the cell contents in place. In addition, gases diffuse in and out through the cell membrane.
- The nucleus controls the cell.

- Food vacuoles secrete acids and enzymes to kill and then digest the prey. Digested material is absorbed from the food vacuole into the cytoplasm.
- The pseudopodia extend in the direction *Amoeba* wishes to move. The cytoplasm (in particular the endoplasm) moves or flows into the pseudopodia, causing the cell to move. The pseudopodia are also used to surround (engulf) the prey.
- *Amoeba* lives in fresh water. This means its cytoplasm is more concentrated than its external environment. As a result, water enters *Amoeba* by osmosis.

  The contractile vacuole collects water that enters *Amoeba*. It then expands, touches the cell membrane and bursts to expel the water. It is said to be responsible for osmoregulation. Without a contractile vacuole, *Amoeba* would expand and burst.

Plant and animal kingdoms

Chapter 20 dealt with organisms (bacteria) from the Kingdom Monera. Chapter 21 dealt with organisms from the Kingdom Fungi. This chapter deals with an organism *(Amoeba)* from the Kingdom Protista.

  The plant and animal kingdoms will be outlined by reference to flowering plants and humans in most of the following chapters.

22.3 *One* Amoeba *feeding on another*

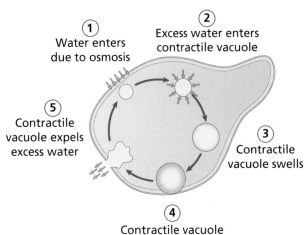

① Water enters due to osmosis

② Excess water enters contractile vacuole

③ Contractile vacuole swells

④ Contractile vacuole touches the cell membrane

⑤ Contractile vacuole expels excess water

22.4 *The function of the contractile vacuole*

Summary

- *Amoeba* is in the kingdom Protista.
- The habitat for *Amoeba* is fresh water.
- The protoplasm consists of the nucleus and surrounding cytoplasm.
- The cytoplasm consists of the outer firm ectoplasm and the inner fluid endoplasm.
- The cell membrane retains the cell contents and allows for gas exchange.
- The nucleus controls the cell.
- The pseudopodia are used for movement and to engulf prey.
- Food vacuoles kill and digest the prey.
- The contractile vacuole eliminates water and prevents the cell from bursting.

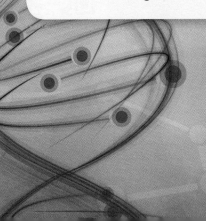

THE ORGANISM

Revision questions

1 (a) State the kingdom to which *Amoeba* belongs.
  (b) What are the main features of this kingdom?
  (c) Why is *Amoeba* considered to be a simple organism?

2 (a) Describe the typical (i) habitat and (ii) size of *Amoeba*.
  (b) Draw a large, labelled diagram of *Amoeba*.

3 Name the structures used by *Amoeba* for each of the following:

(a) Movement
(b) Digestion
(c) Water control
(d) Absorbing oxygen
(e) Controlling the cell.

4 State two differences in each case between *Amoeba* and: (a) Bacteria (b) Fungi (c) A plant cell.

5 Distinguish between:
  (a) Ectoplasm and endoplasm
  (b) Food vacuole and contractile vacuole.

Exam questions

Section A

6 (a) The diagram shows the structure of *Amoeba*.

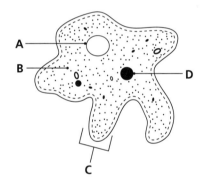

  (i) Name A, B, C, D.
  (ii) To which kingdom does *Amoeba* belong?

(2005 OL Q 6)

7 The diagram shows the structure of *Amoeba*.

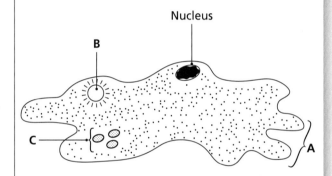

(a) Name the parts labelled A, B and C.
(b) To which kingdom does *Amoeba* belong?
(c) Is the cell of *Amoeba* prokaryotic or eukaryotic?
(d) Give a reason for your answer to part (c).
(e) Give **one** function of A in *Amoeba*.
(f) 1. Give **one** function of B in *Amoeba*.
   2. Suggest **one** reason why B is more active in freshwater amoebae than in marine amoebae.

(2010 HL Q 3)

Previous examination questions

Ordinary level	Higher level
2005 Q 6a	2010 Q 3
2012 Q 2	

Latest questions at www.edco.ie/lcbiologyplus/examhelp

Online test and assessment tracker

Scan the QR code and test yourself on chapter 22
www.edco.ie/lcbiologyplus

Chapter 23 Structure of flowering plants

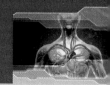

Introduction

In previous chapters we saw that the need for organisation is one of the characteristics of life. Cells are organised into tissues, organs, organ systems and, finally, organisms. This chapter will examine the way in which flowering plants are organised. Later chapters will look at the complex organisation of the human body.

External structure of a flowering plant

There are about 300 000 species of flowering plants (also called angiosperms). This chapter will deal with the general structure of a flowering plant such as a buttercup or a wallflower. Generally these plants are composed of an underground root system and an above-ground shoot system.

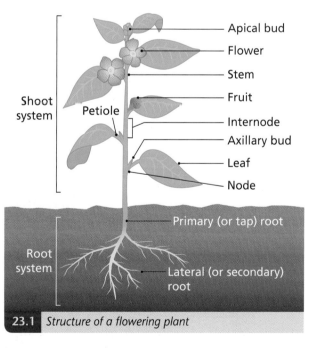

23.1   *Structure of a flowering plant*

Roots

Types of roots

Tap roots consist of a main root that develops from the radicle (which is the initial root that emerged from the seed). The tap root is also called the primary root. Lateral or secondary roots emerge from the primary root. The tips of the lateral roots have thousands of tiny, invisible root hairs. Tap roots are present in most dicotyledons (dicots), e.g. dandelion, wallflower and ash.

THE ORGANISM

23.2 *Types of roots*

Tap root

Fibrous roots

Functions of roots

- Anchor the plant in the soil
- Absorb water and mineral salts from the soil – the root hairs carry out this function
- Transport absorbed materials to the shoots
- Store food in some plants, e.g. carrots, turnips, radish.

The zones in a root

If a root tip is examined it is seen to have four zones, each with a distinct function, as shown in diagram 23.5.

1. **Zone of protection**: the root cap protects the root cells as they push through the soil.
2. **Zone of cell production**, or **meristematic zone**: meristems allow plants to

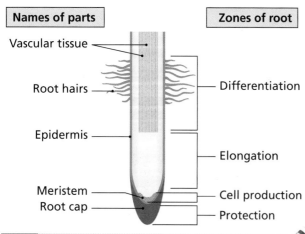

Names of parts

Vascular tissue

Root hairs

Epidermis

Meristem

Root cap

Zones of root

Differentiation

Elongation

Cell production

Protection

23.5 *Longitudinal section (LS) of a root*

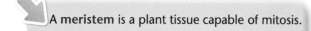

A **meristem** is a plant tissue capable of mitosis.

Fibrous roots form when the radicle dies away to leave a group of equal-sized roots. These roots emerge from the base of the stem. They are most common in monocotyledons (monocots), e.g. grasses and daffodils. (See pages 272–273 later in this chapter for a description of monocots and dicots.)

Adventitious roots are roots that do not develop from the radicle. They are sometimes said to grow in strange places. Examples include fibrous roots, the roots at the base of an onion and the gripping roots of ivy.

23.3 *Tap roots (containing stored food)*

23.4 *Fibrous roots*

grow. Apical meristems are found in the root tip and in the shoot tip. Other meristems are found around the edge of some plant stems and in leaves and fruits. Cells in the root meristem are constantly dividing by mitosis to produce new cells for root growth.

3. **Zone of elongation**: when new cells are formed by the meristem they are very small.

In the zone of elongation, plant growth regulators (such as auxins) stimulate the cells to grow longer.

4. **Zone of differentiation**: in this region, the elongated cells, which are all similar or undifferentiated, develop into different types of tissues:

- **Dermal tissue** (such as epidermis), which surrounds and protects the plant
- **Vascular tissue** (such as xylem and phloem), which transports materials see pages 269–271
- **Ground tissue**, which is found between the dermal and vascular tissues.

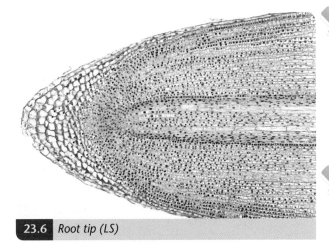

23.6 *Root tip (LS)*

Herbaceous plants do not contain wood (or lignin).

Woody plants contain wood (or lignin).

A **node** is the point on a stem at which a leaf is attached.

An **internode** is the region on a stem between two nodes.

A **bud** is a potential growth point that may develop into a shoot, a leaf or a flower.

A **lenticel** is an opening on a stem for gas exchange.

Stems

The stem is the main part of the shoot. In herbaceous plants (e.g. a daffodil) it is usually soft and green and does not contain wood. In woody plants (e.g. a chestnut tree) it is hard, woody and brown.

The stem carries leaves, which emerge from points called nodes. The part of the stem between two nodes is called an internode.

The tip of the stem has a terminal or **apical bud** (from the Latin *apex*, meaning 'tip').

23.7 *Stems of sycamore in winter or early spring: the buds are about to start growing*

This causes the stem to grow at the growing tip. If the growth tip is removed, a low bushy plant will form.

The **axil** is the angle between a leaf and a stem. Axillary or lateral buds are located at each axil. These buds produce new growth such as branches or flowers.

The structure of a typical shoot is shown in diagram 23.1 on page 265.

Stem in winter

In winter a woody stem may appear as shown in diagram 23.8.

The apical bud will produce the following year's growth. The scale scars mark the locations of previous apical buds. The distance between two sets of scale scars represents one year of growth. The leaf scars indicate where a leaf has fallen.

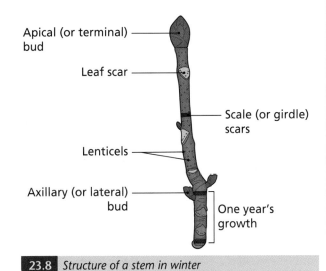

Apical (or terminal) bud

Leaf scar

Scale (or girdle) scars

Lenticels

Axillary (or lateral) bud

One year's growth

23.8 *Structure of a stem in winter*

THE ORGANISM

Functions of stems
- Support the aerial parts of the plant
- Transport water and minerals from the roots to the leaves and flowers
- Transport food made in the leaves to the roots
- Carry out photosynthesis (when they are green)
- May store food.

Leaves

Leaf structure

Leaves are attached to stems at nodes. The stalk of the leaf is called the petiole. Some leaves do not have a petiole (i.e. they are joined directly to the stem). Such leaves are said to be sessile.

The leaf is normally flattened into a thin leaf blade or lamina. The petiole continues through the lamina as the midrib. Veins emerge from the midrib and are clearly seen in the lamina. The petiole, midrib and veins contain vascular or transport tissues called xylem and phloem.

Venation

> **Venation** is the pattern of veins in a leaf.

Two types of venation are common.

1. **Parallel venation** means that the veins run alongside each other. This pattern is found in most monocots, e.g. grasses, daffodils and tulips.
2. **Net** or **reticulate venation** means that the veins form a branching network throughout the lamina. This pattern is most common in dicots, e.g. horse chestnut, rose and buttercup.

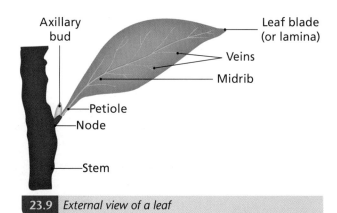

23.9 *External view of a leaf*

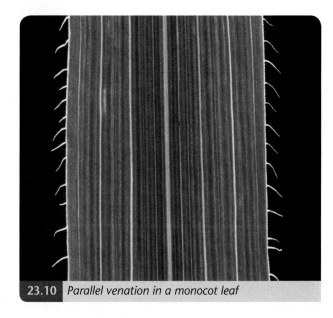

23.10 *Parallel venation in a monocot leaf*

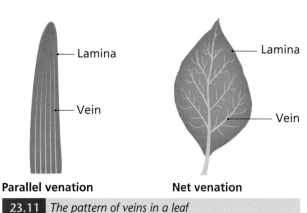

Parallel venation — Lamina, Vein

Net venation — Lamina, Vein

23.11 *The pattern of veins in a leaf*

23.12 *Net venation in a dicot leaf*

Functions of leaves

- Make food (i.e. carry out photosynthesis)
- Exchange gases with the atmosphere (in daylight they take in carbon dioxide and release oxygen and water vapour)
- Lose water (in a process called transpiration) – this allows fresh water and mineral salts to be taken into the plant and it may also cool the plant
- Store food (this is why the leaves of plants such as grasses, lettuce and cabbage are often consumed by animals and humans).

Flowers

The structure and functions of flowers and their parts will be discussed in Chapter 39.

Tissues in flowering plants

When meristematic tissue divides, it produces new cells. Initially, these cells are unspecialised or undifferentiated. They differentiate into three categories of plant tissue: dermal, ground and vascular tissue. These tissues are continuous throughout the plant, but their exact structure and arrangement may vary.

Dermal tissue

Dermal tissue forms the covering layer on a plant. In many respects it is similar to the skin of humans. It is normally called epidermis. Its main function is to protect the plant.

Dermal tissue may have secondary functions, depending on its location.

For example:

- Root hairs are extensions of the epidermis near the tip of a root and are designed to absorb water and minerals
- The epidermis of leaves and most stems is coated with a waxy cuticle to prevent water loss from the plant.

Ground tissue

Ground tissue occupies the area between the dermal and vascular tissues in a plant. Ground tissue makes up most of the bulk of a young plant. It carries out a range of functions such as photosynthesis, storage of food and wastes, and it often gives strength and support to a plant.

Vascular tissue

Vascular tissue consists of xylem and phloem. The main function of vascular tissue is to transport materials throughout the plant.

Xylem

Xylem is made up of two main types of cells: vessels and tracheids. The living contents of tracheids and vessels die before they reach maturity. For this reason, xylem is a dead tissue.

Appearance

Xylem tracheids are long, sloping or tapering cells whose insides are hollow at maturity. They overlap and allow water to pass from tracheid to tracheid through thin parts of the wall called pits.

Tracheids are more primitive than vessels. They are the only type of xylem found in coniferous trees such as pine trees.

THE ORGANISM

> **Lignin** is a strengthening material found in some plant cell walls.

Xylem vessels are tubular structures formed when a number of cells join end-to-end. They are wider than tracheids and their end walls break down to form a continuous tube. They have pits in their side walls to allow water to pass from one vessel to another.

Vessels are more efficient at transporting water than tracheids and are very common in flowering plants.

Cells that contain lignin are said to be lignified. Both tracheids and vessels have thick, lignified cell walls. This gives them great strength. Lignin is laid down in definite patterns, the most common of which is spiral. Lignified xylem forms the wood in trees.

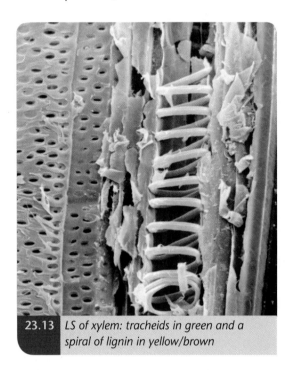

23.13 *LS of xylem: tracheids in green and a spiral of lignin in yellow/brown*

Function

- Xylem transports water and mineral salts from the roots to the leaves.
- Xylem also gives mechanical support to the plant (due to lignin).

Location

Xylem is found in roots, stems, leaves and flowers. It is often found in vascular bundles (special groups of transporting cells).

Phloem

Phloem is mainly composed of sieve tubes and companion cells. As companion cells are alive, phloem is a living tissue.

Appearance

Sieve tubes are long, tubular structures. They form when individual cells, called sieve tube elements, join end-to-end. The end walls develop pores, which allow the passage of materials from one element to another.

The end walls are called **sieve plates** because they resemble plates with numerous pores in them. The cytoplasm of each element remains,

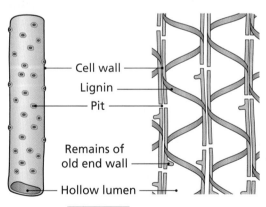

Cell wall
Lignin
Pit

Remains of old end wall

Hollow lumen

Vessels

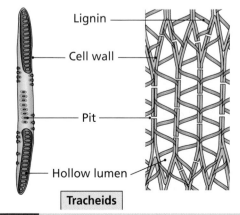

Lignin
Cell wall
Pit
Hollow lumen

Tracheids

23.14 *LS of xylem*

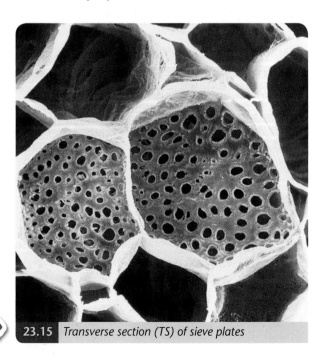

23.15 *Transverse section (TS) of sieve plates*

THE ORGANISM

although the nucleus degenerates. The walls are made of cellulose, but lignin is not present.

Each sieve tube element has an accompanying **companion cell** on its outside. These have a nucleus and dense cytoplasm.

Function

- Sieve tubes transport food made by photosynthesis from the leaves to the rest of the plant.
- Companion cells control the activities of the sieve tube elements.

Location

Phloem is found in the roots, stems, leaves and flowers.

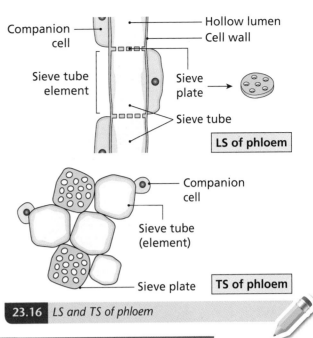

23.16 *LS and TS of phloem*

Differences between xylem and phloem	
Xylem	**Phloem**
Carries water and minerals	Carries food
Is dead	Is living
Has lignin	Has no lignin
Has no companion cells	Has companion cells

Location of plant tissues in roots, stems and leaves

Roots

In a longitudinal section (LS) of a root (as shown in diagram 23.5 on page 266), the dermal tissue forms the epidermis and root hairs. The vascular tissue consists of the xylem and phloem in the centre of the root and the rest of the cells (apart from the meristem) make up the ground tissue.

Diagram 23.18 shows the arrangements of tissues in the transverse section (TS) of a root.

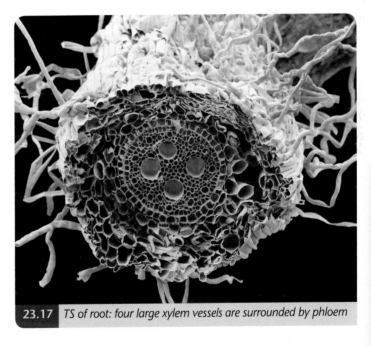

23.17 *TS of root: four large xylem vessels are surrounded by phloem*

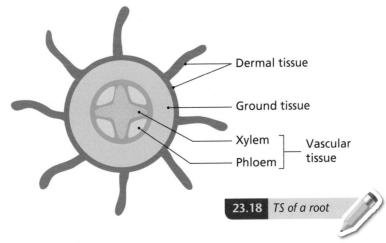

23.18 *TS of a root*

Stems

The location of the three plant tissues in a stem LS and TS are shown in diagram 23.20.

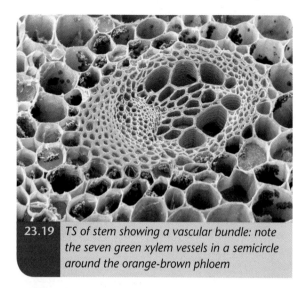

23.19 | TS of stem showing a vascular bundle: note the seven green xylem vessels in a semicircle around the orange-brown phloem

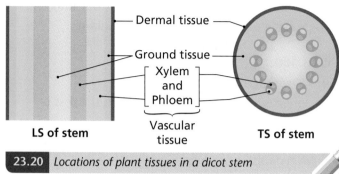

23.20 | Locations of plant tissues in a dicot stem

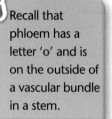

Recall that phloem has a letter 'o' and is on the outside of a vascular bundle in a stem.

Leaves

The location of the three plant tissues in the TS of a leaf is shown in diagram 23.21. A vertical section (VS) of a leaf is shown in diagram 24.4 in the next chapter.

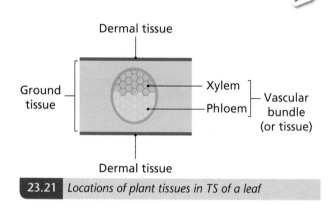

23.21 | Locations of plant tissues in TS of a leaf

Monocotyledons and dicotyledons

Flowering plants are divided into two categories: monocotyledons and dicotyledons. These names are usually shortened to 'monocots' and 'dicots'. Monocots include daffodils, tulips, grasses and cereals such as wheat and barley.

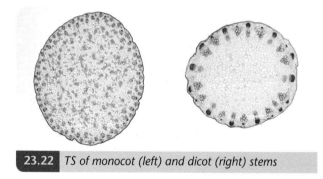

23.22 | TS of monocot (left) and dicot (right) stems

Dicots include beans, peas, peanuts, sunflowers, roses and trees such as chestnut, oak and ash. There are greater numbers and varieties of dicots than there are of monocots.

Monocot features

- Monocots take their name from the fact that they have one cotyledon in the seed. A cotyledon is the first leaf that develops in a seed. It is often specialised for food storage.

A **cotyledon** is a seed leaf.

- Monocots are mostly herbaceous plants. This means they are soft, because they do not contain woody parts.
- Monocot leaves are long and narrow with veins that run parallel along the leaf (this is called parallel venation; see diagrams 23.11 and 23.24).
- Monocot vascular bundles are scattered at random in the stem.
- Monocot flowering parts are arranged in groups of three or multiples of three. For example, there may be either three, six, nine etc. petals in the flower of a monocot.

Dicot features

- Dicots are so named because they have two cotyledons in each seed (see diagram 23.23).
- Dicots may be herbaceous (e.g. peas, sunflowers or tomatoes) or woody (e.g. roses or oak and ash trees).

- Dicot leaves are often broad and they have a network of veins (net venation; see diagrams 23.11 and 23.24).
- The vascular bundles of dicots are arranged in a ring around the inside of the stem.
- The flowering parts in a dicot are arranged in fours or fives, or multiples of these numbers.

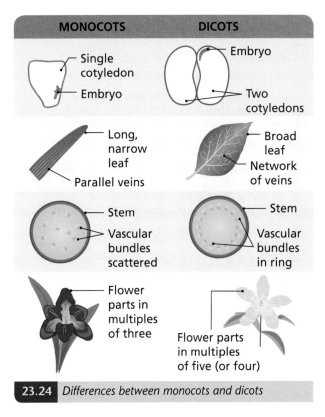

MONOCOTS	DICOTS
Single cotyledon / Embryo	Embryo / Two cotyledons
Long, narrow leaf / Parallel veins	Broad leaf / Network of veins
Stem / Vascular bundles scattered	Stem / Vascular bundles in ring
Flower parts in multiples of three	Flower parts in multiples of five (or four)

23.24 Differences between monocots and dicots

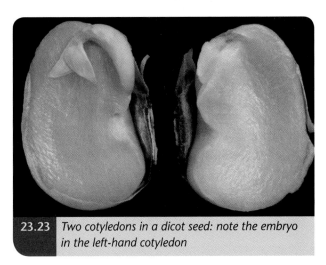

23.23 Two cotyledons in a dicot seed: note the embryo in the left-hand cotyledon

Activity 17 To prepare and examine a transverse section (TS) of a dicot stem

1. Plants that are suitable for this purpose are busy Lizzie, begonia, sunflower or celery (although celery is actually a petiole rather than a stem). As these are herbaceous (i.e. non-woody), they are easier to cut.
2. Cut out a short section of the stem between two nodes using a scalpel or backed blade.
3. Wet the blade (to reduce friction) and cut thin sections of the stem (cutting away from your fingers to prevent injury).
4. Cut the sections at right angles to the stem (i.e. try and avoid wedge-shaped sections). If the stem is too soft and flexible, it can be supported by placing it into a slit that is cut in some elder pith or carrot, which can then be sectioned as shown in diagram 23.25, method B.
5. Store the cut sections in a clock glass or petri dish of water (to prevent them dehydrating).

Section of stem — Finger — Backed blade — Thin sections — **Method A** — Stem section — Water — Internode — Leaf — Backed blade — **Method B** — Finger — Stem — Carrot (for support) — Section of stem

23.25 Cutting sections of a stem for microscopic examination

6. Transfer the thinnest sections onto a microscope slide using a forceps or small paint brush.
7. Add a few drops of water and a cover slip at an angle (to eliminate air bubbles).
8. Observe the section under low power and then under high power of the microscope (as explained in Activities 6 and 7 in Chapter 7) and compare them with diagram 23.20.
9. Draw a diagram of the TS of the stem. Label the position of the dermal tissue, ground tissue and vascular tissue.

THE ORGANISM

Summary

Flowering plants are divided into:
- Underground root systems for anchorage and absorption of water and minerals
- Over-ground shoot systems, which consist of stems, leaves, flowers and fruits.

Roots can be:
- Tap roots (where one main root grows down into the soil)
- Fibrous roots (where a mass of small, branched roots emerge from the stem).

The **zones in a root** are:
- The zone of protection (root cap)
- The zone of cell production (meristem)
- The zone of elongation
- The zone of differentiation.

The **main functions of stems** are:
- To support the aerial parts
- To transport materials to and from the leaves.

Leaf venation (the pattern of veins on a leaf) is of two types:
- Parallel (typical of monocots)
- Reticulate or net (typical of dicots).

The **main functions of leaves** are:
- To make food
- To exchange gases
- To allow water loss (transpiration).

The **three main categories of plant tissues** are:
- Dermal tissue (forms a protective covering layer)
- Vascular tissue (xylem for water transport, phloem for food transport)

- Ground tissue (found between the other two tissues, carrying out a range of functions).

Xylem is a dead tissue that transports water.

Phloem is a living tissue that transports food.

Flowering plants are subdivided into monocots and dicots.

Monocots (such as daffodils and grasses) have:
- One seed leaf, or cotyledon
- Long, narrow leaves with parallel veins
- Scattered vascular bundles in the stem
- Flowering parts arranged in multiples of three.

Dicots (such as beans and oak trees) have:
- Two seed leaves or cotyledons
- Broad leaves with a network of veins
- Vascular bundles arranged in a ring in the stem
- Flowering parts arranged in multiples of four or five.

To prepare and examine a TS of a dicot stem:
- Cut thin sections of a stem
- Prepare a microscope slide using the sections
- Examine the sections under low and then high power of the microscope
- Draw a labelled diagram to show the three categories of tissue.

Revision questions

1 (a) Name the parts labelled A to H on diagram 23.26.

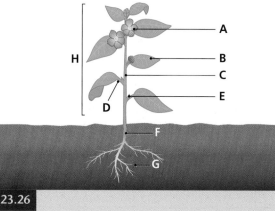

23.26

(b) What evidence is there to suggest that this plant is: **(i)** Photosynthetic **(ii)** A dicot?
(c) Describe the pattern of veins in the leaves.
(d) Give the functions of the parts labelled A and C.

2 Distinguish between the following pairs of terms:
(a) Herbaceous and woody
(b) Node and internode
(c) Root and shoot
(d) Tap and fibrous roots
(e) Dermal and ground tissue.

3 **(a)** What is meant by venation?
  (b) Draw labelled diagrams to show leaves with **(i)** parallel and **(ii)** net venation.
  (c) Name a plant with each type of venation.

4 Give one function for each of the following plant parts: **(a)** Petiole **(b)** Apical bud **(c)** Root hairs **(d)** Stems **(e)** Leaf **(f)** Leaf blade **(g)** Meristem.

5 Plants have three main types of tissue.
  (a) Name the three plant tissues.
  (b) State one function for each tissue.
  (c) Draw a TS of a stem and a root to show the locations of the vascular tissue.

6 **(a)** Name the zones of the root labelled A, B, C and D on Figure 23.27.

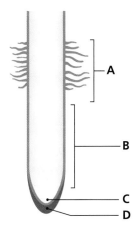

23.27

  (b) Which of the labelled parts do you associate with:
    (i) Absorption of water
    (ii) The formation of xylem and phloem
    (iii) Mitosis
    (iv) Cells becoming longer?

7 **(a)** Name two types of vascular tissue in plants.
  (b) State the function of each of these tissues.

8 Distinguish between xylem and phloem in terms of:
  (a) Whether they are living or dead
  (b) Their functions
  (c) Whether they have lignin or not
  (d) Whether they have pits or not
  (e) Whether they are tapered or not.

9 **(a)** Name a monocot plant.
  (b) Which of the leaves X or Y in diagram 23.28 is typical of a monocot?

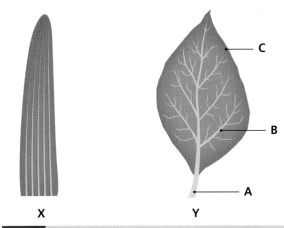

X   Y

23.28

  (c) Name the parts A, B and C of leaf Y.
  (d) Name the type of venation shown by each of the leaves.
  (e) Draw a labelled diagram to show the arrangement of vascular bundles in a TS of the stem of plant X.

10 When examining the TS of a stem under a microscope, give one reason for each of the following:
  (a) Wetting the blade or scalpel
  (b) Cutting very thin sections of the stem
  (c) Storing the cut sections under water
  (d) Cutting the sections at 90° to the stem
  (e) Adding the cover slip at an angle.

11 Choose which of the options (i), (ii), (iii) or (iv) represents the correct answer in each case below.
  (a) Fibrous roots are found in: **(i)** Wheat **(ii)** Dandelions **(iii)** Carrots **(iv)** Ash trees.
  (b) Petioles are attached to: **(i)** Petals **(ii)** Phloem **(iii)** Leaves **(iv)** Internodes.
  (c) Which of the following transports food?
    (i) Xylem vessel
    (ii) Phloem companion cell
    (iii) Xylem tracheid
    (iv) Phloem sieve cell.
  (d) The tissue that transports water in a plant is called: **(i)** Ground tissue **(ii)** Epidermal tissue **(iii)** Xylem **(iv)** Phloem.
  (e) Which of these cells contains lignin?
    (i) Companion cells
    (ii) Xylem vessels
    (iii) Meristematic cells
    (iv) Epidermis cells.

THE ORGANISM

Exam questions

Section A

12 The diagram represents a tomato plant.

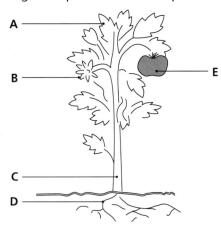

(a) Name the parts labelled B, C and E.
(b) Give **one** main function each for the parts labelled A and D.
(c) What is the role of part E?
(d) Name the tube-like tissue found in part C in which water moves through the plant.
(2007 OL Q 5)

13 The diagrams represent two forms of a vascular plant tissue, as seen under the microscope.

A   B

(a) Name this vascular tissue.
(b) Identify the two forms of this tissue.
(c) The walls of A and B are reinforced with a hard material. Name this material.
(d) Where precisely is this vascular tissue found in the stem of a young dicotyledonous plant?
(e) Name another vascular tissue.
(2007 HL Q 6)

14 The diagram shows a transverse section through the stem of a monocotyledonous (monocot) plant.
(a) What is meant by the term *monocotyledonous*?
(b) Give an example of a monocotyledonous plant.
(c) Name the structures labelled A.

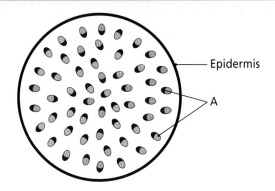

(d) How do you know from the diagram that the section is taken from:
  (i) a stem?
  (ii) a monocot?
(e) How are the veins arranged in the leaves of monocots?
(f) How does the vein arrangement in the leaves of dicot plants differ from that in monocots?
(2012 HL Q 5)

Section B

15 (a) Observation of a transverse section of a dicotyledonous stem reveals vascular and other tissues. Name **two** of the tissues that are not vascular tissues.
  (b) Answer the following questions in relation to the preparation of a microscope slide of a transverse section of a dicotyledonous stem.
   (i) State **one** reason why you used a herbaceous stem rather than a woody one.
   (ii) Explain how you cut the section.
   (iii) Why is it desirable to cut the section as thinly as possible?
   (iv) Draw a diagram of the section as seen under the microscope. Label the vascular tissues that can be seen.
   (v) State **one** precise function of each of the vascular tissues labelled in your diagram.
(2004 HL Q 8)

16 (a) (i) Why is a dicotyledonous (dicot) plant so called?
   (ii) Name a dicotyledonous plant.
  (b) (i) Describe in detail how you prepared a microscope slide of a transverse section of the stem of a dicotyledonous plant.
   (ii) Give an account of the procedures that you followed in order to view your slide under the microscope.

(iii) Draw enough of your section to show and label the location of **each** of the following:
 1. Phloem
 2. Xylem
 3. Ground tissue.
(2009 HL Q 7)

Section C

17 (a) **(i)** What is meant by ground tissue?
 (ii) Give a function of ground tissue.
 (iii) What is a meristem?
 (iv) Give a location for a meristem.
 (v) The diagram shows a transverse section through part of a plant. Is this part the root or the stem? Give **two** reasons for your answer.

 (vi) Copy the diagram into your answer book. Place an X where you would find vascular tissue and place a Y where you would find ground tissue.
(2007 OL Q 14)

18 (b) The diagram shows a transverse section of a dicotyledonous (dicot) root.

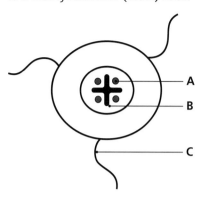

 (i) Name the parts labelled A, B and C.
 (ii) State **two** functions of a root.
 (iii) From what part of a seed does the root develop?
 (iv) Give **one** example of a root modified for food storage.
 (v) Plants can be monocotyledonous or dicotyledonous. Give any **one** difference between a monocotyledonous plant and a dicotyledonous plant.
 (vi) Give **one** example of a monocotyledonous plant and **one** example of a dicotyledonous plant.
(2011 OL Q 15)

Previous examination questions

Ordinary level	Higher level
2004 Q 15c	2004 Q 8
2005 Q 15a	2006 Q 14c
2006 Q 14a,b	2007 Q 6
2007 Q 5, 14a	2008 Q 14c
2008 Q 15a	2009 Q 7
2009 Q 14a	2012 Q 5
2011 Q 15b	
2012 Q 4	

Latest questions at www.edco.ie/lcbiologyplus/examhelp

Online test and assessment tracker

Scan the QR code and test yourself on chapter 23
www.edco.ie/lcbiologyplus

Chapter 24 Transport, storage and gas exchange in flowering plants

The need for a transport system in plants

Plants make their own food in the process of photosynthesis. Organisms that make their own food are said to be **autotrophic**.

Metabolism refers to all the reactions in an organism. Plant metabolism refers to reactions such as photosynthesis and respiration, and to reactions that occur in other processes such as cell division, growth and reproduction.

To allow these processes to occur, plants need to be able to acquire and transport water, carbon dioxide, oxygen and certain minerals. The following sections will deal with how plants acquire and transport these materials.

Water uptake by roots

Many root hairs are found near the tip of small roots. Root hairs are extensions of root epidermis cells and have thin walls that are not covered by a cuticle.

Adaptations of root hairs for absorption

- Thin walls
- Not covered by a cuticle
- Very numerous, which provides a large surface area

Osmosis

The absorption of water into root hairs takes place by osmosis. Soil particles are enclosed by a layer of relatively pure water called capillary water. The cytoplasm of root hairs

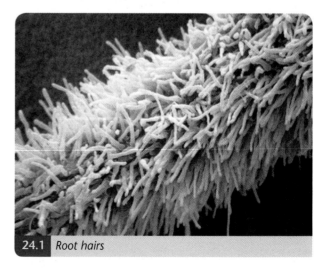

24.1 Root hairs

contains many dissolved solutes. This means that the cytoplasm is more concentrated than the water in the soil. As a result, water enters the cytoplasm of the root hairs by osmosis.

Movement of water into xylem

Water diffuses from the root hair cells into cells in the root. It continues to diffuse across the ground tissue until it reaches the xylem in the centre of the root as shown in diagram 24.2.

Xylem vessels form a continuous hollow pipeline from the roots to all parts of the plant. In particular, water can flow in xylem from the roots, up through the stem, into the petiole and from there into the leaves.

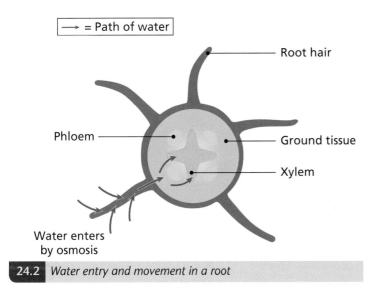

= Path of water

Root hair

Phloem

Ground tissue

Xylem

Water enters by osmosis

24.2 *Water entry and movement in a root*

24.3 *Root pressure: water is sometimes forced out of the plant because of root pressure*

Upward movement of water

There are two mechanisms that combine to cause the movement of water from the roots to the upper parts of a plant: root pressure and transpiration.

Root pressure

When water is drawn into roots by osmosis, the build-up of water causes a pressure. Root pressure pushes water up through the xylem. However, root pressure does not fully explain how water rises in stems, especially in very tall trees.

Root pressure has been measured, and it is not strong enough to push water to the top of very high plants. Also, root pressure is very low in summer – yet this is when most water passes up through the stem.

> **Transpiration** is the loss (by evaporation) of water vapour from the leaves and other aerial parts of a plant.

Transpiration

Most transpiration takes place through openings called stomata (singular, stoma) on the underside of the leaf, as shown in diagram 24.4.

Water evaporates from the cells in the leaf into the air spaces. From the air spaces it diffuses out into the atmosphere through the stomata. When the leaf cells lose water in this way they become less swollen and less turgid. As a result, they become more concentrated than the xylem cells. This means that water passes from the xylem into the cells because of an osmotic gradient.

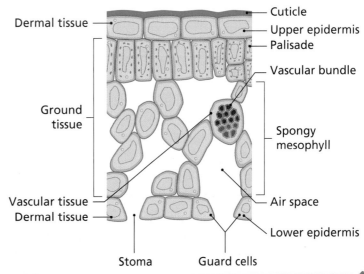

Dermal tissue

Cuticle

Upper epidermis

Palisade

Vascular bundle

Ground tissue

Spongy mesophyll

Vascular tissue

Dermal tissue

Air space

Lower epidermis

Stoma

Guard cells

24.4 *Vertical section (VS) of a leaf, showing the internal structure*

THE ORGANISM

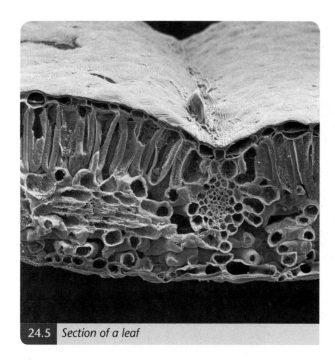

24.5 | *Section of a leaf*

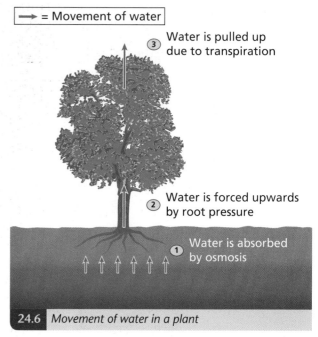

= Movement of water

③ Water is pulled up due to transpiration

② Water is forced upwards by root pressure

① Water is absorbed by osmosis

24.6 | *Movement of water in a plant*

As each water molecule is 'pulled' from the xylem cells by osmosis it pulls the next water molecule. This pulling force is transmitted from water molecule to water molecule all the way down the stem and into the root. In this manner water is said to be pulled up through the plant by transpiration. The flow of water through a plant is known as the transpiration stream.

Control of transpiration in leaves

Leaves may lose more than their weight in water each day due to transpiration. If they do not replace this water they will wilt and may die. At certain times, especially in dry weather, plants may find it difficult to absorb water from the soil.

To prevent wilting it is necessary for plants to reduce their rate of transpiration. They can do this in the following ways.

- Leaves have a waxy cuticle through which water cannot pass. The cuticle is normally thicker on the upper surface of the leaf because more water can evaporate from the upper surface of a leaf than from the lower surface. The cuticle does not cover the stomata on the lower surface of the leaf.

- Stomata are normally located on the lower surface of a leaf. The lower surface is not in direct sunlight and so it is cooler. This helps to reduce water loss by transpiration because the rate of evaporation is higher on the warmer upper surface than on the lower surface.

- Each stoma is surrounded by two guard cells. The guard cells can open or close the stoma by changing shape. Normally stomata are open by day. This allows the leaf to exchange gases for photosynthesis during the day. Stomata generally close at night. This helps to reduce water loss from the leaves at night, when gas exchange is not necessary because there is no photosynthesis in the dark.

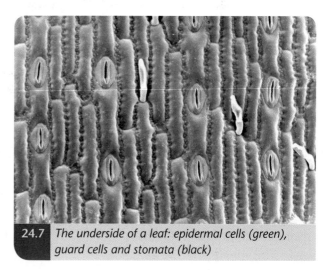

24.7 | *The underside of a leaf: epidermal cells (green), guard cells and stomata (black)*

However, environmental conditions can cause stomata to close during the day. This happens due to the following conditions: (a) if the plant loses too much water, (b) high temperatures and (c) high wind. In these cases the rate of transpiration is too great. By closing the stomata the plant reduces water loss.

In dry conditions (drought) the stomata will remain closed for much of the time. This is why food crop yields are normally substantially reduced in dry weather.

Mineral uptake and transport

Plants require a variety of minerals to function normally. These minerals include calcium (for the formation of cell walls) and magnesium (for the formation of chlorophyll). Minerals are absorbed into roots through root hairs in two ways.

1. Some of the minerals are absorbed by **diffusion**. This method does not require energy and is also called passive transport.

2. Some of the minerals are absorbed by **active transport**. This method uses energy in the form of ATP.

Once inside the root, the minerals are transported to all parts of the plant dissolved in water in xylem.

Uptake and transport of carbon dioxide

Photosynthesis takes place mostly in the ground tissue of the leaf (both palisade and spongy mesophyll). There are two sources of carbon dioxide for photosynthesis.

● Most of the carbon dioxide comes in through the stomata from the atmosphere. This carbon dioxide diffuses into the air spaces in the leaf. From here it diffuses into the photosynthesising cells in the ground tissue of the leaf. The rate of absorption or uptake of carbon dioxide is a measure of the *apparent* rate of photosynthesis.

● Carbon dioxide is produced in leaf cells by the process of respiration. This carbon dioxide may also be used in photosynthesis. The production of carbon dioxide in this way is more substantial at higher temperatures as a result of increased rates of respiration at these temperatures.

The real or true rate of photosynthesis is calculated by combining the carbon dioxide taken in through the stomata with the carbon dioxide formed in respiration.

True rate of photosynthesis = Rate of carbon dioxide absorbed through the stomata
+ Rate of carbon dioxide produced in respiration

The fate of the products of photosynthesis

The leaf is the main photosynthetic organ in a flowering plant. Photosynthesis takes place in the chlorophyll-containing cells of the leaf. Chlorophyll is contained in chloroplasts, and these are mostly located in the ground tissue or mesophyll of the leaf.

The products of photosynthesis are oxygen and glucose.

● Oxygen produced in photosynthesis can diffuse into the air spaces of the leaf.
  ▸ Oxygen can then diffuse out through the stomata into the atmosphere.
  ▸ However, some of the oxygen formed in photosynthesis can be used in leaf cells for respiration.

● Glucose is the main carbohydrate produced in photosynthesis.
  ▸ Glucose may be used immediately for respiration (continued overleaf)

THE ORGANISM

281

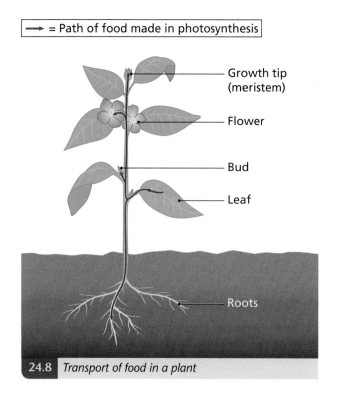

= Path of food made in photosynthesis

Growth tip (meristem)

Flower

Bud

Leaf

Roots

24.8 *Transport of food in a plant*

▶ Glucose may be converted to starch for storage. Some of this starch is stored in leaf cells, especially the spongy mesophyll cells. Starch stored in leaves is an important part of the diet of leaf-eating animals such as horses, cattle, sheep, monkeys and apes.

▶ Some of the glucose may be converted to another carbohydrate called sucrose (which is table sugar). Sucrose enters phloem sieve tube cells in the leaf and is then transported throughout the plant. The solution of sugary water carried in phloem is called phloem sap. The precise mechanism(s) by which food moves in phloem are not yet fully known.

Phloem carries food to all parts of the plant. For example, some of the food is sent to the growth areas of the plant. These growth areas can include buds, leaves, stems, roots or flowers. The food can then be used for respiration, to form new structures in the plant or it can be stored as starch.

Food storage organs in plants

Plants can alter or modify their roots, stems and leaves to act as food storage organs.

Modified root

Some dicots produce a large, V-shaped root that penetrates deep down into the soil. This **tap root** serves to anchor the plant and to absorb water deeper in the soil. In plants such as carrots, turnips and sugar beet, the tap root becomes swollen and fleshy with stored food. The stored food is used in the following year to produce flowers, seeds and fruits.

Modified stem

Potato plants produce an underground stem system. The tips of some of these underground stems become swollen with stored starch. These swollen tips are called stem **tubers**. The standard edible potato is a modified stem or stem tuber.

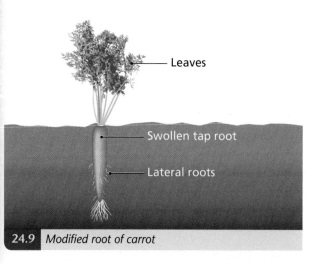

Leaves

Swollen tap root

Lateral roots

24.9 *Modified root of carrot*

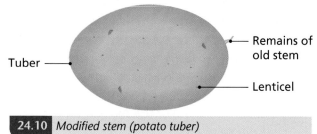

Tuber

Remains of old stem

Lenticel

24.10 *Modified stem (potato tuber)*

Modified leaves

Plants such as onions, garlic, daffodils and tulips produce bulbs.

A **bulb** contains an underground stem that is reduced in size. Swollen fleshy leaves, which are modified to store food, are attached to this stem. The fleshy leaves surround a central apical bud. A number of lateral or axillary buds are located where the leaves meet the reduced stem. The entire bulb is protected by old, dry, scaly leaves on the outside.

Note that celery and rhubarb are leaf **petioles** that are modified to store food.

24.11 *Assorted bulbs: onion (top right) and garlic (lower right)*

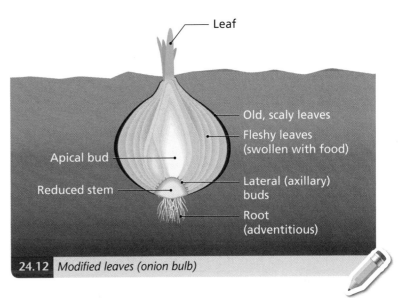

24.12 *Modified leaves (onion bulb)*

Leaf

Old, scaly leaves

Fleshy leaves (swollen with food)

Apical bud

Lateral (axillary) buds

Reduced stem

Root (adventitious)

Although onion and garlic bulbs are edible, the bulbs of daffodils and tulips are poisonous. This is an adaptation to prevent them from being eaten by organisms while in the ground.

24.13 *Section through a red onion*

Gas exchange in the leaf

Carbon dioxide

Plants require carbon dioxide for photosynthesis. In sunlight carbon dioxide diffuses from the atmosphere into leaves through the stomata located on the lower surface of the leaf. The function of the stomata is gas exchange.

The underside of a leaf normally contains a huge number of stomata; many leaves have about 50 000 stomata per cm^2. The large numbers of stomata increase the rate of gas exchange (by increasing the surface area).

Once inside the leaf, carbon dioxide diffuses to the ground tissue through the air spaces between these cells. The air spaces increase the internal surface area of the leaf. In most leaves the internal surface area is about 20 times greater than the outer, visible surface area of the leaf. The increased surface area allows carbon dioxide to diffuse more readily into the ground tissue cells.

Oxygen

Photosynthesis produces glucose and oxygen. Oxygen diffuses from the ground tissue, into the air spaces and out of the leaf through the stomata.

THE ORGANISM

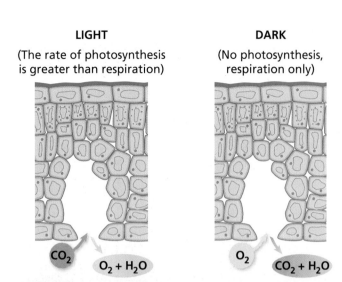

LIGHT
(The rate of photosynthesis is greater than respiration)

DARK
(No photosynthesis, respiration only)

CO_2 $O_2 + H_2O$ O_2 $CO_2 + H_2O$

24.14 *Summary of gas exchange in a leaf (provided stomata remain open)*

When the Earth was formed as a planet, the atmosphere did not contain any oxygen, i.e. it was anaerobic. Oxygen now makes up about 20% of the atmosphere. This oxygen has been produced by plants in photosynthesis and released out of the stomata.

Water vapour

Water vapour also diffuses out of the leaf through the stomata. The loss of water vapour from a plant is called transpiration.

Each stoma is enclosed by a pair of guard cells. The guard cells can open or close the stoma. In general, stomata are open by day (to allow gas exchange for photosynthesis) and closed at night (to reduce water loss).

Gas exchange in stems

Cells in the stems (or trunks) of trees and shrubs require oxygen for respiration. In addition, they produce carbon dioxide as a result of respiration. Normally the epidermis or bark does not permit the passage of gases in or out of the stem.

> **Lenticels** are openings in the stems of plants that allow gas exchange.

Normally oxygen diffuses inwards through a lenticel; carbon dioxide and water vapour diffuse outwards.

The cohesion–tension model of water transport in xylem

Introduction

Some plants have to move large amounts of water very rapidly from their roots to their leaves. For example, in warm conditions a large tree may lose 200 litres of water in an hour. The rate at which this water flows up through the tree is in excess of 15 m per hour.

As mentioned earlier, water moves up through a flowering plant:

● Partly by being pushed up by root pressure
● Mostly by being pulled up by transpiration.

The cohesion–tension model explains how water is transported in plants to great heights against the force of gravity. The model was first put forward in 1894 by two Irish scientists working in Trinity College, Dublin: **Henry Dixon** (1869–1953) and **John Joly** (1857–1933). It is now thought to be the main mechanism for the upward movement of water in plants.

Water has a high cohesion, i.e. water molecules tend to stick together. Water adheres to the walls of xylem, but this force is not as great as the cohesive forces of water.

HIGHER ▼

THE ORGANISM

Outline of the cohesion–tension model

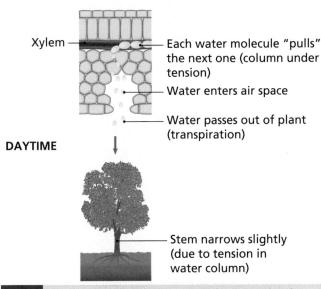

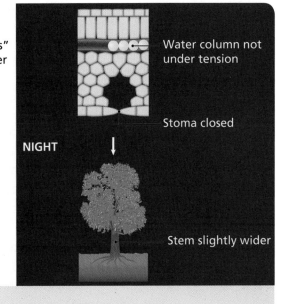

24.15 *Water movement and stem width by day and night*

The cohesion–tension model of water transport in xylem can be outlined as follows:

1. Water evaporates from the xylem into the air spaces of the leaf (and eventually out of the stomata into the air by transpiration). As transpiration pulls each water molecule out of the xylem, the next water molecule is pulled with it, because of their high **cohesion**. This is comparable to sucking water up through a straw.

   Provided there is a continuous column of water in a xylem tube, this pull will be transmitted through the water right down the stem to the root. The ability of water to be pulled upwards in this way only works in narrow tubes such as xylem.

   Transpiration and cohesion combine to generate a 'pulling force' from the top of the plant all the way down to the roots at the bottom of the plant.

2. When water molecules are pulled in this way the entire column of water in the xylem is stretched (like a piece of elastic). The water in the xylem is said to be under **tension**. The cohesive forces between the water molecules are great enough to hold water molecules in a column without breaking, even when tension is applied.

3. The tension in the xylem due to transpiration is great enough to pull water to a height of approximately 150 m. As the tallest trees are only about 100 m high, the cohesion–tension model can easily account for the upward movement of water in plants.

4. Stomata open in daylight and transpiration occurs. The tension produced in the water column causes xylem to become narrower. This in turn causes stems to become slightly narrower by day. To prevent xylem cells collapsing inwards, each xylem cell is strengthened with lignin.

> **Cohesion** is the sticking of similar molecules to each other.
>
> **Adhesion** occurs when different molecules stick together.

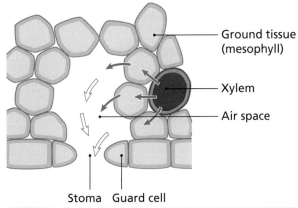

⇒ = Movement of water vapour
→ = Movement of water

24.16 *Movement of water in a leaf*

? Wood is a mixture of cellulose and lignin.

24.17 *Lenticels on the bark of a tree*

HL ▼

5. When transpiration stops (i.e. at night when the stomata close), the lack of tension allows the xylem to return to its original wider shape. This happens as a result of the elasticity of the xylem walls (see diagram 24.15).

Stomatal opening and closing

Each stoma is enclosed by a pair of kidney-shaped guard cells. The guard cells open and close the stoma by changing shape. The walls of the guard cells are especially thickened on the insides. This causes the cells to curve when they absorb water and swell.

When water enters the guard cells by osmosis, they become swollen or turgid. The guard cells are joined at their tips. The increase in size of the guard cells causes them to buckle outwards. The gap between them (which is the stoma) increases in size. When the guard cells lose water they shrink in size. This causes the gap between them (the stoma) to close.

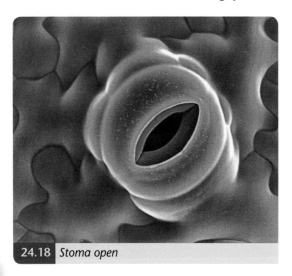

24.18 *Stoma open*

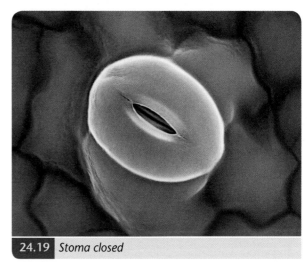

24.19 *Stoma closed*

Control of stomatal opening and closing

A major factor in the process of stomatal opening and closing is the **concentration of carbon dioxide** in the air spaces of the leaf.

HIGHER ▼

High concentration of CO₂

High levels of carbon dioxide in the air spaces cause the stomata to close.

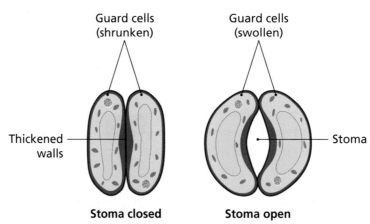

Guard cells (shrunken)   Guard cells (swollen)

Thickened walls   Stoma

Stoma closed   **Stoma open**

24.20 *Stomatal size (as seen on the underside of a leaf)*

THE ORGANISM

HIGHER ▼

The rate of photosynthesis falls in the evenings as a result of decreasing light intensity. As the rate of photosynthesis reduces, less carbon dioxide is absorbed from the air spaces in leaves.

In fact, respiration (which occurs in the plant 24 hours a day) in the leaf cells may increase the level of carbon dioxide. This means that carbon dioxide levels can build up in the air spaces. As a result the stomata close in the evenings.

Low concentration of CO_2

Low levels of carbon dioxide cause the stomata to open.

In the mornings photosynthesis resumes in the leaf because of increased levels of light intensity. The level of carbon dioxide falls because it is absorbed by the cells in the ground tissue. This results in the stomata opening.

If a plant is placed into a dark chamber with no carbon dioxide present, the stomata will open. This shows that carbon dioxide levels (and not light) trigger stomatal opening.

High concentration of CO_2 → stomata close
Low concentration of CO_2 → stomata open

The exact mechanism responsible for stomatal opening and closing is not yet known for certain. Although carbon dioxide levels play a major role in the process, other factors may be involved.

Summary

Plants make their own food and are autotrophic.

Plants need to transport:
- Water
- Carbon dioxide
- Oxygen
- Minerals for their metabolism.

Root hairs absorb water by osmosis.

Minerals are absorbed into roots by diffusion and by active transport.

Water passes from root hairs into root xylem.

Xylem transports water from the roots to all parts of the plant.

The transport of water in a plant is caused by:
- Root pressure, which pushes water up from the roots
- Transpiration (the loss of water from a plant), which pulls water out of the leaves.

The loss of water from leaves is controlled by:
- A waterproof cuticle covering the top and bottom of leaves
- Stomata being on the lower surface of a leaf

- The closing of the stomata at night, and during the day when transpiration rates are high.

Carbon dioxide for photosynthesis can be:
- Absorbed from the atmosphere through the stomata
- Obtained from respiration in leaf cells.

Photosynthesis mainly takes place in the chlorophyll-containing ground tissue.

The products of photosynthesis are glucose and oxygen.

Oxygen formed by photosynthesis may:
- Diffuse out through the stomata
- Be used by leaf cells for respiration.

Glucose formed in photosynthesis may be:
- Used directly in respiration
- Stored as starch
- Transported around the plant as sucrose in phloem sieve tubes.

Modified plant food storage organs include:
- Modified roots such as carrot tap roots
- Modified stems such as potato tubers
- Modified leaves such as onion bulbs.

THE ORGANISM

287

The **function of stomata** is gas exchange.
- Carbon dioxide diffuses inwards through the stomata in daylight.
- Oxygen and water vapour diffuse outwards through the stomata during daylight.

Air spaces increase the surface area for gas exchange inside a leaf.

Lenticels are openings in the stems of plants for gas exchange.

Guard cells change shape to open and close the stoma:
- When the guard cells are full of water they swell to open the stoma
- When the guard cells lose water they shrink to close the stoma.

Carbon dioxide is a controlling factor in gas exchange in leaves.
- High levels of carbon dioxide (at night) cause the stomata to close.
- Low levels of carbon dioxide (by day) cause the stomata to open.

The main method by which water rises in plants is the cohesion–tension model.
- Cohesion means similar molecules sticking together (water has a high cohesion).
- Adhesion means different molecules sticking together (water and xylem have a lower adhesion).
- Water is pulled out of xylem (and leaves) because it evaporates into the air (i.e. transpiration).
- Each water molecule pulls the next one behind it, creating tension in the xylem.
- This tension is caused by transpiration.
- The tension is transmitted down to the root xylem as a result of cohesion between water molecules.
- Tension in the water column causes xylem to become narrow during transpiration.
- When transpiration stops, xylem cells return to their normal wider shape, because of the elasticity of their walls.

Lignin prevents xylem from collapsing inwards.

Revision questions

1 (a) Name three substances transported by plants.
   (b) For each substance named state:
     (i) Where it originates
     (ii) A place to where it is transported.

2 (a) List three adaptations of root hairs for maximum absorption.
   (b) Name the process by which water enters root hairs.

3 Draw a labelled diagram of the TS of a root to show:
   (a) Where water enters the root
   (b) The position of the vascular tissue in the root
   (c) The path of water across the root.

4 (a) What is transpiration?
   (b) Name two adaptations of leaves to reduce the rate of transpiration.
   (c) Distinguish between transpiration and root pressure.

5 The apparatus shown in diagram 24.21 was set up to investigate water movement in a dicot plant.
   (a) Why is a dye added to the water?

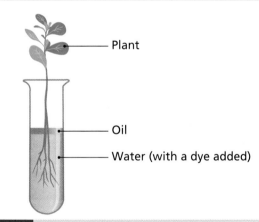

Plant

Oil

Water (with a dye added)

24.21

   (b) What is the purpose of the oil layer?
   (c) What will happen to the level of water in the test tube? Give a reason for your answer.
   (d) Draw simple diagrams to show the areas where the dye will appear in a TS of (i) the root, and (ii) the stem, of this plant.

6 (a) Name two minerals required by plants.
   (b) Give one function for each of these minerals in plants.

(c) Name a process by which these minerals enter a plant.

(d) State how these minerals get into a leaf.

7 Give two possible fates for each of the following:

(a) Carbon dioxide produced in respiration in leaves

(b) Oxygen formed in photosynthesis in leaves

(c) Glucose formed in photosynthesis in leaves.

8 (a) Name the parts labelled A to I in diagram 24.22.

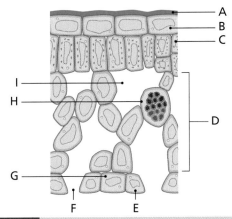

24.22

(b) Which labelled part(s) represent:
  (i) Dermal
  (ii) Ground
  (iii) Vascular tissue?

(c) In which labelled parts does photosynthesis take place?

(d) In which labelled parts are chloroplasts mostly found?

9 Give one reason for each of the following

(a) Chloroplasts are mostly concentrated near the upper surface of a leaf.

(b) There are no stomata on the upper surface of most leaves.

(c) Stomata tend to open during the day.

(d) Stomata close at night.

(e) Air spaces are located directly over stomata.

(f) Leaves have a cuticle but root hairs do not.

(g) Stomata are enclosed by guard cells.

(h) Leaves contain veins.

10 Name a plant in each case in which the following parts are modified for food storage:

(a) A root

(b) A stem

(c) Leaves.

11 (a) Name the tissue responsible for carrying food in plants.

(b) Name the carbohydrate that is normally carried in this tissue.

(c) Name the carbohydrate used by plants for: (i) Respiration (ii) Storage (iii) Cell walls.

12 (a) Why does a leaf require carbon dioxide?

(b) Why do leaves produce oxygen?

(c) How do these gases get in and out of: (i) Leaves (ii) Stems?

13 (a) Draw labelled diagrams to show the structure of the guard cells (i) In bright light (ii) In darkness.

(b) What causes the change in size of the guard cells?

14 (a) Who first proposed the cohesion–tension model of water movement in xylem?

(b) Is this model a push or a pull effect? Explain your answer.

15 Why must the water column be continuous for the cohesion–tension model to work?

16 The diameter of a tree trunk was measured and found to vary as shown by the graph in diagram 24.23. The time between X_1 and X_2 represents 24 hours.

(a) What time of day is represented by X_1 and Y_1?

(b) Describe the results shown in the graph.

(c) What causes the changes in the diameter of the trunk?

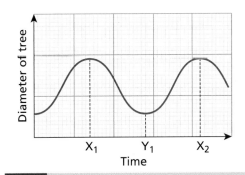

24.23

17 (a) Why is the level of carbon dioxide in the air spaces of a leaf:
  (i) High at night
  (ii) Low by day?

(b) What are the results on stomatal opening or closing of (i) high, and (ii) low, carbon dioxide concentrations?

(c) What is the benefit to a plant of the stomata closing at night?

HIGHER ▼

THE ORGANISM

18 Choose which of the options (i), (ii), (iii) or (iv) represents the correct answer in each case below.
    (a) Mesophyll is an example of: (i) Vascular tissue (ii) Ground tissue (iii) Dermal tissue (iv) Meristematic tissue.
    (b) Stomata are found mostly in the: (i) Stem (ii) Tree (iii) Leaf (iv) Bud.
    (c) Water enters root hairs by a process known as:
         (i) Translocation (ii) Cohesion (iii) Osmosis (iv) Diffusion.
    (d) During drought conditions, stomata are usually: (i) Turgid (ii) Open (iii) Closed (iv) Waxy.

Exam questions

Section A

19 (a) The diagram shows part of the under surface of a leaf as seen through the microscope. A is an aperture. B and C are cells.

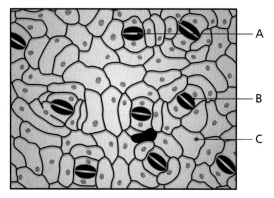

        (i)   Name A, B, C.
        (ii) What is the function of A?
        (iii) Name a factor that influences the diameter of A.
        (iv) Name the apertures in stems that are equivalent to A.
    (b) In some species of flowering plants the leaves are modified for the storage of food.
        (i)   Name a plant in which the leaves are modified for food storage.
        (ii) Name a carbohydrate that you would expect to find in the modified leaves of the plant that you named above.
        (iii) Name a type of modified stem that functions in food storage.

                                    (2004 HL Q 4)

20 The diagram shows the internal structure of a leaf.
        (i)   Name the **one** tissue type that is found at **both** V and Y.
        (ii) The cells at W contain many organelles that carry out photosynthesis. Suggest why the cells at W contain more of these organelles than the cells at X.
        (iii) In layer X, gases can diffuse throughout the leaf. Name **one** such gas.

        (iv) State **one** function of the opening at Z.
        (v)   Name the cells which are responsible for controlling the size of the opening at Z.

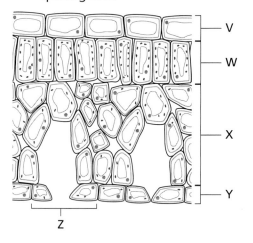

                                    (2010 OL Q 6)

Section C

21 (a) The passage of water through a plant is known as the transpiration stream. Answer the following questions in relation to the transpiration stream.
        (i)   Explain how water enters the plant at the root hair.
        (ii) Do minerals enter the plant by the process that you have indicated in (i)? Explain your answer.
        (iii) How is xylem adapted for its role in water transport?
        (iv) Strong forces of attraction exist between water molecules. Give an account of the importance of these forces in raising water to great height in trees.

                                    (2005 HL Q 14)

22 (b) (i)   Draw a diagram of a section through a leaf. Label a stoma and a guard cell.
        (ii) Give a function of the guard cell.
        (iii) Name **two** gases that enter or leave the leaf.

(iv) Name the process by which the gases move in or out of the leaf.
(2007 OL Q 15)

23 (a) (iii) Name the tissue that transports water from the root to the leaves.

(iv) Mention one way in which the tissue you have named in (iii) is adapted for the transport of water.

(v) The diagram below shows another tissue that is involved in transport in plants. Name this tissue and name a substance that is transported in it.

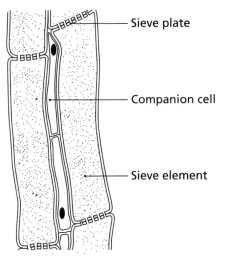

Sieve plate

Companion cell

Sieve element

(2008 OL Q 15)

24 (a) (i) Name the openings in the leaf which allow the entry of carbon dioxide for photosynthesis. State a factor which influences the diameter of these openings.

(c) (i) Draw a large, labelled diagram of a transverse section through a young root.

(v) Describe how minerals such as nitrates enter the root of a plant from the soil.
(2008 HL Q 14)

25 (b) (i) Name the tissue in plant stems through which water rises to the leaves.

(ii) Give **one** way in which this tissue is adapted for the transport of water.

(iii) Give a precise location of this tissue in the stem.

(iv) State another function of the tissue referred to in (i).

(v) The cohesion–tension model of transport attempts to explain water movement in plants against a particular force. Name this force.

(vi) Describe the principal features of the cohesion–tension model.

(vii) Name the two scientists mainly associated with the cohesion–tension model of transport.
(2011 HL Q 15)

Previous examination questions

Ordinary level	Higher level
2006 Q 4	2004 Q 4
2007 Q 15b(iii)–(v)	2005 Q 3h, 14a
2008 Q 15a	2006 Q 6a, 11c
2010 Q 6, 15a	2008 Q 14a(i), c(i)(v)
	2011 Q 15b

Latest questions at www.edco.ie/lcbiologyplus/examhelp

Online test and assessment tracker

Scan the QR code and test yourself on chapter 24
www.edco.ie/lcbiologyplus

THE ORGANISM

Composition of blood

Blood has four parts: plasma, red blood cells (corpuscles), white blood cells and platelets.

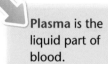

Plasma is the liquid part of blood.

Plasma

Plasma is a pale, golden liquid that makes up about 55% of the blood. The remaining 45% consists of blood cells and platelets.

If blood is specially treated so that it cannot clot and is then left to settle, it will appear as shown in diagram 25.1.

Plasma is made of:

- 90% water
- 7% proteins
- 3% dissolved materials that are being transported.

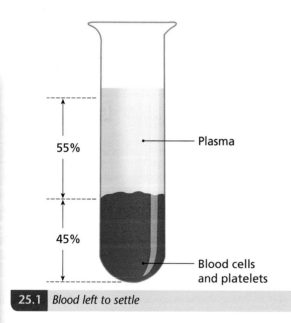

25.1 *Blood left to settle*

(Diagram labels: 55% — Plasma; 45% — Blood cells and platelets)

25.2 *Blood that was spun in a centrifuge, showing plasma in the upper layer*

The main plasma proteins are:

- **Antibodies,** which are produced by white blood cells in order to combine with and neutralise foreign substances
- **Clotting proteins,** which are acted upon to form blood clots.

As these proteins are too large to pass easily through the walls of blood vessels they help ensure that blood plasma has the same concentration as the blood cells.

Role of plasma

The role (or function) of plasma is to **transport** dissolved materials such as glucose, amino acids, minerals, vitamins, salts, carbon dioxide, urea and hormones. Plasma also carries heat.

Serum has no clotting protein but it does contain the other plasma-soluble materials (including antibodies).

Red blood cells

Red blood cells (also called red blood corpuscles or erythrocytes) are produced in the marrow of bones such as the ribs, breastbone, the long bones in the arms and legs, and the vertebrae of the backbone.

Red blood cells are round and very small – about 5 million are found in 1 cubic millimetre (mm^3) of blood. They consist of a flexible membrane containing many molecules of a red protein called haemoglobin.

Red blood cells are broken down (and replaced) at the amazing rate of 3 million cells per second. This is because they become damaged by constantly changing shape in order to pass through narrow blood vessels.

Red blood cells cannot repair themselves and so they live for only about 4 months. Dead red blood cells are broken down in the liver and spleen.

- The iron from the haemoglobin is stored in the liver and may be recycled to make new haemoglobin in bone marrow.
- The rest of the red blood cell and haemoglobin is converted to bile pigments such as biliverdin and bilirubin.

Role of red blood cells

The role (or function) of red blood cells is to **transport oxygen**.

Haemoglobin is based on molecules of iron and can join with oxygen in areas of high oxygen concentration (e.g. the lungs) and release oxygen in areas of low oxygen (e.g. the body cells).

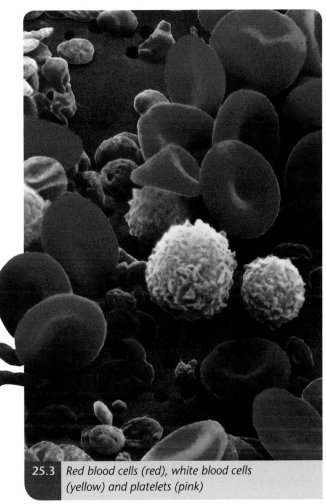

25.3 *Red blood cells (red), white blood cells (yellow) and platelets (pink)*

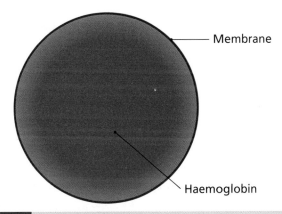

— Membrane

— Haemoglobin

25.4 *A red blood cell*

> **Serum** is plasma from which the clotting proteins have been removed.

Anaemia is a lack of haemoglobin (or red blood cells). The symptoms of anaemia are pale skin colour and a loss of energy.

THE ORGANISM

293

White blood cells

White blood cells (also called leucocytes):

- Are larger than red blood cells
- Have no definite shape
- Have a nucleus
- Live for a few days (but some types live for years)
- Are less numerous than red cells (700 red:1 white).

White blood cells are made in bone marrow (and some of them mature in the lymphatic system).

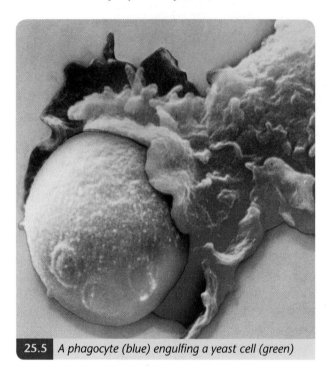

25.5 *A phagocyte (blue) engulfing a yeast cell (green)*

Role of white blood cells

The role (or function) of white blood cells is to **defend** the body against infection and to **fight infections** already present in the body.

There are many types of white blood cells.

- The majority of white blood cells attack bacteria in the body. They surround (engulf) the bacteria (and other invading particles such as viruses) and digest them. The way in which a cell 'eats' solid particles is called phagocytosis. As a result these white blood cells are called **phagocytes**.
- Some white blood cells (called lymphocytes) react to invading particles, such as bacteria and viruses, by producing **antibodies**. Antibodies play an important role in defending the body against infection and are dealt with more fully in Chapter 37.

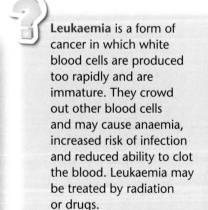

Leukaemia is a form of cancer in which white blood cells are produced too rapidly and are immature. They crowd out other blood cells and may cause anaemia, increased risk of infection and reduced ability to clot the blood. Leukaemia may be treated by radiation or drugs.

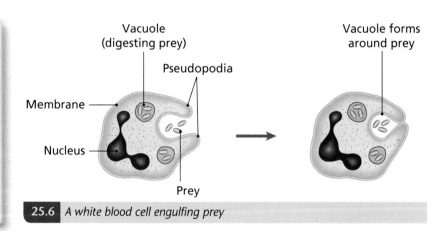

Vacuole (digesting prey)

Vacuole forms around prey

Pseudopodia

Membrane

Nucleus

Prey

25.6 *A white blood cell engulfing prey*

Platelets

Platelets (or thrombocytes) are made in bone marrow from large cells. These large cells break down to produce **cell fragments** called platelets. A platelet is smaller than a red blood cell.

Role of platelets

The role (or function) of platelets is to **clot** the blood. A clot results when damaged body cells produce chemicals that stimulate platelets to form a clot.

THE ORGANISM

Blood clots have two main functions:

- They reduce the loss of blood
- They prevent the entry of micro-organisms.

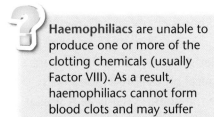

Haemophiliacs are unable to produce one or more of the clotting chemicals (usually Factor VIII). As a result, haemophiliacs cannot form blood clots and may suffer from excessive bleeding.

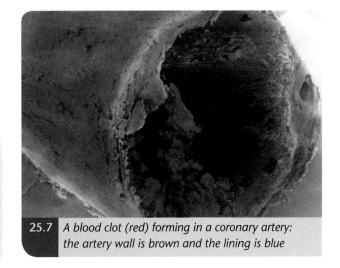

25.7 *A blood clot (red) forming in a coronary artery: the artery wall is brown and the lining is blue*

Clots do not usually form in healthy, undamaged blood vessels. However, if the vessel walls are damaged, a blood clot may form and may block the blood vessel. This is called thrombosis. Examples include clots forming in blood vessels in the brain (causing strokes) or in the vessels of the heart (causing heart attack).

Functions of blood

- Transport of food, waste products and hormones by plasma
- Transport of heat from internal organs by plasma – this helps to maintain a constant body temperature
- Transport of oxygen by red blood cells
- Defence against disease. This is due to:
  - White blood cells (phagocytes), which engulf and digest bacteria
  - White blood cells (lymphocytes), which produce antibodies to destroy 'foreign bodies' such as bacteria and viruses
  - Platelets clotting the blood, which prevents blood loss and the entry of disease-causing organisms.

Blood groups

ABO groups

Red blood cells can be placed in four different categories (or blood groups), depending on the types of chemicals (if any) attached to their cell membranes. The four main (ABO) blood groups are A, B, AB and O.

When blood transfusions are given it is important to match the incoming blood group to the blood group of the recipient. Failure to do this may result in blood clumping in the recipient.

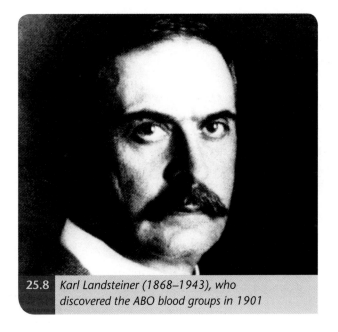

25.8 *Karl Landsteiner (1868–1943), who discovered the ABO blood groups in 1901*

The Rhesus factor

Apart from the ABO blood groups there are many other blood types. The best known of these is the Rhesus factor. This is named after Rhesus monkeys, in which it was first discovered.

About 85% of Irish people have a chemical called the Rhesus factor on the surface of their red blood cells. Those people who have this chemical are said to be Rhesus positive (Rh+). The 15% of the population who do not have the Rhesus chemical on their red cells are said to be Rhesus negative (Rh–).

- People of blood group A may be A positive (also called A+ and A Rh+). This means they are in blood group A and have the Rhesus chemical on their red blood cells.
- Those who are A negative (A– or A Rh–) do not have the Rhesus chemical. A similar situation applies for those who are B+ and B–, AB+ and AB–, O+ and O–.

 The Rhesus factor is important for safe blood transfusions. It may also lead to problems for a Rhesus-negative mother who is pregnant with a Rhesus-positive child. Her first Rhesus-positive baby is normally born safely, but any further Rhesus-positive foetuses may be anaemic, brain damaged or stillborn. Treatment is now available to prevent such complications in pregnancy.

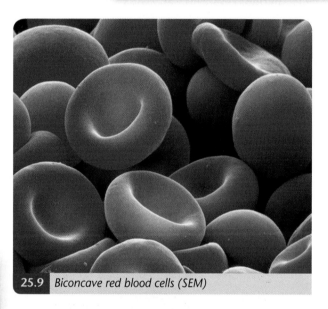

25.9 *Biconcave red blood cells (SEM)*

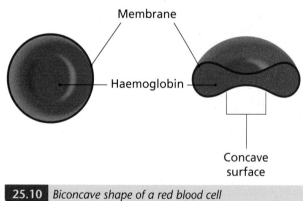

Membrane

Haemoglobin

Concave surface

25.10 *Biconcave shape of a red blood cell*

Haemoglobin (purple) ⇄ Oxyhaemoglobin (bright red)
Lungs / Body cells

25.11 *Relationship between haemoglobin and oxyhaemoglobin*

Further details of red blood cells

HIGHER ▼

Red blood cells have:
- No nuclei (when mature)
- No mitochondria
- Biconcave shape (to give a larger surface area).

When red blood cells (erythrocytes) are first made they have a nucleus. They lose their nuclei within a few days, so mature red blood cells have no nuclei. They are then called red blood corpuscles. They also lack mitochondria.

Red blood cells are said to have a biconcave shape. This gives them a larger surface area over which they can exchange oxygen.

Haemoglobin has an amazing ability to form a loose chemical union with oxygen. In the lungs haemoglobin combines with oxygen to form oxyhaemoglobin. Haemoglobin is a purple colour; oxyhaemoglobin is a bright red colour.

Fortunately, haemoglobin loses oxygen very readily, which allows it to supply the cells in the body with oxygen.

THE ORGANISM

Types of white blood cells

There are a number of categories of white blood cells or leucocytes. Two of the categories are lymphocytes and monocytes.

Lymphocytes

- They are made in bone marrow
- Some of them mature in lymphatic tissue
- All of them are later stored in parts of the lymphatic system, such as the spleen, lymph nodes, tonsils, adenoids and thymus gland
- They comprise 25% of all white blood cells
- They can survive for between 3 months and 10 years
- They have a large round nucleus, with very little cytoplasm.

Function

The main function of lymphocytes is to **make antibodies**. Antibodies help the body to resist infection by micro-organisms (they are discussed in more detail in Chapter 37).

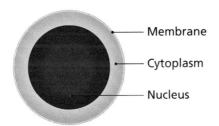

Membrane
Cytoplasm
Nucleus

25.14   *Structure of a lymphocyte*

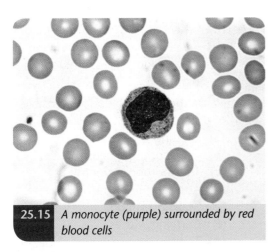

25.15   *A monocyte (purple) surrounded by red blood cells*

Syllabus   Note: lymphocytes and monocytes make up about 30% of white blood cells. The remaining (70%) white blood cells act as phagocytes, but they are not on the Leaving Certificate syllabus.

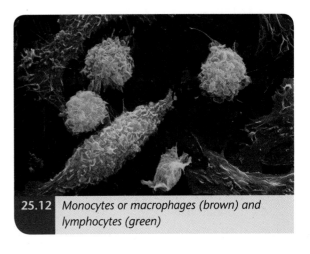

25.12   *Monocytes or macrophages (brown) and lymphocytes (green)*

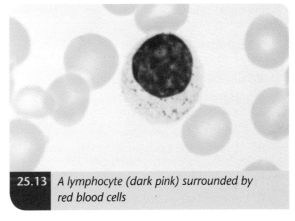

25.13   *A lymphocyte (dark pink) surrounded by red blood cells*

Monocytes

- They are formed in the bone marrow
- They comprise about 5% of white blood cells
- They survive for 6–9 days
- They have kidney-shaped nuclei.

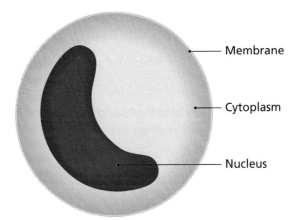

Membrane
Cytoplasm
Nucleus

25.16   *Structure of a monocyte*

Function

The function of monocytes is to scavenge throughout the body and surround and digest bacteria and other particles. In this way they act as phagocytes. They are also called **macrophages** (which means large phagocytes).

THE ORGANISM

297

Summary

Plasma:
- Is the liquid part of blood
- Transports foods, salts, hormones, waste and heat.

Serum is plasma without the clotting proteins.

Red blood cells (erythrocytes):
- Are made in bone marrow
- Contain haemoglobin
- Carry oxygen.

Dead red blood cells are broken down in the liver and spleen.

Haemoglobin is broken down to form bile.

White blood cells (leucocytes):
- Have no definite shape
- Are bigger than red cells but less numerous
- Defend the body against infection.

Platelets (thrombocytes):
- Are cell fragments
- Are formed in bone marrow
- Help to clot the blood.

The **main functions of blood** are:
- Transport
- Body defence.

The **human blood groups** are:
- O, A, B, AB.

Blood groups can be Rhesus positive or Rhesus negative.

Red blood cells have:
- No nuclei
- No mitochondria
- A biconcave shape.

Haemoglobin:
- Gains oxygen in the lungs, forming oxyhaemoglobin.

Oxyhaemoglobin:
- Loses oxygen to body cells, forming haemoglobin.

Two categories of white blood cells (leucocytes) are:
- Lymphocytes (25% of white blood cells, made in bone marrow but found in the lymphatic system, make antibodies)
- Monocytes (5% of white blood cells, made in bone marrow, engulf bacteria).

HIGHER ▼

Revision questions

1 (a) Name the four parts of blood.
   (b) Which of these parts are made of or from cells?
   (c) State one function for each part named.

2 Contrast red blood cells and white blood cells under these headings:
   (a) Shape
   (b) Size
   (c) Function
   (d) Ratio of each type
   (e) Contents
   (f) Site(s) of production.

3 Explain two methods by which white blood cells defend the body against infection.

4 The virus responsible for AIDS attacks and inhibits white blood cells. Suggest why AIDS victims may suffer from increased infections.

5 (a) Name two advantages of blood clotting.
   (b) What causes blood to clot?

   (c) Explain why blood within the circulatory system does not normally clot.

6 (a) Where are red blood cells made?
   (b) Name the main pigment in red blood cells.
   (c) What mineral is essential for this pigment?

7 Name the part of blood responsible for each of the following:
   (a) Clotting
   (b) Transporting glucose
   (c) Transporting oxygen
   (d) Attacking bacteria
   (e) Making antibodies
   (f) Carrying wastes
   (g) Transporting carbon dioxide.

8 (a) Name the four main blood groups.
   (b) What is the basis by which people are allocated to a particular blood group?
   (c) What is meant by the Rhesus factor?

THE ORGANISM

HIGHER ▼

9   (a) What shape are red blood cells?
     (b) What is the advantage of this shape?
     (c) Suggest two reasons why red blood cells have short lives.
     (d) Where are red blood cells broken down?
     (e) Name the end product made from the breakdown of red blood cells.

10 (a) Name two categories of white blood cells.
     (b) Discuss them in terms of their:
          (i)   Site of production
          (ii) Percentage of the total number of white cells
          (iii) Shape of nucleus
          (iv) Function
          (v)   Lifespan.

11 (a) Name seven components of human blood.
     (b) Give one function for each of the components named.
     (c) Distinguish between:
          (i)   The nucleated (i.e. having a nucleus) and non-nucleated parts of blood
          (ii) The cellular and non-cellular components of blood.

Exam questions

Section A

12 (a) Name the liquid part of blood.
     (b) Give **two** components of this liquid.
     (c) Copy and complete the following table in relation to blood cells:

Cell type	One function
Red blood cell	
White blood cell	
Platelet	

(2009 OL Q 5)

Section C

13 (a) (i)   State a precise location in the human body at which red blood cells are made.
          (ii) State **two** ways in which red blood cells differ from typical body cells, e.g. from the cheek lining.

(2006 HL Q 13)

14 (b) Answer the following questions in relation to blood.
          (i)   What is blood plasma? Give a role for blood plasma.
          (ii) Name **two** types of cell found in the blood and give a function for each of them.
          (iii) The ABO blood group system has four blood groups. What are these **four** groups?
          (iv) Suggest a reason why it is important to know a person's blood group.

(2008 OL Q 15)

15 (b) (i)   State **two** ways, other than colour, in which red blood cells differ from white blood cells.
          (ii) Name a group of white blood cells, other than lymphocytes.

(2012 HL Q 15)

Previous examination questions

Ordinary level	Higher level
2008 Q 15b	2005 Q 3f
2009 Q 5	2006 Q 13a
2011 Q 13a	2007 Q 13a(ii)
	2009 Q 13b(iii)
	2012 Q 15b

Latest questions at www.edco.ie/lcbiologyplus/examhelp

Online test and assessment tracker

Scan the QR code and test yourself on chapter 25
www.edco.ie/lcbiologyplus

THE ORGANISM

Chapter 26 The heart and blood vessels

An open circulatory system means blood leaves blood vessels and flows around the cells of the animal's body before re-entering blood vessels again.

A closed circulatory system means blood remains in a continuous system of blood vessels.

Learning objectives

- To describe the structure and organisation of tissues in the heart and vessels of the closed circulatory system of humans
- To explain the role of muscles and valves in the human circulatory system
- To describe the human circulatory system as a two-circuit system
- To draw the structure of the heart and the main blood circulation pathways, including the hepatic portal system
- To describe the supply of blood to the heart
- To understand simply how the heartbeat is controlled
- **HIGHER ▷** To be aware of specialised heart tissue and where the SA and AV nodes are located
- **HIGHER ▷** To describe the heart cycle and the systole and diastole periods
- To understand pulse and blood pressure and the effects that smoking, diet and exercise have on the circulatory system
- To dissect, display and identify an ox or sheep heart
- To investigate the effect that exercise has on breathing rate or pulse rate in humans.

The need for a circulatory system

Small organisms such as *Amoeba* have no need for a circulatory system. Nutrients and oxygen are supplied to their cells and wastes are removed by diffusion. Diffusion is adequate provided that the organisms are only a few cells thick. However, larger organisms need a circulatory system to supply their cells with all the materials they require.

Open and closed blood systems

There are two forms of circulatory system: open systems and closed systems.

In an **open blood system** the heart pumps blood into open-ended blood vessels. The blood later leaves the blood vessels and moves around the cells in the animal's body. The blood then moves back into blood vessels before it flows back to the heart.

Animals with open circulatory systems include crabs, lobsters, insects, spiders, snails and slugs.

In a **closed circulatory system** blood remains in a continuous system of blood vessels. Materials are exchanged between the blood and cells through the thin walls of the smallest blood vessels. The human circulatory system is a closed system.

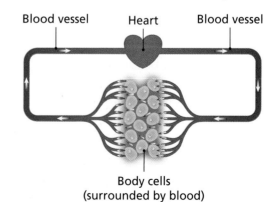

Blood vessel   Heart   Blood vessel

Body cells
(surrounded by blood)

26.1 *An open circulatory system*

A closed system is more efficient than an open system, for two main reasons.

- Blood can be pumped around the body faster. This allows nutrients and, especially, oxygen to be distributed faster to the cells. This in turn allows the animal to be more active (i.e. have a higher metabolic rate).
- A closed system allows the flow of blood to different organs to be increased or decreased. For example, more blood can be supplied to the leg muscles when the animal is running.

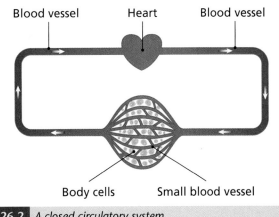

26.2 *A closed circulatory system*

Composition of the closed circulatory system of humans

The human circulatory system consists of:

- Blood (as described in Chapter 25)
- The heart (which pumps the blood)
- Blood vessels (which carry the blood to and from the heart).

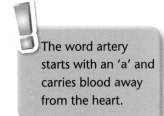

The word artery starts with an 'a' and carries blood away from the heart.

Blood vessels

The three main types of blood vessel are:

- **Arteries**, which carry blood **away** from the heart. Arteries divide into smaller vessels called arterioles.
- **Veins** carry blood **to** the heart. Small veins are called venules.
- **Capillaries** are tiny vessels that link arteries and veins.

26.3 *Different types of blood vessels*

Arteries and veins

Arteries and veins both have three similar layers in their walls. The main difference is that veins have a thinner middle layer. This results in veins having a larger lumen (diagram 26.4).

The three layers are:

1. An outer layer of tough, **inelastic protein** (called collagen), which prevents the walls from over-expansion.
2. A middle layer of **muscle and elastic fibres**. The muscle is involuntary and can alter the size of the vessel.
   - For example, during exercise the arteries leading to muscles expand and allow up to 10 times more blood to flow into the muscle.
   - Also, when we are too hot, blood vessels in the face expand (or dilate), causing blushing. This allows more blood to enter the vessels. As a result more heat is lost, allowing us to cool.
   - The elastic fibres bring the vessel back to shape when the muscle relaxes. The recoil of the artery also helps to pump blood.
3. An inner single layer of living cells called the **endothelium**, which surrounds the lumen.

THE ORGANISM

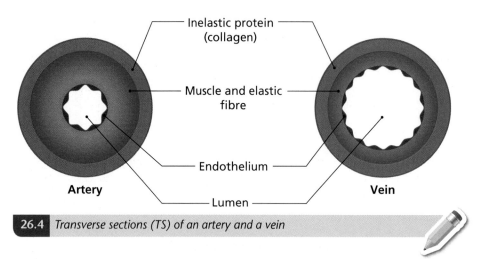

Inelastic protein (collagen)

Muscle and elastic fibre

Endothelium

Artery   **Vein**

Lumen

26.4 *Transverse sections (TS) of an artery and a vein*

Blood pressure is the force the blood exerts against the wall of a blood vessel.

Valves control the direction of blood flow.

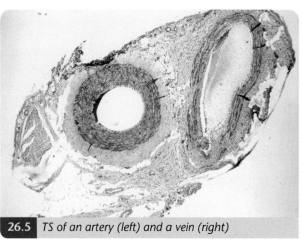

26.5 *TS of an artery (left) and a vein (right)*

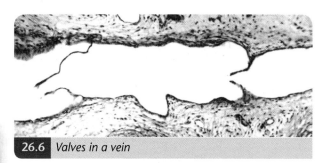

26.6 *Valves in a vein*

Blood pressure and valves

Blood pressure is highest in arteries when the heart contracts. This pressure causes the artery to expand slightly. The expansion can be detected as a pulse.

Pressure in veins is very low. Physical activity helps to push blood in the veins back to the heart. This happens when ordinary body muscles (skeletal muscles) contract. They squeeze the veins and help to return blood to the heart.

The pressure that forces blood through the veins is low. In order to prevent backflow, and to ensure blood flows only towards the heart, veins have valves.

People who stand still for long periods of time often get weak because their muscles do not contract. Blood then collects in veins and the brain suffers from a shortage of blood (and oxygen).

Differences between arteries and veins	
Arteries	**Veins**
Carry blood away from the heart	Carry blood to the heart
Blood under high pressure	Blood under low pressure
Thick wall	Thin wall
Small lumen	Large lumen
Blood flows in pulses	Blood flows smoothly (no pulses)
Valves absent	Valves present
Blood high in oxygen (except pulmonary artery)	Blood low in oxygen (except pulmonary vein)

Capillaries

Capillaries are tiny, much-branched vessels. Their walls are made of a single layer of endothelium cells.

Capillaries allow for the exchange of materials between the blood and body cells. Capillary walls are permeable so they allow exchange of materials between the blood and body tissues. The body has so many capillaries (100 000 km) that there is a capillary close to every body cell.

THE ORGANISM

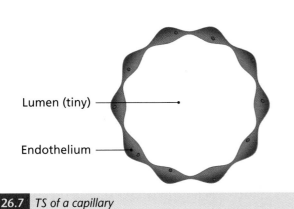

Lumen (tiny) ————

Endothelium ————

26.7 *TS of a capillary*

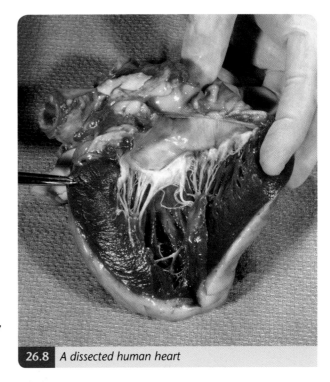

26.8 *A dissected human heart*

The heart

The heart is located between the two lungs (pointing slightly to the left-hand side of the chest, or thorax) and just above the diaphragm.

It is made of cardiac muscle and surrounded by a double membrane called the pericardium. Pericardial fluid between these membranes helps to reduce friction when the heart beats. Cardiac muscle is a special type of involuntary muscle that is slow to fatigue. Like all muscle, cardiac muscle is a contractile tissue, which means that it is capable of shortening.

Structure of the heart

The heart is divided into two sides by a wall called the septum. There are four chambers in the heart.

 The human heart is about the size of a clenched fist. It contracts about 100 000 times every day and pumps between 5 and 20 litres of blood per minute.

Atria

The two upper chambers are the atria (singular: **atrium**). The atria pump blood to the lower chambers or ventricles. Atria have thin walls because they pump blood only a short distance.

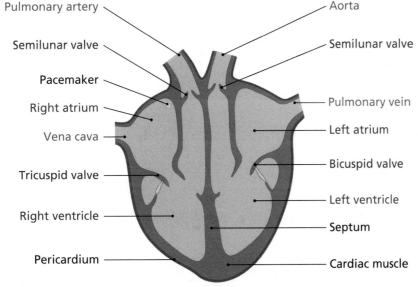

Pulmonary artery
Semilunar valve
Pacemaker
Right atrium
Vena cava
Tricuspid valve
Right ventricle
Pericardium

Aorta
Semilunar valve
Pulmonary vein
Left atrium
Bicuspid valve
Left ventricle
Septum
Cardiac muscle

26.9 *Structure of the heart*

THE ORGANISM

Ventricles

The **ventricles** pump blood out of the heart. The right ventricle pumps blood to the lungs. The left ventricle pumps blood to the head and body. As this is a much longer circuit, the wall of the left ventricle is much thicker (and stronger) than the wall of the right ventricle.

The atria and ventricles are separated by valves. These are held in place by tough cords ('heart strings') called tendons. The tendons are attached to the walls of the heart by small projecting muscles.

Valves

- The valves in the heart ensure that blood can only flow from the atria to the ventricles (i.e. they prevent backflow of blood).
- The valve on the right-hand side of the heart is the **tricuspid valve** (i.e. it has three flaps). The valve on the left is the **bicuspid valve** (i.e. it has two flaps).
- **Semilunar valves** (named because their flaps are shaped like half-moons) allow blood to flow out of the heart into the two main arteries (i.e. the pulmonary artery and the aorta). They prevent blood returning to the heart.

Blood flow in the heart

Deoxygenated blood

Blood that is low in oxygen (deoxygenated) enters the heart through the vena cava. The blood enters the right atrium. This chamber contracts and forces blood down through the tricuspid valve. The vena cava closes to prevent blood flowing back out of the heart. The blood now enters the right ventricle.

When this chamber contracts the tricuspid valve closes. Blood is forced out of the heart to the lungs through the semilunar valve in the pulmonary artery.

Oxygenated blood

Oxygen-rich (oxygenated) blood returns to the heart from the lungs. It enters the left atrium through the pulmonary veins. It is pumped down, through the bicuspid valve, to the left ventricle.

When this chamber contracts, the bicuspid valve closes and blood is pumped out to the body through the semilunar valve in the aorta. The semilunar valves allow blood to pass out of the heart. When the ventricles relax, these valves close to stop blood flowing back into the ventricles.

The oxygen content of the blood in the two sides of the heart can be recalled as follows:

LORD =
Left
Oxygenated
Right
Deoxygenated

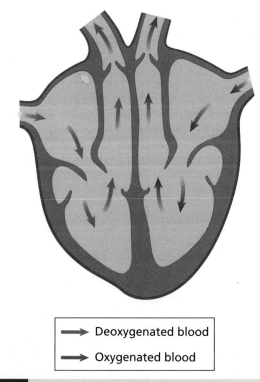

→	Deoxygenated blood
→	Oxygenated blood

26.10 *Blood flow in the heart*

Double circulation

The human heart is really a double pump (see diagram 26.11). The two sides of the heart are separated by the septum. The septum is necessary to separate deoxygenated and oxygenated blood. This separation is a vital part of the two-circuit circulatory system in humans: the pulmonary circuit and the systemic circuit.

Pulmonary circuit (heart → lungs → heart)

The right ventricle pumps blood around the pulmonary circuit. In this circuit, blood gains oxygen (and loses carbon dioxide) in the lungs. This circuit is relatively short, so the walls of the right ventricle are fairly thin.

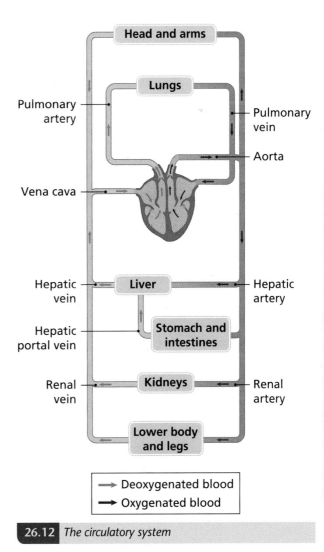

26.11 *Double circulation*

Systemic circuit (heart → body → heart)

The left ventricle pumps oxygenated blood to the head, arms, body and legs. In this circuit, blood loses oxygen (and gains carbon dioxide) to and from all the body cells. This is a much longer route than the pulmonary circuit, so the walls of the left ventricle are thicker and stronger than those of the right ventricle.

Double versus single circulation

A double-circulation system has the following benefits:

- It allows oxygen-rich and oxygen-poor blood to be kept separate.
- It also ensures that the blood pressure is high enough to reach all parts of the body.

In contrast to double circulation, some animals display single circulation. This means that blood is pumped from their heart, around the body and back to the heart again in a single circuit.

A single-circulation system can only produce low blood pressure around most of the body. This restricts the activities (metabolism) of the animal. Examples of animals with single circulation are earthworms and fish.

Portal system

A portal system is a blood pathway that begins and ends in capillaries.

The vessel(s) in a portal system do not connect directly to the heart.

The hepatic portal vein is an example of a portal system. The hepatic portal vein connects the stomach and intestines to the liver. It contains the highest concentration of food soon after a meal.

26.12 *The circulatory system*

THE ORGANISM

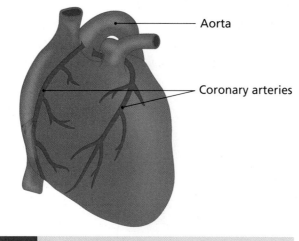

Aorta

Coronary arteries

26.13 *The location of the coronary arteries*

Blood supply to the heart

The muscle of the heart is supplied with blood by the **coronary (or cardiac) arteries**. These branch from the aorta at the point where it leaves the heart. Blood is drained from the muscle of the heart by the **coronary (or cardiac) veins**. These return the blood directly to the right atrium (i.e. not to the vena cava).

Blockage of the coronary arteries is a common cause of heart attack. Such attacks are often preceded by chest pains called angina. The coronary arteries subdivide to form numerous cardiac capillaries. These capillaries exchange materials with the muscular walls of the heart. The cardiac capillaries rejoin to form coronary veins.

Control of heartbeat

If a heart is removed from a body and kept in a nutritive, oxygen-rich fluid it will continue to beat. This shows that heartbeat can occur independently of the brain.

Heartbeat is controlled by a small bundle of specialised tissue called the **pacemaker**. This is located in the wall at the top of the **right atrium**. The pacemaker sends out regular electrical impulses, which initially cause the atria to contract. These impulses then cause the ventricles to contract. This means that blood is first pumped from the atria to the ventricles and a split second later it is pumped from the ventricles out of the heart.

The frequency of these impulses can be increased or decreased by the brain (i.e. the brain can cause the pacemaker to speed up or slow down the rate of heartbeat).

Heartbeat is controlled in the following way:

1. The pacemaker (also called the SA, or sinoatrial node) pulses and causes the atria to contract.

2. The electrical impulse from the pacemaker stimulates the AV (atrioventricular) node. This is similar to the pacemaker but is located further down in the right atrium near to where it joins the ventricle.

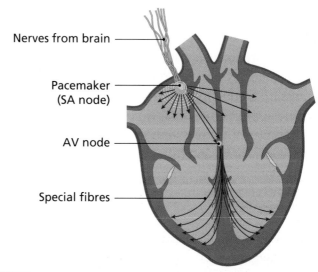

Nerves from brain

Pacemaker (SA node)

AV node

Special fibres

26.14 *Path of nerve impulses in the heart*

HIGHER ▼

3. The AV node sends an impulse down special muscle fibres located in the septum.

4. The impulse is passed out to the walls of the ventricles by thin fibres. The impulses from these fibres cause the ventricles to contract.

THE ORGANISM

HIGHER ▼

The pacemaker controls the rate of heartbeat. However, nerves from the brain (along with hormones) can change the rate at which the pacemaker (and therefore the heart) operates.

- Factors that increase the rate of heartbeat include exercise, temperature, emotions and shock.
- Factors such as relaxation, sleep and alcohol decrease the rate of heartbeat.

Diastole is when the heart chambers relax.

Systole is when the heart chambers contract.

The stages of heartbeat (cardiac cycle)

The events that take place during one heartbeat occur in three stages.

1. Blood enters the heart:
   - The atria and ventricles are both relaxed (diastole)
   - Blood enters the atria
   - All valves are closed.

2. Blood is pumped from the atria to the ventricles:
   - Electrical impulses from the pacemaker cause the atria to contract (atrial systole)
   - Blood is pumped to the ventricles
   - The tricuspid and bicuspid valves open
   - The vena cava and pulmonary veins close to stop blood entering the atria
   - The semilunar valves remain closed.

3. Blood leaves the heart:
   - The atria relax
   - Impulses from the AV node cause the ventricles to contract (ventricular systole)
   - Blood is forced out of the heart into the pulmonary artery and the aorta
   - The pressure forces the semilunar valves to open
   - The pressure closes the tricuspid and bicuspid valves
   - The ventricles now relax again
   - The semilunar valves close, which prevents blood from flowing back into the heart (or ventricles)
   - The vena cava and pulmonary veins open and the cycle starts again.

? The characteristic double sound of heartbeat (called the 'lub-dub' sound) is caused by the valves being forced shut. The low-pitched, quieter, longer-lasting 'lub' sound is due to the bicuspid and tricuspid valves being forced shut when the ventricles contract. The higher pitched, louder, much shorter 'dub' sound is due to the semi-lunar valves snapping shut.

A heart murmur is any abnormal sound associated with heartbeat. A heart murmur may indicate damage to one or more of the valves.

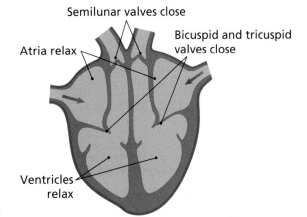

Atrial and ventricular diastole (atria fill with blood)

1

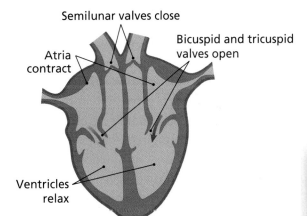

Atrial systole (blood pumped to ventricles)

2

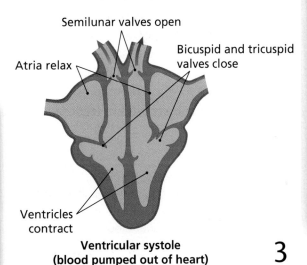

Ventricular systole (blood pumped out of heart)

3

26.15 *Blood flow through the heart*

THE ORGANISM

Pulse

When the left ventricle contracts, the pressure of the blood forced into the aorta causes the aorta to expand. A wave of expansion (followed by contraction) passes down along all the arteries. The contraction is caused by the elastic walls of the arteries.

The pulse can be felt most easily in the wrist or neck. The pulse rate is an indication of the heart rate. The average adult pulse (or heart) rate is 72 beats per minute. Most people have rates between 60 and 100 beats per minute.

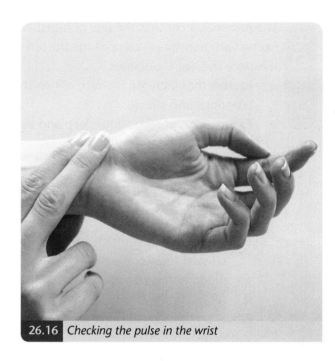

26.16 *Checking the pulse in the wrist*

Blood pressure

Blood entering the aorta is under high pressure due to the contraction of the left ventricle. As the blood passes from the aorta to the arteries, arterioles, capillaries, venules, veins and back to the right atrium of the heart, the pressure of the blood falls.

Blood pressure is different in different parts of the body. Medical professionals record the pressure required to stop the flow of blood in the major artery in the upper arm. Blood pressure readings are given as two values. Normally the higher value records the pressure of blood as a pulse passes through the artery (i.e. when the ventricles contract, or are in systole). It is called the systolic pressure. The lower value usually records the pressure when there is no pulse (i.e. when the ventricles are not contracting, or are in diastole). It is called the diastolic pressure.

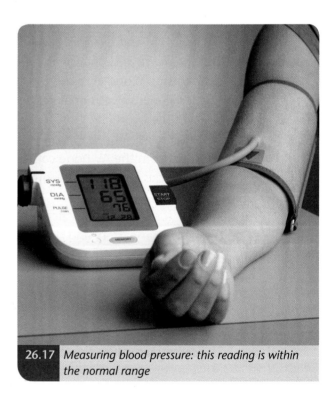

26.17 *Measuring blood pressure: this reading is within the normal range*

Typical blood pressure for a young adult is about $\frac{120}{80}$ mm of mercury (or mm Hg, the units used to record blood pressure). These values normally rise with age.

If the lower of the two blood pressure values (the diastolic pressure) is over 95 mm Hg the person is said to suffer from **high blood pressure** (called hypertension).

High blood pressure is most often caused by blockages in arterioles and small arteries. These blockages mean that the heart has to pump harder and this may lead to a stroke (lack of blood in the brain), heart attack and death.

THE ORGANISM

The effects of smoking, diet and exercise on the circulatory system

Smoking

Tobacco contains about 400 harmful chemicals. These include nicotine (a drug that is more addictive than heroin) and carbon monoxide. Nicotine causes increased heart rates and raises blood pressure, both factors that increase the workload of the heart. Carbon monoxide reduces the amount of oxygen carried by the blood. This results in lower energy production by the body.

Other chemicals in tobacco smoke increase the likelihood of blood clots in blood vessels (thrombosis), lung cancer, bronchitis and many other lung ailments.

Diet

The three main dietary factors affecting the circulatory system are fat intake, salt and being overweight.

Fats

Harmful fats are mostly found in animal products such as red meat and dairy foods (milk, cream, butter and cheese). These fats are high in cholesterol. Cholesterol increases the risk of forming blockages (called plaques) in arteries, especially the coronary arteries and those leading to the brain. These blockages result in heart attacks and strokes.

It is healthier to eat low-fat products (such as low-fat milk and low-fat cheese) and less-harmful fats that are found in margarine, sunflower oil, soya bean oil and oily fish. In addition, it is better to bake or grill food than to fry it.

Salt

High salt intake causes high blood pressure. Very often a single helping of packaged food contains more salt than the recommended salt intake for an entire day. Instead of salting food we should use pepper or other herbal seasonings.

Overweight

Obesity means being more than 20% overweight. Obesity is a contributory factor to causing high blood pressure and heart attacks.

Exercise

Sportspeople who exercise regularly tend to have visibly larger body muscles. In the same way, exercise enlarges and strengthens the heart. Exercise also improves our overall circulation and helps to reduce body weight.

The most beneficial forms of exercise are aerobic exercises. These speed up our intake of oxygen and are maintained for long periods of time. Aerobic exercises include fast walking, jogging, running, cycling, swimming and dancing.

In Ireland about 7000 people a year die from smoking-related causes. On average, smokers die 10 to 15 years earlier than non-smokers.

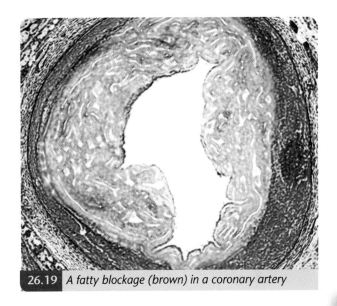

26.18 *A healthy lung (left) and a smoker's lung (right)*

26.19 *A fatty blockage (brown) in a coronary artery*

THE ORGANISM

Activity 18 To dissect, display and identify the parts of a heart

A sheep's heart is smaller than an ox's (or cow's) heart. Dissect an ox's or sheep's heart in the following manner.

1. Rinse the heart in cold water. Wash out any dark-coloured, jelly-like clumps of blood.
2. Place the heart on a dissecting board or tray.
3. Distinguish between the front (ventral) and back (dorsal) surface of the heart in one of the following ways:
   ▸ The front is more rounded and the thick-walled arteries are on this side.
   ▸ The lower part of the left side feels much firmer than the lower part of the right side.
   ▸ One of the coronary arteries runs diagonally from the top right to the bottom left of the heart.
4. Identify the four major blood vessels that enter and leave the heart. (Note that very often the butcher will have removed many of the vessels). Notice how thick-walled the arteries are compared with the veins. Notice the coronary arteries and veins on the surface of the heart. These vessels supply blood to the heart itself.
5. Locate the four chambers of the heart. (Note that the upper chambers or atria are quite small, are very high up and look like 'ears' on the outside of the heart.)
6. Draw a labelled diagram of the external structure of the un-dissected heart.
7. Make eight cuts in the front of the heart using a scalpel or scissors, in the positions shown in diagram 26.21.
8. Cuts 1 and 2 open up the left ventricle. In this chamber you should observe:
   ▸ A very thick wall
   ▸ White 'strings', which are the tendons that hold the valves in place
   ▸ The two flaps of the bicuspid valve.
9. Cuts 3 and 4 open up the right ventricle. In this chamber you should observe:
   ▸ A thinner wall
   ▸ White 'strings', which are the tendons
   ▸ The three flaps of the tricuspid valve.
10. Cuts 5 and 6 open up the atria. In these chambers you should observe:
    ▸ Very thin walls
    ▸ The bicuspid and tricuspid valves.

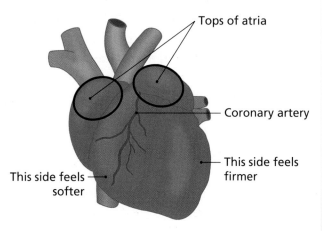

26.20 *Identifying the ventral surface of the heart*

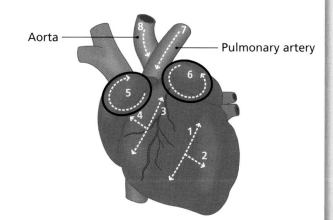

26.21 *Ventral view of the heart, showing the location of the cuts to be made*

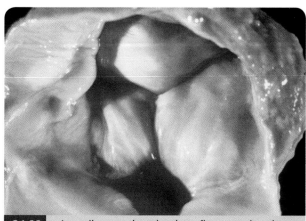

26.22 *A semilunar valve: the three flaps are closed*

11. Cut 7 opens up the pulmonary artery. This should allow you to see:
    ▸ The three flaps of the semilunar valve (at the point where the artery emerges from the heart).
12. Cut 8 opens up the aorta. This should allow you to see:
    ▸ The second semilunar valve
    ▸ The origin or beginning of the coronary artery (just above the semilunar valve). If you squirt water (or a dye) into the coronary artery you will see it flow down to the heart.
13. Identify the septum between the ventricles.
14. Draw a diagram of the dissected heart. This will be similar to diagram 26.9.
15. Using small pins and paper labels, flag-label the parts you have identified.
16. Wash your hands and sterilise the board and dissecting instruments.

26.23	A flag label

Activity 19a To investigate the effect of exercise on the pulse rate of a human

You have a choice between this activity and investigating the effect of exercise on the breathing rate of a human (Activity 19b on page 344).
1. Work in pairs, one person recording the results.
2. Sit down on a chair and rest for a few minutes.
3. Locate a strong pulse in your neck or wrist (just below the thumb).
4. Count the number of pulses per minute while at rest.
5. Repeat this two more times.
6. Calculate your average pulse rate per minute (measured in beats per minute, bpm) at rest by adding the three values and dividing the total by three. This is called the resting heart rate and is used as a control.
7. Walk slowly for 5 minutes.
8. Count your pulse rate per minute immediately after walking.
9. Walk briskly for 5 minutes.
10. Count your pulse rate per minute immediately after walking.
11. Exercise strenuously for 5 minutes (e.g. step up and down on a chair every 3 seconds or run).
12. Count your pulse rate per minute immediately after exercising.
13. Present your results in tables such as those shown below.

Heart rate before exercise					
Before exercise	Trial 1	Trial 2	Trial 3	Total	Average
Resting pulse rate (bpm)					

Heart rate after different types of exercise			
Activity	Gentle walk	Brisk walk	Strenuous exercise
Pulse rate (bpm)			

14. Compare the average resting rate with the rates after each type of exercise.

THE ORGANISM

Summary

Diffusion is sufficient for transport of materials in small animals; large animals need a circulatory system.

An **open circulatory system** means that blood leaves blood vessels.

A **closed circulatory system:**
● Means that blood is always in blood vessels
● Moves blood around the body faster
● Allows alterations in blood flow to different body organs.

Arteries:
● Carry blood away from the heart
● Have high pressure
● Have a thick wall
● Do not have valves
● Have a narrow lumen
● Carry oxygen-rich blood (except for the pulmonary artery).

Veins:
● Carry blood to the heart
● Have low pressure
● Have a thin wall
● Have valves
● Have a large lumen
● Carry oxygen-poor blood (except for the pulmonary vein).

Capillaries:
● Connect arteries to veins
● Have thin walls
● Allow exchange of materials.

Valves prevent backflow of blood.

Double circulation means that blood flows:
● From the heart to the lungs and then back to the heart (pulmonary circuit)
● From the heart to the rest of the body and back to the heart (systemic circuit).

Although heartbeat is usually controlled by the pacemaker, it can be altered by nervous stimulation from the brain or by hormones.

Heartbeat is controlled by:
● The pacemaker (SA node) in the wall of the right atrium, which causes the atria to contract
● The atrioventricular (AV) node, which sends electrical impulses down the septum
● The ventricles, which contract.

Diastole is when the heart is relaxed.

Systole is when the heart contracts.

The stages of heartbeat are:
● Diastole: blood enters the atria
● Atrial systole: blood is pumped to the ventricles
● Ventricular systole: blood is pumped out of the heart.

A **pulse** is caused by:
● The expansion and contraction of an artery as blood is forced through it
● Ventricular systole (ventricles contracting).

Blood pressure is the force of blood against the walls of the arteries.
● Normally the higher value is a measure of the systolic pressure; the lower value is a measure of the diastolic pressure.

Smoking damages the heart and blood vessels by:
● Increasing heart rate
● Increasing blood pressure
● Increasing the risk of blood clots and cancer.

The **main dietary factors** affecting the circulatory system are:
● Animal fats (causing blocked arteries)
● High salt intake (raising blood pressure)
● Being greatly overweight (raises blood pressure and causes heart attacks).

Aerobic exercise (high oxygen intake over a long period):
● Strengthens the heart
● Improves blood circulation
● Reduces body weight.

A heart can be dissected by:
● Cutting into the ventral surface
● Identifying the four chambers, the main blood vessels and the coronary artery.

The **effects of exercise on heartbeat** are investigated by comparing the pulse rate at rest and after exercise.

Revision questions

1 (a) Name the method of transport used by small organisms that do not have a circulatory system.
   (b) Why can humans not rely on the transport method used in small organisms?
   (c) How do humans overcome this problem?

2 (a) Distinguish between an open blood system and a closed blood system.
   (b) Name one animal with each type of circulation system.
   (c) Give one advantage of a closed blood system compared with an open blood system.

3 (a) State two structural differences between an artery and a vein.
   (b) Give two other differences between an artery and a vein.
   (c) State two ways in which a capillary differs from both an artery and a vein.

4 Name the material which (a) gives strength to an artery, (b) allows arteries and veins to change size, (c) lines all blood vessels.

5 (a) Arteries and veins are unsuited to exchanging materials with surrounding tissues. Explain why this is the case.
   (b) Give two reasons why capillaries are suited to exchanging materials.

6 (a) Name the structures labelled A to H in diagram 26.24.
   (b) What structure is located at X?
   (c) Give the functions of the structures labelled C, E, G and X.

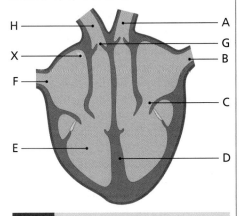

H ——
X ——
F ——
E ——

—— A
—— G
—— B
—— C
—— D

26.24

7 (a) What is a portal system?
   (b) Name a portal system in humans.
   (c) Suggest why the coronary arteries do not form a portal system.

8 (a) Why are the walls of the atria thinner than the walls of the ventricles?
   (b) Why are the walls of the left ventricle thicker than the walls of the right ventricle?

9 (a) Draw a diagram of the heart, about the size of your fist. Label:

    (i) The four chambers
    (ii) Four major blood vessels
    (iii) Four valves
    (iv) Any other four parts associated with the heart.
   (b) Indicate on your diagram the direction of blood flow through the heart. Use blue to show deoxygenated blood and red for oxygen-rich blood.

10 Describe in words the path taken by a blood cell from the time it enters the heart at the vena cava until it leaves the heart in the aorta (e.g. vena cava → right atrium → …).

11 Distinguish between the pulmonary and systemic circuits.

12 With regard to heartbeat, answer the following:
   (a) What structure causes it?
   (b) Where is this structure located?
   (c) What effect has exercise on heartbeat?
   (d) How is heartbeat normally measured?

13 Outline the stages of heartbeat under these headings:
   (a) Where the blood is flowing
   (b) The chambers that are contracted (if any)
   (c) The valves that are closed.

14 (a) Distinguish between systole and diastole.
   (b) What is meant by blood pressure?
   (c) Suggest one reason why high blood pressure is unhealthy.

15 (a) What causes a pulse?
   (b) In terms of blood vessels, why is a pulse often taken at the wrist?
   (c) Why do those who exercise regularly usually have lower pulse rates than those who do not exercise?
   (d) What is the danger in having a very high resting pulse rate?

16 Outline two negative effects on the circulatory system of each of the following:
   (a) Smoking (b) Poor diet
   (c) Lack of exercise.

17 Give a reason for each of the following:
   (a) Standing still may cause a person to feel faint.
   (b) A person with a hole in the heart (septum) often lacks energy.
   (c) Pulses are felt in arteries but not in veins.
   (d) Turning red in the face after exercise.
   (e) Recording the pulse rate a number of times when calculating resting heart rate.
   (f) Arteries blocked with fatty plaques are bad for the heart.
   (g) Smokers are at risk of having strokes.
   (h) Avoiding eating animal fats.

18 What is unusual about blood in the:
   (a) Pulmonary artery
   (b) Pulmonary vein
   (c) Hepatic portal vein?

HIGHER ▼

THE ORGANISM

313

19 **(a)** What is the average resting rate of the human heart in beats per minute?

(b) State one factor that decreases heart rate and one factor that increases it.

20 Diagram 26.25 shows the circulatory system of a mammal.

(a) Name the structures labelled A to H.

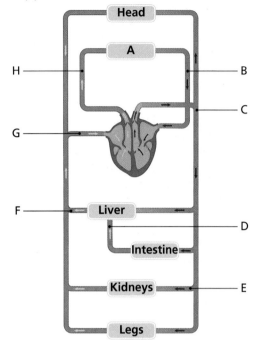

26.25

(b) Name the vessel in each case marked on the diagram which has the highest concentration of **(i)** oxygen, **(ii)** carbon dioxide and **(iii)** glucose, soon after a meal.

(c) Name the chambers of the heart to which the vessels marked B, C, G and H are connected.

21 Choose which of the options (i), (ii), (iii) or (iv) represents the correct answer in each case below.

(a) Pulmonary circulation involves:
(i) An open circulatory system
(ii) The lungs and kidneys
(iii) The hepatic portal vein
(iv) The pulmonary artery and the pulmonary vein.

(b) Inelastic collagen is found in:
(i) Only veins
(ii) Only capillaries
(iii) Arteries and veins
(iv) Only arteries.

(c) The hepatic portal vein contains:
(i) Blood rich in glucose
(ii) Blood rich in hormones
(iii) Blood lacking glucose
(iv) Blood rich in oxygen.

(d) The semilunar valves can be seen:
(i) In the aorta only
(ii) In the septum
(iii) In the pulmonary artery only
(iv) In both the aorta and pulmonary artery.

(e) Smoke that enters the blood in the lungs next enters the:
(i) Liver
(ii) Right atrium
(iii) Vena cava
(iv) Pulmonary artery.

Exam questions

Section A

22 The diagram shows a section through a human heart.

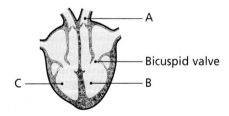

(a) Name blood vessel A.

(b) Is the blood in A oxygenated or deoxygenated?

(c) Name the chamber of the heart labelled B.

(d) Give **one** reason why the wall of chamber B is thicker than the wall of chamber C.

(e) What is the role of the bicuspid valve?

(2008 OL Q 4)

Section B

23 **(a)** **(i)** Cardiac muscle may be described as a <u>contractile</u> tissue. Explain the meaning of the underlined term.

(ii) Which chamber of the heart has the greatest amount of muscle in its wall?

(b) Describe how you dissected a mammalian heart in order to investigate the internal structure of atria and ventricles.
(i) Draw a labelled diagram of your dissection to show the location and structure of the bicuspid and tricuspid valves.
(ii) State the procedure that you followed to expose a semilunar valve.
(iii) What is the function of a semilunar valve?
(iv) Where in your dissection did you find the origin of the coronary artery?

(2004 HL Q 9)

24 **(a)** **(i)** Name the chamber of the heart that receives blood back from the lungs.
(ii) Name the blood vessels that bring this blood back from the lungs.

(b) Answer the following in relation to the dissection of a heart.
(i) What instrument did you use for the dissection?

(ii) Describe how you carried out the dissection.

(iii) Draw a diagram of the dissected heart and on it label the following: bicuspid valve, left ventricle, right atrium, tricuspid valve.

(2006 OL Q 7)

25 (a) (i) Name the cavity of the body in which the heart and lungs are located.

(ii) State **one** way in which heart muscle differs from other muscles in the body.

(b) Answer the following questions in relation to a dissection that you carried out to investigate the structure of an ox's or a sheep's heart.

(i) Describe the steps that you followed in order to identify and display the inner structures of the heart. Use suitably labelled diagrams if necessary.

(ii) What did you do in order to expose a semi-lunar valve?

(iii) Draw and label sufficient of your dissection to show the tricuspid valve, the right atrium and the right ventricle.

(2010 HL Q 7)

26 (b) Answer the following questions about an activity that you carried out to investigate the effect of exercise on your breathing rate or your pulse rate. Tick the rate you will refer to.

Breathing Rate	
Pulse Rate	

(i) The investigation starts by measuring the resting rate. How did you measure the resting rate?

(ii) After measuring your resting rate, what other steps did you carry out to complete the investigation?

(iii) What was the result of your investigation?

(iv) Does this investigation give the same result for both fit and non-fit people?

(v) Give a reason for your answer.

(2012 OL Q 7)

Section C

27 (a) The human circulatory system has two circuits.

(i) Give the name of each of these circuits.

(ii) Which of these circuits involves the pumping of blood by the left ventricle?

(b) (i) Write a short note on **each** of the following:

1. Pulse.
2. Blood pressure.

(ii) Comment on the effect of **each** of the following on the circulatory system:

1. Diet.
2. Exercise.

(iii) Give **two** ways, other than colour, in which a red blood cell differs in structure or composition from a typical body cell such as one in the cheek lining.

(iv) What is the role of the SA (sinoatrial) and AV (atrioventricular) nodes in the heart?

(v) Give the **precise** locations of **both** the SA and the AV nodes in the heart.

(2009 HL Q 13)

28 (b) The diagram shows a section through the human heart.

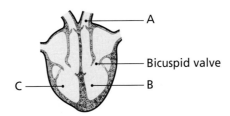

(i) Name the blood vessel labelled A.

(ii) Does A carry blood towards or away from the heart?

(iii) Name the chamber of the heart labelled C.

(iv) Why is the wall of chamber B thicker than the wall of chamber C?

(v) Name the arteries that supply the heart wall with blood.

(vi) What is the role of valves in the heart?

(2011 OL Q 13)

Online test and assessment tracker

Scan the QR code and test yourself on chapter 26
www.edco.ie/lcbiologyplus

THE ORGANISM

Chapter 27 The lymphatic system

Introduction

Along with the blood circulatory system, mammals have a second circulatory system called the lymphatic system. The lymphatic system is a **one-way** system of dead-ending vessels and lymph nodes. These lymph vessels collect the fluid that surrounds each cell in the body and return it to the blood.

Lymph nodes are swellings in the lymph vessels. Lymph nodes help to fight infection in the body.

Formation of lymph

Blood in arteries is under higher pressure than blood in veins. This causes some fluid and small proteins to be forced out of blood plasma in capillaries arising from arterioles. This fluid is called **tissue fluid** (also interstitial fluid or extracellular fluid, ECF). It surrounds all the cells of the body.

Tissue fluid is similar to plasma except it does not have red blood cells or platelets and has smaller amounts of white blood cells and proteins. It acts as an exchange medium, whereby materials entering or leaving cells must pass through it.

As tissue fluid is continuously being formed (i.e. about one litre an hour is produced), it must be removed and returned to the blood. This prevents swelling (called oedema) from developing in the tissues. Tissue fluid is drained away by two routes.

- Most (90%) of it is drawn back into plasma in the capillaries near the veins. This occurs by osmosis and is helped by the reduced blood pressure in the veins.
- About 10% of the fluid enters dead-ending tubes called lymph vessels (or lymphatics). The fluid is now called lymph. Lymph contains large amounts of white blood cells, proteins and fats.

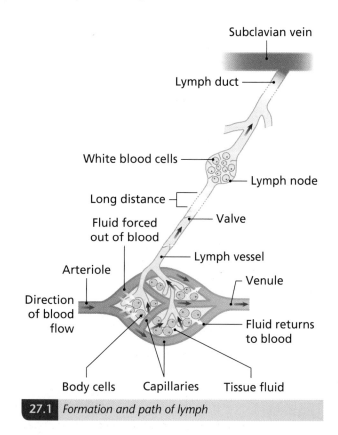

27.1 *Formation and path of lymph*

THE ORGANISM

Lymph vessels

Lymph vessels are found throughout the body. Lymph is moved slowly through lymph vessels by:

- The muscular walls of the vessels
- General body movements pressing on the vessels.

A system of valves ensures that lymph can only flow towards the shoulder regions. Smaller lymph vessels join together to form two main vessels:

- The thoracic duct on the left side of the body
- The right lymphatic duct at the right shoulder.

These ducts empty lymph into the bloodstream at the subclavian veins located near the collar bones at the shoulders.

Lymph nodes

Lymph nodes are small swellings found along the lymph vessels. They contain large numbers of white blood cells (lymphocytes) and have many channels through which lymph flows.

Lymph nodes are found in clusters, which form glands, in areas of the body such as the tonsils, adenoids (in the back of the nose), neck, armpits, thymus (a gland in the chest), spleen and groin (where the legs join the body).

Lymph nodes fight infection in two ways:

- They filter bacteria and other harmful material from lymph as it passes through
- They mature and store large numbers of white blood cells called lymphocytes. Some of these lymphocytes kill micro-organisms directly; others make antibodies, which help to neutralise micro-organisms.

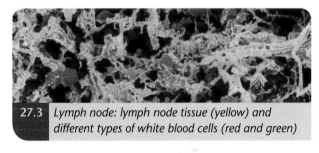

27.2 *The lymphatic system*

27.3 *Lymph node: lymph node tissue (yellow) and different types of white blood cells (red and green)*

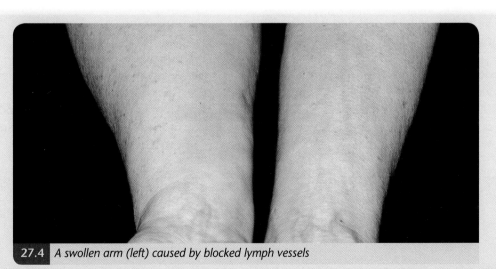

27.4 *A swollen arm (left) caused by blocked lymph vessels*

When lymph nodes are very active in fighting disease (especially in young people) they may become swollen. This results in swollen glands, which indicate that the person has an infection.

If lymph vessels become blocked (or if a person is inactive for several hours), swelling (oedema) may result. This is often seen in the ankles, where gravity adds to the excess tissue fluid.

THE ORGANISM

Functions of the lymphatic system

The lymphatic system forms a link between different parts of the blood (i.e. plasma produces tissue fluid, tissue fluid forms lymph and lymph returns to the plasma).

The lymphatic system has the following functions:

- To collect tissue fluid and return it to the blood.
- To defend the body against infection. It does this by:
  - Filtering micro-organisms in lymph nodes
  - Maturing and storing lymphocytes
  - Destroying micro-organisms by engulfing and digesting them or by antibody production.

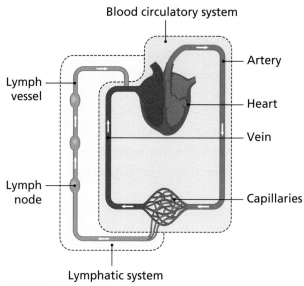

27.5 *The link between the blood and lymphatic circulatory systems*

- To absorb and transport fats in the digestive system. Lymph is found in lacteals (which are in the villi of the small intestine, see diagram 28.15 in the next chapter). Lymph often has a milky appearance because of its high fat concentration.

Summary

The **lymphatic system:**
- Is a secondary transport system
- Returns tissue fluid from around cells to the blood.

Tissue fluid:
- Is plasma without red cells, platelets or large proteins
- Surrounds all body cells and helps transport materials in and out of cells.

Tissue fluid returns to the plasma in two ways:
- Most enters blood capillaries
- Some enters dead-ending lymph vessels, where it is called lymph.

Lymph is made from tissue fluid and contains white blood cells, proteins and fats.

Lymph moves in lymph vessels because of:
- Muscles in the vessel walls
- General body movements.

Valves in lymph vessels control the direction of lymph flow.

Lymph returns to the blood in the subclavian veins (near the collar bones).

Lymph nodes:
- Are swellings found along lymph vessels
- Filter bacteria
- Store lymphocytes (white blood cells). Some of these kill micro-organisms and others produce antibodies.

The lymphatic system's functions are:
- To return tissue fluid to the blood
- To defend the body against infection
- To transport fat.

THE ORGANISM

Revision questions

1 Name two circulatory systems in a human.

2 **(a)** How is tissue fluid made?
  (b) Give one function for tissue fluid.
  (c) What happens to this fluid to prevent too much from accumulating?

3 Give one difference in each case between:
  (a) Plasma and tissue fluid
  (b) Tissue fluid and lymph
  (c) Lymph and plasma.

4 If plasma is leaving the blood at the rate of 1 litre every hour, explain why the volume of blood does not normally fall.

5 **(a)** Name the items labelled A to D in diagram 27.6.
  (b) State, giving a reason, whether X or Y on the diagram represents the arteriole side of the capillary.
  (c) State two pieces of evidence from diagram 27.6 which indicate that structure B is not a blood capillary.

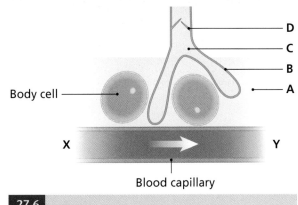

27.6

6 **(a)** Where are lymph nodes mostly located in the body?
  (b) What is their main function?
  (c) State two ways in which they achieve this function.
  (d) Why do they sometimes become swollen?

Exam questions

Section C

7 **(c)** **(i)** Describe the structure of the lymphatic system.
    (ii) Give an account of **three** functions of the lymphatic system.

(2006 HL Q 13)

8 **(b)** **(vii)** The lymphatic system is another series of vessels carrying fluid in the body. Give any **two** functions of the lymphatic system.

(2011 OL Q 13)

Previous examination questions

Ordinary level	Higher level
2011 Q 13b(vii)	2006 Q 13c

Latest questions at www.edco.ie/lcbiologyplus/examhelp

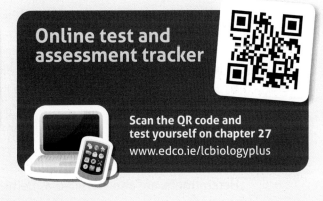

Online test and assessment tracker

Scan the QR code and test yourself on chapter 27
www.edco.ie/lcbiologyplus

THE ORGANISM

Herbivores are animals that feed mainly on plants. Examples are sheep, cattle and rabbits.

Carnivores are animals that feed mainly on animals. Examples are dogs, cats and ladybirds.

Omnivores are animals that feed on plants and animals. Examples are humans, badgers and hedgehogs.

Learning objectives

- To understand heterotrophic organisms and define the terms 'omnivore', 'herbivore' and 'carnivore'
- To define the term 'digestion' and explain why digestion and a digestive system are necessary
- To explain 'ingestion', 'digestion', 'absorption' and 'egestion' in relation to the human digestive tract
- To describe the structure and function of the alimentary canal and associated glands in digesting and transporting nutrients
- To describe the mechanical breakdown of food in the human digestive system, to include the teeth, peristalsis and the stomach
- To describe the chemical breakdown of food in the human digestive system, to include bile salts and an amylase, protease and lipase enzyme
- To describe the basic structure and function of the small and large intestines
- To explain the benefits of dietary fibre
- To describe two functions of symbiotic bacteria in the human digestive tract
- To explain the importance of a balanced diet containing a variety of food from the main food groups.

Introduction

Nutrition is the way in which an organism gets its food. There are two main types of nutrition.

- Autotrophs make their own food. Plants are autotrophic, as they make their own food by photosynthesis.
- Heterotrophs take in food from the environment. Animals, fungi and most bacteria are heterotrophic.

Heterotrophs can be subdivided according to whether they feed on live or dead sources.

- Parasites take in their food from a live source. Fleas and disease-causing bacteria are parasites.
- Saprophytes take in their food from a dead source. Bacteria and fungi that cause decay are saprophytes.

Heterotrophs are also classified as herbivores, carnivores and omnivores.

The need for a digestive system

Some animals, such as sponges and tapeworms, do not have a digestive system. In these animals each cell must have a full range of digestive enzymes.

Most animals do have a digestive system. This allows them to take in large pieces of food and break the food down using structures that need be located in only one place (e.g. teeth in the mouth or enzymes in the small intestine). This means there is no need for every cell in the body to contain all the digestive enzymes.

The tiny particles of digested food are carried to each part of the body, mainly by the blood.

THE ORGANISM

The digestive system

The digestive system (also known as the alimentary canal or gut) is a long tube starting at the mouth and ending at the anus. Attached to the digestive system are the associated glands:

- Salivary glands
- Liver (and gall bladder)
- Pancreas.

> **Digestion** is the physical and chemical breakdown of food.

28.1 *The digestive system*

Main events in human nutrition

Human nutrition involves the following four processes.

1. **Ingestion** is the taking of food into the digestive system. This happens when food is placed in the mouth.
2. **Digestion** is the breakdown of food. There are two types of digestion.
   - Physical digestion is the mechanical breakdown of food. Physical digestion takes place when we chew food or churn it in the stomach. Physical digestion increases the surface area so that chemical digestion can take place more efficiently.
   - Chemical digestion is the breakdown of food using enzymes.
3. **Absorption** occurs when the digested food passes from the digestive system and enters into the blood.
4. **Egestion** is the removal of unabsorbed waste from the digestive system.

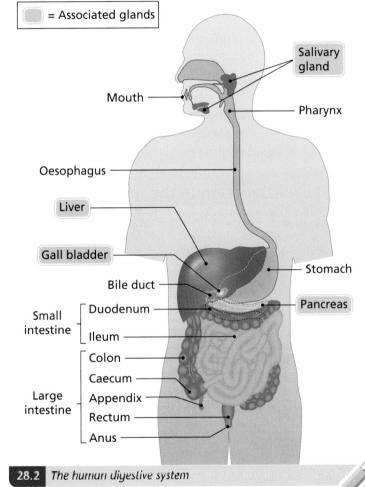

= Associated glands

Salivary gland
Mouth
Pharynx
Oesophagus
Liver
Gall bladder
Bile duct
Stomach
Duodenum
Small intestine
Ileum
Pancreas
Colon
Caecum
Large intestine
Appendix
Rectum
Anus

28.2 *The human digestive system*

Mouth

Types of teeth

- **Incisors** are found at the front of the mouth. They are shaped like chisels and they cut and slice food.
- **Canines** are the long, pointed, fang-like teeth. They are used to grip and tear food.
- **Premolars** have large, flat surfaces and are used to crush and grind food.
- **Molars** are the large teeth located at the back of the jaw. They also crush and grind food.

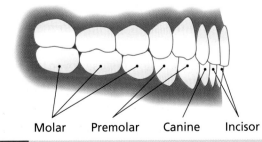

Molar   Premolar   Canine   Incisor

28.3 *Human jaw, showing the different kinds of teeth*

THE ORGANISM

321

Dental formula

The dental formula for an adult human is:

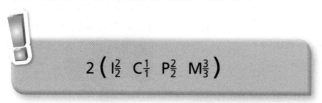

$$2\left(I\frac{2}{2}\ \ C\frac{1}{1}\ \ P\frac{2}{2}\ \ M\frac{3}{3}\right)$$

In this formula the letters represent the four types of teeth. The upper numbers refer to the number of teeth on one side of the upper jaw. The lower numbers refer to the number of teeth on the lower jaw on the same side. The formula refers to one side of the mouth.

The formula means that humans have two incisors on the top right and two incisors on the bottom right of the jaw. They have one canine in the top right and one in the bottom right, two top right and two bottom right premolars and three top right and three bottom right molars.

The formula shows that there are 16 teeth on the right-hand side of the mouth and the same number on the left-hand side. This means humans can have a maximum number of 32 teeth.

Digestion in the mouth

- **Mechanical digestion** takes place in the mouth by the chewing and grinding action of teeth on food.
- **Chemical digestion** occurs in the mouth by the action of the enzyme amylase. Amylase is found in saliva, which is a fluid produced by three pairs of salivary glands (located under the tongue, in the cheeks and at the back of the jaws).

Saliva contains water, salts, mucus (or mucin), lysozyme (an enzyme that destroys micro-organisms) and amylase.

Amylase travels through small tubes or ducts into the mouth where it is active. The pH of the mouth is close to 7 and this allows amylase to work. Amylase is inhibited by the acid pH in the stomach.

In the mouth amylase breaks down starch to form maltose:

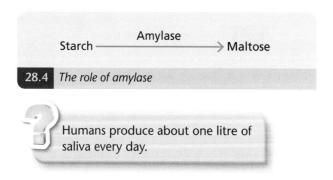

Starch $\xrightarrow{\text{Amylase}}$ Maltose

28.4 *The role of amylase*

Humans produce about one litre of saliva every day.

Syllabus The digestive system has many enzymes. However, the syllabus only requires that you study three enzymes: an **amylase** (for starch digestion), a **protease** (for protein digestion) and a **lipase** (for fat or lipid digestion).

In the mouth, food is formed into a ball, or bolus, and pushed backwards into the pharynx (or throat). The pharynx connects the mouth to the oesophagus. A flap called the **epiglottis** closes over the trachea (or windpipe) and ensures the food passes down the oesophagus.

Oesophagus

The oesophagus (or foodpipe) carries food to the stomach by an involuntary wave of muscular contraction called **peristalsis**. The process of peristalsis continues throughout the length of the alimentary canal.

Peristalsis

In the stomach, peristalsis helps to break down food mechanically. It also mixes food with the secretions of the stomach and then forces the mixture into the small intestine. In the small intestine, peristalsis forces food forwards and backwards, helping the food to be absorbed. In the large intestine about every 30 minutes strong waves of peristalsis force waste into the rectum.

> **Peristalsis** is a wave of muscular action in the walls of the alimentary canal that moves the contents along.

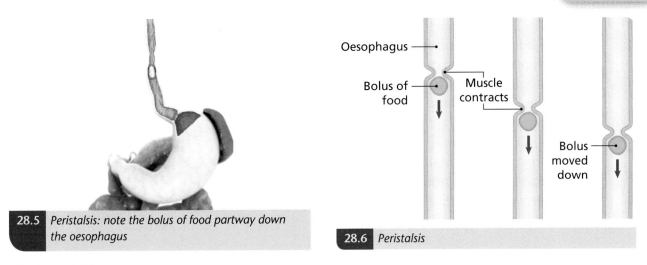

| 28.5 | Peristalsis: note the bolus of food partway down the oesophagus |

| 28.6 | Peristalsis |

Role of fibre

Dietary fibre (also called roughage) is made of cellulose from plant cell walls. Humans cannot digest cellulose. Good sources of fibre in our diet include wholemeal bread, cereals, vegetables and fruit.

Fibre absorbs and stores water. This causes the unabsorbed wastes to expand. The physical increase in the bulk of the waste stimulates the muscles of the intestine to work. In this way **fibre stimulates peristalsis**.

 A high-fibre diet is thought to be helpful in reducing the risk of colon cancer. This is because wastes move more rapidly through the colon, which means that cancer-causing chemicals have less time in contact with the colon.

Stomach

The stomach is a muscular bag that holds and digests food. The lining of the stomach (the mucosa) is heavily folded, forming millions of gastric glands. These glands produce a range of secretions, collectively called gastric juice. This consists of mucus, pepsinogen and hydrochloric acid.

Mucus coats the stomach and prevents self-digestion. **Pepsinogen** is an inactive enzyme and therefore does not digest the cells in the stomach lining that produce it. Pepsinogen is converted to the active enzyme pepsin by acid in the stomach. Pepsin converts proteins to smaller peptides. Pepsin is said to be a protease, i.e. it is an enzyme that digests protein.

Proteins ──── Pepsin ───→ Peptides

| 28.7 | The role of pepsin |

Hydrochloric acid (HCl) gives the stomach a pH of 1 to 2. The acid kills many bacteria, loosens fibrous and cellular foods, activates pepsinogen and denatures salivary amylase.

The contraction of the stomach walls helps to churn and digest the food mechanically. This turns it into a thick, soupy mixture called chyme. Chyme leaves the stomach in small amounts when a muscle at the base of the stomach opens briefly.

The stomach can hold about 1 litre of food for up to 4 hours. An overproduction of acid in the stomach can lead to heartburn. This occurs when acid rises up the oesophagus, which is not as well covered in mucus as the stomach. It may be controlled by neutralising the acid with alkali, e.g. by taking medicines such as Alka-Seltzer or Rennies.

Glands associated with the small intestine

Pancreas

The pancreas secretes the hormone insulin (see Chapter 35) and digestive materials (which form pancreatic juice). Pancreatic juice consists mainly of the salt sodium hydrogen carbonate (or sodium bicarbonate), which neutralises chyme from the stomach, and a range of enzymes such as amylase and lipase. These enzymes enter the duodenum through the pancreatic duct.

Lipase acts on lipids, whereas amylase digests starch. Both enzymes function best at a pH of between 7 and 9, which is the pH of the duodenum.

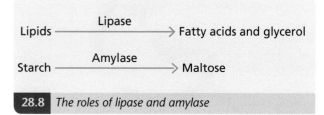

28.8 *The roles of lipase and amylase*

Liver

The liver is a complex organ with many functions. Among the most important functions of the liver are:

- Breaking down red blood cells
- Making bile
- Detoxifying the body, i.e. breaking down poisons such as alcohol and drugs
- Breaking down excess amino acids to form urea
- Converting glucose to glycogen for storage
- Converting excess carbohydrates to fat
- Storing vitamins, such as vitamin D
- Storing minerals (trace elements), such as iron (Fe), copper (Cu) and zinc (Zn)
- Making plasma proteins that are used in blood clotting
- Making cholesterol, which is needed to form many hormones
- Producing heat to warm the blood (and the body).

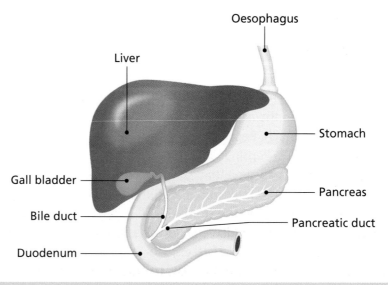

28.9 *The relationship between the alimentary canal and the liver and pancreas*

Bile

Bile is partly formed from the remains of damaged red blood cells. It is a yellow-green viscous liquid. It consists of water, bile salts and bile pigments (it does not contain any enzymes). Bile is made in the liver and stored in the gall bladder. It enters the duodenum through the bile duct.

The functions of bile are:

- To emulsify lipids, i.e. to break down large fats and oils into tiny droplets (this increases the surface area for enzyme digestion)
- To neutralise chyme from the stomach (it contains sodium hydrogen carbonate, which is alkaline)
- To excrete pigments (biliverdin and bilirubin), which are made from damaged red blood cells.

Gallstones can form in the bile duct and prevent the release of bile. This often results in severe indigestion, especially after eating fat-rich foods.

28.10 *Gallstones*

Small intestine

The small intestine consists of two main parts: the duodenum and the ileum.
The duodenum carries out digestion, whereas the ileum is the site of absorption.

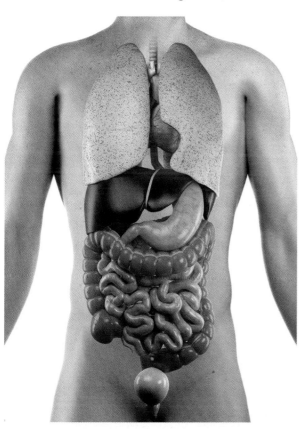

The first 25 cm of the small intestine is the duodenum. The remaining 5.5 m comprise the ileum. Food remains in the small intestine for between 1 and 6 hours.

28.11 *Male thorax and abdomen*

Duodenum

The cells lining the duodenum produce a range of digestive enzymes. In addition, the products of the pancreas and liver enter the duodenum.

The inner lining of the small intestine contains many infoldings called villi (singular: villus). These give the lining a velvety texture. In addition, each villus has many microvilli. The numerous infoldings increase the surface area for either digestion (in the duodenum) or absorption (in the ileum). Intestinal glands between the villi produce a range of enzymes called intestinal juice.

The main function of the **duodenum** is **d**igestion.

A summary of the digestive process is given in the table below.

Summary of digestion (enzymes are in bold)					
Substance	**Made in**	**Active in**	**Substrate**	**Product**	**Preferred pH**
Amylase	Salivary glands	Mouth	Starch	Maltose	7 to 9
Pepsin	Stomach lining	Stomach	Protein	Peptides	2
Hydrochloric acid	Stomach lining	Stomach	Bacteria and fibrous foods	Dead bacteria and softened food	–
Sodium hydrogen carbonate	Pancreas	Duodenum	Acid	Neutralises acid	–
Amylase	Pancreas	Duodenum	Starch	Maltose	7 to 9
Lipase	Pancreas	Duodenum	Lipids	Fatty acids and glycerol	7 to 9
Bile salts	Liver	Duodenum	Lipids	Lipid droplets	–
Sodium hydrogen carbonate	Liver	Duodenum	Acid	Neutralises acid	–

Ileum

> The function of the ileum is to absorb nutrients.

Food entering the ileum is almost fully digested. The end products of digestion are given below.

The end products of digestion	
Food	**Digested to**
Carbohydrates	Monosaccharides (e.g. glucose)
Proteins	Amino acids
Lipids	Fatty acids and glycerol

Villus (plural: villi)

As mentioned earlier, the lining of the duodenum and ileum contains many villi, which increase the surface area for absorption. Food is absorbed by diffusion.

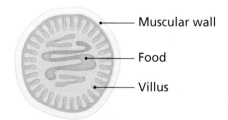

Muscular wall
Food
Villus

(a) TS of small intestine

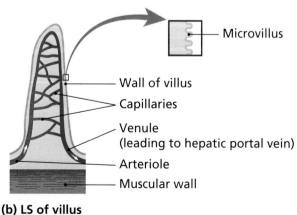

Microvillus
Wall of villus
Capillaries
Venule (leading to hepatic portal vein)
Arteriole
Muscular wall

(b) LS of villus

28.12 (a) Transverse section (TS) of the small intestine
       (b) Longitudinal section (LS) of a villus

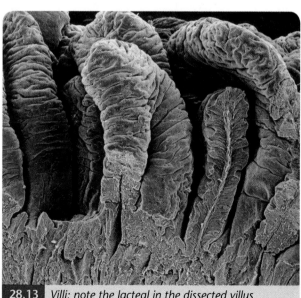

28.13 Villi: note the lacteal in the dissected villus

Adaptations of the villi for absorption

- Large numbers (increase the surface area)
- Large numbers of microvilli (increase the surface area)
- Their walls are only one cell thick
- They have a rich blood supply

The capillaries in each villus absorb water and soluble nutrients such as glucose, amino acids, vitamins and minerals. The capillaries carry the nutrients to the hepatic portal vein, which takes them to the liver. The liver acts as a warehouse, storing some nutrients and releasing others for use throughout the body.

Amino acids cannot be stored in the body (they become toxic). Any amino acids not used by the body are broken down in the liver, forming urea. This process is called **deamination**. Urea and other waste leave the liver in the hepatic vein and eventually pass to the kidneys. Here it forms part of urine, which is then excreted (see Chapter 31).

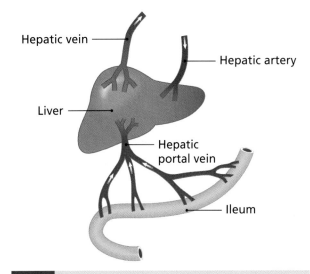

28.14 *The relationship between the ileum and the liver*

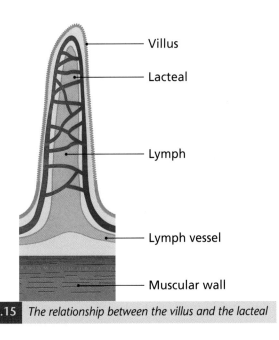

28.15 *The relationship between the villus and the lacteal*

Lacteal

Inside each villus is a **lacteal** (see diagram 28.15). Each lacteal contains a liquid called lymph. Fatty acids and glycerol are absorbed into the cells of the villus lining. Here they re-form into fats. These fats are coated with protein and pass into the lymph in the lacteals.

The fats are transported by the lymph, which carries them to the bloodstream in lymph vessels. The protein coat is dissolved in the blood and the fats are absorbed into cells.

 It takes lymph about 18 hours to pass from the intestine to the bloodstream. Lymph flows into the bloodstream at the subclavian veins near the base of the neck.

Adaptations of the small intestine for absorption

- It is very long
- It has numerous villi and microvilli (which increase the surface area)
- The walls of the villi are very thin
- There is a rich blood supply to carry away water-soluble products
- Each villus has a lymph supply (lacteal) to carry away the fats

THE ORGANISM

Large intestine

 The large intestine is only about 1.5 m long (compared with the small intestine, which is about 6 m long). It is called 'large' due to its greater diameter (about 6 cm, compared with 3 cm for the small intestine). Food stays in the large intestine for between 10 hours and a few days.

Caecum and appendix

The part of the large intestine below its junction with the small intestine is called the caecum. The appendix is found at the end of the caecum. The functions of the appendix and caecum in humans are not fully known.

In many herbivores (e.g. rabbits) the appendix and caecum contain bacteria capable of digesting cellulose. It is thought that our ancestors once needed them for the same reason. We no longer need to digest cellulose as we get our carbohydrate supplies from more easily digested sources such as starch. The caecum and appendix are now **vestigial** organs (i.e. they have lost their former use).

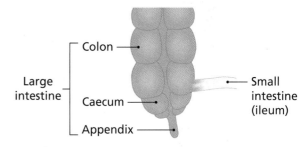

28.16　*The junction of the small and large intestines*

Colon

The function of the colon is to reabsorb water.

The liquid waste that enters the large intestine is converted to semi-solid waste called faeces by the reabsorption of water. Faeces are stored in the rectum before being egested through the anus. (**Note:** Faeces are egested and not excreted. This is because excretion is the removal of the waste products of metabolism from the body. Faeces are not the product of metabolism.)

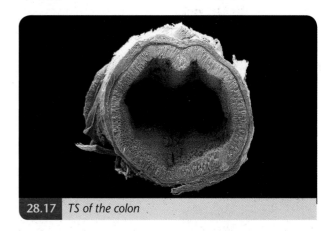

28.17　*TS of the colon*

 Diarrhoea occurs when unabsorbed material moves too rapidly through the colon. Less water is then reabsorbed and the faeces contain more liquid. Constipation is the reverse. It results from unabsorbed material passing too slowly through the colon so that too much water is reabsorbed. It may be controlled by eating more fibre, which stimulates peristalsis.

Symbiotic bacteria in the digestive system

● Bacteria in the colon feed on the waste and produce some B group vitamins and vitamin K. These vitamins are absorbed into the blood from the colon. Bacteria such as these obtain food from humans and provide useful vitamins in return. They are said to be symbiotic bacteria.

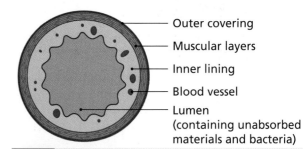

Outer covering
Muscular layers
Inner lining
Blood vessel
Lumen (containing unabsorbed materials and bacteria)

28.18　*TS of the large intestine*

THE ORGANISM

- Bacteria in the digestive system break down food, especially cellulose. Some of the digested nutrients are absorbed into the body from the intestines. These bacteria are also symbiotic.
- The presence of beneficial bacteria prevent the growth of disease-causing (pathogenic) bacteria and fungi.

28.19 *The ileum, caecum and appendix*

Sometimes bacteria gather and grow in the appendix. Their waste products may produce painful inflammation of the appendix. The pain is felt between the navel and the lower right-hand side of the abdomen. If the pain appears and disappears it is called a 'grumbling appendix'. If not treated the appendix may burst and bacterial infection of the abdomen lining results.

Balanced human diet

There are seven components in a balanced diet: carbohydrate, protein, lipid, vitamins, minerals, fibre and water. These components must be present in our diet in the right amounts and should come from a variety of sources. This ensures that the body gets all the necessary energy and nutrients.

> A balanced diet contains all the necessary food types in the correct proportions.

The total amount of food a person requires depends on:
- Age (young people need more food than older individuals)
- Activity levels
- Gender (males need more food than females)
- Health.

Food groups

Foods that contain similar nutrients are arranged into four food groups. These groups are:
- Cereals, bread and potatoes
- Fruit and vegetables
- Milk, cheese and yoghurt
- Meat, fish and poultry.

We should eat a variety of foods from each of these food groups. Suggested numbers of servings of each food group are given in the food pyramid in diagram 28.20.

Sparingly

Drink water regularly

2

4

4+

6+

Number of servings per day

28.20 *The food pyramid*

Summary

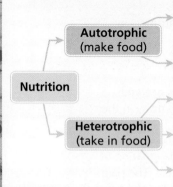

28.21 *Types of nutrition*

Heterotrophic nutrition involves:
- Ingestion (taking in food)
- Digestion (breaking down food)
- Absorption (food entering the body)
- Egestion (removing waste).

In the mouth:
- The four types of teeth are incisors, canines, premolars and molars
- The enzyme amylase digests starch to maltose.

The oesophagus:
- Is a muscular pipe
- Moves food by peristalsis.

Peristalsis is a wave of muscular action that forces food through the intestines.

Fibre stimulates peristalsis.

The stomach:
- Stores and digests food
- Is a muscular bag
- Churns food to make chyme
- The stomach lining makes:
  - (i) Mucus
  - (ii) Pepsinogen (becomes pepsin in acid; pepsin digests protein to peptides)
  - (iii) Hydrochloric acid (pH 1–2), which kills bacteria and softens food.

The pancreas makes:
- Sodium hydrogen carbonate (neutralises acid from the stomach)
- The enzymes:
  - (i) Amylase (starch to maltose)
  - (ii) Lipase (lipid to fatty acid and glycerol).

The **digestive roles of the liver:**
- Makes bile, which emulsifies fat
- Makes sodium hydrogen carbonate to neutralise acid
- Stores many nutrients.

The **duodenum** is the main location for digestion. It makes a range of digestive enzymes.

In the **ileum:**
- Food is absorbed
- There is a lining of numerous villi to increase surface area
- Glucose and amino acids are absorbed into the bloodstream and taken to the liver
- Fatty acids and glycerol enter the lacteals and are transported in lymph and returned to the bloodstream for distribution around the body.

The appendix and caecum are vestigial (i.e. have lost their former use).

The **colon:**
- Reabsorbs water from the waste, forming faeces
- **Symbiotic bacteria in the colon:**
  - (i) Make vitamins and digest cellulose
  - (ii) Break down cellulose
  - (iii) Prevent the growth of disease-causing organisms.

The **rectum** stores faeces.

There are **seven components of a balanced diet:**
- Carbohydrate
- Lipid
- Protein
- Minerals
- Vitamins
- Fibre
- Water.

The **amount of food a person requires** depends on age, activity, gender and health.

The four food groups and their average number of servings per day are:
- Cereals, bread and potatoes (6+)
- Fruit and vegetables (4+)
- Milk, cheese and yoghurt (4)
- Meat, fish and poultry (2).

Revision questions

1 (a) What is nutrition?
   (b) Distinguish between autotrophic and heterotrophic nutrition.

2 (a) Name the four stages in heterotrophic nutrition.
   (b) Give the location for each stage in humans.

3 (a) Name the parts of the alimentary canal in sequence and give a function for each part.
   (b) Name the associated glands.

4 Distinguish between:
   (a) Mechanical and chemical digestion
   (b) Autotrophic and heterotrophic
   (c) Incisor and canine
   (d) Herbivore and carnivore.

5 (a) Name the four types of teeth.
   (b) Give the function for each tooth type.
   (c) Give the full human dental formula.

6 Why is salivary amylase inactive in the stomach?

7 (a) Name the material that makes up the wall of the stomach.
   (b) What enzyme in the stomach digests this substance?
   (c) How does the stomach prevent self-digestion?
   (d) Why does stomach acid not damage the duodenum?

8 Name the functions of each of the following:
   (a) Duodenum (b) Ileum (c) Colon
   (d) Rectum.

9 Answer the following with reference to bile.
   (a) Where is it made?
   (b) What is it made from?
   (c) Where is it stored?
   (d) Where does it act?
   (e) What are its functions?

10 List four features of the small intestine that are adaptations to help it absorb food.

11 Give a biological reason for each of the following statements.
   (a) Chewing food well.
   (b) Certain tablets relieve heartburn.
   (c) An astronaut in space can still swallow.
   (d) Pepsin is not secreted in an active form.
   (e) Chocolate provides energy very rapidly compared with potatoes.
   (f) A person can survive without an appendix.

12 For each of the substances pepsin, bile, amylase and lipase, state:
   (a) Where they are produced
   (b) Where they act

   (c) What they act on
   (d) The result of their action
   (e) Their preferred pH (if any).

13 (a) Name the parts labelled A to N on diagram 28.22.

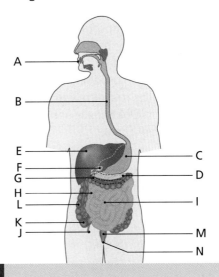

28.22

   (b) Name a part of the diagram:
      (i)   That is acidic
      (ii)   Where chyme is formed
      (iii) Where bile is stored
      (iv)   Where glycogen is stored
      (v)   Where bacteria are killed
      (vi)   Where bacteria live
      (vii) Where villi are found.

14 (a) State the end products of digestion.
   (b) Name the end products of food digestion that are: (i) Soluble (ii) Insoluble in water.
   (c) Explain what happens to the:
      (i)   Water-soluble end products
      (ii) Water-insoluble end products.

15 Choose which of the options (i), (ii), (iii) or (iv) represents the correct answer in each case below.

   (a) Proteins are chemically digested in the:
      (i) Mouth (ii) Stomach (iii) Liver
      (iv) Large intestine.
   (b) Lacteals are used to absorb: (i) Starch
      (ii) Amino acids (iii) Lipids (iv) Proteins.
   (c) The substance produced by the pancreas to neutralise stomach acid is called:
      (i) Chyme (ii) Maltose (iii) Vitamin D
      (iv) Sodium hydrogen carbonate.
   (d) The stomach has a pH of: (i) 6 (ii) 2
      (iii) 8 (iv) 12.
   (e) Symbiotic bacteria in the colon produce:
      (i) Vitamins A and D (ii) Vitamins A and B (iii) Vitamins D and K (iv) Vitamins B and K.

Exam questions

Section A

16 Answer the following questions in relation to the human alimentary canal.
   (a) What is peristalsis?
   (b) State **one** reason why a low pH is important in the stomach.
   (c) Why is fibre important?
   (d) Name an enzyme that is involved in the digestion of fat.
   (e) What are the products of fat digestion?
   (f) What is the role of bile in fat digestion?
   (g) State a role of beneficial bacteria in the alimentary canal.

   (2004 HL Q 6)

17 The diagram shows part of a section of the human small intestine.

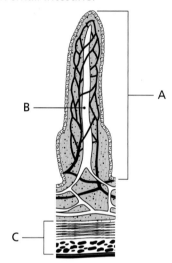

   (a) Name A, B, C.
   (b) State **two** ways in which A is adapted for the absorption of soluble foods.
   (c) Name a process by which soluble foods are absorbed into the blood from the small intestine.
   (d) What type of food is mainly absorbed into B?

   (2005 HL Q 6)

18 The graph shows how the rate of reaction of a carbohydrate-digesting enzyme in the human alimentary canal varies with pH.

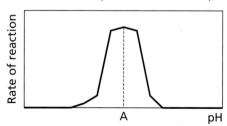

   (a) Name a carbohydrate-digesting enzyme in the human alimentary canal.
   (b) Where in the alimentary canal does this enzyme act?

   (c) State the enzyme's product(s).
   (d) What is the pH at A?
   (e) A is said to be the enzyme's _____ pH.
   (f) Suggest a temperature at which human enzymes work best.
   (g) What term best describes the shape of an enzyme?

   (2006 HL Q 3)

19 (a) (i) What is meant by the term *digestion*?
       (ii) Why is digestion necessary?
       (iii) Distinguish between mechanical and chemical digestion by writing a sentence about each.
   (b) The diagram shows part of the human alimentary canal and associated structures.

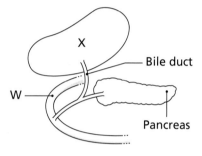

       (i) What part of the alimentary canal is labelled W?
       (ii) The bile duct is connected to X. Name X.
       (iii) From which part of the alimentary canal does food arrive into W?
       (iv) State **one** digestive function of the pancreas.

   (2011 HL Q 5)

Section C

20 (a) Bile is involved in digestion in the human body.
       (i) 1. Where is bile produced?
          2. Where is bile stored?
       (ii) Where does bile act in the alimentary canal?
   (b) The diagram shows the digestive system of the human.

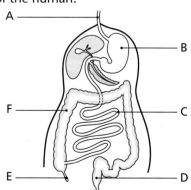

       (i) Name the parts labelled A, B, C, D, E and F.

(ii) What is the role of peristalsis in the digestive system?

(iii) Where do the products of digestion enter the blood?

(iv) How do these products of digestion pass into the blood?

(c) **(i)** For each of the parts labelled B and C in the diagram above, state whether the contents are acidic, neutral or alkaline.

(ii) Amylase is an enzyme that is found in saliva. State the substrate and the product of this enzyme.

(iii) State **two** functions of symbiotic bacteria in the alimentary canal.

(iv) What is meant by egestion? From which labelled part of the diagram does egestion occur?

(2008 OL Q 13)

21 **(b)** **(i)** Draw a labelled diagram to show the relationship between the liver, the small intestine and the hepatic portal vein.

(ii) Name a substance transported to the liver by the blood in the hepatic portal vein.

(iii) Name the blood vessel that brings oxygenated blood to the liver.

(iv) Where in the human body is the liver located in relation to the stomach?

(v) Where is bile stored after it has been made in the liver?

(vi) Give **one** role that the bile salts play in the digestive process.

(vii) Give **two** further functions of the liver, other than the manufacture of bile.

(2010 HL Q 15)

22 **(a)** **(i)** What is meant by a 'balanced' diet?

(ii) Distinguish between autotrophic nutrition and heterotrophic nutrition.

(b) **(i)** Explain the word *digestion*.

(ii) Give **one** role for **each** of the following types of teeth:

1. Incisors
2. Molars.

(iii) Peristalsis begins when food enters the oesophagus. What is meant by *peristalsis*?

(iv) Describe the following changes that happen to food in the stomach:

1. Mechanical changes
2. Chemical changes.

(v) What is the pH of the stomach contents?

(vi) Where does the partially digested food go when it leaves the stomach?

(c) The liver, the gall bladder and the pancreas all play a part in digestion. Digested food is carried to the liver where it is processed. Undigested food enters the large intestine.

(i) State

1. **One** role of the pancreas in digestion.
2. **One** role of the gall bladder in digestion.

(ii) From what part of the digestive system does the digested food enter the blood?

(iii) Name the blood vessel that carries the digested food to the liver.

(iv) State **two** functions of the liver – other than the processing of digested food.

(v) The colon contains many symbiotic bacteria – mostly 'good' bacteria. State **two** benefits we get from these bacteria.

(2010 OL Q 13)

Previous examination questions

Ordinary level	Higher level
2006 Q 12	2004 Q 6
2007 Q 15c	2005 Q 6
2008 Q 13	2006 Q 3, 5
2010 Q 13	2008 Q 12
2012 Q 15c	2010 Q 15
	2011 Q 5
	2012 Q 15a

Latest questions at www.edco.ie/lcbiologyplus/examhelp

Online test and assessment tracker

Scan the QR code and test yourself on chapter 28
www.edco.ie/lcbiologyplus

THE ORGANISM

Learning objectives

- To define the term 'homeostasis'
- To understand why homeostasis is necessary in living organisms in terms of temperature, fluid balance and chemistry.

External and internal environments

The term 'external environment' refers to the surroundings in which an organism lives. The external environment for *Amoeba* is fresh water; for humans it is the air around us. Most organisms (apart from humans) have relatively little ability to control their external environment.

The term 'internal environment' refers to the surroundings of the cells in a multicellular organism. The internal environment of humans is tissue fluid (or intercellular fluid). Tissue fluid surrounds every cell in the human body. All organisms have the ability to control their internal environment, or their cell conditions, to some extent.

Homeostasis

Homeostasis is the ability of an organism to maintain a constant internal environment.

Homeostasis involves a combination of many processes acting together to control the internal environment of an organism. Examples of homeostasis in humans include:

- Maintaining body temperatures very close to 37°C, despite widespread changes in external temperatures
- Keeping the pH of the blood and tissue fluid very close to pH 7.4
- Preventing the build-up of toxic chemicals in the body
- Maintaining sufficient levels of oxygen in the body
- Regulating the level of glucose in the blood plasma so that it stays close to 0.1%.

The control of features such as those listed above requires the involvement of many organs and organ systems. For example:

- Body temperature is controlled mainly by the skin (as described in Chapter 31)
- Blood plasma pH and, consequently, tissue fluid pH, is controlled by the kidneys (as described in Chapter 31)
- Prevention of the build-up of toxic wastes is controlled by the liver and kidneys (Chapter 31)
- Oxygen concentrations are controlled by the respiratory system (Chapter 30)
- The level of glucose is controlled by the hormone insulin produced by the endocrine system (Chapter 35).

The brain co-ordinates the activities of these organs and systems in humans. To allow this to happen, the brain must be continuously informed of conditions, both inside and outside the body, so that it can cause the relevant change(s) to be made.

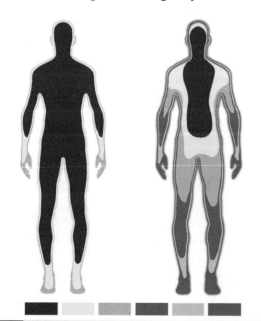

29.1 *Body temperature in hot (left) and cold (right) temperatures: red is 37°C and dark blue is 25°C*

Homeostasis requires exchange

In many cases, homeostasis is dependent on an organism exchanging materials with its environment by diffusion, osmosis and active transport. Diffusion and osmosis do not require energy, but active transport does. For example, materials such as gases, nutrients and toxic wastes have to be exchanged between cells and their external environment.

The rate and efficiency at which exchange can take place depends on the amount of material to be exchanged and the surface area available for diffusion.

- For small, single-celled organisms (such as *Amoeba*), special organs are not required for exchange. This is because there is a large surface area over which a relatively small amount of material can be exchanged.
- In larger, multicellular organisms, such as plants and animals, the problems of exchange are overcome by a range of methods. Some of these methods require the development of exchange systems such as respiratory and excretory systems, as outlined below.

Methods used to improve exchange

- The organ or organism may be flattened, as is the case in the leaves of a plant. This reduces the distance between the two surfaces and allows sufficient materials to be exchanged by diffusion.
- Respiratory systems provide increased surface area for the exchange of gases by diffusion. This is seen in the development of alveoli in the human lungs (see Chapter 30).
- Respiratory and excretory systems take materials to the body surface. This happens in humans where gases pass in and out of the lungs and waste products are excreted from the body (e.g. when salts and water are removed from the body in the form of sweat).

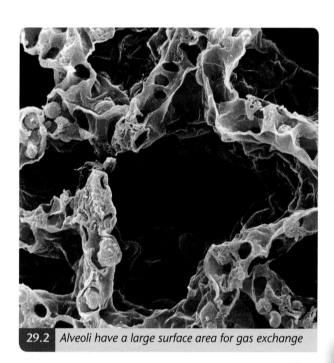

29.2 *Alveoli have a large surface area for gas exchange*

In addition to the methods outlined above, large organisms have another problem. Exchange is only effective over short distances (about 0.5 mm). Therefore, large active animals such as humans have to develop a circulatory system.

A circulatory system transports materials such as gases, nutrients and toxic wastes over long distances. For example, gases are transported by the blood circulatory system from all over the body to and from the lungs. In addition, waste products from all parts of the body are taken to the kidneys in the bloodstream.

The need for homeostasis

Homeostasis allows organisms to function efficiently

Homeostasis controls the environment surrounding the cells. This allows the cells to maintain constant conditions, thus enabling them to function under the most suitable (optimal) conditions. If the cells operate under ideal conditions then the organism will function most efficiently. For example:

- If the temperature of the cells in the human body falls below 37°C, the reactions in the cells will slow down (because the rate of enzyme reactions slows down). This will result in the metabolism of the person slowing down.

THE ORGANISM

● If the temperature of human cells rises above 37°C, the reactions will also slow down (because human enzymes begin to lose their shape and work less efficiently at high temperatures). Each human cell (and as a consequence the human body) works most efficiently at 37°C.

Homeostasis allows organisms to function independently of their external environment

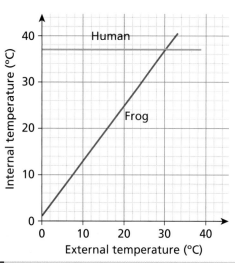

29.3 *The relationship between body temperature and external temperature*

Homeostasis allows organisms to function most efficiently in adverse or unsuitable external conditions.

● For example, humans can continue to function when the external temperature drops in winter because they can control their internal temperature.

● However, frogs, for example, cannot control their internal temperature. Their temperature rises and falls with the temperature of their external environment. As a result, low temperatures cause frogs to slow down their metabolism. In order to avoid slowing down (and dying) in the cold of winter, frogs are forced to hibernate in order to conserve energy.

Homeostasis allows slight changes in internal environments

It is important to realise that conditions in the internal environment of any organism have to be allowed to change or fluctuate **slightly**. For example:

● Human body temperature falls (by about 1°C) at night when we sleep
● Human body temperature rises when we get an infection (this is called a fever and is an attempt by the body to destroy whatever is causing the infection)

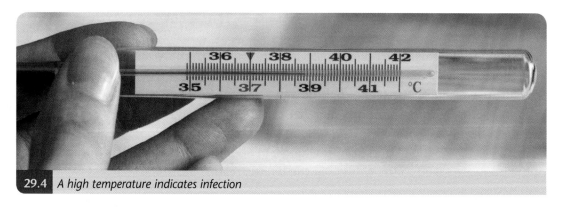

29.4 *A high temperature indicates infection*

● The internal environment of the body changes due to hormonal changes during:
  ▸ The menstrual cycle
  ▸ Puberty
  ▸ Menopause.

In the short term, homeostasis maintains a relatively constant internal environment. However, homeostasis can be adapted to allow for the changing requirements of the body over longer periods of time.

Summary

The **external environment** surrounds the outside of an organism.

The **internal environment** surrounds the cells in an organism.

Homeostasis:
- Is the ability of an organism to maintain a constant internal environment
- Involves many organs and organ systems acting together, co-ordinated by the brain
- Often requires an organism to exchange materials with its environment.

Cells exchange materials with their environment by diffusion, osmosis and active transport.

Special organs of exchange are not needed in small organisms because diffusion is adequate.

To improve their rate of exchange, large organisms require special features such as:
- Flat structures
- A respiratory system with a large surface area
- Respiratory and excretory systems, which take materials from within the body to the body surface.

Large organisms require a circulatory system to carry materials over long distances.

Homeostasis allows:
- Cells, and therefore organisms, to function at their most efficient rate
- Organisms to function independently of external conditions
- Slight changes in internal conditions when necessary.

Revision questions

1. (a) What is homeostasis?
   (b) Distinguish between the external and internal environment of an organism.
   (c) Name the internal environment for humans.

2. (a) Name three organs involved in homeostasis in humans.
   (b) Briefly explain the role of each of the organs you have named.
   (c) State the immediate consequences for a person if each of the named organs ceased to function.

3. (a) Why are circulatory systems found in large animals but not in small ones?
   (b) Suggest one method by which an organism without a circulatory system might transport materials.

4. 'Homeostatic mechanisms allow for temporary changes in the internal environment.' Give two examples in support of this statement.

Exam questions

Section C

5. (a) What is homeostasis? State the role of the kidneys in homeostasis.
   (2004 HL Q 12)

6. (c) (i) What is homeostasis? Note one reason why it is important in the human body.
   (2007 HL Q 15)

7. (c) (i) Explain the term homeostasis.
   (ii) Homeostasis often requires an organism to exchange materials between different tissues, or between itself and the external environment by <u>diffusion</u>, <u>osmosis</u>, and <u>active transport</u>. Explain **each** of the underlined terms.
   (iii) State **one** way in which **each** of the following contributes to homeostasis.
   1. Liver.
   2. Lungs.
   3. Nephrons of kidneys.
   (2012 HL Q 15)

Previous examination questions

Ordinary level	Higher level
n/a	2004 Q 12a
	2007 Q 15c
	2009 Q 15c
	2012 Q 15c

Latest questions at www.edco.ie/lcbiologyplus/examhelp

Online test and assessment tracker

Scan the QR code and test yourself on chapter 29
www.edco.ie/lcbiologyplus

THE ORGANISM

337

Chapter 30 **Human breathing**

Learning objectives

- To describe the structure and function of the breathing system in humans
- To describe the essential features of the alveoli and capillaries as surfaces for gas exchange
- To describe the mechanism of the human breathing system in gas exchange
- To describe asthma or bronchitis in terms of one possible cause, prevention and treatment
- **HIGHER ▶** To explain how carbon dioxide is a controlling factor in the human breathing system
- To investigate the effect of exercise on breathing rate.

The human respiratory system

The human respiratory system is composed of a pair of lungs and a series of tubes. The respiratory system is located in the chest (or thorax or thoracic cavity).

The base of the thorax is formed by a sheet of involuntary muscle called the diaphragm. The diaphragm separates the thorax from the lower abdominal cavity (or abdomen). The ribs and intercostal muscles form the walls of the thorax.

Contraction and relaxation of the diaphragm and intercostal muscles change the size of the thorax and are responsible for ventilation (the movement of air in and out of the lungs).

Parts of the respiratory system

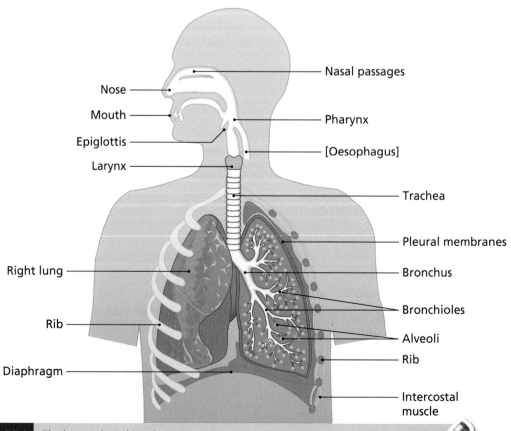

30.1 *The human breathing (respiratory) system*

THE ORGANISM

Nose

Air can be inhaled through the mouth or the nose. The two openings into the nose are the nostrils. The nostrils are separated by the septum. This is made of cartilage at the lower end and bone near to the face. Each nostril leads into the nasal chambers or passages.

Breathing in through the nose is beneficial because the air is:

- Filtered or cleaned by hairs and mucus in the nostrils
- Moistened
- Warmed as it passes through the nasal passages.

Moist, warm air passes more easily from the lungs into the bloodstream.

Pharynx

In the pharynx a flap of tissue called the epiglottis closes over the trachea (or windpipe) when we swallow. This prevents food and drink from passing into the trachea.

> The epiglottis works automatically. If food or drinks get past the epiglottis we say they 'have gone down the wrong way'. In this case we cough, which forces the material back up the windpipe to prevent it blocking the passage of air in and out of the lungs.

The **pharynx** is the throat.

The **larynx** is the voice box.

Just below the epiglottis is the larynx. The larynx (or Adam's apple) contains two vocal cords. These vibrate to produce sound when we force air across them. Our tongue and lips convert the sound to speech.

Trachea and subdivisions

The trachea (or windpipe) and many of its subdivisions (the bronchi and the higher bronchioles) are all made of muscle and elastic fibres along with incomplete (C-shaped) rings of cartilage. Cartilage is a strong, rigid material and it prevents the tubes from closing in when air is drawn in through them.

The walls of the lower, smaller bronchioles do not contain cartilage. They only have muscle and elastic fibres and are flexible. These are the bronchioles that become narrow during an asthma attack.

All the tubes in the respiratory system are lined with mucus and cilia (tiny hairs). These act to defend our lungs from infection.

- The mucus is sticky and traps small particles such as dust, pollen grains, bacteria and viruses.
- The cilia beat and create an upward current. This moves the mucus upwards and past the epiglottis. It then passes down the oesophagus and into the stomach.

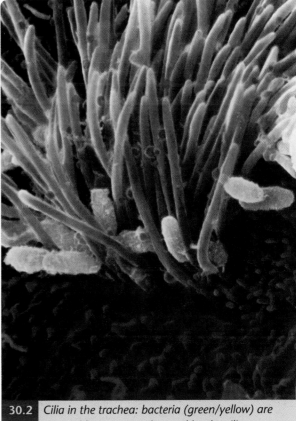

30.2 *Cilia in the trachea: bacteria (green/yellow) are trapped by mucus and moved by the cilia*

> We often cough to clear our throats. This forces mucus away from the vocal cords and up past the epiglottis.

THE ORGANISM

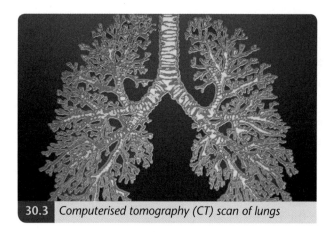

30.3 | *Computerised tomography (CT) scan of lungs*

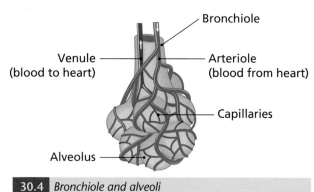

Bronchiole

Venule
(blood to heart)

Arteriole
(blood from heart)

Capillaries

Alveolus

30.4 | *Bronchiole and alveoli*

The function of the alveoli is gas exchange. They are adapted for this function because:

- The huge number of alveoli (over 700 million between the two lungs) provide a huge surface area for gas exchange
- They are thin walled (only one cell thick)
- They have moist surfaces
- They are enclosed in a network of blood capillaries.

Lungs

The lungs are large, pink, spongy structures in which gas exchange takes place. Each lung is enclosed by a pair of pleural membranes (the pleura):

- The outer pleura lines the chest wall and the diaphragm
- The inner pleura lines the lungs.

The pleural cavity is the gap between the two pleura. It contains a liquid which lubricates the membranes and reduces friction during breathing.

Alveoli

Each bronchus subdivides into about one million bronchioles. These end in tiny, hollow, balloon-like air sacs called alveoli (singular alveolus).

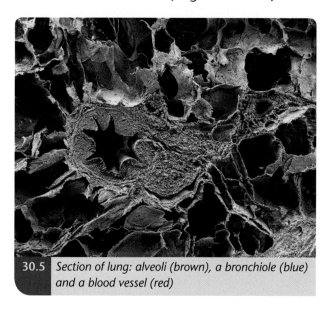

30.5 | *Section of lung: alveoli (brown), a bronchiole (blue) and a blood vessel (red)*

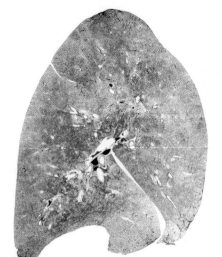

30.6 | *A healthy lung*

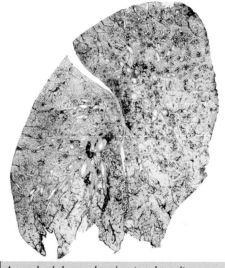

30.7 | *A smoker's lung, showing tar deposits*

THE ORGANISM

Gas exchange

Respiration takes place in body cells in order to supply the cells with energy. As a result body cells use up oxygen and produce carbon dioxide and water.

Carbon dioxide and water

Carbon dioxide and water pass out of body cells by diffusion. This happens because the cytoplasm has a higher concentration of carbon dioxide and water than the blood plasma. In the lungs, carbon dioxide and water diffuse from the blood plasma into the alveoli (i.e. from a high to a lower concentration).

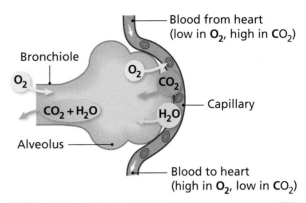

30.8 *Gas exchange in an alveolus*

Oxygen

Oxygen diffuses in the reverse direction. It passes from the alveoli into the blood and then it passes from the blood into the body cells. In each case it is diffusing from a higher to a lower concentration.

Transport of gases

- Oxygen is mainly transported by combining with the red pigment haemoglobin, to form oxyhaemoglobin. Only about 3% of oxygen is carried dissolved in plasma.
- Carbon dioxide and water are both carried in blood plasma.

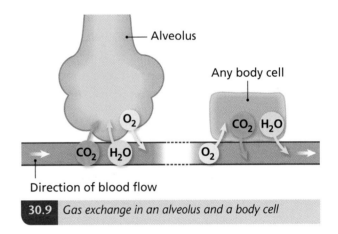

30.9 *Gas exchange in an alveolus and a body cell*

Mechanism of breathing

Breathing (or ventilation) is normally an involuntary process. An adult at rest normally breathes about 12 to 18 times per minute.

The processes responsible for breathing are outlined below.

Inhalation

1. The brain controls the rate of breathing.
2. Normally a message is sent from the brain to the intercostal muscles (located between the ribs) and the diaphragm.
3. These muscles use energy (in the form of ATP) to contract. For this reason inhalation is said to be an **active** process.
4. The ribs are pulled up and out and the diaphragm curves down.
5. The volume or size of the chest cavity (or thorax) increases.
6. The pressure in the chest cavity decreases.
7. The external air pressure is now higher than the air pressure in the chest. As a result air is forced into the lungs. This is called inhalation or inspiration.

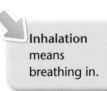

Inhalation means breathing in.

THE ORGANISM

341

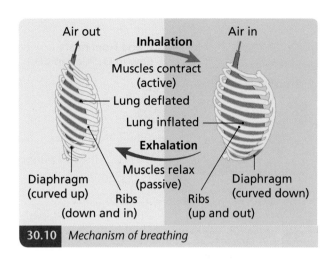

Air out · Inhalation · Air in

Muscles contract (active)

Lung deflated

Lung inflated

Exhalation

Muscles relax (passive)

Diaphragm (curved up) · Ribs (down and in) · Ribs (up and out) · Diaphragm (curved down)

30.10 *Mechanism of breathing*

Exhalation

To exhale, the process is reversed as outlined below in points 1 to 5. Note that nervous control is not necessary for exhalation.

> Exhalation means breathing out.

1. The intercostal muscles and diaphragm relax. As a result exhalation is a **passive** process.
2. The ribs move down and in and the diaphragm curves up.
3. The volume or size of the chest cavity (or thorax) decreases.
4. The pressure in the chest cavity increases.
5. Air is forced out of the lungs.

Effect of exercise on the rate of breathing

Exercise increases the rate of respiration, especially in muscle cells. As a result, the body experiences lower levels of available oxygen. The brain detects the increased level of exercise and increases the level of breathing.

Exhalation, which is normally a passive process, becomes an active process as a result of exercise. In addition extra muscles are used to increase the **depth** of breathing.

> Breathing is normally an involuntary or unconscious process. However, the rate of breathing can be controlled consciously for a short time. This occurs when we control our breathing as we speak, sing or swim.

The composition of inhaled and exhaled air

The composition of inhaled and exhaled air for a person at rest is given in the following table.

Composition of air for a person at rest		
	Inhaled	**Exhaled**
Oxygen %	21	14
Carbon dioxide %	0.04	5.6
Water concentration	Low	High

Syllabus You are required to study **one** breathing disorder, i.e. asthma or bronchitis.

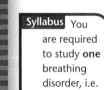

Breathing disorders

Asthma

Symptoms

The symptoms (or signs) of asthma include noisy, wheezy breathing and a feeling of breathlessness.

Cause

External

The exact causes of asthma are not clear, but attacks may be triggered by substances called allergens that are inhaled. Common **allergens** include pollen, animal dander (tiny scales from skin, hair or feathers), house dust and dust mites.

Lung infections, exercise (especially in cold air), stress or anxiety can also contribute to causing asthma.

30.11 *Trachea covered in allergens: cilia are brown/yellow and pollen grains are pink and blue*

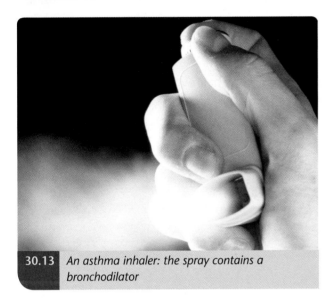

30.12 *An inflamed bronchiole (left) and a normal bronchiole (right)*

Internal

In an asthma attack the lower bronchioles become inflamed and narrow (or constricted).

About 10% of children are asthmatic and the incidence of asthma seems to be rising in developed countries. More than half of children affected by asthma grow out of it in their teenage years.

Prevention

Asthmatic attacks may be prevented by identifying and avoiding those allergens or conditions that trigger attacks. Tests can be undertaken to identify the precise allergens that affect an individual. In addition, preventative inhalers may be used. These prevent the bronchioles from reacting to allergens.

30.13 *An asthma inhaler: the spray contains a bronchodilator*

Treatment

The normal treatment for asthma is to inhale drugs that cause the bronchioles to widen (or dilate; hence they are called bronchodilators). In addition, steroids may be inhaled to reduce inflammation. In severe cases these drugs are given by injection.

Control of human breathing

Earlier in this chapter we saw that the rate of human breathing is controlled by the brain (in the medulla oblongata). The brain controls breathing by monitoring the levels of carbon dioxide in the blood that passes through it.

Carbon dioxide is a slightly acidic gas. It dissolves in water to form a weak acid called carbonic acid. Carbonic acid causes the pH of the blood and tissue fluid to fall slightly from its normal value of 7.4. Special centres in the brain detect the slight drop in pH and react by sending out impulses to the diaphragm and intercostal muscles that cause us to breathe.

Breathing allows gas exchange to take place in the lungs. If we exercise vigorously the level of carbon dioxide in our blood will increase (because of respiration). This will result in a drop in blood pH. The brain will detect this change and cause our breathing rate to increase.

Our brain does not normally respond to low levels of oxygen. It is interesting to note that we breathe in response to high levels of carbon dioxide, rather than responding to low levels of oxygen.

Carbon dioxide controls gas exchange

In Chapter 24 we saw that carbon dioxide causes the opening and closing of the stomata in leaves. We now know that carbon dioxide also causes the rate of breathing in humans to increase. For both of these reasons, we can say that carbon dioxide operates as a controlling factor in gas exchange in both plants and animals.

HIGHER ▼

THE ORGANISM

343

Activity 19b   To investigate the effect of exercise on breathing rate

1. Work in pairs, one person recording the results.
2. Sit down on a chair and rest for a few minutes.
3. Breathing in and breathing out is considered to be one breath.
4. Count the number of inhalations or exhalations per minute while at rest.
5. Repeat this two more times.
6. Calculate your average breathing rate per minute (measured in breaths per minute, or bpm) at rest by adding the three values and dividing the total by three. This is called the resting breathing rate and is used as a control.
7. Walk slowly for 5 minutes.
8. Count your breathing rate per minute immediately after walking.
9. Walk briskly for 5 minutes.
10. Count your breathing rate per minute immediately after walking.
11. Exercise strenuously for 5 minutes (e.g. step up and down on a chair every 3 seconds or run).
12. Count your breathing rate per minute immediately after exercising.
13. Compare your resting rate with the rate immediately after each type of exercise.
14. Present your results in tables such as those shown below.

> **Syllabus** You have a choice to carry out **either** this activity **or** Activity 19a on page 311.

Breathing rates before exercise					
Before exercise	Trial 1	Trial 2	Trial 3	Total	Average
Resting breathing rate (bpm)					

Breathing rates after different types of exercise			
Activity	Slow walk	Brisk walk	Strenuous exercise
Breathing rate (bpm)			

15. After exercise the rate of breathing often falls below the resting rate. This is due to deeper breathing.

Summary

The **respiratory system** is located in the chest cavity (also called the thorax or thoracic cavity).
- Breathing in through the nose causes the air to be filtered, moistened and warmed.
- The epiglottis prevents food and drink entering the trachea.
- The larynx contains vocal cords for speech.
- The trachea (windpipe), bronchi and larger bronchioles are made of muscle, elastic fibres and rigid cartilage.
- Smaller (lower) bronchioles have muscle and elastic fibres only.
- Mucus traps dust and micro-organisms.
- Cilia are tiny hairs that beat to sweep the mucus out of the air pipes (and into the oesophagus).
- Each lung is enclosed by a pair of pleural membranes. These are separated by the pleural cavity.

Alveoli are tiny, thin-walled air sacs that allow gas exchange.
- Oxygen diffuses from the alveoli to the red cells in the blood.
- Carbon dioxide diffuses from the blood plasma into the alveoli.
- These gases diffuse in the reverse direction in the cells of the body.

Breathing in is called inhalation or inspiration.

Breathing out is called exhalation or expiration.

Inhalation involves the following:
- The brain controls the rate of breathing
- The intercostal muscles and diaphragm contract
- The chest cavity gets bigger
- The air pressure decreases in the chest cavity
- Air is forced into the lungs by the higher external air pressure.

THE ORGANISM

344

Asthma is:
● A breathing disorder
● Triggered by outside agents called allergens
● Caused by the smaller bronchioles becoming narrower
● Controlled by avoiding known allergens
● Treated by drugs (usually taken from inhalers).

Human breathing is controlled by the brain.

High levels of carbon dioxide in the blood:
● Form an acid

● Decrease the pH
● Trigger the brain to cause breathing.

Carbon dioxide is a controlling factor in gas exchange in leaves and in human breathing.

Exercise increases the rate and the depth of breathing.
● The effect of exercise on breathing rate can be shown by comparing breathing rates at rest with those after exercise.

Revision questions

1 Distinguish between:
   (a) Nose and nostril
   (b) Pharynx and larynx
   (c) Oesophagus and trachea
   (d) Bronchus and bronchioles
   (e) Thorax and abdomen.

2 List two ways by which the respiratory system protects itself from infection.

3 (a) What are the functions of: (i) The epiglottis (ii) Alveoli (iii) Intercostal muscles (iv) Nasal passages?
   (b) Why are there so many alveoli?

4 'Gas exchange in the alveoli is the reverse of gas exchange in muscle cells.' By reference to two named gases explain why this statement is true.

5 Name three adaptations shown by the alveoli that enable them to exchange gases efficiently.

6 (a) Name the parts labelled A to G in diagram 30.14.

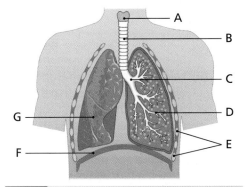

30.14

   (b) What are the functions of A and G?
   (c) Does the position of F suggest it is contracted? Explain your answer.

7 Name the type of blood vessel taking blood:
   (a) To the lungs (b) Around the alveoli
   (c) From the lungs.

8 (a) Exhalation is usually a passive process, but inhalation is active. Explain why.
   (b) Why is the right lung bigger than the left lung?

9 Diagram 30.15 represents the respiratory system.

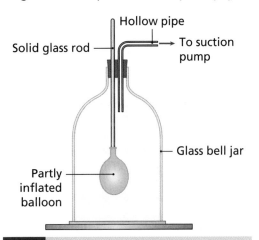

30.15

   (a) What parts of the respiratory system do the following represent:
       (i) The balloon (ii) The bell jar?
   (b) What happens to the balloon when air is withdrawn through the hollow pipe?
   (c) Explain your answer to part (b).
   (d) What phase of breathing does this represent?

10 (a) Explain what happens to the smaller bronchioles to cause asthma.
   (b) Why does this not happen to larger (higher) bronchioles in an asthma attack?

11 (a) What are the symptoms of asthma?
   (b) What are allergens?
   (c) Name three common substances that may trigger asthma.
   (d) Give details regarding any (i) cure, (ii) prevention or (iii) treatment, for asthma.

THE ORGANISM

12 (a) Name the gas that causes humans to breathe.
   (b) What process (i) increases, and (ii) decreases, the concentration of this gas in the bloodstream?
   (c) What effect has this gas on the pH of the blood?
   (d) Where in the body is the concentration of this gas monitored?
   (e) What is the result of high levels of this gas in the body?

13 In investigating how exercise affects the rate of breathing:
   (a) How is the breathing rate measured?
   (b) Why should the rate/minute be taken a number of times?
   (c) State the expected results of the experiment.
   (d) Sometimes after exercise the rate of breathing is often lower than it was before the exercise started. Suggest a reason for this.

14 Choose which of the options (i), (ii), (iii) or (iv) represents the correct answer in each case below.
   (a) Another name for the voice box is: (i) Larynx (ii) Pharynx (iii) Thorax (iv) Epiglottis.
   (b) The correct percentage of CO_2 in exhaled air for a person at rest is about: (i) 0.04% (ii) 20% (iii) 5.6% (iv) 78%.
   (c) The rate of breathing is controlled by: (i) The lungs (ii) The thoracic cavity (iii) The brain (iv) The diaphragm.
   (d) The flap of tissue that prevents food 'going down the wrong way' is called: (i) The pleura (ii) The larynx (iii) The epiglottis (iv) The oesophagus.

Exam questions

Section B

15 (a) Answer the following in relation to human breathing rate OR pulse rate. State which of these you will refer to.
   (i) What is the average rate at rest?
   (ii) State a possible effect of smoking on the resting rate.
   (b) (i) How did you measure the resting rate?
   (ii) Describe how you investigated the effect of exercise on this rate.
   (iii) Using the axes below draw a graph to show how rate is likely to vary as the exercise level increases.

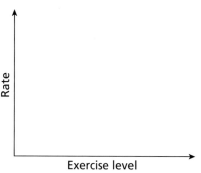

(2004 OL Q 9)

16 (a) State the location in the human body of the following muscles which are used for breathing:
   (i) Diaphragm
   (ii) Intercostals.

(b) Answer the following questions about an activity that you carried out to investigate the effect of exercise on the breathing rate or pulse of a human.
   (i) At the start of the investigation you asked the person who was about to do the exercise to sit down for a few minutes. Explain the purpose of this.
   (ii) How did you measure the breathing rate or the pulse?
   (iii) Describe how you conducted the investigation after the period of rest.
   (iv) State the results of your investigation.
   (2008 OL Q 8)

Section C

17 (a) (i) Name the blood vessel that returns blood to the heart from the lungs.
   (ii) Name the main gas transported in the blood vessel that you have named in (i). How is this gas transported?
   (b) (i) Draw a large diagram of the human breathing system. Label the trachea, bronchus and lung.
   (ii) State the function of the following: epiglottis, larynx.
   (iii) Describe briefly the role of the diaphragm and intercostal muscles in inhalation. In your answer refer to volume and thoracic air pressure.

(c) **(i)** Give **three** ways in which an alveolus is adapted for efficient gas exchange.

(ii) Name the process involved in the passage of gas between the alveolus and the blood.

(iii) Name a breathing disorder.

(iv) In the case of the breathing disorder that you have named in (iii) state:

1. A cause
2. A means of prevention
3. A treatment.

(2007 HL Q 13)

18 **(c)** The diagram shows microscopic detail from a human lung.

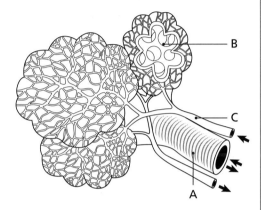

(i) Name the parts labelled A, B and C.

(ii) Give **two** features of the structures in the diagram that allow for efficient gas exchange.

(iii) Name a disorder of the breathing system and say how it may be:

1. Caused.
2. Prevented.
3. Treated.

(iv) Which gas, dissolved in the blood, can trigger deeper or faster breathing?

(2009 HL Q 13)

19 **(c)** The diagram shows part of the human breathing system.

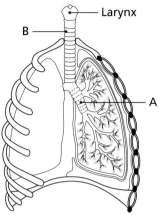

(i) Name the parts labelled A and B.

(ii) In what structures in the lungs does gaseous exchange take place?

(iii) Give **one** feature of the structures referred to in (ii) above that allows efficient exchange of gases.

(iv) What is the function of the larynx?

(v) Outline the steps involved in inhalation.

(2011 OL Q 13)

Previous examination questions

Ordinary level	Higher level
2004 Q 9	2007 Q 13
2005 Q 12	2009 Q 13c
2008 Q 8, 14c	
2011 Q 13c	
2012 Q 7	

Latest questions at www.edco.ie/lcbiologyplus/examhelp

Online test and assessment tracker

Scan the QR code and test yourself on chapter 30
www.edco.ie/lcbiologyplus

THE ORGANISM

Chapter 31 **Excretion**

Learning objectives
- To describe the role of leaves as excretory organs in plants
- To describe the role of the excretory system in homeostasis
- To describe the structure and basic function of the skin and the human urinary system, including the kidney, ureters, urinary bladder and urethra
- To describe the role of the kidney in regulating body fluids, including filtration and reabsorption
- To describe how urine passes from the kidney to the urethra
- HIGHER ▶ To describe the structure and associated blood supply of the nephron
- HIGHER ▶ To describe the process of urine production in detail
- HIGHER ▶ To describe the role of ADH in the reabsorption of water.

Excretion in plants

Excretion is the elimination of metabolic waste from the body. It is a term that is generally applied to animals.

Plants do not have as great a need for excretion as animals, because plants make their own food. Consequently, they do not produce surplus amounts of food (which reduces the amount of waste they produce). In addition, the products of some plant reactions are reused by the plant. For example, some of the oxygen produced in photosynthesis is used in respiration. Also, carbon dioxide and water produced in respiration are used in photosynthesis.

Many plant waste products are stored in vacuoles in living plant cells and within dead cells (such as old xylem) in the plant. Sometimes these stored waste products are removed when the plant loses its leaves, bark, petals, seeds and fruit.

Role of leaves (stomata) and lenticels in excretion

Plants lose oxygen and water vapour, especially during daylight. These products are mostly lost through the stomata on the lower surface of the leaf, but also through lenticels on the stem. At night-time plants lose carbon dioxide through the same openings. These losses may be described as 'excretion' in plants.

Homeostasis

Homeostasis is the maintenance of a constant internal environment in an organism. In particular, this means that humans must maintain a constant temperature, fluid balance and chemical composition.

Temperature regulation in animals

The need to control body temperature is determined by the fact that temperature regulates the rate of chemical (especially enzyme-controlled) reactions. High temperatures can damage enzymes; low temperatures will slow down reactions.

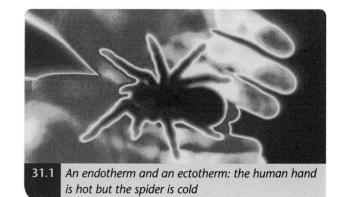

31.1 *An endotherm and an ectotherm: the human hand is hot but the spider is cold*

Animals use two different methods to control their temperature: ectothermy and endothermy. Ectotherms were formerly known as cold-blooded animals. Examples include fish, frogs, snakes and lizards.

Endotherms generate most of their own heat from respiration and were formerly called warm-blooded animals. Examples include birds and other animals such as dogs, cats, mice and humans.

The skin

The skin plays a major part in regulating human body temperature. It consists of two layers: the outer epidermis and the inner dermis. Beneath these layers is the subcutaneous tissue (or adipose tissue), which contains fat-rich cells.

> **Ectotherms** gain or lose heat from or to their external environment.
>
> **Endotherms** generate their own heat from metabolic reactions.

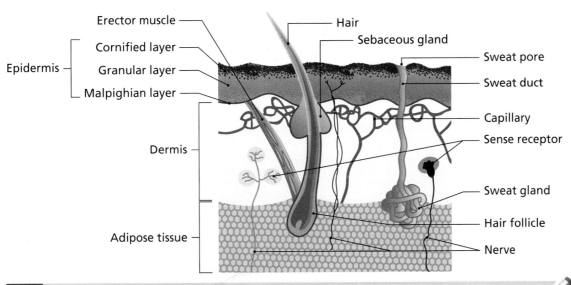

31.2 *Vertical section (VS) of the skin*

31.3 *A hair on the skin (scanning electron micrograph): keratin sections are seen on the hair and some skin cells are peeling off*

Epidermis

The epidermis is the outer layer of the skin. Cells in the Malpighian layer (see diagram 31.2) are constantly dividing by mitosis to produce new epidermis cells. As the new cells are pushed out through the granular layer, they produce a waterproof protein called keratin (this is the material from which nails, claws, hooves, horns, scales, feathers and hair are made). The build-up of keratin causes the cells to become hardened, or cornified.

Excess keratin, along with a lack of blood capillaries, causes the cells in the cornified layer to die as they reach the surface of the skin. The dead outer cells are continuously worn away (as skin flakes or dandruff).

Specialised cells in the Malpighian layer produce a brown or black pigment called **melanin**. This gives colour to the skin, hair and the coloured part of the eye (the iris). Freckles and moles are areas where melanin is very concentrated. Melanin protects the skin against the harmful effects of ultraviolet radiation. Production of melanin increases following exposure to sunlight.

THE ORGANISM

Dermis

The dermis is the inner layer of skin, located just inside the epidermis. It consists of connective tissue containing a strengthening protein called collagen. It also contains a variety of specialised structures such as sweat glands, hair follicles, sebaceous glands (which produce an oil called sebum), blood vessels and nerve receptors.

Functions of the skin

Protection

- The **epidermis** protects the body from damage and acts as a barrier to prevent the loss of water and the entry of pathogens.
- The **dermis** protects internal organs from damage due to bumps and bangs.
- **Melanin** protects the skin from ultraviolet radiation (which can cause skin cancers).
- **Sebum** is an oil produced by sebaceous glands that are located alongside hair follicles. It passes out of the hair follicle and onto the epidermis. Sebum keeps hair moist and flexible and also prevents the skin from drying up and becoming cracked. For this reason sebum can be considered to protect the body.

 Sebaceous glands are especially concentrated on the face and scalp of humans. At puberty excessive production of sebum, due to hormonal influences, may cause acne.

Vitamin production

Vitamin D is produced in the skin following exposure to ultraviolet radiation. This vitamin helps to absorb calcium in the intestines.

Food store

Fat stored in the adipose tissue acts as a food store.

Sense organ

The skin contains a variety of receptors that allow it to act as a sense organ. For example, the skin can detect sensations of touch, pain and temperature.

Excretion

Sweat glands act as organs of excretion. Sweat contains water and salts. When sweat passes out of the skin these wastes are removed from the body.

31.4 *Droplets of sweat on the skin*

Temperature regulation

Cold conditions

In cold conditions, the skin helps to retain heat in two ways.

- Erector muscles contract (forming goose bumps). This causes the hairs to stand up on the skin, in a process called **piloerection**. A layer of warm air is trapped close to the skin by the hairs. This air helps to reduce heat loss from the body.

- Blood vessels in the skin contract when we are cold. This is called **vasoconstriction** and it reduces heat loss through the skin.

A third mechanism also helps us to maintain our temperature in cold conditions. A part of the brain responds to low blood temperature by causing muscles throughout the body to contract and relax very rapidly. This results in shivering, which produces heat to raise our temperature.

Note that fat stored under the skin insulates the body from heat loss.

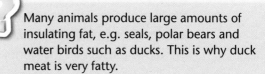

Many animals produce large amounts of insulating fat, e.g. seals, polar bears and water birds such as ducks. This is why duck meat is very fatty.

Warm conditions

In warm conditions, the skin acts in two ways to reduce our temperature.

- Sweat is produced and released onto the skin. When the water evaporates it lowers our body temperature. At normal room temperature we can lose as much as one litre of sweat in a day. In hot weather and during exercise, the loss of water and salts in the form of sweat is much greater. It is important to drink water and salts before, during and after exercise to maintain the salt/water concentration of the body. Salt tablets are often taken before competing in sports events in very warm weather to replace salt that will be lost in sweat.
- When we are too hot, blood vessels in the skin (especially in the face) expand (or dilate). This increases heat loss through the skin and reduces body temperature. This is why we turn red in the face after exercise.

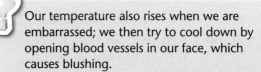

Our temperature also rises when we are embarrassed; we then try to cool down by opening blood vessels in our face, which causes blushing.

Excretion and homeostasis

The role of the excretory system in homeostasis can be summarised as:

- Regulating body temperature
- Controlling osmosis (i.e. controlling the salt and water balance of the body)
- Controlling the concentration of body fluids
- Removing waste products of metabolism from the body.

Organs of excretion

The main organs of excretion are:

- **Lungs.** The lungs excrete water and carbon dioxide.
- **Skin.** The skin excretes water and salts (in the form of sweat).
- **Kidneys.** These are the main excretory organs in humans. They excrete water, salts and urea (in the form of urine). By controlling the amount of water and salts that are excreted, the kidneys play a major role in the homeostasis of the fluid and chemical composition of the blood (and of the body).

The urinary system

Kidneys

The urinary system consists of two kidneys, two ureters, the bladder and the urethra. The kidneys are fist-sized, bean-shaped

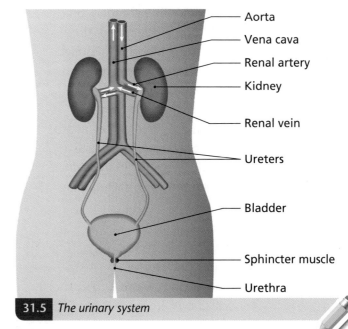

- Aorta
- Vena cava
- Renal artery
- Kidney
- Renal vein
- Ureters
- Bladder
- Sphincter muscle
- Urethra

31.5 *The urinary system*

THE ORGANISM

organs located just below the diaphragm in the small of the back.

Blood in the aorta contains waste products collected from all over the body. Some of this blood enters the kidneys through the two renal arteries. Every minute about 20% of our blood passes into the kidneys.

Main processes in the kidneys

Filtration

In the kidneys the incoming blood is filtered. This takes place in the outer **cortex** of each kidney. Filtration results in small substances (both useful and waste) being forced out of the bloodstream into the kidney.

Reabsorption

Some of the useful materials are then taken back into the blood. This is called reabsorption. It occurs in the **cortex** and **medulla** of each kidney.

Secretion

Some substances are secreted from the blood into the **cortex** of the kidney. These substances include potassium and hydrogen ions. (Too much potassium in the body prevents nerve impulses travelling correctly and reduces the strength of muscular contraction.)

By controlling the hydrogen ion concentration of the blood, the kidneys control blood pH. Purified blood leaves the kidneys through the renal veins. The renal veins take the blood to the vena cava.

When these three processes are complete only unwanted waste and toxic products are left in the kidney. These form the liquid called urine.

Urine

Urine is typically composed of:

● Water (96%)
● Nitrogenous waste (2.5%, mostly urea)
● Salts (1.5%).

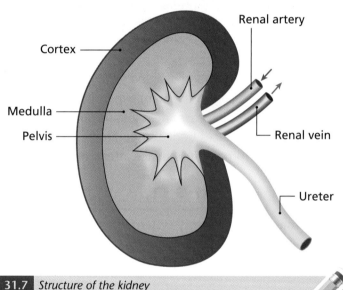

31.6 Computerized tomography (CT) scan of a section of human kidney

Cortex — Renal artery

Medulla —

Pelvis — Renal vein

Ureter

31.7 Structure of the kidney

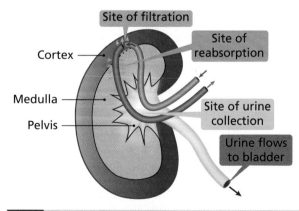

Site of filtration

Site of reabsorption

Cortex —

Medulla —

Pelvis —

Site of urine collection

Urine flows to bladder

31.8 Simplified diagram to show the location of the main events in urine production

THE ORGANISM

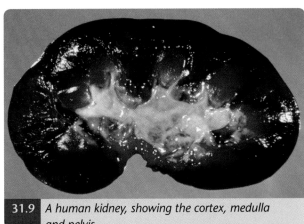

31.9 *A human kidney, showing the cortex, medulla and pelvis*

Urea is produced in the liver. It is formed when excess proteins are broken down (de-aminated).

Urine flows from the medulla into the renal pelvis. This is shaped like a funnel and collects waste and carries it into the ureter. The waste (called urine) is then carried by the two ureters to the bladder.

Bladder

The bladder stores urine. It is a muscular organ that is not under voluntary control. Two sphincter muscles are located at the junction of the bladder and urethra. In babies, these muscles open automatically by reflex action when the bladder becomes about half full. The bladder then contracts to force urine out into the urethra. The urethra emerges through the penis in males and close to the vagina in females.

Control of urination is caused by the ability to control the sphincter reflex. Up to about 2 years of age children cannot control this reflex and urination is automatic. Once the reflex is controlled, even though the bladder may be very full, urine can be retained for some time.

Normal urine is sterile, but it is easily decomposed by bacterial action outside the body. This results in the formation of ammonia, which is the cause of nappy rash in young children.

Functions of the kidneys

Excretion

The kidneys remove waste products from the bloodstream and convert them to urine. Urine is sent to the bladder for storage and is excreted through the urethra.

Osmoregulation

Water content

The kidneys control the water content of the body. They do this by varying the water content of the urine. For example, on hot days the kidneys conserve water by producing low volumes of urine.

Salt concentration

The kidneys control the salt concentration of the body fluids. They achieve this by varying the amount of salt released in the urine. For example, if we consume too much salt the kidneys will increase the amount of salt excreted in urine.

By controlling water and salt concentrations, the kidneys ensure that the blood plasma (and, as a result, all body fluids) has the same concentration as normal body cells. This means that the cells bathed by these fluids do not have problems gaining or losing water by osmosis. For this reason the kidneys are said to regulate osmosis, or to be osmoregulatory.

pH control

The kidneys control the pH of the body fluids. They do this by producing urine that is either more or less acidic. This allows the pH of the blood to remain at its normal value of 7.4.

THE ORGANISM

The nephron

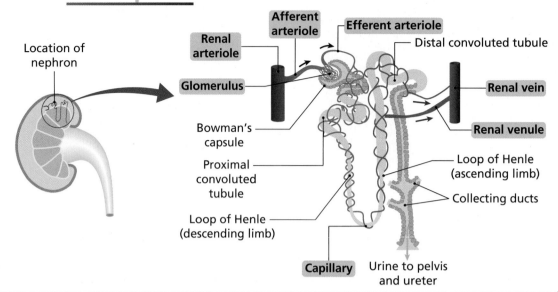

Location of nephron

Renal arteriole

Afferent arteriole

Efferent arteriole

Distal convoluted tubule

Glomerulus

Renal vein

Bowman's capsule

Renal venule

Proximal convoluted tubule

Loop of Henle (ascending limb)

Collecting ducts

Loop of Henle (descending limb)

Capillary

Urine to pelvis and ureter

31.10 *Structure of the nephron, with its associated blood supply highlighted in blue*

Each kidney contains more than a million nephrons. A nephron is a tube about 3 cm long, located in the cortex and medulla of the kidney as shown in diagram 31.10.

Nephrons are the functional units of the kidney, i.e. they make urine. To understand the workings of the kidney it is necessary to understand what happens in each nephron.

Blood supply to the nephron

Blood enters each kidney through the renal artery. Once inside the kidney, this vessel divides to form many renal arterioles, which then split, forming many smaller afferent (incoming) arterioles. Each afferent arteriole in turn divides to form a cluster of capillaries called a glomerulus. A glomerulus is found in each Bowman's capsule, which is a cup-shaped structure at one end of the nephron.

Blood leaves the glomerulus in the efferent (outgoing) arteriole. This then divides to form the capillaries that surround the rest of the nephron. These capillaries eventually re-join to form renal venules, which then combine and emerge from the kidney as the renal vein.

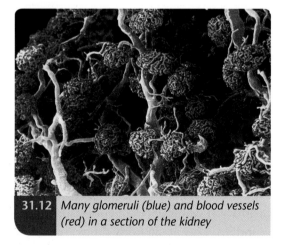

31.11 *Scan of a nephron, showing the glomerulus (red), part of Bowman's capsule (white-brown, at top right) and parts of the tubule (blue)*

31.12 *Many glomeruli (blue) and blood vessels (red) in a section of the kidney*

Urine production

Urine is produced in the nephron. There are three main processes involved in urine production: filtration, reabsorption and secretion.

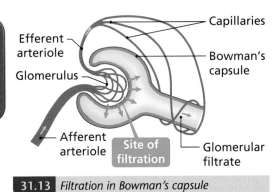

Efferent arteriole

Glomerulus

Afferent arteriole

Capillaries

Bowman's capsule

Site of filtration

Glomerular filtrate

31.13 *Filtration in Bowman's capsule*

Filtration

1. Blood entering the nephron in the afferent arteriole contains waste products.
2. Filtration takes place in the glomerulus. Small molecules such as glucose, amino acids, vitamins, some hormones, urea, salts and water are forced out of the plasma and into Bowman's capsule (diagram 31.13). Here they form a dilute solution called **glomerular filtrate**.
3. The structure of the glomerulus helps filtration in three ways:
   ▸ The pressure in the glomerulus is greater than normal blood pressure. This is caused by the already high pressure of the afferent arteriole being increased due to the efferent arteriole being narrower. Filtration in Bowman's capsule is called **ultra-filtration** because of the high pressure.
   ▸ The surface area of capillaries in the glomerulus is large. This increases the area for filtration.
   ▸ The walls of the glomerular capillaries are more porous than normal capillaries. In addition, the wall of Bowman's capsule is only one cell thick.
4. Larger substances do **not** enter the glomerular filtrate. These include red and white blood cells, platelets, antibodies, clotting proteins and some hormones.

Filtration means that water and small molecules pass (under high pressure) from the blood into the nephron.

Reabsorption means that molecules pass from the nephron back into the blood.

Active transport means that energy (in the form of ATP) is used to move molecules, often against a concentration gradient, i.e. from low concentrations to high concentrations.

> About 180 litres of glomerular filtrate are formed every 24 hours. This is 4.5 times the fluid content of the body. Obviously not all of this liquid can leave the body as urine.

Reabsorption

In the rest of the nephron (beyond Bowman's capsule), water, most salts and useful substances are reabsorbed into the blood. About 99% of the glomerular filtrate is reabsorbed. This leaves about 1.5 litres of urine to be excreted in a normal day.

1. In the proximal convoluted tubule:
   ▸ Most of the water is reabsorbed by osmosis
   ▸ All of the useful molecules such as glucose, amino acids and vitamins are reabsorbed by a combination of diffusion and active transport
   ▸ Most of the salts are reabsorbed by active transport or diffusion.
   In contrast to active transport, diffusion and osmosis do not require energy.
   To help in the process of reabsorption the proximal tubule:
   ▸ Is thin-walled, only one cell thick
   ▸ Is long (14 mm)
   ▸ Has numerous infoldings (called microvilli) in its cells
   ▸ Has a high concentration of mitochondria to provide energy for active transport.

2. The descending limb of the loop of Henle is permeable to water. In this section of the loop of Henle a small amount of the water is reabsorbed by osmosis. Also some minerals are reabsorbed.

3. The ascending limb of the loop of Henle is permeable to salts. In this region salts move out of the nephron into the fluid of the medulla. Initially the movement of salts is by diffusion, but at the top of the ascending limb

THE ORGANISM

sodium is pumped out by active transport. The addition of salts makes the medulla more concentrated than the fluid in the tubule. This helps to remove water (by osmosis) from both the descending limb of the loop of Henle and the collecting ducts. For this reason, the function of the loop of Henle is to reabsorb water.

4. The distal convoluted tubule is involved in the delicate, precise control of the water, salt and pH values of the blood. Some water and salts can be reabsorbed from the tubule into the blood in this region.

5. The collecting duct is permeable to water. A small amount of water is reabsorbed from the filtrate in the collecting duct. This occurs by osmosis, due to the high salt concentration in the medulla.

6. The liquid passing from the collecting duct is called urine. It flows into the pelvis of the kidney and on to the bladder through the ureters.

> Secretion means that some substances pass from the blood into the nephron.

Secretion

Secretion of potassium ions (K^+) and hydrogen ions (H^+) in the distal tubule help to maintain the pH of blood.

Summary of nephron functions

The functions of the regions of the nephron, and the materials reabsorbed in each, are summarised in the following table and in diagram 31.14.

Functions of the regions of the nephron		
Region	**Substances reabsorbed**	**Amount of water reabsorbed**
Proximal convoluted tubule	Most salts, glucose, amino acids and vitamins	Most
Loop of Henle (descending limb)	Some minerals	A little
Loop of Henle (ascending limb)	Some salts	None
Distal convoluted tubule	Some salts	Some
Collecting duct	None	A little

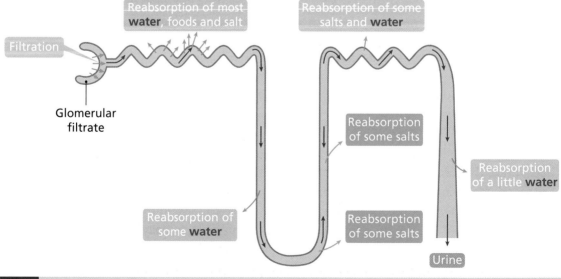

31.14 *Summary of the functions of the nephron*

HIGHER ▼

Glomerular filtrate compared with urine

Glomerular filtrate differs from urine in the following ways:
- It has more water (i.e. is more dilute) than urine
- It contains many useful molecules, e.g. glucose and amino acids that are not normally found in urine.

Control of urine volume

ADH

The volume of urine produced is controlled by a hormone called anti-diuretic hormone (ADH, also called vasopressin). ADH:
- Is produced in a part of the brain (the hypothalamus) and stored in the pituitary gland
- Is released from the pituitary gland into the bloodstream
- Affects the distal convoluted tubule and the collecting duct
- Causes more water to be reabsorbed from the nephron
- Controls osmoregulation.

Blood plasma too concentrated

1. Blood plasma becomes too concentrated when we:
   ▸ Drink too little water
   ▸ Lose too much water as sweat or faeces
   ▸ Consume too much salt.
2. The pituitary gland releases ADH.
3. ADH travels to the kidneys in the bloodstream. In the kidneys, ADH causes the walls of the distal tubule and the collecting ducts to become more permeable to water.
4. More water is reabsorbed from the nephron. This causes a reduction in:
   ▸ The salt concentration of the plasma
   ▸ The volume of urine produced.

Blood plasma concentration normal or too dilute

1. Blood plasma concentration is normal or too dilute when we:
   ▸ Consume a great deal of water
   ▸ Eat a low-salt diet.
2. In this situation ADH is not released.
3. The distal tubules and collecting ducts become relatively impermeable to water.
4. Very little water is reabsorbed from the distal tubules and collecting ducts. This causes:
   ▸ The concentration of the plasma to remain relatively unchanged
   ▸ The production of a large volume of urine.

31.15 *How ADH controls urine volume*

The effects of different conditions on urine production are shown in the table overleaf.

THE ORGANISM

Effects of different conditions on urine production				
Condition	Effect on blood	ADH	Distal tubule and collecting duct	Urine
Thirsty or Salty diet or Hot day or Exercise or Sweating	Low water content and high salt concentration	Released	More permeable to water	Low volume of water; higher salt concentration (i.e. a low volume of concentrated urine)
Excessive water intake or Very low-salt diet	High water content and low salt concentration	Not released	Less permeable to water	High volume of water; lower salt concentration (i.e. a high volume of dilute urine)
High protein diet	Normal water content and increased concentration of urea	No effect	No effect	Same volume of water; increased urea concentration (i.e. the same volume of concentrated urine)

HIGHER ▼

Summary

Excretion is the getting rid of the waste products of metabolism.

Plants:
- Produce very little waste
- Store some wastes and lose more when dead structures fall off
- Lose waste gases through their stomata and lenticels.

Homeostasis is the maintenance of a constant internal environment in an organism.

Ectotherms are animals that obtain their heat from external sources.

Endotherms generate their heat from their own body reactions.

Skin is composed of:
- **Epidermis**
  ‣ The outer layer is dead, cornified and full of waterproof keratin.
  ‣ The inner layer has living, granular cells.
  ‣ The base of the granular layer is the Malpighian layer. This makes new cells and contains many pigment (melanin) cells.

- **Dermis**
  ‣ These cells contain a strong protein called collagen.
  ‣ Has many blood vessels, sweat glands, hairs, sebaceous glands and nerve receptors.
- Subcutaneous layer contains fat in adipose tissue.

The **functions of skin** are:
- **Protection:**
  ‣ Epidermis protects against damage, water loss and the entry of pathogens
  ‣ Melanin protects against ultraviolet radiation
  ‣ Sebum (oil) keeps the epidermis intact.
- **Vitamin production** (vitamin D is made in the skin)
- **Food store** (fat stores energy)
- **Sense organ** (the skin senses touch, pain and temperature)
- **Excretion** (sweat removes water and salts from the body)
- **Temperature regulation:**
  ‣ **Cold conditions** cause:
    (i) Hairs to stand up to keep skin warm
    (ii) Blood vessels become narrow (constrict) to retain heat
    (iii) Shivering.

THE ORGANISM

> **Warm conditions** cause:
>   (i) Sweating, which cools the body due to evaporation
>   (ii) Blood vessels to widen (dilate) to lose heat.

The **main excretory organs** are:
- Lungs (water and carbon dioxide)
- Skin (water and salts)
- Kidneys (water, salts, and urea).

The **urinary system** consists of two kidneys, two ureters, the bladder and urethra.

The **kidneys make urine** in the following way:
- Blood (containing waste) enters the kidneys through the renal arteries
- The kidneys filter waste and useful materials from the blood
- Useful materials are reabsorbed from the kidneys back into the blood
- Some materials are secreted from the blood into the kidneys
- Urine formed in the kidneys flows to the bladder through the ureters
- Blood (low in waste) leaves the kidneys in the renal veins.

The **bladder stores urine.**

Urine is excreted through the urethra.

The **functions of the kidneys** are:
- Excretion of water, salts, and urea
- Osmoregulation:
  > To control the water content of the blood (and body fluids)
  > To control the salt concentration of the blood (and body fluids)
- Control of the pH of the blood (and body fluids).

Nephrons:
- Carry out the functions of the kidneys

● Are located in the cortex and medulla of the kidney.

HIGHER ▼

A **nephron makes urine** as follows:
● **Filtration:**
  > Blood enters the nephron in the afferent arteriole
  > This forms many capillaries called the glomerulus
  > High pressure in the glomerulus forces water and small molecules out of the blood
  > Glomerular filtrate is a dilute solution of waste and useful molecules.
● **Reabsorption** takes place in the following parts of the nephron:
  > **Proximal tubule** = most water by osmosis, useful molecules and most salts by diffusion and active transport
  > **Loop of Henle**
    (i) descending limb = water by osmosis
    (ii) ascending limb = salts by diffusion and then by active transport.
  > **Distal tubule** = water by osmosis and some salts by active transport
  > **Collecting ducts** = water by osmosis
● **Secretion** into the nephron of some substances
● **Urine flows** from the collecting ducts to the ureters and then to the bladder.

A hormone (ADH):
● Is released from the pituitary gland
● Controls the volume of urine formed
● Is released when plasma has too little water or too much salt.

ADH causes:
● Increased reabsorption of water in the distal tubule and collecting ducts
● A low volume of urine.

ADH is not released when we drink sufficient water or consume a low-salt diet.

THE ORGANISM

Revision questions

1 What is meant by **(a)** Excretion **(b)** Metabolism **(c)** Homeostasis?

2 **(a)** Why have plants less need for excretion than animals?
  (b) Name two places in each case where plants **(i)** store, and **(ii)** reuse, the products of metabolism.
  (c) Name two materials released from openings in plants.

(d) Name the two openings in plants from which these materials are released.

3 **(a)** Why do living things need to control their temperatures?
  (b) Distinguish, naming two animals in each case, between: **(i)** Ectotherms **(ii)** Endotherms.

4 **(a)** Name the parts of the skin labelled A to J on diagram 31.16.

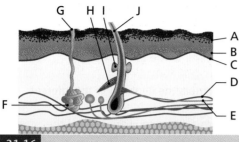

31.16

(b) In which labelled region would you expect to find the greatest rate of mitosis?

(c) Explain how the parts labelled D, G and H help to regulate the temperature of the body.

(d) How do parts A and I help the body to resist infection?

5 (a) State six functions carried out by the skin.

(b) Name one part of the skin associated with each of the functions listed and explain how each part named carries out its function.

6 Give a biological reason for each of the following:

(a) We shiver when we are cool.

(b) We blush when we are embarrassed.

(c) Whales have a lot of blubber.

(d) We sweat heavily after exercise.

(e) A boxer is fanned with a towel between rounds.

7 (a) Name three human excretory organs.

(b) State the main substances excreted by each organ.

(c) Why is faeces not considered to be excreted?

8 (a) Name the parts labelled A to I in diagram 31.17.

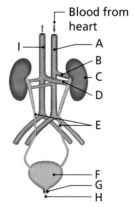

31.17

(b) State the part in the diagram that carries out each of the following:

(i) Makes urine

(ii) Stores urine

(iii) Carries blood to the kidney

(iv) Takes blood from the kidney

(v) Controls the release of urine

(vi) Excretes urine.

9 (a) Why are the kidneys referred to as osmoregulatory structures?

(b) Name two ways by which the body gains water.

(c) Name six ways by which water is lost from the body.

10 (a) From what food type is urea made?

(b) In what organ is urea made?

(c) Where does urea enter the blood?

(d) Where does urea leave the blood?

(e) Where does urea leave the body?

11 Where in the body is urine **(a)** Made **(b)** Stored **(c)** Excreted?

12 (a) Draw a labelled diagram to show the location of a nephron in the kidney.

(b) Redraw diagram 31.18 twice the size shown here.

(c) On your diagram name the parts A to K labelled on diagram 31.18.

(d) Give one function carried out by each part labelled.

HIGHER ▼

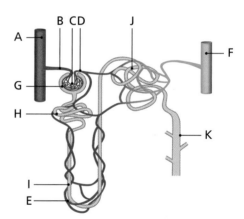

31.18

13 (a) Why is the blood pressure in the glomerulus higher than normal?

(b) Why do the cells lining some parts of the nephron contain many mitochondria?

14 The table below shows the composition of plasma, glomerular filtrate and urine.

Substance	% in plasma	% in glomerular filtrate	% in urine
Protein	8	0	0
Glucose	0.2	0.2	0
Urea	0.03	0.03	2
Salts	0.7	0.7	1.5

(a) Why is there no protein in the glomerular filtrate or urine?

(b) Explain why the urine has no glucose.

HIGHER ▼

(c) According to these figures, the urea concentration in the urine is much greater than that in the glomerular filtrate. Explain why this is so.

(d) Why does the salt concentration only increase by a factor of about 2 (i.e. 0.7% to 1.5%) while urea concentration increases by a factor of 67 (i.e. 0.03% to 2%)?

15 Describe the effects on the composition and volume of urine of the following:
   (a) A hot day
   (b) Drinking a lot of water quickly
   (c) Eating a protein-rich meal.

16 (a) Name a hormone that controls urine volume.
   (b) From which gland is this hormone released?

(c) State two situations that might cause it to be released.

(d) Name the parts of the nephron affected by the hormone.

(e) What effect has a high level of the hormone on (i) Urine (ii) Blood plasma?

17 The functions of the nephron can be summarised as <u>filtration</u>, <u>reabsorption</u> and <u>secretion</u>.

(a) Explain the meaning of each of the underlined terms.

(b) State a location and name two substances involved in filtration and reabsorption.

HIGHER ▼

Exam questions

Section A

18 The diagram shows a section through human skin.

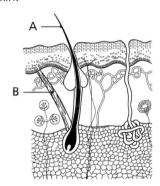

(a) Name parts A and B.
(b) Place X on the diagram to show where sweat reaches the skin surface.
(c) Apart from water, name **one** other substance which is found in sweat.
(d) Describe briefly one way by which the skin helps to retain heat in cold conditions.

(2008 OL Q 6)

Section C

19 (b) Use your knowledge of the human vascular and excretory systems to answer the following.
   (i) Explain the terms, plasma, glomerular filtrate.
   (ii) Explain why red blood cells are normally absent from glomerular filtrate.
   (iii) The concentration of glucose is the same in plasma and glomerular filtrate. Why is this?
   (iv) Why is glucose normally absent from urine?

(v) Following a period of heavy exercise an athlete may produce only a small volume of concentrated urine. Explain this observation and give an account of the process that concentrates the urine.

(2006 HL Q 13)

20 (b) (i) What is meant by excretion?
   (ii) Name **two** products excreted by the human.
   (iii) Name **one** organ of excretion, other than the kidney, in the human body.
   (iv) What is meant by osmoregulation?

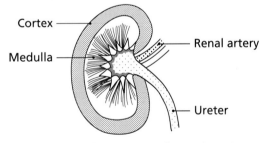

(v) Study the diagram of a section through the kidney and answer the following questions.
   1. Where does filtration of blood take place?
   2. Where does reabsorption of salt take place?
   3. To what organ does the ureter link the kidney?
   4. To which main blood vessel does the renal artery link the kidney?

(vi) Name the fluid present in the ureter.

(2007 OL Q 14)

21 **(a)** **(i)** What is meant by excretion?

(ii) Urea and carbon dioxide are excretory products of the human body. In the case of each product name a substance from which it is derived.

(b) The diagram shows the structure of a nephron and its associated blood supply.

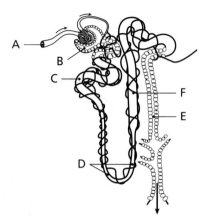

(i) Name the parts A, B, C, D, E and F.

(ii) From which blood vessel is A derived?

(iii) Where in the kidney is B located?

(iv) Give the part of the nephron in which each of the following takes place:

1. filtration,

2. reabsorption of amino acids.

(v) Give **two** features of the nephron that aid filtration.

(vi) Name a group of biomolecules in the blood which are too large to pass through the filtration system of the nephron.

(c) **(i)** Suggest **two** situations which may result in a drop in the water content of the blood.

(ii) When the water content of the blood drops a hormone is released. Name this hormone and the endocrine gland from which it is secreted.

(iii) Give a precise target area for this hormone. How does the hormone reach the target area?

(iv) Explain the role of the hormone at its target area, when the water content of the blood is low.

(2008 HL Q 13)

22 **(c)** Suggest a biological explanation for **each** of the following observations:

(iv) After a long session of heavy exercise, an athlete's urine is likely to be concentrated and low in volume.

(v) A person's fingers may turn white when exposed to low temperature for a period of time.

(2010 HL Q 15)

23 **(c)** **(i)** Explain the term excretion.

(ii) Name **two** substances excreted by the kidneys.

(iii) The diagram shows the human urinary system. Name the parts labelled A, B and C.

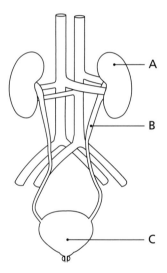

(iv) Name the parts of the kidney in which **each** of the following takes place:

1. Filtration

2. Reabsorption.

(v) Name **one** other excretory organ in the body.

(2011 OL Q 14)

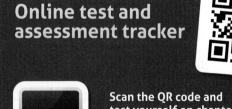

Previous examination questions

Ordinary level	Higher level
2005 Q 14a	2004 Q 12b, c
2006 Q 15a	2005 Q 3a
2007 Q 14b	2006 Q 13b
2008 Q 6	2007 Q 15c
2009 Q 14b	2008 Q 13
2011 Q 14c	2010 Q 15c (iv), (v)
2012 Q 15a	2012 Q 15c

Latest questions at www.edco.ie/lcbiologyplus/examhelp

Online test and assessment tracker

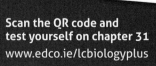

Scan the QR code and test yourself on chapter 31
www.edco.ie/lcbiologyplus

Chapter 32 **Plant responses**

A **stimulus** (plural: **stimuli**) is anything that causes a reaction in an organism or in any of its parts.

A **response** is the activity of a cell or organism as a result of a stimulus.

Stimulus and response

Animal stimuli include hearing a loud noise, seeing a pleasant sight, smelling nice perfume or feeling pain or hunger. Plant stimuli include light, gravity, water and chemicals.

Animal responses include movement, production of enzymes or hormones and feeding. Plant responses include growth, flowering, fruit formation and production of plant enzymes.

The structures required for response

The structures needed by organisms in order to allow them to respond include:
- A chemical or hormonal system (present in plants and animals)
- A nerve and sense organ system (only found in animals)
- A method of movement, which includes growth along with muscular and skeletal systems (a muscular and skeletal system is only found in animals)
- A defence or immune system.

The structures required by animals for responding will be dealt with in Chapters 33–37.

Plants do not possess nervous systems. Instead, they depend on chemical coordination for their responses. Chemical coordination is much slower than nervous coordination. Plant responses often involve growth and changes in growth. These responses cause plants to move, but their movement is much slower than that of animals.

Responses in flowering plants

Growth regulation

The growth of flowering plants can be controlled by external and internal factors. Normally the external factors operate by causing, or controlling, the production of internal factors.

THE ORGANISM

External factors

- **Light** affects plant growth by providing the energy needed for photosynthesis. This in turn supplies the energy-rich molecules needed by plants for growth. In addition, light is needed to produce chlorophyll, fully formed chloroplasts, normal-sized leaves and strong stems.
- **Day length** plays a very significant role in causing plants to flower. It may also have a role in fruit and seed formation, dormancy, leaf loss and germination of some seeds.
- **Gravity** can cause roots to grow down into the soil, while shoots grow upwards, away from gravity.
- **Temperature** affects the growth of plants mainly by affecting the rate of enzyme reactions. As a result, plants grow faster at higher temperatures. In addition, some plants will only produce flowers if they are exposed to low temperatures for a number of days or weeks.

Internal factors

Plants produce a range of chemicals called growth regulators. These growth regulators are produced in the meristematic regions of the plant, such as in the root tip or shoot tip regions.

Tropisms

A **tropism** is a change in the growth of a plant in response to an external stimulus.

A **positive tropism** occurs when the growth is towards the stimulus.

A **negative tropism** occurs when the growth is away from the stimulus.

The main advantage of tropisms is that they allow plants to obtain more favourable growing conditions. For example:
- Stems grow towards light so they can produce more food by photosynthesis
- Roots grow towards gravity so they can penetrate deeper into the soil for better anchorage and absorption.

The main types of tropisms are outlined below.

Phototropism

Phototropism is the change in growth of a plant in response to light, usually from one direction (i.e. unidirectional light).

Stems are positively phototropic (i.e. they grow towards light). This allows the stem (and the leaves) to get more light. In this way they can carry out more photosynthesis and produce more food.

Many roots are negatively phototropic. This is clearly seen in the roots of climbing plants such as ivy, where the roots grow away from light and towards the wall or surface to which they are attached.

32.1 *Phototropism: a stem growing towards light*

Geotropism

Roots usually grow towards gravity (positively geotropic) and stems grow away from gravity (negatively geotropic).

If the roots grow towards gravity they can anchor the plant more efficiently in the soil. In addition they can absorb more water and minerals. By growing away from gravity, stems grow towards the light. This allows plants to produce more food.

> **Geotropism (or gravitropism)** is the change in growth of a plant in response to gravity.

32.2 *Geotropism: a stem growing away from gravity*

32.3 *Thigmotropism: tendril growing around a supporting stem*

Thigmotropism

Climbing plants (e.g. ivy, vines, peas, tomatoes) produce specialised parts, called tendrils, which wrap around supporting structures. Tendrils exhibit positive thigmotropism, i.e. they grow around any object they touch.

> **Thigmotropism** is a change in growth of a plant in response to touch.

Hydrotropism

Roots and pollen tubes grow towards water.

> **Hydrotropism** is a change in growth of a plant in response to water.

Chemotropism

> **Chemotropism** is a change in growth of a plant in response to chemicals.

Roots grow towards minerals (e.g. calcium and magnesium and fertilisers such as nitrogen, phosphorous and potassium) in the soil. Pollen tubes grow towards chemicals released by the ovule. These are examples of positive chemotropism. However, most roots are negatively chemotropic to acids or heavy metals (e.g. lead and zinc) in the soil.

Growth regulators

> **A growth regulator** is a chemical that controls the growth of a plant.

Most growth regulators are produced in small amounts in one part of a plant (mainly in meristems) and transported to another part where they cause an effect. For this reason they are often called hormones. The exact way that growth regulators are transported is not known. Most, however, are transported in the vascular tissues (xylem and phloem).

It is difficult to establish the exact role of plant regulators. This is due to the following reasons:

- They are active in very small amounts.
- Their effects depend on their concentration. This means the same regulator can have opposite effects at high or low concentrations.
- Their effects depend on the location in the plant in which they are acting. For example, the same concentration of plant regulator can have opposite effects in the stem and root.

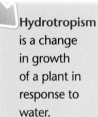

THE ORGANISM

● Different regulators interact in different ways. Some regulators support each other to produce a greater effect. Others interfere with each other and the combination may have no effect.

Growth regulators can act as growth promoters or growth inhibitors.

Growth promoters

Auxins are examples of growth promoters in plants.

Auxin as an example of a growth regulator

Auxins and IAA

There are a number of auxins, the most important of which is indoleacetic acid (IAA). IAA, which is often simply called auxin, is made in shoot tips, young leaves and seeds. It moves down the stem by an unknown mechanism. Auxins cause stem and root growth and stimulate fruit formation (at certain concentrations).

Production sites

Auxin is produced in the meristematic tissue in the tips of shoots. It is also produced in young leaves and in developing seeds.

Functions of auxin

The functions of auxin include:
● Stimulating stem elongation
● Stimulating root growth
● Causing cells to form into different structures (e.g. in the zone of differentiation in the root)
● Developing fruit
● Inhibiting side branching in stems
● Causing phototropism
● Causing geotropism.

Effects of auxins

Tropisms

Auxins cause cell elongation and growth or bending, as described opposite, on page 367.

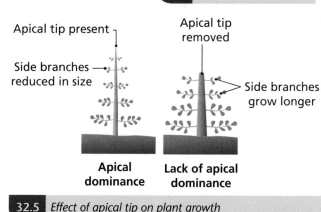

32.4 *Apical dominance: the plant on the right has had its growth tip removed and shows more side branching*

HIGHER ▼

Apical dominance

The apex is the tip (top) of the plant. If the apical bud is intact, auxin produced in the tip will pass down the stem and inhibit (prevent the growth of) lateral buds and any side branching. This form of growth is clearly seen in cacti (which have very few side branches) and conifers

Apical tip present
Side branches → reduced in size

Apical dominance

Apical tip removed
Side branches grow longer

Lack of apical dominance

32.5 *Effect of apical tip on plant growth*

(where the inhibition decreases down the stem, allowing lower branches to grow more strongly). If the apical tip is removed side branches are allowed to develop. The plant will then develop as a low, bushy form.

Farmers often cut down hedges to stimulate side branching and form a livestockproof barrier.

THE ORGANISM

HIGHER ▼

Fruit formation

IAA is made in developing seeds. It stimulates food to form in the fruit that surrounds the seed(s).

Root growth

At low concentrations, IAA causes roots to grow (whereas at higher concentrations IAA causes stems to grow). IAA can be applied artificially to stimulate rooting. However, commercially prepared growth promoters (i.e. synthetic ones) are more efficient at this process.

The mechanism of a plant response to light (i.e. mechanism of phototropism)

> **Syllabus** You are required to know the mechanism of a plant response to any **one** external stimulus.

Auxin and cell elongation

Auxin loosens cell walls, which allows them to expand. Cell elongation is essential for normal growth and tropisms.

Role of auxin (IAA) in phototropism

1. IAA is produced in the growth tips (meristems) of the stem.
2. If the stem is exposed to light from one side IAA will diffuse down the shaded side (i.e. the side furthest from the light source).
3. The concentration of IAA present in the shaded cells causes them to elongate more than the cells on the bright side of the stem.
4. As a result of the uneven elongation, the stem bends towards the light (phototropism will result).

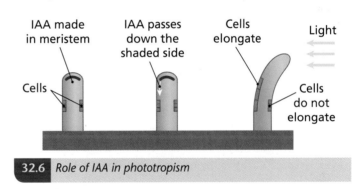

32.6 *Role of IAA in phototropism*

Growth inhibitors

A **growth inhibitor** is a chemical that causes a reduction in growth of plants.

Ethene and abscisic acid are examples of growth inhibitors in plants.

Ethene

Ethene (formerly called ethylene) is the only growth regulator that is a gas. It is made by plants in stem nodes, ripe fruits and decaying leaves. The functions of ethene include:

- Ripening fruits
- Causing fruit colour to form, fruit flavour to develop and fruit tissues to soften
- Stimulating leaves to fall in autumn
- Ageing of plants
- Stimulating more ethene production (i.e. ethene stimulates more ethene).

Ethene is used commercially to ripen bananas. Bananas are harvested while they are still green and are exported to consumer countries. They are exposed to ethene to stimulate ripening (i.e. they turn yellow and soften) just before distribution to shops.

The saying 'one bad apple rots the barrel' is true because damaged fruit releases ethene, which will ripen (and soon over-ripen) surrounding fruit. If ripe fruit is put in a plastic bag with green tomatoes, ethene will cause the tomatoes to turn red faster than normal.

THE ORGANISM

Abscisic acid

Abscisic acid is produced in leaves, stems and root caps. It is often called the stress regulator of plants. The functions of abscisic acid include:

- Causing plants to respond to harmful conditions
- Causing stomata to close in dry conditions (to retain water)
- Causing the production of bud scales, which protect the buds in winter
- Inhibiting seed germination, which allows the seeds to remain dormant in the soil during winter.

> **Syllabus** You are required to know **two** uses of commercially prepared plant growth regulators.

Although it was thought that abscisic acid caused leaf fall (abscission) in autumn, this is now known to be caused by ethene (in combination with auxins).

Commercially prepared growth regulators

32.7 *Dipping a cutting in rooting powder*

Plant growth regulators can be produced outside of plants by artificial or synthetic methods.

- **Rooting powders** often contain a synthetic growth regulator such as naphtylacetic acid (NAA). This stimulates rapid root formation on stem cuttings. Horticulturists (people who grow plants) use NAA to produce roots on cuttings more quickly than would naturally be the case.
- In **tissue culturing** (or micropropagation), pieces of plant material are grown to form entire new plants. If a piece of plant tissue is grown in a high auxin concentration, it will develop into a mass of similar (undifferentiated) cells, called a callus. By adding different concentrations of auxins, the callus can be stimulated to form roots, shoots or an entire plant, as outlined in Chapter 8.
- **Ethene** ripens bananas and other fruits.

Plant adaptations for protection

> **Syllabus** You are required to know **four** methods of plant protection.

Plants are subject to a large range of potentially harmful environmental conditions. These include being eaten by herbivores, being infected with disease-causing micro-organisms, losing water and the danger of overheating. To protect themselves, plants have a large number of adaptive features. Some of these features are anatomical (or structural); others are chemical.

Anatomical protective features

- Plants are enclosed by a physical barrier consisting of epidermis or bark. These protective layers prevent the entry of pathogens and reduce the loss of water from the plant. In addition, the epidermis is often covered with a protective cuticle. In some plants, the epidermis cells are adapted to form thorns (e.g. blackberry bushes) or stinging hairs (e.g. nettle leaves).
- A shortage of water in a plant causes the guard cells to shrivel. This has the effect of closing the stomata and therefore reducing any further loss of water by transpiration.

Chemical protective features

- Excessive heat may cause plant enzymes to lose shape and become denatured. This may harm or even kill plants. Many plants form special heat-shock proteins once the temperature rises above about 40°C. These heat-shock proteins normally surround other proteins (especially enzymes) and help them to maintain their shape. Heat-shock proteins are also formed by animals and micro-organisms that are subjected to high temperatures (such as during fevers in humans).

- When a plant is infected by a micro-organism the plant is sometimes able to produce stress proteins. Some of these stress proteins are called **phytoalexins**. Stress proteins act in different ways, some of which include:
  - Damaging the micro-organisms by attacking their cell walls
  - Stimulating the formation of specialised plant cell walls that prevent the spread of the micro-organism
  - Stimulating nearby plant cells to respond to the micro-organism.

Activity 20 To investigate the effect of IAA growth regulator on plant tissue

Preparing a stock solution

This step is often carried out by the teacher, as IAA is irritant, toxic and may cause mutations.

1. Dissolve a small amount of IAA in a small volume of ethanol. Note that although pure IAA may be toxic, dilute solutions do not carry much risk. Ethanol is flammable. (IAA is dissolved in ethanol first because it does not easily dissolve in water.)

2. When the IAA is fully dissolved in the ethanol, bring the volume up to 1 litre using distilled water. If the correct weight of IAA is dissolved in 1 litre a stock solution of IAA is prepared with a concentration of 10^2 parts per million (ppm) (see diagram 32.8).

Distilled water — IAA dissolved in ethanol

1 litre —

Stock solution of IAA (10^2 ppm)

32.8 *Preparing a stock solution of IAA*

Carrying out a serial dilution

3. Label eight small bottles or petri dishes A to H.

4. (a) Transfer 10 ml of the stock solution into dish A.

   (b) Using a clean pipette, place 9 ml of distilled water into each of the dishes labelled B to H. (**Note:** do not add any distilled water to dish A.)

   (c) Use a clean pipette to transfer 1 ml of IAA solution from dish A to dish B and stir to mix thoroughly.

   (d) Using a clean pipette each time and stirring to mix the contents thoroughly, transfer 1 ml of IAA solution from B to C, C to D, D to E, E to F and F to G (see diagram 32.9).

   (e) Remove 1 ml of solution from dish G and dispose of it down the sink. (The procedure carried out in step 4 is called a serial dilution. It produces a range of IAA solutions, each one of which is one-tenth the concentration of the previous solution.)

5. Do not transfer any IAA solution to dish H. It acts as a control (containing no IAA, only distilled water).

THE ORGANISM

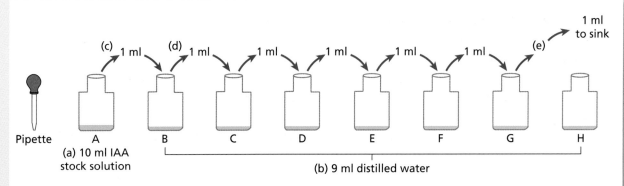

32.9 *Preparing a serial dilution of IAA*

6. The final concentration of IAA in each dish is shown in the table below.

Dish	A	B	C	D	E	F	G	H
Concentration of IAA (ppm)	10^2	10^1	10^0	10^{-1}	10^{-2}	10^{-3}	10^{-4}	0 (no IAA)

Investigating the effect of IAA on plant tissue

7. Photocopy a sheet of graph paper on to acetate sheets. (The acetate will be used to measure the length of the roots or shoots.)

8. Place a circular acetate grid in the **lid** of each of eight petri dishes.

9. Place five radish or cress seeds along one of the lines on each of the acetate sheets.

10. Place filter paper on top of the seeds in the lids of the petri dishes.

11. Use a clean dropper to add about one-quarter of each IAA solution to each filter paper.

12. Cover the filter papers with a layer of cotton wool.

13. Sprinkle the remaining IAA solutions onto each piece of cotton wool.

14. Put the base of the petri dish over the cotton wool and tape it shut.

15. Stand the petri dishes on their edges with the seeds horizontal, as in diagram 32.11. (This ensures that the roots grow down and the shoots grow up.)

16. Leave the dishes in a warm place (20–25°C), such as an incubator, for 2 or 3 days.

32.10 *The set-up in a petri dish*

Observing the results

17. If you can see the roots and shoots through the lid of the petri dish then you can leave the petri dish sealed shut. If not, remove the tape and the base of the petri dish. Carefully remove the filter paper (be careful that the plant tissue does not remain attached to the filter paper).

18. Use the acetate grid to measure the lengths of the roots and shoots of the seedlings in each dish. Record the results as shown in the table opposite. Use a similar table for the length of the shoots.

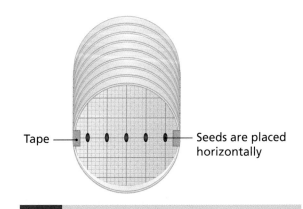

32.11 *Incubating the petri dishes*

THE ORGANISM

19. Calculate the percentage increase or decrease according to the formula shown in diagram 32.12.

20. Draw a graph (using graph paper) of the percentage increase or decrease vs. IAA concentration. Put IAA concentration on the horizontal axis. The graph may be similar to the one shown in revision question 15 on page 373.

$$\text{Percentage stimulation or inhibition} = \frac{\text{(Average length} - \text{Average length of controls)}}{\text{Average length of controls}}$$

32.12 *The formula for calculating the percentage increase or decrease in root and shoot growth*

Note: IAA causes cell elongation or inhibition in roots and shoots, depending on the concentration of IAA. Roots are much more sensitive to IAA than shoots.

Dish	Concentration of IAA (ppm)	Length of roots (number of squares on acetate grid)					Total length	Average length	% stimulation or inhibition
		Seed 1	Seed 2	Seed 3	Seed 4	Seed 5			
A	10^2								
B	10^1								
C	10^0								
D	10^{-1}								
E	10^{-2}								
F	10^{-3}								
G	10^{-4}								
H (Control)	0								

The possible results are:

- The roots or shoots in the control dish are seen to have grown (due to IAA produced by the seeds themselves)
- Depending on the IAA concentration the roots may grow longer or shorter than the roots in the control
- Depending on the IAA concentration the shoots may grow longer or shorter than the shoots in the control
- At some concentrations the roots or the shoots (or both) may not grow at all.

Summary

A **stimulus** is anything that causes a reaction in an organism or in any of its parts.

A **response** is the activity of a cell or organism as a result of a stimulus.

Plant responses often involve growth and changes in growth due to:
- External factors such as light, gravity, water and chemicals
- Internal factors such as growth regulators.

A **tropism** is the change in growth of a plant in response to an external stimulus.
- A positive tropism means the growth is towards the stimulus.
- A negative tropism means that the growth is away from the stimulus.

The **benefit of tropisms** is that they help the plant to achieve the best growing conditions.

The **most common tropisms** are:
- Phototropism (response to light)
- Geotropism (response to gravity)
- Thigmotropism (response to touch)
- Hydrotropism (response to water)
- Chemotropism (response to chemicals).

Growth regulators are chemicals that control growth in a plant.
- Growth promoters (auxins) cause increased plant growth.
- Growth inhibitors (ethene and abscisic acid) reduce or stop growth.

Auxins are the best-known growth promoters.

THE ORGANISM

HIGHER ▼

Indoleacetic acid (IAA) is the best-known auxin.

The **effects of auxins** are to cause:
● Tropisms (i.e. growth and bending responses)
● Apical dominance (i.e. they allow the tip of the stem to grow, but inhibit side branches)
● Fruit formation
● Root formation and growth.

IAA affects phototropism as follows:
● IAA is made in the tip of the stem
● It diffuses down the stem
● It causes stem cells to elongate
● It diffuses down the shaded side of a stem
● The cells on the shaded side elongate, causing the stem to bend towards light.

Growth inhibitors include:
● Ethene (or ethylene), which is a gas that ripens fruit, and causes ageing and leaf fall

● Abscisic acid, which responds to stress in plants by closing stomata, forming bud scales and inhibiting seed germination.

Commercial growth regulators are used to:
● Stimulate root formation in cuttings
● Stimulate the formation of new plants in tissue culturing
● Ripen bananas and other fruits.

Plant protective methods may be:
● Anatomical or structural (e.g. epidermis, bark, cuticle, closure of stomata)
● Chemical (heat-shock proteins, stress proteins).

To investigate the effect of IAA on plant tissues:
● Different concentrations of IAA are prepared
● Seeds are grown in the IAA concentrations
● Changes in length of roots and shoots are recorded.

Revision questions

1 (a) What is meant by a: **(i)** Stimulus **(ii)** Response?
   (b) Give two examples in each case for animal and plant stimuli and responses.

2 Name two external factors that control growth in plants.

3 (a) What is a tropism?
   (b) Distinguish between positive and negative tropisms.
   (c) What is the significance of tropisms for plants?

4 (a) Name one positive tropism in each case that affects: **(i)** Shoots **(ii)** Roots.
   (b) Outline one benefit to a plant in each case of: **(i)** Phototropism **(ii)** Geotropism.

5 (a) What is a growth regulator?
   (b) How are growth regulators transported in plants?
   (c) Give three reasons why it proved difficult for scientists to discover the role of growth regulators.

6 (a) Distinguish between growth promoters and growth inhibitors.
   (b) Name one growth promoter and one growth inhibitor.

7 With regard to auxin, state:
   (a) A precise location where it is produced
   (b) Two ways in which it acts as a growth regulator
   (c) One way in which it acts as a growth inhibitor
   (d) Its effects on: **(i)** Fruit formation **(ii)** Side branching.

8 Describe, with the aid of a labelled diagram, the role of auxin (IAA) in the change in growth of a stem in response to light from one side.

HIGHER ▼

9 Some oat seedlings were grown in the dark and then treated as follows:
   Group A: no treatment given, left intact
   Group B: tips of seedlings covered with metal foil
   Group C: tips of seedlings cut off.
   The seedlings were then exposed to light from one side as shown in diagram 32.13.

   Group A   Group B   Group C Light

   32.13

   (a) Which group of seedlings will respond to the light?
   (b) Explain why the other groups will not respond.
   (c) Name the response that is produced.
   (d) What is the value of this response to a plant?
   (e) Name the substance causing the response.

10 In an experiment three groups of oat seedlings were set up and illuminated from one side only (unilateral light). Group A were untreated; members of

THE ORGANISM

HL ▼

HIGHER ▼

Group B had black paper sleeves around them except at their tips; Group C had black paper caps over their tips. The results are shown in diagram 32.14.

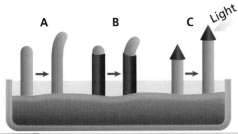

A   B   C   Light

32.14

HIGHER ▼

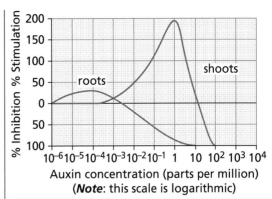

32.15

(a) Explain the reason for the results in Group A.
(b) Suggest why the stems in Group C do not bend?
(c) What result would you expect for Group C if the caps were transparent?
(d) Why do the stems in Group B bend?

11 (a) State two ways in which plant growth regulators may be used commercially.
(b) State the benefit for each example given.

12 In investigating the effect of a growth regulator on plant tissue:
(a) Name the growth regulator used.
(b) Name the plant used.
(c) Why was the growth regulator dissolved in ethanol first?
(d) Why were five seeds (rather than a single seed) placed in each dish?
(e) Why was there no growth regulator in one dish?
(f) How was the effect of the regulator on the plant tissue judged?

13 (a) Give two examples in each case of anatomical and chemical methods by which plants protect themselves.
(b) Explain why a nettle sting is a combination of anatomical and chemical protection.

14 The graph in diagram 32.15 shows the effect of IAA concentration on roots and shoots.

(a) What concentration of IAA:
  (i) Has the same effect on roots and shoots?
  (ii) Causes maximum root elongation?
  (iii) Has no effect on shoots?
(b) Suggest the effect of the following IAA concentrations:
  (i) 10^4 ppm on roots
  (ii) 1 ppm on shoots
  (iii) 10^{-2} ppm on roots
  (iv) 10^{-6} ppm on roots and shoots.

15 Choose which of the options (i), (ii), (iii) or (iv) represents the correct answer in each case below.
(a) The response of a plant to touch is called:
  (i) Thermotropism
  (ii) Chemotropism
  (iii) Thigmotropism
  (iv) Geotropism.
(b) Phototropism is caused by cell elongation in:
  (i) The bright side of the stem tips
  (ii) The shady side of the stem tips
  (iii) The base of the stem
  (iv) All the cells in the stem.
(c) Auxin such as IAA may act as:
  (i) A growth inhibitor
  (ii) A form of plant protection
  (iii) Either a growth promoter or a growth inhibitor
  (iv) A growth promoter.

HIGHER ▼

Exam questions

Section A

17

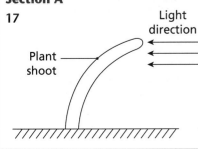

Light direction

Plant shoot

(a) Give the term used for the growth response shown by the plant shoot in the diagram.
(b) Why is this growth response of benefit to plants?
(c) Name the group of substances that controls such responses.
(d) Name the tissue through which the substances named in (c) are transported in the plant.
(e) Name another growth response found in plants.

(2009 OL Q 6)

THE ORGANISM

Section B

18 Growth regulators in plants can promote growth or inhibit it.
   (a) Give an example of each of the following:
       (i) A growth regulator that promotes growth.
       (ii) A growth regulator that inhibits growth.
   (b) In the course of your studies you investigated the effect of a growth regulator on plant tissue. Answer the following questions in relation to that investigation.
       (i) Name the plant that you used.
       (ii) Describe how you carried out the investigation.
       (iii) Give a safety precaution that you took while carrying out the investigation.
       (iv) State the results that you obtained.
       (2008 HL Q 8)

Section C

19 (b) (i) What is an auxin? State a site of auxin secretion. How may the action of an auxin be considered similar to the action of a hormone in the human body?
       (ii) Define tropism. List **three** types of tropism.
       (iii) Relate the role of an auxin to one of the tropisms that you have listed in (ii).
       (2004 HL Q 15)

20 (b) The graph shows the effect of varying auxin concentration on the root and shoot of a plant.

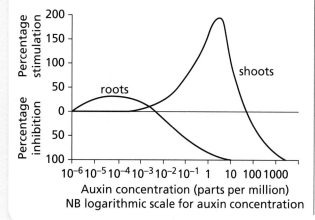

Auxin concentration (parts per million)
NB logarithmic scale for auxin concentration

   (i) What is an auxin?
   (ii) At what approximate auxin concentration does the root receive maximum stimulation?
   (iii) At what approximate auxin concentration does the shoot receive maximum stimulation?
   (iv) What is the effect on the root of an auxin concentration of 10^{-2} parts per million?
   (v) Give two examples of uses of synthetic (man-made) auxins.
   (vi) Describe three methods used by plants to protect themselves from adverse external environments.
   (2005 HL Q 14)

21 (a) (i) What do you understand by the term *adverse external environment*?
       (ii) Give **two** ways in which plants protect themselves from adverse external environments.
   (b) (i) Name the group of substances in plants which control responses to external stimuli.
       (ii) 1. What name is given to the regions in plants in which these substances are produced?
           2. Give locations for two of these regions.
       (iii) Most plant shoots are <u>positively phototropic</u>. Explain the underlined term.
       (iv) How does the plant benefit from this response?
       (v) Explain the mechanism of response by a plant to a **named** external stimulus.
       (2011 HL Q 11)

22 (b) (ii) In relation to plant responses:
           1. What name is given to a plant's response to light?
           2. Name **one** growth regulator produced in plants.
           3. Where in a plant are growth regulators produced?
           4. Give **one** way by which plants can protect themselves from attack.
           (2012 OL Q 15)

Previous examination questions

Ordinary level	Higher level
2009 Q 6	2004 Q 15b
2012 Q 15b(ii)	2005 Q 14b
	2006 Q 6, 7b
	2008 Q 8
	2009 Q 2
	2010 Q 9
	2011 Q 11a,b

Latest questions at www.edco.ie/lcbiologyplus/examhelp

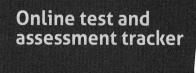

Online test and assessment tracker

Scan the QR code and test yourself on chapter 32
www.edco.ie/lcbiologyplus

THE ORGANISM

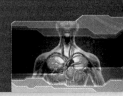

Chapter 33 The nervous system

Introduction

In animals, the nervous system and the endocrine system (Chapter 35) are responsible for the coordination of activities in the body. They allow the animal to respond to internal and external changes called stimuli.

The nervous system is specially adapted for the rapid responses that an animal makes. It is divided into:

- The central nervous system (CNS), which consists of the brain and spinal cord
- The peripheral nervous system (PNS), which consists of a vast network of nerves (in the form of nerve fibres) that carry messages between the CNS and the rest of the body.

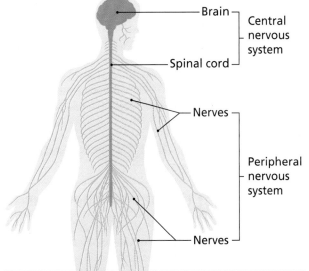

33.1 *The parts of the nervous system*

In order to carry out the correct response to a stimulus, four processes are involved.

- **Reception.** The stimulus must be detected. This is the function of receptors, neurons (nerve cells) and sense organs.
- **Transmission.** The message passes along the neurons. The neurons in the PNS carry messages from receptors to the CNS and from the CNS to effectors, such as muscles or glands.

A **neuron** (or neurone) is a nerve cell.

A **sensory** (or afferent) **neuron** takes a message from a sense organ to the CNS.

A **motor** (or efferent) **neuron** takes a message from the CNS to a muscle or a gland.

- **Integration**. The incoming messages are sorted and processed and a response decided upon. This occurs in the CNS, especially in the brain.
- **Response**. This is carried out by the effectors (i.e. muscles or glands) when they are stimulated by neurons.

Neurons

Neurons are the basic units of the nervous system and are specialised to carry information (as electrical impulses) from one place to another.

There are three types of neuron: sensory, motor and interneurons. Not only do neurons vary in type, they also differ in size. Neurons in the brain are very tiny, whereas neurons connecting the spine and the feet may be over 1 metre long.

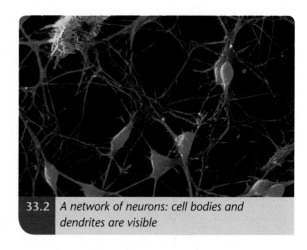

33.2 *A network of neurons: cell bodies and dendrites are visible*

Structure of neurons

The typical structure of a sensory and a motor neuron is shown in diagram 33.4.

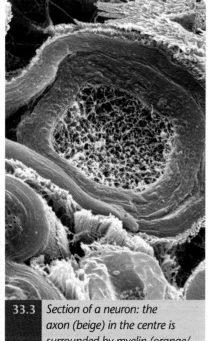

33.3 *Section of a neuron: the axon (beige) in the centre is surrounded by myelin (orange/green), which in turn is enclosed by a Schwann cell (green)*

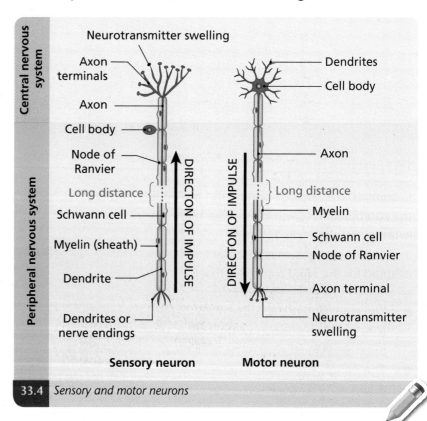

33.4 *Sensory and motor neurons*

Functions of the parts of neurons

- A **receptor** is a cell or group of cells that detects a stimulus.
- **Nerve endings** connect sensory neurons to receptor cells or sense organs.
- **Dendrites** are fibres (often highly branched) that carry impulses **towards** the cell body.
- **Axons** carry impulses **away from** cell bodies.
- **Schwann cells** produce the myelin sheath.
- The **myelin sheath** is a fat-rich layer that insulates the electrical impulses.

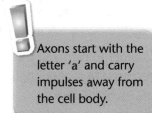

Axons start with the letter 'a' and carry impulses away from the cell body.

THE ORGANISM

- The **cell body** contains a nucleus and cell organelles. In particular cell bodies contain mitochondria, which provide energy for the movement of nerve impulses. Each cell body forms the dendrites and axons that may emerge from it as well as neurotransmitter chemicals. The cell bodies of sensory neurons are located outside the CNS. The cell bodies of motor neurons are located within the CNS.
- **Axon terminals** are branches formed by the splitting of an axon. Each of these small branches carries an impulse to a swelling called a neurotransmitter swelling.
- **Neurotransmitter swellings** release chemicals that carry the impulse from one nerve cell to another. The chemicals are called neurotransmitters. Neurotransmitters are stored in vesicles in the swellings.

A **ganglion** (plural: ganglia) is a group of cell bodies located outside the CNS.

An **interneuron** (also called an intermediate, relay or association neuron) carries information between sensory and motor neurons.

 In multiple sclerosis (MS), patches of myelin degenerate in the CNS. As a result, the passage of nerve impulses is impeded and the person suffers symptoms ranging from numbness and tingling to difficulty in moving or paralysis and loss of bladder control.

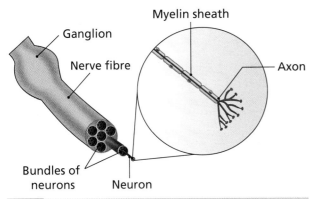

33.5 *Relationship between a nerve fibre and neurons*

Nerve fibres

Many axons or dendrites often combine to form nerve fibres (sometimes simply called a nerve). Axons can be very long, e.g. those that run from the spine to the feet may be over 1 metre in length.

Interneurons

Interneurons are short neurons found between motor and sensory neurons in the CNS. They are not enclosed in myelin sheaths.

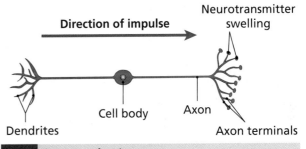

33.6 *Structure of an interneuron*

Transmission of nerve impulses

A stimulus of sufficient strength arriving at a neuron causes an electrical current or impulse to travel along the dendrite and axon to the neurotransmitter swellings. The movement of the electrical impulse along a neuron involves the movement of ions (charged particles) in and out of neurons. This movement uses energy and is an active process.

Features of nerve impulses

Resting neuron

A resting neuron is a neuron that is not carrying an impulse.

Threshold

The **threshold** is the minimum stimulus needed to cause an impulse to be carried in a neuron.

A stimulus below the threshold has no effect, but one that is at or above the threshold causes an electrical impulse to travel along the axon. Some people are said to have a higher threshold for pain or for high temperatures. This means they can tolerate more pain or higher temperatures before their nervous system reacts.

THE ORGANISM

> The 'all or nothing' law states that if the threshold is reached an impulse is carried, but if the threshold is not reached no impulse is carried.

'All or nothing' law

The 'all or nothing' law means that an impulse is either carried or not carried. If the threshold is reached a message is sent. No matter how strong the stimulus is, once it is above the threshold level, the same impulse is carried. This means that a mild stimulus or a severe stimulus will cause the same impulse to be sent along any axon. Sensitivity to different degrees of stimulation (e.g. mild versus severe pain) depends on the number of neurons stimulated and the frequency with which they send their impulses.

Movement of impulse

Once the threshold is reached the axon (or dendrite) changes its permeability to ions. This allows for the transmission of an impulse. An impulse will cause a section of a neuron to change its permeability to ions. This will cause the next section to change its permeability and the impulse will 'jump' to that section. Once the impulse has moved along, the area behind is restored to the original state. This pattern of movement of ions continues along the entire length of the neuron.

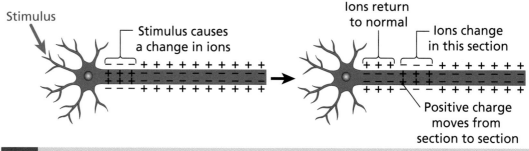

33.7 *Movement of an impulse in a neuron*

Refractory period

> The **refractory period** is a short time span after a neuron has carried an impulse during which a stimulus fails to cause a response.

There has to be a slight delay of a fraction of a second between any two impulses. This time span is necessary to allow the impulse to pass from one neuron to a second neuron (at a synapse, as explained later in this chapter). This tiny time span is called the refractory period.

The transmission of a nerve impulse can be compared to a set of dominoes lined up, as shown in diagram 33.8.
- If the first domino is touched lightly the dominoes do not fall. This is the equivalent of the threshold not being reached, and so no impulse is carried.
- If the first domino is pushed hard enough, it and all the other dominoes will fall. The threshold was reached and an impulse was carried.

The refractory period can be compared to the time needed to stand the dominoes up again after they have fallen down.

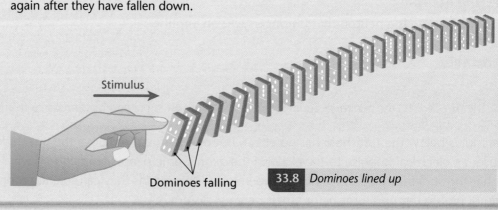

Dominoes falling   **33.8** *Dominoes lined up*

378

Speed of impulse

The speed at which an electrical impulse travels along a neuron depends on whether myelin is present or absent around the neuron.

- When myelin is present the impulse 'jumps' from one node of Ranvier to the next. This means the impulse travels very fast.
- When myelin is absent the impulse must travel along the entire length of the neuron. This slows down the speed of the impulse.

The speed at which the electrical impulse travels is also dependent on the diameter of the dendrite or axon. The larger the diameter, the faster the impulse travels.

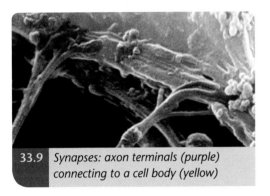

33.9 *Synapses: axon terminals (purple) connecting to a cell body (yellow)*

Synapse

Synapses are commonly found between the axon terminals of one neuron and the dendrites of another neuron. Normally the gap is as small as 0.00002 mm. The number of synapses associated with each neuron is very large, ranging from 1000 for a cell body in the spinal cord up to 10 000 for cell bodies in the brain.

> A synapse is a region where two neurons come into close contact.
>
> A synaptic cleft is the tiny gap between the two neurons at a synapse.

Passage of an impulse across a synapse

Activation of neurotransmitter

Electrical impulses cannot cross a synapse. Instead, the impulse stimulates the neurotransmitter swellings (at the end of the axon) in the pre-synaptic neuron to release a chemical substance that diffuses rapidly across the synaptic cleft. These chemicals are called **neurotransmitters**.

Some neurotransmitters are made in the cell bodies of the neurons, whereas others are formed in the neurotransmitter swellings. The enzymes needed to make these latter neurotransmitters are made in the cell body and transported to the swellings. Over 60 different neurotransmitters are known, the most common being **acetylcholine (ACh)**, **noradrenalin** (also called norepinephrine) and **dopamine**.

Inactivation of neurotransmitter

The neurotransmitter diffuses across the synaptic cleft. It then combines with receptors on the post-synaptic neuron and is broken down by enzymes. The digested neurotransmitters are reabsorbed back into the neurotransmitter swellings. This allows them to be recycled and reused upon the arrival of the next impulse. The breakdown of the neurotransmitters causes the electrical impulse to be regenerated and to be transmitted onwards.

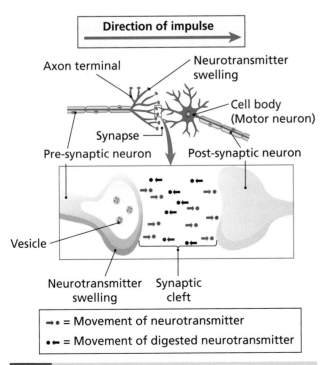

33.10 *Events at a synapse*

Electrical impulse → Chemical impulse → Electrical impulse

33.11 *The interchange that occurs at a synapse*

THE ORGANISM

Functions of synapses

1. They **transmit impulses** from one neuron to another neuron or to an effector (muscle or gland).

2. They **control the direction of the impulse**. This is due to neurotransmitter swellings being found only on the pre-synaptic side of the synapse. In this way they act as valves (i.e. they allow only a one-way flow).

3. They **prevent overstimulation** of effectors. This happens when the neurotransmitter ceases to be produced due to constant stimulation. The impulse is therefore inhibited and the effector ceases to be stimulated.

   This is why we tend to get used to stimuli such as pain and noise and are stimulated only by changes in these inputs.

4. The **impulse can be blocked** by certain chemicals (drugs). This is important in controlling pain and some psychiatric disorders.

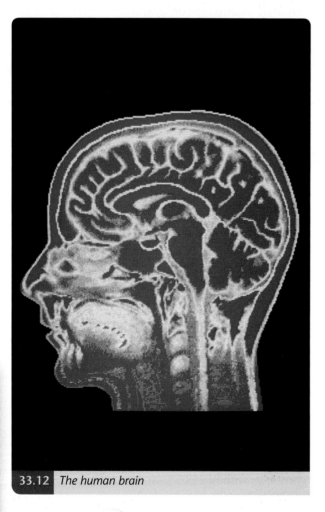

33.12 *The human brain*

The central nervous system (CNS)

The brain

The senses and individual sensory neurons act as receptors for incoming stimuli. Electrical impulses are passed along the sensory neurons (dendrites and axons) to the CNS, and in particular to the brain. The brain acts as an interpreting centre to sort and process the incoming impulses and decide on a response.

The human brain is composed of about 85 000 million (85 billion) neurons. The cell bodies and synapses form the grey matter of the brain, with the nerve fibres (dendrites and axons) forming the white matter. The brain uses about 20% of the body's energy.

Both the brain and spinal cord are protected by bone (the cranium and vertebral column respectively) and are covered by three membranes called **meninges**. The space between the inner two meninges is filled with cerebrospinal fluid. This fluid acts as a protective shock absorber and as an exchange medium between the blood and brain.

Meningitis is an inflammation of the meninges that enclose the brain and also the nerves in the spinal cord. Meningitis occurs more commonly in children than adults, but can occur at any age. There are two causes of meningitis: a virus and a bacterium.
- Viral meningitis is a more common and less severe infection. It causes irritability, headache and fever. In severe cases it results in neck ache. There is no specific treatment and the symptoms normally disappear within a week or two.
- Bacterial meningitis is much more dangerous. Along with the symptoms described above, it causes skin rash, vomiting, intolerance of bright light, inability to bend the neck down, convulsions and even coma and death. Bacterial meningitis is treated with antibiotics. Vaccines are available for some forms of bacterial meningitis.

Structure of the brain

Cerebrum

The cerebrum is the largest part of the brain. It contains about 75% of the neurons in the brain. It is divided into two halves: the right and left cerebral hemispheres.

The functions of the cerebrum include:

- Controlling voluntary movements
- Receiving and interpreting impulses from the sense organs
- Thinking
- Intelligence
- Memory
- Language
- Emotions
- Judgement
- Personality.

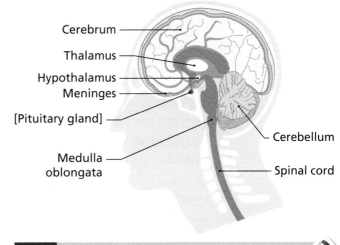

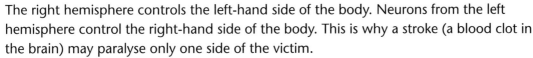
33.13 *Structure of the brain*

The right hemisphere controls the left-hand side of the body. Neurons from the left hemisphere control the right-hand side of the body. This is why a stroke (a blood clot in the brain) may paralyse only one side of the victim.

Each hemisphere is specialised to function in different ways.

- In general, the left side is dominant for hand use (i.e. most people are right-handed), language, mathematics, analysis and logic.
- The right side specialises in art, music, shape recognition and emotional responses.

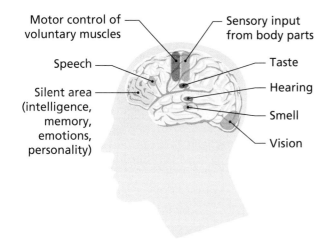

33.14 *Functions of the cerebrum*

The functions associated with different parts of the cerebrum are shown in diagram 33.14.

The outer part of the cerebrum, called the cerebral cortex, is grey. The inner, white matter of the cerebrum contains millions of nerve fibres. These connect different areas of the cortex and the two sides of the brain (which are connected by a structure called the corpus callosum).

Cerebellum

The cerebellum is the second largest section of the brain. It is heavily **folded**. The cerebellum controls:

- Muscular coordination (and allows smooth, refined muscular action)
- Balance.

The responses of the cerebellum are **involuntary**, once the process has been learned. For example, walking is originally controlled by the cerebrum, but once we learn to walk the cerebellum takes over and walking is controlled involuntarily.

Medulla oblongata

The medulla oblongata connects the spinal cord with the rest of the brain. It controls involuntary actions such as:

- Breathing
- Blood pressure
- Swallowing
- Coughing
- Salivation
- Vomiting
- Sneezing.

THE ORGANISM

381

Thalamus and hypothalamus

The **thalamus** is located below the cerebrum.

● It acts as a sorting centre for the brain (by sending all incoming impulses to the correct part of the brain).

The **hypothalamus** lies below the thalamus. Its functions are to:

● Regulate the internal environment of the body (homeostasis) by monitoring body (blood) temperature, appetite, thirst, osmoregulation and blood pressure
● Link with the pituitary gland to regulate the production of many hormones.

The hypothalamus is thought to be the link between the mind (or brain) and the body.

Pituitary gland

The pituitary gland is not a part of the brain. It is located below the hypothalamus, to which it is attached. It produces numerous hormones and is described in Chapter 35.

Nervous system disorder

Parkinson's disease

Cause

Parkinson's disease is a disorder of the nervous system. It is caused by the failure (for reasons unknown) to produce a neurotransmitter called **dopamine** in a part of the brain.

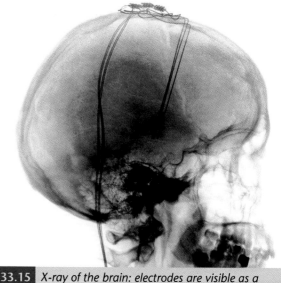

33.15 *X-ray of the brain: electrodes are visible as a treatment for Parkinson's disease*

Symptoms

The failure to produce dopamine results in the inability to control muscle contraction. This results in symptoms such as:

● Trembling of the hands and/or legs
● Stiff and rigid muscles and body
● A shuffling unbalanced gait when walking
● A fixed, unblinking stare
● Difficulty with everyday activities such as dressing, washing and eating.

Thought processes are not affected until late in the course of the disease. Parkinson's disease is normally found in the elderly and is more common in men than in women.

Prevention

There is no known way to prevent Parkinson's disease.

Treatment

Initial treatment involves physiotherapy and special exercises along with the provision of special aids and home help to patients. Treatment with drugs to stimulate or mimic dopamine can reduce the symptoms but cannot stop the degeneration of the brain. Recent research suggests that electrical stimulation or implanting dopamine-secreting tissue (stem cells) into the brain may prove beneficial.

Spinal cord

The spinal cord is composed of nerve tissue. It is surrounded by bony vertebrae, which protect it. The spinal cord transmits impulses to and from the brain. It also controls many reflex actions.

The spinal cord is located in the neural canal of the vertebrae. The neural canal is lined by the meninges.

In cross-section the spinal cord appears as an outer ring of **white matter** (axons only) surrounding an inner H-shaped region of **grey matter** (cell bodies). At the centre of the grey matter is the central canal, which contains cerebrospinal fluid.

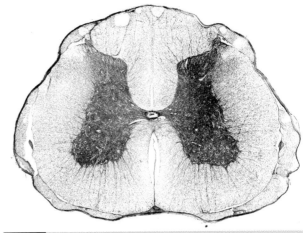

33.16 *Section through the spinal cord: the grey matter (red) is surrounded by white matter*

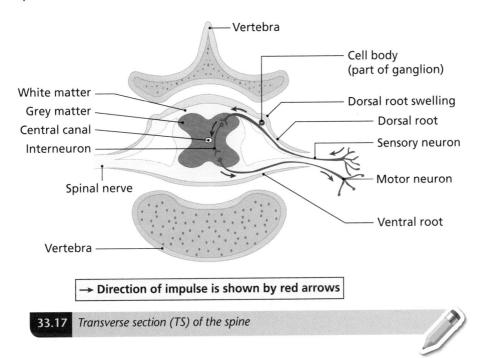

Vertebra — Cell body (part of ganglion)
White matter — Dorsal root swelling
Grey matter — Dorsal root
Central canal — Sensory neuron
Interneuron —
Spinal nerve — Motor neuron
Vertebra — Ventral root

→ **Direction of impulse is shown by red arrows**

33.17 *Transverse section (TS) of the spine*

The dorsal root carries sensory neurons into the spinal cord and the ventral root carries motor neurons out. These neurons are usually linked by numerous interneurons in the grey matter. The dorsal root swellings contain ganglia, i.e. groups of cell bodies of sensory neurons. The dorsal and ventral roots combine to form 31 pairs of spinal nerves, which take impulses to and from the spinal cord.

Peripheral nervous system

The peripheral nervous system (PNS) mostly consists of nerve fibres outside the brain and spinal cord. These are made up of long dendrites or axons taking impulses to or from the CNS.

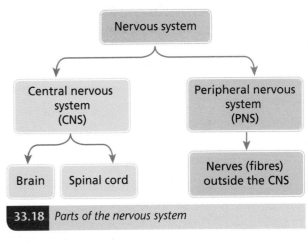

33.18 *Parts of the nervous system*

- The cell bodies of sensory nerves are located in ganglia in the PNS (i.e. in the dorsal root ganglia just outside the spinal cord).
- The cell bodies of motor neurons are found in the CNS (i.e. in the grey matter of the brain and spinal cord).

THE ORGANISM

Reflex action

The simplest form of activity in the nervous system is a reflex action.

Examples of reflex actions

Many of the activities of the body are reflex and are controlled by reflex arcs. Examples include:

- The grasp reflex in children
- The movement of the iris of the eye
- Blinking the eyes for protection
- Breathing
- Control of blood pressure
- The protective actions we take when falling
- The knee jerk.

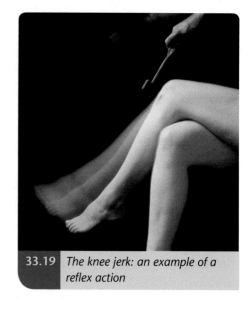

33.19 *The knee jerk: an example of a reflex action*

Dorsal root ganglion — Neuron to brain

Neuron from brain

Sensory neuron

Receptors

Interneuron

Flame —

Effector (muscle)

Spine

Ventral root

Motor neuron —

→ **Direction of impulse is shown by red arrows**

33.20 *A reflex arc*

Advantages of reflex actions

The advantage of reflex actions is that they are fast responses and so can **protect** the body from damage.

This is best understood by considering a relatively simple, 3-neuron withdrawal reflex, such as pulling the hand back from a hot flame.

Reflex arc

A **reflex arc** is the pathway taken by a nerve impulse in a reflex action

A reflex arc is the unit of function of the nervous system.

Withdrawal reflex

1. Receptors in the finger are stimulated by the hot flame.
2. Sensory neurons carry an impulse into the spinal cord through the dorsal root.
3. In the spinal cord numerous synapses are made with other neurons.
   (i) An interneuron carries the impulse across the spinal cord to a motor neuron.
   (ii) Another neuron takes the impulse up to the brain.
4. Motor neurons take the impulse straight out of the spine (through a ventral root) to the effector (i.e. a muscle or gland). This causes us to pull our hand back from the hot flame.
5. At the same time as the hand withdraws, the impulse reaches the brain. This makes us aware of what has happened and we feel some pain. However, the action was involuntary, it was **not** controlled by the brain.

This account is a simplification of the process. Extra connections and pathways exist to add further complexity to the process. For example, we pull our arm **up** from a hot cooker, but **down** when changing a hot overhead bulb. Also, reflex actions can be inhibited, e.g. we drop a hot plate but we attempt to place an expensive hot dish down gently.

THE ORGANISM

Summary

The **nervous system** is divided into:
- The central nervous system (CNS) = brain and spinal cord
- The peripheral nervous system (PNS) = the nerves outside the CNS.

Nervous coordination involves:
- Reception (detecting a stimulus)
- Transmission (movement of the impulse)
- Integration (impulses are sorted, processed and decisions made)
- Response (a muscle or gland carries out the effect).

A **neuron** is a nerve cell. There are three types of neurons:
- Sensory (afferent) neurons take messages to the CNS
- Motor (efferent) neurons take messages from the CNS
- Interneurons connect motor and sensory neurons in the CNS.

The **main parts of a neuron:**
- Nerve endings connect to receptors or sense organs
- Dendrites (can be long or short, are branched) carry impulses to a cell body
- Axons carry nerve impulses away from cell bodies
- Schwann cells make myelin
- Myelin insulates the electrical impulses
- The cell body forms neurotransmitters and the different parts of the neuron.

Features of a nerve impulse:
- A resting neuron is not carrying an impulse
- The threshold is the minimum stimulus needed for an impulse to travel
- The 'all or nothing' law says that:
  - If the threshold is reached, an impulse travels
  - If the threshold is not reached, no impulse travels.
- There is a delay (or refractory) period between two impulses
- The myelin sheath speeds up the passage of an impulse.

A **synapse** is the region where two neurons come into close contact.

A **synaptic cleft** is a tiny gap between two neurons.

A **nerve impulse** involves the following:
- Neurotransmitter swellings produce neurotransmitters such as acetylcholine (ACh)
- ACh diffuses across the synapse
- ACh causes the production of an electrical impulse at the other side where it is broken down by enzymes.

Synapses control the direction of impulses.

Functions of the parts of the brain
- Cerebrum:
  - Controls voluntary muscles
  - Receives impulses from sense organs
  - Intelligence
  - Memory
  - Language
  - Emotions
  - Judgement
  - Personality.
- Cerebellum:
  - Controls muscular coordination
  - Balance.
- Medulla:
  - Controls involuntary actions.
- Thalamus:
  - Sends messages to different parts of the brain.
- Hypothalamus:
  - Controls internal environment of the body.

Parkinson's disease:
- Is a nervous disorder caused by a lack of dopamine in the brain
- Results in trembling limbs, a rigid body and inability to walk properly
- Cannot be prevented
- Is treated by physiotherapy and drugs.

The **spinal cord** carries impulses to and from the brain and controls many reflex actions.

In the spinal cord:
- Sensory neurons enter through dorsal roots
- The dorsal root ganglion contains the cell bodies of the sensory neurons
- White matter contains axons
- Grey matter contains cell bodies and dendrites
- Interneurons connect sensory and motor neurons
- Motor neurons emerge through ventral roots.

The **peripheral nervous system** is mostly made of nerve fibres (i.e. long dendrites or axons).

A **reflex action** is an automatic response to a stimulus.

Reflex actions are:
- Fast responses
- Designed to protect the body.

A **reflex arc** is the basic unit of function of the nervous system.
- Reflex arcs consist of receptors, nerves and effectors.
- The route taken along a reflex arc is: receptor → sensory neuron → spinal cord → interneuron → motor neuron → effector.
- At the interneuron stage an impulse is also sent to the brain. The brain is made aware of the action, but does not control it.

THE ORGANISM

Revision questions

1 (a) Name the three types of neurons.
   (b) Distinguish between the three types of neurons in terms of where they carry impulses to and from.

2 (a) Name the type of neuron shown in diagram 33.21.

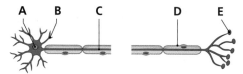

33.21

   (b) Name, and give one function for, all the parts labelled A to E.
   (c) In what form does the impulse travel along structure C?
   (d) In what direction does the impulse travel at C?
   (e) Name the other two types of neurons and draw similar labelled diagrams for each.

3 (a) What is a synapse?
   (b) Give two benefits of synapses.

4 Describe how an impulse arriving at one side of a synapse can continue across the synapse.

5 (a) What is the function of neurotransmitters?
   (b) Name two neurotransmitters.

6 Distinguish between:
   (a) The central and peripheral nervous systems
   (b) Afferent and efferent neurons
   (c) Dendrites and axons
   (d) Synapse and synaptic cleft.

7 (a) Name the parts of the CNS labelled A, B, C and D in diagram 33.22.
   (b) Give two functions for each part named in answer (a).
   (c) Assign each of the following abilities to one of the regions labelled X, Y or Z: eyesight, speech, hearing.

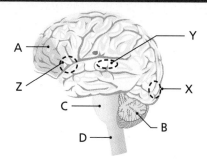

33.22

8 Give a location and function for each of the following: (a) Meninges (b) Cerebrospinal fluid (c) Corpus callosum (d) Hypothalamus (e) Pituitary gland.

9 (a) Name a disorder of the nervous system.
   (b) Give three symptoms of this disorder.
   (c) Name one way in which the disorder may be treated.

10 (a) Name the parts labelled A to J in the TS of the spinal cord shown in diagram 33.23.

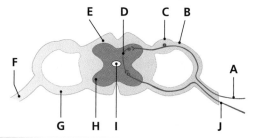

33.23

   (b) Describe the direction of the impulse in each of the structures labelled A, D and J.
   (c) Name the substance in the part labelled I.

11 (a) Give three examples of reflex actions.
    (b) What is the advantage of a reflex action?

Exam questions

Section A

12 The diagram shows a motor neuron.

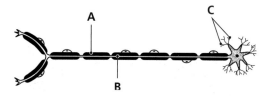

   (a) Identify parts A, B and C.
   (b) Give a function of A.
   (c) Place an arrow on the diagram to show the direction of the impulse.
   (d) Give a function of C.

   (e) Place an X on the diagram at a point at which a neurotransmitter substance is secreted.
   (f) What is the role of the motor neuron?

   (2008 HL Q 4)

Section C

13 (a) (i) Draw and label sufficient of two neurons to show a synaptic cleft.
         (ii) Describe the sequence of events that allows an impulse to be transmitted across a synapse from one neuron to the next.

(iii) Suggest a possible role for a drug in relation to the events that you have outlined in (ii).

(2004 HL Q 15)

14 (b) (i) What is a neuron?

(ii) Distinguish between sensory, motor and interneurons (association neurons).

(iii) Briefly explain the role of neurotransmitter substances.

(iv) State a function for:
   1. Schwann cells,
   2. Myelin sheath.

(v) In relation to Parkinson's disease or paralysis give:
   1. A possible cause,
   2. A method of treatment.

(2006 HL Q 14)

15 (a) The diagram shows part of a reflex arc.

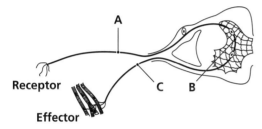

(i) Name neurons A, B and C.

(ii) In which direction is the impulse transmitted A → B → C or C → B → A?

(iii) Name the small gaps between neurons.

(iv) Neurons produce neurotransmitter substances. What is their function?

(v) Give an example of a reflex action in humans.

(vi) Why are reflex actions important in humans?

(2007 OL Q 15)

16 (b) (ii) In relation to animal responses:
   1. Name the **two** main parts of the central nervous system in humans.

2. Messages are carried around the body by neurons (nerve cells). Name any **two** types of neuron.

3. What name is given to the area where one neuron ends and another begins?

4. Name the type of chemical that carries messages between two neurons.

5. What happens to this chemical once the messages have been transmitted?

(2012 OL Q 15)

17 (a) (i) Distinguish between the central nervous system and the peripheral nervous system. Include a clear reference to each in your answer.

(ii) Give **one** way in which a nervous response differs from a hormonal response.

(b) (i) Draw a large labelled diagram of a motor neuron.

(ii) Give one function **each** of any **two** parts found **only** in neurons.

(iii) Place an arrow on or near your diagram to indicate the direction of impulse transmission.

(iv) Name **and** state the role of any **two** types of neuron, other than the motor neuron.

(c) (i) State **one** function for **each** of the following parts of the human brain.
Cerebrum;
Hypothalamus;
Cerebellum;
Medulla oblongata.

(ii) In relation to the nervous system, distinguish between grey matter and white matter. Include a clear reference to each in your answer.

(iii) In the case of either paralysis or Parkinson's disease state:
   1. a possible cause, other than accident;
   2. a method of treatment.

(2012 HL Q 13)

Previous examination questions

Ordinary level	Higher level
2007 Q 15a	2004 Q 15a
2012 Q 15b(ii)	2005 Q 3b, 14c(iii)
	2006 Q 14b
	2008 Q 4
	2009 Q 15c(ii)
	2010 Q 11a,b
	2012 Q 13

Latest questions at www.edco.ie/lcbiologyplus/examhelp

Online test and assessment tracker

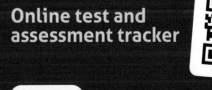

Scan the QR code and test yourself on chapter 33
www.edco.ie/lcbiologyplus

THE ORGANISM

Chapter 34 **The senses**

Introduction

Humans were said to have five senses: touch, taste, smell, sight and hearing. It is now thought that balance is also a sense. In addition, touch is seen as a complex sense because its functions include detecting pressure, pain, hot and cold.

This chapter will focus on the five senses: touch, taste, smell, sight and hearing. The senses are based on receptor cells or groups of receptors that form a sense organ. Receptor cells may be neuron endings or specialised cells in close contact with neurons. Receptors are specialised to respond to various stimuli such as heat, light, pressure and chemicals. All these stimuli are forms of energy that the receptors absorb. They convert this energy into electrical impulses that travel along neurons.

All neurons carry similar electrical impulses. We distinguish between sight or hearing as a result of the part of the brain to which the neuron connects. The brain interprets the impulses arising from the appropriate sense organ. Sensations occur in the brain.

Touch

The structure of the skin is shown in diagram 34.1.

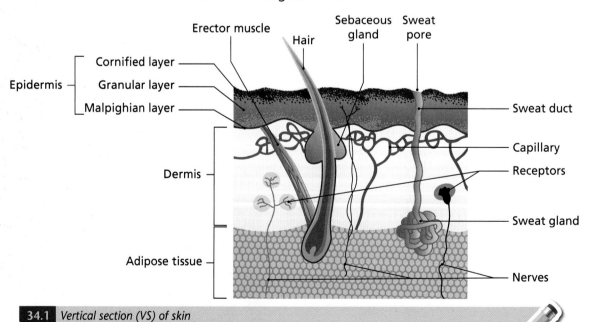

34.1 *Vertical section (VS) of skin*

The skin contains receptors for pain, touch and temperature. These receptors are found in different concentrations in skin at various locations around the body. For example, there are few touch receptors in the skin at the heel of the foot, but there are many temperature receptors at the elbow (which is why the elbow is often used when testing the temperature of a baby's bath).

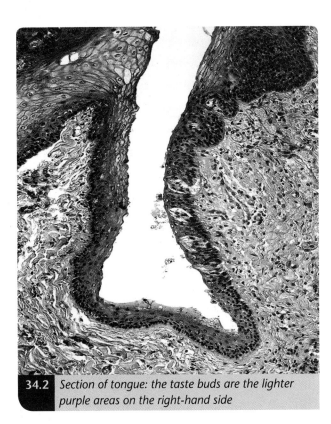

34.2 *Section of tongue: the taste buds are the lighter purple areas on the right-hand side*

Taste

Receptors for taste are located in taste buds. These are found on the top and sides of the tongue and in some parts of the lining of the throat.

There are four basic taste receptors:

- Sweet
- Sour
- Bitter
- Salt.

Recently a fifth taste, called umami, has been suggested. An example of this taste is monosodium glutamate (MSG), which is a flavour enhancer sometimes used in Chinese cooking and processed snack foods such as crisps.

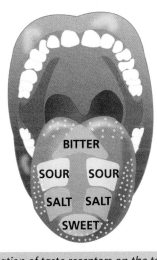

34.3 *The location of taste receptors on the tongue*

Different areas of the tongue have greater numbers of each of these receptors, as shown in diagram 34.3. Tastes often persist due to substances dissolving and lodging in the grooves of the taste buds.

The flavour of food is a combination of taste, smell, texture and temperature. When we have a cold the sense of smell is reduced and food loses much of its flavour.

Smell

The roof of the nasal cavity has millions of neurons to detect smell (olfactory neurons). These neurons respond to about 50 different chemicals in the gaseous state. The responses combine to produce about 10 000 different smells (as opposed to only four different tastes).

Smell receptors are extremely sensitive. They also adjust very quickly to a smell and stop responding. Within the first second of detecting a new smell about half of the sensations disappear. This is why we get used to smells so quickly.

THE ORGANISM

389

Sight

Structure of the eye

Diagram 34.4 shows the structure of the eye.

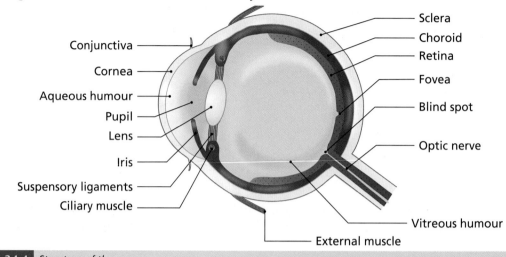

Conjunctiva

Cornea

Aqueous humour

Pupil

Lens

Iris

Suspensory ligaments

Ciliary muscle

Sclera

Choroid

Retina

Fovea

Blind spot

Optic nerve

Vitreous humour

External muscle

| 34.4 | *Structure of the eye* |

Functions of the parts of the eye

Conjunctiva

This is a thin membrane protecting the sclera. Inflammation of this membrane is called conjunctivitis.

Sclera (or sclerotic coat)

This is the white of the eye. It is very tough and opaque (lets no light through). It holds the eye in shape.

Cornea

This is the transparent part of the sclera at the front of the eye. It lets light into the eye and bends it towards the retina.

Choroid

This is a dark-coloured layer. It contains blood vessels to nourish the eye and black pigment (melanin) to absorb light in the eye. It ensures that there is no internal reflection of light inside the eye.

Retina

It is here that the light receptors (rods and cones) are located (see the table below).

| Comparison of rods and cones ||
Rods	Cones
120 million per eye	6 million per eye
Detect black and white	Detect colours (red, green, blue)
Work in dim light	Work in bright light
Found all over retina	Found mostly at fovea

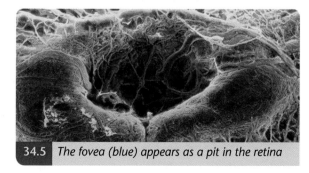

| 34.5 | *The fovea (blue) appears as a pit in the retina* |

Fovea

This area of the retina contains only cones. It is the region of sharpest vision and it is here that most images are focused. When we stare at, or concentrate on, an object its image forms on the fovea (also called the yellow spot).

Blind spot

Nerve fibres from the rods and cones are located on the surface of the retina. This means that they impede incoming light rays and therefore obstruct vision. The reason why the eye is structured in this way is not known (it is thought to be an evolutionary 'mistake').

Nerve fibres leave the eye through a part of the retina called the blind spot. There are no rods or cones at the blind spot and it is not sensitive to light.

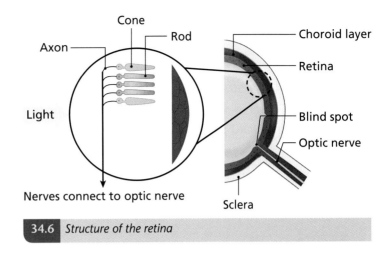

34.6 *Structure of the retina*

Optic nerve

This contains 126 million axons that carry impulses from the rods and cones to the back of the brain (cerebrum). The optic nerve is white and about the diameter of a ballpoint refill.

Lens

This is an elastic, transparent structure. It changes shape to focus light on the retina.

 The lens contains a clear protein. Cataracts occur when this protein becomes cloudy, just as egg white becomes less transparent when cooked. Cataracts are often caused by exposure to ultraviolet radiation. This is why it is advisable to wear protective sunglasses in sunny climates.

Ciliary muscle

This surrounds the lens and causes the shape of the lens to change when we look at near or far objects. The changing of shape of the lens is a reflex action and is called **accommodation**.

The ciliary muscle is connected to the lens by suspensory ligaments.

Iris

This is a coloured, muscular part of the eye. The amount of light entering the eye is controlled by the iris. It may be pigmented with melanin (i.e. giving the person dark-coloured eyes). Blue-eyed people have no melanin in the iris.

Pupil

The opening in the iris is called the pupil. It lets light into the eye. The pupil is black because no light normally emerges from the inside of the eye (i.e. all the incoming light is absorbed by the retina or the choroid). The changing of shape of the iris is a reflex action carried out in response to light intensity.

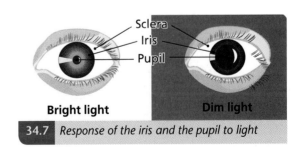

34.7 *Response of the iris and the pupil to light*

- In bright light, the size of the pupil is reduced so that less light can enter the eye.
- In dim light, the size of the pupil enlarges (dilates) to allow more light to enter the eye.

 The size of the pupil has psychological significance. When we observe an object that we admire (for example, mothers looking at their babies), our pupils dilate. Also, large pupils are considered a warm, friendly sign. Advertisements often have faces with large, dark pupils to highlight the appeal of the person's face.

THE ORGANISM

Aqueous humour

This is a salt solution that holds the front of the eye in shape.

Vitreous humour

This is a more viscous fluid (similar to raw egg white). It supports the eye by exerting an outward pressure on the eyeball.

External muscle

The eye is moved by the use of six external muscles.

Hearing

Functions of the ear

The functions of the ear are **hearing** and **balance**.

The ear is composed of three sections: the outer, middle and inner ear. The outer and middle ear are filled with air; the inner ear is filled with a fluid called lymph.

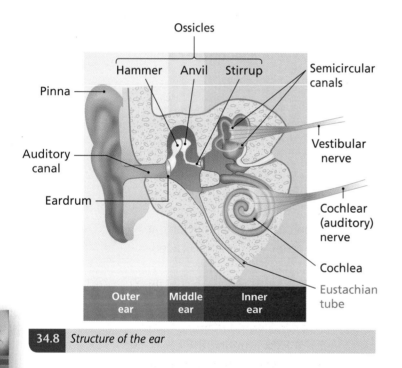

| Outer ear | Middle ear | Inner ear |

34.8 *Structure of the ear*

Structure of the ear

The structure of the ear is shown in diagram 34.8.

The ear and hearing

Sound is caused by vibrations in the air (or in the medium in which an organism is located, e.g. water). Vibrations are collected by the outer ear, passed through the middle ear (where the vibrations are amplified or increased) and transferred to fluid (lymph) in the cochlea of the inner ear.

The cochlea contains receptors that are stimulated by pressure waves in lymph. These receptors cause electrical impulses to be sent to the brain, which interprets them as sound.

Functions of the parts of the ear

Pinna

This is mostly made of cartilage. It helps to collect and channel vibrations into the auditory canal.

Auditory canal

This tube carries vibrations to the eardrum. Wax is secreted outside the eardrum to trap dust particles and protect the ear.

Eardrum

This is a small, tightly stretched membrane that separates the outer ear from the middle ear. It vibrates as a result of the vibrations that reach it.

Ossicles

The ossicles are three tiny bones in the middle ear called the hammer, the anvil and the stirrup.

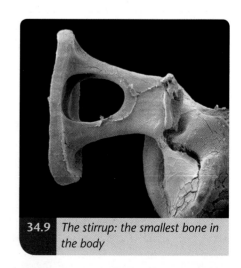

34.9 *The stirrup: the smallest bone in the body*

THE ORGANISM

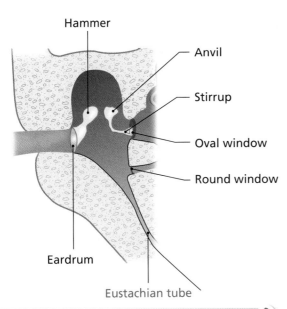

Hammer

Anvil

Stirrup

Oval window

Round window

Eardrum

Eustachian tube

34.10 *Structure of the middle ear*

The stirrup is the smallest bone in the body. These bones transmit vibrations from the outer to the inner ear and amplify (increase) the vibrations.

Eustachian tube

Strictly speaking, the Eustachian tube is not part of the ear. It runs from the middle ear to the pharynx (throat). It equalises pressure on either side of the eardrum. This prevents damage to the eardrum caused by differences in pressure between the outer and middle ear.

The Eustachian tube is usually closed, but opens with a 'pop' when we yawn or swallow. When we go up a mountain the external air pressure falls. As a result there is a danger that the eardrum might be forced outwards. In this case the Eustachian tube opens and air moves out of the middle ear. If we dive underwater the reverse happens, i.e. air moves into the middle ear to equalise the increased pressure caused by the water.

It is common for infections to travel between the throat and the middle ear along the Eustachian tube. This results in an association between ear, nose and throat (ENT) infections (which is why hospitals have ENT departments).

34.11 *The cochlea (scanning electron micrograph)*

Cochlea

This is a spiral tube, 3.5 cm long, which resembles a snail's shell. It is responsible for hearing because it converts pressure waves caused by sound vibrations into electrical impulses that travel to the brain. The cochlea works in the following manner.

- Vibrations arrive at the cochlea from the stirrup. This bone attaches to a membrane in the cochlea called the oval window.
- The vibrations pass through the oval window and form pressure waves in lymph in the cochlea.

- The pressure waves stimulate receptors in the cochlea. These receptors are hairs that are attached to 24 000 sensory cells located along the length of the cochlea. The sensory cells collectively form a structure called the **Organ of Corti**.
- The receptors cause electrical impulses to be sent to the brain. These impulses travel along the auditory or cochlear nerve.
- The round window allows the pressure waves to dissipate out of the cochlea into the air of the middle ear.

THE ORGANISM

The ear and balance

Balance is largely detected in the vestibular apparatus in the inner ear, although it is also maintained due to vision, receptors in muscles, ligaments and tendons and pressure receptors in the soles of the feet. The vestibular apparatus mainly consists of three semicircular canals. A person suffering damage to the vestibular apparatus loses his/her sense of balance. After some time the person may learn to use other receptors to redevelop a sense of balance.

The structure of the vestibular apparatus is shown in diagram 34.12. The vestibular apparatus is filled with a liquid called lymph. Receptors located in different parts of the vestibular apparatus detect whether the head is vertical or not. Other receptors in the vestibular apparatus can detect movement of the head. All these receptors send impulses to the cerebellum of the brain through the vestibular nerve.

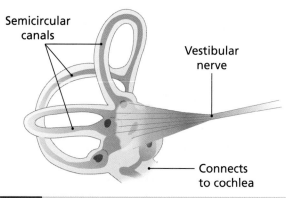

34.12 *Structure of the vestibular apparatus*

Corrective measures for a hearing disorder

Syllabus You are required to know corrective measures for either long and short sight **or** a hearing defect.

Disorder

Glue ear is a common hearing disorder in children. It is caused by surplus sticky fluid collecting in the middle ear (often due to overproduction of fluid as a result of infection or blockage of the Eustachian tubes). The fluid prevents the free movement of the eardrum and of the small bones in the middle ear. This results in some degree of discomfort and deafness.

Correction

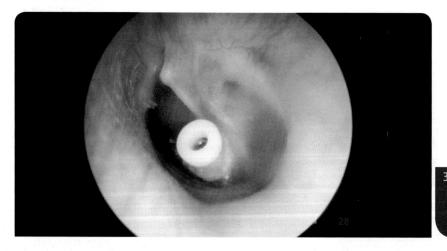

34.13 *A grommet (white) in the surrounding eardrum*

In mild cases, nose drops are taken to decongest and unblock the Eustachian tube. In more severe cases, small grommets are inserted into the eardrum. Grommets allow air into the middle ear and this forces fluid down the Eustachian tube. In time the grommets normally fall out of the eardrum by themselves.

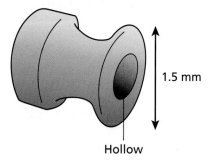

34.14 *A typical ear grommet*

THE ORGANISM

Summary

The five traditional senses are:
- Touch
- Sight
- Smell
- Hearing.
- Taste

The skin is the organ of touch.

The tongue is the organ of taste. Taste buds in the tongue can detect the following tastes:
- Sweet (at the tip)
- Salt (at the sides, near the front)
- Sour (at the sides, near the back)
- Bitter (across the back).

The nose is the organ of smell. Olfactory neurons in the nose detect many smells.

The eye is the organ of sight. The main parts of the eye and their functions are as follows.
- The **conjunctiva** is the membrane around the eye. It protects the eye.
- The **sclera** is a tough, white coat that holds the eye in place.
- The **cornea** is the front part of the sclera. It allows light into the eye and bends it to help focus it on the retina.
- The **choroid** nourishes the eye and prevents internal reflection of light.
- The **retina** is light sensitive. It contains light receptors, rods (for black-and-white vision, work in dim light) and cones (for colour vision, work in bright light).
- The **fovea** is the part of the retina where most images are focused.
- The **blind spot** is where the optic nerve leaves the retina. It has no rods or cones.
- The **optic nerve** carries impulses to the brain.
- The **lens** focuses light on the retina.
- The **iris** is the coloured part of the eye. It controls the amount of light entering the eye.

- The **pupil** is the black circle at the front of the eye. It lets light into the eye.
- **Ciliary muscles** change the shape of the lens (called accommodation) to focus light on the retina.
- The **aqueous** and **vitreous humours** keep the eye in shape.

The ear is the organ of hearing and balance. The functions of the parts of the ear associated with **hearing** are as follows.
- The **pinna** collects vibrations.
- The **auditory canal** carries vibrations to the eardrum.
- The **eardrum** carries the vibrations to the middle ear.
- The **ossicles** (the hammer, anvil and stirrup) amplify (increase) the vibrations and pass them on to the cochlea in the inner ear.
- The **Eustachian tube**, although not part of the ear, connects the middle ear with the pharynx and equalises pressure between the middle and outer ear.
- The **cochlea** is responsible for hearing. It converts vibrations into electrical impulses that are sent to the brain along the auditory nerve.
- The **Organ of Corti** in the cochlea contains receptor cells that allow hearing.

Balance is detected by the vestibular apparatus in the inner ear.
- The main parts of the vestibular apparatus are the semicircular canals.

Glue ear is:
- A hearing disorder
- Caused by too much sticky fluid in the middle ear
- Corrected by decongestants or grommets.

Revision questions

1. (a) Name the five senses.
   (b) Name the organ responsible for each sense.
2. Give a biological explanation for each of the following.
   (a) Testing the temperature of milk from a baby's bottle on the inside of the wrist.
   (b) A pin sticking into the toe causes more pain than a pin in the heel.
   (c) Pain receptors are very numerous in the extremities of the body, e.g. toes and fingertips.
   (d) The taste of food can remain in the mouth long after the food is swallowed.
   (e) Colds and flu reduce our appetite.
   (f) A person does not notice the smell of his/her own deodorant but a stranger can.
   (g) A clean lollipop stick that touches different parts of the tongue may taste sweet, sour, salty or bitter.
3. (a) Name four tastes to which the tongue is sensitive.
   (b) Draw a labelled diagram to illustrate the part of the tongue that is most sensitive to each taste.
4. (a) Name the parts of the eye labelled A to M in diagram 34.15.

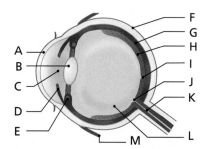

34.15

(b) Give one function for each of the labelled parts.
(c) Name the types of receptors in structure H.
(d) To what part of the brain does structure K connect?

5 Diagram 34.16 represents the front view of an eye.

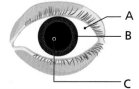

34.16

(a) Name the parts labelled A, B and C.
(b) What is the evidence that this eye is adapted to dim light?
(c) Draw a similar diagram to show how this eye would appear in bright light.

6 Distinguish between rods and cones in terms of:
(a) Numbers (b) Shape (c) Location
(d) Operating conditions (e) What they detect.

7 Explain the likely results of damage to the following structures: (a) The optic nerve (b) Suspensory ligaments (c) The fovea (d) The iris.

8 Give a reason for each of the following.
(a) The pupil is normally black.
(b) People with cataracts have obscured vision.
(c) A person may be born with blue eyes but later develops dark-coloured eyes.
(d) It is difficult to detect colour at dusk.
(e) Sunglasses increase the size of the pupils.

9 (a) State two functions of the ear.
(b) Name the parts of the inner ear associated with each of the stated functions.

10 Name (a) Three parts of the outer ear (b) Three parts of the middle ear (c) Two parts of the inner ear.

11 (a) Name the parts labelled A to I on diagram 34.17.

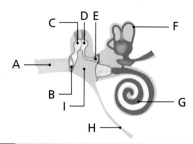

34.17

(b) Give a function for each part named.
(c) Draw a similar diagram of the ear, twice this size, and mark on it:
   (i) The outer, middle and inner ear
   (ii) The auditory and vestibular nerves
   (iii) The pinna
   (iv) The oval window.
(d) Name two structures on the diagram that contain fluid.
(e) What substance is found in the part labelled I?
(f) Suggest the likely effect(s) of damage to the parts labelled F and G.

12 How can throat infections gain entrance to the ear?

13 (a) Name a hearing disorder.
(b) What is the cause of the disorder you have named?
(c) What are the effects of the disorder?
(d) How may the disorder be corrected?

14 Choose which of the options (i), (ii), (iii) or (iv) represents the correct answer in each case below.
(a) The function of the lens in the eye is:
   (i) Vision (ii) Reflection (iii) Focus
   (iv) Dilation.
(b) Protection of the eyeball is the function of:
   (i) The fovea (ii) The sclera (iii) The cornea
   (iv) The choroid.
(c) The inner ear is filled with: (i) Fluid (ii) Air
   (iii) Protein (iv) Lipid.
(d) Which of the following is connected to the brain by the olfactory nerve? (i) The ear (ii) The skin (iii) The eye (iv) The nasal cavity.
(e) The flavour of glucose can be detected by taste receptors in which part of the tongue?
   (i) The back (ii) The bottom (iii) The sides at the front (iv) The tip.

Exam questions

Section A

15 The diagram shows the external and internal structure of the human ear.
   (i) Name the parts labelled A and B.
   (ii) What is the function of B?
   (iii) What is connected to the middle ear by the Eustachian tube?
   (iv) What is the function of the Eustachian tube?

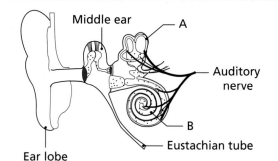

THE ORGANISM

(v) Name **one** disorder of the ear **or** of the eye and give a corrective measure for the disorder you have named.

(2010 OL Q 5)

Section C

16 (b) The diagram shows a vertical section through the human eye.

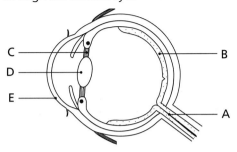

(i) Name A, B, C, D and E.

(ii) In which of these parts would you find rods and cones?

(iii) Give **one** function of rods and **one** function of cones.

(iv) What is the function of A?

(v) What type of lens is used to correct long sight?
(**Note:** This part of the question was unfair as asked. Students who attempted any part of this question were given full marks for part (v) no matter what they answered.)

(2006 OL Q 15)

17 (b) (i) Copy the diagram of the front of the eye into your answer book and label the iris and the pupil.

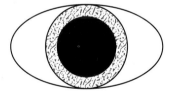

(ii) Is the eye shown in the diagram above adapted for dim light or bright light? Explain your answer.

(iii) Where in the eye is the retina located?

(iv) Two types of cells that receive light are found in the retina. Name each of these.

(v) Give **one** difference between the two types of cell that receive light.

(vi) The optic nerve is attached to the eye. What is the function of the optic nerve?

(2008 OL Q 14)

18

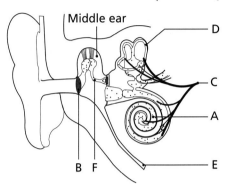

(a) (i) The diagram above shows the internal structure of the human ear.

   1. Name the structures labelled A, B, C.

   2. Give the functions of parts D and E.

   3. Which letters denote the parts of the ear in which nerve impulses are generated?

(ii) In what part of *the eye* are nerve impulses generated?

(iii) Suggest **one** way by which the ear may be protected.

(iv) Explain how a corrective measure for a **named** defect of hearing **or** vision works.

(2011 HL Q 15)

Previous examination questions

Ordinary level	Higher level
2004 Q 15a	2009 Q 15b
2006 Q 15b	2011 Q 15a
2008 Q 14b	
2010 Q 5	
2011 Q 6	

Latest questions at www.edco.ie/lcbiologyplus/examhelp

Online test and assessment tracker

Scan the QR code and test yourself on chapter 34
www.edco.ie/lcbiologyplus

Chapter 35 **The endocrine system**

Nervous and endocrine coordination

Two systems are used to coordinate body responses: the nervous and endocrine (hormonal) systems. These systems interact in the manner shown in the table below.

Comparison of the nervous and endocrine systems		
Feature	**Nervous system**	**Endocrine system**
Example	Catching an object	Growth
Speed of response	Fast-acting	Slower-acting
Method by which messages are carried	Mostly electrical	Chemical
Duration of response	Short-lived	Long-lasting
Location affected	Localised (i.e. one effector reacts)	Effects may be widespread

Glands

Glands are structures that secrete substances. There are two types of gland: exocrine and endocrine.

 Exocrine glands release their product into ducts or tubes.

Examples of exocrine glands include salivary glands, sweat glands, tear glands in the eye, gastric glands in the stomach, sebaceous glands in the skin and mammary glands in the breasts.

 An endocrine gland is a ductless gland that produces hormones, which are released directly into the bloodstream.

Endocrine glands secrete hormones into tissue fluid and from there the hormones pass into the bloodstream. For this reason endocrine glands have a rich supply of capillaries, because their hormones are transported by the blood.

Hormones

Although hormones are carried to all parts of the body in the bloodstream, they affect only specific areas, called target tissues or organs. Hormones are sometimes said to be chemical messengers.

Most hormones are made of **protein**. However, some hormones are steroid-based (especially male and female reproductive hormones). A steroid is a form of lipid.

Hormones are usually slow to act. For example, sex hormones may take many years to cause all the changes that occur during puberty. Once produced, however, hormones remain active for long periods of time. Hormones are said to be slow-acting but sustained in their effects.

> A **hormone** is a chemical messenger produced by an endocrine gland and carried by the bloodstream to another part of the body, where it has a specific effect.

Hypothalamus
Pineal
Pituitary
Parathyroids
Thyroid
Thymus
Adrenal
Pancreas
Ovary (in females)
Testis (in males)

35.1 *Location of the principal endocrine glands*

Traditionally there are 10 major endocrine glands. In addition, hormones can be made by other organs such as the stomach, intestines, kidneys, heart, brain and placenta. The locations of the 10 major endocrine glands are shown in diagram 35.1.

Role of principal endocrine glands

Pituitary

The pituitary is often called the master gland. This is because it produces a range of hormones that regulate other endocrine glands. The pituitary gland produces hormones such as follicle-stimulating hormone (FSH) and luteinising hormone (LH). These hormones regulate the activity of other glands and are described in Chapter 41.

> **Syllabus** For **each** of the principal endocrine glands you must know the location of the gland and the name and function of **one** hormone.

● Among a range of other hormones produced by the pituitary gland is **growth hormone (GH)**. This causes body cells to absorb amino acids and form proteins. In this way it causes growth. In particular, it causes the elongation of the bones of the skeleton.

35.2 *Robert Wadlow (died 1940) was the tallest person ever, at 8 feet 11 inches (2.7 m): he had an overproduction of growth hormone*

THE ORGANISM

Hypothalamus

The hypothalamus links the nervous and endocrine systems. It secretes hormones that control the pituitary gland in response to messages from the brain and other hormones.

● An example of a hormone produced in the hypothalamus is **anti-diuretic hormone (ADH)**. This hormone is then stored in the pituitary and released from there when needed. ADH causes water to be reabsorbed in the kidneys (it controls osmoregulation).

Pineal

The pineal is a tiny gland located within the brain. It was once thought to be the site of the soul.

● It produces a number of hormones, the best known of which is **melatonin**. This hormone is mainly produced when we are asleep. The function of melatonin is not fully understood, but it seems to be involved in biological rhythms such as ovulation, sleep, activity patterns and sexual maturity.

Thyroid

Syllabus For any **one** hormone you must give a description of its deficiency symptoms, excess symptoms and corrective measures.

The thyroid is an H-shaped gland located on the trachea in the neck.

● It produces the hormone **thyroxine**. This is made when an amino acid (tyrosine) combines with iodine. Thyroxine controls the rate of all the body's reactions, i.e. it controls metabolism.

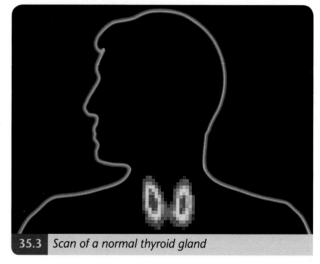

35.3 *Scan of a normal thyroid gland*

Thyroxine deficiency

Symptoms

Underproduction of thyroxine in young children results in low metabolic rates and retarded mental and physical development. This condition is called cretinism.

Deficiency of thyroxine in an adult results in a reduced metabolic rate. This is seen as tiredness, lack of energy, slow mental and physical activity and weight gain caused by the build-up of fluid under the skin. These symptoms are collectively called myxoedema. Deficiency of thyroxine also causes the thyroid gland to swell, a condition known as goitre.

Corrective measures

Newborn babies are tested for low thyroxine levels as part of what is called the 'heel test'. If necessary, thyroxine can be administered to prevent the occurrence of cretinism. In adults, thyroxine tablets or iodine can be taken to prevent myxoedema.

Thyroxine excess

Symptoms

Overproduction of thyroid hormone results in an increased metabolic rate (often 60% higher than normal). This causes symptoms such as bulging eyes, hunger, loss of weight, heat production, nervousness, irritability and anxiety. The metabolic condition is called Graves' disease.

Corrective measures

Graves' disease can be cured by surgically removing part of the thyroid or by killing part of the gland using radioactive iodine.

THE ORGANISM

Parathyroids

The four parathyroid glands are embedded in the thyroid gland.

● They make **parathormone**, which stimulates the release of calcium from bones into blood plasma.

Thymus

The two lobes of the thymus gland are located behind the breastbone in the upper chest.

● The thymus gland produces a hormone called **thymosin**, which causes lymphocytes (white blood cells) to mature and become active. The activated white blood cells are involved in the body's immune system.

The thymus begins to degenerate around puberty (which is why it is associated with childhood) but some tissue remains until middle age.

Adrenals

The two adrenal glands are located on top of the kidneys. They produce hormones that help the body cope with stress.

● The adrenal glands produce **adrenaline**. This is called the fright/fight/flight hormone.

Adrenaline is produced when we are frightened or under stress. It affects the body in a number of ways that help us to respond more efficiently to stress.

Pancreas

The pancreas is both an exocrine and an endocrine gland.

Exocrine function

The bulk of the pancreas cells produce enzymes (such as amylase). These flow to the duodenum through ducts. In this respect, the pancreas is an exocrine gland.

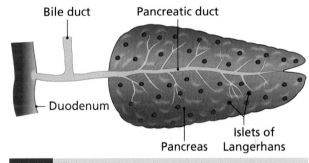

35.4 *The pancreas*

Endocrine function

The pancreas also contains about a million groups of cells called **islets of Langerhans** (after the German biologist Paul Langerhans).

● These cells produce the hormone **insulin**, which is carried away by the bloodstream. In this respect, the pancreas (or the islets of Langerhans) is an endocrine gland.

Insulin is a vital hormone, because it is the only hormone that reduces blood glucose levels. It causes cells, especially muscle and fat cells, to absorb glucose from the blood. The absorbed glucose is either used in respiration or converted to glycogen. Glycogen is mostly stored in the liver and muscles.

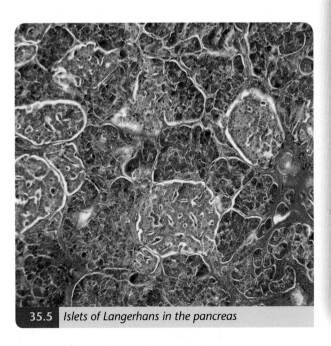

35.5 *Islets of Langerhans in the pancreas*

THE ORGANISM

401

Ovaries and testes

The role of these glands will be discussed in Chapter 41 in the context of human reproduction.

Hormone supplements

Insulin

Low insulin production, or an inability of cells to take up insulin, results in a disorder called diabetes. If this develops in young people, it is normally caused by the failure of the islets of Langerhans in the pancreas to work properly. The symptoms of diabetes are high glucose concentration in the blood and urine, the production of large amounts of urine, severe thirst, loss of weight and tiredness.

Severe diabetes is controlled by regular (between one and four times daily) **injections** of insulin. Alternatively an insulin pump can be used, which reduces the need for frequent injections. In addition to injections or a pump, the intake of carbohydrate is controlled, physical activity is increased and normal weight is maintained.

Insulin cannot be taken into the digestive system, because it is a protein and would be broken down by digestive enzymes.

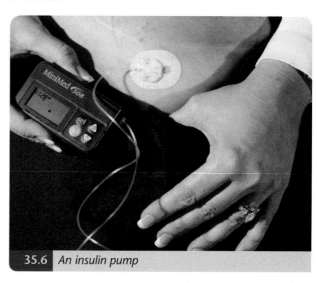

35.6 An insulin pump

Anabolic steroids

Anabolic steroids are drugs that build up protein (or muscle). They are similar to the male sex hormone testosterone. They are normally taken in tablet form or by injection.

Anabolic steroids build up muscle, speed up muscle recovery after injury and help to strengthen bones. For these reasons they allow for more severe training methods and increase the size and strength of muscles.

These drugs have been widely abused in sport (particularly in track and field events, cycling, bodybuilding and weight lifting). Their use is illegal because they give an unfair advantage and they endanger the health of those who take them.

Risks associated with abuse of anabolic steroids include liver and adrenal gland damage, infertility (the inability to produce offspring), failure of males to achieve erections (impotence) and the production of male traits in female abusers.

Anabolic steroids are sometimes given to animals to promote increased muscle (meat) production. They also produce low-fat (lean) meat. This procedure is banned in EU countries because of the risk of the hormones entering the human food chain.

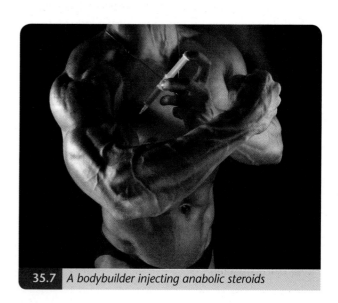

35.7 A bodybuilder injecting anabolic steroids

HIGHER ▼

Control of thyroxine level

Control of thyroxine level (and of many other hormones) is similar to the control used in a central heating system.

- If the temperature of the water in the system falls too low, the thermostat causes the boiler to switch on.
- If the temperature is sufficiently high the boiler shuts off.

This method of control is called **negative feedback**, i.e. the correct level of one item has a negative effect on a previous step in the cycle.

Normal concentrations of thyroxine

If thyroxine concentration is normal, it inhibits the pituitary from releasing thyroid-stimulating hormone (TSH). This means no further thyroxine is made.

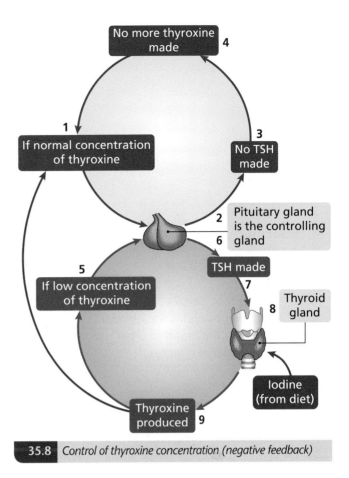

35.8 *Control of thyroxine concentration (negative feedback)*

Low concentrations of thyroxine

When thyroxine concentrations fall below the required level, the pituitary gland produces TSH. TSH causes more thyroxine to be made by the thyroid gland, until thyroxine concentration is returned to normal. Iodine is essential for the production of thyroxine.

Goitre

Goitre normally indicates the underproduction of thyroxine. This is usually caused by a lack of iodine in the diet (sources of iodine are seafood and iodised table salt). A low concentration of thyroxine in the blood causes the pituitary to produce TSH. TSH is carried by the blood to the thyroid.

Normally TSH combines with iodine in the thyroid to produce thyroxine. However, if this cannot happen (due to a shortage of iodine) then TSH is stored in the thyroid. This causes the thyroid to swell, causing goitre. This form of goitre can be treated by increasing the intake of iodine in the diet.

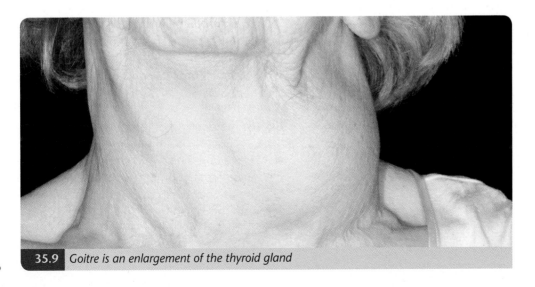

35.9 *Goitre is an enlargement of the thyroid gland*

THE ORGANISM

403

Summary

Body coordination is controlled by the nervous and endocrine systems.

The **endocrine system:**
● Is slow-acting
● Is based on chemicals (hormones)
● Produces long-lasting, widespread effects.

Exocrine glands have ducts.

Endocrine glands are ductless and make hormones.

A **hormone** is:
● A protein or steroid
● Produced by endocrine glands
● Carried in the blood to other parts, where it has a special effect.

The **pituitary** gland:
● Is located in the middle of the head, just below the brain
● Makes growth hormone, which controls body growth.

The **hypothalamus:**
● Is located at the base of the brain
● Makes anti-diuretic hormone, which controls osmoregulation.

The **pineal gland:**
● Is located in the brain
● Makes melatonin, which controls body rhythms.

The **thyroid gland:**
● Is located on the trachea in the neck
● Makes thyroxine, which controls metabolism.

Deficiency of thyroxine:
● Causes cretinism in young children (mental and physical retardation)
● Causes goitre, swelling and reduced rates of metabolism in adults
● Is controlled by taking thyroxine or iodine.

Excess thyroxine:
● Causes increased rates of metabolism, weight loss, large appetite, nervousness (Graves' disease)
● Is controlled by removing part of the thyroid or killing it with radioactive iodine.

The **parathyroids** (4):
● Are located in the thyroid
● Make parathormone, which controls the release of calcium from bones.

The **thymus gland:**
● Is located in the chest
● Makes thymosin, which matures white blood cells.

The **adrenal glands** (2):
● Are located on top of the kidneys
● Make adrenaline, which causes us to respond to stress.

The **pancreas (islets of Langerhans):**
● Is located in the abdomen just below the stomach
● Make insulin, which reduces blood sugar levels.

The **pancreas** is:
● An exocrine gland (releases enzymes into ducts)
● An endocrine gland (releases insulin into bloodstream).

Inability of the islets of Langerhans to make sufficient insulin is called diabetes.
● Diabetes can be controlled by regular injections of insulin (and by controlling the intake of carbohydrates).

Anabolic steroids are sometimes used in sport to enhance muscle growth.
● Abuse of anabolic steroids can result in liver and adrenal disorders and a number of sexual disorders.

Hormone levels are often controlled by negative feedback mechanisms.
● Normal concentrations of thyroxine inhibit TSH production. This means no more thyroxine is made.
● Reduced concentrations of thyroxine allow TSH to be made. New thyroxine is then produced until its concentration returns to normal.

Goitre is a swelling of the thyroid gland in the neck. It is normally caused by:
● A lack of iodine, which results in an underproduction of thyroxine. In this case the thyroid swells due to storing large amounts of TSH.

HIGHER ▼

THE ORGANISM

Revision questions

1 Distinguish between the nervous and endocrine systems in terms of:
  (a) Speed of action
  (b) Method by which the message is carried
  (c) Duration of effect
  (d) Areas affected.

2 (a) Distinguish between exocrine and endocrine glands, giving two examples of each type.
  (b) Name a gland that is both exocrine and endocrine and name a product in each case.

3 (a) Name the glands labelled A, B and C in diagram 35.10.

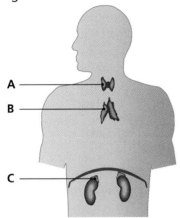

35.10

  (b) Name one hormone produced by each of these glands, and give a function for this hormone.
  (c) Make a copy of this diagram and indicate on it the positions of the following glands: (i) Pituitary (ii) Parathyroids (iii) Pancreas.

4 In the case of the thyroid:
  (a) Name a hormone it secretes.
  (b) Give the function of this hormone.
  (c) Name two disorders associated with abnormal activity of this gland.
  (d) Give three symptoms for each disorder.
  (e) Suggest a correction for each disorder.

5 (a) Name a hormone that lowers blood sugar concentration.
  (b) Name the cells that produce this hormone.
  (c) Name the condition associated with a lack of this hormone.

6 (a) Name one endocrine gland in each case located in the (i) Head (ii) Thorax (iii) Abdomen.
  (b) Name one endocrine gland found only in males and one found only in females.

7 (a) Name two hormone supplements that can be taken by humans.
  (b) State one reason why each hormone is taken.

8 State a biological reason for each of the following:
  (a) Taking extra iodine in the diet.
  (b) Testing newborn babies for thyroxine levels.
  (c) Testing urine samples for glucose.
  (d) Insulin is not taken in tablet form.
  (e) Endocrine glands have rich blood supplies.
  (f) Diabetics often carry a sugar sweet or some chocolate.

9 (a) Name two substances needed to produce thyroxine.
  (b) What hormone causes thyroxine to be produced?
  (c) Where is the hormone you have named in (b) produced?
  (d) Under what condition is this named hormone made?
  (e) What normally prevents the production of this named hormone?
  (f) Name the process by which thyroxine concentrations are controlled.

10 (a) What is goitre?
  (b) Describe the normal cause of goitre.
  (c) Historically goitre was associated with inland areas or countries. Explain why this was the case.

11 Choose which of the options (i), (ii), (iii) or (iv) represents the correct answer in each case below.
  (a) Adrenaline is produced by: (i) The thymus gland (ii) The parathyroid gland (iii) The adrenals (iv) The testes.
  (b) Which of the following glands has both an exocrine and an endocrine function? (i) Ovary (ii) Pituitary (iii) Adrenal (iv) Pancreas.
  (c) Hormones are sometimes called: (i) Biological catalysts (ii) Stimulators (iii) Coordinators (iv) Chemical messengers.
  (d) The hormone thyroxine contains: (i) Salt (ii) Iodine (iii) Iron (iv) Calcium.
  (e) One of the following glands is sometimes called 'the master gland': (i) Pituitary (ii) Pancreas (iii) Pineal (iv) Thymus.

HIGHER ▼

THE ORGANISM

Exam questions

Section C

12 (b)
(i) What is a hormone?
(ii) Draw an outline diagram of the human body and indicate on it the location of the following hormone-producing glands by using the following letters:
W Pituitary
X Thyroid
Y Pancreas (Islets of Langerhans)
Z Adrenals
(iii) In the case of **one** of the hormone-producing glands that you have located in your diagram, state:
1. the gland and a hormone that it produces.
2. a function of this hormone.
3. a deficiency symptom of this hormone.
(iv) State **one** way in which hormone action differs from nerve action.

(2004 OL Q 15)

13 (c) Answer the following questions in relation to systems of response to stimuli in the human body.
(i) The pancreas is both an <u>exocrine</u> gland and an <u>endocrine</u> gland. Explain the underlined terms.
(ii) Name a product of the endocrine portion of the pancreas and state one of its functions.

(2005 HL Q 14)

14 (b)
(i) Other than the secretion of hormones, how does an endocrine gland differ from an exocrine gland?
(ii) State **two** ways in which hormone action differs from nerve action.
(iii) Copy the following table into your answer book and fill each of the empty boxes.

Endocrine gland	Location	Hormone	Role of hormone
	Pancreas	Insulin	
Thyroid gland			
			'fight or flight'

(iv) In the case of a named hormone give:
1. a deficiency symptom,
2. a corrective measure.

(2007 HL Q 15)

15 (c)
(i) What term is used to describe the glands that secrete hormones in the human body?
(ii) 1. Name a hormone-producing gland in the human body.
2. Where in the body is the gland located?
3. Name a hormone that this gland secretes.
4. State a role of this hormone.
5. Describe what happens if the body experiences a deficiency of this hormone.
(iii) Give **two** examples of the use of hormone supplements.

(2010 HL Q 11)

16 (c)
(i) What is a hormone?
(ii) State **two** ways in which hormones are similar to the group of substances in plants which control responses to external stimuli.
(iii) 1. What is meant by feedback in relation to hormone action?
2. Give a brief account of the feedback mechanism for a **named** hormone.
(iv) Describe **one** deficiency symptom of a **named** hormone.

(2011 HL Q 11)

Previous examination questions

Ordinary level	Higher level
2004 Q 1d, 15b	2005 Q 3c, 14c(i), (ii)
2011 Q 14b	2007 Q 15b
	2010 Q 11c
	2011 Q 11c

Latest questions at www.edco.ie/lcbiologyplus/examhelp

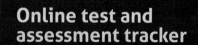
Online test and assessment tracker

Scan the QR code and test yourself on chapter 35
www.edco.ie/lcbiologyplus

THE ORGANISM

Chapter 36 The skeleton and muscles

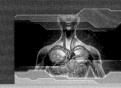

Learning objectives

- To describe the structure and function of the human skeleton
- To describe the parts of the human axial skeleton and the position and function of the intervertebral discs
- To describe the parts of the human appendicular skeleton
- To describe the anatomy of long bone, to include the medullary cavity, compact bone, spongy bone and cartilage
- **HIGHER** ▶ To describe bone growth, development and replacement in detail
- To describe the classification, location and function of different types of joint
- To describe the role of cartilage, ligaments and tendons in the human musculoskeletal system
- To describe one possible cause, prevention and treatment of arthritis or osteoporosis
- To describe muscles and how they work in antagonistic pairs, giving one example.

Introduction

The skeletal and muscular systems work together in most animals to form the musculoskeletal system. This system is controlled by the nervous system.

Muscles associated with the skeleton are called skeletal muscle. Other types of muscles are found in the heart (cardiac muscle) and in places such as blood vessels, intestines, the bladder and the uterus (smooth muscle).

Functions of the skeleton

- **Support:** the bones of the skeleton provide a rigid framework that holds the body upright.
- **Protection:** the skull protects the brain, the vertebrae protect the nerves of the spinal cord and the ribs protect the heart and lungs.
- **Movement:** bones provide a system of rigid levers against which muscles can pull. Without rigid bones, movement would not be possible.
- **Shape:** the shape of the body is determined to a large extent by the skeleton. If a person has long bones they are tall; the bones in the feet determine the width of the foot.
- **Manufacture of blood components:** bone marrow makes red blood cells, white blood cells and platelets.

Structure of the human skeleton

The adult human skeleton has 206 bones and is divided into the axial and appendicular skeletons.

THE ORGANISM

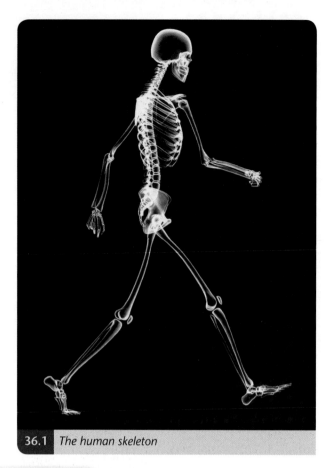

36.1 *The human skeleton*

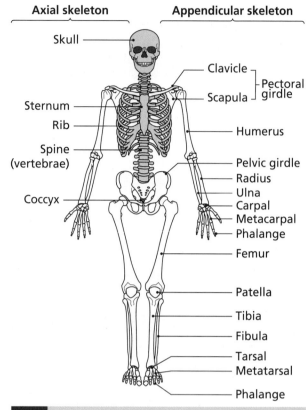

36.2 *The human skeleton, showing the parts of the axial skeleton and the appendicular skeleton*

The **axial skeleton** consists of the skull, spine, ribs and sternum (breastbone).

Parts of the axial skeleton

Skull

The skull, or cranium, consists of over 20 bones fused together.

Spine

The spine is made of 33 bones called **vertebrae**. These are arranged into five regions, as shown in diagram 36.3.

The top 24 vertebrae are held together by ligaments and can **move slightly** relative to one another. They are separated by (intervertebral) discs of cartilage. These discs have a hard outer layer and a soft, jelly-like centre. They act as shock absorbers and protect the vertebrae.

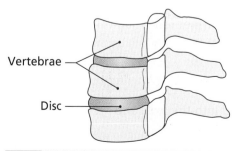

Vertebrae

Disc

36.4 *The position of the discs in relation to the vertebrae*

Region	Number of vertebrae
Cervical (neck)	7
Thoracic (chest)	12
Lumbar (back)	5
Sacrum (hip)	5
Coccyx (tail)	4

36.3 *Regions of the spine and the number of vertebrae*

The last nine vertebrae are **fused** together and there are no discs between them. No movement occurs between these vertebrae. Together they form the sacrum and coccyx.

THE ORGANISM

Sometimes the soft centre of a disc bulges out and compresses some spinal nerves. This may result in pain in the back or leg (i.e. the region to which the nerve is attached). This condition is often called a 'slipped disc'.

In addition it is known that people are taller in the mornings when their discs are fully expanded. During the day the discs become compressed (due to gravity) and people become slightly shorter.

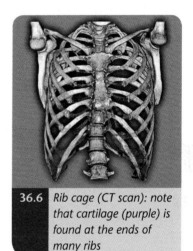

Neural spine (for muscular attachment)
Transverse process (for muscular attachment)
Facet (where next vertebra rotates against)
Neural canal (contains the spinal cord)
Centrum (gives strength)

36.5 *Transverse section (TS) of a typical vertebra*

Vertebrae have different shapes, depending on where they are located in the spine. The general shape of a vertebra is shown in diagram 36.5.

Rib cage

The rib cage consists of the sternum (breastbone) and 12 pairs of ribs. All ribs are attached to the vertebrae of the spine.

- The top seven ribs are attached to the breastbone at the front of the body. They are called **true ribs**.
- The next three ribs (i.e. numbers 8, 9 and 10 from the top) are attached to each other at the front of the chest by cartilage. They are called **false ribs**.
- The bottom two ribs, called **floating ribs**, are only attached to the spine (i.e. they do not attach to anything at the front of the body).

36.6 *Rib cage (CT scan): note that cartilage (purple) is found at the ends of many ribs*

Parts of the appendicular skeleton

Pectoral girdle

The pectoral girdle forms a connection with the vertebral column and with the arms (i.e. the humerus, radius, ulna, carpals, metacarpals and digits (fingers), which contain the phalanges).

Pelvic girdle

The **pelvic girdle** is composed of two halves of the hip joined to the sacrum.

Each half of the pelvic girdle consists of three fused bones. The two halves are joined by a band of flexible cartilage.

The pelvic girdle is fused (joined firmly) to the spine (at the sacrum). The hollow cavity where the hip bones attach to the sacrum is called the pelvis. The pelvic girdle is also connected to the legs (the femur, patella, tibia, fibula, tarsals, metatarsals and digits (toes), which contain the phalanges).

Limbs

The arms and legs have a similar design pattern, as shown in diagram 36.7.

The **appendicular skeleton** is composed of the limbs (arms and legs), the pectoral (shoulder) girdle and the pelvic (hip) girdle.

The **pectoral girdle** consists of the collarbone (or clavicle) and the shoulder blade (or scapula).

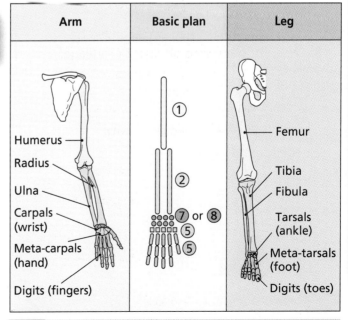

Arm	Basic plan	Leg
Humerus	①	Femur
Radius	②	Tibia
Ulna	⑦ or ⑧	Fibula
Carpals (wrist)	⑤	Tarsals (ankle)
Meta-carpals (hand)	⑤	Meta-tarsals (foot)
Digits (fingers)		Digits (toes)

36.7 *Bones of the arm and leg*

THE ORGANISM

409

Each limb ends in five digits (fingers or toes). For this reason they are called **pentadactyl limbs**. The phalanges are the individual bones of the fingers and toes. Each finger and toe has three phalanges, except the thumb and big toe, which only have two phalanges.

An important feature of the limbs of great apes (orang-utan, gorilla and chimpanzee) and humans is that they have opposable thumbs. This means that the thumb can be pushed against all the other four digits. This gives much greater powers of grip and manipulation.

Cartilage

Cartilage contains a firm but flexible fibrous protein called collagen. Cartilage is lacking in blood vessels and nerves. For transport it depends on materials diffusing through to the cells that form it (compared with bone, which has a rich blood supply). This is why cartilage is slower to heal than bone.

Cartilage is found in the pinna of the ear, the nose, the trachea and in the discs between the vertebrae. Cartilage also covers the ends of bones.

Function of cartilage

Cartilage protects bones (by acting as a shock absorber) and allows friction-free movement.

Structure of long bone

External structure

Long bones such as the femur are enclosed by a membrane called the periosteum. This membrane contains blood vessels and nerves. The long shaft of a bone is the diaphysis and the head of a bone is called the epiphysis.

Internal structure

The inside of a bone has three main regions: compact bone, spongy bone and the medullary cavity.

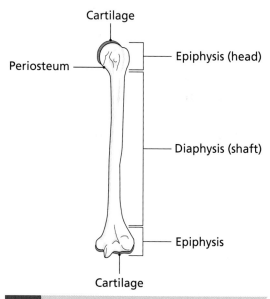

36.8 *External structure of a long bone*

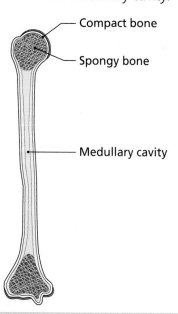

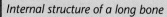

36.9 *Internal structure of a long bone*

Compact bone

Compact bone is made of bone-forming cells embedded in a surrounding medium or matrix. The matrix is composed of 70% inorganic (non-living) salts such as calcium phosphate and 30% protein (called collagen). Bone cells are supplied with nutrients by blood vessels. Nerve fibres also run throughout a bone.

Compact bone is mostly found in the shaft (diaphysis) of a bone. It is also located as a layer around the end (epiphysis) of a bone.

Function of compact bone

The calcium salts give compact bone its strength and protein gives bone its flexibility. Bone cells and protein are both organic (living) materials.

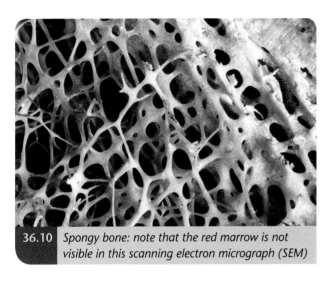

36.10 *Spongy bone: note that the red marrow is not visible in this scanning electron micrograph (SEM)*

Spongy bone

Spongy bone is like compact bone that contains numerous hollows (similar to Aero chocolate). Spongy bone consists of a network of thin, bony bars separated by different-sized spaces. The spaces in spongy bone are filled with red bone marrow, which produces blood cells. Spongy bone is found mostly in the ends (epiphyses) of bones.

Function of spongy bone

Spongy bone makes blood cells and also gives strength and rigidity to the skeleton.

Medullary cavity

The medullary cavity contains bone marrow.

- In young people, bone marrow is full of active, red marrow. Red marrow makes blood components.
- In adults, active marrow is confined to the spongy bone. The medullary cavity of adults contains inactive, yellow, fat-rich marrow. This marrow can convert to red marrow if the body requires increased blood cell formation.

HIGHER ▼

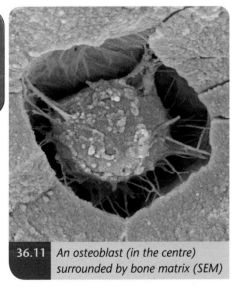

36.11 *An osteoblast (in the centre) surrounded by bone matrix (SEM)*

Bone growth

Embryonic cartilage begins to be replaced with bone around the eighth week of development in the uterus. Bone-forming cells called **osteoblasts** produce a protein called collagen. A hard compound (mainly calcium phosphate) forms around the collagen fibres. The osteoblasts become trapped in this hard compound and become dormant bone cells.

An **osteoblast** is a bone-forming cell.

The **growth plate** is the area between the epiphysis and the diaphysis in a long bone within which bone growth occurs.

Growth plate

The increase in the length of a bone is due to a **growth plate** made of cartilage. This plate is found between the epiphysis and diaphysis of the bone. In the growth plate, cartilage is continually formed and turned into bone (ossified).

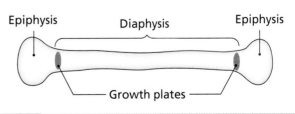

Epiphysis   Diaphysis   Epiphysis

Growth plates

36.12 *The location of growth plates*

THE ORGANISM

411

The growth plate ceases to function when the person becomes an adult. This limits the growth of the bones and the height of the individual. The inactivation of the growth plate is said to terminate the development of adult height.

36.13 *Cartilage (pale blue, on the right) covers the epiphysis; spongy bone contains marrow (purple); the growth plate is dark blue*

Bone development

Throughout life bone is being dissolved and replaced. This happens at least 10 times during the life of each bone. The restructuring of bone involves bone material being removed from the interior of the medullary cavity and extra bone material being deposited on the outside of the bone. This ensures that as bones become larger they do not become too heavy.

Large bone-digesting cells (called **osteoclasts**) move about in the medullary cavity. They digest the bone that lines the cavity and deposit calcium from the bone into blood vessels. These are catabolic cells.

> An osteoclast is a bone-digesting cell.

The activity of bone-digesting cells alone would cause bones to become thin and weak. Osteoblasts form new bone to replace the bone that is destroyed. Bone-digesting cells and osteoblasts work in conjunction to enlarge the medullary cavity and thicken the compact bone lining it.

Renewal of bone

Continual renewal of bone is dependent on physical activity, hormones and diet.

● When bones are stressed by physical activity they become thicker and stronger (the osteoblasts are stimulated). This happens especially at the sites where muscles attach to the bone. Lack of stress on bones causes them to become thin.

● The main hormones affecting bone development are growth hormone, sex hormones and parathormone.

▸ Growth hormone and many sex hormones increase the size of bones. This can be seen clearly at puberty when bone mass in the body may increase rapidly.

▸ Parathormone removes calcium from bone. This happens so that the level of calcium in the blood can be raised (a constant level of calcium in the blood is essential for muscles and nerves to work properly). It is essential to have sufficient supplies of calcium in the diet to replace the calcium lost from bones.

Osteoporosis is the loss of protein (collagen) material from bone. It causes bones to become brittle and easily broken. It should not be confused with **osteomalacia**, which is the loss of minerals (calcium) from bone due to the lack of vitamin D.

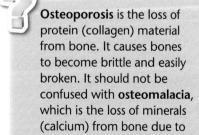

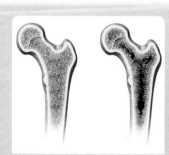

36.14 *A normal bone (left) and a bone showing osteoporosis*

Joints

Joints may be classified according to the degree of movement they allow.

A joint is where two or more bones meet.

Immovable joints

Immovable (fixed or fused) joints include the skull and pelvic girdle. The junction between fused bones is called a suture. These joints provide strength, support and protection.

Slightly movable joints

The joints between the vertebrae in the upper spinal column are slightly movable. In these joints the bones are separated by a disc of cartilage and the bones are held in place by ligaments. These ligaments limit the amount of movement possible in order to protect the nerves of the spinal cord.

Freely movable (synovial) joints

In synovial joints, the ends of the bones are covered with cartilage and the bones are separated by a cavity. The bones are held in place by ligaments, which prevent excessive movement of bones at joints.

Synovial fluid is produced in movable joints to lubricate and reduce friction.

These joints are enclosed in a synovial membrane. The membrane secretes synovial fluid, a clear sticky liquid resembling egg white. This fluid lubricates the joint and reduces friction in the joint.

Examples of synovial joints include ball-and-socket joints and hinge joints.
- **Ball-and-socket joints** (e.g. the shoulder and hip) allow movement in all directions. They are unable to support heavy loads.
- **Hinge joints** (e.g. the elbow and knee) allow movement in one direction only. They can support heavy loads.

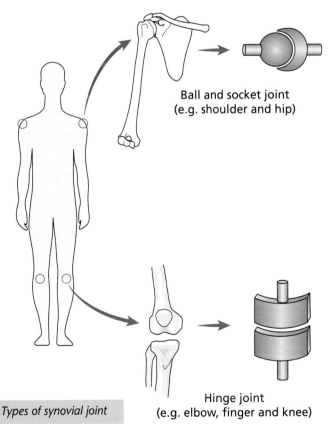

Ball and socket joint
(e.g. shoulder and hip)

Hinge joint
(e.g. elbow, finger and knee)

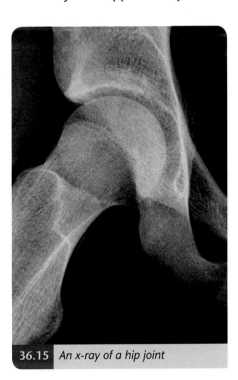

36.15 *An x-ray of a hip joint*

36.16 *Types of synovial joint*

THE ORGANISM

Excessive fluid in joints often occurs because of an injury. As a result of the injury, the synovial membrane secretes more fluid and the joint swells. The usual treatment for excess fluid is summarised by the word **RICE** (i.e. **r**est; **i**ce or cold treatment applied as soon as possible; **c**ompression with a bandage or sock; **e**levation of the limb to allow the fluid to drain away). Occasionally anti-inflammatory drugs may be needed.

> **Ligaments** are strong, fibrous, slightly elastic tissues that connect bone to bone.
>
> **Tendons** are strong, flexible, inelastic fibres that connect muscle to bone.

Syllabus You are required to study **either** arthritis **or** osteoporosis as an example of a musculoskeletal disorder.

Ligaments

Ligaments are more flexible when warm; hence the need for warming-up exercises before physical activities, to prevent ligaments from being damaged.

Tendons

Tendons are mostly composed of collagen and contain some blood vessels.

Musculoskeletal disorders

Arthritis

Cause

Arthritis is a skeletal disorder resulting from inflammation (swelling) of a joint. There are over 100 types of arthritis.

The most common type of arthritis is **osteoarthritis**. This usually occurs from 50 years of age onwards. It is caused by the cartilage in synovial joints wearing down. The underlying bones enlarge and more synovial fluid forms. The joint(s) become sore and stiff. Osteoarthritis affects about half a million people in Ireland.

Rheumatoid arthritis is the most severe form of joint inflammation. It is caused genetically by the body's immune system turning on itself (i.e. it is an autoimmune disease).

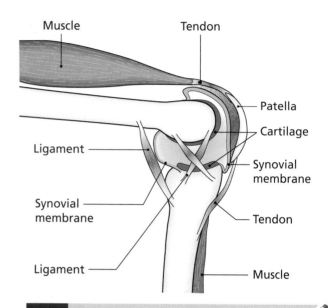

36.17 *A typical synovial joint (the knee)*

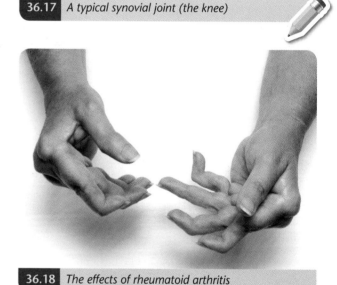

36.18 *The effects of rheumatoid arthritis*

The synovial membranes are attacked first. The joint swells and in time may become damaged and deformed. Up to 3% of Irish people have some signs of this disease (75% of whom are females). It can occur at any age.

Prevention

As osteoarthritis is caused by wear and tear on the cartilage in joints, it may be prevented by reducing damage to joints. This may involve using proper footwear when running, avoiding running on hard surfaces (especially roads) and perhaps exercising by walking or swimming instead of running.

Treatment

There is no cure for either form of arthritis. Treatments include rest, exercises to maintain mobility and strength, weight loss, anti-inflammatory medications, steroids, drugs to reduce the immune response and possibly surgery to replace the joint.

Muscles

There are three types of muscle: skeletal, smooth and cardiac muscle.

Skeletal muscle

Skeletal muscle is also called striated, striped or voluntary muscle. There are over 600 skeletal muscles in the body, and they make up 50% of body weight.

Skeletal muscle is concerned with body movements. It can contract quickly, but tires very easily (try opening and closing your fist for 1 minute!). This type of muscle is under **voluntary** or conscious control.

Smooth muscle

Smooth muscle is also called unstriped or involuntary muscle. It is found in internal structures such as the digestive system, blood vessels, bladder and uterus. It contracts slowly and is slow to tire. It is under **involuntary** or unconscious control.

Cardiac muscle

Cardiac muscle is found in the heart. It has many mitochondria, contracts strongly and **does not tire** as easily as skeletal muscle. It is **involuntary**, i.e. not under conscious control.

Antagonistic pairs

Muscular contraction is an active process and requires energy in the form of ATP. Muscles are connected to bones by tendons. When the muscle contracts, the tendon pulls on the bone, causing it to move.

Muscles can only pull (by contracting or shortening). They cannot push. For example, in the forearm a muscle on top of the humerus called the **biceps** contracts to pull the lower arm up. A second muscle is required to straighten the lower arm. This is a smaller, weaker muscle

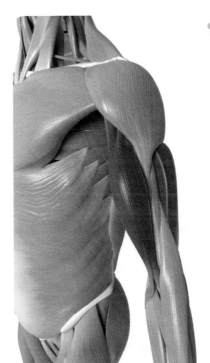

> An **antagonistic pair** is two muscles that have opposite effects to each other.

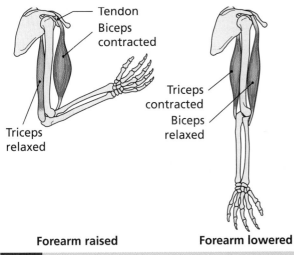

| 36.19 | *A model showing the biceps (larger) and triceps* |

Tendon
Biceps contracted
Triceps contracted
Biceps relaxed
Triceps relaxed

Forearm raised **Forearm lowered**

| 36.20 | *An antagonistic pair in the arm* |

(called the **triceps**), located at the back of the humerus. It contracts to straighten the arm.

In this example, the biceps is a flexor (i.e. it closes the joint) and the triceps is an extensor (it opens the joint).

THE ORGANISM

? Generally flexors are stronger than extensors. The palm of the hand has many flexors (i.e. the front of the hand is fleshy), but the back of the hand has smaller, weaker extensors (the back of the hand has less 'padding'). The same effect is seen on the back and front of the shins and thighs.

Summary

The **skeleton and muscles** work together to form the musculoskeletal system.

The **functions of the skeleton** are:
- Support
- Protection
- Movement
- Shape
- Blood cell manufacture.

The **axial skeleton** is made up of the:
- Skull
- Spine
- Ribs
- Breastbone (sternum).

The **appendicular skeleton** contains the:
- Arms
- Legs
- Pectoral (shoulder) girdles
- Pelvic (hip) girdles.

The **regions of the spine** and the **number of vertebrae** in each are:
- Cervical or neck (7)
- Thoracic or chest (12)
- Lumbar or back (5)
- Sacrum, near the hips (5)
- Coccyx or tail (4).

Vertebrae are separated by discs of cartilage.

The **12 pairs of ribs** are arranged as follows:
- The top seven are true ribs (attached to the spine and breastbone)
- The next three are false ribs (attached to the spine and a higher rib)
- The lowest two are floating ribs (only attached to the spine).

The **long shaft of a bone** is the diaphysis.

The **enlarged end of a bone** is the epiphysis.

The **internal structure of a bone** shows:
- Compact bone is hard and strong; it has bone cells in a matrix of salts (strength) and protein (flexibility)
- Spongy bone is more porous; it has hollow spaces containing bone marrow
- The medullary cavity is a hollow tube located at the centre of the shaft of a bone.

Bone marrow is a soft material.
- Red marrow makes blood cells.
- Yellow marrow is inactive.

Osteoblasts are cells that form bone.

Bones grow longer due to a **growth plate** between the epiphysis and diaphysis.

Bones change during life as a result of:
- Bone-digesting cells (osteoclasts) removing bone material from inside the medullary cavity
- Osteoblasts making new bone material.

Renewal of bone is affected by physical activity, certain hormones and diet.

A **joint** is where bones meet.

The **types of joint** are:
- Immovable (fixed or fused) joints such as the skull
- Slightly movable joints such as those between vertebrae
- Freely movable (synovial) joints, which include:
  - Ball-and-socket joints (shoulder and hip)
  - Hinge joints (elbow and knee).

Cartilage:
- Protects the ends of bones
- Forms structures such as the ear, nose and trachea.

Ligaments join bone to bone.

Tendons join muscle to bone.

Arthritis:
- Is a disorder of the musculoskeletal system
- Results from inflammation in joints
- May be prevented by reducing damage to joints in sports
- Is treated by rest, exercise, drugs and surgery.

There are **three types of muscle:**
- Skeletal, striped or striated muscle is attached to bones; it is under voluntary control
- Smooth, unstriped muscle is involuntary; it is found in internal organs
- Cardiac muscle is in the heart.

Muscle contraction needs energy (ATP).

An **antagonistic pair** is two muscles that produce opposite effects.
- The biceps contracts to raise the forearm. It is a flexor.
- The triceps contracts to straighten the forearm. It is an extensor.

Revision questions

1 (a) State the functions of the skeleton.
(b) Explain briefly how each function is carried out.

2 Name the parts of:
(a) The axial skeleton
(b) The appendicular skeleton.

3 (a) Name the parts labelled A to D in the TS of a vertebra shown in diagram 36.21.
(b) What is the common function of the structures labelled A and B?
(c) What is found in C during life?
(d) What is the function of E?

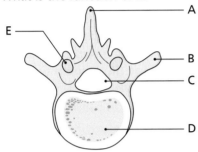

36.21

4 Distinguish between:
(a) True, false and floating ribs
(b) Pectoral and pelvic girdles
(c) Compact and spongy bone
(d) Ligaments and tendons
(e) Red and yellow marrow.

5 (a) What are vertebrae?
(b) Name the regions of the spine and say how many vertebrae are located in each region.
(c) Name the structures located between the vertebrae.
(d) What is the function of these structures?

6 (a) Name the bones labelled A, B, C and D shown in diagram 36.22.
(b) What types of joint are found at X and Y?
(c) Name the muscle labelled E. Say if this muscle is contracted or relaxed.

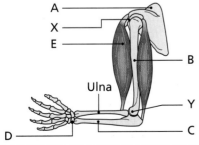

36.22

7 (a) How many ribs are normally present in a complete rib cage?

(b) Outline the attachment of the ribs:
  (i) At the back
  (ii) In the chest region.

8 Diagram 36.23 represents the hip.
(a) Name the parts labelled A to D.
(b) What function is common to parts B and C?
(c) What type of joint is represented by the diagram?

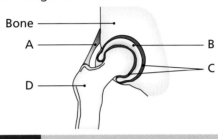

36.23

9 Draw a long section of a bone to show the positions of:
(a) Compact bone
(b) Spongy bone
(c) Medullary cavity
(d) Red marrow
(e) Periosteum
(f) Epiphysis
(g) Diaphysis.

10 (a) Name the parts labelled A to F in diagram 36.24 of the knee.
(b) What type of joint does the knee represent?
(c) Is the muscle, labelled M, a flexor or extensor? Explain your answer.
(d) Is the antagonistic partner of muscle M located at position X, Y or Z?

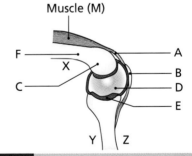

36.24

11 Give one function for each of the following:
(a) Cartilage **(b)** Ligament **(c)** Tendon
(d) Synovial fluid.

12 In adults bone is continually being broken down and replaced.
(a) Explain how this process takes place.
(b) Suggest one reason why this happens.

13 (a) Name the structure responsible for bone elongation.
(b) Why is exercise good for bones?
(c) Name one hormone that increases and one that reduces bone mass.

HIGHER

THE ORGANISM

14 **(a)** What is arthritis?
(b) Name and distinguish between two types of arthritis.
(c) Name two methods by which the effects of arthritis may be relieved.

15 Give a biological reason for each of the following:
(a) A slipped disc in the back often causes pain in the leg.
(b) Ligaments and tendons are slow to heal.
(c) People may be slightly shorter in the evenings than they are in the mornings.
(d) Osteoporosis causes bone to become more brittle.
(e) In the jaw, flexor muscles are stronger than extensor muscles.
(f) Loss of cartilage may lead to arthritis in the knee.
(g) The joints between vertebrae are not freely movable.

16 **(a)** What is meant by an antagonistic pair?
(b) Name an antagonistic pair of muscles.
(c) Why must muscles usually work in pairs?
(d) Distinguish between flexor and extensor.

17 Choose which of the options (i), (ii), (iii) or (iv) represents the correct answer in each case below.

(a) The human forelimb contains the following number of long bones:
(i) 3 **(ii)** 30 **(iii)** 8 **(iv)** 5.
(b) The function of a transverse process is for:
(i) Articulation **(ii)** Muscular attachment **(iii)** Ossification **(iv)** Strength.
(c) Osteoporosis is a skeletal disorder caused by a loss of: **(i)** Collagen **(ii)** Marrow **(iii)** Calcium **(iv)** Cartilage.
(d) The wall of the alimentary canal contains which type of muscle? **(i)** Striped **(ii)** Cardiac **(iii)** Smooth **(iv)** Antagonistic.
(e) The shin bone is usually called the:
(i) Humerus **(ii)** Fibula **(iii)** Femur **(iv)** Tibia.

Exam questions

Section A

18 Study the diagram of a synovial joint and then answer the following questions.

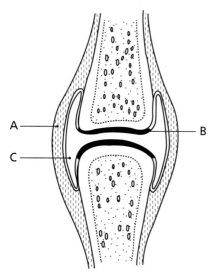

(a) Name tissue A.
(b) Give a function of A.
(c) Name tissue B.
(d) Name the fluid in C.
(e) Give a function of the fluid in C.
(2007 OL Q 6)

19 **(a)** The diagram shows the macroscopic structure of part of a long bone.
(i) Name a long bone in the human body.

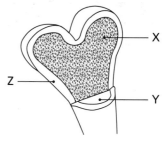

(ii) Name parts X, Y and Z in the diagram.
(iii) State a function of X.
(iv) State a function of Y.
(b) **(i)** Show clearly on the diagram where you would expect to find cartilage.
(ii) State **one** role of **this** cartilage.
(2012 HL Q 3)

Section C

20 **(c)** **(i)** State **two** functions of the human skeleton.
(ii) The vertebrae form part of the axial skeleton. Name the vertebrae found in:
1. The neck,
2. The small of the back.
(iii) Name the part of the central nervous system that runs through the vertebrae.
(iv) Name the **three** bones that form the human arm.

THE ORGANISM

(v) Write a short note (about five lines) on **one** of the following: arthritis or osteoporosis.

(2006 OL Q 15)

21 (a) (i) Draw a diagram to show the structure of a synovial joint. Label **three** parts of the joint that you have drawn, other than bones.

(ii) Explain the functions of the three parts that you have labelled.

(iii) Name a disorder of the musculoskeletal system.

(iv) Give a possible cause of the disorder that you have named in (iii) and suggest a treatment for it.

(2006 HL Q15)

22 (a) Answer the following questions in relation to the human musculoskeletal system.

(i) Give **three** roles of the skeleton.

(ii) Explain what is meant by the axial skeleton.

(iii) Give a function for each of the following:

1. Red marrow,

2. Cartilage,

3. Tendon.

(iv) Explain what is meant by an antagonistic muscle pair and give an example in the human body.

(v) Suggest a treatment for a <u>named</u> disorder of the musculoskeletal system.

(2008 HL Q 15)

23 (b) The diagram shows the bones of the human arm.

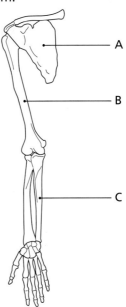

(i) Name the parts labelled A, B and C.

(ii) What structures attach a muscle to a bone?

(iii) Which upper arm muscle contracts to raise the lower arm?

(iv) What is meant by the term *antagonistic pair* in reference to muscles?

(v) Name the type of joint at the elbow.

(vi) Apart from movement, give **one** other function of the skeleton.

(vii) Suggest **one** reason why the bones of birds are almost hollow.

(2010 OL Q 15)

Previous examination questions

Ordinary level	Higher level
2004 Q 1b, 4	2005 Q 3d
2006 Q 15c	2006 Q 15a
2007 Q 6	2008 Q 15a
2010 Q 15b	2009 Q 4
	2012 Q 3

Latest questions at www.edco.ie/lcbiologyplus/examhelp

Online test and assessment tracker

Scan the QR code and test yourself on chapter 36
www.edco.ie/lcbiologyplus

THE ORGANISM

Learning objectives

- To describe the general defence system in humans, including the skin, mucous membranes and phagocytic white blood cells
- To describe the specific defence system (immune system) in humans and define the term 'induced immunity'
- To describe vaccination and immunisation
- **HIGHER ▶** To describe the role of lymphocytes in the immune system, including B cells in antibody production and the four types of T cell.

A **pathogen** is an organism that causes disease.

Immunity is the ability to resist infection.

The **general defence system** acts as a barrier to all pathogens attempting to gain entry to the human body.

Introduction

The human body defends itself against bacteria, fungi and viruses that cause disease.

The human defence system allows the body to resist infection. It has two parts: the general defence system and the specific defence system.

The **general defence system** is non-specific. This means that it acts against **all** pathogens. There are two parts to the general defence system.

- The first part consists of the skin, mucous membranes and their secretions. These features attempt to prevent the entry of all pathogens.
- The second part consists of white blood cells and chemicals that destroy any pathogens that penetrate the body.

The **specific defence system** is also called the immune system. It attacks **particular** (or specific) pathogens, either by producing antibodies against them or by killing infected cells.

General defence system

First line of general defence

The first line of general defence consists of the skin, mucous membranes that line the respiratory, digestive, urinary and reproductive tracts and secretions produced by the skin and mucous membranes.

Examples of how the first line of the general defence system operates include the following.

Skin

The skin provides a structural barrier to infection. This means it is a physical barrier that prevents pathogens from entering the body.

Clotting

If the skin is broken, blood clotting prevents the entry of further pathogens (as well as preventing blood loss).

Lysozyme

Lysozyme is an enzyme found in sweat, tears and saliva. It attacks and dissolves the cell walls of many bacteria.

Sebaceous glands

Sebaceous glands in the skin produce sebum (oil). Sebum contains chemicals that kill bacteria.

Mucus

Many body systems are lined with sticky mucus. Pathogens are trapped by this mucus and prevented from entering the body.

Cilia

The respiratory system is lined with tiny hairs called cilia. These beat and create a current, which moves mucus back up the respiratory system so that it can be swallowed into the stomach. When we cough to clear our throats we are clearing mucus (and pathogens) from the larynx.

Acid

Hydrochloric acid in the stomach kills many pathogens.

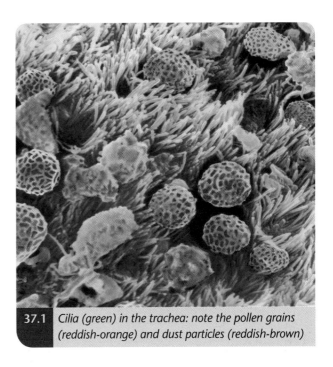

37.1 *Cilia (green) in the trachea: note the pollen grains (reddish-orange) and dust particles (reddish-brown)*

Beneficial bacteria

Bacteria in the vagina produce lactic acid. This acid prevents the growth of pathogens.

Second line of general defence

The second line of general defence consists of the destruction by white blood cells of pathogens that have entered the body, the production of proteins that kill or prevent pathogens from reproducing and the inflammatory response. The ways by which these mechanisms work are outlined below.

Phagocytic white blood cells

When cells are damaged by invading micro-organisms they release a large number of chemicals. These chemicals attract white blood cells from the bloodstream. The white blood cells engulf (surround) and destroy any bacteria, viruses or other micro-organisms that they meet. These white blood cells are called **phagocytes** because they surround and ingest pathogens.

Some phagocytes are very large and are called **macrophages**.

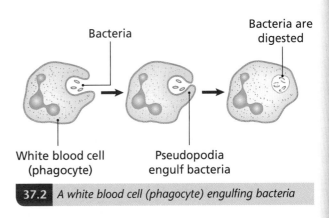

37.2 *A white blood cell (phagocyte) engulfing bacteria*

- Some macrophages move around the body in body fluids and act as scavengers for pathogens.
- Other macrophages remain fixed in places such as the spleen, lymph nodes and other lymphatic tissues such as the tonsils, adenoids and appendix. These macrophages filter out and destroy any pathogens that are present in lymph.

THE ORGANISM

421

Defence proteins

Complement is a set of about 20 proteins found in the blood plasma. The proteins in complement are activated by infection. Once activated these proteins destroy viruses and other pathogens.

Interferons are another set of defence proteins. They prevent viral multiplication and help to limit the spread of virus infections such as colds and influenza.

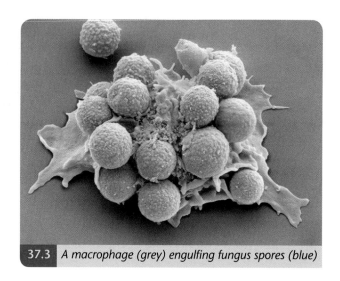

37.3 *A macrophage (grey) engulfing fungus spores (blue)*

Inflammation

When cells are infected they release a chemical that results in blood capillaries opening wider (dilating) and becoming more porous. This causes localised swelling, redness, heat and pain. In addition, it brings more white blood cells to the area to fight the infection.

Sometimes inflammation occurs over the whole body. In this case it causes increased body temperature, called fever. The higher temperature interferes with the ability of some bacteria and viruses to reproduce.

Specific defence system (the immune system)

> The specific defence system attacks particular (or specific) pathogens.

The specific defence system works by:
- The production of antibodies
- White blood cells destroying body cells that have been infected with a particular pathogen.

Monocytes and lymphocytes

Monocytes and lymphocytes are two types of white blood cell (or leucocyte). Both monocytes and lymphocytes are formed in bone marrow. Once they are produced, these cells move from the bone marrow into blood vessels and into parts of the lymphatic system such as lymph vessels, lymph nodes, the spleen (located beside the stomach) and the thymus gland in the chest. Monocytes and lymphocytes react to pathogens in different ways.

Monocytes

Monocytes develop into white blood cells called **macrophages**. Macrophages recognise foreign molecules (called antigens) that are present on the surface of pathogens. When a macrophage digests a pathogen, antigens from the pathogen are normally displayed on the surface of the macrophage. These antigens then stimulate the production of antibodies.

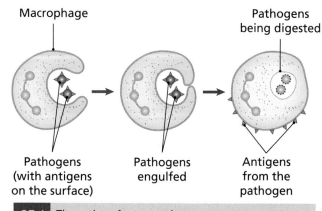

Macrophage

Pathogens being digested

Pathogens (with antigens on the surface)

Pathogens engulfed

Antigens from the pathogen

37.4 *The action of a macrophage*

Lymphocytes

Lymphocytes fight infection in two different ways.

- Some lymphocytes attack body cells that display antigens on their surface. These cells may be infected with a pathogen or they may be cancer cells (cancer cells produce abnormal molecules that are identified as 'foreign' by lymphocytes).
- Other lymphocytes produce antibodies.

Antigens and antibodies

The word **antigen** is based on the words **antibody gen**erating. Antigens include molecules from the coats of viruses and the cell walls of bacteria, fungi and other micro-organisms. Antigens are also found on foreign cells such as pollen grains, incompatible blood transfusions, transplanted tissues or organs and cancer cells.

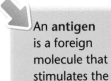

An **antigen** is a foreign molecule that stimulates the production of antibodies.

An **antibody** is a protein produced by white blood cells (called lymphocytes) in response to a specific antigen.

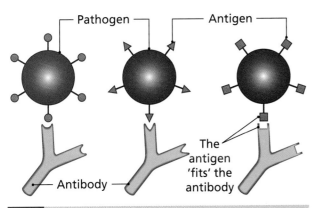

Pathogen — Antigen —

The antigen 'fits' the antibody

Antibody —

37.5 *Pathogens, antigens and antibodies*

The antigen–antibody reaction is a highly specific reaction. This means there is a precise fit between the antigen and the antibody. Just like enzymes and substrates, each antibody is complementary to a single antigen. Each antigen stimulates the production of only one specific antibody.

Antibodies bind to antigens and allow the pathogens to be destroyed by lymphocytes.

Antibodies also trigger the complement system, which results in the pathogenic cells being burst.

Allergies are inappropriate immune responses. In an allergy the body reacts to a substance that is not a pathogen, e.g. food, dust, a drug or a chemical in washing powder.

Sometimes antibodies are produced against our own body cells. This results in autoimmune disorders such as rheumatoid arthritis (where joints are attacked) and multiple sclerosis (where the myelin sheath on nerves is attacked).

After a transplant the recipient is given medication to reduce their immune response. This reduces the risk that the transplanted tissue will be attacked (rejected). Of course the reduction in the immune response may result in more infections.

Duration of immunity

After an infection is fully overcome, some of the antibody-producing lymphocytes remain in the body for a long time. These long-lived cells are called **memory cells**. If a second, similar antigen enters the body later, these memory lymphocytes can rapidly produce large amounts of that specific antibody much more quickly. This is why we usually do not suffer from the same infection for a second time.

We can suffer from colds or influenza more than once. This is because there are many different forms of cold and flu viruses (each with different antigens). New cold and flu viruses develop by mutations.

On first contact with an antigen (or pathogen), the body takes about 14 days to produce the maximum number of antibodies. On subsequent contact with the same antigen, antibodies are produced in large numbers in about 5 days. This prevents the re-infection from producing symptoms.

THE ORGANISM

Induced immunity is the ability to resist disease caused by specific pathogens by the production of antibodies.

Active immunity involves the production of a person's own antibodies in response to foreign antigens that enter the body.

Natural active immunity occurs when a pathogen enters the body in the normal way (i.e. when you get an infection).

Summary of the human defence system		
General defence system (non-specific)		**Specific (immune) system**
First line of defence	**Second line of defence**	**Third line of defence**
Skin	Phagocytes	Monocytes destroy antigens
Mucous membranes	Defence proteins	Antibodies
Secretions from skin and mucous membranes	Inflammation	

Induced immunity

There are two types of induced immunity: active and passive immunity.

Active immunity

Active immunity develops after a person is infected by a virus or bacterium or after vaccination. Active immunity gives **long-term** resistance to infection because the lymphocytes responsible for producing the particular antibody live for a long time in the body.

Active immunity can occur in two ways: naturally or artificially.

Natural active immunity

When we get a cold, flu or chickenpox, we develop natural resistance to these infections by producing antibodies against them. This is natural active immunity.

Artificial active immunity

Introducing a pathogen into the body medically is a form of immunisation that is often called **vaccination**. A vaccine is taken in oral form or by injection.

Artificial active immunity occurs when a pathogen is medically introduced into the body.

A **vaccine** is a non disease-causing dose of a pathogen (or its toxin), which triggers the production of antibodies.

A vaccine may contain pathogens that are killed or treated so that they cannot reproduce. In some cases only the outer wall or coat of the pathogen is used, as these contain the antigens needed to produce antibodies. The person who receives a vaccine produces antibodies without suffering the full symptoms of the infection. The ability to form these antibodies persists in the body, conferring long-term immunity (often for life).

Children are usually vaccinated (or immunised) for tuberculosis (BCG injection), diphtheria, whooping cough and tetanus, polio (given by mouth on a sugar lump) and measles, mumps and rubella (MMR injection). Vaccinations for influenza, cervical cancer and some forms of meningitis are also available. Booster vaccinations strengthen the effect of the first treatment.

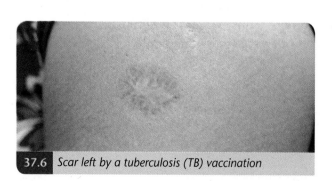

37.6 *Scar left by a tuberculosis (TB) vaccination*

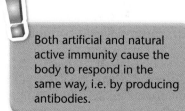

Both artificial and natural active immunity cause the body to respond in the same way, i.e. by producing antibodies.

Passive immunity

In the case of passive immunity an individual does not have to be infected with the pathogen. Passive immunity provides **short-term** resistance to infections. The immunity lasts until the antibodies are broken down in the recipient's body. This usually happens somewhere between a few weeks and about 6 months.

Passive immunity can occur in two ways: naturally or artificially.

Natural passive immunity

Antibodies can be passed from the mother to her child either:
● Across the placenta while the child is in the womb or
● In the mother's colostrum that is produced in the first 2 to 3 days of breastfeeding and later in the milk if the child continues to breastfeed.

These antibodies give the child immunity to most common diseases for the first few months of life (or for a few months after the child stops breastfeeding).

Artificial passive immunity

Antibodies are injected into a person when the person has an infection that requires an immediate response. This might be the case because the pathogen grows so fast that the body does not have time to produce antibodies fast enough. The introduced antibodies act very rapidly to control the disease. However, they do not last very long in the recipient.

An example of artificial passive immunity is when a person gets an anti-tetanus injection. The antibodies are extracted from blood samples taken from horses that have been infected with tetanus bacteria. The horse antibodies are then given by injection to an infected human.

Passive immunity occurs when individuals are given antibodies that were formed by another organism.

Natural passive immunity occurs when a child gets antibodies from its mother.

Artificial passive immunity occurs when a person is given an injection containing antibodies made by another organism.

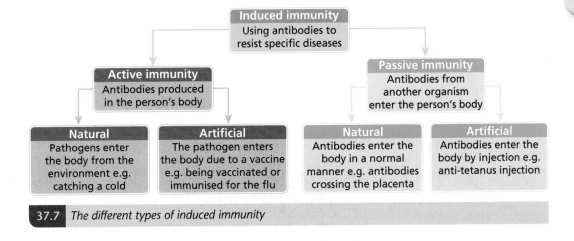

37.7 *The different types of induced immunity*

Vaccination and immunisation

Vaccination is the administration (usually by injection) of a non-disease-causing dose of a pathogen (or its toxin) to stimulate the production of antibodies.

Immunisation occurs when we produce or are injected with antibodies against a pathogen.

Vaccination is designed to result in immunisation (i.e. when the person produces their own antibodies).

THE ORGANISM

Role of lymphocytes in the immune system

Lymphocytes are white blood cells or leucocytes. They are formed in bone marrow. Each lymphocyte has a large, round nucleus with very little cytoplasm.

There are two types of lymphocyte: B lymphocytes (B cells) and T lymphocytes (T cells). These lymphocytes are distinguished according to the location in which they mature. B cells continue to mature in the bone marrow. T cells move from the bone marrow and mature in the thymus gland, which is located in the top of the chest.

Cell membrane

Nucleus

Cytoplasm

37.8 *A typical lymphocyte*

The difference between the two types of lymphocyte can be recalled by the first letters, B and T:

B cells mature in **B**one marrow

T cells mature in the **T**hymus gland

B cells

Plasma B cells

Plasma B cells produce antibodies.

When they have matured in the bone marrow, B cells move out into lymphatic tissue, especially the spleen and lymph nodes.

There are many millions of different B cells. However, each B cell is adapted to recognise only **one** specific antigen, which is usually present on the surface of a macrophage. Each B cell produces only one type of antibody in response to that specific antigen.

When a B cell comes into contact with the antigen that it is specific to, it multiplies to produce large amounts of the required antibody. B cells that produce antibodies are called plasma B cells (see diagram 37.9).

Antibodies inactivate antigens by attaching to them. This allows the cell that carries the antigen to be disposed of by phagocytes or by activating the complement system, which causes the cells to burst.

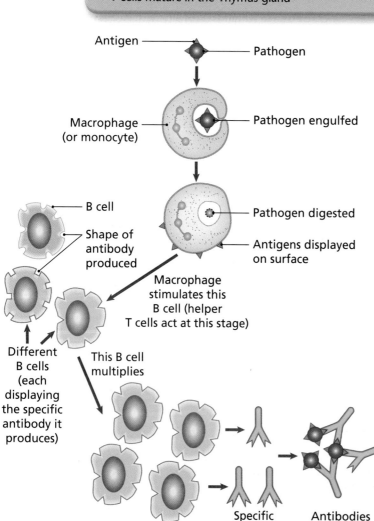

Antigen — Pathogen

Macrophage (or monocyte) — Pathogen engulfed

B cell

Shape of antibody produced — Pathogen digested

Antigens displayed on surface

Macrophage stimulates this B cell (helper T cells act at this stage)

Different B cells (each displaying the specific antibody it produces)

This B cell multiplies

Plasma B cells

Specific antibodies produced

Antibodies disable pathogens

37.9 *How B cells work*

HIGHER ▼

Memory B cells

Most of the B cells die off once the infection has been overcome. However, some remain alive for many years. It is these surviving memory B cells that allow the body to respond if the same antigen enters the body again. In this case the memory B cells convert to plasma B cells, which produce the specific antibody.

This so-called secondary response is much more effective for the following reasons:

- It produces antibodies in response to much smaller amounts of antigen
- It produces antibodies much faster (in 5 days rather than 14 days)
- It produces much greater numbers of antibodies than is the case with a first-time infection.

These three factors prevent us from being infected more than once by the same pathogen.

> Memory B cells survive for years after the infection is eliminated and can make the specific antibody if the same infection later enters the body.

T cells

T cells move from the bone marrow into the thymus gland, where they become activated (by the hormone thymosin found in the thymus gland). The activation of T cells is especially important in the early months and years of life. The thymus gland is most active in the first few weeks before and after birth. It remains relatively active (and enlarges) up to puberty, when it begins to shrink in size.

T cells **do not** produce antibodies. Instead they act against most viruses and some bacteria in one of four ways. The functions of T cells are explained by reference to the four types of T cell: helper T cells, killer T cells, suppressor T cells and memory T cells.

Helper T cells

Helper T cells recognise antigens on the surface of other white blood cells, especially macrophages. Helper T cells stimulate the multiplication of those B cells that produce the antibody that is specific to the recognised antigen. These B cells, in turn, produce the specific antibodies. Along with stimulating B cells, helper T cells also stimulate killer T cells to reproduce.

> Helper T cells stimulate B cells and killer T cells.

Helper T cells are the main types of cells that are infected by human immunodeficiency virus (HIV).

HIV severely reduces the efficiency of the entire immune system by preventing helper T cells from functioning properly. In this way HIV is responsible for the condition known as AIDS (see Chapter 38).

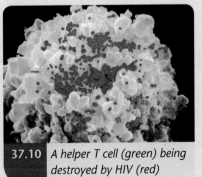

37.10 *A helper T cell (green) being destroyed by HIV (red)*

Killer T cells

Killer T cells are stimulated by chemicals that are produced by helper T cells. Killer T cells attack and destroy abnormal body cells. Abnormal body cells include virus-infected cells or cancer cells.

Killer T cells release a protein called **perforin**, which forms pores in the membrane of the abnormal cell. Water and ions (charged particles) flow into the abnormal cell through

> Note that killer T cells destroy human cells, not pathogens. They should not attack normal human cells, only human cells that have viruses in them or that are cancerous.

> **Killer T cells** destroy abnormal human body cells.

THE ORGANISM

427

these pores. The abnormal cell swells and bursts, as shown in diagram 37.12.

Killer T cells are said to be cytotoxic cells (from the Greek *kytos* meaning 'hollow' 'cell' and *toxikon* meaning 'poison').

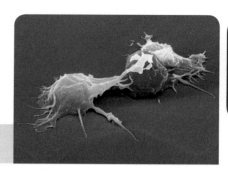

| 37.11 | *Two killer T cells (brown) with long protrusions destroying a cancer cell (red)* |

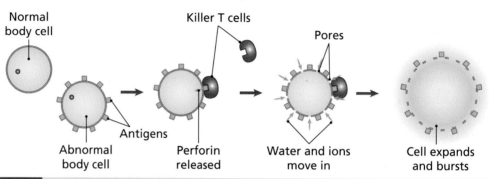

| 37.12 | *The role of killer T cells* |

Suppressor T cells

> **Suppressor T cells inhibit the immune response.**

Suppressor T cells are stimulated to grow by specific antigens. They grow more slowly than the other T or B cells. Suppressor T cells usually become active after the antigen (and pathogen) has been destroyed.

Suppressor T cells inhibit plasma B cells, other T cells (such as helper T cells and killer T cells) and macrophages. In this way they turn off the immune response when the infection is over.

Memory T cells

> **Memory T cells survive for years after the infection is eliminated and can stimulate the specific B cells and killer T cells if the same infection later enters the body.**

Memory T cells can survive for a long time; many of them often survive for many decades. If the same pathogen re-enters a person's body, the memory T cells very quickly stimulate memory B cells to produce huge amounts of the specific antibody. Memory T cells also trigger the production of killer T cells.

Memory T cells (along with memory B cells) are responsible for lifelong immunity from infections.

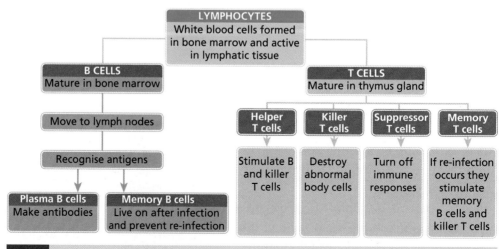

| 37.13 | *The different types of lymphocytes* |

Summary

A pathogen is an organism that causes disease.

The **general defence system:**
- Acts against all pathogens
- Is not specific to any one pathogen.

The **specific defence system:**
- Acts against only one particular type of pathogen
- Is called the immune system
- Acts by forming antibodies and by killing infected cells.

The **general defence system** involves two lines of defence:
- Skin, blood clotting, lysozyme, chemicals in sebum, mucous membranes, cilia, stomach acid and lactic acid in the vagina
- White blood cells that act by phagocytosis, defensive proteins (interferons and complement) and inflammation.

Monocytes and lymphocytes:
- Are white blood cells
- Are found in lymphatic tissue
- Both react to antigens.

Monocytes (which develop into macrophages) destroy pathogens and display antigens on their membranes.

Lymphocytes:
- Attack body cells displaying antigens
- Produce antibodies.

The **organs of the immune system** are the spleen, thymus and lymph nodes.

An **antigen** is a foreign molecule that stimulates the production of antibodies.

An **antibody** is a protein produced by lymphocytes in response to an antigen.
- Each type of antibody is highly specific (complementary) to a single antigen.
- Antibodies inactivate antigens and allow the pathogen to be destroyed.

Some lymphocytes survive for many years as memory cells, allowing long-term immunity.

Induced immunity is the ability to resist disease (by producing antibodies) caused by specific antigens.

Active immunity means that a person makes his/her own antibodies.

Active immunity provides long-term immunity in two ways:
- When pathogens naturally enter the body
- When antigens are artificially placed in the body by vaccination.

Passive immunity occurs when foreign antibodies are introduced into the body.

Passive immunity provides short-term immunity in two ways:
- A child getting antibodies in a natural manner from the placenta or mother's milk
- Getting an injection of foreign antibodies.

B cells (or B lymphocytes) mature in the bone marrow.

T cells (or T lymphocytes) mature in the thymus gland.

B cells:
- Recognise an antigen
- Produce antibodies.

The **four types of T cell** all recognise specific antigens:
- Helper T cells stimulate B cells (to produce antibodies) and killer T cells
- Killer T cells (cytotoxic cells) produce perforin, which causes abnormal body cells to burst
- Suppressor T cells turn off immune responses
- Memory T cells survive a long time to trigger immunity to the same antigen in later years.

HIGHER ▼

THE ORGANISM

Revision questions

1 **(a)** What does the defence system protect the body against?
 (b) Distinguish between:
  (i) The general and specific defence systems
  (ii) The first and second lines of general defence.

2 Suggest one way in which each of the following help to defend the body:
 (a) Skin
 (b) Blood clotting
 (c) Mucous membranes
 (d) Cilia
 (e) Acid in the stomach
 (f) Phagocytes
 (g) Complement
 (h) Interferons
 (i) Inflammation
 (j) Lactic acid.

3 **(a)** Distinguish between:
  (i) An antigen and an antibody
  (ii) An antigen and a pathogen.
 (b) What type of cell makes antibodies?
 (c) Why do adults have a greater variety of antibodies than children do?

4 Why is the antibody–antigen reaction said to be specific? Explain your answer with the aid of a labelled diagram.

5 **(a)** What is meant by induced immunity?
 (b) Distinguish between active and passive induced immunity.
 (c) Why does active immunity last longer than passive immunity?

6 **(a)** Explain what is meant by each of the following types of immunity:
  (i) Natural active immunity
  (ii) Natural passive immunity
  (iii) Artificial active immunity
  (iv) Artificial passive immunity.
 (b) Which of the above types of immunity do not work in people with AIDS?

7 Give a biological reason for each of the following:
 (a) Young children do not normally get common infections for the first few months of life.
 (b) Breastfed babies tend to get fewer infections than bottle-fed babies.
 (c) A person feels ill for a day or two after receiving a vaccination.
 (d) A sting becomes inflamed.
 (e) A dog licking a wound helps prevent infection.
 (f) Some forms of immunity last longer than others.
 (g) Booster injections are sometimes given.
 (h) People suffering from AIDS do not respond to vaccines.
 (i) Some people suffer allergic reactions.
 (j) Transplant patients are given drugs to inhibit their immune systems.
 (k) People can suffer influenza infections more than once.

8 **(a)** Distinguish between B and T lymphocytes.
 (b) Outline the role of B cells in fighting infection.

9 The graph in diagram 37.14 shows the response to injecting the same antigen at two different times labelled X and Y.

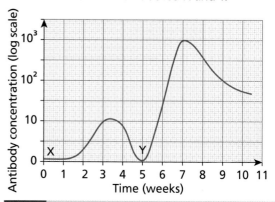

37.14

 (a) What is meant by: **(i)** Antigen **(ii)** Antibody?
 (b) Name the particular type of white blood cell responsible for the production of antibodies.
 (c) How long did it take to start producing antibodies: **(i)** After injection X **(ii)** After injection Y?
 (d) What evidence is there on the graph to indicate that the reaction to injection Y was: **(i)** Greater **(ii)** More rapid?
 (e) Suggest one reason why the antibody concentration declined around the fourth week.
 (f) Copy the graph and show on it the graph you would expect if a **different** antigen was injected at time Y.

10 **(a)** Name four types of T lymphocyte.
 (b) Give one function for each of the four types of T lymphocyte.

11 Name one way in which helper T cells are:
 (a) Stimulated **(b)** Inhibited.

12 Give two reasons why helper T cells are considered to be crucial to the working of the specific defence system.

13 **(a)** Name the type of lymphocyte that attacks cancer cells.
 (b) Suggest one reason why these cells attack cancer cells but not other body cells.

14 What is the significance of memory cells in the immune system?

15 **(a)** **(i)** What is meant by the term 'immunity'?
  (ii) Distinguish between active and passive immunity.
 (b) Describe two ways in which the skin helps to defend the body against pathogenic micro-organisms.

THE ORGANISM

HIGHER ▼

(c) Lymphocytes play a vital role in the body's immune system.
- (i) To which group of blood cells do lymphocytes belong?
- (ii) Name two types of lymphocyte and state a role of each.

(d) What is the purpose of vaccination?

16 Choose which of the options (i), (ii), (iii) or (iv) represents the correct answer in each case below.
- (a) A pollen grain that enters a person's nose is an example of:
  (i) An antibody (ii) An antigen
  (iii) An antibiotic (iv) A pathogen.

(b) Lysozyme is an enzyme found in: (i) Lymph glands (ii) Bacteria (iii) Viruses (iv) Tears.

(c) Monocytes develop into:
(i) Micro-organisms (ii) Lymphocytes (iii) Antibodies (iv) Macrophages.

(d) B cells become mature in the:
(i) Blood (ii) Lymph
(iii) Thymus gland (iv) Bone marrow.

(e) Killer T cells produce this chemical:
(i) Perforin (ii) Allergen
(iii) Interferon (iv) Lysozyme.

Exam questions

Section C

17 (a) (iii) Name **two** types of lymphocyte and state a role of each when viruses or other micro-organisms enter the blood.

(iv) "Immunity that results from vaccination is effectively the same as the immunity that develops following an infection." Do you agree with this statement? Explain your answer.

(2005 HL Q 15)

18 (c) (i) What is meant by the term immunity?

(ii) Outline briefly the role of B lymphocytes in the human immune system.

(iii) Distinguish between active and passive immunity.

(iv) "Vaccination gives rise to active immunity." Explain this statement.

(v) In certain situations a person is given a specific antibody rather than being vaccinated.
1. Is this an example of active or passive immunity?
2. Under what circumstances might an antibody, rather than a vaccination, be given?

3. Comment on the duration of immunity that follows the administration of an antibody.

(2007 HL Q 14)

19 (c) (iii) What is meant by the term *immunity*?

(iv) The skin is an important part of our immune system. Outline **two** ways in which the skin provides immunity.

(v) To help the immune system, many people receive vaccinations during their lifetime. What is meant by the term *vaccination*?

(2011 OL Q 15)

20 (b) (i) State **two** ways, other than colour, in which red blood cells differ from white blood cells.

(ii) Name a group of white blood cells, other than lymphocytes.

(iii) Lymphocytes may be divided into B cells and T cells. B cells produce antibodies.
1. What is the role of antibodies in the body?
2. Name any **three** types of T cell.
3. State a role of **each** of the T cell types that you named in part 2.

(2012 HL Q 15)

Previous examination questions

Ordinary level	Higher level
2011 Q 15c(iii)–(v)	2005 Q 15a(iii), (iv)
	2006 Q 6e
	2007 Q 14c
	2009 Q 15c(i)
	2012 Q 15b

Latest questions at www.edco.ie/lcbiologyplus/examhelp

Online test and assessment tracker

Scan the QR code and test yourself on chapter 37
www.edco.ie/lcbiologyplus

Chapter 38 **Viruses**

Introduction

Viruses are tiny, non-cellular structures. They cannot be seen with a light microscope, only with an electron microscope.

 A virus is about 50 times smaller than a bacterium. This means that approximately 50 000 viruses, but only 1000 bacteria, could fit across the width of the full stop at the end of this sentence.

Virus structure

Viruses have an outer protein coat called a capsid. In some viruses (e.g. the influenza virus) the capsid is enclosed in a complex outer membrane.

Inside the capsid is a nucleic acid: either DNA or RNA (*never both*). In either case there are very few genes. Viruses contain from four to several hundred genes, unlike more complex organisms, which have tens of thousands of genes. Viral genes carry instructions for the formation of new viruses.

Viruses do not have ribosomes, mitochondria or other cytoplasmic organelles. They do not carry out any metabolic reactions on their own. They require the organelles and enzymes of a host cell to carry out their limited number of reactions.

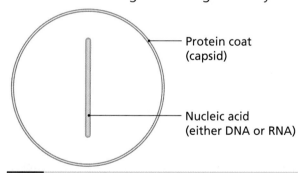

38.1 *Structure of a typical virus*

Viruses: living or dead?

Viruses are on the border between living and non-living. They show some features of living things but lack many others. The evidence relating to whether viruses are living or non-living is summarised in the following table.

The living and non-living features of viruses	
Living	**Non-living**
1 Contain genetic material (DNA or RNA)	1 Are non-cellular
2 Have a protein coat	2 Cannot reproduce by themselves
3 Can replicate (inside a living cell)	3 Do not have ribosomes, mitochondria or other cell organelles
	4 Only have one type of nucleic acid (living things have both DNA and RNA)

Viruses are not included in any of the five kingdoms of living things. This is because viruses are non-cellular and do not carry out any metabolic reactions on their own.

Shapes of viruses

Viruses are classified into three groups according to their shapes. The main virus shapes are:

- Round
- Rod-shaped
- Complex.

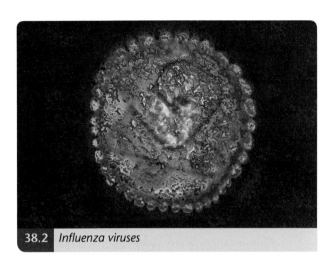

38.2 *Influenza viruses*

Replication

As viruses are not cells, the term 'replication' is used instead of 'reproduction'. Viruses cannot replicate themselves; they only multiply by using the energy and structures of a live host cell. For this reason viruses are said to be **obligate parasites**.

 A **bacteriophage** (or phage) is a virus that infects bacteria.

Bacteriophages are the most complex and best studied viruses. The replication cycle of a typical bacteriophage such as the T-phage takes about 30 minutes and is outlined in diagram 38.3. This is also the way in which most viruses infect human cells.

Stages in viral replication

Attachment

The virus attaches to the host cell. Proteins on the virus match up with receptor sites on the host wall or membrane. This is why viruses are often specific to one particular host cell.

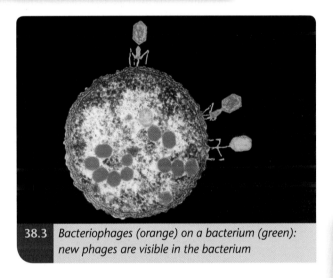

38.3 *Bacteriophages (orange) on a bacterium (green): new phages are visible in the bacterium*

Entry

The virus forms a hole in the host cell and viral nucleic acid is pushed through. The protein coats of bacteriophages stay outside the bacterium cell. When viruses enter animal cells the protein coats also enter, but are digested.

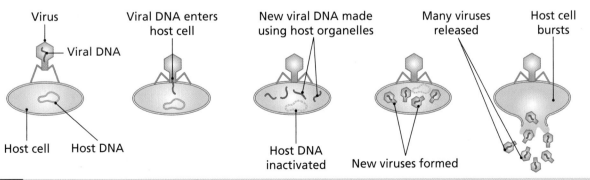

38.4 *Viral replication*

Synthesis

The host nucleic acid (DNA) is made inactive. The viral nucleic acid uses the host's organelles to produce new viral nucleic acid and proteins.

Assembly

New viruses are made inside the host cell using the viral molecules that have been produced.

Release

Very often the host cell bursts to release between 100 and 100 000 new viruses. The bursting of the host cell is called lysis.

 Retroviruses contain RNA (instead of DNA) and an enzyme that converts the virus RNA to DNA. This DNA then makes new copies of the virus RNA and new viruses inside the host cell. The virus that causes acquired immune deficiency syndrome (AIDS) – human immunodeficiency virus, or HIV – is a retrovirus.

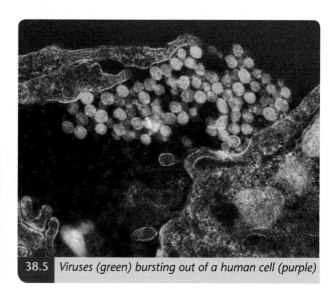

38.5 *Viruses (green) bursting out of a human cell (purple)*

Syllabus You are required to know **two** harmful examples and **one** beneficial example of viruses.

Medical and economic importance of viruses

Disadvantages of viruses

1. Human diseases

Viruses are responsible for causing a wide range of human diseases. These include common colds, influenza (flu), polio, rabies, mumps, measles, German measles (rubella), chickenpox, one form of meningitis, warts, cold sores, hepatitis, AIDS and some cancers.

2. Plant diseases

Plant diseases caused by viruses include tobacco mosaic disease (in which the leaves of the plant develop a spotted, mosaic appearance), potato mosaic disease and tomato mosaic disease.

3. Animal diseases

Common animal diseases caused by viruses are foot and mouth, rabies, distemper, cowpox and myxomatosis.

Benefits of viruses

1. Genetic engineering

Viruses are sometimes used to transfer genes from one organism to another in genetic engineering. Such viruses are called vectors.

2. Control of infections

Bacteriophages may be used to control bacterial infections. In this way, they may help to reduce infections by antibiotic-resistant bacteria.

THE ORGANISM

AIDS

Cause

AIDS is a disorder in which the person cannot make antibodies. This is due to infection with HIV.

Transmission

HIV enters the body in fluids such as blood and semen. The most common methods of transmission are sexual intercourse, infected blood products and shared needles. It can also be passed from mother to child across the placenta or in breast milk.

HIV is not contracted by touching, embracing, kissing where saliva is not exchanged, sharing utensils such as cups or from toilet seats.

Effects

Once the virus enters the body, it may enter a white blood cell and either remain dormant and produce no effects, or disable the white blood cell.

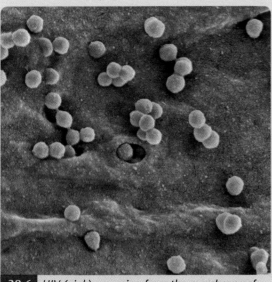

38.6 *HIV (pink) emerging from the membrane of an infected white blood cell*

When the virus is dormant a person can be identified as having HIV by testing his/her blood for antibodies against HIV. If these antibodies are present, it indicates that the person has the virus, and is said to be HIV-positive. Unfortunately, these antibodies do not disable the virus. This is because the virus mutates (changes) very rapidly to a different form.

The type of white blood cell affected by HIV is a lymphocyte called a helper T cell. The virus disables these cells, which results in the person being unable to produce antibodies.

The result of not producing antibodies is that the ability to resist infection is severely reduced. Consequently, AIDS sufferers die of opportunistic infections (e.g. pneumonia), which they would normally be able to fight off.

While accurate figures are difficult to obtain, it is thought that about 34 million people worldwide suffer from AIDS. The number of AIDS cases is growing by about 2.5 million every year (especially in developing countries). There are about 6000 people in Ireland living with AIDS.

Control and prevention

At present there is no cure or vaccine for AIDS. However, recent discoveries in medication can reduce the complications and prolong life for those with AIDS.

Prevention is vital in controlling the spread of AIDS. The main methods of prevention are:

- Avoid sexual intercourse
- Confine sexual intercourse to one faithful partner
- Use a condom during intercourse
- Do not use shared needles, toothbrushes or razors
- Avoid contact with blood and body fluids (i.e. wear gloves when treating another person's wounds)
- Those with AIDS or who have tested positive for HIV antibodies should not donate blood, semen or body organs.

Control and immunity

- Viruses are controlled by the body's general defence system (e.g. skin, mucus, stomach acid and phagocytes) and the specific defence system (i.e. antibodies are produced to disable viruses).
- In addition, immunity to many virus infections can be produced artificially by vaccination or by injecting antibodies.
- Antibiotics kill bacteria but do *not* affect viruses.
- Interferons are a range of substances produced by virus-infected cells to protect healthy cells. They can be made artificially and can help to treat colds and other virus infections.
- A wide and growing range of antiviral drugs are used to treat virus infections. These drugs interfere with viruses without affecting the host (a difficult objective as the two are so closely linked).

THE ORGANISM

Summary

Viruses:
- Are tiny
- Consist of a protein coat (capsid) and nucleic acid (either DNA or RNA)
- Are non-cellular
- Do not have cell organelles
- Are borderline between living or non-living
- Can be round, rod-shaped or complex in shape
- Are obligate parasites.

Retroviruses have a protein coat, RNA, and an enzyme to convert RNA to DNA.

A **bacteriophage** (or phage) is a virus that infects a bacterium.

A **virus replicates** by sending its nucleic acid into a live host cell and using the host to produce new viruses.

The **disadvantages of viruses** are that they cause:
- Human diseases
- Plant diseases
- Animal diseases.

The **advantages of viruses** are that they:
- Transfer genes from one organism to another
- Can be used to control bacterial infections.

Viruses may be controlled by:
- The general body defences
- The production of antibodies
- Vaccination
- Drugs (partially).

Revision questions

1 Describe the structure of viruses.

2 'Viruses have no ribosomes, but have got protein walls.'
   (a) Why is this statement an apparent contradiction?
   (b) Explain how it can be true.

3 List five differences between viruses and bacteria.

4 (a) What name is given to virus multiplication?
   (b) How does this process differ from reproduction?
   (c) Outline how viruses increase in numbers.
   (d) 'We give ourselves the flu.' Explain why this statement can be considered to be true.
   (e) Why are viral diseases so difficult to treat with drugs?

5 Explain (a) bacteriophage, (b) retrovirus and (c) obligate parasite, in terms of viruses.

6 Explain why viruses are sometimes considered to be non-living.

7 Say whether the following diseases are caused by a virus, bacterium or fungus: wheat rust, rabies, ringworm, colds, lockjaw, potato mosaic, apple mildew, cold sores, pneumonia, athlete's foot, AIDS, syphilis, myxomatosis, thrush, mumps, measles, potato blight, foot and mouth.

8 (a) Distinguish between HIV and AIDS.
   (b) How can AIDS be prevented?
   (c) Explain why a person could be HIV-positive but not suffer from AIDS.
   (d) Name the type of blood cell attacked by HIV.
   (e) Explain why AIDS patients suffer from so many other infections.

9 (a) Why do viruses not cause decay?
   (b) Why are viruses not grown on agar plates in laboratories?
   (c) Suggest why it might be dangerous to work with viruses in a laboratory.

Exam questions

Section A

10 The diagram shows a virus attached to a host cell.

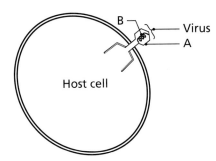

(a) **(i)** What is part A made of ?

(ii) What is part B made of?

(b) Briefly describe how viruses reproduce

(c) During 2009 swine flu spread through the population of many countries. Younger people were more at risk of becoming ill with swine flu than older people. Using your knowledge of the immune system, suggest a reason for this.

(2010 HL Q 6)

Section C

11 (a) **(i)** Comment briefly on the difficulty in classifying viruses as living organisms.

(ii) Name **two** diseases of humans caused by viruses.

(2005 HL Q 15)

12 (b) Just over fifty years ago the myxoma virus was brought to Ireland. The disease for which it is responsible in rabbits, myxomatosis, quickly decimated the wild population. Now, however, the disease is much less common and is responsible for far fewer deaths.

(i) Why do you think that the rabbit population was decimated when the myxoma virus was first brought to Ireland?

(ii) Suggest a reason why myxomatosis is no longer a major threat to the Irish rabbit population.

(iii) The use of one species to control the population of another species is called biological control. Suggest **one** advantage and **one** disadvantage of biological control.

(iv) The human immunodeficiency virus (HIV) is responsible for AIDS in the human population. Would you expect a similar trend to that shown by myxomatosis as time passes? Explain your answer.

(v) Outline briefly how a virus replicates (reproduces).

(2008 HL Q 15)

13 (c) The diagram shows the structure of a type of virus.

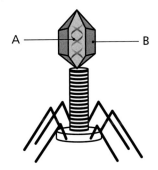

(i) Name the parts labelled A and B.

(ii) State **two** harmful effects of viruses.

(iii) What is meant by the term *immunity*?

(iv) The skin is an important part of our immune system. Outline **two** ways in which the skin provides immunity.

(v) To help the immune system, many people receive vaccinations during their lifetime. What is meant by the term *vaccination*?

(vi) Antibiotics are usually not given to a person suffering from a viral infection. Suggest a reason for this

(2011 OL Q 15)

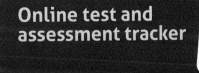

Previous examination questions

Ordinary level	Higher level
2009 Q 12c	2005 Q 15a
2011 Q 15c	2007 Q 14b
	2008 Q 15b
	2009 Q 15c
	2010 Q 6

Latest questions at www.edco.ie/lcbiologyplus/examhelp

Online test and assessment tracker

Scan the QR code and test yourself on chapter 38
www.edco.ie/lcbiologyplus

THE ORGANISM

Chapter 39 Sexual reproduction in flowering plants

Introduction

The ability to produce offspring of the same species as the parent is one of the characteristics of life. Reproduction ensures that the traits of the parent and species are transmitted to succeeding generations.

Reproduction has two basic functions.

- It replaces those organisms that die. This maintains the continuity of the species.
- It allows for an increase in numbers when conditions are suitable.

Asexual and sexual reproduction

Asexual reproduction

Asexual reproduction involves only one parent.

Asexual reproduction does not require meiosis and **does not involve sex cells** (gametes).

In asexual reproduction, the offspring are genetically identical to the parent. This is because all the cell divisions are by **mitosis**. Genetically identical offspring produced by asexual reproduction form a family called a clone.

Sexual reproduction

Sexual reproduction **involves two parents**. Each parent typically produces sex cells called gametes. In order to halve the chromosome number in the formation of gametes, **meiosis is essential for sexual reproduction**.

Two gametes fuse to form a diploid cell called a zygote.

The offspring produced as a result of sexual reproduction show **variations** due to the mixing of genes from two parents. As variations are the basis for evolution, sexual reproduction is more advantageous to a species than asexual reproduction.

> **Sexual reproduction** involves the union of two sex cells or gametes.
>
> **Gametes** are haploid cells capable of fusion.

Structures and functions of the parts of a flower

Receptacle

The receptacle is the part of the flower from which the flowering parts arise. It supports these parts.

Sepals

Sepals are originally green, leaf-like structures. Once the flower opens out the sepals often turn brown. The function of sepals is to protect the flower when it is a bud.

Petals

In animal-pollinated plants, petals are large and brightly coloured to attract animals (especially insects). In wind-pollinated plants, petals are small (or absent) and green.

Stamens

> **Stamens** are the male parts of the flower.

Each stamen consists of a thin stalk or filament. This contains a vascular bundle to bring food and water up to the anther. The anther produces pollen grains on its inside as a result of meiosis.

Carpels

> **Carpels** are the female parts of the flower.

Each carpel has three parts:
- A **stigma** where the pollen lands
- A **style** through which the pollen tube grows
- An **ovary**, which contains one or more ovules.

> Note the spelling difference between a carpel (part of flower) and a carpal (a bone in the wrist).

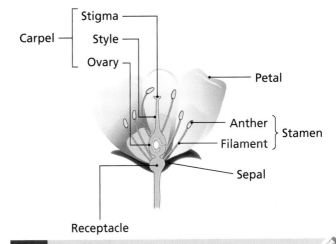

39.1 *Structure of a flower*

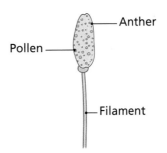

39.2 *Structure of a stamen*

39.3 *Anthers surrounding a stigma and style*

THE ORGANISM

439

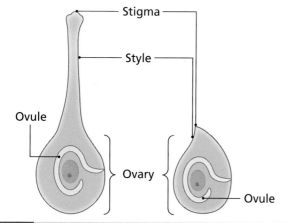

39.4 Structure of two different carpels

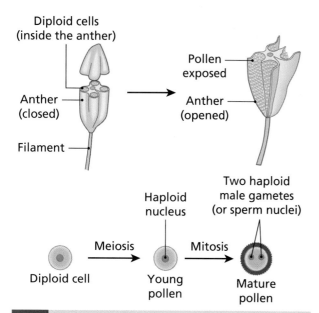

39.5 Development of anther and pollen

Meiosis occurs in the ovule to produce a structure called the embryo sac. After fertilisation the ovule becomes the seed and the ovary becomes the fruit.

Formation of sex cells (or gametes)

Male gamete formation

The cells lining the inside of the anther are diploid. Meiosis takes place in some of these cells to produce **pollen grains** containing a single haploid nucleus. Each pollen grain divides by mitosis to form the male sex cells or male gamete nuclei (also called sperm nuclei).

Pollen grains are formed on the inside of the anther. When the pollen grains are fully developed, the anther splits and peels back so that the pollen grains are exposed on the outside of the anther.

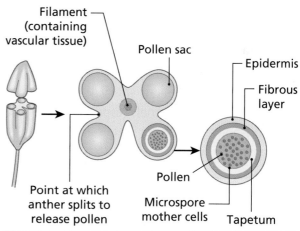

39.6 Transverse section (TS) of an anther

Structure of pollen sac

An anther consists of four chambers called pollen sacs. Each pollen sac is enclosed by a protective epidermis and fibrous layer. The tapetum is a nutrient-rich layer of cells located just inside the fibrous layer.

Pollen grain development

Inside each pollen sac are a number of diploid microspore mother cells, also called pollen mother cells. These cells divide by meiosis to produce a cluster of four haploid cells called a tetrad. Each tetrad soon breaks up to form four separate haploid pollen grains. Pollen grains are also called microspores.

39.7 Pollen grains from different plant species

THE ORGANISM

HIGHER ▼

HIGHER ▼

Each pollen grain divides by mitosis while still in the pollen sac, to produce two haploid nuclei, the tube and generative nuclei. Both the tube and generative nucleus are haploid. The tube nucleus will form the pollen tube (as described later) and will then degenerate. The generative nucleus will divide by mitosis to form the male gametes (this last division may happen in the pollen sac or in the pollen tube as described later).

Structure of mature pollen grain

Each pollen grain has a thick outer wall called the **exine**. The exine often has a very distinctive pattern, which is specific to the type of plant. The exine is made of a very durable material that allows it to survive for long periods of time. The **intine** is a thin, inner coat on a pollen grain.

Pollen grains are not gametes, as they do not join with other cells (i.e. they are not involved in fertilisation). In fact, the pollen grains form the male sperm nuclei, which are the gametes.

When the pollen grains have matured, the walls of the anther become dry and they shrivel. This results in the splitting (dehiscing) of the anther walls. The pollen grains are then exposed on the outside of the anther.

Female gamete formation

Development of the embryo sac

Each ovule is composed of a number of diploid cells. One of these cells divides by meiosis to form a single haploid cell called the **embryo sac**. This cell then undergoes mitosis three times to form eight haploid nuclei.

The embryo sac has eight nuclei. Five of these die. The others are the egg cell and the two polar nuclei.

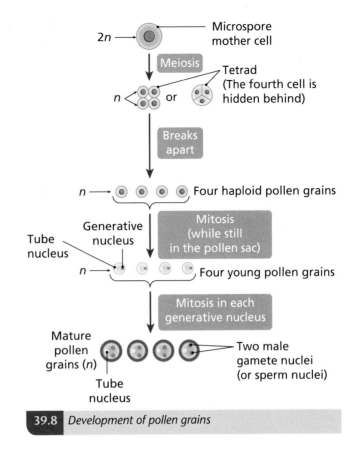

39.8 *Development of pollen grains*

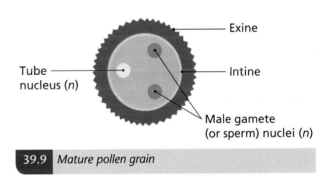

39.9 *Mature pollen grain*

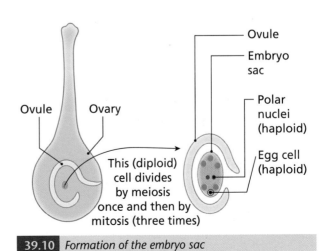

39.10 *Formation of the embryo sac*

THE ORGANISM

441

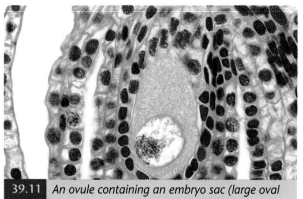

39.11 *An ovule containing an embryo sac (large oval in centre), which in turn contains a megaspore mother cell (white circle)*

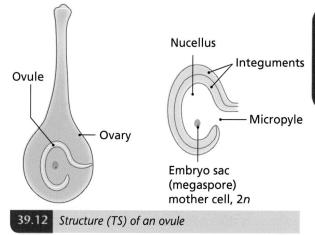

39.12 *Structure (TS) of an ovule*

Structure of the ovule

Each ovary contains one or more ovules. An ovule has two walls, called integuments. The integuments have a small opening, the micropyle, through which a pollen tube can enter. The bulk of the ovule consists of diploid nucellus cells that supply nutrients for later growth in the ovule. One cell, low down in the ovule, is called the megaspore mother cell (or the embryo sac mother cell).

Formation of the embryo sac

The megaspore (or embryo sac) mother cell is diploid and divides by meiosis to form four haploid cells. Three of these cells degenerate and die off. The remaining cell is the embryo sac (also called the megaspore because it is large).

The haploid nucleus of the embryo sac divides by mitosis three times to form eight haploid nuclei. These are contained in the embryo sac, which swells using food supplied by the nucellus. Of the eight nuclei, five take no further part in reproduction and degenerate. The three remaining nuclei form the female gametes.

- Two of the female gametes form the polar nuclei in the embryo sac.
- The remaining female gamete forms a thin cell wall and becomes the egg cell.

By the time the embryo sac is mature the carpel will appear as shown in diagram 39.14.

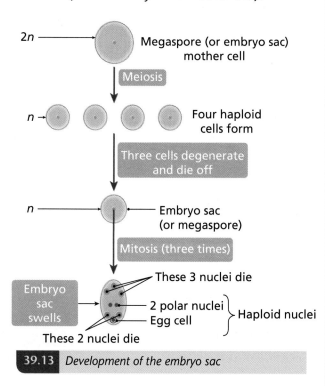

39.13 *Development of the embryo sac*

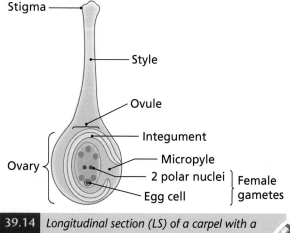

39.14 *Longitudinal section (LS) of a carpel with a mature embryo sac*

Pollination

Self-pollination leads to self-fertilisation, which is an extreme form of inbreeding. The resulting seeds may be less sturdy and vigorous. Some cereals are self-pollinated.

Cross-pollination results in cross-fertilisation and the seeds formed show more variation and vigour. Plants use many techniques to ensure cross-pollination occurs.

Methods of pollination

Plants cannot move from place to place. In order to get the male gametes to reach the female gametes, plants use either wind or animals (self-pollination does not need any external agents in order to take place).

Wind

Wind was the original form of pollination used by plants. It is very wasteful of pollen. Examples of wind-pollinated plants are conifers, grasses, oak, hazel and alder.

Animals

Animals provide a more advanced form of pollination. They are more precise in carrying pollen directly to a stigma and so less pollen is wasted. The most common animal pollinators are insects. However, bats and birds can also carry pollen. Examples of insect-pollinated plants are orchids, dandelions, primroses, snapdragons, daisies and buttercups.

39.15 *Pollen (yellow) with developing pollen tube on a stigma (pink)*

39.16 *Wind pollination*

39.17 *A bee covered in yellow pollen*

Pollination is the transfer of pollen from an anther to a stigma of a flower from the same species.

Self-pollination involves the transfer of pollen from an anther to a stigma on the same plant.

Cross-pollination involves the transfer of pollen from an anther to a stigma on a different plant.

	Adaptations of flowers to wind and insect pollination	
	Wind pollination	**Animal pollination**
Petals	Small (or absent), not brightly coloured (green), no scent, no nectaries	Large, brightly coloured, scented, have nectaries (these contain nectar, i.e. sugary water)
Pollen	Large amounts, light, small, dry, smooth	Small amounts, heavy, large, sticky
Anthers	Large, outside petals, loosely attached to filament	Usually small, inside petals, firmly attached to filament
Stigmas	Large and feathery, outside petals	Usually small and sticky, inside petals

THE ORGANISM

443

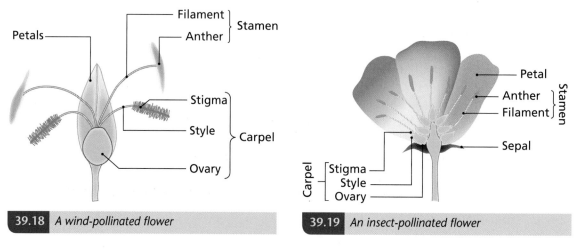

| **39.18** | *A wind-pollinated flower* |

| **39.19** | *An insect-pollinated flower* |

Flowers show many adaptations to suit their method of pollination. Some of these adaptations are outlined in the previous table and shown in diagrams 39.18 and 39.19.

> Hay fever is an allergic reaction to the inhalation of particles of certain harmless substances. The substance that triggers the allergic reaction is called an allergen. The most common allergens are pollen grains, but others include fungus spores, animal skin or scales, house dust and house dust mites.
>
> The normal symptoms of hay fever (also called allergic rhinitis) are inflammation of the mucous membranes in the nose, sneezing and a blocked and runny nose, along with watery and irritated eyes.
>
> Hay fever affects up to 10% of the population. It can be reduced by avoiding the allergen (which can be identified by skin tests). Treatments include decongestant drugs to clear the nose, antihistamines to reduce inflammation and other drugs that partially inhibit the allergic response.

Fertilisation

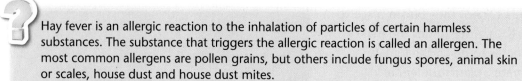

Fertilisation is the union of the male and female gametes to form a diploid zygote.

When a pollen grain lands on a stigma it is stimulated to grow by sugars produced by the stigma. A pollen tube grows down through the style towards the ovule.

The growth of the pollen tube is controlled by a nucleus, which degenerates when the pollen tube reaches the opening of the ovule (the micropyle).

The pollen tube grows towards chemicals released from the ovule. This is an example of chemotropism.

The two haploid male gamete nuclei move down through the pollen tube. The presence of a pollen tube means that the male gametes of flowering plants can move towards the egg without the need for external water. This is a major adaptation towards life on dry land.

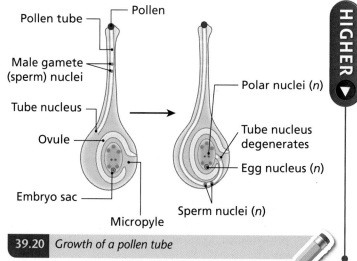

| **39.20** | *Growth of a pollen tube* |

HIGHER

THE ORGANISM

Double fertilisation

Flowering plants are unique in having a double fertilisation.

- One sperm nucleus (n) joins with the egg nucleus (n) to form a diploid ($2n$) zygote. This zygote will develop into an embryo (i.e. the young plant).

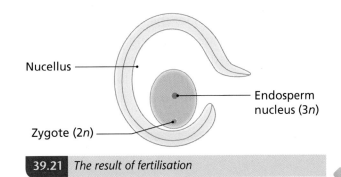

39.21 *The result of fertilisation*

- The second sperm nucleus (n) joins with the two polar nuclei (both n) to form a triploid ($3n$) endosperm nucleus.

Seeds

Seed formation

The fertilised ovule becomes the seed. The walls of the ovule (integuments) dry up to become the wall of the seed (testa).

The zygote ($2n$) grows repeatedly by mitosis. It forms a group of cells that give rise to the embryo ($2n$) or young plant. The embryo consists of the future root (the radicle) and the future shoot (the plumule).

39.22 *An immature seed*

Some of the embryo cells grow to form one or two leaves. These embryonic leaves are the seed leaves or cotyledons. Monocots have one cotyledon and dicots have two. Cotyledons are simple seed leaves, which may become swollen with stored food, especially in dicots.

At the same time, the endosperm nucleus ($3n$) divides repeatedly by mitosis to produce many endosperm cells ($3n$). These expand and absorb the nucellus. The endosperm acts as a food store. The main foods stored by seeds are fats (or oils), protein and starch.

The **radicle** is the part of the plant embryo that develops into a root.

The **plumule** is the part of the plant embryo that develops into the shoot.

A **cotyledon** is a seed leaf.

A **non-endospermic seed** has no endosperm when fully formed.

An **endospermic seed** contains some endosperm when fully formed.

Endospermic and non-endospermic seeds

In time, the cotyledons will continue to grow and absorb the endosperm. If all the endosperm is absorbed by the cotyledons, the seed is said to be **non-endospermic** (e.g. broad bean, peanut, sunflower).

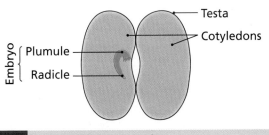

39.23 *A non-endospermic seed*

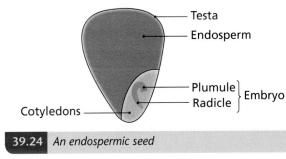

39.24 *An endospermic seed*

If the cotyledons only absorb some of the endosperm, the seed is said to be **endospermic**, i.e. some endosperm remains in the seed. Examples of endospermic seeds are maize and corn.

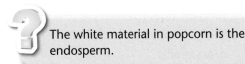
The white material in popcorn is the endosperm.

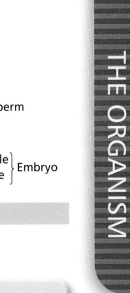
THE ORGANISM

The energy needed for the growth of a seed comes from the nucellus (which is absorbed by the endosperm, and then by the cotyledon or cotyledons) and from food that enters the seed from the parent plant.

When a seed is fully formed it loses most of its water. This slows down the development of the embryo and allows dormancy to begin.

39.25 *A whole peanut (left) and a split peanut: note the embryo at the top of the cotyledon in the middle image*

Monocot and dicot seeds

Number of cotyledons

- As explained in Chapter 23, monocots (monocotyledons) are plants in which the seed has only one cotyledon, e.g. cereals, grasses, daffodils.
- Dicots (dicotyledons) have two cotyledons in each seed, e.g. peanuts, broad beans, sunflowers.

Food storage

Monocots and dicots also differ in the way they store food in the seed.

- In monocots, food is stored in the endosperm (and is rarely stored in the cotyledons). The growing embryo absorbs food stored in the endosperm. Endospermic seeds are mostly monocots.
- In dicots, food is stored in the cotyledons. This means that most dicots have non-endospermic seeds.

Fruit

Fruit formation

As the seed is developing, the surrounding ovary becomes the fruit. The process of fruit formation is stimulated by growth regulators (auxins) produced by the seeds.

The wall of the ovary becomes the wall of the fruit (the pericarp). Fruits are designed to protect the seed(s) and to help in seed dispersal.

Some fruits are succulent or fleshy, e.g. tomatoes, grapes, peaches and plums.

Other fruits are dry. These include pea pods, green beans, monkey nuts (peanuts in the shell), popcorn grains and grass grains.

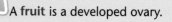
A **fruit** is a developed ovary.

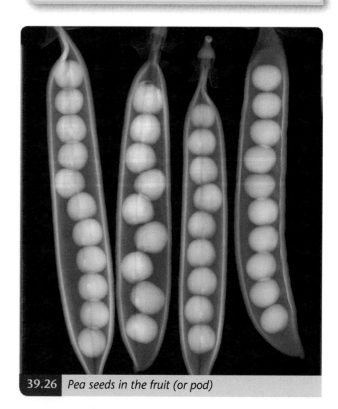

39.26 *Pea seeds in the fruit (or pod)*

Grains (such as grass and cereals) are called fruits because they have an internal seed and the fruit wall is attached to the seed wall.

Once the fruit forms, the rest of the flower parts die and fall away.

	Before fertilisation	After fertilisation
	Changes in flower after fertilisation	
1	Ovule	Seed
2	Integuments	Testa (seed coat)
3	Nucellus	Endosperm → cotyledon(s)
4	Egg	Zygote → embryo (plumule, radicle, cotyledon(s))
5	Polar nuclei	Endosperm
6	Ovary	Fruit
7	Ovary wall	Pericarp (fruit coat or wall)

Seedless fruit

The development of a fruit without a seed is called parthenocarpy (or parthenocarpic fruiting). This is a form of virgin birth, in that the egg is not fertilised.

Seedless fruit can be formed in two ways.

- Some seedless fruits arise genetically, either naturally or by special breeding programmes. Examples include bananas, grapefruit, pineapples, seedless oranges and grapes.
- Another way to produce seedless fruit is to spray plants with growth regulators. If large concentrations of growth regulators (e.g. auxins) are sprayed on flowers, fruits may form without fertilisation or the production of seeds. Examples include seedless grapes, peppers, cherries, apricots, peaches and some types of seedless tomato.

In addition to stimulating seedless fruits, growth regulators also cause fruits and vegetables to grow larger.

Ethene as a growth regulator

Along with the role of plant growth regulators in producing seedless fruits with more stored food, the plant growth regulator ethene (or ethylene) is used commercially to ripen many fruits. For example, ethene gas is pumped into large storage containers where it ripens fruits such as bananas, melons and tomatoes.

Ethene is also used to 'de-green' fruits by causing the breakdown of chlorophyll. This process takes place in the three previously named fruits as well as in oranges, lemons and grapefruit.

 Carbon dioxide inhibits the production of ethene. For this reason fruits such as apples can be stored in containers through which carbon dioxide is circulated. This allows apples to be picked in autumn and stored for use in the following summer.

Fruit and seed dispersal

 Dispersal is the transfer of a seed or fruit away from the parent plant.

Dispersal is necessary to:
- Avoid large numbers of seeds competing with each other and with the parent plant
- Increase the chance of survival for the plant
- Find new areas for growth
- Increase the numbers of the species.

THE ORGANISM

447

39.27 *Wind dispersal in a dandelion*

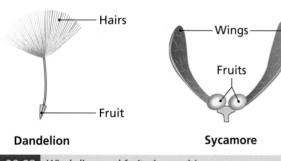

Hairs

Wings

Fruits

Fruit

Dandelion

Sycamore

39.28 *Wind-dispersed fruits (or seeds)*

39.29 *A plant burr (containing many fruits) attached to wool: the hooks were the inspiration for 'Velcro-like' fasteners*

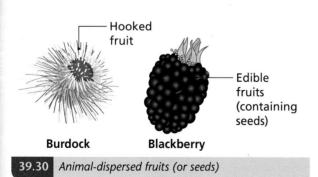

Hooked fruit

Edible fruits (containing seeds)

Burdock

Blackberry

39.30 *Animal-dispersed fruits (or seeds)*

The main methods of seed dispersal are wind, water, animal and self-dispersal.

Wind dispersal

- Orchids produce small, light seeds. This is an advantage because they are easily dispersed. However, the young plant (embryo) has very little food supply to nourish it in the early days of growth.
- Dandelions, thistles and clematis produce parachute devices that help to disperse the seeds more widely.
- Sycamore and ash produce fruit with wings. These fruits spiral down to the ground and increase the distance over which the seeds may be dispersed.

Water dispersal

Coconut trees, alders and water lilies have light, air-filled fruits that float. This allows them to be dispersed by rivers or streams, or even by the sea (as happens with coconuts).

Animal dispersal

Animal dispersal is very successful because animals can carry seeds or fruits long distances and tend to live where seeds have a chance of growing. Fruits dispersed by animals have either of two major adaptations.

1 Sticky fruits

Fruits with hooks (called burrs) may cling to an animal's hair or fur and be carried away. These seeds are dispersed by attaching to the external surface of the animal. Examples of these fruits include burdock, goose grass and buttercup.

2 Edible, fleshy or succulent fruits

These fruits attract animals by being brightly coloured with strong scents and plenty of food. The animal eats and digests the fruit but the seeds pass through the intestine unharmed. These seeds are released with the faeces, which even acts as a fertiliser for them. Examples include strawberries, tomatoes, blackberries, acorns and other nuts (which are dispersed when they are accidentally dropped).

Self-dispersal

Some fruits have explosive mechanisms that catapult the seeds away. These fruits often have pods that dry out and split open (dehisce). Examples are peas, beans and gorse.

THE ORGANISM

Seeds flung out

Seeds

Fruit wall splits open

Dries out

Fruit (pea-pod)

39.31 *Self-dispersal*

Dormancy

Dormancy is brought about in a number of ways.

- Growth inhibitors (such as abscisic acid) may be present in the outer part of the seed. These inhibitors delay growth until they are broken down by water, cold or decay.
- The testa (seed coat) may be impermeable to water or

> **Dormancy** is a resting period when seeds undergo no growth and have reduced cell activity or metabolism.

oxygen. Eventually the testa decays and breaks down, allowing water and oxygen to enter the seed.

- The testa may be too tough to allow the embryo to emerge.
- There may be a lack of a suitable growth regulator needed to stimulate growth. The regulator may be produced due to increased light or temperatures in spring.

Dormancy in agriculture and horticulture

Many seeds need a cold period to break dormancy. The cold may cause the breakdown of growth inhibitors or the production of growth promoters such as auxins.

Special conditions may be necessary to break dormancy in seeds before they are planted for agricultural or horticultural use. These conditions include:

- Soaking the seeds in water
- Physical damage (e.g. scraping them with fine sandpaper) to break the testa
- Exposing the seeds to light or dark
- Exposing the seeds to cold temperatures (e.g. placing them in a fridge).

Advantages of dormancy

- It allows the plant to avoid the harsh conditions of winter.
- It gives the embryo time to develop fully.
- It provides time for the seed to be dispersed.
- It maximises the growing season for the young seedling, i.e. by starting growth in spring the plant is well developed by autumn.
- It helps the survival of the species because the duration of dormancy varies. This means that some seeds always remain dormant in the soil and form what is called a **seed bank**. These dormant seeds can grow following the elimination of the mature plants by natural (or human-made) disasters.

Germination

> **Germination** is the regrowth of the embryo, after a period of dormancy, if the environmental conditions are suitable.

Germination involves the regrowth of the embryo, because the zygote initially grows to form the embryo, which then remains dormant for some time. When germination occurs, the embryo resumes its growth.

39.32 *A germinating seed: the radicle (with many root hairs) is growing towards gravity (geotropism)*

THE ORGANISM

Conditions necessary for germination

- **Water** is needed to allow enzyme reactions to occur. The seed absorbs water from the soil. This causes the seed to swell (and increase in weight) and allows enzymes to function.
- **Oxygen** is needed for aerobic respiration. It is absorbed from the soil.
- A **suitable temperature** is needed to allow enzyme reactions to take place. Each species has its own preferred temperature for germination. Suitable temperatures are usually between 5 and 30°C.
- Dormancy must be complete.

Events in germination

Seeds store food in the form of oils, starch (especially in cereals and grasses) and protein (especially in legumes such as peas and beans).

1. Germination begins when the seed absorbs water. Water is absorbed through a tiny hole called the micropyle and through the testa. Water allows enzymes to be activated in the seed.
2. In germinating seeds, oils are digested to fatty acids and glycerol, starch is digested to glucose (which involves the enzyme amylase) and proteins are digested to amino acids.
3. The products of digestion are moved to the growing embryo (i.e. the plumule and radicle).
4. Glucose and amino acids are used to make new structures such as cell walls and enzymes.
5. The fats and some of the glucose are used in respiration to produce energy.
6. The dry weight (mass) of the seed falls due to the foods used in respiration.
7. As the weight of the food stores (i.e. the endosperm and/or cotyledon(s)) falls, the weight of the embryo increases.
8. The radicle bursts through the testa.
9. The plumule emerges above ground and leaves are produced.
10. Once the first leaves start to photosynthesise, the dry weight of the seedling increases again.

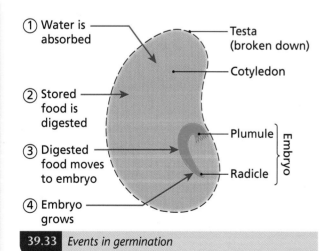

39.33 *Events in germination*

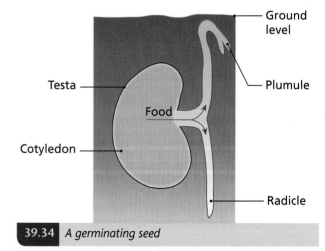

39.34 *A germinating seed*

Changes in the dry weights of germinating seeds

When weighing plant material, dry weight (or mass) is normally used. This is the weight without water. Dry weight is measured by placing the plant in an oven at 100°C until the weight remains constant. Normally about 20 seeds are used and the average weight (or mass) is calculated. This allows for the different sizes of the seeds.

The changes in the dry weights of the parts of a germinating seed can be seen on graphs, as shown in diagram 39.35.

In graph A, the weight (mass) of the seed falls between days 0 and 9, due to respiration. From day 9 on, it increases due to photosynthesis taking place in the newly formed leaves.

In graph B, the loss of weight of the cotyledon is matched by a rise in the weight of the embryo. This suggests that food is passing from the cotyledon to the embryo.

The stages in seedling growth

Cotyledons remain below soil

Broad beans are an example of germination in which the cotyledons remain below the soil.

- In this type of germination, the seed absorbs water, enzymes become active and the radicle begins to grow.
- The radicle bursts out through the testa (seed coat) and grows down due to geotropism.
- The plumule emerges.
- The plumule grows up through the soil and its delicate leaves are protected by the plumule being hooked over.
- The cotyledons (and endosperm, if present) shrivel as food is transferred from them. The radicle develops into the primary (or tap) root, which forms many side roots.
- Once above the ground, the plumule straightens up and produces the first true leaves. These soon become green and start to photosynthesise.

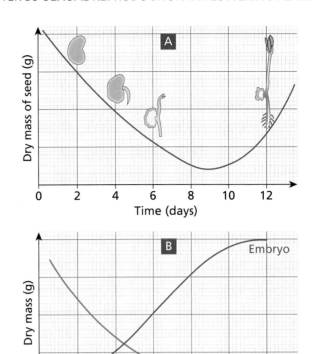
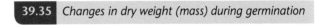

39.35 *Changes in dry weight (mass) during germination*

39.36 *Germination in a broad bean*

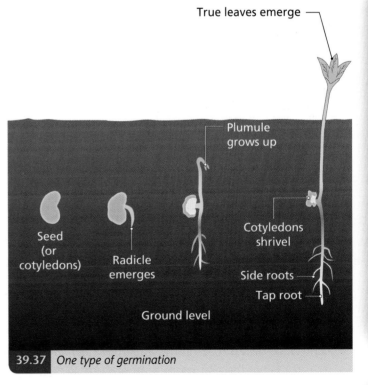

39.37 *One type of germination*

Cotyledons move above the soil

Sunflower seeds are an example of germination in which cotyledons move above the soil. (Sunflower 'seeds' are in fact fruits, with the fruit wall (pericarp) and the seed wall (testa) being fused.)

This form of germination is similar to the previous form of germination, with the following differences.

- The cotyledons are forced above the soil.
- Once above the soil, the fruit wall (pericarp) falls to the ground. The cotyledons open out, become green and photosynthetic. The plumule emerges from between the cotyledons and forms the first true leaves.

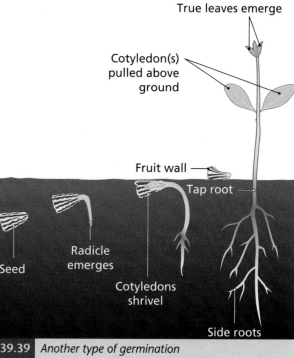

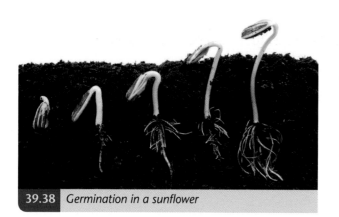

| 39.38 | *Germination in a sunflower* |

| 39.39 | *Another type of germination* |

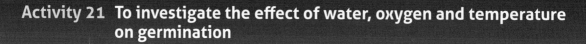

Activity 21 To investigate the effect of water, oxygen and temperature on germination

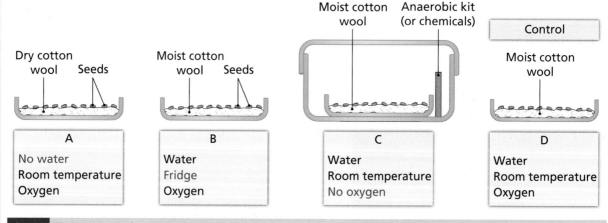

| 39.40 | *To investigate the conditions needed for germination* |

1. Place equal amounts of cotton wool in the base of four petri dishes.
2. Label the dishes A, B, C and D.
3. Add water to the cotton wool in dishes B, C and D. Leave dish A dry.
4. Place 10 small seeds (e.g. radish or cress) on the surface of the cotton wool in each dish.
5. Place dish B in a fridge (low temperature).
6. Place dish C in an anaerobic jar, activate the anaerobic-producing chemical and seal the jar.
7. Place dishes A, C (in the anaerobic jar) and D, which is the control, in an incubator at 25°C (or leave them at room temperature, 20°C).

8. Check the dishes each day for 2 to 3 days. The seeds in the control dish should germinate, while those in the other dishes should not germinate as result of each dish missing one vital condition.
9. Record the results as shown below.

Results			
Dish	Conditions present	Conditions absent	Germination (yes/no)
A	Suitable temperature Oxygen	Water	
B	Water Oxygen	Suitable temperature	
C	Water Suitable temperature	Oxygen	
D	Water Suitable temperature Oxygen	None (control)	

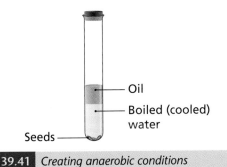

Oil
Boiled (cooled) water
Seeds

Note 1: Test tubes can be used instead of petri dishes.
Note 2: Anaerobic conditions can be created in another way. To remove oxygen, boil water vigorously and allow it to cool. Place seeds in the boiled water and add a layer of oil to prevent oxygen diffusing into the water.

39.41 *Creating anaerobic conditions*

Activity 22 To use starch agar or skimmed milk plates to show digestive activity during germination

Note: This activity allows the use of starch agar or skimmed milk plates. Starch agar plates are used in the following account.
Seeds contain the enzyme amylase. In this activity, amylase breaks down starch in the agar plates.
1. Soak four large seeds (e.g. broad bean) in water for a day or two.
2. Wash the bench with disinfectant (to kill bacteria and fungi).
3. Kill two of the seeds by boiling them in water for 5 minutes (these will act as controls).
4. Use a backed blade (for safety) to split the four seeds in half. Cut away from your fingers (to prevent cutting yourself).
5. Sterilise the half seeds by soaking them in alcohol or mild disinfectant for 10 minutes.
6. Wash off the alcohol or mild disinfectant with water.
7. Flame a forceps using a bunsen burner and allow it to cool (this sterilises it).
8. Barely open a petri dish containing starch agar (to prevent bacteria or fungi from entering).
9. Using the forceps, place four of the cut, **unboiled**, half seeds face down onto the starch agar in one dish. (This allows the amylase in the seed to come in contact with starch in the petri dish). Label this dish A.
10. Re-flame the forceps and use it to place four cut, **boiled**, half seeds face down in another dish. Label this dish B. (These act as controls).
11. Place the covered dishes in a warm place for 2 days.
12. Remove the half seeds and add dilute iodine solution to the dishes (to test for starch).
13. After 2 minutes pour off the iodine.

THE ORGANISM

453

14. Observe the results.

- In dish A the agar under the seeds will stay clear, while the rest of the agar will turn blue-black. This is due to the digestive action of the enzyme amylase formed by the germinating seeds. The enzyme breaks down starch so that there is no reaction with iodine.
- In dish B all the agar will turn blue-black. This is because amylase was denatured by boiling. Starch is not broken down.

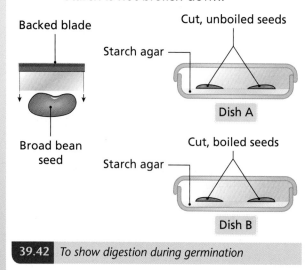

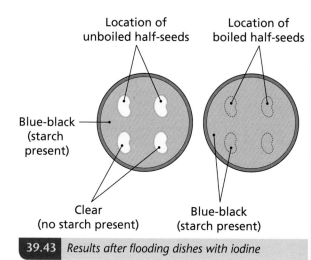

39.42 *To show digestion during germination*   **39.43** *Results after flooding dishes with iodine*

Summary

Asexual reproduction:
- Involves only one parent
- Produces identical offspring.

Sexual reproduction:
- Involves the fusion of two sex cells (gametes)
- Produces non-identical offspring.

The **main parts of a flower**
- The receptacle supports the flower parts.
- Sepals protect the flower when it is a bud.
- Petals may attract animals (especially insects).
- Stamens (male) consist of a filament and anther. The anther produces pollen.
- Carpels (female) consist of a stigma, style and ovary. The ovary contains the ovule(s), which produce(s) the embryo sac.

Pollen grains produce male gametes.

Pollen development involves:
- Meiosis occurring in the pollen sac (part of the anther) to produce haploid pollen grains
- Each pollen grain later producing two male gametes and a tube nucleus.

The **embryo sac** produces female gametes called the egg cell and the (two) polar nuclei.

Embryo sac development involves:
- Meiosis occurring in the ovule to produce a haploid embryo sac
- The embryo sac later producing eight haploid nuclei by mitosis:
  - Five of these nuclei die
  - Two nuclei form the polar nuclei
  - The remaining nucleus forms the egg cell
  - The polar nuclei and egg cell are the gametes.

The **food supply in the ovule** is the nucellus.

The **integuments** are the walls of the ovule.

Pollination is the transfer of pollen from an anther to a stigma.
- Self-pollination occurs when the anther and stigma are on the same plant.
- In cross-pollination, the anther and stigma are on different plants.

Methods of cross-pollination are wind and animals (especially insects).

Wind-pollinated flowers have:
- Small, green petals with no scent or nectar
- Huge amounts of light, dry pollen
- Large, loosely held anthers, outside petals
- Large, external feathery stigmas.

HIGHER

THE ORGANISM

Animal-pollinated flowers have:
- Large, coloured petals with scent and nectar
- Small amounts of heavy, sticky pollen
- Small, firmly held anthers, inside petals
- Small, internal stigmas.

Fertilisation is the union of male and female gametes.

The **pollen tube** grows down the style to the embryo sac.

Double fertilisation occurs in flowering plants as follows:
- A sperm nucleus (n) + the egg nucleus (n) → zygote ($2n$)
- The second sperm nucleus (n) + the two polar nuclei (n) → endosperm ($3n$).

After fertilisation:
- The ovule becomes the seed
- The integuments become the testa
- The endosperm ($3n$) absorbs the nucellus ($2n$)
- The zygote ($2n$) grows into the young plant (or embryo, $2n$)
- The ovary forms the fruit
- The wall of the ovary forms the fruit wall (pericarp).

The **embryo** has the following parts:
- The plumule (future shoot)
- The radicle (future roots)
- Cotyledon(s) (seed or embryonic leaf or leaves).

In monocots:
- One cotyledon develops from the embryo
- The food is normally stored in the endosperm.

In dicots:
- Two cotyledons emerge from the embryo
- The cotyledons usually absorb food from the endosperm
- If all the endosperm is absorbed, the seed is non-endospermic
- If some of the endosperm remains, the seed is endospermic.

Fruits protect and disperse seeds.
Fruits may be:
- Fleshy or succulent (tomatoes, grapes, oranges)
- Dry (pea pods, cereal grains).

Seedless fruits form due to:
- Genetic breeding programmes
- Treating flowers with growth regulators.

Ethene is a growth regulator used to:
- Remove the green colour from fruits
- Ripen fruits.

Dispersal is the carrying of the seed as far as possible from the parent plant.

The **methods of seed dispersal** are:
- Wind ● Water ● Animal ● Self.

Dormancy is a resting period when seeds reduce their metabolism and do not grow.

Dormancy is brought about:
- By growth inhibitors
- If the testa is impermeable to water or oxygen
- If the testa is too tough
- By the lack of a growth promoter.

The **advantages of dormancy** are:
- The seedling avoids growing in winter
- The embryo has time to develop
- There is time for dispersal
- It allows the seedling the maximum growing season
- It allows some seeds to survive in the soil.

Germination is the regrowth of the embryo after dormancy, under suitable conditions.

The **conditions required for germination** are:
- Water ● Suitable temperature
- Oxygen ● Dormancy completed

The **main events in germination** are:
- The seed absorbs water
- Stored foods are digested to simpler forms by enzymes in the seed
- Digested foods are transferred from the endosperm or cotyledon(s) to the embryo
- Some digested foods make new structures; some are used in respiration
- The radicle grows and bursts out through the testa
- The plumule emerges above ground and new leaves develop.

In **one form of germination** the cotyledons stay below ground, e.g. broad bean.

In **another form of germination** the cotyledons move above ground to form the first leaves, e.g. sunflower.

To investigate the effect of water, oxygen and temperature on germination:
- Grow a number of small seeds (e.g. radish) on damp cotton wool in a warm place (these seeds should germinate and act as a control)
- Grow three different sets of radish seeds:
  ‣ On dry cotton wool
  ‣ In a cold fridge
  ‣ In anaerobic conditions.

THE ORGANISM

- The three sets of seeds described do not germinate due to the lack of water, a suitable temperature and oxygen, respectively.

To show that germinating seeds produce digestive enzymes:
- Place halved, sterile, soaked seeds on starch agar
- Leave in a warm place
- Remove the halved seeds and add iodine after a few days

- The starch is digested by enzymes in live seeds (clear areas occur, surrounded by blue-black agar)
- The starch is not digested by dead (boiled) seeds (no clear areas occur, i.e. all the agar is blue-black).

Revision questions

HIGHER ▼

1. (a) Distinguish between asexual and sexual reproduction.
   (b) State the type of cell division involved in each type of reproduction.
   (c) Say which type of reproduction is more advanced and give a reason for your answer.

2. State whether the following parts are male or female:
   (a) Stamen   (e) Ovule
   (b) Style   (f) Stigma
   (c) Ovary   (g) Carpel
   (d) Filament   (h) Anther.

3. (a) What is the function of a flower?
   (b) Name the structures labelled A to E on the flower in diagram 39.44.

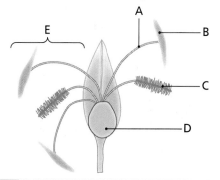

39.44

   (c) Is this flower wind- or insect-pollinated? Give two reasons, visible on the diagram, to support your answer.
   (d) In which two labelled parts does meiosis occur?

4. Name the cell in each case in which
   (a) male gametes and
   (b) female gametes are formed.

5. Distinguish between:
   (a) Microspores and megaspores
   (b) Tapetum and tetrad
   (c) Tube and generative nucleus
   (d) Exine and intine.

6. (a) Name the cell division at X and Y in diagram 39.45.

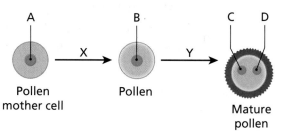

39.45

   (b) What is the ratio between the chromosome number of the nuclei at A and B?
   (c) Name the nuclei at C and D.
   (d) One of the nuclei labelled C and D will divide again. Name the type of cell division involved and state the significance of the products.

7. Explain why cross-pollination is of more advantage than self-pollination.

8. Which of the three pollen grains shown in diagram 39.46 is most likely to be animal-pollinated? Explain your reasoning.

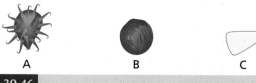

39.46

9. What structure in flowering plants has reduced the need for external water in fertilisation?

THE ORGANISM

10 (a) What is meant by double fertilisation in flowering plants?
    (b) Name the products of double fertilisation.
    (c) State the location of double fertilisation.

11 If a plant has a diploid number of 20 chromosomes, state how many chromosomes are present in each of the following:
    (a) A pollen nucleus
    (b) The egg nucleus
    (c) A cell from the stigma
    (d) The zygote
    (e) A nucellus cell
    (f) An endosperm nucleus
    (g) A cotyledon cell
    (h) A cell from the fruit.

12 (a) What is a cotyledon?
    (b) Distinguish between the number of cotyledons in monocots and dicots.

13 Name the structures from which each of the following develop prior to fertilisation:
    (a) Seeds   (d) Fruit
    (b) Testa   (e) Pericarp.
    (c) Endosperm

14 (a) What is the advantage of seedless fruit to humans?
    (b) What is the disadvantage of such fruit to the plant?

15 Name one growth regulator in each case responsible for:
    (a) Forming seedless fruit
    (b) Breaking down chlorophyll in fruit walls
    (c) Producing larger fruit.

16 (a) What is seed dispersal?
    (b) Suggest one advantage of seed dispersal.
    (c) Name three methods of seed dispersal and name one plant example in each case.

17 (a) What is dormancy?
    (b) State two methods used by plants to ensure their seeds remain dormant.
    (c) List two advantages of dormancy.

18 Suggest one reason in each case for each of the following practices used in sowing seeds.
    (a) Placing the seeds in a fridge or cold place overnight
    (b) Making a small cut in the seed coat
    (c) Soaking the seeds in water
    (d) Not sowing the seeds too closely
    (e) Storing seeds for a year before sowing them.

19 (a) What is germination?
    (b) Name the three main conditions necessary for germination.
    (c) Suggest one reason why each of the named conditions is necessary.

20 When investigating the need for certain factors in germination:
    (a) Name the three factors investigated.
    (b) Outline how you removed each factor.
    (c) What factors were present in the control apparatus?
    (d) Why was a control apparatus necessary?
    (e) Why were a number of seeds used in each apparatus rather than single seeds?

21 Choose which of the options (i), (ii), (iii) or (iv) represents the correct answer in each case below.
    (a) The nucellus provides nutrients for:
        (i) The nucleus (ii) The ovary
        (iii) The ovule (iv) The integuments.
    (b) The wall of a fruit is called:
        (i) The testa (ii) The parthenocarpy
        (iii) The pod (iv) The pericarp.
    (c) Which of the following conditions is not normally required for germination? (i) Light (ii) Oxygen
        (iii) A suitable temperature (iv) Water.
    (d) The triploid part of a seed is called:
        (i) The testa (ii) The cotyledon
        (iii) The zygote (iv) The endosperm.
    (e) During fertilisation, the tube nucleus degenerates as soon as the pollen tube arrives at: (i) The micropyle
        (ii) The cotyledons (iii) The ovary
        (iv) The style.

THE ORGANISM

Exam questions

Section A

22 The diagram shows the external structure of a stamen.

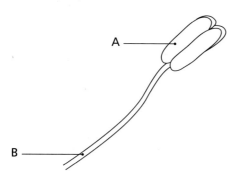

(a) Name A and B.
(b) Where is pollen produced, in A or in B?
(c) To which part of a flower is pollen carried?
(d) What is meant by cross-pollination?
(e) Name two methods of cross-pollination.

(2005 OL Q 3)

Section B

23 (a) (i) What is meant by the germination of seeds?
       (ii) Seeds may remain inactive for a period before germination. What term is used to describe this period of inactivity?
    (b) Answer the following questions about an investigation that you carried out on the effect of water, oxygen and temperature on germination.
       (i) What seeds did you use?
       (ii) Explain how you set up a control for the investigation.
       (iii) How did you deprive some of the seeds of oxygen?
       (iv) How did you ensure that some of the seeds were deprived of a suitable temperature for germination?
       (v) State the results of the investigation, including those of the control.

(2008 OL Q 9)

24 (a) (i) What is meant by *germination*?
       (ii) Why is digestion necessary in a germinating seed?
    (b) (i) Digestive activity during germination can be demonstrated by using agar plates. What is an agar plate?
       (ii) An extra food material is added to the agar plate for this demonstration. Give an example of such an extra food material.
       (iii) Outline the procedures that you carried out in setting up this demonstration.
       (iv) What control did you use for this demonstration?

(v) What procedure did you carry out in order to show that digestive activity had taken place?
(vi) Describe the results that you obtained in:
  1. The experimental plate.
  2. The control plate.

(2009 HL Q 8)

25 (b) (iii) What type of agar plates did you use when investigating the digestive activity of seeds?
       (iv) How did you demonstrate that digestive activity had taken place in the investigation referred to in part (iii)?

(2012 HL Q 7)

Section C

26 (a) The diagram shows a vertical section through a carpel.

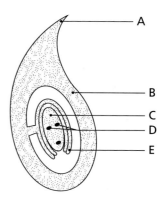

(i) Name A, B, C, D, E.
(ii) What happens to the two nuclei labelled D?
(iii) In the case of B and E state what may happen to each of them after fertilisation.
(iv) Copy the diagram into your answer book and add a pollen tube that has completed its growth. Label the nuclei in the pollen tube.

(2004 HL Q 14)

27 (a) (i) From what structure in the carpel does the seed develop?
       (ii) State **two** locations in the seed where food may be stored.
       (iii) The embryo plant within the seed has a number of parts. List **two** of these parts, apart from food stores, and give a role for each of them.
       (iv) Following dispersal, the seed undergoes a period of dormancy. What is dormancy?
       (v) Suggest **two** advantages of dormancy.

(2007 HL Q 14)

THE ORGANISM

28 (a) The diagram shows the structure of a flower.

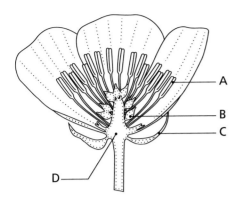

     (i) Name the parts labelled A, B, C, D.
    (ii) In which labelled part is pollen produced?
   (iii) What is meant by pollination?
   (iv) From the list below, choose **three** characteristics in each case of:
      1. an insect-pollinated flower,
      2. a wind-pollinated flower.
      brightly coloured petals, feathery stigmas, anthers within petals, anthers outside petals, nectaries, petals reduced or absent.
    (v) What process follows pollination in the life cycle of a flowering plant?

                        (2008 OL Q 14)

29 (a) Give a role for **each** of the following parts of a flower: sepals, anther, stigma.
   (b) (i) Describe the development of pollen grains from microspore mother cells.
     (ii) What is meant by the term *fertilisation*?
    (iii) Give a brief account of the process of fertilisation in flowering plants.
   (c) (i) What is meant by the *dormancy* of seeds?
     (ii) Give **one** way in which the dormancy of seeds is of benefit to plants.
    (iii) Suggest **one** way in which a knowledge of dormancy is useful to farmers and gardeners.
    (iv) Water, oxygen and a suitable temperature are all required for the germination of seeds. In the case of **each** of these factors describe its effect on the process of germination.
    (v) Which part of the embryo in a germinating seed gives rise to each of the following parts of the seedling?
      1. The root   **2.** The shoot.

                        (2010 HL Q 13)

30 (a) (i) Name the **two** main types of reproduction.
     (ii) Explain the term *fertilisation*.
   (b) The flower is the organ of reproduction in many plants.
     (i) What part of the flower produces pollen?
     (ii) After fertilisation, what part of the flower becomes the fruit?
    (iii) Give **two** methods of seed dispersal in plants.
    (iv) Why is it necessary for plants to disperse their seeds?
    (v) What is the advantage of dormancy to seeds?
    (vi) Give **three** conditions necessary for seeds to germinate.

                        (2012 OL Q 12)

31 (a) (i) Give a brief account of the role of **each** of the following in flowering plant reproduction.
      1. Petal.   **2.** Anther.
      3. Stigma.
     (ii) Name **one** structure through which the pollen tube grows in order to reach the embryo sac.
    (iii) Within the pollen tube the generative nucleus divides to form two male gametes.
      1. What type of division takes place?
      2. With what does **each** male gamete fuse in the embryo sac?
      3. Name the product of **each** fusion.
    (iv) As the seed forms following fertilisation, a food store develops in one of two structures. Name any **one** of these structures.

                        (2012 HL Q 14)

Previous examination questions

Ordinary level	Higher level
2004 Q 14	2004 Q 14a
2005 Q 3, 9	2005 Q 3g, j
2006 Q 9, 14c	2006 Q 7, 14a
2007 Q 14c	2007 Q 14a
2008 Q 9, 14a	2009 Q 8, 15c
2009 Q 9, 14c	2010 Q 13
2010 Q 14c	2012 Q 7b(iii), (iv), 14a
2011 Q 15a	
2012 Q 12a, b	

Latest questions at www.edco.ie/lcbiologyplus/examhelp

Online test and assessment tracker

Scan the QR code and test yourself on chapter 39
www.edco.ie/lcbiologyplus

THE ORGANISM

Chapter 40 Vegetative propagation

> **Vegetative propagation (or vegetative reproduction)** is asexual reproduction in plants.
>
> **Natural vegetative propagation** involves forming new plants from a stem, root, leaf, or bud.

Introduction

Vegetative propagation does not involve gametes, flowers, seeds or fruits. Only one plant is involved, so the offspring are produced by a single parent plant.

Generally a specialised part of the plant separates from the parent and grows by mitosis to form a new plant. The offspring formed in this way are genetically identical to the parent.

Natural vegetative propagation

Sometimes in natural vegetative propagation the structures that are used are altered or modified for reproduction; sometimes they are not altered.

Methods of natural vegetative propagation

40.1 *A runner in a strawberry plant*

Stem

> **Runners** are horizontal stems that run (or grow) above ground and from which new plants grow.

Runners normally have long internodes. Buds are formed at each node. Each bud may give rise to a new plant, complete with its own root system. In time, the new plant will continue the process by producing its own runners (see diagram 40.2). Examples of plants with runners are strawberries and buttercups.

Root

> A **root tuber** is a swollen, underground root that remains dormant during winter and from which new plants may grow.

New shoots grow from the buds at the base of the old stem, which has withered away (see diagram 40.4). Examples of plants that have root tubers are dahlia, yam and sweet potato.

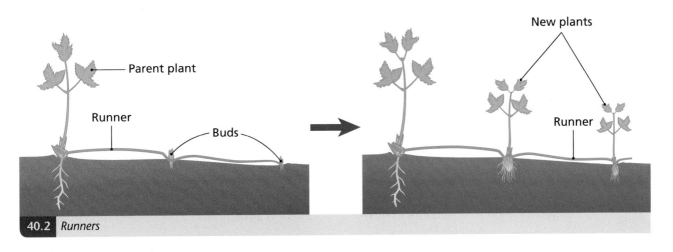

40.2 *Runners*

40.3 *Dahlia tubers*

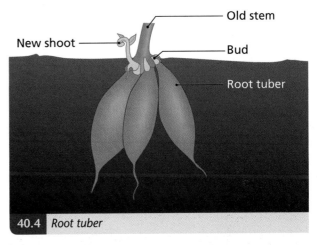

40.4 *Root tuber*

Leaf

The leaves of some plants will readily grow into new plants if they are detached from the parent plant and land in soil. Examples of plants that can be propagated from leaves are begonia, cactus and succulent plants (such as Kalanchoe).

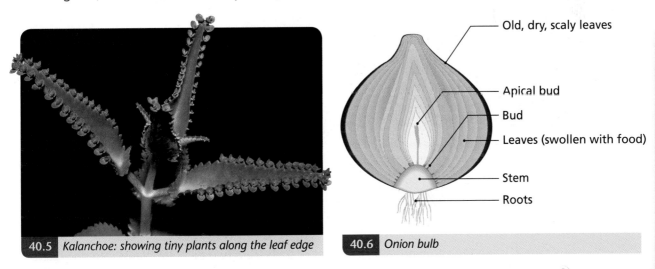

40.5 *Kalanchoe: showing tiny plants along the leaf edge*

40.6 *Onion bulb*

Buds

A bulb contains an underground stem reduced in size. Numerous leaves are attached to this stem. Each leaf is swollen with stored food. The centre of the bulb has an apical bud, which can produce leaves and a young flower. Lateral buds are located between the stem and each leaf. These buds can each form a new shoot in spring. The old leaves become dry and scaly and serve to protect the new bulb(s) inside. Examples of plants with bulbs include onion, daffodil and tulip (see diagram 40.6).

A bulb is a modified bud.

THE ORGANISM

461

Each bulb contains one or more buds. If more than one bud grows, each one will form a new shoot. Each new shoot will form a new bud at the end of its growing season. In this way, the bulbs increase in number by asexual reproduction.

Gardeners often have to dig up bulbs in autumn and replant some of them, in order to prevent overcrowding when the plants emerge from the ground.

Syllabus You are required to know any **four** methods of artificial vegetative propagation.

Artificial vegetative propagation

Apart from the natural methods of vegetative reproduction, a number of artificial methods are employed to reproduce plants by vegetative methods. These methods are widely used in horticulture (growing plants) and agriculture to propagate (reproduce) new plants that are identical to the parent.

Methods of artificial vegetative propagation

Cuttings

A cutting is a portion of a plant that is removed from the parent plant and grown into a new, independent plant.

Cuttings are parts of a plant (usually shoots) that are removed from the parent plant and allowed to form new roots and leaves. The shoot is cut at an angle and is often treated with rooting powder (a growth promoter) to speed up root formation. Plants produced from cuttings will be similar to the parents. Propagation by cuttings is a simple, cheap method of producing large numbers of similar plants. Examples of the many plants that can be propagated by cuttings are busy Lizzie, geranium and willow.

40.7 | *Geranium cutting growing in water*

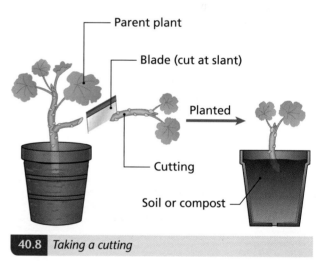

Parent plant

Blade (cut at slant)

Planted

Cutting

Soil or compost

40.8 | *Taking a cutting*

Grafting

Grafting is the joining and uniting of part of one plant with a second plant.

Grafting is used to combine useful qualities or traits from two different plants into one plant. When grafting plants, part of one plant is removed and attached to a healthy, rooted part of a second plant. To be successful the graft has to achieve good contact between the growth areas (meristems) and vascular tissue of both plants.

In roses, a plant with large flowers (but a poor root system) can be grafted to a wild rose with large roots (but with small, insignificant flowers). In this way the best features of both plants can be combined (see diagram 40.10).

Eating-apple trees can be grafted to crab-apple plants. This produces well-rooted plants that produce good-quality eating apples.

40.9 *Grafting two apple plants*

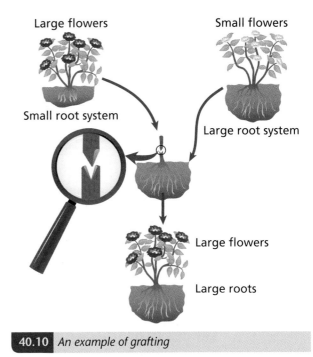

40.10 *An example of grafting*

Layering

In layering, a branch of a parent plant is bent down and covered in soil, except at the tip. The covered part forms roots and the exposed tip forms new shoots. In time the two plants may be separated. Examples of plants that may be propagated by layering are blackberries, climbing roses and spider plants. Many plants propagate naturally by layering, e.g. strawberries.

> **Layering** is the growth of a new plant from a stem that is still attached to the parent plant.

40.11 *Layering: a wire pin holds down the stem and white rooting powder is used to stimulate fast root growth*

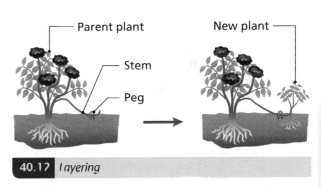

40.12 *Layering*

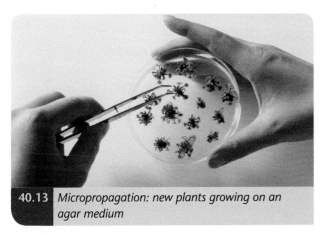

40.13 *Micropropagation: new plants growing on an agar medium*

Micropropagation

> **Micropropagation** is the growth of plants from small pieces of tissue under sterile conditions on a specially selected medium.

Micropropagation is also called tissue culturing (and is outlined in Chapter 8). It involves growing large numbers of plants from small pieces (often single cells) of a parent plant. It is an expensive and very specialised process. It is often used to produce large numbers of newly developed plants or plants that do not reproduce from seeds.

THE ORGANISM

Advantages of artificial vegetative propagation

- It is a simple and reliable process
- New plants form fast
- New plants are the same as the parents.

Disadvantages of artificial vegetative propagation

- There is a lack of variation
- Diseases can be passed from the parent to the offspring plant
- If it is carried out repeatedly the plants may lack vigour.

Comparing sexual (seed) reproduction with asexual reproduction

Sexual and asexual methods of plant propagation both have their advantages and disadvantages.

Sexual reproduction

The main advantage of seed or sexual reproduction is that the offspring possess **variations**. These variations may assist the new plants to survive in a habitat by being better adapted. For example, some of the seedlings may be resistant to a pathogen, or may be able to survive if climatic conditions change.

Additional advantages of seed reproduction include the ability of seeds to be **dispersed** widely and the possibility that some seeds may **survive** in the soil and grow when unsuitable environmental conditions improve.

Asexual reproduction

Asexual reproduction allows plants to produce many copies of themselves in a short space of time. This helps asexually reproducing plants to establish themselves very rapidly in new habitats.

In addition, the new plants are very strong because they can draw nutrients from the parent plant while they are still attached to it.

The advantages and disadvantages of each method of reproduction are outlined in the table below.

Comparison of sexual (seed) and asexual (vegetative) reproduction in plants	
Sexual (seed)	**Asexual (vegetative)**
Advantages	**Advantages**
Offspring show variations from parents (allowing evolution)	Simple process (more reliable)
Some plants may be resistant to disease	No outside agents are needed
There is less competition due to seed dispersal	Rapid growth, as young plants are attached to the parent
Some seeds may remain dormant in the soil	No waste
Disadvantages	**Disadvantages**
Complex process (less reliable)	There are no variations (although this may be an advantage to the grower)
May depend on outside agents, e.g. for pollination and dispersal	If one plant is susceptible to a disease then all plants are susceptible
Slow growth of the young plants to maturity	There is overcrowding and competition
Wasteful (e.g. petals, nectar, pollen, fruit)	No seeds are formed (i.e. no dormant structures in soil)

Summary

Vegetative propagation:
- Is asexual reproduction in plants
- Produces genetically identical offspring.

Vegetative propagation may form new plants from the following structures:
- Stems, such as runners in strawberries
- Roots, such as root tubers in dahlias
- Leaves, in cacti
- Buds, in bulbs such as onions or daffodils.

Artificial methods of vegetative propagation include:
- Cuttings – shoots that are removed from a plant and allowed to form new plants
- Grafting – a section from one plant is attached to a section of another plant
- Layering – a stem of a plant is fixed into the soil to allow it to form roots and a new plant
- Micropropagation – the growth of new plants from tiny pieces of a parent plant.

The **advantages of seed (sexual) reproduction** are:
- Variation in offspring
- More disease resistance
- Less overcrowding due to seed dispersal
- Dormant seeds survive in soil.

The **advantages of vegetative (asexual) reproduction** are:
- It is a simple process
- No external agents are needed
- Young plants show fast growth
- There is little waste.

Revision questions

1 (a) Explain what is meant by:
    (i) Asexual reproduction
    (ii) Vegetative propagation.
  (b) Name the type of cell division involved in vegetative reproduction.

2 (a) Give three examples of natural vegetative propagation.
  (b) In each case name the part of the plant that is used and give an example of a plant that reproduces in that way.

3 (a) Name three methods of artificially propagating plants.
  (b) Name one plant in each case that is propagated by the methods named.

4 Suggest a biological reason for each of the following:
  (a) Growing plants from cuttings rather than from seeds
  (b) Using growth regulators when growing cuttings
  (c) Grafting cultivated roses onto wild rose rootstock
  (d) Cherry blossom trees may have white flowers on some branches and pink flowers on other branches

  (e) Growing plants by micropropagation
  (f) Plants that reproduce vegetatively in nature may become overcrowded.

5 Give three reasons why seed reproduction is more complex than vegetative reproduction.

6 Explain why seed-grown plants often show more resistance to disease than plants that arise from vegetative propagation.

7 (a) In relation to flowering plants explain what is meant by vegetative propagation.
  (b) Clones are genetically identical individuals. Are the products of vegetative propagation clones? Explain your answer.
  (c) Give two examples of natural vegetative propagation that involve different parts of a plant.
  (d) Describe two techniques of artificial vegetative propagation that are used for flowering plants.
  (e) Suggest a benefit of artificial propagation.

THE ORGANISM

Exam questions

Section C

8 (b) (i) What is vegetative propagation?
   (ii) Give **one** example of vegetative propagation and state whether it involves a stem, a root, a leaf or a bud.
   (iii) How does vegetative propagation differ from reproduction by seed?
   (iv) Artificial propagation is widely used in horticulture. Give **two** examples of artificial propagation.
   (v) Suggest **one** advantage and **one** disadvantage of artificial propagation.
   (2005 OL Q 15)

9 (a) (i) What is meant by *vegetative propagation*?
   (ii) Horticulturists use a number of methods to artificially propagate plants. Suggest **one** advantage of artificial propagation.

   (iii) Describe **two** methods used by horticulturists to artificially propagate plants.
   (iv) Give **two** differences between vegetative propagation and propagation involving seeds.
   (v) Seeds and fruits need to be dispersed. Give:
      1. Two methods of dispersal.
      2. Two advantages of dispersal to the plant.
      (2009 HL Q 15)

10 (a) (v) Sometimes artificial methods are used to propagate (reproduce) plants. Name any **two** methods of artificially propagating plants.
   (2011 OL Q 15)

Previous examination questions

Ordinary level	Higher level
2005 Q 15b	2009 Q 15a
2011 Q 15a(v)	

Latest questions at www.edco.ie/lcbiologyplus/examhelp

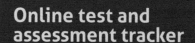

Online test and assessment tracker

Scan the QR code and test yourself on chapter 40
www.edco.ie/lcbiologyplus

Chapter 41 **Human reproduction**

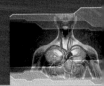

Learning objectives

- To describe the general structure and function of the male and female reproductive systems and the functions of their main parts
- To describe the role of meiosis in the production of sperm cells and egg cells (ova)
- To define the term 'secondary sexual characteristics'
- To describe the roles of oestrogen, progesterone and testosterone in human reproduction
- To describe the events of the menstrual cycle and the roles of oestrogen and progesterone
- **HIGHER** ▶ To describe the menstrual cycle in detail, including hormonal control
- **HIGHER** ▶ To describe one possible cause, prevention and treatment of endometriosis or fibroids
- To describe copulation and the four types of birth control
- To describe where fertilisation occurs
- To describe one cause in each case and the availability of corrective measures for male and female infertility
- To describe in-vitro fertilisation and implantation
- To describe implantation and the formation and function of the placenta
- **HIGHER** ▶ To describe in detail the sequence of embryonic development up to the third month
- To describe the process of birth
- To describe milk production and breastfeeding, including the biological benefits of breastfeeding.

Introduction

The human reproductive systems (male and female) are composed of three structural levels of organisation:

1. A pair of structures in both males and females to produce sex cells (gametes):
   - The testes produce the male sex cells called sperm
   - The ovaries produce the female gametes called eggs or ova (the singular is ovum).
2. A series of transport tubes.
3. A number of glands to secrete hormones that control human reproduction.

The male reproductive system

Testes

The male gonads, called the testes, develop inside the body cavity. A few weeks before birth they descend out of the body cavity into a pouch called the scrotum. The temperature in the scrotum is maintained at 35°C. At this temperature meiosis can occur, producing sperm. (Meiosis does not take place properly in males at normal body temperature, i.e. 37°C).

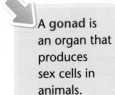

A **gonad** is an organ that produces sex cells in animals.

THE ORGANISM

467

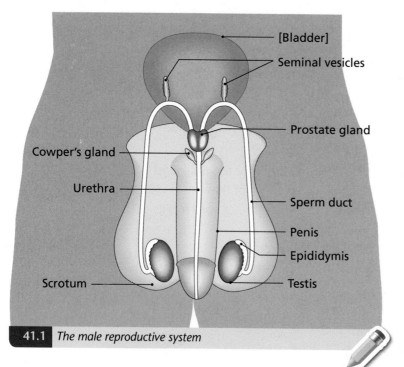

41.1 *The male reproductive system*

Each testis consists of a coiled mass of tubules (about 50 cm long in total). These tubules are lined with diploid sperm-producing cells. It is in these cells that meiosis occurs to produce haploid sperm. Cells located between the tubules produce the hormone testosterone.

Epididymis

The tubules in the testes combine to form the epididymis, which is located outside each testis (as shown in diagram 41.2). Sperm mature in the epididymis and are stored (for up to 6 weeks). If sperm are not released they are broken down in the epididymis and taken back into the bloodstream – a process called resorption.

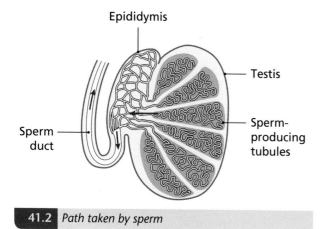

41.2 *Path taken by sperm*

Sperm duct

The epididymis leads into the sperm duct (or vas deferens). The sperm ducts carry sperm to the urethra.

 A **vas**ectomy is an operation performed to cut and seal each sperm duct or **vas** deferens. Vasectomy is a form of male sterilisation.

Urethra

The urethra is the tube located in the centre of the penis. It has the dual function of carrying urine or sperm out of the body at different times.

Associated glands

The **seminal vesicles**, the **prostate gland** and **Cowper's glands** produce a liquid called seminal fluid. When seminal fluid is added to sperm cells the resulting liquid is called **semen**. Seminal fluid provides a medium for the sperm to swim in and also nourishes the sperm (as it contains fructose).

Semen is a fluid containing sperm and seminal fluid.

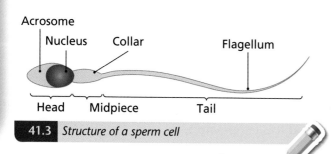

41.3 *Structure of a sperm cell*

Sperm

Sperm are produced by **meiosis**. Sperm-producing cells are diploid, i.e. they contain 46 chromosomes. They divide by meiosis to form sperm cells. Meiosis halves the number of chromosomes and so sperm cells (spermatozoa) are haploid, i.e. they contain only 23 chromosomes.

Each sperm cell contains:

- An acrosome (a region containing enzymes that can digest the membrane of the egg)
- A nucleus (containing 23 chromosomes)
- A midpiece (containing many mitochondria)
- A tail (to allow the sperm to swim).

Sperm cells are first produced in the testes at the onset of sexual maturity, called **puberty**. This occurs at about 12 or 13 years of age in males. Sperm are formed continually throughout a man's lifetime.

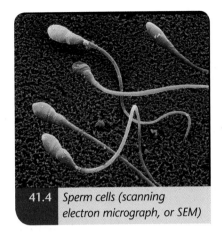

41.4 *Sperm cells (scanning electron micrograph, or SEM)*

> **Puberty** is the beginning of sexual maturity.

Penis

The penis is a structure adapted to introduce sperm into the female reproductive system. The swollen tip of the penis is called the glans. A fold of skin called the foreskin (or prepuce) partially covers the glans.

During sexual arousal more blood flows into the penis than can flow out of it. This causes the penis to become erect. In this state it can be used to place sperm into the female system.

Hormones in the male reproductive system

At puberty two hormones are produced by the male pituitary gland:

- **FSH** (follicle stimulating hormone) causes the diploid sperm-producing cells in the testes to divide by meiosis and produce haploid sperm
- **LH** (luteinising hormone) stimulates the testes to produce testosterone.

Testosterone

Androgens are male hormones. Testosterone is the main androgen. It is produced in small amounts by the testes before puberty (and by the female ovaries throughout life). Testosterone causes the primary male sex characteristics early in life, i.e. the growth of the penis and other male reproductive parts and the descent of the testes into the scrotum.

The production of testosterone increases enormously at puberty, causing the enlargement of the penis, testes and other reproductive parts. Testosterone also causes the secondary male characteristics.

Secondary male characteristics

- Growth of pubic, underarm, facial and body hair
- Enlargement of the larynx, causing the voice to break and deepen
- Increased muscular and bone development
- Widening of the shoulders
- Growth spurt (body weight may double)
- Increased secretion of sebum in the skin

> **Secondary sexual characteristics** are those features that distinguish males from females, apart from the sex organs themselves.

Male infertility

> **Infertility** is the inability to produce offspring.

> **Syllabus** You are required to know **one** cause of male infertility from the following: low sperm count, low sperm mobility or endocrine gland failure.

The main type of male infertility is the production of low numbers of sperm.

THE ORGANISM

Low sperm count

Cause

Low sperm counts may arise due to persistent smoking of cigarettes, alcohol abuse, use of marijuana or anabolic steroids or low levels of male hormones. If males suffer from mumps in adult life, this may also destroy the ability of the testes to produce sperm.

Recent evidence suggests that contact with certain chemicals used in detergents and plastics may reduce sperm counts.

Corrective measures

Treatment to correct a low sperm count consists of changes in diet and lifestyle. These include stopping smoking cigarettes, not taking any drugs, stopping or reducing alcohol consumption and reducing stress levels.

If the cause of the infertility is hormonal then hormone supplements may be administered. Sometimes in-vitro (artificial) fertilisation can be tried. This process is described later in this chapter.

Female reproductive system

Ovaries

The ovaries produce eggs and female hormones. The ovaries of a female foetus may contain up to one million potential eggs at birth. These potential eggs have not yet divided by meiosis. As a result, they are diploid, containing 46 chromosomes.

Puberty, the onset of sexual maturity, occurs in females at about 11 or 12 years of age. By the age of puberty, the number of potential eggs has fallen to about 40 000. Each potential egg is enclosed in a cluster of cells, forming what is called a follicle in the ovary. After puberty, about 20 eggs are produced by **meiosis** each month. Usually only one egg continues to grow; the rest die off.

Once meiosis is complete, a haploid egg (ovum) is surrounded by a **Graafian follicle**. The Graafian follicle produces the female hormone oestrogen. As the Graafian follicle matures, it forms a swelling (like a blister) on the surface of the ovary. The follicle bursts at ovulation to release the egg.

> **Ovulation** is the release of an egg from the ovary.

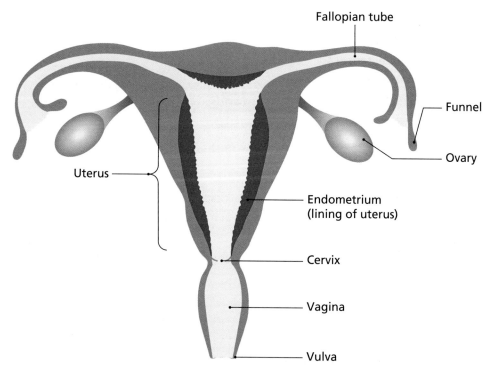

41.5 *The female reproductive system*

THE ORGANISM

After ovulation, the follicle fills with yellow cells and becomes the **corpus luteum** (or yellow body). This secretes the hormone progesterone.

Fallopian tubes

The **oviduct** is a collective term for the Fallopian tubes and the funnel. The ends of the Fallopian tubes have funnels that catch the egg after ovulation. The egg is moved along the Fallopian tube by cilia and muscular peristalsis. The egg is either fertilised or dies in the Fallopian tube.

Uterus (womb)

The uterus is a muscular structure about the size of the fist. The outer wall is made of involuntary muscle. The inner lining is called the **endometrium**. This lining thickens each month with cells and blood vessels in order to nourish the embryo in the event of pregnancy. The opening into the uterus is called the cervix.

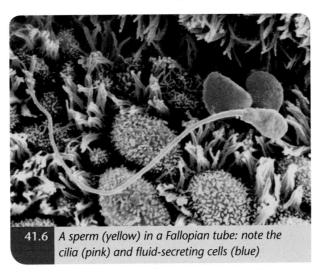

41.6 *A sperm (yellow) in a Fallopian tube: note the cilia (pink) and fluid-secreting cells (blue)*

Vagina

The vagina is an elastic, muscular tube about 10 cm long. It allows the entry of sperm into the female system and also serves as the birth canal to allow the exit of the baby.

The vagina is lined with mucous-producing cells. The urethra, which carries urine from the bladder, opens near the vagina. The labia are folds of skin that protect the vagina. Collectively they form the vulva.

The hymen is a ring of tissue that may partially block the vagina entrance. It is stretched or torn by the use of tampons or at first sexual intercourse.

The menstrual cycle

The menstrual cycle (*mensis* is the Latin for 'month') begins at puberty and continues until the **menopause**, which is the end of a woman's reproductive life (usually between the ages of 45 and 55).

> The **menstrual cycle** is a series of events that occurs every 28 days on average in the female if fertilisation has not taken place.
>
> The **menopause** is when ovulation and menstruation stop happening in a female.

The events of a typical menstrual cycle can be summarised as follows:

Days 1–5

- The old lining of the uterus (the endometrium) breaks down and is shed from the body. The loss of this blood and tissue through the vagina is called menstruation (or a period).
- Meiosis occurs in an ovary to produce a new egg. The new egg is surrounded by the Graafian follicle.

Days 6–14

- The developing Graafian follicle produces the hormone **oestrogen**. This hormone causes the endometrium to thicken again.
- Oestrogen also prevents new eggs from developing, so that normally only one Graafian follicle develops during each menstrual cycle.

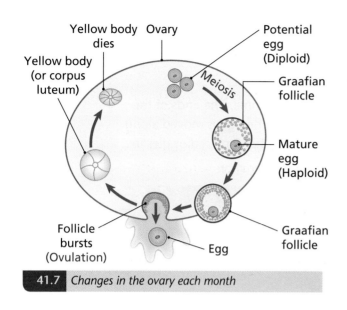

41.7 *Changes in the ovary each month*

Day 14

- Ovulation occurs when the Graafian follicle bursts to release the egg from the ovary. The egg passes into the abdomen of the female and on into the funnel of the Fallopian tube. The egg is then moved along the Fallopian tube.
- The egg is normally only available for fertilisation for up to 48 hours after ovulation.

Days 14–28

- The remains of the Graafian follicle develop into the corpus luteum (yellow body).
- The yellow body makes the hormone **progesterone** (and some oestrogen), which causes the endometrium to thicken even more.
- Progesterone also prevents new eggs from forming. The egg that was released will die by day 16 if it is not fertilised.
- If fertilisation has not taken place, the yellow body (corpus luteum) starts to degenerate around day 22. This results in a reduction in progesterone levels, which causes the lining of the uterus to break down on day 28.
- On day 28 the spongy, nutritive lining of the uterus breaks down and is released from the body through the vagina. This bleeding is called menstruation or 'a period'. The bleeding lasts for about 5 days. The onset of bleeding marks the start of a new monthly (menstrual) cycle.

> **Menstruation** is the discharge of the lining of the uterus (the endometrium) and the unfertilised egg.

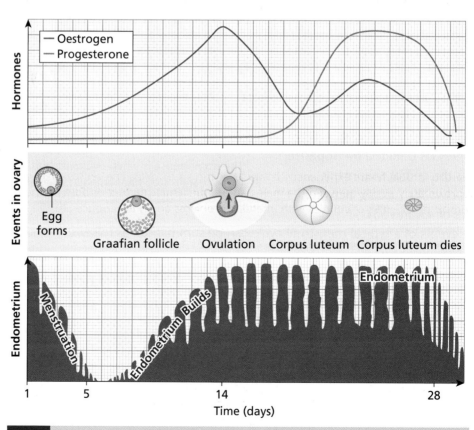

41.8 *Events during a single menstrual cycle*

Functions of oestrogen and progesterone

- Oestrogen causes the endometrium to thicken in the first half of the cycle.
- Progesterone continues this process in the second 14 days.
- Both hormones prevent (inhibit) eggs from developing. For this reason they are used in contraceptive pills.

The high levels of oestrogen produced at puberty cause the primary female sexual characteristics. These are the growth of the sex organs. The combination of oestrogen and progesterone at puberty causes the secondary female characteristics.

Secondary female characteristics

- The maturing and enlargement of the breasts
- Widening of the pelvis (to allow for birth)
- Increased body fat
- Growth of pubic and underarm hair
- Growth spurt (which is also stimulated by testosterone produced by the adrenal glands)

Female infertility (e.g. endocrine gland failure)

As mentioned earlier, infertility is the inability to produce offspring.

The most common type of female infertility is the failure to ovulate (i.e. release the egg from the ovary) due to endocrine gland failure.

Endocrine gland failure
Cause

If the pituitary gland fails to produce FSH or LH (or produces too much of either hormone) then eggs may not be produced or released by the ovaries. A lack of FSH results in the failure of eggs to form. A lack of LH results in failure to ovulate.

Corrective measures
The treatment given involves the use of hormone supplements (normally by injection of the missing hormone). As a last resort, in-vitro fertilisation may be used to achieve pregnancy (as explained later in this chapter).

Syllabus You are required to know **one** cause of female infertility from the following: blockage of the Fallopian tube or endocrine gland failure.

 Infertility problems are experienced by up to one in six couples. The causes are divided approximately evenly between the male partner, the female partner or both partners. Approximately 50% of couples with infertility problems go on to produce offspring when properly treated.

Hormonal control in the menstrual cycle

HIGHER ▼

There are four hormones involved in the menstrual cycle. Each one tends to cause the production of the hormone following it and to inhibit the preceding hormone. In the following account, each hormone is dealt with in three categories: (1) site of production, (2) time of production and (3) functions.

FSH (follicle-stimulating hormone)
1. Produced by the pituitary gland.
2. Produced early in the cycle (days 1 to 5).
3. It stimulates a few potential eggs to develop, surrounded by Graafian follicles. Only one follicle (and egg) normally survives.

THE ORGANISM

473

FSH is sometimes used in fertility treatments to stimulate the ovaries to produce eggs. Often a number of eggs develop, resulting in multiple births.

Each Graafian follicle will secrete oestrogen, so that FSH can be said to cause the production of oestrogen.

Oestrogen

1. Produced by the Graafian follicle (in the ovary).
2. Produced from days 5 to 14 (mainly).
3. It causes the endometrium to develop. It also inhibits FSH by negative feedback (ensuring no further eggs develop; hence its use in the contraceptive pill).

High levels of oestrogen just before day 14 stimulate the release of the next hormone, LH.

LH (luteinising hormone)

1. Produced by the pituitary gland.
2. Produced on day 14.
3. It causes ovulation. It then causes the remains of the Graafian follicle to develop into the corpus luteum. The corpus luteum makes the final hormone in the cycle, progesterone (along with small amounts of oestrogen).

Progesterone

1. Produced by the corpus luteum (in the ovary).
2. Produced from days 14 to 28.
3. It maintains the structure of the endometrium. It inhibits (by negative feedback) the production of FSH, which prevents further eggs from developing. It also inhibits LH so that further ovulation and pregnancies are prevented. Progesterone also prevents contractions of the uterus.

If pregnancy does not occur, the corpus luteum starts to degenerate around day 22. By day 28, low levels of progesterone (and oestrogen) produce the following effects.

- FSH secretion by the pituitary gland is no longer inhibited. As the FSH level rises, new eggs begin to develop.
- The uterus contracts and the endometrium is shed from the body. Menstruation and a new cycle have begun.

Menstrual disorder

> **Syllabus** You have to know about **one** menstrual disorder: either endometriosis or fibroids.

Fibroids

Fibroids are benign tumours of the uterus. This means they result from the overproduction of cells but they do not invade other tissues and do not spread. Fibroids are slow growing and range from the size of a pea to the size of a large grapefruit. They are most common between the ages of 35 and 45.

Small fibroids often produce no symptoms. As they enlarge they cause heavy and prolonged menstrual bleeding (which in turn leads to anaemia). They can also cause pain, miscarriage or infertility.

Cause

The cause of fibroids is uncertain. They may be an abnormal response to oestrogen. For this reason they tend to be larger in women taking the contraceptive pill.

Prevention and treatment

Small fibroids require no treatment apart from frequent examinations to check on their growth. Larger fibroids are removed by surgery. If there are large numbers of fibroids it may be necessary to remove the entire uterus, in a process called hysterectomy.

The stages of copulation

Sexual arousal

Sexual arousal in the male causes the flow of blood into the penis to increase and the blood flow out of the penis to decrease. Spongy tissue in the penis fills with blood and the penis becomes erect. In this state the penis can be inserted into the vagina.

Arousal in females results in the vagina becoming lubricated, elongated and wider.

Copulation

Copulation is also called coitus or sexual intercourse. During this process, the penis moves inside the vagina. Breathing and heart rates increase in both partners.

Orgasm

Physical and mental sensations resulting from copulation may lead to a climax in sexual excitement called orgasm. This may last from a few seconds in males to up to a minute in females.

During orgasm, muscles in the pelvis of both partners contract and heart rates, respiration and blood pressures rise dramatically. In females, the outer vagina and uterus contract. In males, the sphincter muscle from the bladder closes and contraction of the involuntary muscles in the epididymis, sperm ducts, glands and urethra discharge semen out of the penis. The propelling of semen from the penis is called ejaculation.

Normally males release 200–300 million sperm at each ejaculation. However, recent evidence suggests that males are producing and therefore releasing fewer sperm in their semen.

Copulation is the act of sexual intercourse.

Orgasm is the physical and emotional sensations experienced at the peak of sexual excitement.

Ejaculation is the release of semen from the penis.

Insemination is the release of semen into the vagina, just outside the cervix.

Behaviour of sex cells

Contractions of the uterus and Fallopian tubes can move the sperm along the Fallopian tubes within 5 minutes of insemination. If ovulation has occurred and an egg is present, it releases a chemical that attracts the sperm. The sperm swim towards the chemical released by the egg. This process is called **chemotaxis**.

Fertilisation

Events leading to fertilisation

Fertilisation occurs when the nucleus of the sperm fuses with the nucleus of the egg, forming a diploid zygote.

Many of the sperm die in the female system. This is due either to the acidic conditions in the vagina or to being attacked (as foreign objects) by white blood cells in the female system. Some sperm enter the wrong Fallopian tube, i.e. the tube that does not contain an egg.

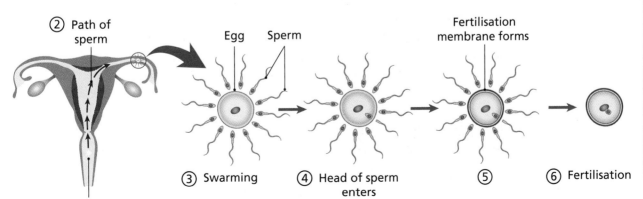

THE ORGANISM

However, many sperm reach the egg in the Fallopian tube. These sperm swarm around the egg. Acrosomes at the front end of the sperm contain enzymes that are used to digest an opening through the membrane of the egg. One sperm loses its tail and the head of the sperm enters the egg. Once the sperm has entered, the membrane of the egg undergoes a rapid chemical change, forming a fertilisation membrane. This prevents further sperm from entering.

Survival times for sperm and eggs

- The egg survives for up to 2 days.
- Sperm are nourished in the female reproductive system. This lengthens the survival time for sperm and increases the chance of fertilisation. Sperm can survive for up to 7 days in the female system.

41.10 *Sperm attempting to fertilise an egg*

Fertilisation normally takes place in the Fallopian tube. Fertilisation may result if copulation takes place in the interval from up to 7 days before ovulation to 2 days after ovulation (as the egg dies 2 days after ovulation).

In a typical menstrual cycle the most fertile time is normally considered to be days 12 to 16. However, fertilisation can sometimes occur if intercourse happens before or after these days.

Many women do not have regular menstrual cycles. Also it is common for irregular cycles to occur in women whose cycle is normally very regular. For these reasons fertilisation may occur if intercourse happens between days 7 and 18.

> Implantation is the embedding of the fertilised egg into the lining of the uterus.

Implantation

Implantation happens about 6 to 9 days after fertilisation. By this time the zygote has grown to form an **embryo**.

During implantation a membrane called the amnion develops around the embryo. The amnion secretes amniotic fluid, which will surround and protect the embryo (by acting as a shock absorber). For the first 4 weeks the developing embryo gets nutrients directly from the lining of the uterus (the endometrium). As the embryo gets bigger nutrients are supplied by the placenta.

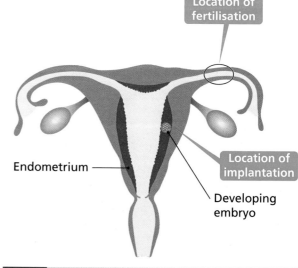

Location of fertilisation

Endometrium

Location of implantation

Developing embryo

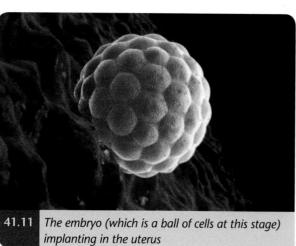

41.11 *The embryo (which is a ball of cells at this stage) implanting in the uterus*

41.12 *Locations of fertilisation and implantation*

THE ORGANISM

In-vitro fertilisation and implantation

IVF may be used for females whose Fallopian tubes are blocked or who fail to release eggs naturally. It is also used to allow males with low sperm counts to have offspring.

IVF involves giving the female fertility drugs in the first week of her menstrual cycle. These drugs stimulate several eggs to develop. On day 14 the eggs are surgically removed from the ovary. They are then mixed with sperm in a dish (often a glass petri dish is used). The term 'in-vitro fertilisation' literally means fertilisation *in glass*.

Two days later the eggs are examined microscopically to see if they have developed into embryos. If embryos have formed, a number of these embryos are put into the uterus to allow them to implant naturally. The woman

> **In-vitro fertilisation (IVF) involves removing eggs from an ovary and fertilising them outside the body.**

41.13 | *IVF: eggs being added to sperm in a petri dish*

is checked regularly in the following days to ensure that implantation has occurred. Once implantation is successful the pregnancy normally proceeds in the usual way.

> Women treated with IVF often have multiple births (i.e. twins or triplets) because a number of the embryos implant and develop. Babies born as a result of IVF are often (wrongly) called test-tube babies. While fertilisation may take place 'in glass', the baby develops normally in the uterus for 9 months (exactly as naturally fertilised babies do).

Placenta

Placenta formation

Soon after implantation, the embryo forms an outer membrane called the chorion. This completely surrounds the amnion and the embryo. The chorion develops large chorionic projections called villi, which, together with the blood vessels of the mother in the endometrium, form the placenta.

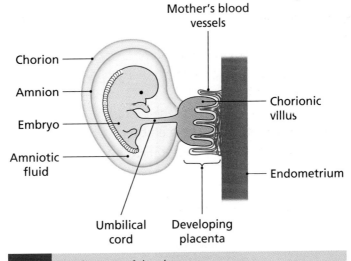

41.14 | *Development of the placenta*

The placenta starts to function after 4 weeks and becomes fully functional about 3 months into the pregnancy. The placenta is the only animal organ that is formed from the tissues of two different individuals (i.e. the embryo and the mother).

The umbilical cord connects the embryo (at the navel) with the placenta. It contains blood vessels that take blood from the embryo out to the placenta and back to the embryo again.

THE ORGANISM

477

Functions of the placenta

Exchange

The placenta allows gases, nutrients, waste, antibodies, drugs and some hormones and micro-organisms to be exchanged between the blood of the mother and of the embryo. This exchange happens mainly by diffusion.

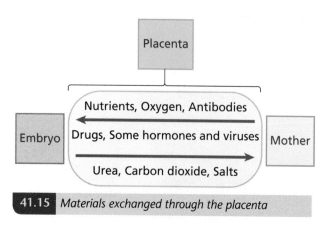

41.15 *Materials exchanged through the placenta*

Prevents bloods from mixing

The blood supplies of the mother and embryo do **not** mix. The separation of the two blood supplies is essential for two reasons.

1. The blood groups might not be compatible, which would lead to damage to red blood cells.
2. The blood pressure of the mother's system would cause damage to the embryo.

Hormone production

The placenta also produces the hormone progesterone (as outlined on page 481).

Early development of zygote

Day 1

Fertilisation occurs on day 1. The fertilised egg or zygote contains 46 chromosomes. Half of these are from the egg and half from the sperm. However, most of the cytoplasm (and all of the mitochondria) in the zygote comes from the egg.

> A **morula** is a solid ball of cells formed from a zygote by mitosis.

Day 3

During the first 3 days the zygote divides rapidly by a series of mitotic divisions to produce two cells, then four, eight, sixteen, etc. After about 3 days, a solid clump of cells, called the **morula**, has formed.

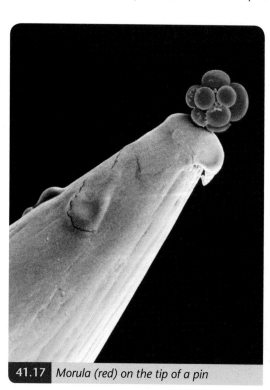

41.17 *Morula (red) on the tip of a pin*

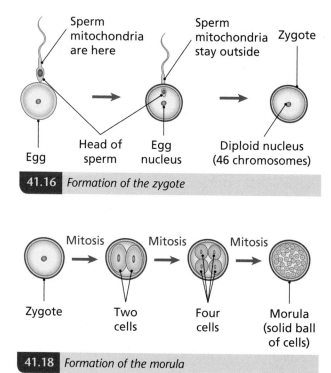

41.16 *Formation of the zygote*

41.18 *Formation of the morula*

HIGHER ▼

Day 5

Around 5 days after fertilisation, the morula forms a hollow ball of a few hundred cells called the **blastocyst**.

The outer cells of the blastocyst form the trophoblast. This will later form the membranes around the embryo. The inner cells of the blastocyst (called the inner cell mass) will later form the embryo.

The blastocyst is pushed down the Fallopian tube into the uterus.

> A blastocyst (or blastula) is a hollow ball of cells formed from a morula.

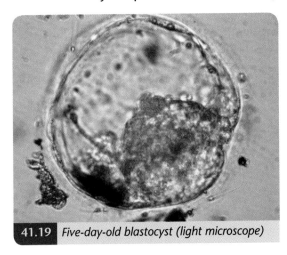

41.19 *Five-day-old blastocyst (light microscope)*

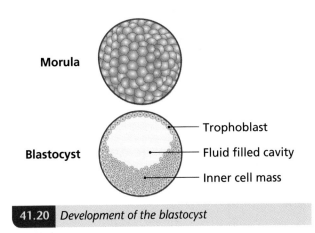

Morula

Blastocyst — Trophoblast
— Fluid filled cavity
— Inner cell mass

41.20 *Development of the blastocyst*

Embryonic development

Day 10

About 10 days after fertilisation, the cells of the inner cell mass of the blastocyst form three layers of cells called primary **germ layers**: the ectoderm, mesoderm and endoderm.

In humans, the middle layer of cells (the mesoderm) is divided into an outer and inner layer. The gap between them is called a coelom and it allows space for complex organs such as the heart, lungs and kidneys to develop.

Each germ layer gives rise to specific structures in the developing embryo (as shown in the table below). Animals (such as humans) that arise from three germ layers have more complex organ systems than those that arise from only two cell layers (e.g. jellyfish, which lack a mesoderm).

> Germ layers are basic layers of cells in the blastocyst from which all adult tissues and organs will form.

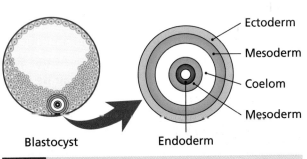

Ectoderm
Mesoderm
Coelom
Mesoderm

Blastocyst   Endoderm

41.21 *The three germ layers of the embryo*

Embryonic development	
Germ layer	**Organ or system produced**
Ectoderm	Skin, nails, hair, nervous system
Mesoderm	Muscles, skeleton, excretory system, respiratory system, circulatory system, reproductive system
Endoderm	Inner lining of digestive, respiratory and excretory systems; liver and pancreas

Stem cells are unspecialised (undifferentiated) cells that can give rise to many different types of tissue. They are found in the blastocyst (and also in red bone marrow and other places in the body). Research is ongoing into the use of stem cells to form, renew or repair damaged body parts.

THE ORGANISM

Embryonic development up to 8 weeks

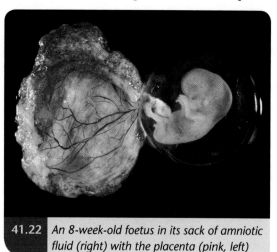

41.22 *An 8-week-old foetus in its sack of amniotic fluid (right) with the placenta (pink, left)*

The heart forms and starts to beat in the embryo in the first 4 weeks after fertilisation. The brain develops and the umbilical cord forms. By the fifth week, the internal organs and the limbs have started to form. By the sixth week, the eyes are visible and the mouth, nose and ears are forming.

By the eighth week, the tail has diminished. The face is human and the major body organs are formed. Ovaries or testes are distinguishable. Bone is beginning to replace cartilage. At this stage the embryo is recognisably human and is called a **foetus**.

Embryonic development up to 3 months

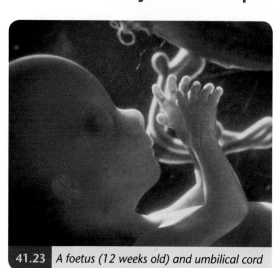

41.23 *A foetus (12 weeks old) and umbilical cord*

From the eighth week onwards the foetus grows and refines the structures already formed. During the remainder of the pregnancy the foetus does not produce any more organs. The last 7 months of the pregnancy involve the growth of the foetus (along with the enlargement of the mother's uterus and abdomen).

By the end of the third month (12 weeks) the eyes are low in the face and are widely spaced. Bones grow to replace cartilage (called ossification). The nerves and muscles become coordinated, allowing the arms and legs to move. The foetus sucks its thumb, kicks and forms milk teeth beneath the gums.

Although it is exchanging gases and excreting waste through the placenta, the foetus is seen to take amniotic fluid in and out of its mouth. It even urinates and releases faeces into the amniotic fluid. At this stage the external sex organs have formed and the gender of the foetus can be seen in scans.

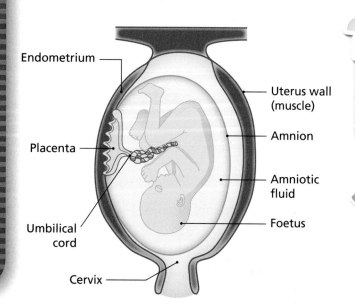

Endometrium

Placenta

Umbilical cord

Cervix

Uterus wall (muscle)

Amnion

Amniotic fluid

Foetus

41.24 *Foetus in the uterus*

? The embryo and foetus are particularly sensitive to radiation and drugs (including alcohol and smoke) in the first 3 months of development. This is due to the formation of tissues, organs and systems in this time.

Gestation

➤ **Gestation** is the length of time spent in the uterus from fertilisation to birth.

In humans gestation lasts 266 days (38 weeks, or 9 months) from the date of fertilisation.

Birth

Hormones associated with birth

Throughout pregnancy the hormone **progesterone** is produced in greater and greater amounts.

- For the first 10–12 weeks progesterone is made by the corpus luteum in the ovary of the mother.
- After 12 weeks it is made by the placenta, which means the placenta acts as an endocrine gland.

The factors that cause childbirth (also called parturition) to begin are not fully understood. It is thought that many hormones are involved in the onset of labour. The two main hormonal changes are as follows.

- Immediately before birth the placenta stops producing progesterone. The walls of the uterus begin to contract when levels of progesterone are low.
- At the same time, the pituitary gland of the mother produces a hormone called **oxytocin**. Oxytocin causes stronger contractions of the uterus muscle, resulting in the onset of labour. Labour begins when the uterus starts to contract involuntarily.

 Oxytocin is often called the 'love hormone'. It is produced when people are in love or emotionally attracted (such as when a mother is with her baby). It increases trust and attachment, improves levels of optimism and self-esteem, reduces inflammation (and may help in healing), improves digestion, reduces stress and increases generosity.

Stages of birth

See diagram 41.27 for the three stages of birth.

Stage 1 (normally lasts about 12 hours). The contractions of the uterus push the foetus down towards the cervix. A mucous plug that blocks the cervix is expelled, along with some blood. The membranes around the foetus break to allow the loss of about 1 litre of amniotic fluid from the vagina (the 'waters' are said to break).

Stage 2 (normally lasts about 20 minutes to an hour). The cervix dilates (opens) enough to allow the baby to be born. The foetus is pushed out through the cervix and vagina of the mother, usually head first. The umbilical cord is still attached to the baby. The cord is clamped or tied (near the baby's body) and then cut. The baby is now independent of the mother.

Stage 3. Within 5 to 30 minutes of the birth, continuing uterus contractions expel the placenta and foetal membranes (called the afterbirth) from the mother.

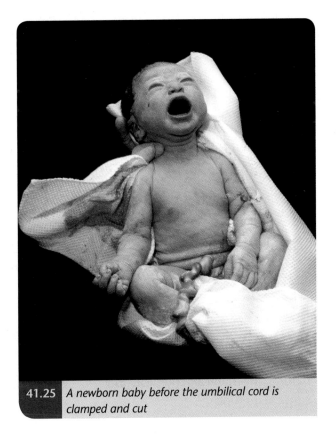

41.25 *A newborn baby before the umbilical cord is clamped and cut*

 Cutting the umbilical cord does not hurt the baby as there are no nerves in the umbilical cord.

THE ORGANISM

481

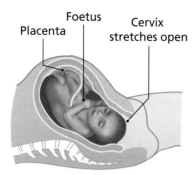

Placenta · Foetus · Cervix stretches open

The birth begins

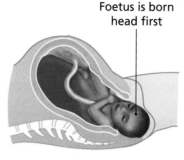

Foetus is born head first

The baby is born

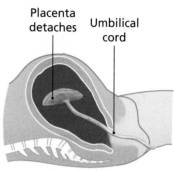

Placenta detaches · Umbilical cord

The afterbirth is expelled

41.26 *The process of birth*

Breastfeeding

Colostrum

The breasts produce a thick, yellow fluid called colostrum for the first few days after birth. Mothers are encouraged to breastfeed, at least for a few days, because colostrum has less fat and sugar than breast milk, but is higher in minerals, proteins and antibodies. Colostrum helps to nourish the baby and provides protection against infection.

Prolactin

> Lactation is the secretion of milk by the mammary glands (breasts) of the female.

During pregnancy, progesterone prevents the production of a hormone called prolactin. Progesterone levels fall around the time of birth. The inhibition is removed and the mother's pituitary gland produces **prolactin**.

Prolactin stimulates milk production. Prolactin (and therefore milk) continues to be produced as long as the baby breastfeeds. Once breastfeeding stops, the breasts of the mother will soon cease to produce milk.

Biological benefits of breastfeeding

- Human milk contains the ideal balance of nutrients needed by the baby.
- Breastfeeding provides a continuing supply of antibodies in the milk produced by the mother. This means the baby has extra resistance to most common infections.
- Breastfeeding is safer for the baby as breast milk is sterile, i.e. there is less danger of infection from micro-organisms than if bottles are used.
- Breastfeeding helps the mother's body to recover from the effects of pregnancy and birth. It does this by causing the uterus to contract and it may help her body to lose excess fat.
- Breastfeeding may help to reduce the risk of breast cancer in the mother.

Birth control

Methods of contraception

There are four methods of contraception: natural, mechanical, chemical and surgical methods.

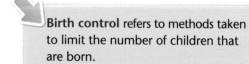

> **Birth control** refers to methods taken to limit the number of children that are born.
>
> **Contraception** is the deliberate prevention of fertilisation or pregnancy.

Natural contraception

Natural contraception involves not having intercourse at those times in the menstrual cycle when pregnancy is possible. Natural methods of contraception try to identify the time of ovulation based on:

- Body temperature (which rises after ovulation)
- Mucus secreted in the cervix (which changes its texture after ovulation)

THE ORGANISM

- Past menstrual cycles (this is called the rhythm method and it presumes that in women with regular 28-day cycles ovulation will occur 14 days after the last period, which cannot always be relied upon).

Mechanical contraception

Mechanical contraception involves using mechanical (physical) barriers to prevent sperm from reaching the egg. These barriers include:
- Condoms (male condoms cover the penis, female condoms are placed in the vagina)
- Diaphragms (dome-shaped rubber devices fitted into the vagina before intercourse)
- Caps (small rigid rubber devices that cover the cervix).

Chemical contraception

Chemical contraception involves the use of spermicides or hormones. **Spermicides** (substances that kill sperm) are normally used along with the mechanical methods of contraception.

Hormones such as progesterone and oestrogen prevent ovulation. These hormones may be taken in tablet form (the so-called 'pill') every day for the first 21 days in each menstrual cycle. They are not taken for the full cycle to allow 1 week for a 'false' menstruation to take place. Longer-acting hormones can be implanted under the skin or given by injection.

Hormonal contraceptives may produce side effects such as sickness, weight gain and headaches. More serious side effects include increased risk of blood clots, high blood pressure, heart disease and liver disorders.

Surgical contraception

Surgical methods of contraception involve sterilisation for females and vasectomy for males. Both methods are difficult to reverse and so are considered to be permanent methods of contraception.

Female sterilisation involves cutting or tying (called tubal ligation) the Fallopian tubes so that sperm cannot reach an egg. In a vasectomy each vas deferens (sperm duct) in the male is cut and sealed shut. The male will continue to ejaculate but there are no sperm present in the semen.

Apart from never having sexual intercourse, sterilisation is the only method of contraception that is 100% guaranteed. All the other contraceptive methods have some level of failure.

Summary

The male and female reproductive systems consist of:
- Gamete-producing structures (ovaries and testes)
- Gamete transport tubes
- Hormone-secreting structures.

The testes produce sperm and testosterone.
- Meiosis occurs in tubules in the testes. Haploid (23 chromosomes) sperm are produced.
- Cells between the tubules make testosterone.

The **epididymis** matures and stores sperm.

Sperm ducts carry sperm to the urethra in the penis.

The **urethra** allows the passage of either urine or sperm.

The **associated glands** (seminal vesicles, the prostate gland and Cowper's glands) produce seminal fluid that feeds the sperm and allows them to swim.

Sperm and seminal fluid form **semen**.

THE ORGANISM

The **male reproductive hormones** are:
- FSH, made by the pituitary gland, stimulates sperm production
- LH, made by the pituitary gland, causes testosterone production to increase greatly
- Testosterone, which causes:
  - The primary male characteristics (growth of penis and descent of testes from body cavity)
  - The secondary male characteristics (increased body hair, enlargement of the larynx, muscle and bone growth).

Infertility is the inability to produce offspring.

Male infertility:
- Can be due to the production of low numbers of sperm
- Can be caused by lack of hormones, smoking, drugs, mumps or chemicals
- Can be treated by hormones, by treating the cause (smoking, alcohol or drugs) or by in-vitro fertilisation.

Puberty is the onset of sexual maturity (about 11 or 12 years of age in females and 12 or 13 in males).

The **menopause** is the time at which the reproductive life of a female ends.

After puberty, the ovary produces eggs and female hormones.

Each month the ovary allows one potential egg to mature (by meiosis) into an egg (ovum).

The **egg** is enclosed in a Graafian follicle, which makes oestrogen.

Ovulation is the release of an egg from the Graafian follicle in the ovary.

After ovulation, the empty follicle becomes the corpus luteum, which makes progesterone and some oestrogen.

The **funnel of the Fallopian tube** catches the egg; then cilia and muscles push it along the tube.

The **uterus** is a muscular structure with a spongy lining (called the endometrium) that is enriched with blood vessels to nourish the embryo.

The **vagina** allows the entry of sperm and the exit of the baby at birth.

The **events of an average menstrual (monthly) cycle** are:
- **Days 1–5:** menstruation (loss of old endometrium); meiosis occurs in the ovary, forming a new egg in a Graafian follicle
- **Days 6–14:** the endometrium thickens (due to oestrogen)
- **Day 14:** ovulation (i.e. an egg is released from the Graafian follicle in the ovary)
- **Days 14–28:** the endometrium continues to develop; the egg dies by day 16 if it is not fertilised.

If fertilisation does not occur, the cycle starts again.

Increased oestrogen at puberty causes the growth of the female sex organs (primary female traits).

Oestrogen and progesterone also cause the following effects:
- In the menstrual cycle they both cause the development of the endometrium and they both inhibit egg formation
- At puberty they cause secondary female traits such as breast enlargement, widening of the pelvis, increase in body fat, body growth and production of body hair.

Female infertility (inability to produce offspring):
- Is often due to the failure to release an egg from the ovary (ovulate)
- Can be caused by a lack of LH
- Is treated by injections of LH or by in-vitro fertilisation.

Hormonal control in the menstrual cycle involves four hormones:
- FSH is made by the pituitary gland between days 1 and 5; it stimulates egg development
- Oestrogen is made by the Graafian follicle on days 5 to 14; it causes the endometrium to develop, inhibits secretion of FSH and, in high concentrations, stimulates secretion of LH
- LH is made by the pituitary on day 14; it stimulates ovulation and causes the corpus luteum to form
- Progesterone and oestrogen are made by the corpus luteum on days 14 to 28; they continue the enlargement of the endometrium, inhibit the secretion of FSH and LH, and inhibit uterine contraction
- If pregnancy has not occurred approaching day 28, the lack of progesterone allows

HIGHER ▼

contractions of the uterus (resulting in menstruation) and FSH to be formed (resulting in a new egg).

Fibroids:
- Are benign tumours of the uterus
- Are of unknown cause (although they may be associated with oestrogen)
- Produce no symptoms when small but cause heavy and prolonged periods, pain, miscarriage or infertility if they are large
- Are not treated if they are small but are removed by surgery when they are large.

The **stages in copulation** are:
- Sexual arousal, which causes the penis to become erect and the vagina to enlarge and produce lubricants
- Copulation (sexual intercourse)
- Orgasm, which is the climax of sexual excitement
- Ejaculation, which is the emitting of semen from the penis.

Insemination is the release of sperm (semen) into the female.

Sperm are pushed (and swim) to an egg (if one is present) in the Fallopian tube.

Fertilisation is the union of the sperm and egg nuclei to produce a diploid zygote.

Implantation is the burrowing of the fertilised egg into the endometrium.

The **placenta** separates the blood of the embryo and mother.

The **functions of the placenta** include the exchange of materials between the embryo and mother:
- Oxygen, food, antibodies, drugs, some hormones and micro-organisms enter the embryo
- Carbon dioxide, salts and urea enter the mother.

Embryonic development includes (length of time since fertilisation given in brackets):
- Rapid mitosis to form a solid ball of cells, called a morula (3 days)
- The formation of a hollow blastocyst (day 5)
- Implantation, which is the burrowing of the blastocyst into the endometrium (day 7)
- The blastocyst forms three germ layers (day 10)

HIGHER ▼

- Each germ layer forms specific structures in the embryo
- The outer wall of the blastocyst (trophoblast) forms the chorion, which surrounds the embryo and the amnion (day 10)
- The heart, brain and umbilical cord form (by the fourth week)
- The chorion and the mother's blood vessels in the endometrium make the placenta (about the fourth week)
- Internal organs start to form (fifth week)
- By the eighth week, all the organs and systems are formed; the shape is now recognisably human and the embryo is called a foetus
- By the 12th week bones are replacing cartilage; the foetus sucks its thumb and kicks its legs
- For the rest of the pregnancy (up to the 38th week), the foetus grows in size.

Gestation is the length of time spent in the uterus from fertilisation to birth (38 weeks, or 9 months).

Birth (or parturition) has three stages:
- **Stage 1:** contractions of the uterus push the head of the foetus towards the cervix; the amnion bursts and amniotic fluid is released
- **Stage 2:** the head of the baby is forced out through the vagina
- **Stage 3:** the afterbirth (placenta and foetal membranes) are expelled from the vagina.

The **main hormones at birth** are:
- A sudden drop in the level of progesterone, which allows the uterus to contract
- Oxytocin (produced by the pituitary of the mother), which stimulates uterus contractions.

Lactation is the production of milk by the mother's breasts. It is stimulated by breastfeeding.

Prolactin (produced by the pituitary of the mother after the birth of the child) stimulates milk production.

The **benefits of breastfeeding** include:
- Ideal nutrients
- Antibodies to fight infection
- Safe, as it is sterile
- Improves recovery in the mother
- Reduces risk of breast cancer.

Birth control involves taking steps to reduce the number of children born.

THE ORGANISM

Contraception involves using methods to prevent fertilisation or pregnancy.

Contraceptive methods include:
- Natural methods, i.e. intercourse is avoided at times in the menstrual cycle when it may result in fertilisation
- Mechanical methods use physical barriers to stop sperm and eggs from uniting
- Chemical methods use chemicals to kill sperm or hormones to prevent egg formation or ovulation
- Surgical methods involve closing the Fallopian tubes or sperm ducts (sterilisation).

Revision questions

1 (a) Name the parts labelled A to I in diagram 41.28 of the male reproductive system.

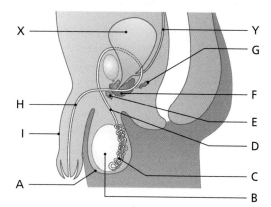

41.27

(b) Structure B is kept at a different temperature to body temperature.
- **(i)** State the ideal temperature for structure B.
- **(ii)** Why is this temperature necessary?

(c) Name four labelled parts that help to make semen.

(d) Name two liquids that can pass through part H.

(e) Name and give the functions of parts X and Y.

2 State three differences between a sperm and a normal body cell.

3 Give one function for each of the following:
- **(a)** Acrosome
- **(b)** Prostate gland
- **(c)** Testes
- **(d)** Epididymis
- **(e)** Seminal fluid.

4 (a) Name two hormones made by the pituitary gland in the male at puberty.

(b) State one function for each of the named hormones.

5 (a) Draw a diagram of a sperm and label four major parts.

(b) Give one function for each part named.

6 (a) Distinguish between primary and secondary male traits.

(b) Name the hormone responsible for these traits in males.

7 (a) What is meant by infertility?

(b) Name one type of male infertility.

(c) Suggest two causes for your answer to part (b) of this question.

(d) How may this disorder be treated?

8 State **(a)** two similarities and **(b)** two differences between an egg and a sperm.

9 (a) Name the parts labelled A to G in the side view of the female reproductive system shown in diagram 41.29.

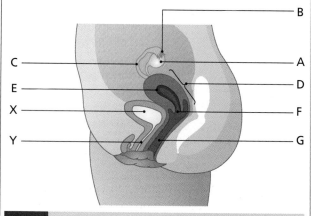

41.28

(b) (i) In which labelled part does meiosis occur?

(ii) What does meiosis produce?

(iii) Name two hormones produced in the same labelled part.

(c) Name and give the functions of the structures labelled X and Y.

10 (a) What is meant by the term 'menstrual cycle'?

(b) State one important event that occurs on the following days in a typical cycle:
(i) Day 1 **(ii)** Day 14 **(iii)** Day 28.

(c) Name a hormone associated with:
(i) Days 5 to 14 **(ii)** Days 14 to 28.

HIGHER ▼

11 **(a)** State one function common to oestrogen and progesterone in the menstrual cycle.
   (b) Name the hormone that causes the primary female traits.
   (c) What hormones cause the secondary female traits?
   (d) Name three of these traits.

12 **(a)** State one type of female infertility.
   (b) State two possible causes for this type of infertility.
   (c) Outline two possible treatments for the disorder named.

HIGHER ▼

13 Diagram 41.30 shows the changes taking place in the reproductive system of a female over 28 days.

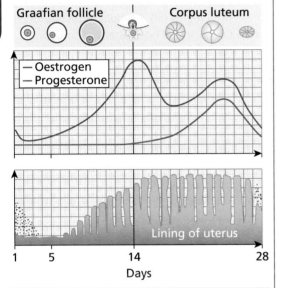

Graafian follicle   Corpus luteum

— Oestrogen
— Progesterone

Lining of uterus

1   5   14   28
           Days

41.29

   (a) What name is given to the events of the 28 days shown?
   (b) What name is given to what happens to the lining of the uterus from days 1 to 5?
   (c) What structure causes oestrogen production up to day 14?
   (d) Name the event that occurs in the Graafian follicle on day 14.
   (e) Why does the level of oestrogen fall just after day 14?
   (f) What structure makes progesterone after day 14?
   (g) Why does the level of progesterone fall just before day 28?
   (h) What effect does this fall have on the lining of the uterus?
   (i) Does this diagram indicate that pregnancy has occurred? Explain your answer.

14 **(a)** Name the four hormones involved in the menstrual cycle in the order in which they are produced.

   (b) State the approximate days on which each hormone is produced.
   (c) Outline two effects of each hormone within the cycle.

15 **(a)** Name one menstrual disorder.
   (b) Suggest how the named example may affect the menstrual cycle.
   (c) Suggest a treatment for this disorder.

16 **(a)** What do you understand by:
      (i) Copulation **(ii)** Insemination
      (iii) Fertilisation **(iv)** Implantation?
   (b) Draw a diagram of the female reproductive system to show the location of events (ii), (iii) and (iv) above.

17 **(a)** List six structures through which sperm must pass from where they are produced to where fertilisation takes place.
   (b) List three structures through which the egg must pass from where it is made to where fertilisation takes place.

18 State the normal survival times for:
   (a) Sperm in the female system
   (b) An egg after ovulation.

19 **(a)** Name the normal location in the female reproductive system for fertilisation.
   (b) State the events that occur from the time the sperm reaches an egg until fertilisation takes place.

20 Explain the terms: **(a)** Gamete **(b)** Zygote **(c)** Morula **(d)** Blastocyst **(e)** Trophoblast **(f)** Amnion **(g)** Chorion **(h)** Germ layer **(i)** In-vitro fertilisation.

HIGHER ▼

21 **(a)** Name the three primary (germ) layers from which humans develop.
   (b) Name two structures produced by each layer.

22 In carrying out in-vitro fertilisation:
   (a) Why is the female given hormonal treatment in advance?
   (b) Why are several eggs removed from the ovary?
   (c) Why are the fertilised eggs put back into the uterus?
   (d) Why does the procedure often result in the birth of more than one baby?

23 **(a)** Name two substances in each case that pass in the following directions:
      (i) From the foetus to the mother's blood
      (ii) From the mother's blood to the foetus.
   (b) Name two harmful substances that could pass from the mother to the foetus.

THE ORGANISM

24 **(a)** Name the parts labelled A to G in diagram 41.31.

(b) Who makes the part labelled C?

(c) What is the function of the liquid labelled E?

(d) To what part of the foetus does structure D attach?

(e) What flows through part D?

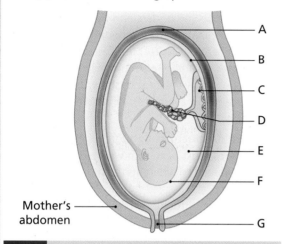

Mother's abdomen

41.30

25 **(a)** State two reasons why the blood of the mother and foetus should not mix.

(b) Give a reason why the placenta can be considered to be an endocrine gland.

26 State two hormonal changes that occur in a mother just before childbirth.

27 **(a)** What is colostrum?

(b) What hormone causes milk production?

(c) What causes this hormone to be produced?

(d) For how long is this hormone produced?

(e) Suggest why breastfed babies should get fewer infections than bottle-fed babies.

28 **(a)** What is meant by contraception?

(b) Give one example from each of the following categories of contraception and state how your named example works:
(i) Natural **(ii)** Mechanical **(iii)** Chemical **(iv)** Surgical.

(c) Which of your named examples is most reliable in preventing fertilisation?

29 Choose which of the options (i), (ii), (iii) or (iv) represents the correct answer in each case below.

(a) After the eighth week of pregnancy, the baby is called: **(i)** An embryo **(ii)** A foetus **(iii)** A zygote **(iv)** A blastocyst.

(b) Oxytocin is a hormone that causes: **(i)** Ovulation **(ii)** Meiosis **(iii)** Labour **(iv)** Milk production.

(c) The structure that matures and stores sperm is the: **(i)** Testis **(ii)** Epididymis **(iii)** Scrotum **(iv)** Sperm duct.

(d) In males, FSH is the hormone that is responsible for: **(i)** Mitosis **(ii)** Meiosis **(iii)** Ejaculation **(iv)** Secondary male features.

(e) The lungs of the developing baby arise from cells in this layer:
(i) Endoderm
(ii) Periderm
(iii) Mesoderm
(iv) Ectoderm.

Exam questions

Section A

30 The graphs below illustrate changes in the levels of two hormones, A and B, which are involved in the development of the endometrium, during the human female menstrual cycle.

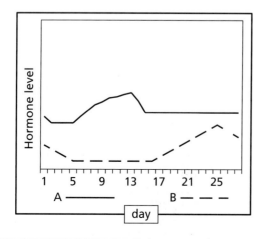

(a) Name one of these hormones.

(b) What happens in the ovary around day 14 of the cycle?

(c) Apart from the two hormones illustrated, another hormone called FSH has a role in the cycle.
(i) Where is FSH produced?
(ii) Give one function of FSH.

(d) Which graph, A or B, represents the hormone secreted by the corpus luteum (yellow body)?

(e) Draw a line graph in the space above A and B to illustrate the changes that take place in the thickness of the endometrium over the course of the cycle.

(2007 HL Q 4)

31 The diagram shows the female reproductive system.

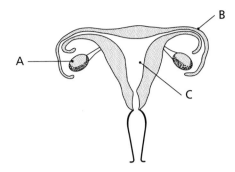

(a) Identify parts A, B and C.

(b) Using the letters X, Y and Z and arrows, identify each of the following on the diagram: endometrium (X), where fertilisation normally occurs (Y), where meiosis occurs (Z).

(c) Which part of the system is influenced by both FSH and LH?

(d) Give **two** biological advantages of breastfeeding.

(2008 HL Q 6)

Section C

32 (a) What are secondary sexual characteristics? Give an example of a human secondary sexual characteristic.

(b) The diagram shows the reproductive system of the human male.

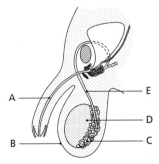

(i) Name the parts A, B, C, D, E.

(ii) Where are sperm produced?

(iii) What is the function of the prostate gland?

(iv) State **one** way in which a sperm differs from an ovum (egg).

(c) (i) What is meant by infertility? State **one** cause of infertility in the human male.

(ii) Name **three** methods of contraception and, in each case, explain how the method prevents conception.

(2004 OL Q 11)

33 (a) (i) Where is testosterone secreted in the body of the human male?

(ii) Give a brief account of the role of testosterone.

(b) (i) Draw a large, labelled diagram of the reproductive system of the human male.

(ii) Where are sperm produced?

(iii) State **two** ways in which sperm differ from ova (eggs).

(iv) Name a gland that secretes seminal fluid.

(v) State a function of seminal fluid.

(c) (i) What is meant by contraception?

(ii) Give an example of a surgical method of male contraception. Suggest an advantage and a disadvantage of the method that you have named.

(iii) List **three** methods of contraception other than surgical. In your answer you may refer to either or both sexes.

(iv) Suggest a possible effect on a human population that may result from an increased availability of contraception.

(2005 HL Q 13)

34 (a) (i) Draw a detailed diagram of the reproductive system of the human male. Label the following parts on your diagram: testis, seminal vesicle, urethra, sperm duct (vas deferens), epididymis, prostate gland.

(ii) Place an X on your diagram where meiosis occurs.

(iii) Place a Y on your diagram where sperm are stored.

(iv) State **two** functions of testosterone.

(v) Give a cause of male infertility and suggest a corrective measure.

(2007 HL Q 15)

35 (a) (i) Draw a diagram of the reproductive system of the human female. On your diagram indicate where the following occur:

1. Meiosis.
2. Fertilisation.
3. Implantation.

(ii) Give an account of the role of either oestrogen or progesterone in the menstrual cycle.

(iii) Name a human female menstrual disorder. In the case of this disorder give:

1. A possible cause.
2. A method of treatment.

(b) (i) Give an account of the importance of the placenta during human development in the womb.

(ii) From what tissues is the placenta formed?

(iii) Outline how birth occurs.

(iv) What is meant by *in-vitro fertilisation*?

(v) After implantation, the embryo first develops into a *morula* and then into a *blastocyst*. Explain the terms in italics.

(2009 HL Q 14)

THE ORGANISM

36 (a) (i) Draw a large labelled diagram of the human female reproductive system.
(ii) Indicate clearly on your diagram where each of the following events takes place:
1. Ovulation
2. Fertilisation.
(iii) What does the term *infertility* mean?
(iv) *In vitro* fertilisation is a method used to treat infertility. What is meant by the term *in vitro* in relation to fertilisation?
(v) Give **one** cause of infertility in women.
(vi) As a result of fertility treatment, an embryo develops successfully from an *in vitro* fertilisation. What is the next step for the embryo?

(2011 OL Q 14)

37 (b) Answer the following questions from your knowledge of early human development in the womb.
(i) 1. Name the **three** germ layers in the early human embryo.
2. For **each** germ layer name a structure in the adult body that develops from it.
(ii) From which tissues does the placenta develop?
(iii) 1. What is the amnion?
2. Explain the importance of the amnion for the foetus.

(2012 HL Q 14)

Previous examination questions

Ordinary level	Higher level
2004 Q 11	2004 Q 14b, c
2005 Q 14b	2005 Q 13
2006 Q 5	2006 Q 15c
2010 Q 14a, b	2007 Q 4, 15a
2011 Q 14a	2008 Q 6
2012 Q 12a, c	2009 Q 14a, b
	2010 Q 15a, c(i)
	2012 Q 14b

Latest questions at www.edco.ie/lcbiologyplus/examhelp

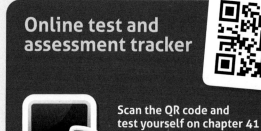

Online test and assessment tracker

Scan the QR code and test yourself on chapter 41
www.edco.ie/lcbiologyplus

Glossary

abiotic factors non-living factors. *page 34*

acquired variations are not inherited but are learned or developed during life. *page 213*

active immunity the production of a person's own antibodies in response to foreign antigens that enter the body. *page 424*

active site the part of an enzyme that combines with the substrate. *page 114*

active transport energy (in the form of ATP) is used to move molecules, often against a concentration gradient, i.e. from low concentrations to high concentrations. *page 355*

adaptation any alteration that improves an organism's chances of survival and reproduction. *page 68*

adhesion occurs when different molecules stick together. *page 285*

aerobic respiration the controlled release of energy from food using oxygen. *page 133*

alleles different (or alternative) forms of the same gene. *page 191*

all or nothing law states that if the threshold is reached an impulse is carried, but if the threshold is not reached no impulse is carried. *page 378*

anabolic reactions use energy to convert smaller molecules into larger molecules. *page 24*

anaerobic respiration the controlled release of energy from food without the use of oxygen. *page 135*

antagonistic pair two muscles that have opposite effects to each other. *page 415*

antibiotics chemicals produced by micro-organisms that stop the growth of, or kill, other micro-organisms without damaging human tissue. *page 244*

antibody a protein produced by white blood cells (called lymphocytes) in response to a specific antigen. *page 423*

anticodon a sequence of three bases (a triplet) on tRNA that are complementary to a sequence of three bases on mRNA. *page 182*

antigen a foreign molecule that stimulates the production of antibodies. *page 423*

appendicular skeleton composed of the limbs (arms and legs), the pectoral (shoulder) girdle and the pelvic (hip) girdle. *page 409*

artificial active immunity occurs when a pathogen is medically introduced into the body. *page 424*

artificial passive immunity occurs when a person is given an injection containing antibodies made by another organism. *page 425*

aseptic or **asepsis** means that measures are taken to exclude unwanted micro-organisms. *page 256*

asexual reproduction involves only one parent. *pages 14, 438*

autotrophic (organism) one that makes its own food. *page 241*

axial skeleton consists of the skull, spine, ribs and sternum (breastbone). *page 408*

bacteriophage (or **phage**) a virus that infects bacteria. *page 433*

balanced diet contains all the necessary food types in the correct proportions. *page 329*

batch culture the growth of cells in a sealed container (or bioreactor) over a short period of time and under ideal conditions until all the nutrients are used up. *page 246*

biogenesis living things arise from other living things of the same type. This is also called **continuity of life**. *page 11*

biology the study of living things. *page 2*

biomolecules chemicals that are made inside a living thing. *page 16*

bioprocessing the use of enzyme-controlled reactions to produce a product. *page 105*

bioreactor a vessel or container in which living cells or their products are used to make a product. *pages 105, 247*

biosphere that part of the planet containing living organisms. *page 32*

biotechnology the use of living things or their components (especially cells and enzymes) to manufacture useful products or to carry out useful reactions. *page 136*

biotic factors living factors. *page 34*

birth control methods taken to limit the number of children that are born. *page 482*

blastocyst (or **blastula**) a hollow ball of cells formed from a morula. *page 479*

blood pressure the force exerted by the blood against the walls of the blood vessels (mainly the arteries). *pages 302, 308*

bud a potential growth point that may develop into a shoot, a leaf or a flower. *page 267*

bulb a modified bud. *page 461*

cancer a group of disorders in which certain cells lose their ability to control both the rate of mitosis and the number of times mitosis takes place. *page 160*

carnivores animals that feed mainly on animals. Examples are dogs, cats and ladybirds. *page 320*

carpels the female parts of the flower. *page 439*

catabolic reactions release energy when a complex molecule is broken down to a simpler form. *page 24*

catalyst a substance that speeds up a reaction, without itself being used up in the reaction. *page 103*

cell continuity all cells develop from pre-existing cells. *page 155*

cell cycle the changes that take place in a cell during the period between one cell division and the next. *page 157*

cellular energy the energy stored in the bonds of biomolecules. *page 102*

centromere the point at which the chromosomes are attached in a double-stranded chromosome. *page 162*

characteristics traits or features that are inherited genetically. *page 170*

chemosynthesis the production of food using energy released from chemical reactions. *page 241*

chemotropism a change in growth of a plant in response to chemicals. *page 365*

chromatin the name given to chromosomes when they are elongated and not dividing. *page 87*

chromosomes coiled threads of DNA (which forms genes) and protein that become visible in the nucleus at cell division. *page 155*

chromosome mutation a large change in the structure or number of one or more chromosomes. *page 215*

classification placing objects into groups based on similar characteristics. *page 212*

climatic factors refer to weather over a long period of time. *page 34*

cloning the production of identical copies of the bacterium (containing the target gene). *page 226*

closed circulatory system blood remains in a continuous system of blood vessels. *page 300*

codon (or **triplet**) a sequence of three bases in DNA (or RNA) that act as a code for an amino acid. *page 172*

cohesion the sticking of similar molecules to each other. *page 285*

community all the different populations in an area. *page 33*

competition occurs when organisms actively struggle for a resource that is in short supply. *page 51*

conclusion a summary of the results of an experiment. *page 3*

conservation the wise management of the existing natural resources in an ecosystem, in order to maintain a wide range of habitats and prevent the death and extinction of organisms. *page 42*

consumers organisms that take in food from another organism. *page 36*

contest competition an active physical contest between two individual organisms. *page 52*

continuity of life living things arise from other living things of the same type. This is also called **biogenesis**. *page 11*

continuous flow (food processing) the growth of cells in an open container (or bioreactor), where nutrients are added and the end products are removed all the time at a rate that maintains the volume of liquid and the number of cells. *page 247*

contraception the deliberate prevention of fertilisation or pregnancy. *page 482*

control used to provide a comparison (or standard) against which the actual experiment can be judged. *page 5*

copulation the act of sexual intercourse. *page 475*

cotyledon a seed leaf. *pages 272, 445*

cross-pollination the transfer of pollen from an anther to a stigma on a different plant. *page 443*

cutting a portion of a plant that is removed from the parent plant and grown into a new, independent plant. *page 462*

cytoplasm the living material in a cell outside the nucleus. *page 85*

data the measurements, observations or information gathered from experiments. *page 3*

decomposers organisms that feed on dead organic matter. *page 36*

denatured enzyme one that has lost its shape and can no longer carry out its function. *pages 104, 115*

denitrification the conversion of nitrates to nitrogen gas. *page 40*

detritus feeders organisms that feed on small pieces of dead organic matter. *page 36*

diastole when the heart chambers relax. *page 307*

diffusion the spreading out of molecules from a region of high concentration to a region of low concentration. *page 147*

dihybrid cross involves the study of two characteristics. *page 197*

diploid cell one that has two sets of chromosomes, i.e. it has two of each type of chromosome in the nucleus. *page 156*

dispersal the transfer of a seed or fruit away from the parent plant. *page 447*

DNA profile (also called a DNA or genetic fingerprint) a method of making a unique pattern of bands from the DNA of a person, which can then be used to compare with the DNA profile of another person. *page 174*

dominant the allele that prevents the recessive allele from being expressed. *page 191*

dormancy a resting period when seeds undergo no growth and have reduced cell activity or metabolism. *page 449*

double blind both the investigator and the participant are unaware of the nature of the treatment the participant is receiving. *page 6*

ecological niche (of an organism) the functional role it plays in the community. *page 38*

ecology the study of the interactions between living things (organisms) and between organisms and their environment. *page 32*

ecosystem a group of clearly distinguished organisms that interact with their environment as a unit. *page 32*

ectotherms gain or lose heat from or to their external environment. *page 349*

edaphic factors relate to soil. *page 34*

ejaculation the release of semen from the penis. *page 475*

endocrine gland a ductless gland that produces hormones, which are released directly into the bloodstream. *page 398*

endospermic seed contains some endosperm when fully formed. *page 445*

endotherms generate their own heat from metabolic reactions. *page 349*

enzymes proteins that speed up a reaction without being used up in the reaction. *page 103*

enzyme specificity each enzyme will react with only one particular substrate. *page 115*

ethics relates to whether conduct is right or wrong. *page 8*

eukaryotic cells have a nucleus and cell organelles, all of which are enclosed by membranes. *page 89*

evolution the way in which living things change genetically to produce new forms of life over long periods of time. *page 216*

excretion the removal of waste products of metabolism from the body. *page 13*

exhalation breathing out. *page 342*

exocrine glands release their product into ducts or tubes. *page 398*

experiment a test for a hypothesis. *pages 3, 4*

expression the formation of the product by the organism with the recombinant DNA. *page 226*

facultative parasite can get its food from a live or a dead host. *page 251*

fauna all the animals in an ecosystem. *page 36*

fermentation another name for anaerobic respiration. *page 135*

fertilisation the union of the male and female gametes to form a diploid zygote. *pages 190, 444, 475*

filtration water and small molecules pass (under high pressure) from the blood into the nephron. *page 355*

flora all the plants in an ecosystem. *page 36*

food chain (grazing food chain) a sequence of organisms in which each one is eaten by the next member in the chain. *page 36*

food web two or more interlinked food chains. *page 37*

forensic medicine the way in which medical knowledge is used in legal situations. *page 175*

fossil the remains of something that lived a long time ago (or some indication of something that lived a long time ago). *page 218*

frequency the chance of finding a named species with any one throw of a quadrat. *page 73*

fruit a developed ovary. *page 446*

gametes haploid cells capable of fusion. *pages 190, 439*

ganglion (plural: ganglia) a group of cell bodies located outside the CNS. *page 377*

gene a section of DNA that contains the instructions for the formation of a protein. *pages 156, 169*

gene expression the way in which the genetic information in a gene is decoded in the cell and used to make a protein. *page 169*

gene (or **point**) **mutation** a change in a single gene. *page 215*

general defence system acts as a barrier to all pathogens attempting to gain entry to the human body. *page 420*

genetic code the sequence of bases in DNA that provide the instruction for a cell (using RNA) to form a protein. *page 172*

genetic engineering the artificial manipulation or alteration of genes. *page 223*

genetic screening testing DNA for the presence or absence of a particular gene or an altered gene. *page 177*

genotype the genetic make-up of an organism, i.e. the genes that are present. *page 191*

geotropism (or **gravitropism**) the change in growth of a plant in response to gravity. *page 365*

germination the regrowth of the embryo, after a period of dormancy, if the environmental conditions are suitable. *page 449*

germ layers basic layers of cells in the blastocyst from which all adult tissues and organs will form. *page 479*

gestation the length of time spent in the uterus from fertilisation to birth. *page 480*

glycolysis the conversion of glucose into two molecules of pyruvic acid. *page 138*

gonad an organ that produces sex cells in animals. *page 467*

grafting the joining and uniting of part of one plant with a second plant. *page 462*

growth inhibitor a chemical that causes a reduction in growth of plants. *page 367*

growth plate the area between the epiphysis and the diaphysis in a long bone within which bone growth occurs. *page 411*

growth promoter a chemical that causes increased growth in plants. *page 366*

growth regulator a chemical that controls the growth of a plant. *page 365*

habitat the place where a plant or an animal lives (and is also the local area of study). *pages 33, 65*

haploid cell one that has one set of chromosomes, i.e. it has only one of each type of chromosome in the nucleus. *page 156*

helper T cells stimulate B cells and killer T cells. *page 427*

herbaceous plants do not contain wood (or lignin). *page 267*

herbivores animals that feed mainly on plants. Examples are sheep, cattle and rabbits. *page 320*

heredity the passing on of features from parents to offspring by means of genes. *page 169*

heterotrophic (organism) one that takes in food made by other organisms. *page 241*

heterozygous the alleles are different. *page 192*

homeostasis the ability of an organism to maintain a constant internal environment. *page 334*

homologous pair two chromosomes of similar size with the same sequence of genes. *page 156*

homozygous two alleles that are identical. *page 192*

hormone a chemical messenger produced by an endocrine gland and carried by the bloodstream to another part of the body, where it has a specific effect. *page 399*

hydrotropism a change in growth of a plant in response to water. *page 365*

hypha a tube or filament in a fungus. *page 251*

hypothesis an educated guess based on observations. *page 3*

immobilised enzymes are attached, or fixed, to each other, or to an inert material. *page 105*

immunisation occurs when we produce or are injected with antibodies against a pathogen. *page 425*

immunity the ability to resist infection. *page 420*

implantation the embedding of the fertilised egg into the lining of the uterus. *page 476*

incomplete dominance neither allele is dominant or recessive with respect to the other. Both alleles are equally expressed in the heterozygous genotype to produce an intermediate phenotype. *page 193*

induced immunity the ability to resist disease caused by specific pathogens by the production of antibodies. *page 424*

infertility the inability to produce offspring. *page 469*

inhalation breathing in. *page 341*

inherited variations are controlled by genes. *page 213*

insemination the release of semen into the vagina, just outside the cervix. *page 475*

interneuron (also called an **intermediate, relay** or **association neuron**) carries information between sensory and motor neurons. *page 377*

internode the region on a stem between two nodes. *page 267*

interphase the phase in the cell cycle when the cell is not dividing. *page 157*

inter-specific competition occurs between members of different species. *page 51*

intra-specific competition occurs between members of the same species. *page 51*

in-vitro fertilisation (IVF) removing eggs from an ovary and fertilising them outside the body. *page 477*

isolation the removal of the chromosome (containing the target gene) from the human cell and the plasmid DNA from the bacterium. *page 225*

joint where two or more bones meet. *page 413*

key a means of naming organisms by answering a series of questions with alternative answers. *page 69*

killer T cells destroy abnormal human body cells. *page 427*

lactation the secretion of milk by the mammary glands (breasts) of the female. *page 482*

larynx the voice box. *page 339*

law or **principle** arises from a theory that has been shown to be valid when fully tested over a long period of time. *page 4*

law of independent assortment states that: when gametes are formed either of a pair of alleles is equally likely to combine with either of another pair of alleles. *page 197*

law of segregation (Mendel's first law) states that:
- Inherited characteristics are controlled by pairs of alleles.
- These alleles segregate (or separate) from each other at gamete formation, with only one member of the pair being found in each gamete. *page 196*

layering the growth of a new plant from a stem that is still attached to the parent plant. *page 463*

lenticels openings in the stems of plants that allow gas exchange. *pages 267, 284*

life the possession of all the following characteristics: organised, requiring nutrition and excretion, capable of responding and reproducing. *page 12*

ligaments strong, fibrous, slightly elastic tissues that connect bone to bone. *page 414*

ligation the joining of two sections of DNA to form a single strand. *page 225*

lignin a strengthening material found in some plant cell walls. *page 270*

linkage genes are located on the same chromosome. *page 200*

locus (of a gene) its position on a chromosome. *page 191*

meiosis a form of nuclear division in which the four daughter nuclei contain half the chromosome number of the parent nucleus. *page 161*

memory B cells survive for years after the infection is eliminated and can make the specific antibody if the same infection later enters the body. *page 427*

memory T cells survive for years after the infection is eliminated and can stimulate the specific B cells and killer T cells if the same infection later enters the body. *page 428*

menopause when ovulation and menstruation stop happening in a female. *page 471*

menstrual cycle a series of events that occurs every 28 days on average in the female if fertilisation has not taken place. *page 471*

menstruation the discharge of the lining of the uterus (the endometrium) and the unfertilised egg. *page 472*

meristem a plant tissue capable of mitosis. *page 266*

metabolism the sum of all the chemical reactions in an organism. *page 11*

micro-organisms small living things. *page 237*

micropropagation the growth of plants from small pieces of tissue under sterile conditions on a specially selected medium. *page 463*

mitosis a form of nuclear division in which one nucleus divides to form two nuclei, each containing the same number of chromosomes with identical genes. *page 157*

monohybrid cross involves the study of a single characteristic. *page 197*

morula a solid ball of cells formed from a zygote by mitosis. *page 478*

motor (or **efferent**) **neuron** takes a message from the CNS to a muscle or a gland. *page 376*

mutagens agents that cause mutations. *page 214*

mutation a spontaneous (or sudden) change in the amount or structure of DNA. *page 214*

mycelium a (usually) visible mass of hyphae. *page 251*

natural active immunity occurs when a pathogen enters the body in the normal way (i.e. when you get an infection). *page 424*

natural passive immunity occurs when a child gets antibodies from its mother. *page 425*

natural selection the process by which those organisms with genetically controlled characteristics that allow them to be well adapted to their environments will survive and reproduce to pass on their genes to following generations. *page 217*

natural vegetative propagation involves forming new plants from a stem, root, leaf or bud. *page 460*

negative tropism occurs when the growth is away from the stimulus. *page 364*

neuron (or **neurone**) a nerve cell. *page 376*

nitrification the conversion of ammonia and ammonium (NH_4^+) compounds to nitrite and then to nitrate. *page 40*

nitrogen fixation the conversion of nitrogen gas into ammonia (NH_3), ammonium (NH_4^+) or nitrate (NO_3^-). *page 40*

node the point on a stem at which a leaf is attached. *page 267*

non-endospermic seed has no endosperm when fully formed. *page 445*

nutrient recycling the way in which elements (such as carbon and nitrogen) are exchanged between the living and non-living components of an ecosystem. *page 38*

nutrition the way organisms obtain and use food. *page 12*

obligate parasite can only take its food from a live host. *page 251*

observation when something is noticed. *page 3*

omnivores animals that feed on plants and animals. Examples are humans, badgers and hedgehogs. *page 320*

open circulatory system blood leaves blood vessels and flows around the cells of the animal's body before re-entering blood vessels again. *page 300*

optimum pH the pH value at which the enzyme works best. *page 115*

organ a structure composed of a number of tissues that work together to carry out one or more functions. *page 98*

organisation living things are composed of cells, tissues, organs and organ systems. *page 12*

organism a living thing. *page 11*

organ system a number of organs working together to carry out one or more functions. *page 99*

orgasm the physical and emotional sensations experienced at the peak of sexual excitement. *page 475*

osmosis the movement of water molecules across a semi-permeable membrane from a region of high water concentration to a region of low water concentration. *page 148*

osteoblast a bone-forming cell. *page 411*

osteoclast a bone-digesting cell. *page 412*

ovulation the release of an egg from the ovary. *page 470*

parasites organisms that take in food from a live host and usually cause harm. *page 242*

parasitism when two organisms of different species live in close association and one organism (the parasite) obtains its food from, and to the disadvantage of, the second organism (the host). *page 53*

passive immunity occurs when individuals are given antibodies that were formed by another organism. *page 425*

pathogen an organism that causes disease. *page 420*

pathogenic bacteria bacteria that cause disease. *page 244*

pectoral girdle consists of the collarbone (or clavicle) and the shoulder blade (or scapula). *page 409*

pedigree a diagram showing the genetic history of a group of related individuals. *page 194*

pelvic girdle composed of two halves of the hip joined to the sacrum. *page 409*

percentage cover an estimate of the amount of ground in a quadrat covered by each species. *page 72*

peristalsis a wave of muscular action in the walls of the alimentary canal that moves the contents along. *page 323*

pharynx the throat. *page 339*

phenotype the physical make-up, or appearance, of an organism. *page 191*

phospholipids fat-like substances in which one of the fatty acids is replaced by a phosphate group or has a phosphate group added to it. *page 19*

photolysis the splitting of water by light. *page 125*

phototropism the change in growth of a plant in response to light, usually from one direction (i.e. unidirectional light). *page 364*

plasma the liquid part of blood. *page 292*

plasma B cells produce antibodies. *page 426*

plumule the part of the plant embryo that develops into the shoot. *page 445*

pollination the transfer of pollen from an anther to a stigma of a flower from the same species. *page 443*

pollutants harmful additions to the environment. *page 41*

pollution any harmful addition to the environment. *page 41*

population all the members of the same species living in an area. *page 33*

portal system a blood pathway that begins and ends in capillaries. *page 305*

positive tropism occurs when the growth is towards the stimulus. *page 364*

predation the catching, killing and eating of another organism. *page 53*

predator an organism that catches, kills and eats another organism. *page 53*

prey the organism that is eaten by a predator. *page 53*

principle (or **law**) arises from a theory that has been shown to be valid when fully tested over a long period of time. *page 4*

producers organisms that carry out photosynthesis. *page 36*

product the substance(s) formed by an enzyme. *page 103*

progeny offspring that are produced. *page 192*

prokaryotic cells do not have a nucleus or membrane-enclosed organelles. *page 89*

protoplasm all the living parts of a cell. *page 85*

puberty the beginning of sexual maturity. *page 469*

pulse the alternate expansion and contraction of the arteries. *page 308*

punnett square a grid used to show the ratio of the genotypes of the progeny in a genetic cross. *page 192*

purines (double-ring molecules) adenine (A) and guanine (G). *page 180*

pyramid of numbers represents the numbers of organisms at each trophic level (or stage) in a food chain. *page 38*

pyrimidines (single-ring molecules) thymine (T) and cytosine (C). *page 180*

qualitative study records the presence or absence of organisms. *page 66*

quantitative study records the numbers of organisms that are present. *page 66*

radicle the part of the plant embryo that develops into a root. *page 445*

reabsorption molecules pass from the nephron back into the blood. *page 355*

recessive the allele is prevented from being expressed by a dominant allele. *page 191*

reflex action an automatic, involuntary, unthinking response to a stimulus. *page 384*

reflex arc the pathway taken by a nerve impulse in a reflex action. *page 384*

refractory period a short time span after a neuron has carried an impulse during which a stimulus fails to cause a response. *page 378*

replicate a repeat of an experiment. *page 6*

reproduction the production of new individuals. *page 14*

response the activity of a cell or organism as a result of a stimulus. *page 363*

root tuber a swollen, underground root that remains dormant during winter and from which new plants may grow. *page 460*

runners horizontal stems that run (or grow) above ground and from which new plants grow. *page 460*

saprophytes organisms that take in food from dead organic matter. *page 241*

scientific method a process of investigation in which problems are identified and their suggested explanations are tested by carrying out experiments. *page 3*

scramble competition all of the competing individuals get some of the resource. *page 52*

secondary sexual characteristics those features that distinguish males from females, apart from the sex organs themselves. *page 469*

secretion some substances pass from the blood into the nephron. *page 356*

selectively permeable membrane allows some but not all molecules to pass through. *page 147*

self-pollination the transfer of pollen from an anther to a stigma on the same plant. *page 443*

semen a fluid containing sperm and seminal fluid. *page 468*

sensory (or **afferent**) **neuron** takes a message from a sense organ to the CNS. *page 376*

serum plasma from which the clotting proteins have been removed. *page 293*

sex linkage a characteristic is controlled by a gene on a sex (or X) chromosome. *page 202*

sexual reproduction the union of two sex cells or gametes. *pages 14, 439*

solar energy energy from the Sun. *page 102*

speciation the production of new species as a result of evolution. *page 217*

species a group of similar organisms that are capable of naturally interbreeding with each other to produce fertile offspring. *page 212*

specific defence system attacks particular (or specific) pathogens. *page 422*

sporulation the process of making spores. *page 253*

stamens the male parts of the flower. *page 439*

sterile all micro-organisms are destroyed, i.e. there is nothing living. *page 256*

stimulus (plural: stimuli) anything that causes a reaction in an organism or in any of its parts. *page 363*

substrate the substance with which an enzyme reacts. *page 103*

suppressor T cells inhibit the immune response. *page 428*

symbiosis occurs when two organisms of different species live (and have to live) in close association and at least one of them benefits. *page 54*

synapse a region where two neurons come into close contact. *page 379*

synaptic cleft the tiny gap between the two neurons at a synapse. *page 379*

systole when the heart chambers contract. *page 307*

taxonomy the science of classifying organisms. *page 212*

tendons strong, flexible, inelastic fibres that connect muscle to bone. *page 414*

theory a hypothesis that has been supported by many different experiments. *page 4*

thigmotropism a change in growth of a plant in response to touch. *page 365*

threshold the minimum stimulus needed to cause an impulse to be carried in a neuron. *page 377*

tissue culture the growth of cells in or on a sterile nutrient medium outside an organism. *page 97*

tissue a group of similar cells that are modified (or adapted) to carry out the same function(s). *page 95*

transcription the copying of a sequence of genetic bases from DNA onto messenger RNA (mRNA). *page 178*

transformation the uptake of DNA into a cell. *page 226*

translation the conversion of a sequence of genetic bases on messenger RNA into a sequence of amino acids. *page 179*

transpiration the loss (by evaporation) of water vapour from the leaves and other aerial parts of a plant. *page 279*

triplet (or **codon**) a sequence of three bases in DNA (or RNA) that act as a code for an amino acid. *page 172*

trophic level a feeding stage in a food chain. *page 36*

tropism a change in the growth of a plant in response to an external stimulus. *page 364*

turgor (or **turgor pressure**) the outward pressure of the cytoplasm and vacuole against the cell wall of a plant. *page 149*

ultrastructure the detail of a structure as seen using an electron microscope. *page 85*

vaccination the administration (usually by injection) of a non-disease-causing dose of a pathogen (or its toxin) to stimulate the production of antibodies. *page 425*

vaccine a non disease-causing dose of a pathogen (or its toxin), which triggers the production of antibodies. *page 424*

valves control the direction of blood flow. *page 302*

variable a factor that may change in an experiment. *page 4*

variation (within a species) in a group of successfully interbreeding organisms the individual members show different characteristics. *page 213*

vegetative propagation (or **vegetative reproduction**) asexual reproduction in plants. *page 460*

venation the pattern of veins in a leaf. *page 268*

woody plants contain wood (or lignin). *page 267*

Index

499